ISBN 978-1-5283-4607-8
PIBN 10921809

1 MONTH OF
FREE
READING

at

www.ForgottenBooks.com

By purchasing this book you are eligible for one month membership to ForgottenBooks.com, giving you unlimited access to our entire collection of over 1,000,000 titles via our web site and mobile apps.

To claim your free month visit: www.forgottenbooks.com/free921809

THE

LAW OF COPYRIGHT,

IN WORKS OF LITERATURE AND ART:

INCLUDING THAT OF THE

DRAMA, MUSIC, ENGRAVING, SCULPTURE, PAINTING, PHOTOGRAPHY,
AND ORNAMENTAL AND USEFUL DESIGNS;

TOGETHER WITH

INTERNATIONAL AND FOREIGN COPYRIGHT,

WITH THE STATUTES RELATING THERETO,

AND

REFERENCES TO THE ENGLISH AND AMERICAN DECISIONS.

BY

WALTER ARTHUR COPINGER,

OF THE MIDDLE TEMPLE, ESQ., BARRISTER-AT-LAW.

AUTHOR OF 'INDEX TO PRECEDENTS IN CONVEYANCING;' 'A TREATISE ON THE CUSTODY
AND PRODUCTION OF TITLE DEEDS;' 'TABLES OF STAMP DUTIES,' ETC.

" Non equidem hoc studeo, bullatis ut mihi nugis
Pagina turgescat, dare pondus idonea fumo."—*Pers.*

SECOND EDITION.

LONDON:

STEVENS AND HAYNES,

Law Publishers,

BELL YARD, TEMPLE BAR.

1881.

LONDON:
PRINTED BY WILLIAM CLOWES AND SONS, LIMITED,
STAMFORD STREET AND CHARING CROSS.

TO

THE RIGHT HONOURABLE

HUGH McCALMONT EARL CAIRNS,

K.B., D.C.L., LL.D., &c.,

FORMERLY LORD HIGH CHANCELLOR OF GREAT BRITAIN,

This Work

IS

BY HIS LORDSHIP'S KIND PERMISSION

RESPECTFULLY DEDICATED

BY

THE AUTHOR.

PREFACE TO THE SECOND EDITION.

TEN years have elapsed since this, the first of the Author's literary adventures, was placed before the public. The favourable manner in which it was then received, and the undeserved terms in which it has been so frequently referred to by his professional brethren, has induced the Author to revise the whole work and make the volume as complete a treatise on the subject of copyright as was in his power, and any failure in this respect must be attributed rather to his want of skill than to lack of labour.

Though the legislative changes during the last ten years have been few, yet many cases have been decided involving principles of great magnitude.

Matters, too, of great value were evolved in the evidence given before the Royal Commissioners on Copyright, and where in their valuable report they have suggested alterations and amendments in the existing law, these have invariably been referred to throughout the present work.

The Author's best thanks are due to his friend S. Moore, Esq., of Lincoln's Inn, for his kind assistance in the chapter on Foreign Copyright, the greater part of the additions to which have been compiled by him.

It is hoped that the forms in the Appendix, especially those under the Fine Arts Copyright Act, 1862, may prove of use to authors, artists, and others.

The Index has been compiled by the Author with great care, and has been made as comprehensive as the case seemed to require ; for the Author is one of those who consider that many of our best law books are rendered far less valuable than they otherwise would prove to the professional man, by reason of their meagre index, while on the other hand many an indifferent treatise is rendered comparatively valuable by reason of the exhaustive character of its index, whereby reference is easily found to general principles and particular cases on the point in question.

W. A. COPINGER.

LINCOLN CHAMBERS,
    18 *South King Street, Manchester.*
      December 1880.

PREFACE TO THE FIRST EDITION.

THE decisions of our Courts of Law and Equity on the subject of Copyright during the last few years have been numerous; and so severely has been experienced the want of a work embodying these decisions, and presenting an exposition of the principles on which they have been determined, that little apology will be deemed necessary for introducing to the profession a digest of the Copyright Laws.

If I have, by the classification adopted, in any way facilitated the lawyer in his search for the principles of law as applicable to particular circumstances, and have proved of assistance to the literary man or the artist in the acquirement of that peculiar knowledge of the law which, for the due protection of his production is so requisite, I shall have attained an object at once gratifying to myself, and sufficiently compensative for my labour.

W. A. COPINGER.

MIDDLE TEMPLE LANE, TEMPLE.
September 1870.

CONTENTS.

—◆—

CHAPTER I.

HISTORICAL VIEW OF THE COPYRIGHT LAWS.

CHAPTER II.

WHAT MAY BE THE SUBJECT OF COPYRIGHT.

CHAPTER III.

TERM OF COPYRIGHT, AND IN WHOM VESTED.

CHAPTER IV.

REGISTRATION OF COPYRIGHT.

CHAPTER V.

ASSIGNMENT OF COPYRIGHT.

CHAPTER VI.

INFRINGEMENT OF COPYRIGHT.

CHAPTER IX.

CROWN COPYRIGHT.

CHAPTER X.

UNIVERSITY AND COLLEGE COPYRIGHT.

CHAPTER XI.

MUSICAL AND DRAMATIC COPYRIGHT.

CHAPTER XII.

COPYRIGHT IN ENGRAVINGS, PRINTS, AND LITHOGRAPHS.

CHAPTER XIII.

COPYRIGHT IN SCULPTURE AND BUSTS.

CHAPTER XIV.

COPYRIGHT IN PAINTINGS, DRAWINGS AND PHOTOGRAPHS.

CHAPTER XV.

COPYRIGHT IN DESIGNS.

CHAPTER XVI.

NEWSPAPERS.

CHAPTER XVII.

INTERNATIONAL COPYRIGHT.

CHAPTER XVIII.

COPYRIGHT IN FOREIGN COUNTRIES.

France.

Belgium.

Holland.

CHAPTER XIX.

ARRANGEMENTS BETWEEN AUTHORS AND PUBLISHERS.

Arrangement between authors and publishers—The reward due to the authors— Contracts between authors and publishers should be in writing—What neces- sary to satisfy the Statute of Frauds—An action maintainable for not

---

APPENDICES.

TABLE OF CASES.

THE LAW OF COPYRIGHT.

CHAPTER I.

HISTORICAL VIEW OF THE COPYRIGHT LAWS.

COPYRIGHT may be defined as the sole and exclusive liberty of multiplying copies of an original work or composition (a). Definition and nature of copyright.

The right of an author to the productions of his mental exertions may be classed among the species of property acquired by occupancy; being founded on labour and invention (b).

A literary composition, so long as it lies dormant in the author's mind, is absolutely in his own possession. Ideas drawn from external objects may be communicated by external signs, but words demonstrate the genuine operations of the intellect. The former are so identical with himself, that when by the author resolved into the latter, they lose not their original characteristic; and whether

---

(a) 14 M. & W. 316. The term "copyright" may be understood in two different senses. The author of a literary composition, which he commits to paper belonging to himself, has an undoubted right at common law to the piece of paper on which his composition is written, and to the copies which he chooses to make of it for himself, or for others. If he lends a copy to another his right is not gone; if he sends it to another under an implied undertaking that he is not to part with it, or publish it, he has a right to enforce that undertaking. The other sense of that word is, the exclusive right of multiplying copies; the right of preventing all others from copying, by printing or otherwise, a literary work which the author has published. This must be carefully distinguished from the other sense of the word. (Per Baron Parke, in Jefferys v. Boosey, 4 H. L. C. 920.)

(b) Hoffman's 'Legal Outlines,' sect. iii.; Locke on Gov. pt. 2, c. 5.

B

CAP. I.

or not they be regarded as of pecuniary value in the way of recital or sale, he ought to be the sole arbiter to authorize or to prohibit their publication, and have full control over them, before they are actually submitted to public inspection. In ancient times orations, plays, poems, and even philosophical discourses, were usually orally communicated, and all ages have allotted to the composers the profits which arose from this mode of publication. They were rewarded by the contributions of the audience or by the patronage of those illustrious persons in whose houses they recited their works. A recompense of some sort was regarded as a natural right, and any one contravening it, was esteemed little better than a robber. Terence sold his 'Eunuchus' to the ædiles, and was afterwards charged with stealing his fable from Nævius and Plautus. "*Exclamat furem, non poetam, fabulam dedisse*" (a). He sold his 'Hecyra' to Roscius, the player. Statius would have starved had he not sold his tragedy of 'Agave' to Paris, another player:

> "*Esurit, intactam Paridi nisi vendat Agaven*" (b).

These sales were founded upon natural justice. No man could possibly have a right to make a profit by the publication of the works of another, without the author's consent. It would be converting to one's own emolument the fruits of another's labour.

In later times the method of publication was usually by writing, or describing in characters those words in which an author had clothed his ideas. Characters are but the signs of words, and words the vehicle of sentiments. Here the value which distinguishes the writing arises merely from the matter it conveys. The sentiment is, therefore,

---

(a) *Prologus ad* ' *Eunuchum* ' :

> "Exclamat, furem, non poetam, fabulam
> Dedisse, et nihil dedisse verborum tamen ;
> *Colacem* esse Nævi, et Plauti veterem fabulam,
> Parasiti personam inde ablatam et militis."

(b) Juvenal, *Sat.* vii. 87.

the thing of value from which the profit must arise. No man has a right to give another's thoughts to the world, or to propagate their publication beyond the point to which the author has given consent. His reputation is concerned and he has a right to defend it. This is natural justice, and dictated by reason; consequently, as *Lex est ratio summa, quæ jubet quæ sunt utilia et necessaria et contraria prohibet* (a), we may obviously assume that though copyright, as *a species of property*, was in a strictly accurate sense unknown to, or at least was not by precedent established at common law, yet, "the novelty of the question did not bar it of the common law remedy and protection" (b).

Distinct properties were not adjusted at the same time and by one single act, but by successive degrees, according as either the condition of things or the number and genius of men seemed to require. When once established, the same law which pointed out and settled the line of demarcation commands the observance of everything that may be conducive to the end for which these various boundaries were erected. "*Nequaquam autem omnes res,*" says Puffendorf (c), "*statim ab initio humani generis, aut ubique locorum ex definito aliquo præcepto juris naturalis debuerunt proprietatem subire; sed hæc est introducta, prout pax mortalium id requirere visa fuit.*"

The necessary consequence of being a distinguishable property was its having a determinate owner. As property must precede the violation of property, so the rights must be instituted before the remedies for their violation; and the seeking for the law of the right of property in the law of procedure relating to the remedies is a mistake similar to supposing that the mark on the ear of an animal is the cause, instead of the consequence, of property therein.

Property in literary compositions.

(a) Co. Lit. 319 b. Jenk. Cent. 117.
(b) 4 Burr. 2345. . *Nihil quod est contra rationem est licitum :* Co. Lit. 97 b. *Sou le ley done chose, la ceo done remedie a vener a ceo :* 2 Roll. R, 17. *In novo casu, novum remedium apponendum est :* 2 Inst. 3.
(c) *De Jure Nat. et Gen.* lib. iv. c. iv. s. 14. *Vide ibid.* s. 6.

If the essential principle for one source of property be production, the mode of production is unimportant; the essential principle is applicable alike to the steam and gas appropriated in the nineteenth century, and the printing introduced in the fifteenth, and the farmers' produce of the earlier ages. The importance of the interest dependent on words advances with the advance of civilization. If the growth of the law be traced with respect to the words that make and unmake a simple contract, and with respect to the words that are actionable or justifiable as defamation, and with respect to the words that are indictable as seditious or blasphemous, it will be thought reasonable that there should be the same growth of the law in respect of the interest connected with the investment of capital in words. In the other matters the law has been adapted to the progress of society according to justice and convenience, and by analogy it should be the same for literary works, and they would become property with all its incidents, on the most elementary principles of securing to industry its fruits and to capital its profits (a).

In the vast complications of human affairs, requiring new applications of old principles continually to be made; in the measureless range of human thought, bringing new doctrines out of the mass of new and old events; in the immense fields of human exploration, luminous with the light of every species of science, over which the race of man is always travelling ; in the unlimited expansibility of human society, developing new aspects, new relations, new wants ; in the fact that, although the reported decisions of the courts are numerically great, they embrace but comparatively few even of the questions which have arisen heretofore ; in the known fact, also, that evermore the surges of time are driving the shores of human capability farther towards the infinite,—we read the truth, pervading every system of jurisprudence, that whenever a matter comes before the courts, it is really a call for a new enunciation of legal doctrines, and that from the past we

(a) *Per* Mr. Justice Erle in *Jefferys* v. *Boosey*, 4 H. L. C. 870.

only gather a few rules to guide us in the future. We learn that both the olden and the new light point to the way of principle for the settlement of all new cases, when particular precedents fail (a).

What property could be more emphatically a man's own than his literary works? Is the property in any article or substance accruing to him by reason of his own mechanical labour denied him? Is the labour of his mind less arduous, less worthy of the protection of the law? When the right could not be combated on the ground of common sense or simple reason, the lawyers were forced to fly to what Lord Coke styles "*summa ratio*," or the *legal* reason, and they contended that from the very nature of literary productions no property in them could exist. For, said they, to claim a property in anything it is necessary that it should have certain qualities; it should be of a *corporeal substance*, be capable of occupancy or possession, it should have distinguishable proprietary marks, and be a subject of sole and exclusive enjoyment. Now, none of these indispensable characteristics were possessed by a literary production.

To this it was replied, that such definition of property was too narrow and confined; (for the rules attending property must ever keep pace with its increase and expansibility, and must be adapted to every particular condition;) that a distinguishable existence in the thing claimed as property, and an actual value in such thing to the true owner, are its essentials; and that the best rule of reason and justice seemed to be, to assign to everything capable of possession a legal and determinate owner.

Ideas, being neither capable of a visible possession nor of sustaining any one of the qualities or incidents of property, inasmuch as they have no bounds whatever, cannot be the subject of property. Their whole existence is in the mind alone; incapable of any other mode of acquisition or enjoyment than by mental possession or

No copyright in mere ideas.

(a) Bishop's 'Criminal Law.'

apprehension, safe and invulnerable from their own immateriality, no trespass can reach, no tort affect, no fraud or
violence diminish or damage them (a). They are of a
nature too unsubstantial, too evanescent, to be the subject
of proprietary rights.

Copyright however in the material that has embodied the ideas. When, however, any material has embodied those ideas,
then the ideas, through that corporiety, can be recognised
as a species of property by the common law. The claim
is not to ideas, but to the order of words, and this order has
a marked identity and a permanent endurance. The order
of each man's words is as singular as his countenance, and
although, if two authors composed originally with the same
order of words, each would have a property therein, still
the probability of such an occurrence is less than that
there should be two countenances that could not be dis-
criminated. The permanent endurance of words is obvious
by comparing the words of ancient authors with other
works of their day ; the vigour of the words is unabated,
though other works have mostly perished (b). It is true
that property in the order of words is a mental abstraction, but so also are many other kinds of property ; for
instance, the property in a stream of water, which is not
in any of the atoms of the water, but only in the flow of
the stream. The right to the stream is not the less a
right of property, either because it generally belongs to the
riparian proprietor, or because the remedy for a violation
of the right is by action on the case, instead of detinue or
trover (c).

Author's right to the first publication of his own manuscript. "Ideas," says Mr. Justice Yates, "are free. But while
the author confines them to his study, they are like birds
in a cage, which none but he can have a right to let fly ;

(a) Yates, J., in *Millar* v. *Taylor*, 4 Burr. 2362; *Abernethy* v. *Hutchinson*,
1 Hall & Tw. 28; S. C. in 3 L. J. (Ch.) 209, 213, 219 : and see Sir G. Turner,
V.C., in *Morison* v. *Moat*, 9 Hare, 257.

(b) The intellectual creations of the ancient Greeks and Romans have
come to us through many centuries in better preservation than their great
works of art; and while many of their stupendous monuments of stone and
brass can no longer be distinguished, the identity of their intellectual
labours remain unaffected by time.

(c) Mr. Justice Erle, in *Jefferys* v. *Boosey*, 4 H. L. C. 869.

for, till he thinks proper to emancipate them, they are under his own dominion. It is certain every man has a right to keep his own sentiments, if·he pleases; he has certainly a right to judge whether he will make them public, or commit them only to the sight of his friends. In that state, the manuscript is, in every sense, his peculiar property; and no man can take it from him or make any use of it which he has not authorized, without being guilty of a violation of his property. And as every author or proprietor of a manuscript has a right to determine whether he will publish it or not, he has a right to the first publication; and whoever deprives him of that priority is guilty of a manifest wrong, and the court have a right to stop it " (a).

Thus we see that every man has the right at common law to the first publication of his own manuscript, it cannot without his consent be even seized by his creditors as property (b). He has in fact, supreme control over his own productions, and may either exclude others from their enjoyment, or may dispose of them as he pleases. He may limit the number of persons to whom they shall be imparted, and impose such restrictions as he pleases upon their use. He may annex conditions, and proceed to enforce them, and for their breach he may claim compensation (c).

(a) Yates, J., in *Millar* v. *Taylor*, 4 Burr. 2378; 1 Mac. & Gor. 36; *Forrester* v. *Walker*, cited 2 Bro. P. C. 138; *Manley* v. *Owen*, 4 Burr. 2329; *Webb* v. *Rose*, 4 Burr. 2330; *Southey* v. *Sherwood*, 2 Mer. 435; *Wheaton* v. *Peters*, 8 Peters, S. C. R. (Amer) 591; Eden on Injunc. 285; 2 Story, Eq. Jur. s. 943; Curtis on Copy, 84, 150, 159; *Woolsey* v. *Judd*, 4 Duer (Amer.) 385.

(b) See *Little* v. *Hall*, 18 How. (Amer.) 170; *Bartlette* v. *Crittenden*, 4 McLean (Amer.) 300; S. C. 5 *ibid.* 32; *Webb* v. *Rose*, *supra*; *Pope* v. *Curl*, 2 Atk. 342; *Manley* v. *Owen*, *supra*; *Macklin* v. *Richardson*, Amb. 694; *Donaldson* v. *Becket*, 4 Burr. 2408; *Abernethy* v. *Hutchinson*, 1 Hall & Tw. 28; *Prince Albert* v. *Strange*, 2 De G. & Sm. 652: 1 Mac. & G. 25; *Turner* v. *Robinson*, 10 Ir. Ch. 121, 510; *Wheaton* v. *Peters*, *supra*. See *Dudley* v. *Mayhew*, 3 Coms. (Amer.) 12; *Clayton* v. *Stone*, 2 Paine (Amer.) 383; *Jones* v. *Thorne*, 1 N. Y. Leg. Obs. 409; *Parton* v. *Prang*, 3 Cliff. (Amer.) 537; *Carter* v. *Bailey*, 64 Me. (Amer.) 458; *Boucicault* v. *Wood*, 16 Amer. Law Reg. 529; *Keene* v. *Wheatley*, 23 Law Rep. 440; *Roberts* v. *Dyer*, *ibid.* 396; *Stone* v. *Thomas*, 2 Amer. Law Reg. 228; *Woolsey* v. *Judd*, *supra*; *Beckford* v. *Hood*, 7 T. R. 616; *Palmer* v. *Dewitt*, 23 L. T. N. S. 823.

(c) Lord Mansfield described his right as "an incorporeal right to print a set of intellectual ideas, or modes of thinking, communicated in a set of words, or sentences, and modes of expression. It is equally detached from the manuscript, or any other physical existence whatsoever," 4 Burr. 2396.

Suppose therefore, that a man, with or without leave to peruse a manuscript work, transcribes and publishes it, the offence would not be within the Copyright Acts; it would not be larceny, nor trespass, nor a crime indictable (the physical property of the author, the original manuscript, remains), but it would be a gross violation of a valuable right. Again, suppose the original or a transcript be given or lent for a man to read, and he were to publish it, such publication would be a violation of the author's common law right to the copy (a).

Lord Clarendon's 'History.'   In the case of the *Duke of Queensbury* v. *Shebbeare*, before Lord Henley, an injunction was granted against printing the second part of Lord Clarendon's 'History,' Lord Clarendon lent to a person of the name of Gwynne a copy of his 'History;' his son and representatives insisted that he had a right to print and publish this 'History,' but the court were of opinion that Gwynne might make every use of it except the profit of multiplying in print. The presumption was that Lord Clarendon never intended that when he gave him the copy. The injunction was acquiesced under (b); and Dr. Shebbeare recovered, before Lord Mansfield, a large sum against Gwynne for repre-

---

(a) "The nature of a right of an author in his works is analogous to the rights of ownership in other personal property, and is far more extensive than the control of copying after publication in print, which is the limited meaning of copyright in its common acceptation, and which is the right of an author, to which the statute of Anne relates. Thus, if after composition the author chooses to keep his writings private, he has the remedies for wrongful abstraction of copies analogous to those of an owner of personalty in the like case. He may prevent publication; he may require back the copies wrongfully made; he may sue for damages if any are sustained; also if the wrongful copies were published abroad, and the books were imported for sale without knowledge of the wrong, still the author's right to his composition would be recognised against the importer, and such sale would be stopped. . . . Again, if an author choses to impart his manuscript to others without general publication, he has all the right for disposing of it incidental to personalty. He may make an assignment either absolute or qualified in any degree. He may lend, or let, or give, or sell any copy of his composition, with or without liberty to transcribe, and if with liberty of transcribing, he may fix the number of transcripts which he permits. If he prints for private circulation only, he still has the same rights, and all these rights he may pass to his assignee. About the rights of the author before publication at common law, all are agreed." Erle J., *Jeffreys* v. *Boosey*, 4 H. L. C. 867; see *Parton* v. *Prang*, 3 Cliff. (Amer.) 548.

(b) 2 Eden, 329; *Knaplock* v. *Curle*, 4 Vin. Abr. 278.

senting "that he had a right to print." But where the plaintiff, as residuary legatee under the will of Miss Mitford, claimed to be entitled to an account against the defendant Bentley for the profits of the publication of the letters and papers of the testatrix, without the plaintiff's authority ; and it appeared that after the date of her will, Miss Mitford had addressed an unattested letter to her executor, W. Harness, saying, that in case anybody should print her letters or life, she wished that a part at least of the produce should go to the plaintiff; and some years afterwards Harness arranged with one of the defendants to edit the said letters and papers, and requested him to pay £20 to the plaintiff, in compliance with Miss Mitford's wish, and the editor entered into an agreement with Bentley for the publication of a work containing the letters and papers which he had edited, and offered the plaintiff the sum of £20, which was not accepted, the Master of the Rolls held that the letter of Miss Mitford to Harness was tantamount to a gift to him of her letters and papers, and that on Bentley offering and undertaking to pay to the plaintiff the sum of £20, before offered by the editor, the bill must be dismissed, but without costs (a).

In the cases of Webb and Forrester (b), the Court of Chancery again interposed by injunction. It appears that the plaintiff in the former case had his 'Precedents of Conveyancing' stolen out of his chambers and printed ; and in the latter he had his notes copied by a clerk of a gentleman to whom he had lent them, and printed. In *Macklin* v. *Richardson* (c) the defendant had employed a short-hand writer to take down the farce of ' Love à la mode,' upon its performance at the theatre, and inserted one act in a magazine, giving notice that the second act would be published in the magazine of the following month. Upon an application to Lord Camden for an

CAP. I.

'Precedents of Conveyanc-ing.'

'Love à la mode.'

(a) *Sweetman* v. *Bentley*, W. N. (1871) 162.
(b) Cited Ambl. 695
(c) *Ibid.*

injunction, he directed the case to stand over until that of *Millar* v. *Taylor,* which was then pending, should be determined; and after the decision had been given in that case the injunction was granted by the Lords Commissioners Smythe and Bathurst. The former, referring to the play, saying, "it has been argued to be a publication by being acted, and therefore the printing is no injury to the plaintiff; but that is a mistake; for, besides the advantage of the performance, the author has another source of profit from the printing and publishing, and there is as much reason that he should be protected in that right as any other." Bathurst adding, "The printing it before the author is doing him a great injury."

This was the opinion also of Lord Cottenham in a case subsequently referred to (a). "The property," said he, "of an author or composer of any work, whether of literature, art, or science, in such work unpublished, and kept for his private use or pleasure, cannot be disputed after the many decisions upon which that proposition has been affirmed or assumed. I say 'assumed,' because in most cases which have been decided, the question was not as to the original right of the author, but whether what had taken place did not amount to a waiver of such right; as, in the case of letters how far the sending of the letter, in the case of dramatic composition how far the permitting performance, and in the case of Mr. Abernethy's lectures how far the oral delivery of the lecture, had deprived the author of any part of his original right and property;—a question which could not have arisen if there had not been such original right or property."

The statutes
do not affect
right before
publication.

The statutes with reference to copyright do not in any manner affect the common law ownership of literary compositions before publication, and therefore until publication

---

(a) *Prince Albert* v. *Strange,* 18 L. J. (N. S.) Cb. 120; 1 Hall & Tw. 1; 1 Mac. & Gor. 25; *Turner* v. *Robinson,* 10 Ir. Ch. Rep. 121, 510; *Southey* v. *Sherwood,* 2 Mer. 435; *Gee* v. *Pritchard,* 2 Swans. 402.

an author and his assignees have a proprietary right in his production, of which he is not deprived by the statute, and which the court will protect against invasion (a). The copyright laws are merely ancillary to the common law rights of authors (b). They continue them after publication in print, but in no way impair such rights, so long as the literary composition remains in manuscript, or is not printed.

These principles were clearly developed in Prince Prince Albert's case (c), a case possessed of peculiar interest from Albert's case. the high position of the parties. It appeared that the Queen and the plaintiff had occasionally, for their amusement, made drawings and etchings, being principally of subjects of private and domestic interest to themselves, and that they had made impressions of those etchings for their own use, and not for publication; that, for greater privacy, such impressions had been, for the most part, made by means of a private press kept for that purpose, and the plates themselves had been ordinarily kept by her Majesty under lock, and the impressions had been placed in some of the private apartments of her Majesty at Windsor, and in such apartments only; that the defendants Strange and Judge had in some manner obtained some of such impressions, which had been surreptitiously taken from some of such plates, and had thereby been enabled to form, and had formed, a gallery or collection of such etchings, of which they intended to make a public exhibition without the permission of her Majesty and the plaintiff, or either of them, and against their will; that the defendants had compiled and prepared a work, which had been printed and published by the defendant Strange, of which the title page or cover was as follows:—" A Descriptive Catalogue of the Royal Victoria and Albert Gallery of Etchings."

(a) *Palmer* v. *Dewitt* (American case), 23 L. T. (N. S.) 823.
(b) Mr. Edward Jenkins, M.P., in his separate report as a member of the copyright commission says, "The statute law *creates*, it does not *recognise* copyright," but it is conceived that this is a position which could not be supported.
(c) *Prince Albert* v. *Strange*, 1 Hall & Tw. 1; 1 Mac. & Gor. 25, 18 L. J. (N. S.) Ch. 120; 13 Jur. 45, 109, 507.

"Every purchaser of this catalogue will be presented (by permission) with a facsimile of the autograph of either her Majesty or of the Prince Consort engraved from the original, the selection being left to the purchaser, price sixpence;" that this work had been compiled, printed, and published without the consent of her Majesty and the plaintiff, or either of them, and against their will; that, in fact, among the etchings were portraits of the plaintiff, the Prince of Wales, the Princess Royal, and other members of the Royal Family, and personal friends of her Majesty, from life, and afterwards transferred to copper and etched by her Majesty and the plaintiff, and among such etchings were portraits of their favourite dogs, taken by them from life, and etchings from old and rare engravings in the possession of her Majesty, and several from such original designs as in the catalogue mentioned; and among such etchings there were several portraits of the Princess Royal, and such scenes in the Royal nursery as in the said catalogue mentioned; and that the said descriptive catalogue comprised sixty-three several etchings; that the catalogue could not have been made except from impressions surreptitiously obtained; that the impressions were intended for private use, and not for publication, and very few had been given away, and those only to private friends. The bill then, as amended, charged that certain of the plates were given to Brown, a printer, at Windsor, for the purpose of printing off certain impressions thereof for her Majesty and the plaintiff, and that Brown employed therein a person of the name of Middleton, who, without Brown's consent or knowledge, and in violation of the confidence reposed in him, took impressions thereof for himself; and that Judge had bought or in some manner obtained the same from Middleton. It was then prayed that the defendants might be ordered to deliver up to the plaintiff all impressions and copies of the several etchings respectively made by the plaintiff; and that they, their servants, &c., might be restrained by injunction from ex-hibiting the said gallery or collection of etchings, or from

making engravings or copies of them, or in any manner pub-
lishing them, or from parting with or disposing of them,
and also from selling, publishing, or printing, the descriptive
catalogue in the bill mentioned or any work being or purporting to be a catalogue of the said etchings, and that
the copies of the catalogue in the possession of the defendants might be given up to the plaintiff. An injunction
was immediately granted against Strange until he had
answered the bill, or the court should make order to the
contrary, which injunction was afterwards extended to
the other defendants. Strange subsequently put in an
answer denying that he had in any manner, either
surreptitiously or otherwise, obtained any impressions
of the etchings or copies of them. He stated that he
believed that Judge purchased certain impressions of
the etchings from Middleton; that Judge had proposed
to him to exhibit them if her Majesty and the Prince
did not object; and that he then believed that the
impressions had not been improperly obtained; that
Judge afterwards wrote the catalogue, which Strange
printed, but struck off fifty-one copies only, and then
broke up the type; that this catalogue had never been
exposed for sale, and that as soon as he learnt that the
exhibition was disapproved of by the Queen and the
Prince, he determined to abandon the scheme, and had
offered to give up all copies of the catalogue in his possession if the bill were dismissed against him and his costs
paid, but that the solicitor for the plaintiff refused to pay
the defendant's costs. He insisted by his answer that, as
a matter of strict right, he was entitled to publish the
catalogue; and so far as the injunction related to the
publication of the catalogue he moved to dissolve it
before Vice-Chancellor Knight Bruce. It was contended
by the defendants that a man acquiring knowledge
of another man's property without his consent, is not
by any rule or principle which a Court of Justice
can apply—however secretly that other man may have
kept or endeavoured to keep his property—forbidden,

without consent, to communicate or publish that knowledge to the world, to inform the world what the property
is, or to describe it publicly, whether orally or in print or
writing. That there were distinct properties, independent
of each other, in the owner of portraits; first, there was the
right of property in the canvas; secondly, in the face that
adorned the canvas; thirdly, the knowledge of the existence
of what he possessed. That supposing that the owner of
a collection of pictures allowed the public on certain days
to view his collection, and by this means one of the visitors
acquired a knowledge of the paintings, the same as the
owner, that such person had in the absence of contract to
the contrary a right to make use of that knowledge. It
was admitted that he might be restrained from using the
form, but contended that he could not be restrained from
describing the attributes created by the form. That there
was no greater right of property in the knowledge, in the
owner of the collection, than in any stranger who might
have had access to them. But both the Vice-Chancellor
Knight Bruce in the first instance, and Lord Cottenham on
appeal, refused to give effect to this argument. The former
saying (a), "The author of the manuscripts, whether he is
famous or obscure, high or low, has a right to say of them,
whether light or heavy, saleable or unsaleable, that they
shall not, without his consent, be published; and I think
to use a dishonest knowledge of them, for the purpose of
composing and publishing, and so to compose and publish
a catalogue of them, amounts to a publication of them
within the principle and the rule. Assuming the law to
be so, what is its foundation in this respect? It has not
reference to any considerations peculiarly literary. Those
with whom our common law originated, had not, probably,
among their many merits, that of being patrons of letters,
but they knew the duty and necessity of protecting
property, and, with that general object, laid down rules
providently expansive—rules capable of adapting themselves to the various forms and modes of property that

(a) 13 Jur. 57.

peace or cultivation might discover or introduce. The produce of mental labour, thoughts, and sentiments recorded and preserved by writing, became, as knowledge went onwards and the culture of man's understanding advanced, a kind of property which it was impossible to disregard. . . . Upon the principle, therefore, of protecting property, it is that the common law, in cases not aided nor prejudiced by the statute, shelters the privacy of thoughts and sentiments committed to writing, designed by the author to remain not generally known. This has been, in effect, judicially declared, not by any judge more distinctly than by Lord Eldon, on several occasions, particularly in Mr. Southey's case. He says, 'It is to protect the exclusive property of the writer that injunctions are granted.' And again: 'I have examined the cases I have been able to meet with containing precedents for injunctions, and I find that they all proceed upon the ground of title to property in the plaintiff.' Such being, as I believe, the nature and foundation of the common law as to manuscripts, independently of Parliamentary additions and subtractions, its operation cannot, of necessity, be confined to literary subjects; that would be to limit the rule by the example. Wherever the produce of labour is liable to invasion in an analogous manner, there must be, I suppose, a title to analogous protection or redress. Such I consider the case of mechanical works or works of art executed by a man for his private use. Whatever protection those, or some of those, may have by the Act of Parliament, they are not, I apprehend, deserted by the common law. The principles and rules which it applies to literary compositions and manuscripts must, to a considerable extent, be applicable to these also." And the latter, assuming the right of property, says (a): 'If, then, such right and property exist in the author of such works, it must so exist exclusively of all other persons. Can any stranger have any right or title to, or interest in, that which belongs exclusively to another?—and yet

(a) 13 Jur. 112.

this is precisely what the defendant claims, although, by a strange inconsistency, he does not dispute the general proposition as to the plaintiff's right and property; for he contends that, admitting the plaintiff's right and property in the etchings in question, and, as incident to it, the right to prevent publication or exhibition of copies of them, yet he insists that some persons having had access to certain copies, and having, from such copies, composed a description and list of the originals, he, the defendant, is entitled to publish such list and description —that is, that he is entitled, against the will of the owner, to make such use of his exclusive property. It being admitted that the defendant could not publish a copy—that is, an impression—of the etchings, how, in principle, does the case of a catalogue, list, or description differ? A copy or impression of the etchings could only be a means of communicating knowledge and information of the original; and does not a list and description do the same? The means are different, but the object and effect are similar: it is to make known to the public, more or less, the unpublished works and compositions of the author, which he is entitled to keep wholly for his private use and pleasure, and to withhold altogether, or so far as he may please, from the knowledge of others. Cases of abridgments, translations, extracts, and criticisms of published works, have no reference whatever to the present question. They all depend on the extent and right under the Acts with respect to copyright, and have no analogy to the exclusive right of the author in unpublished compositions, which depend entirely on the common law right of property . . . . Upon the first question, therefore—that of property—I am clearly of opinion that the exclusive right and interest of the plaintiff in the compositions and works in question being established, and there being no right or interest whatever in the defendant, the plaintiff is entitled to the injunction of this Court to protect him against the invasion of such right and interest by the defendant, which the publication of any catalogue would undoubtedly be."

What amounts to publication sufficient to defeat the common law right is a question of some nicety. The property which a composer of a piece of music ordinarily has in his composition is the pecuniary value which it has to him, and not merely the amount of fame he may acquire; and such pecuniary value is necessarily and wholly dependent upon the means which he may lawfully employ to bring his production before the public, and the approval of the public of his work; and there is no other property in that description of literary composition.

"When a right of property in the invention or creation of an author is recognised as an inherent right by the common law," says Mr. Judge Monell in a late American case (a), "it assumes that the thing to be secured and protected is of value to the owner. The law does not regard as property a thing entirely worthless. If a literary composition, therefore, derives its value from, and becomes property because of, the use which can be made of it before the public, and such value is increased or diminished in proportion to the extent of its use, then it becomes very important to know where and when the author's literary property in it terminates. To give it value, or to make it property, recognised by the common law, the author must be allowed to use it before the public; and if, having submitted it once to a public hearing, it is to be deemed a publication, so as to take away the proprietary right, and to deprive the author of the benefit of copyright laws, then, obviously, the common law means nothing, and there is no such thing as property in literary work. Can it be said that once delivering a lecture upon a scientific or literary subject, before a public audience, will for ever thereafter deprive the author of his property in the ideas invented or created, and which represent, by a combination of words his meaning? If so, then any one who can obtain the

(a) *Palmer* v. *Dewitt* 23 L. T. (N.S.), 823, 825.

C

manuscript, or access to it, or who, by employing the art of stenography, or by the exercise of memory, can carry it out of a public lecture-room, may, without the consent or knowledge of the author, appropriate and use, for his own emolument, the literary production of another person. I cannot believe there is so little foundation for, or so narrow a limit to, the proprietary rights of an author in his literary labours. I believe the law intended to secure to him the *beneficial* results of his labours, and to protect him from any piratical invasion of his rights, until he has done some act inconsistent with an exclusive ownership, and which shall amount, in judgment of law, to a publication. There can be no fixed rule determining when an author has surrendered his literary property."

What does not amount to publication.   The publication of a work for private purposes and private circulation is not a publication sufficient to defeat the common law right of an author (a). Accordingly, it has been determined that a copyright in a piece of music is not lost, although it had been published in manuscript a year before being printed. The words "printed and published," used in the statutes, have reference only to the time at which the author's exercise of the right is to be dated; and therefore, the circumstance of an author having previously published in manuscript any composition which is afterwards printed, only varies the period of time from which the term of protection is to be calculated. The delivery of a lecture to an audience of persons admitted on payment of a fee, is not deemed a publication (b); neither is the exhibition of a picture at a public exhibition or gallery, where copying is expressly or impliedly forbidden, nor the exhibition of a picture for the purpose of obtaining subscribers to an engraving (c).

(a) *White* v. *Geroch*, 1 Chitt. 26, 2 B. & Ald. 298; *Prince Albert* v. *Strange*, 2 De G. & Sm. 686; 1 Mac & Gor. 42; 1 Hall & Tw. 1; *Jefferys* v. *Boosey*, 4 H. L. C. 816.

(b) *Abernethy* v. *Hutchinson*, 3 L. J. (Ch.) 209.

(c) *Turner* v. *Robinson*, 10 Ir. Ch. 510. But see *Dalglish* v. *Jarvie*, 2 Mac. & Gor. 231, 2 H. & T. 437, cited Kerr on Injunc. 184, and 25 & 26 Vict. c. 68.

On publication, no more passes to the public than an CAP. I.
unlimited use of every advantage that the purchaser can The effect of
reap from the doctrines and sentiments which the work publication.
contains. The property in the composition does not pass;
for those things which are peculiarly and appropriately
his, must remain his until he agrees or consents to part
with them by compact or donation; " because no man can
deprive him of them without his approbation; but the
depriver must use them as his when they are not his, in
contradiction to truth." For "to have the property" in
any thing, and "to have the sole right of using and
disposing of it," is the same thing. They are equipollent
expressions (a).

It was only since the introduction of printing that any Primary re-
question of the extent and duration of copyright could be cognition of copyright.
expected to occur in a court of justice. For the period of
about a century from the time of this discovery we have
no evidence of the recognition in any public form of the
copyright of authors, or of the remedies by which its
infraction might be redressed (b). The earliest evidence
which occurs is to be found in the charter of the Stationers'
Company and the decrees of the Star Chamber.

The original charter of the Stationers' Company was The original
granted by Philip and Mary in 1556. It was the declared charter of the Stationers'
object of the Crown at that time to prevent the propagation Company.
of the reformed religion, and it seems to have been thought
that this could most effectually be brought about by im-
posing the severest restrictions on the press. About this
period there are several decrees and ordinances of the
Star Chamber regulating the manner of printing, the
number of presses throughout the kingdom, and prohibiting all printing against the force and meaning of any of
the statutes or laws of the realm. Until the year 1640
the Crown through the instrumentality of the Star
Chamber, exercised this restrictive jurisdiction without
limit, enforcing by the summary powers of search, confis-

(a) Author of 'The Religion of Nature Delineated,' p. 136.
(b) Maugham, Lit. Prop.

cation, and imprisonment, its decrees, without the least obstruction from Westminster Hall or the Parliament in any instance.

In 1556, by a decree of the Star Chamber, it was forbidden, among other things, to print contrary to any ordinance, prohibition, or commandment in any of the statutes or laws of the realm, or in any injunction, letters-patent, or ordinances set forth, or to be set forth by the queen's grant, commission, or authority.

By another decree, dated June 23rd, 1585, every book was required to be licensed, and all persons were prohibited from printing "any book, work, or copy against the form or meaning of any restraint contained in any statute or laws of this realm, or in any injunction made by her Majesty, or her Privy Council; or against the true intent and meaning of any letters-patent, commissions or prohibitions under the great seal, or contrary to any allowed ordinance set down for the good government of the Stationers' Company."

In 1623, a proclamation was issued to enforce this decree; reciting that it had been evaded, among other ways "by printing beyond sea such allowed books, works, or writings as have been imprinted within the realm, by such to whom the sole printing thereof by letters-patent or lawful ordinance or authority doth appertain."

In 1637, the Star Chamber again decreed that "no person is to print or import (printed abroad) any book or copy which the Company of Stationers, or any other person, hath or shall, by any letters-patent, order or entrance in their register book, or otherwise, have the right, privilege, authority, or allowance, solely to print" (a).

(a) 4 Burr. 2312. "It is natural to suppose," says Mr. Hallam (1 Const. History, 238), "that a government thus arbitrary and vigilant must have looked with extreme jealousy on the diffusion of free inquiry through the press. The trades of printing and bookselling, in fact, though not absolutely licensed, were always subject to a sort of peculiar superintendence. Besides protecting the copyright of authors, the council frequently issued proclamations to restrain the importation of books, or to regulate their sale. It was penal to utter, or so much as to possess, even the most learned works on the Catholic side; or, if some connivance was usual in favour of educated men, the utmost strictness was used in sup-

In 1640, however, the Star Chamber was abolished; the King's authority was set at nought; all the regulations of the press, and restraints previously imposed upon unlicensed printers by proclamations, decrees of the Star Chamber, and charter powers given to the Stationers' Company, were deemed and certainly were illegal. The licentiousness of libels induced Parliament to make an ordinance which prohibited printing unless the book was first licensed. The ordinance prohibited printing without the consent of the owner, or importing (if printed abroad), upon pain of forfeiting the same to the owner or owners of the *copies* of the said books, &c. This provision necessarily presupposed the property to exist; it would have been nugatory if there had been no admitted owner. An owner could not at that time have existed otherwise than by common law. In 1649 the Long Parliament made another ordinance; and in 1662 was passed

Marginal notes: Cap. I. On abolition of Star Chamber all restraints on printing deemed illegal. — The Licensing Act of Car. 2.

---

pressing that light infantry of literature—the smart and vigorous pamphlets with which the two parties arrayed against the Church assaulted her opposite flanks. Stow, the well-known chronicler of England, who lay under a suspicion of an attachment to popery, had his library searched by warrant, and his unlawful books taken away; several of which were but materials for his history. Whitgift, in this as in every other respect, aggravated the rigour of preceding times. At his instigation, the Star Chamber in 1585, published ordinances for the regulation of the press. The preface to these recites ' enormities, and abuses of disorderly persons professing the art of printing and selling books,' to have more and more increased, in spite of the ordinances made against them, which it attributes to the inadequacy of the penalties hitherto inflicted. Every printer, therefore, is enjoined to certify his presses to the Stationers' Company, on pain of having them defaced, and suffering a year's imprisonment. None to print at all, under similar penalties, except in London, and one in each of the two universities. No printer who has only set up his trade within six months to exercise it any longer, nor any to begin it in future until the excessive multitudes of printers be diminished and brought to such a number as the Archbishop of Canterbury and Bishop of London for the time being shall think convenient; but whenever any addition to the number of master printers shall be required, the Stationers' Company shall select proper persons to use that calling, with the approbation of the ecclesiastical commissioners. None to print any book, matter, or thing whatsoever, until it shall have been first seen, perused, and allowed by the Archbishop of Canterbury or Bishop of London, except the Queen's printers, who shall require the license only of the chief justices. Every one selling books printed contrary to the intent of this ordinance, to suffer three months' imprisonment. The Stationers' Company empowered to search houses and shops of printers and booksellers, and to seize all books printed in contravention of this ordinance, to destroy and deface the presses, and to arrest and bring before the council those who shall have offended therein."

the Licensing Act (13 & 14 Car. 2, c. 33), which interdicted the printing of any book unless first licensed and
entered in the registry of the Stationers' Company. It
ordered that no person should presume to print "any
heretical, seditious, schismatical or offensive books or
pamphlets, wherein any doctrine or opinion shall be asserted or maintained which is contrary to the Christian
faith, or the doctrine or discipline of the Church of England,
or which shall, or may tend or be to the scandal of religion
or the church, or the government or governors of the church,
state, or commonwealth, or of any corporation or particular person or persons whatever." It further prohibited
the publication of unlicensed books, prescribed regulations
as to printing, and empowered the King's messengers, and
the master and wardens of the Stationers' Company, to seize
books suspected of containing matters hostile to the Church
or Government. It was necessary to print in the beginning
of every licensed book the certificate of the licenser to
the effect that the books contained nothing "contrary to
the Christian faith, or the doctrine or discipline of the
Church of England, or against the state and government
of this realm, or contrary to good life or good manners, or
otherwise, as the nature and subject of the work shall
require." To prevent fraudulent changes in a book after
it had been licensed, a copy was required to be deposited
with the licenser when application was made for a license.

The Act further prohibited any person from printing or
importing without the consent of the owner, any book
which any person had the sole right to print by virtue of
letters-patent, or "by force or virtue of any entry or
entries thereof duly made or to be made, in the register
book of the said Company of Stationers, or in the register
book of either of the universities." The penalty of piracy
was forfeiture of the book and six shillings and eightpence
for each copy : half to go to the king, and half to the
owner."

The sole property of the owner is here acknowledged in
express terms as a common law right ; and the legislature

which passed that Act could never have entertained the most distant idea "that the productions of the brain were not a subject matter of property." To support an action on this statute ownership had to be proved or the plaintiff could not have recovered, because the action was to be brought by the owner, who was to have a moiety of the penalty. The various provisions of this Act effectually prevented piracies, without actions at law or bills in equity. But cases arose of disputed property. Some of them were between different patentees of the Crown; some, whether the property "belonged to the author, from his invention and labour, or the king, from the subject-matter."

The ordinance of 1643 prohibited the printing or importing of any book that had been lawfully licensed and entered in the register of the Stationers' Company, "for any particular member thereof, without the license and consent of the owner." The penalty prescribed was forfeiture of the book to the owner, "and such further punishment as shall be thought fit." This clause was repeated in the ordinances of 1647, 1649, and 1652.

It has been questioned whether these clauses were applicable to any than members of the Stationers' Company—in fact bylaws for the regulation of the members *inter se*, but it is doubtful whether any such restriction can be put upon their scope.

The Licensing Act of Car. 2 was continued by several Acts of Parliament, but expired May, 1679; soon after which there is a case in Lilly's 'Entries of Hilary Term,' 31 Car. 2, B. R. (*a*). In this case an action was brought for printing 4000 copies of the 'Pilgrim's Progress,' of which the plaintiff was the true proprietor, whereby he lost the profit and benefit of his copy. There is no account, however, of the case having been proceeded with.

In 1681, all legislative protection having ceased, the Ordinance of

---

· (*a*) *Ponder* v. *Bradyl*, Lilly's ' Entries,' 67 ; see Carter, 89 ; 4 Burr. 2317 ; Skinner, 234 ; 1 Mod. 257.

Stationers' Company adopted an ordinance or bylaw, which recited that several members of the company had *great part of their estates in copies*, that by ancient usage of the company, when any book or copy was duly entered in their register to any member, such person had always been reputed and taken to be the proprietor of such book or copy, and ought to have the sole printing thereof. The ordinance further recited that this privilege and interest had of late been often violated and abused; and it then provided a penalty against such violation by any member or members of the company, where the copy had been duly entered in their register. The true view of this ordinance would seem to be, that the members of the Stationers' Company, finding their estates in copies, which belonged to them by the common law, no longer under the protection of the Licensing Act (the repeal of which had incidentally withdrawn the protection that had always been inserted in it, though it had necessarily no connection with the system of licensing), undertook to provide for the failure of legislation, as far as they could, by an ordinance applicable of course to their own members only. The ordinance is not to be cited as any other proof of what the common law right was than that it shows, in connection with other historical proof, what it was then supposed to be. It was much the same as if an association of persons were to agree that any one of their number should pay a penalty for violating the acknowledged rights of property of any other person in the association, provided such rights were duly entered in their common records. It would not be an attempt to create the right, but it would justly be regarded as an acknowledgment of the existence of such a right (a).

A bylaw of
the Stationers'
Company in
1694.
In another bylaw, passed in 1694 (b), it was stated that copies were constantly bargained and sold amongst the members of the company as their property, and devised to

---

(a) Curtis on Copy, p. 38.
(b) In this year expired finally the Licensing Act of 13 & 14 Car. 2, which had been revived by 1 Jac. c. 7, and continued by 4 W. & M. c. 24.

their children and others for legacies and to their widows
for maintenance; and it was ordained, that if any member
should, without the consent of the member by whom the
entry was made, print or sell the same, he should forfeit
for every copy twelve-pence.

For many years successively attempts were made to
obtain a new Licensing Act. Such a bill once passed the
upper house, but the attempt miscarried upon constitutional objections to a licence. Proprietors of copyright had
so long been protected by summary measures, that they
regarded an action at law as an inadequate remedy. A
bill in equity was never even thought of: no hope of its
success appears at that time to have been entertained.

In one of the petitions presented to the House in support A petition
of applications to Parliament in 1709, for a bill to protect presented to
Parliament in
copyright, the last clause or paragraph was as follows: 1709 for pro-
"The liberty now set on foot of breaking through this tection of
copyright.
ancient and reasonable usage is no way to be effectually
restrained but by an Act of Parliament. For by common
law, a bookseller can recover no more costs than he can
prove damage; but it is impossible for him to prove the
tenth, nay, perhaps, the hundredth part of the damage he
suffers; because a thousand counterfeit copies may be dispersed into as many hands all over the kingdom, and he
not be able to prove the sale of them. Besides, the defendant is always a pauper, and so the plaintiff must lose
his costs of suit. (No man of substance has been known
to offend in this particular, nor will any ever appear in it.)
Therefore, the only remedy by the common law is to confine a beggar to the rules of the King's Bench or Fleet,
and there he will continue the evil practice with impunity. We therefore pray that confiscation of counterfeit copies be one of the penalties to be inflicted on
offenders" (a).

In response to these applications the Act 8 Anne, c. 19, The first
was passed. It recites that printers, booksellers, and other Copyright
Act, 8 Anne,
persons had of late frequently taken the liberty of printing, c. 19.

(a) 4 Burr. 2318.

reprinting, and publishing books and other writings without the consent of the authors or proprietors, to their very great detriment, and too often to the ruin of them and their families. For preventing, therefore, such practices for the future, and for the encouragement of learned men to compose and write useful books, it was enacted, that the authors of books already printed who had not transferred their rights, and the booksellers or other persons who had purchased or acquired the copy of any books in order to print or reprint the same, should have the sole right and liberty of printing them for a term of twenty-one years from the 10th of April, 1710, and no longer; and that authors of books not then printed, should have the sole right of printing for fourteen years and no longer. It also provided that any person who should publish, import, or sell piratical copies should forfeit such copies to the owner of the copyright, to be by him destroyed, and pay one penny for every sheet found in his possession. One half of this penalty was to go to the Queen and the remainder to any person who should sue for it. There was a proviso, however, which permitted the importation and sale of "any books in Greek, Latin, or any other foreign language, printed beyond the seas." That no person might offend against the Act through ignorance, it was provided that no book should be entitled to protection unless the title to the copy had been entered before publication in the register book of the Stationers' Company, which book should be kept open for inspection at any time without fee. The Act further required that nine copies of each book should be delivered to the warehouse-keeper of the said company for the use of the royal library in London, the Universities of Oxford and Cambridge, the four Universities in Scotland, Sion College in London, and the library of the Faculty of Advocates in Edinburgh, inflicting a penalty in default of such delivery, besides the value of the said printed copies, of the sum of £5 for every copy not so delivered (a). If any bookseller or

(a) The number was extended to eleven copies by 41 Geo. 3, c. 107,

printer should offer for sale a book at such a price or rate as should be conceived by any person to be too high or unreasonable, the price might be reduced and fixed at a reasonable figure by the Archbishop of Canterbury, the Chancellor or Lord Keeper of the Great Seal, the Bishop of London, the Chief Justices of the Queen's Bench and Common Pleas, or other designated officials (a).

The Act prohibited any one from importing a book which had been printed without the written consent of the owner of the copyright. And lastly it provided, that after the expiration of the said term of fourteen years the sole right of printing or disposing of copies should return to the authors thereof, if they were then living, for another term of fourteen years Thus by the Act of Anne two classes of books were protected, first, those already published, in which copyright was acknowledged for twenty-one years; second, those not then published, for which a term of fourteen years was secured, with a further term of fourteen years in the event of the author being then living.

The general question upon the common law right to old copies of works could not arise until the expiration of the full term conferred by the Act of Anne, that is, until twenty-one years from the 10th of April, 1710. Shortly after the expiration of this period, in 1735, in the case of *Eyre* v. *Walker* (b), Sir Joseph Jekyll granted an injunction to restrain the defendant from printing the 'Whole Duty of Man,' the first publication of which had been made in December, 1657; and this was acquiesced under.

The common law right to old copies.

Injunctions issued in support of this right.

In the same year, in the case of *Motte* v. *Falkner* (c), an injunction was granted for printing Pope's and Swift's 'Miscellanies.' Many of the pieces had been published in 1701, 1702, and 1703, and the counsel strongly pressed the objection as to these pieces. Lord Talbot, however,

---

s. 6; amended by 54 Geo. 3, c. 156, s. 2, and the number was limited to five by the 6 & 7 Will. 4, c. 110.

(a) This provision was repealed by the 12 Geo. 2, c. 36.

(b) Cited 4 Burr. 2325; 3 Swans. 673; 1 W. Bl. 331; see 2 Eden, 328.

(c) Cited in *Millar* v. *Taylor*, 4 Burr, 2325; *Tonson* v. *Walker*, 3 Swans. 672.

continued the injunction as to the whole, and it was acquiesced under.

In the following year, in the case of *Walthoe* v. *Walker*, an injunction was granted for printing Nelson's ' Festivals and Fasts,' though the bill set forth that the original work was printed in the lifetime of Robert Nelson, the author, and that he died in 1714. This also was acquiesced under.

In 1739 Lord Hardwicke granted a fourth injunction to restrain the defendant from printing Milton's ' Paradise Lost.' The plaintiffs derived their title under an assignment of the copy from the author in 1667. This injunction was also acquiesced under (a). In 1751 Milton's poem again came before Lord Hardwicke, in the form of an application for an injunction to restrain the defendants printing the same with the notes of Dr. Newton and other commentators, all of which belonged to the plaintiff. The bill, as in the former application, derived a title to the poem from the author's assignment in 1667, and a title to the life by Fenton, published in 1727, to Bentley's notes, published in 1732, and to Dr. Newton's notes, published in 1749. The defendants put in an answer, and set up notes of their own, of which it appeared there were twenty-eight, while the notes of the other commentators, belonging to the plaintiffs, and included in the defendants' edition, numbered 1500. Lord Hardwicke gave judgment in 1752, and held that the plaintiffs' notes were within the protection of the statute; and as to the poem, although he said that the general question had never been determined, and there was a doubt, yet he granted the injunction until the hearing (a).

Principle on which the injunctions were issued. All these injunctions were issued and acquiesced in under the presumption that at common law copyright was perpetual and that such common law right remained unaffected by the statute of Anne; had there been a reasonable doubt in the minds of the judges the injunc-

(a) *Tonson* v. *Walker*, 3 Swans. 672; 4 Burr. 2325, 2327, 2379, 2380; 1 W. Bl. 345; 2 Eden, 328; 1 Cox. 285.

tions would have been improper (a), for no reparation CAP. I.
could be afforded to the defendants for the damage sustained thereby, in the case of their being unimpeachable
in respect of the piracies complained of. Speaking of
these injunctions, Lord Mansfield said, "I look upon them
as equal to any final decree" (b).

The common law right was at length disputed and fully *The celebrated*
discussed in the celebrated case of *Millar* v. *Taylor* (c). *cases of Millar*
The work in controversy was Thomson's 'Seasons,' and the *v. Taylor*
copyright secured by the statute of Anne had expired. The *Donaldson v. Becket.*
action was brought in 1766, and was decided by the Court
of King's Bench 1769, judgment being given for the
plaintiff on the ground that the common law right to
copyright was unaffected by the statute of Anne. However, in a case (d) determined on the authority of the
last mentioned, the defendant appealed to the House of
Lords, on which occasion the following questions were
propounded to the judges:

> 1st. Whether, at common law, an author of any book
> or literary composition had the sole right of
> first printing and publishing the same for sale,
> and might bring an action against any person
> who printed, published, and sold the same
> without his consent?
>
> 2nd. If the author had such right originally, did the
> law take it away upon his printing and pub-
> lishing such book or literary composition? And
> might any person afterwards reprint and sell,

(a) *Hill* v. *The University of Oxford*, 1 Vern. 275; *Grierson* v. *Jackson*,
Ir. Term R. 304; *Univers. of Oxf. and Cam.* v. *Richardson*, 6 Ves. 689;
Bruce v. *Bruce*, cited 13 Ves. 505; *Harmer* v. *Plane*, 14 Ves. 130; *Hogg*
v. *Kirby*, 8 Ves. 224. And see Lord Erskine in *Gurney* v. *Longman*, 13
Ves. 505; *The Assignees of Robinson* v. *Wilkins*, cited 8 Ves. 224.

(b) *Millar* v. *Taylor*, 4 Burr. 2399.

(c) 4 Burr. 2303.

(d) *Donaldson* v. *Becket*, 4 Burr. 2408; 2 Bro. Parl. Cas. 129. Lord
Kenyon expressed a decided opinion that no such right existed: *Beckford*
v. *Hood*, 7 T. R. 620. Lord Ellenborough inclined to the same view:
Cambridge Univ. v. *Bryer*, 16 East, 317; and a majority of the judges in
Wheaton v. *Peters*, 8 Peters (Amer.) 591, arrived at the same conclusion.
See *Jefferys* v. *Boosey*, 4 H. L. C. 815.

for his own benefit, such book or literary composition, against the will of the author?

3rd. If such action would have lain at common law, is it taken away by the statute of 8th Anne? And is an author, by the said statute, precluded from every remedy except on the foundation of the said statute and on the terms and conditions prescribed thereby?

4th. Whether the author of any literary composition, and his assigns, had the sole right of printing and publishing the same in perpetuity by the common law?

5th. Whether this right · is in any way impeached, restrained, or taken away by the statute, 8th Anne.

Eleven judges delivered their opinions *seriatim;* ten to one for the affirmative on the first question; eight to three for the negative on the second question; six to five for the affirmative on the third question; seven to four for the affirmative on the fourth question; and six to five for the affirmative on the fifth question; so that it was declared that, although an author had by common law an exclusive right to print his works, and does not lose it by the mere act of publication, yet the statute of Anne had completely deprived him of the right. It was notorious that Lord Mansfield concurred with the ten upon the first question, with the eight upon the second, with the five upon the third, with the seven on the fourth, and with the five on the fifth; but it being very unusual (from reasons of delicacy) for a peer to support his own judgment upon an appeal to the House of Lords, he did not speak (a).

(a) In Scotland this question had been tried as early as 1748, and decided against the author's right: *Midwinter* v. *Hamilton*, June 7, 1748; Mor. Dict. of Dec. 19, 20, 8305. On appeal the case went off upon informality in the original summons: Feb. 11, 1751; 1 Cr. & St. 488. The same decision was pronounced in *Hinton* v. *Donaldson*, July 28, 1773, Mor. Dict. of Dec. 19, 20, 8307; 5 Brown's Sup. 508; and in *Cadell & Davies* v. *Robertson*, Dec. 18, 1804, Mor. Dict. of Dec., App., Lit. Prop. 5, as delivered in the House of Lords, July, 16, 1811 (5 Paton, 493), the

The more general opinion is certainly now against the common law right after publication. For though in the case of *Jefferys* v. *Boosey* (a), the decision of the question was not necessary to the point at issue, yet it being somewhat implicated, many of the judges pronounced their opinion with reference to the right. Of the ten common law judges who delivered their opinions, Erle, J, believed in the existence of the common law right; but Parke, B., Pollock, C.B., and Jervis, C.J., announced the contrary opinion; while Crompton, Williams, Wightman, Maule, Coleridge, and Alderson, expressed no opinion on the point. Lords Cranworth, Brougham, and St. Leonards were unanimous against the right, the last saying: "Upon the claim of common law right, I confess I never have, at least for many years, been able to entertain any doubt. It is a question which I have often, in my professional life, had occasion to consider, and upon which I have arrived, long since, at the conclusion, that no common law right exists after publication. I never could, in my own mind, distinguish between the right to an invention after the publication of that invention, and the right to the description of that invention after the publication of that description. If a mechanical genius should invent a machine of the greatest importance to mankind, it is admitted, nobody attempts to insist or to argue otherwise, and it has always been considered as settled, that after he has disposed of even a single copy of it, it may, so far as the common law is concerned, be copied and made use of without restriction by the purchaser, or by any person who properly obtains possession of it. Now, I do not see how you are to estimate differently different kinds of genius; or how you can say that a man who invents a machine of the greatest importance to the State, shall not have any right the moment he disposes of a single copy of that article,

---

author's right was held to depend entirely on the Act of Queen Anne: Bell's Com. See *Payne* v. *Anderson*, Mor. Dict. of Dec. vols. 19, 20, p. 8316; and *Cadell* v. *Anderson*, Mor. Dict. of Dec. 19, 20, 834, cited Philips on Copy, 43.

(a) 4 H. L. C. 815.

but that a man whose mind brings forth a certain collection of words, shall be entitled to an absolute property in it in all time, even after he has published it, and let the world at large have it. It appears to me, therefore, and always has so appeared, that there is no such common law right either in the one case or in the other; and I agree with my noble and learned friend who has last addressed your lordships, that the patent law is decidedly against the common law right in this particular instance, because it shows that the inventor had not the right. . . . Now, when we are talking of the right of an author, we must distinguish (as has been already very accurately done) between the mere right to his manuscript, and to any copy which he may choose to make of it, as his property, just like any other personal chattel, and the right to multiply copies to the exclusion of every other person. Nothing can be more distinct than these two things. The common law does give a man who has composed a work, a right to that composition, just as he has a right to any other part of his personal property; but the question of the right of excluding all the world from copying, and of himself claiming the exclusive right of for ever copying his own composition, after he has published it to the world, is a totally different thing."

Notwithstanding the admission that the general current of opinion is against the common law right, there can be no doubt that until 1774 when the case of *Donaldson* v. *Becket* was decided, the universal opinion was the other way, and it has the support of some of the ablest judges who ever adorned the bench.

The point came before the court in a subsequent case (a) in which Dr. Reade claimed damages for the infringement of his novel, "It is Never too Late to Mend." Mr. Justice Williams in delivering the judgment of the court, said: "The main reliance of the plaintiff was placed on the general ground that even if his statutable right had not been infringed, yet that as an author, he

(a) *Reade* v. *Conquest*, 9 C. B. N. S. 768; 9 W. R. 434.

had a copyright at common law, concurrently with, but
more extensive than, his right under that statute, and that
such common law right had been invaded by the act of
the defendant.

" Now, it is not necessary, in order to decide the present
case, to consider the question upon which so much learning has been exhausted; viz. whether anterior to the
statute of Anne there existed a copyright at common law
in published books, more extensive in its nature and duration than the right conferred or expressed by that statute.
There can, we think, be no doubt that the weight of
authority in the time of Lord Mansfield was in favour of
the existence of such a right, although the doctrine has
found less favour in modern times; but the continued
existence of any such right, after the passing of the
statute of Anne, was distinctly denied by the majority of
the judges in *Donaldson* v. *Becket* (a), and the case itself
expressly decides that no such right exists after the expiration of the period prescribed by the Act.

" The question therefore seems to us narrowed to this,
viz. whether the statute of Anne having expressly put an
end to such a right if it ever existed after the period it
prescribes, has yet preserved it during the currency of
such period. That it has done so is a proposition which
we think it difficult for the plaintiff to maintain. That a
common law right of action attaches upon the invasion of
the copyright created by statute, was decided in the case
of *Beckford* v. *Hood* (b), and followed in several other cases,
but we are not aware of any case since *Millar* v. *Taylor* (c)
was overruled by the House of Lords, which decides and
recognises that an author of a published work has any
other than the statutable copyright therein.

" In the case of *Murray* v. *Elliston* (d), (before the 3 & 4
Will. 4, c. 15) Lord Byron's tragedy of ' Marino Faliero,'
the copyright of which belonged to the plaintiff, had been

(a) 4 Burr. 2408 ; 2 Bro. P. C. 129.
(b) 7 T. R. 620.
(c) 4 Burr. 2303.
(d) 5 Barn. & Ald. 657.

D

abridged by curtailing the dialogues and soliloquies, and publicly represented in that form by the defendant at Drury Lane Theatre for profit, the advertisements describing it as Lord Byron's tragedy. A bill for an injunction having been filed, a case was sent for the opinion of the Court of Queen's Bench, whether the plaintiff could maintain an action against the defendant under the circumstances. The argument for the plaintiff there was put upon the same ground as in the present case, but the court certified that no action would lie, a decision which appears in point against the plaintiff upon this record.

"That much might be urged in favour of the common law right if the question were *res integra* cannot be doubted by any one who has read the learned judgments of the majority of the court in *Millar* v. *Taylor*, and (on the part of my brother Keating and myself, I must be allowed to add) of Mr. Justice Erle in the case of *Jeffreys* v. *Boosey* (a). But it was the opinion of a large majority of the judges and law lords in that case, that the time was passed when the question was open to discussion, and that it must now be considered to be settled, that copyright in a published work only exists by statute.

"The learned counsel for the plaintiff in his argument cited a case of *Turner* v. *Robinson* (b), in which it was supposed that the Master of the Rolls in Ireland had taken a view favourable to the plaintiff's claim in the present case. Upon looking to the report, however, it will be found that the opinion of that learned judge is directly opposed to such a claim. In that case the plaintiff had applied for an injunction to prevent the defendant from pirating an original picture of 'The Death of Chatterton,' of which the plaintiff was proprietor, by means of stereoscopic apparatus. The Master of the Rolls being of opinion upon the facts that there had been no publication of the picture, and that the imitation was a piracy, granted the injunction, but his opinion upon the

(a) 4 H. of Lords Cas. 876.
(b) 10 Ir. Ch. Rep. 121 ; on appeal 510.

point involved in the claim of the plaintiff upon this record was thus expressed:—'It is not necessary,' said that learned judge, 'to go through the authorities collected in the cases to which I have referred (a), as I apprehend it is clear that by the common law copyright or protection exists in favour of works of literary art or science to this limited extent only, that while they remain unpublished no person can pirate them, but that after publication they are by common law unprotected. There has been much difference of opinion on the subject among the judges in England, but the law is now considered to be as I have stated it.' The opinion of the Master of the Rolls in Ireland, may therefore be added to the weight of authority in this country in favour of the position, that copyright or protection to the works of literature after they have been published, exists only by statute."

The universities, alarmed at the consequence of the decision in *Donaldson* v. *Becket*, applied for and obtained an Act of Parliament (15 Geo. 3, c. 53) establishing in perpetuity their right to all the copies given or bequeathed them theretofore or which might thereafter be given to or acquired by them (b). *The universities obtain an Act for the protection of their copyrights.*

The period for which copyright was capable of existing was somewhat varied by the 54 Geo. 3, c. 156, s. 4, which enacted that instead of enduring for fourteen years, and contingently for fourteen more, authors should have the sole liberty of printing and reprinting their works for the term of twenty-eight years, to commence from the day of the first publication of the same; and further, if the author should be living at the expiration of that period, for the residue of his natural life (c).

All these Acts have been repealed by an Act of Parliament of the present reign—the 5 & 6 Vict. c. 45, on which the law of literary copyright now depends. To *The present Literary Copyright Act, 1842.*

(a) *Prince Albert* v. *Strange*, 1 McN. & Gor. 25; 1 Hall & Twells 1; *Jefferys* v. *Boosey*, 4 H. of Lords Cas. 815.
(b) *Vide post.*
(c) An author whose works had been published more than twenty-eight years before the passing of this statute was held not to be entitled to the copyright for life: *Brooke* v. *Clarke*, 1 B. & Ald. 396.

Mr. Serjeant Talfourd is due the honour of obtaining this piece of legislative justice. From 1837 to 1842 he used his best endeavours and expended his most eloquent strains to accomplish its passing. In contending for an extension of the period during which protection was afforded to literary works, he bursts forth:—"There is something peculiarly unjust in bounding the term of an author's property by his natural life, if he should survive so short a period as twenty-eight years. It denies to age and experience the probable reward it permits to youth— to youth, sufficiently full of hope and joys to slight its promises. It gives a bounty to haste, and informs the laborious student, who would wear away his strength to complete some work which 'the world will not willingly let die,' that the more of his life he devotes to its perfection, the more limited shall be his interest in its fruits. It stops the progress of remuneration at the moment it is most needed; and when the benignity of nature would extract from her last calamity a means of support and comfort to the survivors—at the moment when his name is invested with the solemn interest of the grave—when his eccentricities or frailties excite a smile or a shrug no longer—when the last seal is set upon his earthly course, and his works assume their place among the classics of his country—your law declares that his works shall become your property, and you requite him by seizing the patrimony of his children."

CHAPTER II.

WHAT MAY BE THE SUBJECT OF COPYRIGHT.

THERE can be no copyright in an intellectual creation The subject of however defined in the author's mind, unless embodied in copyright. written or spoken language, then only can it possess the attributes of property.

The copyright is not in the form of words which are expressive of the intellectual creation, but in the intellectual conception which is so expressed.

In order to acquire a copyright in a work it is necessary Work must be that it should be original. If any part of the composition original. is copied or adopted by the writer from a prior-existing work, of course the title fails *quoad hoc*, as the writer cannot have been the author of what he has borrowed from another. "It is difficult," says Mr. Curtis (a), "to lay down any legal definition of originality in a literary composition that may be resorted to as a universal test. Many intellectual productions present no more difficulty upon the question of their originality than some inventions, or discoveries. The poems of the great masters in every language, and a vast body of other writings, however freely their authors may have used the thoughts of others, are at once seen to be just as original in a legal as they are in a critical sense. But in every species of composition, in all literatures, there is of necessity a constant reproduction of what is old, mixed with more or less that is new, peculiar, and original. There are also large classes of works the materials of which are common to all

(a) ' Copyright,' chap. 5.

Cap. II. writers, existing in nature, art, science, philosophy, history,
statistics, &c., where there must be considerable resemblances, however independently of each other the different
authors may have written.   Over this vast field it is
impossible to erect an unvarying general rule, which can
be fitted to all cases and capable of determining whether a
particular work exhibits the degree of originality necessary
to a valid copyright.   The laws which protect literary
property are designed for every species of composition,
from the great productions of genius that are to delight
and instruct mankind for ages, to the humble compilation
that is to teach children the art of numbers for a few
years and then to disappear for ever.

"Hence these laws must be so administered that every
literary labourer shall find in them an adequate protection
to whatever he can show to be the product of his own
labour.   Something he must show to have been produced
by himself; whether it be a purely original thought or
principle unpublished before, or a new combination of old
thoughts, and ideas, and sentiments, or a new application
or use of known and common materials, or a collection,
the result of his industry and skill.   In whatever way he
claims the exclusive privilege accorded by these laws, he
must show something which the law can fix upon as the
product of his, and not another's, labour.   But in order
that the law should do this ample justice, in the great
variety of claimants, it is necessary that its rules should
be capable of adaptation to the objects of their labours.
They must include in their range everything that can be
justly claimed as the peculiar product of individual efforts;
otherwise they would exclude from the benefit of literary
property objects which are as clearly the product of individual labour as the most original thoughts ever written,
namely, new and important combinations and arrangements or collections of materials known and common to
all mankind."

Copyright   The law does not require that the subject of a book
may exist in a should be new, but that the method of treating should

have some degree of originality about it (*a*). Copyright may be claimed by an author of a book who has taken existing materials, from sources common to all writers, and arranged and combined them in a new form, and given them an application unknown before. For in making the selection, arrangement, and combination, he has exercised skill and discretion, and in producing thereby something that is new and useful he is entitled to the exclusive enjoyment of his production.

Books made and composed in this manner are therefore the proper subjects of copyright; and the author of such a book has as much right in his plan, arrangement, and combination of the materials collected and presented, as he has in his thoughts, sentiments, reflections and opinions, or in the modes in which they are therein expressed and illustrated; but he cannot prevent others from using the old material employed in such combination for a different purpose (*b*).

In the case of 'Gray's Poems,' which had been for many years published and were afterwards collected by a Mr. Mason, and reprinted with the addition of several new poems, the Lord Chancellor granted an injunction against a defendant who had copied the whole, though the plaintiff had but a copyright in the additions (*c*).

But where the plaintiff had published a book of roads of Great Britain, comprising Patterson's book, to the copyright of which the plaintiff was not entitled, with improvements and additions obtained by actual survey and otherwise, the court refused an injunction to restrain a publication of an edition of Patterson comprising the plaintiff's improvements and additions. The Lord Chan-

Marginal notes: Cap. II. new arrangement or in novel additions. 'Gray's Poems.' 'Patterson's Road Book.'

(*a*) *Cary* v. *Longman*, 1 East, 358; *Sayre* v. *Moore, ibid.* 361; *Tonson* v. *Walker*, 3 Swans. 672; *Tonson* v. *Collins*, 1 W. Bl. 321; *Cary* v. *Faden.* 5 Ves. 24; *Motte* v. *Falkner*, cited 1 W. Bl. 331; *King* v. *Reed*, 8 Ves. 223, n.; *Hogg* v. *Kirby*, 8 Ves. 215; *Longman* v. *Winchester*, 16 Ves. 269; *Lewis* v. *Fullarton*, 2 Beav. 6; *Leader* v. *Purday*, 7 C. B. 4; *Barfield* v. *Nicholson*, 2 Sim. & Stu. 1; *Jarrold* v. *Houlston*, 3 K. & J. 708; *Emerson* v. *Davies*, 3 Story (Amer.) 768; *Atwill* v. *Ferrett*, 2 Blatch. (Amer.) 46; *Bartlett* v. *Crittenden*, 5 McLean (Amer.) 32. As to musical compositions see *Reed* v. *Carusi*, 8 Law Rep. O.S. (Amer.) 411.

(*b*) Clifford, J., *Lawrence* v. *Dana* 2 Am. L. T. R. (N.S.) 423.

(*c*) *Mason* v. *Murray*, cited 1 East, 360.

cellor asked what right had the plaintiff to the original work, and said that if he were to do strict justice he should order the defendants to take out of their book all they had taken from the plaintiff, and, reciprocally, the plaintiff to take out of his all he had taken from Patterson (a).

Accounts of natural curiosities, &c.   If a person compiles an account of natural curiosities or of works of art, or of mere matters of statistical or geographical information, his own description may be the subject of copyright (b). It is equally competent, however, for any person to compile and publish a similar work; but it must be made substantially new and original, like the first work, by resort to the original sources, and must not be simply a copy or adaptation from the other, under the impression that the subject is common (c).

(a) Cary v. Faden, 5 Ves. 24.
(b) In like manner, the Court of Cassation, in France, decided that a compilation may be the subject of copyright, under the law of July 19, 1793. The book was a devotional work, consisting of extracts from the devotional writings of eminent churchmen, arranged in a particular manner, with reference to the festivals of the Church. The correctional tribunal at Lyons decided that the law of July 19, 1793, extended the privileges of authorship only to those who can strictly be called authors—to those who could claim the first conception of a work of literature or art—and not to one who had only copied from the works of others. They held that the compiler of this book, had only copied passages from the works of others, with slight verbal alterations and additions, and that neither these nor the plan and arrangement of the book gave it the character of a new work, because the greater part of it, which was copied, and was therefore publici juris, drew to itself the lesser part, which was really new, and attached to it the same condition of publicity. From this decree the proprietor appealed to the Court of Cassation: and M. Merlin, arguing against the decree, contended that the law applied not merely to works the fruit of the conceptions of genius, but also to the productions of intelligence; and that the decree confounded a compilation which is the fruit of taste, intelligence, and exquisite and ingenious combination and arrangement, with a compilation which implied nothing but an expenditure of time and research, and an indefatigable patience in copying word for word. He maintained that under this decree the Pandects of Pothier would be no subject of property, but would be open to the first occupant. The court held that the law extends to selections, compilations, and other works of that nature, when they require in their execution, discernment, taste, learning, and intelligent labour; when, in short, instead of being simply copies from one or more other books, they are at the same time the pro-duct of conceptions foreign and of conceptions peculiar to the author, in the union of which the matter receives a new form and a new character. The work in question possessed these characteristics, and the decree of the court of first instance was therefore annulled: Merlin, Rep. de Jurisp. tit. Contrefaçon, tom 3, pp. 701, 708, cited Curtis on Copyright, p. 184.
(c) Bogg v. Kirby, 8 Ves. 215; Hotten v. Arthur, 1 H. & M. 603; 32 L. J. (Ch.) 771; 11 W. R. 934; 9 L. T. (N.S.) 199; and in a Scotch case it was

If a man makes an actual survey of certain roads, and depicts such roads on a map, though his map might, and probably would, correspond with many which had previously been published, it would be hard to say that it was not a new work. In such a case it is not a question of the mind, like the 'Essay on the Human Understanding;' it lies *in medio*; every man with eyes can trace it, and the whole merit depends upon the accuracy of the observation; every description will therefore be in a great measure original (*a*). If this be so, every edition will be a new work if it differs as much from the last edition as it does from the last precedent work; either all are original works or none of them. It is an extremely difficult thing to establish identity in a map or a mere list of distances; but there may be originality in casting an index, or pointing out a ready method of finding a place in a map (*b*).

The composing receipts or arranging them in a book   Receipt books. will give a copyright to the compiler; but the mere collecting them and handing them over to a publisher will not (*c*); nor will the mere copying that which is public property, for there is nothing in such case to represent authorship on the part of the editor. However, if there be some new arrangement or classification of the subject, or the copy be at all varied, then a copyright may exist in it (*d*), provided the variation be not merely colourable (*e*).

Thus, where the defendant had used four charts pub-   Similitude between maps.

---

held that the directors of the Customs Annuity and Benevolent Fund have a copyright or right of property in the publication· 'The Clyde Bill of Entry and Shipping List,' entitling them to protection against piracy: *Walford* v. *Johnston*, 3rd June, 1846; 20 Sess. Cass. 1160. See *Maclean* v. *Moody*, 23 June, 1858, 20 Sess. Cas. 1154.

(*a*) See Lord Jeffrey's observations in *Alexander* v. *Mackenzie*, 9 Sess. Cass. (N.S.) 758; *Blunt* v. *Patten*, 2 Paine (Amer.) 393.

(*b*) *Carnan* v. *Bowles*, 2 Bro. C. C. 80; *Taylor* v. *Bayne*, Mor. Dict. of Dec. in Ct. Sess. vols. 19, 20, 8308; *ibid.* App. pt. 1, 7; *Alexander* v. *Mackenzie, supra.*

(*c*) *Rundal* v. *Murray*, Jac. 314, *per* Lord Eldon; *Matthewson* v. *Stockdale*, 12 Ves. 270.

(*d*) *Newton* v. *Cowrie*, 4 Bing. 234.

(*e*) *Matthewson* v. *Stockdale, supra*; *Barfield* v. *Nicholson*, 2 Sim. & Stu. 1.

CAP. II.

lished by the plaintiff in making one large map, but there were very important differences between them, much in favour of the defendant's, and the evidence showed the plaintiff's charts to be founded on a wrong principle, Lord Mansfield left it to the jury to say whether the alteration was colourable or not. "There must be such a similitude," said he, "as to make it probable and reasonable to suppose that one is a transcript of the other, and nothing more than a transcript. So in the case of different prints; no doubt different men may take engravings from the same picture. The same principle holds with regard to charts; whoever has it in his intention to publish a chart may take advantage of all prior publications." "You are told, that there are various and very material alterations—the chart of the plaintiff is upon a wrong principle, inapplicable to navigation—the defendant, therefore, has been correcting errors, and not servilely copying. If you think so, you will find for the defendant; if you think it is a mere servile imitation, and pirated from the other, you will find for the plaintiff" (a). And in *Matthewson* v. *Stockdale* (b) Lord Eldon said, "I admit that no man can monopolize such subjects as the English Channel, the Island of St. Domingo, or the events of the world; and every man may take what is useful from the original work, improve, add, and give to the public the whole, comprising the original work, with the additions and improvements" (c).

Component parts of a compilation not protected apart from the arrangement.

Protection is not given to the component parts of a compilation independently of their arrangement and combination. Of the component parts the compiler is not the author, and he could not acquire an exclusive right to that which is common to all, neither can the arrangement or combination apart from the materials arranged or combined be the subject of protection (d). The copyright vests in

(a) *Sayre* v. *Moore*, 1 East, 361, n.
(b) 12 Ves. 275; *Wilkins* v. *Aikins*, 17 Ves. 422.
(c) And see Sir L. Shadwell in *Martin* v. *Wright*, 6 Sim. 298. This case can scarcely be reconciled with subsequent decisions, see *Mawman* v. *Tegg.* 4 Russ. 385, and Mr. Justice Story in *Emerson* v. *Davies*, 2 Story, 768, 797.
(d) Thus a subsequent writer cannot be held to have infringed a book

the materials as arranged and combined, not in the form CAP. II. or the substance apart the one from the other, but in the union of the two.

It follows from what has been said above, that a person Mathematical tables. may have copyright in mathematical tables *actually calculated by himself,* although on a fresh calculation the same tables would result from the same *data* and the same principles, and although they may have previously been published before his appeared (*a*).

Selections of poems or prose compositions, and collections Selections of poems, &c. of proverbs, maxims, quotations, hymns, &c., may be the subjects of copyright.

The copyright of private letters forming literary com- Copyright in private letters. positions is in the composer, and not in the receiver, who has only a special property in them; " possibly the property of the paper may belong to him, but this does not give a licence to any person whatever to publish them to the world, for at most the receiver has but a joint property with the writer " (*b*). The right of the writer of the letter to prevent its publication is not founded on considerations of policy or social ethics, but on the principle of property. "The question will be," said Lord Eldon, " whether the bill has stated facts of which the court can take notice as a case of civil property which it is bound to protect. The injunction cannot be maintained on any principle of this sort, that if a letter has been written in the way of friendship, either the continuance or the discontinuance of that friendship affords a reason for the

---

where he has not borrowed any of the materials of which his book is composed, but has simply adopted the same arrangement.

(*a*) *Bailey* v. *Taylor*, 3 L. J. 66 ; 1 Russ. & My. 73.

(*b*) *Per* Lord Hardwicke, *Pope* v. *Carl*, 2 Atk. 342 ; *Perceval* v. *Phipps*, 2 V. & B. 19 ; *Forrester* v. *Walker*, 4 Burr. 2331 ; *Webb* v. *Rose, ibid.* 2330 ; *Macklin* v. *Richardson*, Amb. 694 ; *Duke of Queensbury* v. *Shebbeare*, 2 Eden, 329 ; *Millar* v. *Taylor*, 4 Burr. 2303 ; *Donaldson* v. *Becket*, 2 Bro. P. C. 129 ; *Oliver* v. *Oliver*, 11 C. B. (N. S.) 139 ; *Cadell* v. *Stewart*, Mor. Dict. of Dec. vols. 19, 20, App., Lit. Prop. 13 ; *Palin* v. *Gathercole*, 1 Coll. 565 ; *Folsom* v. *Marsh*, 2 Story (Amer.) 100 ; *Boosey* v. *Jeffreys*, 6 Exch. 583, *per* Lord Campbell. See *Hopkinson* v. *Lord Burghley*, L. R. 2 Ch. 447. If the solicitor of a company writes a letter apparently on behalf of the company, he is not entitled to prevent its publication, although he swears it was written in his private capacity : *Howard* v. *Gunn*, 32 Beav. 462.

interference of the court (a)." If a letter by any means gets back into the hands of the sender the receiver is entitled to recover it from him by action. In *Oliver* v. *Oliver* the facts were as follows. The plaintiff and defendant were brothers. The letters for the recovery of which the action was brought, related to family affairs. They were written and sent by the defendant to the plaintiff,—had been given back by the plaintiff to the defendant, and proof was given of a demand and refusal to restore them. There was contradictory evidence as to whether the letters had been given by the plaintiff to the defendant to be kept by him as his own property, or whether they had been merely handed to the defendant as custodian, to be re-delivered to the plaintiff on request. The learned judge told the jury that the receiver of a letter had such a property in the paper as to entitle him to maintain an action against the sender, if, by any means, it got back into his hands; and that it was for them to say whether the letters in question had been given to the defendant that he might retain them as his own property, in which case the defendant would be entitled to their verdict, or whether they were merely deposited with him to take care of them for the plaintiff, in which case the latter would be entitled to the verdict. Erle, C.J., in refusing a rule for a new trial, upheld this direction, and said: "In the case of letters, the paper at least becomes the property of the persons receiving them. Of course it is necessary to distinguish between the property in the paper and the copyright. The former is in the receiver, the latter is in the writer" (b).

The letters of Pope (c), Swift, and others, and the letters of Lord Chesterfield (d), were prevented from a surreptitious and unauthorized publication by injunction, on the ground of copyright in their authors. Lord Hardwicke, in *Pope's Case*, thought it would be extremely

(a) *Gee* v. *Pritchard*, 2 Swans. 413.
(b) See *Howard* v. *Gunn*, 32 Beav. 462 ; 2 N. R. 256.
(c) 2 Atk. 342.
(d) *Thompson* v. *Stanhope*, Amb. 737.

mischievous to draw a distinction between a book of letters, which came out into the world either by the permission of the writer or the receiver of them, and any other learned work. The same objection would, he thought, hold good against sermons which the author may never have intended to be published, but have been obtained from loose papers and brought out after his death.

In the case of the *Earl of Granard* v. *Dunkin* (a) the executors of Lady Tyrawley obtained an injunction in the first instance against the defendant publishing letters to Lady Tyrawley from different correspondents, and which he had got possession of by being permitted to reside in her house, and continuing to do so after her death. In 1804 the Court of Session in Scotland interdicted, at the instance of the children, the publication of the manuscript letters of the poet Burns (b).

In the case of *Perceval* v. *Phipps*, though the Vice- Chancellor, Sir Thomas Plumer, held that private letters having the character of literary compositions were within the spirit of the Act protecting literary property, and that by sending a letter the writer did not give the receiver the right to publish it, yet the court would not interfere to restrain the publication of *commercial* or *friendly letters*, except under circumstances (c); "for," said he, " though the form of familiar letters might not prevent their approaching the character of literary works, every private letter, upon any subject, to any person, is not to be described as a literary work, to be protected upon the principle of copyright. The ordinary use of correspondence by letters is to carry on the intercourse of life between persons at a distance from each other in the prosecution of commercial or other business, which it would be very

Distinction between commercial or friendly letters and literary compositions.

(a) 1 Ball & Beattie, 207.
(b) *Cadell & Davies* v. *Stewart*, cited 1 Bell's Com. 116, n., cited 2 Kent's Com. 381.
(c) 2 V. & B. 19; see *Wetmore* v. *Scoville*, 3 Edw. Ch. (Amer.) 515; *Hoyt* v. *Mackenzie*, 3 Barb. Ch. (Amer.) 320; but see *Woolsey* v. *Judd*, 4 Duer (N. York) 379; and *Eyre* v. *Higbie*, 35 Barb. (N. York) 502.

extraordinary to describe as a literary work in which the writers have a copyright (a).

Non nostrum est tantas componere lites; yet this distinction appears to us to have but little foundation, and seems to have existed merely in the imagination of Sir Thomas Plumer. It is true that a court of equity cannot interfere to prevent the publication of private letters simply on the ground that such a publication, without the consent of the writer, as a breach of confidence, and social duty, is injurious to the interests of society; but solely on the ground that the writer has an exclusive property which remains in him, even where the letters have been transmitted to the person to whom they were addressed. A court of equity is not the general guardian of the morals of society. It has not an unlimited authority to enforce the performance or prevent the violation of every moral duty. It would be extravagant to say that it may restrain by an injunction the perpetration of every act which it may judge to be corrupt in its motives or demoralising or dangerous in its tendency. An injunction can never be granted unless it is apparent to the court that the personal legal rights of the party who seeks its aid are in danger of violation, and, as a general rule, that the injury to result to him from such violation, if not prevented, will be irreparable.

The sole foundation is the right which every man has to the exclusive possession and control of the product of his own labour. Why should a writing of inferior composition be precluded from being a subject of property (b)?

(a) " Another class is the correspondence between friends or relations, upon their private concerns ; and it is not necessary here to determine how far such letters falling into the hands of executors, assignees of bankrupts, &c., could be made public in a way that must frequently be very injurious to the feelings of individuals. I do not mean to say that would afford a ground for a Court of Equity to interpose to prevent a breach of that sort of confidence independent of contract and property." *Perceval* v. *Phipps,* 2 V. & B. 19.

(b) School books for teaching children are entitled to protection. See *Lennie* v. *Pillans,* 5 Sess. Cas. 2nd series, 416; *Constable & Co.* v. *Brewster,* 3 S. 215 (N. E. 152). So are abstracts and indices of title to land, so long as the compiler retains the ownership of the unpublished manuscript: *Banker* v. *Caldwell,* 3 Min. (Amer.) 94.

To establish a rule that the quality of a composition must be weighed previous to investing it with the title of property, would be forming a very dangerous precedent. What reason can be assigned why the illiterate and badly spelt letters of an uneducated person should not be as much the subject of property as the elegant and learned epistles of a well-known author? The essence of the existence of the property is the labour used in the concoction of the composition, and the reduction of ideas into a tangible and substantial form; and can it be contended that the labour is less in the former than the latter case? Every letter is, in the general and proper acceptation of the term, a literary composition. It is that, and nothing else; and it is so, however defective it may be in sense, grammar, or orthography. Every writing in which words are so arranged as to convey the thoughts of the writer to the mind of the reader is a literary composition; and the definition applies just as certainly to a trivial letter as to an elaborate treatise or a finished poem. Literary compositions differ widely in their merits and value, but not at all in the facts from which they derive their common sense (a).

Printing and publishing cannot make a book "literary" which was not so in manuscript; and consequently, the author of a book (for the same doctrine would apply to a book as to a private letter) which may be of a private nature, and not considered as "a literary composition," ought to be excluded from the benefit of the Acts conferring copyright. But surely it is not contended that the copyright of an author should be liable to impeachment and frustration by reason of an inquiry into the merits or value of his work as published.

The exclusive right which alone a court of equity is bound to protect, and which, from its nature can only be protected by an injunction, is the author's right of property in the words, thoughts, and sentiments which, in their connection, form the written composition—which his

The author's right of property alone protected by the Court.

(a) 2 Story's Rep., cited *Woolsey* v. *Judd*, 4 Duer (N. York) 379.

manuscript embodies and preserves. This composition—whether, as such, it has any value or not, is immaterial—is his work, the product of his own labour, of his hand, and his mind; and it is this fact which gives him the right to say that, without his consent, it shall not be published, and makes it the duty of a court of equity to protect him in the assertion of that right by a permanent injunction. Of this it is a conclusive proof that the right to control the publication of a manuscript remains in the author and his representatives, even when the material property has, with his own consent, been vested in another. The gift of the manuscript, it is settled, unless by an express agreement, carries with it no licence to publish (a).

Lord Eldon intimates in *Gee* v. *Pritchard* (b) that he does not understand the Vice-Chancellor, in the case of *Perceval* v. *Phipps*, as denying the property of the writer in the letters, but that he appears to have inferred, from the particular circumstances of that case, that the plaintiff had authorized, and for that reason could not complain of, the publication. " I will not say," he adds, " that there may not be a case of exception, but if there is, the exception must be established on examination of the letters; and I think that it will be extremely difficult to say where that distinction is to be found between private letters of one nature and private letters of another nature."

Mr. Justice Story strongly asserts the propriety of the jurisdiction by injunction for the purpose of restraining the publication of private letters. He thinks the doctrine but sound and just. that a court of equity ought to interfere where a letter, from its very nature, as in the case of matters of business, or friendship, or advice, or family or private confidence, imports the implied or necessary intention and duty of privacy and secrecy ; or where the publi-

(a) *Duke of Queensbury* v. *Shebbeare*, 2 Eden, 329 ; *Thompson* v. *Stanhope*, Amb. 737.
(b) 2 Swans. 418, 426, 427. See *Brandreth* v. *Lance*, 8 Paige's R. (Amer.) 24, 26.

cation would be a violation of *trust* or *confidence* founded Cap. II. in contract, or implied from circumstances (*a*). Cicero has with great force thus spoken of the grossness of such offences against common decency: " *Quis enim unquam, qui paulum modo bonorum consuetudinem nosset, literas, ad se ab amico missas, offensione aliquâ interpositâ, in medium protulit, palamque recitavit? Quid est aliud tollere e vitâ vitæ societatem, tollere amicorum colloquia absentium? Quam multa joca solent esse in epistolis, quæ, prolata si sint, inepta videantur! Quam multa seria, neque tamen ullo modo divulganda!*" (*b*)

With these natural feelings on the breach of epistolary Principles on which the determina-tions of the Court of Session have proceeded. confidence the determinations of the Court of Session in Scotland have accorded (*c*); but it must be borne in mind that that court is held to have jurisdiction by interdict to protect, not property only, but reputa-tion from injury, and private feelings from outrage and invasion (*d*).

Courts of equity will, notwithstanding what we have Ground on which a court of equity will frequently interfere. already intimated, sometimes interfere to stay the publi-cation of letters, on the ground that the publication is a *breach of contract* or *confidence;* and *à fortiori,* when they are intended to be made a source of *profit;* for then it is not a mere breach of confidence or contract, but it is a violation of the exclusive copyright of the writer.

Thus, upon the principle of *breach of contract,* an injunc-tion was granted to prevent the publication of letters written by an old lady to a young man, to whom she had been foolishly attached, there being an agreement not to

(*a*) Story's Com. on Eq. Jur. ss. 947–949.
(*b*) Cic. *Orat. Philipp.* ij. c. 4. See Sir S. Romilly, 2 Swans. 419.
(*c*) So it was held in *Dodsley* v. *M'Farquhar,* Feb. 27, 1775, relative to the publication of Lord Chesterfield's Letters: Mor. Dict. of Dec., Lit. Prop., App. 1, 5; Br. Sup. 509; and again more solemnly in *Cadell and Davies* v. *Stewart,* June 1, 1804, Mor. Dict. of Dec., Lit. Prop., App. 4. *Ibid.* But see, 5 Pat. 493. Here letters written by Burns to a lady whom he distinguished by the name of *Clarinda,* had been by her given to Stewart, a bookseller, who published them. The family of Burns, as interested in his literary reputation, were found entitled to an interdict: Bell's Com.
(*d*) Bell's Com. b. 2, pt. 2, c. 4.

E

CAP. II.   publish the letters, but to deliver them up for a valuable
consideration (a).

Were the court to interfere on any other principle
than that already stated, individuals would be deprived
of their defence in proving agency, orders for goods, the
truth of an assertion, or some other fact, merely because
the testimony establishing the true and genuine circumstances was contained in letters in which a pretended
copyright was claimed (b).

Instances in
which the
publication of
private letters
has been
permitted.

Accordingly an injunction obtained on account of agency
and confidence was dissolved by the court when the answer
denied confidence, and avowed that the defendant's object in publishing them in a newspaper, of which he was
the proprietor, was not to obtain profit, but to *vindicate
his own character* from the imputation of having published false intelligence publicly cast on him by the
plaintiff; for defective and injurious indeed would be the
effect of a law permitting not the publication or production of business letters when necessary for one's own
defence (c).

Not permis-
sible for the
purpose of
representing
that to be true
which has
been admitted
to be false.

The receiver of a letter, however, will not be permitted
to publish it for the purpose of representing to the public
as true that which he has, in legal proceedings upon that
very question, admitted to be false.   The case of *Palin* v.
Gathercole (d) elucidated this point.   The circumstances
of that case were these : Palin, the plaintiff, had written
to Gathercole, the defendant, who was the editor of a
newspaper, certain letters containing information respecting one Noakes, and Gathercole from these letters drew
up an article which he published in his newspaper.   Noakes
brought an action against him for libel, and he compro-
mised the action, paying Noakes' costs, and apologizing.

(a) *Anon.* v. *Eaton*, cited 2 V. & B. 27 ; *Perceval* v. *Phipps*, 2 V. & B. 27 ;
Earl of Granard v. *Dunkin*, 1 Ball. & B. 247 ; Story's Eq. Jur. vol. 2,
ss. 944–950 ; *Denis* v. *Laclerc*, 1 Martin (Amer.), 297 ; *Woolsey* v. *Judd*,
4 Duer. (N. York) 379 ; *Eyre* v. *Higbie*, 35 Barb. (N. York) 502.
(b) See Godson on Copy. p. 330.
(c) *Folsom* v. *Marsh*, 2 Story (Amer.) 100 ; see *Howard* v. *Gunn*, 32
Beav. 462.
(d) 1 Coll. 565.

Gathercole then claimed of Palin half the costs that he, Gathercole, had so incurred, and Palin refusing to pay them, Gathercole published in his newspaper a statement that the libel upon Noakes was communicated to him, Gathercole, by Palin. Palin thereupon brought an action against Gathercole; and Gathercole pleaded that the matter, however libellous as between Noakes and Gathercole, was matter of which, as between Palin and Gathercole, Palin was the author; but before trial Gathercole submitted to what was, in effect, a general verdict, establishing in substance, as Vice-Chancellor Knight Bruce expressed it in his judgment, that the libel published by Gathercole on Noakes was not a libel which Palin had communicated to Gathercole. Gathercole then proceeded to shew Palin's letters to third persons, upon which Palin filed his bill for an injunction to restrain Gathercole from publishing or showing the letters, and obtained an *ex parte* injunction. The use which Gathercole desired to make of the letters was, it will be observed, to establish the fact that Palin was the author of the libel upon Noakes, the very fact which he had, by submitting to the general verdict in Palin's action, admitted not to exist. Under those circumstances, the court refused to dissolve the injunction, permitting, however, the defendant to exhibit the letters to his solicitors and counsel in the cause.

Communications received from correspondents by editors or proprietors of periodical publications (if sent impliedly or expressly for the purpose of publication) become the property of the person to whom they are directed, and cannot be published by any other person obtaining possession of them (*a*). The editor or proprietor, however, of any such periodical may not publish them if, previous to publication, the writer expresses his desire to withdraw them (*b*); but though the editor may not publish them

Communications sent to editors of periodicals.

(*a*) 8 Ves. 215.
(*b*) *Davis* v. *Miller*, July 28, 1855; 17 Dec. of Ct. of Sess. 2nd Series, 1166. See 1 Jur. (N.S.) pt. 2, 523.

he is not bound to preserve them for the benefit of the writers, but may destroy them.

To make any public use of the production is to publish it. Hence a letter may be published not only by printing it, but also by reading it in public, or by circulating copies of it, though such copies be in manuscript. Any such public use of the letter, without the consent of the writer, is a violation of his rights. But the receiver may, if he wish, destroy the letter as soon as received, and there is nothing to prevent him giving them to another, or reading them to others, or lending them to others to be read, provided such reading or lending does not amount to a publication.

Letters written by one person employed by another, and relating to the business affairs of the latter, will rightly be considered as the property of the employer who pays the writer for his services. Thus it has been held that the letters which an officer of an insurance company had written in the discharge of his official duties became the property of the company (a). "If the solicitor of an assurance company, established in London," said the Master of the Rolls in the case cited; "by the direction of the directors, wrote a letter to one of the shareholders in the country, it is clear that such letter is not the property of the solicitor, and that he cannot say that the company have not a right to publish it. Take it a step further, and assume that the solicitor wrote a letter, but not by the direction or on behalf of the directors, though it had all the appearance of being written on their behalf, and by their direction. Thus, if it were written to a person who proposed to take shares in the company, and it related to the affairs of the company, and contained authoritative information on behalf of the company in answer to an application for shares, and the person who receives it treats it as such, and sends back to the company, objecting to its contents, shall the solicitor be allowed to complain of its publication, and to insist that it is a private letter, though

(a) *Howard* v. *Gunn*, 32 Beav. 462.

it appears to be written on behalf of the directors? The answer is, if that be so, it ought not to have been written. It has all the appearance of having been written by the plaintiff on their behalf, and Jamieson [the person to whom it was written] so treats it, for he writes to the manager in answer to it. Can the plaintiff be allowed to say that the company have no right to publish it? and if they have, is not the defendant entitled, as regards the plaintiff, to bring it forward? It is obvious that this was not a private letter, and was not intended to be a private letter."

The government has, moreover, a right to publish or to withhold all letters addressed to the public offices (a). This exception in favour of the government is not supposed to make such communications common property, to be published by any person who may see fit, without the sanction of the government, nor to take away the property of the writers or their representatives. "In respect to official letters addressed to government," observed Mr. Justice Story in *Folsom* v. *Marsh* (b), "or any of its departments, by public officers, so far as the right of the government extends from principles of public policy to withhold them from publication, or to give them publicity, there may be a just ground of distinction. It may be doubtful whether any public officer is at liberty to publish them, at least in the same age, when secrecy may be required by the public exigencies, without the sanction of the government. On the other hand, from the nature of the public service, or the character of the documents, embracing historical, military, or diplomatic information, it may be the right, and even the duty, of the government, to give them publicity, even against the will of the writers. But this is an exception in favour of the government, and stands upon principles allied to, or nearly similar to the right of private individuals, to whom letters are addressed by their agents, to use them, and publish

Power of government to publish or withhold letters.

(a) Curtis on Copy. 98.
(b) 2 Story (Amer.) 100.

them, upon fit and justifiable occasions. But assuming the right of the government to publish such official letters and papers, under its own sanction, and for public purposes, I am not prepared to admit that any private persons have a right to publish the same letters and papers without the sanction of the government for their own private profit and advantage. Recently the Duke of Wellington's despatches have, I believe, been published by an able editor, with the consent of the noble duke and under the sanction of the government. It would be a strange thing to say, that a compilation involving so much expense and so much labour to the editor in collecting and arranging the materials, might be pirated and republished by another bookseller, perhaps to the ruin of the original publisher and editor. Before my mind arrives at such a conclusion, I must have clear and positive lights to guide my judgment, or to bind me in point of authority."

Copyright in lectures.

Copyright may be had in lectures. Lectures are generally more or less literary productions—frequently the result of much thought and research. They are continually being published in the form of books and pamphlets—such publications being in many cases of great value, and it would be unjust and impolitic to deprive lecturers or other persons of the power of securing an exclusive right to their addresses, scarcely less so than to deprive authors generally of copyright in their productions. If a lecture has been reduced wholly or partially into writing, the author has a right of property in it; but when a court of equity is called upon to restrain the publication of such a lecture, the writing must be produced, that the court may compare the original composition with the piracy.

The admission of persons to hear such a lecture affords no presumption that the speaker intends to give them a right to publish the information they may acquire. When the lecture is orally delivered it is difficult to say that an injunction can be granted upon the same principle as that upon which an injunction is issued in the case of a literary composition; because the court must be satisfied that the publication complained of is an invasion of the written work, and this can only be done by comparing the composition with the piracy. It does not, however, follow that because the information communicated by the lecturer is not committed to writing, but orally delivered, it is therefore within the power of the person who hears it to publish it (a). On the contrary, Lord Eldon, in *Abernethy* v. *Hutchinson*, observed that he was clearly of opinion that, whatever else might be done with it, the lecture could not be published for profit. When persons are admitted as pupils or otherwise to listen to lectures orally delivered, although they may go to the extent, if desirous and capable, of taking down the whole by means of shorthand, yet they can do that only for the purpose of their own information; they may not publish.

The right of property in lectures, whether written or oral, has now been confirmed by statute. The Lecture-Copyright Act is the 5 & 6 Will. 4, c. 65. It provides that, from and after the 1st of September, 1835, the author of any lecture, or the person to whom he has sold or otherwise conveyed the copy in order to deliver the same in any school, seminary, institution, or other place, or for any other purpose, shall have the sole right and liberty of printing and publishing such lecture; and that if any person shall, by taking down the same in shorthand, or otherwise in writing, or in any other way, obtain or make a copy of such lecture, and shall print or lithograph or otherwise copy and publish the same, or cause the same to be printed, lithographed, or otherwise copied and published, without leave of the author thereof, or of the person to whom the author has sold or otherwise conveyed the same, and every person who knowing the same to have been printed or copied and published without such consent, shall sell, publish, or expose to sale, or cause to be sold, published, or exposed to sale, any such lecture, shall forfeit such printed or otherwise copied lecture or

(a) *Per* Lord Eldon, in *Abernethy* v. *Hutchinson*, 3 L. J. (Ch.) 209.

parts thereof, together with one penny for every sheet thereof which shall be found in his custody, either printed, lithographed, or copied, or printing, lithographing, or copying, published, or exposed to sale, contrary to the true intent and meaning of the Act, the one moiety thereof to His Majesty, his heirs or successors, and the other moiety thereof to any person who shall sue for the same. The 2nd section provides that any printer or publisher of any newspaper who shall without such leave as aforesaid print and publish in such newspaper any lecture shall be deemed to be a person printing and publishing without leave within the provisions of the Act, and liable to the aforesaid forfeitures and penalties in respect of such printing and publishing. The 3rd section declares that no person, allowed for a certain fee and reward or otherwise to attend and be present at any lecture delivered at any place, shall be deemed and taken to be licensed, or to have leave to print, copy, and publish such lecture on account merely of having permission to attend the delivery.

Lectures not within the meaning of the Act. Lectures published by authority, since the publication of which the period of copyright therein given by 8 Anne, c. 19, and 54 Geo. 3, c. 156, has expired, and lectures printed and published before September, 1835, are excluded from the protection afforded by the above Act; likewise lectures of the delivery of which notice in writing shall not have been given two days previously to two justices living within five miles of the place of delivery (a); and those delivered in any university, or public school, or college, or on any public foundation, or by any individual in virtue of or according to any gift, endowment, or foundation.

In consequence of these provisions few lectures are protected by this Act, for seldom is the requisite notice given. And, under this latter clause, it would appear

(a) The notice must be given every time such lecture is delivered, and therefore the omission in any one instance to give the requisite notice would render any person at liberty to obtain a copy, which the lecturer would be unable to prevent his publishing.

that sermons delivered by clergymen of the Established Church, in endowed places of public worship, are deemed public property.

It is questionable whether copyright applies under this Act to lectures merely orally delivered even when reduced previously into writing; but with regard to speeches properly so called, or speeches not reduced into writing, there can be no doubt (a).

There is nothing in this statute to prevent any person from delivering in public an unpublished lecture without the consent of the author, it only prohibits the printing, copying, publishing, and exposing for sale, though the delivery would seem to be an infringement of the author's common law rights in the manuscript (b).

In France, the *cour royale* of Paris had before it in 1828 the interesting question whether, when a course of oral lectures is merely the reproduction of a work previously published by the professor, a person who publishes the lectures from notes taken by a stenographer, can be made responsible for a piracy to the publisher of the work thus reproduced, the decision of the question was given in the affirmative (c).

The alterations in the law suggested by the recent report of the Royal Commissioners on Copyright are set forth in the 84th and three following paragraphs. *Alterations suggested by Copyright Commissioners.*

They are of opinion that the author's copyright should extend to prevent re-delivery of a lecture without leave as well as publication by printing, though this prohibition as to re-delivery they consider should not extend to

---

(a) See ' Edinburgh Review,' October, 1854.

(b) In an American case, *Keene* v. *Kimball,* 16 Gray (82 Mass.) 551. Hoar, J., said: " The student who attends a medical lecture may have a perfect right to remember as much as he can, and afterwards to use the information thus acquired in his own medical practice, or to communicate it to students or classes of his own, without involving the right to commit the lecture to writing, for the purpose of subsequent publication in print or by oral delivery. So any one of the audience at a concert or opera may play a tune which his ears have enabled him to catch, or sing a song which he may carry away in his memory, for his own entertainment or that of others, for compensation or gratuitously, while he would have no right to copy or publish the musical composition."

(c) See Renouard, tom. 2, p. 146, cited Curtis on Copy. 103.

lectures which have been printed and published. They also recommended that the term of copyright in lectures should be the same as in books, namely, the life of the author and thirty years after his death.

"In the course of our inquiry," they report, "it has been remarked that, in the case of popular lectures, it is the practice of newspaper proprietors to send reporters to take notes of the lectures for publication in their newspapers, and that, unless this practice is protected, it will become unlawful. It does not seem to us desirable that this practice should be prevented, but on the other hand the author's copyright should not in any way be prejudiced by his lectures being reported in a newspaper. The author should have some sort of control, so as to prevent such publication if he wishes to do so; and we, therefore, suggest that though the author should have the sole right of publication, he should be presumed to give permission to newspaper proprietors to take notes and report his lecture, unless, before or at the time when the lecture is delivered, he gives notice that he prohibits reporting.

" By the present law, a condition is imposed of giving notice to two justices. Without entering into the origin of this provision we find that it is little known, and probably never or very seldom acted upon; so that the statutory copyright is practically never or seldom acquired. We therefore suggest that this provision should be omitted from any future law.

" We do not suggest any interference with the exception made in the Act as to lectures delivered in universities and elsewhere, wherein no statutory copyright can be acquired."

The commissioners also thought that in case of piracy either by publication or re-delivery without the author's consent, there should be penalties recoverable by summary process, and that the author should be capable of recovering damages by action in case of serious injury, and of obtaining an injunction to prevent printed publication or re-delivery. If the piracy were committed by printed publication they were of opinion that the author should also have power to seize copies (a).

Copyright may likewise exist in a genuine and just abridgment, for it is said that an abridgment may with great propriety be called a new book (b).

Copyright in abridgments.

To constitute a true and equitable abridgment the entire work must be preserved in its precise import and exact meaning, and then the act of abridgment is an exertion of the understanding, employed in moulding and transfusing a large work into a small compass, thus rendering it less expensive, and more convenient both to the time and use of the reader. Independent labour must be apparent, and the reduction of the size of a work by copying some of its parts and omitting others, confers no title to authorship; and the result will not be an abridgment entitled to protection. To shorten a work by leaving out the unimportant parts is not to abridge it in a legal sense. To abridge in the legal sense of the word is to preserve the substance, the essence of the work, in language suited to such a purpose; language substantially different from that of the original. To make such an abridgment requires the exercise of the mind; labour, skill, and judgment are brought into play, and the result is not merely copying.

What constitutes an abridgment.

In the case known as *Newbery's* (c), Lord Chancellor Apsley, having spent some hours in consultation with Mr. Justice Blackstone, decided that an abridgment, where the understanding is employed in retrenching unnecessary and uninteresting circumstances which rather deaden the narration, is not an act of plagiarism upon the original work, nor against any property of the author in it, but an allowable and meritorious work. It requires both invention and judgment, and displays frequently a deal

(a) Para. 181.
(b) *Bell* v. *Walker*, 1 Bro. C. C. 451. An abstract also was held no piracy: *Dodsley* v. *Kinnersley*, Amb. 403; 4 Esp. 168; 1 Camp. 94.
(c) Lofft. 775; *Dodsley* v. *Kinnersley, supra; Butterworth* v. *Robinson*, 5 Ves. 709.

of learning. Lord Hardwicke thus states the rule (a):—
"Where books are colourably shortened only, they are
undoubtedly within the meaning of the Act of Parliament,
and are a mere evasion of the statute, and cannot be called
an abridgment. But this must not be carried so far as to
restrain persons from making a real and fair abridgment;
for abridgments may, with great propriety, be called a new
book, because not only the paper and print, but the invention, learning, and judgment of the author is shewn
in them, and in many cases are extremely useful (b),
though in some instances, prejudicial, by mistaking and
curtailing the sense of an author."

On these considerations the Master of the Rolls refused
an injunction to restrain the publication of an abridgment
of Dr. Johnson's 'Rasselas,' it appearing that not one-
tenth part of the first volume had been abstracted, and
that the injury alleged to be sustained by the author arose
from the abridgment containing the narrative of the tale,
and not the moral reflections (c).

Considerations in discriminating a bonâ fide abridgment from a piracy.
The question in such a case must be compounded of
various ingredients: whether it be a *bonâ fide* abridgment,
or only an evasion by the omission of some important
parts, whether it will in its present form prejudice or
supersede the original work, whether it will be adapted
to the same class of readers, and many other considerations
of the same sort, which may enter as elements, in ascertaining whether there has been a piracy or not. Although
the doctrine is often laid down in the books, that an
abridgment is not piracy of the original copyright, yet
this proposition must be received with many qualifications.

Impropriety of the rule respecting abridgments.
The rule appears very unreasonable, and has been the
subject of much criticism by late writers. Why should an
abridgment, tending to injure the reputation, and to lessen
the profits of the author, not be considered an invasion

(a) *Gyles* v. *Wilcox*, 2 Atk. 141. See also the case of *Read* v. *Hodges*, referred to in *Tonson* v. *Walker*, 3 Swans. 672, *per* Lord Eldon; *Bell* v. *Walker*,
1 Bro. C. C. 451; *Tinsley* v. *Lacy*, 11 W. R. 877; 1 H. & M. 747.
(b) See *Hodges* v. *Walsh*, 2 Ir. Eq. Rep. 266.
(c) Amb. 403.

of his property? (a). In many cases the question may naturally turn upon the point, not so much of the quantity as of the value of the selected materials. As was significantly said on one occasion: *Non numerantur; ponderantur.* The quintessence of a work may be practically extracted so as to leave a mere *caput mortuum*, by a selection of all the important passages in a comparatively moderate space.

In a late case (b), the Vice-Chancellor, Sir W. P. Wood, considered that the court had gone far enough in the sanction it had given to abridgments, and that it was difficult to acquiesce in the reason sometimes given, that a compiler of an abridgment is a benefactor to mankind, by assisting in the diffusion of knowledge.

In the case of *Bramwell* v. *Halcomb* (c) it was held that the question whether one author has made a piratical use of another's work does not necessarily depend upon the quantity of that work which he has quoted, or introduced into his own book. On that occasion Lord Cottenham said, " When it comes to a question of quantity, it must be very vague. One writer might take all the vital part of another's book, though it might be but a small proportion of the book in quantity. It is not only quantity, but value, which is looked at. It is useless to look to any particular case about quantity."

Quantum but little criterion of piracy.

The general principle is, that the proper object of the copyright is the *peculiar expression of the author's ideas,* meaning by this, the structure of the work, the sequence of his remarks, and, above all, his language; and that this peculiarity is always distinguishable, as, by a law of nature, every human production is stamped with the idiosyncrasy of the author's mind. If these views be correct, it follows that any abridgment of the work, in the original author's language, is an infringement of his right; and

(a) Lord Campbell's ' Lives of the Chancellors,' vol. 5, chap. 131.
(b) *Tinsley* v. *Lacy,* 1 H. & M. 747, 754.
(c) 3 My. & Cr. 737; *Bell* v. *Whitehead,* 3 Jur. 68 ; *Sweet* v. *Shaw,* 3 Jur. 217; *Saunders* v. *Smith,* 3 My. & Cr. 711, 728 ; *Wheaton* v. *Peters,* 8 Peters. (Amer.) 591 ; *Gray* v. *Russell,* 1 Story (Amer.) 11 ; *Mawman* v. *Tegg,* 2 Russ. 385 ; *Butterworth* v. *Robinson,* 5 Ves. 709.

CAP. II.   indeed any quotation will be, *pro tanto*, a violation, unless
excused on the ground of its inconsiderable extent, or on
the presumed assent of the author, which, in works of
criticism, might be justly implied (a).

Copyright in
digests.

Copyright may also be had in a digest. A digest, or a
compilation differs from an abridgment. A digest or a
compilation consists of selected extracts from different
authors; an abridgment is a condensation of the views of
the author. The former cannot be extended so as to convey the same knowledge as the original work ; the latter
contains an epitome of the work abridged, and consequently conveys substantially the same knowledge. The
former cannot adopt the arrangement of the works cited;
the latter must adopt the arrangement of the work abridged
to be a faithful abridgment. The former infringes the
copyright if the matter transcribed when published im-
pairs the value of the original book, while a fair abridgment, though it may injure the original, is, as we have
seen, lawful.

Head-notes of
reports.

The digest of a report, usually included in and known
as the head-note, is a species of property which will receive protection. " The head-note, or the side or marginal
note of a report," said Mr. Justice Crowder, in *Sweet* v.

(a) 2 Kent's Com. 382, note; Curtis on Copy. 252. On the subject of
abridgments the Royal Commissioners on Copyright in their recent report
say : " Questions frequently arise, with regard to literary works, as to what
is a fair use of the works of other authors in the compilation of books. In
the majority of cases these are questions that can only be decided, when
they arise, by the proper legal tribunals, and no principle which we can
lay down, or which could be defined by the legislature, could govern all
cases that occur. There is one form of user of the works of others, however, to which we wish specially to draw attention as being capable of some
legislative control in a direction we think desirable. We refer to abridgments.

" At present an abridgment may or may not be an infringement of copyright, according to the use made of the original work and the extent to
which the latter is merely copied into the abridgment; but even though
an abridgment may be so framed as to escape being a piracy, still it is
capable of doing great harm to the author of the original work by interfering with his market ; and it is the more likely to interfere with that
market and injure the sale of the original work if, as is frequently the case,
it bears in its title the name of the original author.

" We think this should be prevented, and upon the whole we recommend,
that no abridgments of copyright works should be allowed during the
term of copyright, without the consent of the owner of the copyright." Par.
67-69.

Benning (a), "is a thing upon which much skill and exercise of thought is required, to express in clear and concise language the principles of law to be deduced from the decision to which it is prefixed, or the facts and circumstances which bring the case in hand within the same principle or rule of law or of practice." It may indeed be considered, perhaps, as in itself a species of brief and condensed report, the reporter furnishing in each case two reports, in one of which he gives the facts, the arguments, and the judgment at length; and in the other, an abstract of the decision, conveying the principle upon which it is founded and the pith and substance of the case. But whether thus regarded, or viewed in the manner adopted by Mr. Justice Maule, in the above cited case, namely, in the nature of an independent deduction from the report, and a succinct statement of the legal principles involved, or of the doctrine of law established by the decision, there is a sufficient exertion of mental power in the formation to render it substantially a subject of copyright.

The right of selecting passages from books of reports (including entire judgments) in treatises upon particular subjects is not disputed. Had it been otherwise decided, the greater part of our law libraries would be much thinned and attenuated, and we should be deprived of many valuable works; for a considerable portion consists of mere transcripts from books of report (b). *Selections from reports and judgments.*

What would become of the elaborate commentaries of modern scholars upon the classics, which, for the most part, consist of selections from the works and criticisms of various former authors, arranged in a new form, and combined together by new illustrations? What would become of the modern treatises upon astronomy, mathematics, natural philosophy and chemistry? What would

(a) 16 C. B. 491; 1 Jur. (N.S.) 543. *Vide D'Almaine* v. *Boosey,* 1 Y. & C. 288, 301; 4 L. J. (N.S.) Ch. 21; but there Lord Lyndhurst referred to digests such as Viner's 'Abridgment' and Comyns' 'Digest.'
(b) See *Butterworth* v. *Robinson,* 5 Ves. 709; Evans' 'Statutes,' 2nd ed. vol. 2, p. 25.

become of the treatises in our own profession, the materials of which, if the work be of any real value, must essentially depend upon faithful abstracts from the reports, and from juridical treatises, with illustrations of their bearing. 'Blackstone's Commentaries' is but a compilation of the Laws of England drawn from authentic sources, open to the whole profession; and yet it was never deemed that it was not a work which, in the highest sense, might be considered an original work, since never before were the same materials so admirably combined and exquisitely wrought out, with a judgment, skill and taste absolutely unrivalled (a).

Copyright in forms or precedents.
In a Scotch case the validity of the complainant's copyright in a collection of legal forms or "styles" was questioned, on the ground that in preparing them he had simply followed the directions prescribed by the statute; and that under the circumstances the forms prepared by two or more persons must be substantially the same. The Court held that if the statute had contained the forms themselves and the complainant had simply copied them, his copyright would have failed through want of originality. But, as the statute gave simply directions, it was an act of authorship to prepare the forms pursuant to such directions (b). Lord Fullerton in the case referred to observed: "It is said that owing to the particular nature of the styles they cannot be the subject of copyright, because they are drawn up precisely after the form prescribed in the statute, and because any styles relating to the same subjects as those given by the complainer must, if the directions of the statutes and phraseology of conveyancers were used, be expressed in the same manner exactly as those proposed by the complainer. Now it may be quite true that if the statute had supplied certain forms by which the operations intended to be thereby regulated were to be done, if the statute had contained, as such statutes sometimes do, an

(a) Story, J., in *Gray* v. *Russell*, 1 Story (Amer.) 17.
(b) *Alexander* v. *Mackenzie*, 9 Sc. Sess. Cas. 2nd Ser. 748.

appendix exhibiting certain schedules of forms which it Cap. II. was only necessary for any one to copy in order to avail himself of the provisions of the Act, then I hold that the reprinting of such forms in a separate publication would not give him a copyright in these forms. But the case here is different, for the statute only gives very general directions and descriptions of the styles that are to be used. The schedules are very general in their terms, and it is no doubt of great practical importance to suit these general directions to each case falling under the statute as it may arise. The preparing and adjusting of such writings require much care and exertion of mind. As to invention, that is a different thing : it does not require the exercise of original or creative genius, but it requires industry and knowledge."

The question has been raised whether there can be copyright in a work not claiming originality in the doctrines contained therein (a). And this argument was put forth in the case of *Jarrold* v. *Houlston* (b) respecting Dr. Brewer's ' Guide to Science,' in which work the author does not profess to have made any discovery in science, or to do more than to provide for the young and other persons who have not been in the habit of making observations for themselves, information by which some of the ordinary phenomena of common life may be explained to them on scientific principles, and that they may themselves be led to observe and to reflect upon those wonderful laws of nature, by which the most ordinary phenomena are governed. And it was determined that, if any one by pains and labour collects and reduces into the form of a systematic course of instruction those questions which he may find ordinary persons asking in reference to the common phenomena of life, with answers to those ques- *As to whether copyright may exist in a work not claiming originality in the doctrines contained therein.*

(a) As to the amount of originality required in a musical composition in America, see *Jollie* v. *Jaques*, 1 Blatch. (Amer.) 626. It has been there held that a good title to copyright is acquired by representing on a map boundaries of townships which are fixed by statute : *Farmer* v. *Calvert Lithographic Engraving and Map Publishing Co.*, 5 Am. L. T. R. 168.

(b) 3 K. &. J. 708 ; 3 Jur. (N.S.) 1051.

tions, and explanations of those phenomena, whether such explanations and answers are furnished by his own re-collection of his former general reading, or out of works consulted by him for the express purpose, the reduction of the questions so collected, with such answers, under certain heads and in a scientific form, is amply sufficient to constitute an original work of which the copyright will be protected.

No copyright in that which has no present existence. Copyright can only exist in respect of some already published or some composed and not yet published literary production. Therefore there can be no copyright in the prospective series of a newspaper. Copyright may attach upon each successive publication; but that which has no present existence as a composition cannot be the subject of this species of property (a).

The mere declaration of the intention to publish any articles bearing a particular name or mark, even though made public by registration at Stationers' Hall, cannot create a right to the exclusive use of such name or mark. So in the cases of *Maxwell* v. *Hogg*, and *Hogg* v. *Maxwell*. Messrs. Hogg, in 1863, registered an intended new maga-zine to be called 'Belgravia.' In 1866, such magazine not having appeared, Mr. Maxwell, in ignorance of what Messrs. Hogg had done, projected a magazine with the same name, and incurred considerable expense in pre-paring it, and extensively advertising it in August and September as about to appear in October. Messrs. Hogg knowing of this, made hasty preparations for bringing out their own magazine before that of Mr. Maxwell could appear, and in the meantime accepted an order from Mr. Maxwell for advertising his (Mr. Maxwell's) magazine on the covers of their own publications, and the first day on which they informed Mr. Maxwell that they objected to his publishing a magazine under that name was the 25th of September, on which day the first number of Messrs. Hogg's magazine appeared. Mr. Maxwell's magazine appeared in October. Under these circum-

(a) *Platt* v. *Walter*, 17 L. T. (N.S.) 157.

stances, on a bill filed by Mr. Maxwell, it was held, that CAP. II. Mr. Maxwell's advertisements and expenditure did not give him any exclusive right to the use of the name 'Belgravia,' and that he could not restrain Messrs. Hogg from publishing a magazine under the same name, the first number of which appeared before Mr. Maxwell had published his; and on a bill filed by Messrs. Hogg, that the registration by them of the title of an intended publication could not confer upon them a copyright in that name, and that, in the circumstances of the case, they had not acquired any right to restrain Mr. Maxwell from using the name as being Messrs. Hogg's trade-mark (a).

In *Maxwell* v. *Hogg*, Lord Cairns seemed to think that there could not be what is termed copyright in a single word, although the word were used as a fitting title for a book. He considered that the copyright contemplated by the Act must be not in a single word, but in some words in the shape of a volume or part of a volume, which is communicated to the public, by which the public are benefited, and in return for which a certain protection is given to the author of the work (b). But his lordship was dealing with a case in which the defendant had nothing but the name, publication not having been effected.

The title of a periodical or newspaper was held under Copyright in the former statutes to be a proper subject of copyright, a title. as characterising the particular publication (c); that it cannot therefore be assumed by another with impunity although a similar title distinguishable may be assumed (d). Even if innocently assumed, and unconsciously made use

---

(a) *Maxwell* v. *Hogg*; *Hogg* v. *Maxwell*, 15 L. T. 204; 15 W. R. 84, 464; 36 L. J. (Ch.) 433; Law Rep. 2 Ch. Ap. 307, 12 Jur. (N.S.) 916.

(b) See *Maxwell* v. *Hogg*, L. R. 2 Ch. 307.

(c) *Hogg* v. *Kirby*, 8 Ves. 215; *Keene* v. *Harris*, cited 17 Ves. 338; *Constable & Co.* v. *Brewster*, 3 Sess. Cas. 215 (N. E. 152). *Prowett* v. *Mortimer*, 2 Jur. (N.S.) 414; *Ingram* v. *Stiff*, 5 Jur. (N.S.) 947; see *Bradbury* v. *Dickens*, 27 Beav. 53; *Correspondent Newspaper Co.* v. *Saunders*, 11 Jur. (N.S.) 540; 13 W. R. 804; *Kelly* v. *Hutton*, L. R. 3 Ch. Ap. 703; *Clowes* v. *Hogg*, W. N. (1870) 268; and see *Bradbury* v. *Beeton*, W. N. (1869) 221; 18 W. R. 33.

(d) 8 Ves. 222. Where assumed for the purpose of deceiving the public, see *Bell* v. *Locke*, 8 Paige R. (Amer.) 75; and see *Cruttwell* v. *Lye*, 17 Ves. 335.

of, to the injury of another, the owner is entitled to protection (a). On the point nothing is said in the Copyright Act, 1842, unless the words " sheet of letterpress " or " part of a volume," be held to include a title; yet there is, at least, nothing to sanction any alteration of the grounds upon which the former judgments stood (b).

The titles to books, newspapers, and periodicals, though often coming before the courts on the question of copyright therein, seem not to be in themselves the proper subjects of this right. A title is no doubt, in one sense, a part of the work itself, for one cannot read a book or turn over the title page without finding that the title is at the commencement of the work and sometimes on every page, yet it is rather the index to the whole than part thereof —and certainly when registered before the publication, or perhaps even before the creation of the work whereof it is intended to be the title, could hardly be deemed to be part of the same; and if it were, then as copyright could not subsist in that which has no actual existence, the right to the title would fail on this ground, except it could be argued that the title being part of the work, and the only part in existence, could be registered as having an intrinsic value of its own.

However intimately connected with the copyright in the work to which it is prefixed, the title is more properly a trade-mark (c). It is not protected on the ground of any intrinsic merit or value possessed by itself, but, like other trade-marks, is protected for the purpose of insuring the genuineness of the article to which it is attached.

There can be no doubt that there is in a title a right

(a) *Clement* v. *Maddick*, 1 Giff. (Ch.) 98 : 5 Jur. (N.S.) 592.
(b) Bell's Com. 6th ed. 549.
(c) Lord Cottenham in *Spottiswoode* v. *Clarke*, 2 Ph. 154, seems to have thought that the title-page of an almanack was quite a different thing from a trade-mark, but his reasoning is not convincing, and hardly capable of being sustained in view of subsequent decisions. And in *Mack* v. *Petter*, L R. 14 Eq. 431, 20 W. R. 964, Lord Romilly used the word " copyright " as applied to the title of a book; " but it is impossible," says V.-C. Bacon in *Kelly* v. *Byles*, 40 L. T. (N.S.) 633, "to read his judgment and to doubt that the injunction he granted was to restrain the defendant's colourable imitation of the actual book which the plaintiff had first sent into the world."

capable of protection, and in the case of ' Bell's Life ' this Cᴀᴘ. II.
right was asserted by Vice-Chancellor Stuart to be a right
of property (a).

The registered proprietors of 'Bell's Life in London Titles in-
and Sporting Chronicle,' published weekly, at the price fringed.
of 5d., filed a bill against the proprietors and publishers
of a new newspaper, called 'The Penny Bell's Life and
Sporting News,' which was published at the price of a
penny. The evidence produced shewed that from the
similarity of the two names mistakes had occurred, and
were likely to occur, on the part of the public, and that
inquiries had been made at the office of ' Bell's Life
in London,' for ' The Penny Bell's Life.' On motion on
behalf of the plaintiffs, the Court granted an injunction
to restrain the defendants from the use of the words
' Bell's Life ' in the title of their newspaper (b). So also in
Ingram v. *Stiff* (c) an injunction was granted by Sir
W. P. Wood, V.C., to restrain the defendant from printing,
publishing, or selling any newspaper or other periodical
under the name of ' The Daily London Journal,' or under
any other name or style of which the words 'London
Journal' should form part, and from doing or committing
any act or default which might tend to lessen or diminish
the sale or circulation of the plaintiff's periodical called
' The London Journal.' The facts of the case were these :
In October 1857, A., being the proprietor of a weekly publication called ' The London Journal,' the price of which was
a penny, assigned his copyright and interest therein to B.
for value, and entered into a covenant with B. not to publish,
either alone, or in partnership with any other person, any
weekly periodical of a nature similar to ' The London
Journal.' In May 1859, A. issued an advertisement
announcing the publication by him on June 1st following
of a daily newspaper, to be called ' The Daily London

(a) See *Clement* v. *Maddick*, 1 Giff. 98 ; *Kelly* v. *Hutton*, L. R. 3 Ch.
703 ; 16 W. R. 1182 ; *Leather Cloth Company* v. *American Leather Cloth
Company*, 12 W. R. 289 ; 4 De G. J. & S. 137 ; *Maxwell* v. *Hogg*, L. R. 2
Ch. 307, 15 W. R. 467.
(b) *Clement* v. *Maddick*, 1 Giff. (Ch.) 98 ; 5 Jur. (N.S.) 592.
(c) 5 Jur. (N.S.) 947.

Journal,' which he intended should be sold at a penny. B. thereupon filed a bill against A. for an injunction to restrain A. from publishing, which was granted by the Vice-Chancellor in the terms before referred to. Upon appeal Sir J. L. Knight Bruce, L.J. (*dissentiente* Sir G. J. Turner, L.J.) confirmed the order for an injunction, upon B. undertaking to abide by any order the Court might make as to damages, and to bring an action against B. within one week.

In the case of the *Correspondent Newspaper Company* v. *Saunders* (a), where the publishers of 'The Correspondent' newspaper sought to restrain the defendant from publishing another paper under the name of 'The Public Correspondent,' Lord Hatherley, when Vice-Chancellor, after holding that registration of a newspaper was of no avail without actual publication, went on to express a doubt whether in any case registration would protect the title of the paper as being included in the copyright.

And in a later case (b) the same judge, when Lord Justice, said that there appeared to him to be nothing analogous to copyright in the name of a newspaper; but that the proprietor had a right to prevent any other person from adopting the same name for any other similar publication.

Where the precisely same title taken.   In the more recent case of *Weldon* v. *Dicks* (c) the question as to whether there could be copyright in a title, again came before the court. In the year 1874, the plaintiff, Mr. Weldon, bought the copyright of a portion of a work called 'The Parlour Library,' which was a series of volumes consisting partly of original works, and partly of works which had been previously published. The particular novel, 'Trial and Triumph,' was originally published in 1854, in a separate form in three volumes. It was not an unsuccessful publication, and Mr. Darton, the proprietor of the 'Parlour Library' at that time, arranged

(a) 13 W. R. 804 ; 11 Jur. (N.S.) 540.
(b) *Kelly* v. *Hutton*, L. R. 3 Ch. 703 ; 16 W. R. 1182.
(c) 10 Ch. D. 247 ; 27 W. R. 369.

with the publishers to make it part of that work, and it was published about the year 1860 in the 196th number. In 1876 the copyright in the 'Parlour Library' series was assigned to the plaintiff, and an entry made accordingly at Stationers' Hall. The plaintiff immediately after the assignment to him of the copyright commenced to re-issue the series, and had published a new edition of eleven of the books in such series, and was preparing for publication a new edition of ' Trial and Triumph,' which would shortly be published by him at the price of two shillings. The defendant had recently commenced to issue a series of books and novels under the general title of ' Dick's English Novels,' and he had since the date of the assignment to the plaintiff, published in such series a novel under the title of ' Trial and Triumph,' at the price of sixpence. And the plaintiff claimed an injunction to restrain the defendant from publishing or selling any book or publication under the title 'Trial and Triumph.' It was stated by the defendant that in the year 1873 the Rev. Henry V. Palmer offered him the manuscript of an entirely original work in the form of a novel with the proposed title of 'True to the Core,' but before purchasing the work the defendant discovered that the title ' True to the Core ' had already been used as a title of a drama, and he therefore requested the author to choose another title, and ' Trial and Triumph ' was then proposed and adopted by the defendant in entire ignorance that it had ever been used by any other person or applied to any other work. The defendant's work was entirely distinct in its plot and subject matter from the plaintiff's book. It also appeared that both before and after the date of the first publication by the plaintiff of his books, more than one book was published by other persons under the same title or one substantially the same. Vice-Chancellor Malins held that the plaintiff was entitled to an injunction.

But when the exact title is not copied, an injunction will not be granted unless the title and appearance of the defendant's publication are designed to deceive persons who are ordinarily intelligent and careful. Thus in a case where the well-known title of 'Punch' was taken, with the addition thereto of 'Judy,' although the court held that the defendant would not be at liberty to use 'Punch' or 'Judy' singly as a title, yet it refused to restrain the use of a title made up of the two words, on the ground that in combination they did not form such a title as to deceive persons of ordinary intelligence. "The defendants," said Vice-Chancellor Malins, "clearly have no right to use a name which is calculated to mislead or deceive the public in purchasing ; and if I thought, on the whole, that their journal was calculated to mislead persons of ordinary intelligence (for these are the persons I must consider) I should grant the injunction. Now 'Punch' is well known both in name and appearance, and its price is threepence. Could any one be misled into buying this other paper instead, which has the words 'Punch and Judy,' printed on it in distinct letters with a different frontispiece, and its price a penny ? I am clearly of opinion that the mass of mankind would not be so misled "(a).

So where the proprietor of the 'Era' newspaper sought to restrain the use of his title with the addition of 'New,' by a rival publication, the Lord Justices reversed the decision of Vice-Chancellor Bacon, and held that there was no ground for granting any injunction. They considered that the real question was this, " Is what appears on the front of the paper calculated to deceive an ordinary purchaser into the belief that the article sold to him is other than what it is, and what it seeks to imitate ? "

The law on this subject cannot be considered to be in a satisfactory state, for it is perfectly clear that a publication may be seriously injured by the similarity of name of a rival publication, without the wrappers or general style or appearance being in any way copied. Thousands of copies are purchased through advertisements, and without the purchaser until delivery seeing the subject of his purchase.

It is usually considered that as the injury caused by

(a) *Bradbury* v. *Beeton*, 18 W. R. 33.

the infringement is an injury to property, the fraudulent
intent is not necessary to prove. This is true so far as it
goes, but at the same time it must be remembered that
unless fraud in a sense is proved, or at least a probability
of deception or imposition on the public is established (*a*),
a plaintiff cannot well succeed. Where there is a close
resemblance in general style and arrangement of the
contents of the book itself (*b*), or a claim of certain
attributes which are known to belong to the original
work (*c*), or a sudden change from an unobjectionable
title, style of publication, and arrangement of contents to
a style more closely resembling the plaintiff's (*d*), an intention to deceive may be established.

Thus in *Hogg* v. *Kirby* (*e*) the proprietor of 'The Wonderful Magazine' succeeded in stopping the publication
of 'The Wonderful Magazine, New Series, Improved.' So
in *Chappell* v. *Sheard* (*f*), and *Chappell* v. *Davidson* (*g*),
where the plaintiff's song was entitled 'Minnie,' and
those of the respective defendants 'Minnie Dale,' and
'Minnie, Dear Minnie;' and where the purchaser of 'The
Britannia' newspaper incorporated it with the 'John
Bull,' under the name of 'The John Bull and Britannia,'
and the former publisher of 'The Britannia' began
to publish 'The True Britannia' (*h*), injunctions were
issued.

But, as already stated, the taking of *part of the title* of a
registered work without fraud, and without any circumstances from which an *animus furandi* could be inferred,
and where no deception is to be apprehended, will
not be deemed an offence, and this is clearly shown in a

(*a*) See *Hall* v. *Barrons*, 4 De G. J. & S. 150; 12 W. R. 322; *Chappell*
v. *Davidson*, 2 K. & J. 123.
(*b*) *Mack* v. *Petter*, L. R. 14 Eq. 431: 20 W. R. 964: *Corns* v. *Griffiths*,
W. N. (1873) 93.
(*c*) *Chappell* v. *Sheard*, 2 K. & J. 177.
(*d*) *Corns* v. *Griffiths*, *supra*. *Metzler* v. *Wood*, 8 Ch. D. 606; 26 W. R.
577.
(*e*) 8 Ves. 215.
(*f*) 2 K. & J. 117; 3 W. R. 646.
(*g*) 2 K. & J. 123.
(*h*) *Prowett* v. *Mortimer*, 4 W. R. 419; see *Edmonds* v. *Benbow*, Seton
on Decrees, 3rd ed. 905.

recent case. It was an action by the proprietor of a book entitled 'Post Office Directory of West Riding of Yorkshire,' which included the town of Bradford, to restrain the intended publication by the defendants of a directory of Bradford with the words 'Post Office' forming part of the title. It appeared that many years ago an officer of the London Post Office published, with the assistance of the letter carriers, a directory which he called 'Post Office' Directory. Subsequently a brother of the plaintiff became the publisher and proprietor of the work, which was carried on by him till 1846, with the assistance of the letter carriers as before. After 1846 the plaintiff's brother was prohibited by the Post Office authorities from employing the letter carriers, and he thereupon employed a large staff of private agents to obtain the information necessary for the continuance of his directory, which was still called the 'Post Office' Directory. In 1852 the plaintiff began publishing country directories, making use of his brother's staff of agents, and, with his brother's consent, called his directories 'Post Office' Directories. The plaintiff alleged that his directories were distinguished and known in the trade and to the public as 'Post Office Directories,' and that the term 'Post Office' was a very valuable trade distinction. The defendants had received assistance of the post-master at Bradford, and it was not alleged that there had been any copying or colourable imitation of any part of the text of the plaintiff's work, neither was there any similarity in price or appearance between the two directories, and the only question was as to the plaintiff's exclusive right to the use of the word 'Post Office' as applied to directories. Vice-Chancellor Bacon was of opinion that to support a claim to restrain the use by another of a name on the ground of it being a *quasi* trade-mark, it was necessary to shew that the wares offered for sale were so nearly identical that the use of the particular trade-mark or name might mislead unwary purchasers. He considered that the defendants were clearly entitled to publish a directory of Bradford, and as no person wishing to possess the plaintiff's 'Post Office Directory for the West Riding of Yorkshire' could be misled or deceived into buying the defendant's 'Post Office Bradford Directory,' judgment must be given for the defendants (a), and on appeal the court affirmed the judgment of the Vice-Chancellor (b).

Should a periodical change its name for another, there Assuming a would be no ground for preventing another periodical title which has been assuming the name which has been thus cast off, after a disused. reasonable lapse of time, provided the latter periodical did not hold itself out to the world as a continuation of the periodical whose title it had adopted (c).

With regard to encyclopædias, periodicals, and works Copyright in published in series, reviews, or magazines (d), it is provided encyclopædias and period- by the Copyright Act, 1842, that the copyright in every icals. article shall belong to the *proprietor* of the work for the same term as is given by the Act to authors of books, whenever any such article shall have been or shall be

(a) *Kelly* v. *Byles*, 46 L. T. (N.S.) 623, on appeal 13 Ch. Div. 682; see *Barnard* v. *Pillow*, W. N. (1868) 94; *Snowden* v. *Noah*, Hopk. (Amer.) 347; *Bell* v. *Locke*, 8 Paige (Amer.) 75; *Stephens* v. *De Cento*, 30 N. Y. Sup. Ct. 343; *Tallcot* v. *Moore*, 13 N. Y. Sup. Ct. 106.

(b) *Jollie* v. *Jaques*, 1 Bl. C. C. (Amer.) 618, was a suit to restrain an imitation of a musical composition entitled 'The Serious Family Polka'; it having been decided that the plaintiff's claim to copyright could not be supported, it was held that the plaintiff not being entitled to the copyright in the composition, he was not entitled to protection in respect of the title. Nelson, J., said, "The title or name is an appendage to the book or piece of music for which the copyright is taken out, and if the latter fails to be protected, the title goes with it, as certainly as the principal carries with it the incident." So in another American case, where the plaintiffs were the proprietors and publishers of a monthly magazine for the young, published at Boston, Mass., under the title 'Our Young Folks; an Illustrated Magazine for Boys and Girls,' and the defendant began to advertise and publish, and sell at Augusta, Maine, a fortnightly illustrated paper for the young, under the title 'Our Young Folks' Illustrated Paper.' A suit being instituted for an injunction to restrain the defendant from using the words 'Our Young Folks' as the title of the publication, the Court held that the title of a copyrighted publication was not capable of protection as copyright, except in conjunction with the publication which it was used to designate, and that the copyright in the paper not having been infringed, that in the title had not been: *Osgood* v. *Allen*, 1 Holmes (Amer.) 185; 6 Am. L. T. 20.

(c) The *Cour Royale* at Paris in 1834 sanctioned the publication of a journal under the title of *Gazette de Santé*, which another journal had formerly borne, but which it had for seven months abandoned for the title *Gazette Médicale de Paris*. Renouard, tom. 2, p. 128, cited Curtis on Copy. 297.

(d) See *Henderson* v. *Maxwell*, 4 Ch. Div. 163.

composed on the terms that the copyright therein shall belong to such proprietor and be paid for by him; but payment must be actually made by the proprietor before the copyright can vest in him (a). There is a special proviso in the case of essays, articles, or portions forming part of, and first published in reviews, magazines, or other periodical works of a like nature, to the effect that after the term of twenty-eight years from the first publication of any such article the right of publishing the same in a separate form shall revert to the author for the remainder of the term given by the Act; and during such term of twenty-eight years the proprietor shall not publish any such article separately, without the previous consent of the author or his assigns, unless the article was written on the express terms that the copyright therein should belong to the proprietor, for all purposes (b). But any author may reserve to himself the right to publish any such composition in a separate form, and he will then be entitled to the copyright in such composition, when published separately, without prejudice to the right of the proprietor of the encyclopædia, review, or other periodical in which it may have first appeared (c).

Reservation by author of right to separate publication.

In order to give the proprietor of a periodical a copyright in articles composed for him by others, it is not necessary that there should be an express contract that he should have the property in the copyright. The fact of the author being paid by the proprietor for articles supplied expressly for the periodical, raises the presumption that the copyright is intended to be the property of the proprietor (d). Otherwise, the articles might be published by

(a) A contract for payment is not sufficient: *Richardson* v. *Gilbert*, 1 Sim. (N.S.) 336; 20 L. J. (Ch.) 553; 15 Jur. 389. See *Brown* v. *Cooke*, 11 Jur. 77; 16 L. J. (N.S.) Ch. 140.

(b) *Hereford (Bishop of)* v. *Griffin*, 16 Sim. 190; 17 L. J. (Ch.) 210. See 1 J. & H. 112; 3 L. T. (N.S.) 466. As to the course to be adopted on dissolution of partnership, and the withdrawal of one partner from the periodical publication by the firm, see *Bradbury* v. *Dickens*, 27 Beav. 53; 28 L. J. (Ch.) 667, cited Philips on Copy. 181, note.

(c) 5 & 6 Vict. c. 45, s. 18.

(d) Where the publishers of a magazine employ and pay an editor, and the editor employs and pays persons for writing articles in the magazine, *semble*, the copyright in such articles is not vested in the publishers: *Brown*

the writers thereof simultaneously, or shortly afterwards; possibly to the detriment and injury of the purchasers of the articles for particular periodicals.

Consent that the proprietor of a periodical should have the copyright for all purposes may be implied from the attending circumstances. Thus, in *Sweet* v. *Benning* (a) the plaintiffs were the publishers of 'The Jurist,' and had employed various lawyers to prepare reports of cases for that periodical. Nothing was said as to the copyright. The Court of Common Pleas held that there must be presumed an implied agreement that the copyright was to be the property of the employers. " It was urged," said Maule, J., " that these reports were not written on the terms that the copyright therein should belong to the proprietors of ' The Jurist,' because there were no express words in the contract under which they were written conferring upon them the right to the copyright. But, though no express words to that effect are stated in this special case, I think that where a man employs another to write an article, or to do anything else for him, unless there is something in the surrounding circumstances, or, in the course of dealing between the parties, to require a different construction, in the absence of a special agreement to the contrary, it is to be understood that the writing or other thing is produced upon the terms that the copyright therein shall belong to the employer, subject of course, to the limitation pointed out in the 18th section of the Act."

This case was decided by reason of the particular circumstances attending it, amounting in the opinion of the court to an implied consent on the part of the author to relinquish his copyright. And it is clear that where no consent is expressed, and no consent from the surrounding circumstances can be implied, the copyright continues in the author.

Thus, in the *Bishop of Hereford* v. *Griffin* (b), where it

v. *Cooke*, 16 L. J. (N.S.) Ch. 140; 11 Jur. 77; *Richardson* v. *Gilbert*, 1 Sim. (N.S.) 336.

(a) 16 C. B. 459.

(b) 16 Sim. 190 ; *Boucicault* v. *Fox*, 5 Blatchf. (Amer.) 87.

appeared that the plaintiff, at the request of the publishers, had written an article on Thomas Aquinas for the 'Encyclopædia Metropolitana,' and no special agreement had been made as to the copyright, Vice-Chancellor Shadwell held that the publishers had acquired merely the right to publish the article in the encyclopædia. He said: "Then the defendants say that they believe that the ordinary terms of contract were adopted between the plaintiff and the publishers of the encyclopædia, and that no special agreement was entered into with respect to the reservation of any right of publication by the plaintiff. But it must be observed that, according to the law, the copyright was in the plaintiff, except so far as he parted with it; therefore no reservation was necessary to constitute a right in him."

Right of separate publication, in whom vested. 　If the absolute copyright vests in the owner of the periodical, he alone is entitled to publish the production in a separate form. If he has acquired merely the right of publication in a specified work, the ownership of the copyright continues in the author, and the owner is a mere licensee without authority to publish the production in a separate form.

In the case of *Smith* v. *Johnson*, where the plaintiff had composed certain tales, under the common title of 'The Chronicles of Stanfield Hall,' for the defendant to publish in the 'London Journal,' of which he was the proprietor, it was held that the subsequent publication of such tales in a weekly supplementary number, for sale with or without the current number, was "a publication separately," within the meaning of the 18th section of the Copyright Act. And Vice-Chancellor Stuart then adopted the same view as did the Vice-Chancellor of England, in the *Bishop of Hereford* v. *Griffin*, and also that subsequently taken by Vice-Chancellor Wood, who considered that the meaning of the proviso in the 18th section, taken with the whole clause, was, not to vest a copyright in the proprietors or publishers of a periodical work, but simply to give them a licence to use the matter for a particular purpose. "Keep-

ing in view," says the Vice-Chancellor, " this principle of
construction—that the Act of Parliament was intended to
give a licence only to the proprietors of periodical works
purchasing and paying for a literary composition to be
published as a part or portion of a periodical work—the
construction of the words in the proviso which prohibit
them from publishing these parts or portions which ' alone '
are the property of the author—from publishing these portions 'separately and singly,' seems reasonably plain.
' Publishing separately ' must mean publishing separately
from something. What is that ' publishing ' which the
Act of Parliament says shall not be separately made? It
must be the publishing of the part or portion separately
from that which has been before published. That is the
view which has been previously taken, and the language
in the case of *Mayhew* v. *Maxwell* was to the effect that
the defendant should be prohibited from publishing the
literary work then in question, otherwise than as part of
the Christmas number of the ' Welcome Guest.' Now,
that Christmas number was a thing called ' a part ' in the
Act of Parliament, which describes these periodical works
as being published in a series of parts and numbers. The
Christmas number is part or portion of the other composition. The order of this court peremptorily prohibited the
defendant Maxwell from publishing it separately from the
other part or number. What has the defendant in this
case done? He has acquired, under the first clause of the
Act of Parliament, an actual property in this literary
composition, which is called ' The Stanfield Hall Tales,'
published in portions or parts of a certain periodical work.
The Act of Parliament says the publishers shall not publish
these portions separately from those parts for the publication of which they have obtained a licence already. What
they have done is to print the portions already published
of these antecedent parts in what is called a supplementary number, and which may be purchased with or without
the number in which the ' portions ' were originally pub-

CAP. II. lished. That is a separate publication; separate from the
'parts' in which it was originally published. To reprint
in numbers, which may be had with or without the concurrent number of the work, is an act not permitted by the
legislature " (a).

Proprietors of periodicals may acquire copyright by contract of employment. The proprietor of a review, magazine, or like periodical,
as well as the proprietor of any other publication em-
braced within the 18th section, as a cyclopædia or a work
published in a series of books or parts may acquire by
virtue of the contract of employment the copyright in
an article, and in such case his rights will not be restricted to the use of the article in the periodical only
for which it was written. .But the copyright in the case
of a magazine, or like periodical, will revert to the author
at the end of twenty-eight years; whereas in the case of
any work not included in the proviso above quoted the
copyright will continue in the proprietor during the
entire term given by the statute.

Suggestions of Copyright Commis-sioners as to periodicals, &c. The report of the Royal Commissioners on Copyrights
thus deals with this subject: "It has been provided that
in the case of encyclopædias, reviews, magazines, periodical
works, and works published in a series of books or parts, for
which various persons are employed by the proprietor to
write articles—if the articles are written and paid for on
the terms that the copyright therein shall belong to the
proprietor of the work, the same rights shall belong to
him as to the author of a book, except in one particular,
in which particular a difference is made between essays,
articles, or portions of reviews, magazines, or other periodical works of a like nature, and articles in encyclopædias. In the case of the former (but not of encyclopædias) a right of separate publication of the articles
reverts to the author after twenty-eight years for the
remainder of the period of copyright, and during the

(a) Vice-Chancellor Stuart, *Smith* v. *Johnson,* 4 Giff. 637; 33 L. J.
(Ch.) 137; 9 Jur. (N.S.) 1223; 12 W. R. 122; 9 L. T. (N.S.) 437; *Mayhew*
v. *Maxwell,* 1 J. & H. 312. See *Wallenstein* v. *Herbert,* 15 W. R. 838; 16
L. T. (N.S.) 453.

twenty-eight years the proprietor of the work cannot publish the articles separately without the consent of the author or his assigns. Authors can, however, by contract reserve to themselves, during the twenty-eight years, a right of separate publication of the articles they write, in which case the copyright in the separate publication belongs to them, but without prejudice to the rights of the proprietor of the magazine or other periodical. We think some modification in this provision is required as regards the time when the right of separate publication should revert to the authors of the articles, and that three years should be substituted for twenty-eight. As we have reason to believe that proprietors of periodicals have not, as a rule, insisted on the right given them by the existing law, we think there would be no objection to making this provision retrospective.

" It has been pointed out to us that, under the existing law, the author of an article in a magazine or periodical cannot, until the right of separate publication reverts to him, take proceedings to prevent piracy of his work; so that, unless the proprietor of the magazine or periodical be willing to take such proceedings (which may very likely not be the case when the right of the author is about to revive), the result would practically be to deprive the author of the benefit of the right reserved to him. We recommend, therefore, that during the period before the right of separate publication reverts to the author, he should be entitled, as well as the proprietor of the magazine or periodical, to prevent an unauthorized separate publication."

The 19th section of the Copyright Act, 1845, provides that the proprietor of the copyright in any encyclopædia, review, magazine, periodical work, or a work published in a series of books or parts, shall be entitled to all the benefits of the registration at Stationers' Hall under the Act, on entering in the registry the title of such encyclopædia, review, periodical work, or other work published in a series of books or parts, the time of the first publication of

Registration of periodicals.

CAP. II. the first volume, number, or part thereof, or of the first number or volume first published after the passing of this Act in any such work which shall have been published before the passing of the Act, and the name and place of abode of the proprietor thereof, and of the publisher thereof when he is not also the proprietor. Under this section it is clear that as each part of a periodical is a book within the meaning of the Act, and copyright runs from the date of publication of any book, that the copyright in each part accrues from the publication of each part, so that if a subsequent part be published twelve years after the publication and registration of the first part all the benefit of registration will accrue for forty-two years from the publication of the subsequent part, notwithstanding that registration has only been effected of the first part.

Copyright in translations.

Copyright may exist in a translation, whether it be the result of personal application and expense, or donation (a). In the case of *Wyatt* v. *Barnard* (b), Lord Eldon states this to be the law : The plaintiff was the proprietor of a periodical called ' The Repository of Arts, Manufacture, and Agriculture.' He claimed the sole copyright of the work, containing, amongst other articles, translations from foreign languages. The defendants were publishers of another periodical which contained various articles, being translations from foreign languages, copied or taken from the plaintiff's work without his consent. The defendants, by their affidavit, stated that it was the usual practice among publishers of magazines, &c., to take from each other articles translated from foreign languages, or become public property by reason of their having appeared in other works. They relied on the custom of the trade, and contended that neither of the works was original, both being mere compilations; that it had never been decided

---

(a) *Wyatt* v. *Barnard*, 3 V. & B. 77. If a foreigner translates an English work, and then an Englishman re-translates the foreign work into English, that is an infringement of the original copyright: *Murray* v. *Bogue*, 17 Jur. 219; 1 Drew. 353; 22 L. J. (Ch.) 457.

(b) 3 V. & B. 78. *Vide Stowe* v. *Thomas*, 2 Amer. L. Reg. 231.

that a translator might have a copyright in a translation, supposing, what was not proved, that these translations were made by the plaintiff himself. The Lord Chancellor said that the custom among booksellers could not control the law ; and upon an affidavit stating that all the articles were translated by a person employed and paid by the plaintiff, and were translated from foreign books imported by the plaintiff at considerable expense, his Lordship granted an injunction.

The work from which the translation was taken in the present case was, of course, unprotected by the copyright law in existence here, and the cases which have treated translations from foreign works, having no copyright in this country, as original, would not necessarily form a precedent in the case of a translation of an English copyright work. But in the case above cited, Lord Eldon drew no *Every fair* distinction between translations of works unprotected and *translation an original work.* those protected in this country, indeed it was not necessary to do so for the decision of the point involved in the case before him. This case is sometimes cited for the purpose of shewing that every translation is an original work and entitled to protection, whether made from an unprotected or a protected work. But it does not go to this extent, and notwithstanding the dicta of Mr. Justice Yates, in *Millar* v. *Taylor* (a), and Lord Macclesfield, in *Burnett* v. *Chetwood* (b), and of the late Lord Justice Knight Bruce, when Vice-Chancellor (c), it appears to be the better opinion that a work in which copyright is still subsisting cannot be translated without the consent of the proprietor of the copyright. Lord Justice Knight Bruce, in the well-known case of *Prince Albert* v. *Strange* (d), thought that a work lawfully published, in the popular sense of the term, stood in this respect differently from a work which had never been in that situation. The former was liable to be translated, abridged,

(a) 4 Burr. 2348.
(b) 2 Mer. 441.
(c) *Prince Albert* v. *Strange*, 2 De G. & Sm. 693.
(d) 2 De G. & Sm. 693.

Cap. II.   analyzed, exhibited in morsels, complimented, and otherwise treated in a manner that the latter was not.   There
has been a decision in America in accordance with the
opinion of Lord Justice Knight Bruce (a), but it is not
likely to be followed in this country.   It is unsupported
by authority and opposed to the principles of the copyright law.

The Queen may now direct that the authors of books
published after a specified day in any foreign country,
their executors, administrators, or assigns, shall have the
power (subject to the provisions of the 15 & 16 Vict. c. 12)
to prevent the publication in the British dominions of any
translations of such books as are not authorized by them,
for a period (to be specified by her Majesty) not exceeding
five years from the first publication of an authorized translation; and in the case of books published in parts, for
a period not exceeding, as to each part, five years from
the first publication of an authorized translation of that
part (b).

No copyright   Copyright cannot exist in a work of libellous, immoral,
in a libellous,
immoral, or   obscene, or irreligious tendency (c); because in order to
obscene work. establish such a claim the author must, in the first place,
shew a right to sell; and this he cannot possibly do, he
himself not being able to acquire a property therein.   *Nemo
plus juris ad alium transferre potest quam ipse haberet (d).*

The property here referred to is that consisting in the
right to take the profits of the work when published.
But in *Southey* v. *Sherwood* (e) Lord Eldon seems to have
carried the rule still further, and refused to admit a right
in the author of a work of a non-innocent nature to the

(a) *Stowe* v. *Thomas,* 2 Wall. Ir. 547; 2 Am. Law Reg. 210.
(b) 15 & 16 Vict. c. 12, s. 2.
(c) *Stockdale* v. *Onwhyn,* 5 B. & C. 173; 7 D. & R. 625; *Hime* v. *Dale,*
2 Camp. 28; *Walcot* v. *Walker,* 7 Ves. 1; *Poplett* v. *Stockdale,* 1 R. & M.
337; *Gee* v. *Pritchard,* 2 Swans. 413; *Southey* v. *Sherwood,* 2 Mer. 435;
Murray v. *Benbow,* 1 Jac. 474; *Lawrence* v. *Smith, ibid,* 471; *Forbes* v.
Johnes, 4 Esp. 97; *Gale* v. *Leckie,* 2 Stark. N. P. C. 107; and see an
article in ' Quarterly Review ' for April, 1822, and ' Blackwood's Magazine '
for July, 1822; *Dodson* v. *Martin,* Sol. Journ. 29th of May, 1880.
(d) Ulpian : *Nemo potest plus juris ad alium transferre quam ipse habet;*
Co. Lit. 309; Wing. 56.
(e) 2 Mer. 435.

possession and control of his manuscript. He appears to
have overlooked the fact that the law recognised two
kinds or degrees of property in a literary work. There is
a right of property which consists in the right to take
the profits of a book when published : and 'there is also
a right to the exclusive possession and control of a manuscript, or the right to publish or to withhold from publication altogether (a).

"The first of these rights," says Mr. Curtis, in his
examination of Lord Eldon's judgment in the last-mentioned case (b), "depends now in England and in America
upon statute. The other is a right at common law, independent of the property created or recognised by statute.
The law of England has never said that an author has no
property in his manuscript *quâ* manuscript, or in the
ideas and sentiments written upon it before publication.
If it had, it would only be necessary to steal a manuscript
in order to be able to print it with impunity ; and the
author could only take the profits, or obtain an injunction,
by shewing that he himself intended to publish and to
take the profits. It has long been settled, however, that
the author and proprietor of a manuscript has the sole
dominion over it, and may obtain an injunction to prevent its publication by another: and in no case has it
been considered that his right depends on his intention
to publish and to make a profit. But the cases proceed
upon the ground of *a right of property* : and what seems
to be intended by this is a right to the possession and
control of the manuscript, and to publish or to withhold
from publication. In the great case of *Donaldson* v.
Becket, in the House of Lords, in which the perpetual
right of authors after publication was held to have been
taken away by the Act of Anne, eleven of the judges
(including those who decided against some of the claims
of authors) affirmed the sole right and dominion of an
author over his own manuscript, as a right at common

(a) See *Wheaton* v. *Peters*, 8 Peters, S. C. R. (Amer.) 591; cited Curtis
Copy. 158.
(b) Copyright, p. 158.

law. When, therefore, an author has not published, or does not intend to publish a work existing in manuscript, but on the contrary desires and intends to withhold it from publication, the question as to its innocence cannot arise, because that question, according to principle and the decisions, affects only so much of his right of property as consists in the right to take the profits of the publication. It is in this sense that the law declares there can be no property in an immoral, irreligious, or seditious publication; and not that there can be no right to the exclusive possession and control of whatever a man writes, before publication, unless it be innocent."

Lord Eldon's decision in *Southey* v. *Sherwood* has been severely criticised by Lord Campbell, who states that in consequence of the refusal of the injunction asked for, hundreds of thousands of copies of Wat Tyler, the poem the publication of which was sought to be restrained, at the price of one penny were circulated over the kingdom (a).

Not to protect such works, it has been argued, is to increase the circulation by allowing the publication of pirated editions; but it is an open question whether the circulation is not more effectually restrained by holding that there can be no property in such a work, than by protecting it; for the inducement to the publisher will be less if other persons may copy and publish *ad infinitum*.

In answer to the remark, that by refusing to interfere in cases where the work is of an evil tendency, the court virtually promotes, in some instances, the multiplication of mischievous productions, it must be borne in mind, that a court of equity professes to decide only upon questions of property, concerning itself merely with the civil interests of the parties, and disclaiming interference to prevent or to punish injuries of a criminal nature; and it therefore leaves the offending person to be dealt with at law (b). And adopting such a course is not merely to act in conformity with its own general principles, but

(a) 'Lives of Chancellors,' vol. 10.
(b) *Vide* 7 Ves. 2; 2 Mer. 438; 2 Swans. 413; 1 Jac. 473.

also with the constitution of the country ; for, to assist a person who has exerted himself to the prejudice of national or of individual welfare, by deciding upon questions of a criminal character, the court would be assuming a power of adjudication in instances which, according to our notions of political freedom, ought not to be determined without the intervention of a jury.   And it is also observable, that although interposition is refused in cases of this kind, except upon the plaintiff's right receiving the sanction of a court of law, the court of equity does not thereby bereave the party applying, of any redress which he might otherwise obtain, or of the means of seeking it, but merely withholds that extraordinary relief which is adapted to other cases (a).

The first case establishing the doctrine that there could not be property in a work of the above description, is that known as Dr. Priestley's.   The plaintiff brought an action against the hundred to recover damages for injury sustained by him in consequence of the riotous proceedings of a mob at Birmingham, and, among other property alleged to have been destroyed, claimed compensation for the loss of certain unpublished manuscripts, offering to produce booksellers as witnesses to prove that they would have given considerable sums for them.   On behalf of the hundred it was alleged that the plaintiff was in the habit of publishing works injurious to the government of the State ; but no evidence was produced to that effect.   Upon this the Lord Chief Justice Eyre remarked, that if any such evidence had been produced, he should have held it was fit to be received as against the claim made by the plaintiff. Several passages were read from the work itself in support of the charge as to its tendency.

Though Lord Eldon appears to base his decision in *Southey* v. *Sherwood* upon this case before Lord Chief Justice Eyre, yet it will be at once perceived that there is a material difference between them, for in the case before Lord Eldon, Southey claimed the right to prevent

Dr. Priestley's case.

(a) Jer. Eq. Jur. bk. 3, ch. 2.

CAP. II. publication, whereas in the case before Lord Chief Justice
Eyre, Dr. Priestley sued for the loss of profits, which he
alleged he might have realised by publication—a point to
which he never could have lawfully proceeded.

No copyright   The above cases were followed in *Walcot* (*Peter Pindar*)
in a work of   v. *Walker* (a), and in *Lawrence* v. *Smith* (b).   In the latter
an irreligious
tendency.   case the doctrine was carried very far.   The plaintiff
having published a work under the title of ' Lectures on
Physiology, Zoology, and the Natural History of Man,'
filed a bill to restrain the defendant from selling a pirated
edition, and obtained an injunction upon motion made *ex
parte*.   The defendants then moved to dissolve the injunction, and argued that the nature and general tendency of
the work in question was such that it could not be the
subject of copyright, and in support of this argument
several passages in it were referred to, which, it was contended, were hostile to natural and revealed religion,
and impugned the doctrines of the immateriality and
immortality of the soul.   Lord Eldon, in dissolving the
injunction, said: "I take it for granted that when the
motion for the injunction was made, it was opened as quite
of course; nothing probably was said as to the general
nature of the work, or of any part of it; for we must look
not only to the general tenor, but at the different parts;
and the question is to be decided, not merely by seeing
what is said of materialism, of the immortality of the soul,
and of the Scriptures, but, by looking at the different
parts, and inquiring whether there be any which deny, or
which appear to deny, the truth of Scripture; or which
raise a fair question for a court of law to determine
whether they do or do not deny.   Looking at the general
tenor of the work, and at many particular parts of it,
recollecting that the immortality of the soul is one of the
doctrines of the Scripture, considering that the law does
not give protection to those who contradict Scripture (c),

(a) 7 Ves. 1. See *Stockdale* v. *Onhwyn*, 5 B. & C. 173; *Poplett* v. *Stockdale*, Ry. & M. 337.   (b) 1 Jac. 471.
(c) " Christianity is part and parcel of the law of the land :" Kelly,
C.B., in *Cowan* v. *Milbourn*, L. R. 2 Ex. Div. 230.

and entertaining a doubt, I think a rational doubt, whether
this book does not violate the law, I cannot continue the
injunction. The plaintiff may bring an action, and when
that is decided, he may apply again." From a note by the
editor, we learn that in 1822, in *Murray* v. *Benbow*, Mr.
Shadwell, on the part of the plaintiff, moved for an injunction to restrain the defendants from publishing a pirated
edition of Lord Byron's poem of 'Cain.' The Lord Chancellor, after reading the work, refused the motion, on
grounds similar to those stated in the above judgment.
He said "that the Court of Chancery, like other courts of
justice in this country, acknowledged Christianity as part
of the law of the land; that the jurisdiction of the court
in protecting literary property was founded on this: that,
where an action would lie for pirating a work, then the
court, attending to the imperfection of that remedy,
granted its injunction, because there might be publication
after publication, which one might never be able to hunt
down by proceeding in other courts. But where such an
action did not lie, he did not apprehend that it was according to the course of the court to grant an injunction
to protect the copyright. That the publication, if it were
one intended to vilify and bring into discredit that portion
of Scripture history to which it related, was a publication
with reference to which, if the principles on which that
case at Warwick (Dr. Priestley's) was decided were just
principles of law, the party could not recover damages in
respect of a piracy of it. That the court had no criminal
jurisdiction; it could not look on anything as an offence;
but in those cases it only administered justice for the protection of the civil rights of those who possessed them, in
consequence of being able to maintain an action. Milton's
immortal work had been alluded to; it so happened that
in the course of the previous long vacation, amongst the
solicitæ jucunda oblivia vitæ, he had read that work from
beginning to end; it was therefore quite fresh in his
memory, and it appeared to him that the great object of
its author was to promote the cause of Christianity; there

CAP. II.   were, undoubtedly, a great many passages in it of which, if
that were not its object, it would be very improper by law
to vindicate the publication; but, taking it altogether, it
was clear that the object and effect were not to bring into
disrepute, but to promote, the reverence of our religion.
That the real question was, looking at the work before
him, its preface, the poem, its manner of treating the
subject, particularly with reference to the Fall and the
Atonement, whether its intent was as innocent as that of
the other with which it had been compared; or whether it
was to traduce and bring into discredit that part of sacred
history. This question he had no right to try, because it
had been settled, after great difference of opinion among
the learned, that it was for a jury to determine that point;
and where, therefore, a reasonable doubt was entertained
as to the character of the work (and it was impossible for
him to say he had not a doubt, he hoped it was a reasonable one), another course should be taken for determining
what was its true nature and character" (a).

"Don Juan."   In a case which came before the Vice-Chancellor in
1823, an injunction which had been obtained to restrain
the publication of a pirated edition of a portion of the
poem of 'Don Juan,' was dissolved on a similar principle.
His Honour ordered that the defendant should keep an
account.

Referring to Lord Eldon's decisions in the above cases,
Mr. Justice Story says: "The soundness of the general
principle can hardly admit of question. The chief embarrassment and difficulty lie in the application of it to
particular cases. If a court of equity, under colour of its
general authority, is to enter upon all the moral, theo-
logical, metaphysical and political inquiries, which in the
past times have given rise to so many controversies, and
in the future may well be supposed to provoke many
heated discussions, and if it is to decide dogmatically
upon the character and bearing of such discussions, and
the rights of authors growing out of them; it is obvious

(a) *Murray* v. *Benbow*, in Ch. 1822, MS., cited 6 Peters. Abr. 558.

that an absolute power is conferred over the subject of CAP. II. literary property, which may sap the very foundations on which it rests, and retard, if not entirely suppress, the means of arriving at physical as well as at metaphysical truths. Thus, for example, a judge who should happen to believe that the immateriality of the soul, as well as its immortality, was a doctrine clearly revealed in the Scriptures (a point upon which very learned and pious minds have been greatly divided), would deem any work anti-christian which should profess to deny that point, and would refuse an injunction to protect it. So, a judge who should be a Trinitarian might most conscientiously decide against granting an injunction in favour of an author enforcing Unitarian views; when another judge, of opposite opinions, might not hesitate to grant it" (a).

The very case surmised by Mr. Justice Story arose 'Life of Jesus.' a short time since (February, 1874) in the Scotch Courts. A work entitled 'The Life of Jesus re-written for Young Disciples,' by Mr. Page Hopps, Unitarian minister, Glasgow, was published by Messrs. Trübner & Co., London, at 1s. a copy. The defendant Harry Alfred Long, Protestant missionary, about a year after its appearance, issued a review containing the whole of Mr. Hopps's book, with notes and criticisms attached to each chapter, and this publication was sold at 6d. Hopps applied for an interim interdict, which being granted, he subsequently sought to have it declared perpetual. The plea put forward by the defendant was that the pursuer could not claim the protection of the law for the book, as it was blasphemous and heretical, denying tacitly or expressly the divinity of Christ. To this the pursuer replied that apart from the fact that it was written by a Unitarian, and set forth the Unitarian view of the Saviour's life, a more unobjectionable book did not exist. Mr. Sheriff Buntine, of the Sheriff's Court of Lanarkshire, declared the interdict perpetual, and found Long liable in expenses, holding that, though the doctrine that Jesus Christ is

(a) 2 Story's Eq. Jur., p. 938.

CAP. II.

the second person of the Trinity is statute law, yet the public are entitled to criticise and controvert any part of the statute law, provided they do it in such a way as not to endanger the public peace, safety, or morality. Mr. Hopps, the sheriff considered, violated none of these conditions, and was entitled to the protection of the law.

No copyright in a work of a scandalous nature.

In the case of *Hime* v. *Dale*, referred to in *Clementi* v. *Goulding* (a), counsel called attention to the libellous nature of the publication, and contended that it was of such a description that it could not receive the protection of the law. It professed to be a panegyric upon money, but was in reality a gross and nefarious libel upon the solemn administration of British justice. The mischievous tendency of the production would sufficiently appear from the following stanza :

> " The world is inclined
> To think *Justice* blind,—
> Yet what of all that ?
> She will blink like a bat
> At the sight of friend Abraham Newland !
> Oh ! Abraham Newland ! magical Abraham Newland !
> Tho' Justice, 'tis known,
> Can see through a milestone,
> She can't see through Abraham Newland."

Lord Ellenborough, however, stated that though if the composition had appeared on the face of it to be a libel so gross as to affect the public morals, he should advise the jury to give no damages, as he knew the Court of Chancery on such an occasion would grant no injunction, yet he thought the above ought not to be considered one of that kind. But in another case (b) where an action was brought for the purpose of recovering compensation in damages for the loss alleged to have been sustained by the publication of a copy of a book which had been first published by the plaintiff ; and at the trial it was proved

(a) 2 Camp. 30.

(b) *Stockdale* v. *Onhwyn*, 5 B. & C. 173 ; see *Poplett* v. *Stockdale*, Ry. & M. 337, where it was held that the printer of the work, the subject of the last case, could not maintain an action for his bill against the publisher who employed him, Best, C.J., said the defendant was equally guilty with the plaintiff, but that he would not, as Lord Kenyon once said, sit to take an account between two robbers on Hounslow Heath.

that the work was the memoir of Harriette Wilson, which
professed to be a history of the amours of a courtezan,
that it contained in some parts matter highly indecent,
and in others matter of a slanderous nature upon persons
named in the book, Abbott, C.J., directed a nonsuit, and
in refusing a rule nisi for a new trial said: "In order to
establish such a claim (*i.e.* to compensation for infringement
of his copyright), he must, in the first place, shew a right
to sell, for if he has not that right, he cannot sustain any
loss by an injury to the sale. Now I am certain no lawyer
can say that the sale of each copy of this work is not an
offence against the law. How then can we hold that by
the first publication of such a work a right of action can
be given against any person who afterwards publishes it?
It is said that there is no decision of a court of law
against the plaintiff's claim. But upon the plainest
principles of the common law, founded as it is, where
there are no authorities, upon common sense and justice,
this action cannot be maintained. It would be a disgrace
to the common law could a doubt be entertained upon the
subject, but I think that no doubt can be entertained,
and I want no authority for pronouncing such a judicial
opinion."

Neither can there be copyright in works intended to
deceive purchasers, and therefore, in an action for pirating
a work of a devotional character, falsely professing to be a
translation from the German, of an author who had a high
reputation for writings of this kind, the object being to
deceive purchasers, and give the work a value which it
would not otherwise have possessed, judgment was given
for the defendants. Chief Justice Tindal, in the case referred to (a), drew a distinction between such a work and
books of instruction or amusement which have been published as translations, whilst they have, in fact, been
original works, or which have been published under an
assumed instead of a true name. Such, for instance, as
'The Castle of Otranto,' professing to be translated from

No copyright in works intended to deceive the public.

(a) *Wright* v. *Tallis,* 1 C. B. 893 ; 14 L. J. (C.P.) 283 ; 9 Jur. 946.

the Italian, and such the case of innumerable works published under assumed names—voyages, travels, biographies, works of fiction or romance, and even works of
science and instruction; for, in all these instances the
misrepresentation is innocent and harmless.   But the
facts stated in the pleas in the case under consideration
imported a serious design on the part of the plaintiff to
impose on the credulity of each purchaser, by fixing on
the name of an author who had a real existence, and who
possessed a large share of weight and estimation in the
opinion of the public.   The object of the plaintiff was, not
merely to conceal the name of the genuine author, and to
publish opinions to the world under an innocent disguise,
but it was to practise upon some of the best feelings of the
public, namely, their religious feelings; and thus to induce
them to believe that the work was the original work of
the author whom he named, when he knew it not to be so.
The transaction, therefore, ranged itself under the head of
crimen falsi.   It was a species of obtaining money under
false pretences; and as the very act of publishing the
work, and the sale of the copies to each individual purchaser, were each liable to the objection above stated, the
chief justice thought the plaintiff could not be considered
as having a valid and subsisting copyright in the work, the
sale of which produced such consequences, or that he was
capable of maintaining an action in respect of its infringement.   Cases in which a copyright has been held not to
subsist, where the work is one which is subversive of good
order, morality, or religion, did not bear, he thought, on
the case before him, but they had so far analogy, that
the rule which denied the existence of copyright in those
cases, was the rule established for the benefit and protection of the public.

So decided on
the ground of
fraud.
This decision proceeded more on the ground of fraud
than invasion of literary property, and to the principle of
this decision may also be referred the case of *Seeley* v.
Fisher (a), where an injunction was granted to restrain A.

(a) 11 Sim. 581.

from putting forth his work under advertisements which the court below thought tended to produce the impression, contrary to the truth, that it contained matter which was in fact the property of B. But if there be no such fraudulent misrepresentation, but only statements which, whether true or false, tend merely to encourage a belief that the matter contained in A.'s work is truly valuable matter, and that contained in B.'s is spurious and of no value, an injunction will not be granted to restrain such representations; and on the ground that such was the true effect of the advertisements, in the last cited case, the Lord Chancellor dissolved the injunction.

But where the plaintiff was the well-known writer and composer of songs and music called 'Claribel,' the defendants were the music publishers carrying on business under the name of "Sinclair & Co." and it appeared that four songs named respectively 'Under the Willows,' 'Spinning by her Cottage Door,' 'I'll cast my Rose on the Waters,' and "Spring Carol,' the words only of which were written by 'Claribel,' had been published and sold by the defendants, with the name of ' Claribel' appearing on them thus, " 'Under the Willows,' song written by Claribel," no mention being made of the name of the composer of the music of the song; and it was contended by the plaintiff that the above mode of publication was intended to deceive, and had deceived, people into the belief that not merely the words, but also the music of these songs was by 'Claribel,' and he prayed that the defendant might be restrained from so publishing; the Master of the Rolls held that the injunction must be refused, as he was of opinion that the words "written by" referred only to the words of the songs, and did not mean "written and composed," and that ordinary purchasers using ordinary caution could not be deceived into thinking that the music was composed by 'Claribel' (a).

Where a publisher advertised for sale certain poems, which he represented to be the work of Lord Byron, who

(a) *Barnard* v. *Pillow*, W. N. (1868) 94.

CAP. II. was abroad, an injunction was granted until answer or further order to restrain the publication, Lord Byron's agents deposing to their belief that the poems were not Lord Byron's work, and to circumstances rendering it highly improbable that they were so, and the defendant refusing to swear to his belief that they were written by Lord Byron (a).

No copyright in a dry catalogue of names.

There can be no copyright in specifications of patents (b), nor in a catalogue consisting of a mere dry list of names. But where a bookseller's catalogue contained a description of the books offered for sale, with short anecdotes relating to them, protection was afforded (c).

Wood, V.C., opinion on copyright in descriptive catalogues.

And in the case referred to, Sir W. Page Wood, V.C., said that he could not conceive on what principle it was supposed that there was no copyright in a catalogue such as the one in the case before him. It was not a mere dry list of names, like a Postal Directory, Court Guide, or anything of that sort, which must be substantially the same by whatever number of persons issued and however independently compiled. It was a case of a bookseller who issues an account of his stock, containing short descriptions of the contents of the books, calculated to interest either the general public or the persons who might take an interest in the questions treated of by particular books. "For example," continues the learned judge, "suppose one of the books to be a History of Cheshire; then he gives you a slight account of it, from which it appears that it contains a number of anecdotes respecting county families and other things of that nature, it might well be that a person who did not 'previously know anything of the work, would be guided by the description and induced to purchase the work. There is another point of view in which this case appears to me to be even clearer. Suppose the case of a professional

(a) *Lord Byron* v. *Johnston,* 2 Meriv. 29.
(b) *Wyatt* v. *Barnard,* 3 V. & B. 77.
(c) *Hotten* v. *Arthur,* 1 H. & M. 603; 32 L. J. (Ch.) 771; 11 W. R. 934; 9 L. T. (N.S.) 199. So there may be copyright in a descriptive catalogue of tricks and magical apparatus: *Bland* v. *Hiam,* 'Times,' 15th Jan. 1873.

writer (there may well be such), whose peculiar department it is to make out "Catalogues Raisonnés" of this Catalogues
kind, and to write such abstracts of the noticeable raisonnés.
points in the various books of the catalogue as we have
here. A man who is an author for this purpose would
naturally expect that the very fact that he had printed
such notes for one publisher would lead to his employment for a similar purpose by another. Suppose now this
other to say to him, ' I have no occasion for your
services, paste and scissors work will give me all I want,'
would it be denied that he would have a right to come
here to prevent this unremunerative use of his labour? In
this case the plaintiff is both author and publisher; but
I do not see any reason for putting him in any worse
position on that account. True, the principal value may
be in the books themselves, but I cannot therefore refuse
to recognise the property which this gentleman has in
the product of his mental exertion; mental exertion used
for this particular purpose, and in print. So soon as
these notes are printed, I consider them completely
protected by the Copyright Acts."

This case was followed by Sir Charles Hall, V.C., in Tradesmen's
Grace v. *Newman* (a). The plaintiff there was a " cemetery catalogues.
stone and marble mason," and had published a book containing, with some letterpress, lithographic sketches of
monumental designs taken from tombstones in cemeteries.
The publication was intended to serve as an advertisement
of the plaintiff's business, and to enable customers to
whom it was given to select designs to be executed by the
plaintiff, yet the court held it to be a proper subject of
copyright.

But an advertisement which has no other use or value No copyright
than to make known the place and kind of business of the in advertisement of place
advertiser is not within the scope of the copyright law. and kind of
business only.
The point to be determined is whether the advertisement
is merely such, useful for no other purpose than to make

(a) L. R. 19 Eq. 623; see also *Hogg* v. *Scott*, 18 Id. 444; *Collender* v.
Griffith, 11 Blatchf. (Amer.) 212.

H

known the business of the advertiser, or if it has any value as a contribution to knowledge. The matter came before the court in the case of *Cobbett* v. *Woodward* (a) The plaintiff, an extensive dealer in upholstery and house furniture, had published and registered an illustrated guide for furnishing houses, and circulated it as an advertisement of his business. The defendant, who was engaged in the same line of business, copied fifty-five of the illustrations and a large portion of the text. In defence it was contended that the plaintiff's book was a mere advertisement, and was, therefore, not within the Copyright Act. The court held that the drawings in the plaintiff's book were not entitled to protection, on the ground that they were mere advertisements. With regard to the text, a distinction was drawn between that part " which bears the trace of original composition," and that which " simply describes the contents of a warehouse, the exertions of the proprietors, or the common mode of using familiar articles." The court held that matter of the latter kind was not entitled to protection : but that the plaintiff was entitled to an injunction restraining the defendant from publishing about sixty words of " original composition " which had been copied. In the case referred to, Lord Romilly considered that the distinction between directories, concordances, dictionaries, &c. and the work then in question was, that such works were compiled and published for the information and use of the public, and were bought by the public without any reference to individual benefit—nothing in the shape of advertisements of articles specified in the work forming a part of the work, whereas in the case before him the work was a mere advertisement for the sale of particular articles which any one might advertise for sale. " If a man," said he, " not being a vendor of any of the articles in question, were to publish a work for the purpose of informing the public of what was the most convenient species of articles of house furniture, or the most graceful

(a) L. R. 14 Eq. 407.

species of decorations for articles of house furniture, what they ought to cost, and where they might be bought, and were to illustrate his work with designs and with drawings of each article he described—such a work as this could not be pirated with impunity, and the attempt to do so would be stopped by the injunction of the Court of Chancery; yet, if it were done with no such object, but solely for the purpose of advertising particular articles for sale, and promoting the private trade of the publisher by the sale of articles which any other person might sell as well as the first advertiser, and if in fact it contained little more than an illustrated inventory of the contents of a warehouse, I know of no law which, while it would not prevent the second advertiser from selling the same articles, would prevent him from using the same advertisement, provided he did not in such advertisement by any device suggest that he was selling the works and designs of the first advertiser. At the same time, I am bound to say that where it is shewn that the second advertiser has been making use literally of the drawings of the first advertiser and copying them precisely, I think that the court, though it could not stop him from taking that course, must feel that a use has been made of the works of the first advertiser which would not be considered fair amongst gentlemen, nor (for the rules are the same as regards the usual intercourse of life) amongst fair traders, and would not give costs to the man who deliberately endeavoured to profit by the exertions of his fellow-tradesmen.

"But at the last it always comes to this, that in fact there is no copyright in an advertisement. If you copy the advertisement of another, you do him no wrong, unless in so doing you lead the public to believe that you sell the articles of the person whose advertisement you copy. A different rule applies to the letterpress which is said to be copied. Wherever this letterpress bears the trace of original composition it is entitled to protection, but not where it simply describes the contents of a warehouse, the exertions of the proprietor, or the common mode of using familiar articles."

Principles on which copyright in an advertising medium depends.

The principles to be extracted from this decision are not very obvious, but the only consistent view which can be drawn from it seems to be that there may be copyright in matter, whether pictorial or literary, designed or used as an advertisement, provided it be original, and have a value *apart from its use as a mere advertising medium.*

It is submitted that the distinction drawn in the above decision between the different sources from which the work may emanate is not sound. The question whether an author of a work is entitled to copyright therein, depends neither upon the vocation of the author or the purpose for which he has designed or may use it, but on the character, the inherent qualities of the production itself.

Copyright in a diagram.

It has been held in America that a diagram with directions for cutting garments, printed on a single sheet, is a book within the meaning of the statute, and the author entitled accordingly to copyright (a), but that a mere label, capable of no other use than to be pasted on a bottle, is not a book and does not entitle the author to copyright (b); and in this country it has been held that a **Scoring-tablet.** scoring sheet or "tablet," used in the game of cricket, is not a book, and the author thereof is not entitled to copyright therein (c).

No copyright in a mere plan.

There can be no copyright in the mere plan of a work; nor any exclusive property in a general subject or in the particular method of treating it. Any number of persons may use the same common materials, in a like manner and for a similar purpose. Their productions may contain the same thoughts and ideas; and resemblance to each other is immaterial so long as there is no unlawful copying.

Copyright in newspaper telegrams.

There can of course be copyright in newspaper

(a) *Drury* v. *Ewing*, 1 Bond (Amer.) 540.
(b) *Scoville* v. *Toland*, 6 West. Law Jour. 84.
(c) *Page* v. *Wisden*, 20 L. T. (N.S.) 435.

telegrams. A case not long since came before the CAP. II.
Supreme Court in Melbourne. It appeared that the proprietors of the 'Melbourne Argus' pay a large sum for the
purpose of obtaining the latest telegrams from Europe,
and any newspaper proprietors who may wish to publish
the telegrams so obtained can do so by paying a contribution towards the expenses incurred. The proprietor
of the 'Gipps' Land Mercury' made an agreement to pay
for the right of republishing the telegrams, but after
carrying out the arrangement for some months cancelled
the agreement. The European telegrams received by the
'Argus' were, however, re-published in another form, as
from a Melbourne correspondent of the 'Mercury,' with
the preliminary words "It is reported," or "The news
about town is." This was considered a breach of the
copyright which the proprietors of the 'Argus' possessed in
the telegrams, and a suit was instituted in the Equity
Court to restrain the proprietor of the 'Mercury' from republishing the telegrams. It was argued for the defendant that, as the telegrams were matters of news, any
one could re-publish them without breach of the Copyright Act; but Mr. Justice Molesworth held that the
plaintiff had a property in the telegrams, and that no one
could re-publish them without the permission of the
person to whom they had been sent in the first instance.
An injunction was, therefore, granted to restrain the
defendant from publishing the telegrams.

Questions of great nicety and difficulty may arise as to How far new
editions the
subject of
copyright.
how far a new edition of a work is a proper subject for
copyright. A new edition of a book may be a reprint of
the original edition, which does not entitle the author to
a new term of copyright running from the new edition;
or it may be so enlarged and improved as to constitute in
reality a new work; for example, a scientific work twenty
or thirty years old may be comparatively worthless,
owing to the progress of science in the interval: but a
new edition, particularly if it be the production of the
original author, would be as valuable at a later period as

the original edition of the book was at the time it was published. There are many courses which lay between the two extremes, and the difficulty would be to lay down any general rule as to what amount of additions, alterations, or new matter would entitle the second or new edition of a book to the privilege of copyright, or whether the copyright extends to the book as amended or improved, or is confined to the additions and improvements themselves as distinguished from the rest of the book (a).

The general rule is, that each successive edition, which is substantially different from the preceding ones, or which contains new matter of substantial amount or value, becomes entitled to copyright as a new work, and it is immaterial whether the new edition is produced by condensing, expanding, correcting, re-writing, or otherwise altering the original work; or by introducing notes, citations, or other additions. Nor is it essential that the new edition should be an improvement on the old, the sole question is whether it is substantially different. A few mere colourable alterations in the text or the addition of a few unimportant notes will not be enough to sustain copyright as in a new work. As Lord Kinloch said in *Black* v. *Murray* (a), to create a copyright by alterations of the text, these must be extensive and substantial, practically making a new book. With regard to notes, in like manner, they must exhibit an addition to the work which is not superficial or colourable, but imparts to the book a true and real value, over and above that belonging to the text. This value may perhaps be rightly expressed by saying that the book will procure purchasers in the market on special account of these notes. There is involved in such annotation, and often in a very eminent degree, an exercise of intellect and an application of learning which place the annotator in the position and character of author in the proper sense of the

(a) 9 Sc. Sess. Cas. 3rd Ser. 341; *Hedderwick* v. *Griffin*, 3 Sc. Sess. Cas. 2nd Ser. 383.

word. It will still of course remain open to publish the
text, which *ex hypothesi* is the same as in the original
edition. But to take and publish the notes will be a
clear infringement of copyright.

An action was raised in the Scotch Court of Session at
the instance of Messrs. Black against Messrs. Murray &
Son for a breach of copyright, and the infringement was
said to be contained in a book published by the defenders
in 1869, which purported to be an edition of the
'Minstrelsy of the Scottish Border,' collected by Sir Walter
Scott, and it was stated in the title page to be a reprint
of the original edition. The peculiarity of the case was
that the original edition of the 'Minstrelsy of the Scottish
Border' was no longer protected by copyright; and
therefore, if the book was what its title represented it to
be, a mere reprint of the original edition, the complaint
of the pursuers could not be maintained. But they
alleged that this was a false pretence on the face of the
title page, and that while all the poems and ballads
contained in the original edition of the 'Minstrelsy' were
reproduced in this volume, there was a considerable
amount of other matter borrowed from works the copyright of which had not expired. The Lord President said
that in the first complaint the pursuers alleged that the
defenders had illegally copied and pirated from the copyright edition of the 'Minstrelsy of the Scottish Border'
the advertisement, or part thereof, prepared by Mr.
John Gibson Lockhart, and that they had printed the
same, or part thereof, as a preface to their volume, and,
further, that they had copied from the 'Minstrelsy' the
notes, quotations, illustrations, and references, or the
essential parts thereof. The defenders could have no excuse,
if this were the case, for it was distinctly stated in that
advertisement that this copyright edition contained
matter which was not to be found in the original edition.
That there might be a copyright of notes, even when the
text was not copyright, was a fixed principle in law, and

CAP. II. most deservedly so; for there was no doubt that the addition of good notes to a standard work was a task worthy of the highest literary talent and reputation; and it must be remembered that Mr. Lockhart stood in a position of peculiar advantage as the editor and annotator of Sir Walter Scott's works, being his son-in-law and literary executor, and having opportunities during the lifetime of Sir Walter Scott to collect materials for the performance of such a task. His lordship, after quoting numerous passages, said there was no doubt that the editor of the defenders' book of 1869 had copied these notes of Mr. Lockhart in the most slavish manner, without even verifying or attempting to make them more accurate than Mr. Lockhart's. It was quite clear to his mind that there had been an appropriation of original matter and quotations, and therefore he held that this part of the pursuers' case had been completely made out. In the said complaint it was alleged that the defender had used notes from 'Old Mortality' with reference to the skirmish of Drumclog, and a letter written by Claverhouse to the Earl of Linlithgow, and also a description of the Battle of Drumclog on Loudon-hill. He was of opinion that the note with the reference to the Battle of Drumclog stood in the same position as the notes to the 'Minstrelsy,' and there again he held that piracy had been committed. In regard to the next complaint—that the defender had copied from volume 8 of the poetical works, containing the 'Lady of the Lake' and other poems, and an account of the 'Massacre of Glencoe'—he was of opinion that there had been the same kind of piracy as in the notes to the 'Minstrelsy.' The Court granted costs to the plaintiffs (a).

Copyright in each edition.   The copyright in each edition will extend from the date of that edition, and will be wholly independent of the copyright in any preceding one. Copyright may be obtained for any number of editions and it is immaterial

(a) *Black* v. *Murray*, Sol. Journ. Dec. 31, 1870.

whether copyright has existed or not in any previous one. And though no person but the proprietor of the copyright may bring out a new edition of the work, supposing the copyright to be subsisting, without his consent; yet if the work be not protected there is nothing to prevent any person from bringing out a new edition of the work and obtaining a valid copyright therein.

CHAPTER III.

TERM OF COPYRIGHT, AND IN WHOM VESTED.

Term of copy-right.

MANY have agitated for the establishment of a perpetual copyright, together with the bestowal upon authors of the exclusive power of abridging, dramatizing, and metamorphosing their own works at will, turning prose into poetry, romances into plays, and *vice versâ*. The claim of authors resulting from the principles of natural right involves the perpetual duration of the property. But in order that such property should be of value, it is necessary that society should interfere actively for its protection. Society will not ordinarily be willing to apply penal remedies in favour of an exclusive right, further than it finds such a course beneficial to its own interests, in the broadest sense of the term. It is argued, however, that the concessionary allowance of a perpetuity in copyright would encourage publication, and tend greatly to the promotion and furtherance of science and literature. But, admitting that learning and science should be encouraged, that everything tending or conducible to the advancement of knowledge, and consequently to the happiness of the community, should be favoured and tenderly cherished by the legislature, and that the labour of every individual should be properly recompensed, it does not follow that the same or a similar end might not be obtained by different and less objectionable means.

If the individual is a gainer by the existence of perpetual copyright, society is a loser. The absurdity of the assertion that authors are alone inclined to make known their

works from the specific benefit arising from an absolute CAP. III.
perpetual monopoly, is manifest. What a studied indignity
to those who have devoted their lives to the advancement
of every science that adorns the annals of literature!
Ambition cannot be deemed a cipher; benevolence will
ever exist in the heart of man, and they at least act as
powerfully by way of conducives to the communication
of knowledge between man and man, as avaricious or
mercenary motives.

Considera-
tions respect-
ing a per-
petuity in
copyright.

A perpetuity in copyright would have the effect of
impeding the progress of literature and science, and
among other serious inconveniences we will mention one.
The text of an author, after two or three generations, if
the property be retained so long by his descendants,
would belong to so many claimants, that endless disputes
would arise as to the right to publish, which in all probability might prevent the publication altogether. The
Emperor Napoleon is reported to have stated this objection in council with his characteristic practical wisdom
as follows:—

The effect of
a perpetuity
in copyright.

" *Napoléon dit que la perpétuité de la propriété dans les
familles des auteurs aurait des inconvénients. Une propriété littéraire est une propriété incorporelle qui, se trouvant
dans la suite des temps et par le cours des successions divisée
entre une multitude d'individus, finirait; en quelque sorte,
par ne plus exister pour personne ; car, comment un grand
nombre de propriétaires, souvent éloignés les uns des autres,
et qui, après quelques générations, se connaissent à peine,
pourraient-ils s'entendre et contribuer pour réimprimer
l'ouvrage de leur auteur commun? Cependant, s'ils n'y
parviennent pas, et qu'eux seuls aient le droit de le publier, les
meilleurs livres disparaîtront insensiblement de la circulation.*

The Emperor
Napoleon's
opinion of a
perpetuity.

" *Il y aurait un autre inconvénient non moins grave. Le
progrès des lumières serait arrêté, puis qu'il ne serait plus
permis ni de commenter, ni d'annoter les ouvrages ; les
gloses, les notes, les commentaires ne pourraient être séparés
d'un texte qu'on n'aurait pas la liberté d'imprimer.*

" *D'ailleurs, un ouvrage a produit à l'auteur et à ses*

CAP. III.   *héritiers tout le bénéfice qu'ils peuvent naturellement en
attendre, lorsque le premier a eu le droit exclusif de le vendre
pendant toute sa vie, et les autres pendant les dix ans qui
suivent sa mort. Cependant, si l'on veut favoriser davantage
encore la veuve et les héritiers, qu'on porte leur propriété à
vingt ans* " (a).

Though we could not, therefore, uphold a perpetual
copyright, believing that its existence would by no means
tend to the spread or encouragement of literature, we would
willingly offer our support to the extension of the period
during which literary copyright is at present protected.

Present term
of copyright.

The 3rd section of the 5 & 6 Vict. c. 45, enacts that
the copyright in every book which shall after the passing
of that Act be published in the lifetime of its author
shall endure for the natural life of such author, and for
the further term of seven years, commencing at the time
of his death, and shall be the property of such author and
his assigns; provided always, that if the said term of seven
years shall expire before the end of forty-two years from
the first publication of such book, the copyright shall in
that case endure for such period of forty-two years; and
that the copyright in every book which shall be published
after the death of its author shall endure for the term of
forty-two years from the first publication thereof, and
shall be the property of the proprietor of the author's
manuscript from which such book shall be first published,
and his assigns.

As to copy-
right subsist-
ing at the time
of passing of
Copyright
Act, 1842.

In case of books published before the passing of the
Act and in which copyright then subsisted, the 4th section
provides that the copyright shall be extended and endure
for the full term provided by the Act in cases of books
thereafter published, and shall be the property of the
person who at the time of the passing of the Act shall be
the proprietor of such copyright. But it is further provided
that in all cases in which such copyright shall belong in
whole or in part to a publisher or other person who shall

(a) Locré, *Législation civile de la France*, tit. ix. pp. 17–19 ; Renouard,
Droits d'Auteurs, tom. 2, p. 387.

have acquired it for other consideration than that of CAP. III. natural love and affection, such copyright shall not be extended by the Act, but shall endure for the term which shall subsist therein at the time of the passing of the Act, and no longer, unless the author of such book if he shall be living, or his personal representative if he shall be dead, and the proprietor of such copyright, shall before the expiration of such term consent to accept the benefits of the Act in respect of such book, and shall cause a minute of such consent in the form in that behalf given in the schedule to the Act to be entered in the registry at Stationers' Hall, in which case such copyright shall endure for the full term provided in cases of books published after the passing of the Act, and shall be the property of such person or persons as in such minute shall be expressed.

The 5th section, in order to provide against the suppression of books of importance to the public, provides that the Judicial Committee of Her Majesty's Privy Council may, on complaint made to them that the proprietor of the copyright in any book after the death of its author has refused to republish or to allow the republication of the same, and that by reason of such refusal such book may be withheld from the public, grant a licence to such complainant to publish such book, in such manner and subject to such conditions as they may think fit (a). Judicial Committee of Privy Council may license republication of certain books.

The Royal Commissioners in their recent report on copyright recommend that the term shall be for life and thirty years from his death in cases of books published in the author's lifetime and with his name; and for thirty years from the date of the deposit of the book for the use of the British Museum as to works published anonymously or after the death of their authors, and as to cyclopædias; but that if the author of an anonymous work publishes in his lifetime an edition bearing his name he should be entitled to copyright therein for his life and thirty years after his death. Suggestion of Copyright Commissioners as to extension of term of copyright.

(a) This section seems to have been put in force with regard to Sir Kenelm Digby's ' Broadstone of Honour.'

CAP. III.

Meaning of
the word
" book."

What is a
publication ?

The term " book " by virtue of the interpretation clause
is to be construed to signify and include every volume,
part, or division of a volume (a), a pamphlet, sheet of
letterpress (b), sheet of music, map, chart, or plan
separately published. But a separate article, advertised
to form part of a periodical publication, is not a book
within the meaning of the Act, and therefore does not
require registration under the 24th section (c).

The copyright is, we have seen, to run from the date
of the publication of the work, consequently it will be
necessary to inquire what, in the eye of the law, may be
regarded as equivalent to publication (d). In *Coleman* v.
Wathen (e), it was said that the acting of a dramatic
composition on the stage was not a publication within the
statute. The plaintiff, it appears, had purchased from
O'Keefe the copyright of an entertainment called the
' Agreeable Surprise,' and the defendant represented this
piece upon the stage. The mere act of repeating such a
performance from memory was held to be no publication.
On the other hand, to take down from the mouths of the
actors the words of a dramatic composition, which the author
had occasionally suffered to be performed, but never printed
or published, and to publish it from the notes so taken
down, was deemed a breach of right; and the publication
of the copy so taken down was restrained by injunction (f).

By the 20th section of the Copyright Act, 1842, it is
declared, that the first public representation or performance of any dramatic piece or musical composition shall be
deemed equivalent to the first publication of any book (g).

(a) See the *University of Cambridge* v. *Bryer*, 16 East. 317 ; *The British
Museum* v. *Payne*, 2 Y. & J. 166 ; *Clayton* v. *Stone*, 2 Paine (Amer.) 383 ;
Scoville v. *Toland*, 6 West. L. J. (Amer.) 84. But a label used in the sale
of an article is not a book : *Coffeen* v. *Brunton*, 4 McLean (Amer.) 517.
(b) See *Clementi* v. *Goulding*, 2 Camp. 25 ; 11 East, 244 ; *Hime* v. *Dale*,
2 Camp. 27 a ; *White* v. *Geroch*, 2 B. & Ald. 298.
(c) *Murray* v. *Maxwell*, 3 L. T. (N.S.) Ch. 466.
(d) The use of letters as evidence in a court is not publication : 7 Byth
& Jarm., by Sweet, 628, note (a).
(e) 5 T. R. 245 : see *Roberts* v. *Myers*, 13 Mo. Law. Rep. (Amer.) 397 ;
Crowe v. *Aiken*, Amer. Law. Rep. L. Jour. vol. 5, No. 226. 1870.
(f) *Macklin* v. *Richardson*, Amb. 694, cited 2 Kent's Com. 378.
(g) *Post.*

A presentation of copies, on the part of the author, CAP. III. may not amount to a publication, but the gratuitous Gratuitous circulation generally would seem to be so (*a*). circulation when a

Abbott, C.J., in *White* v. *Geroch* (*b*) considered that a *sale* publication. of copies of a work in manuscript amounted to a *publication* of the work from which the statutory period would commence to run, and, referring to this opinion, Mr. Sweet, in his notes to Bythewood and Jarman's Conveyancing (*c*), says "this construction, if well founded, would apply to the recent Act." He admits there is no direct authority on the point; but he states that it seems clear that a *gratuitous* circulation of copies of a work among friends and acquaintances would not amount to a publication; quoting in support of this proposition the *Duke of Queensbury* v. *Shebbeare*; and *Dr. Paley's Case*, where the bookseller was restrained from publishing manuscripts left by Dr. Paley for the use of his own parishioners only. The distinction is in the limit of the circulation, if limited to friends and acquaintances it would not be a publication, but if general, and not so limited, it would be.

So the distribution of lithograph copies of music for Private distribution of private use, and not for the purpose of sale or exportation, lithographic has been held to be a publication, but on the other hand it copies. is clear that a private circulation for a restricted purpose is not a publication. Thus, in *Prince Albert* v. *Strange* (*d*), it appeared that her Majesty and the late Prince Consort had given to their intimate friends lithographic copies of drawings and etchings which they had made for their own amusement. This was held to be a private circulation of copies, and hence not a publication.

In an American case (*e*) it appeared that the plaintiff, Circulation who was a teacher of book-keeping, had written his among pupils of a system of system of instruction on separate cards, for the convenience book-keeping.

(*a*) *Vide Novello* v. *Ludlow*, 12 C. B. 177; 16 Jur. 689; 21 L. J. (C.P.) 169; *Dr. Paley's Case* cited 2 V & B. 23; *Alexander* v. *Mackenzie*, 9 Sess. Cas. 2nd series, 748.

(*b*) 2 B. & A. 998; S. C. 1 Chit. Rep. 24.

(*c*) Vol. 7, p. 626.   (*d*) 2 De G. & Sm. 652; 1 Mac. & G. 25.

(*e*) *Bartlett* v. *Crittenden*, 4 McLean, 300; 5 Id. 32; *Rees* v. *Peltzer*, 75 Ill. (Amer.) 475.

of giving instruction to his pupils. He had permitted them to copy these cards for their own convenience, and to enable them to instruct others. The defendant published copies of the cards, which he had obtained while a pupil in the school, and maintained that the plaintiff, by permitting his manuscripts to be so copied, had abandoned them to the public. The court, however, held this to be a private circulation of copies, which did not prejudice' the owner's common law rights. "The students of Bartlett who made these copies," said Mr. Justice McLean, "have a right to them and their use as originally intended. But they have no right to a use which was not in the contemplation of the complainant and of themselves when the consent was first given . . . . The lecturer designed to instruct his hearers, and not the public at large. Any use, therefore, of the lectures which should operate injuriously to the lecturer would be a fraud upon him for which the law would give him redress."

The question of publication does not depend on the number of copies sold or given away; because a sale of one copy only is as clearly a publication as is the sale of ten thousand. Nor can it be essential that a single copy be disposed of before the work can be said to be published, for the work is published when it is publicly offered for sale. The act of publication is the act of the author, and cannot be dependent upon the act of a purchaser. Printing does not amount to publication, for it is obvious that it may be withheld from the public long after it is in print. To constitute publication it is necessary that the work shall be exposed for sale or offered gratuitously to the general public, so that any person may have an opportunity of enjoying that for which copyright is intended to be secured.

Work must be first published in this — The previous publication of a work abroad disqualifies it for copyright in this country (a). If, however, the pub-

(a) See *Clementi* v. *Walker*, 2 B. & C. 861 ; *Guichard* v. *Mori*, 9 L. J. (Ch.) 227 ; *Delondre* v. *Shaw*, 2 Sim. 237 ; *Page* v. *Townsend*, 5 Sim. 395; *Boucicault* v. *Delafield*, 1 H. & M. 597 ; 23 L. J. (N.S.) Ch. 38 ; *Hedderwich* v. *Griffin*, 3 Sess. Cas., 2nd Series, 383.

lication here and abroad be simultaneous, the publication abroad will not stand in the way of copyright in this country (a). The legislature contemplates publication *here* and *here only*, and it contemplates such publication only when made by the author, or with such consent and authority from him as the statute requires; and it contemplates publication of foreign books only when they are capable of advancing literature here, that is to say, before the work is published here by a person who has obtained it fairly and *bonâ fide* under a previous assignment by the author in a foreign country (b).

So where the work was composed before June, 1814, and in that month the author sanctioned a publication of it in France, and five copies of it were deposited in a musical depôt at Paris; in July, 1814, the author made a verbal arrangement with the plaintiff, and the latter published in the September following; it was held, that the publication was not such a publication by the author as to entitle him to the statutory privilege (c).

That the publication must be in the United Kingdom scarcely admits of a doubt. The words of the 3rd section are "every book which shall be published," without saying where; but it would be inconsistent with the usual practice of the Imperial Parliament to create a system of copyright law for all the colonies and dependencies of the empire, many of which have representative institutions of their own, without any consultation with those colonies or dependencies, and without any consideration whether a uniform and arbitrary system, such as that introduced by the Act, would be suitable to the varied circumstances, states of civilization, and systems of jurisprudence and judicature in these different colonies and possessions (d). In deciding this question Lord Cairns

(a). Phillips on Copy. 52, citing Erle, J., in *Cocks* v. *Purday*, 2 Car. & Kirw. 269; *Routledge* v. *Low*, L. R. 3 H. L. 100.
(b) Per Bayley, J., *Clementi* v. *Walker*, 2 B. & C. 861; *Chappell* v. *Purday*, 4 Y. & C. 485; 14 M. & W. 303; *Guichard* v. *Mori*, 9 L. J. (Ch.) 227.
(c) *Clementi* v. *Walker, supra*.
(d) Per Lord Cairns, *Routledge* v. *Low*, L. R. 3 H. L. 100.

said: "But there are, as it seems to me, still clearer indications in the Act of the intention of the legislature on
this point. By the 8th section copies of every book are
to be delivered to various public libraries in the United
Kingdom within one month after demand in writing; an
enactment which in the case of a publication at the
antipodes could not be complied with. By the 10th section
penalties for not delivering these copies are to be recovered before two justices of the county or place where
the publisher making default shall reside, or by action of
debt in any court of record in the United Kingdom. By
the 11th section the book of registry of copyrights and of
assignments is to be kept at Stationers' Hall, in London,
and no registry is provided for the colonies. By the 14th
section a motion to expunge or vary any entry in this
registry is to be made in the Court of Queen's Bench,
Common Pleas, or Exchequer. These clauses are intelligible if the publication is in the United Kingdom, but
hardly so if it may be in India or Australia. Finally by
the 17th section there is a provision against any person
importing into any part of the United Kingdom, or any
other part of the British dominions, for sale or hire, any
copyright book first composed or written, or printed and
published in any part of the United Kingdom, and
reprinted in any country or place out of the British
dominions; a provision shewing clearly, as it appears to
me, that publication in the United Kingdom is indispensable to copyright (a)."

An English-
man resident
abroad may
have a copy-
right.
A residence abroad by an English subject, or the fact
of the work having been composed abroad, either by an
Englishman or a foreigner, would not have the effect of
preventing the author from acquiring a copyright in this
country. On this point there can be no doubt, for inde-
pendent.of the peculiar wording of the copyright statute
and under the old Act of Queen Anne this was decided, the
reason assigned being, that an English subject, though
resident abroad, does not by such residence throw off his

(a) *Per* Lord Cairns, *Routledge* v. *Lowe*, L. R. 3 H. L. 100.

natural allegiance; he cannot be relieved from it, and therefore carries with him the natural rights of a subject of England wherever he goes (a). That gives him, though resident abroad, the right of publishing and acquiring a copyright here, because he has always fulfilled the implied condition of being a subject of, and owing allegiance to, the crown of Great Britain. This of course could not be said of a foreigner who was not actually resident here (b). Nor could he (being resident abroad) under the Act of Queen Anne have acquired a copyright in this country, though, as we shall presently see, there have been conflicting opinions on the point.

Copyright has no existence in the law of nations; it acquires a power simply by the municipal law of each particular community. "As soon," observes Mr. Curtis (c), "as a copy of a book is landed in any foreign country, all complaint of its republication is, in the absence of a treaty, fruitless, because no means of redress exist, except under the law of the author's own country. It becomes public property, not because the justice of the case is changed by the passage across the sea or a boundary, but because there are no means of enforcing the private right."

Copyright no existence in the law of nations.

The only persons who can claim the copyright in a book published before the 1st of July, 1842, are the proprietor on that day of the copyright therein, or his assigns; and in the case of a book since published, the author or his assigns. And as the word "author" is used without limitation or restriction, it is equally applicable to foreigners as to British subjects. There is nothing in any part of the Act to restrict the word "author" to British subjects (d).

Persons who may claim copyright.

As to aliens, the following rules have been laid down at

(a) But British subjects under certain circumstances may, under the Naturalization Act of 33 Vict. c. 13, free themselves from their allegiance, and may resume it again.

(b) Per Lord St. Leonards in *Jefferys* v. *Boosey*, 4 H. L. C. 985; but see *Routledge* v. *Low*, L. R. 3 H. L. 100.

(c) 'Copyright,' 22.

(d) The case of *Jefferys* v. *Boosey* was a decision under the Statute of Anne.

CAP. III.

How aliens may acquire copyright in this country.

Whether a foreigner resident abroad can obtain a copyright in a work first published in this country.

various times, though not without much discussion and difference of opinion :—That an alien may acquire copyright in this country on three conditions: first, publication must be in the United Kingdom; secondly, there must have been no previous publication; and, thirdly, the author must be at the time of publication within the British dominions (a).

In *D'Almaine* v. *Boosey* (b) the two principal questions that arose were, whether the law would protect the assignee of foreign copyright at all, and whether any protection could exist where the work had been first published abroad. Alluding to *Delondre* v. *Shaw*, Lord Abinger said, " If the Vice-Chancellor had decided expressly that a foreigner, *quâ* foreigner, had no protection in England in regard to copyright, I confess I should have doubted the correctness of that decision; though, certainly, I should not have decided in opposition to him, but should have put this case to the course of further investigation, out of respect to his authority. But the case which has been cited upon the subject does not go that length; it is in principle not quite intelligible; but there was clear ground for an injunction independently of the question of copyright. Besides, that was a case where one of the parties resided abroad. Now, the Acts give no protection to foreigners resident abroad in respect of works published abroad; and all the Vice-Chancellor said was, that the publisher of a work at Paris could not protect himself in a court of justice in England, either by action or injunction."

Again, in *Bentley* v. *Foster* (c), Vice-Chancellor Shadwell said, that if an alien friend wrote a book, whether abroad or in this country, and gave the British public the advantage of his industry and knowledge by first publishing the

---

(a) The United Kingdom embraces England and Wales, Scotland and Ireland; while the British dominions include "all parts of the United Kingdom of Great Britain and Ireland, the islands of Jersey and Guernsey, all parts of the East and West Indies, and all the colonies, settlements, and possessions of the Crown which now are or hereafter may be acquired." 5 & 6 Vict. c. 45, s. 2.

(b) 1 Y. & C. 288.

(c) 10 Sim. 329 : see also *Page* v. *Townsend*, 5 Sim. 395 ; *Tonson* v. *Collins*, 1 W. Bl. 301 ; *Bach* v. *Longman*, 2 Cowp. 623 ; *contrà*, *Chappell* v. *Purday*, 14 M. & W. 303.

work here, he was entitled to the protection of the laws relating to copyright in this country.

The question was fully discussed in *Bach* v. *Longman* (a). Bach was a musical composer, who had come into this country from Germany. He sued Longman for pirating a sonata, which the latter had published in England, and he was successful in his suit. In accordance with these decisions, in the year 1845, Chief Baron Pollock, in delivering the judgment of the Barons of the Exchequer in *Chappell* v. *Purday* (b), stated the result of the cases at that time decided on the subject to be that if a foreign author, not having published abroad, first publishes in England, he may have the benefit of the statutes ; and on the authority of these cases, and the general rule that an alien may acquire personal rights and maintain personal actions in respect of injuries to them (c), it was determined in *Cocks* v. *Purday* (d), that an *alien amy* resident abroad, the author of a work of which he is also the first publisher in *England*, and which he has not made *publici juris* by a previous publication elsewhere, has a copyright in that work, whether it be composed in this country or abroad. This determination was supported in *Boosey* v. *Davidson* (e), and subsequently considered by the Court

(a) 2 Cowp. 623.
(b) 14 M. & W. 303, 320.
(c) See *Pisani* v. *Lawson*, 8 Scott, 182; 6 Bing. (N.S.) 90; 8 Dowl. 57; *Tuerloote* v *Morrison*, 1 Bulst. 134; Yelv. 198; Dyer, 2 b.

(d) 5 C. B. 860, since overruled.

(e) 18 L. J. (Q.B.) 174; 13 Q. B. 257. In *Buxton* v. *James* (5 De G. & Sm. 80 ; 16 Jur. 15), an alien residing abroad composed three musical pieces in a foreign country, and sold the copyright in this country to the plaintiff, a British subject, who published the work in London. The work was published on the same day in Prussia. On motion in a suit instituted by the purchaser of the copyright against a person who had, without leave, published the musical compositions in this country, the Court granted an injunction restraining the unauthorized publication. And in *Ollendorf* v. *Black* (4 De G. & Sm. 209; 14 Jur. 1088; 20 L. J. (Ch.) 165), it was held that an alien resident abroad might himself have copyright in a work written by himself, and published for the first time in this country, at all events if he were resident here at the time of publication. In this case an alien author had first published a work while resident in this country, and an edition of the same work was published in Frankfort, and copies were imported into this country and sold by a London bookseller, and the alien filed a bill for an injunction to restrain the sale, and on motion the same was granted, the plaintiff undertaking to bring an action if the defendants desired it.

of Exchequer in *Boosey* v. *Purday* (a), when that court heldthat a foreigner had no such capacity.

This last was the case of a foreigner domiciled abroad sending his work to Great Britain for first publication, and endeavouring to confer a valid title upon a British subject. Baron Pollock there said: "Our opinion is that the legislature must be considered *primâ facie* to mean to legislate for its own subjects, or those who owe obedience to its laws; and, consequently, that the Acts apply *primâ facie* to British subjects only in some sense of that term, which would include subjects by birth or residence being authors; and the context or subject matter of the statutes does not call upon us to put a different construction upon them. The object of the legislature clearly is not to encourage the importation of foreign books and their first publication in England as a benefit to this country; but to promote the cultivation of the intellect of its own subjects."

Case of *Jefferys* v. *Boosey*.

In this unsettled state of the law arose the case of *Jefferys* v. *Boosey*, which was ultimately carried on appeal to the House of Lords.

Bellini, a foreign musical composer, resident at that time in his own country, composed a certain work, in which, by the laws there in force, he had a copyright. He then assigned to Ricordi, another foreigner also resident there, according to the laws of their country, his right to the copyright in the composition of which he was the author, and which was then unpublished. The assignee brought the composition to this country, and, before publication, assigned it, according to the forms required by the laws of this country, to an Englishman. The first publication took place in this country. The work was subsequently pirated, and proceedings instituted which ultimately reached the Upper House. The judges were called upon for their opinions, which they delivered *seriatim*, and judgment was finally pronounced by the House in favour of the defendant. The grounds of the decision were that an Act of Parliament of this country,

(a) 4 Ex. 145.

having within its view a municipal operation only, and being therefore limited to this kingdom, cannot be held to extend beyond our own subjects, except as both statutes and common law so provide for foreigners *when they become resident here*, and owe at least a temporary allegiance to the sovereign, and thereby acquire rights just as other persons do; not because they are foreigners, but because being here, they are here entitled, in so far as they do not break in upon certain rules, to the general benefit of the law for the protection of their property, in the same way as if they were natural-born subjects. " Where an exclusive privilege," said Lord Cranworth (a), " is given to a particular class at the expense of the rest of Her Majesty's subjects, the object of giving that privilege must be taken to have been a national object; and the privileged class to be confined to a portion of that community for the general advantage of which the enactment is made. When I say that the Legislature must *primâ facie* be taken to legislate only for its own subjects, I must be taken to include under the word 'subjects,' all persons who are within the Queen's dominions, and who thus owe to her a temporary allegiance. I do not doubt but that a foreigner resident here, and composing and publishing a book here, is an author within the meaning of the statute; he is within its words and spirit. I go further; I think that if a foreigner having composed, but not having published a work abroad, were to come to this country, and the week or day after his arrival, were to print and publish it here, he would be within the protection of the statute. This would be so if he had composed the work after his arrival in this country, and I do not think any question can be raised as to when and where he composed it. So long as a literary work remains unpublished at all, it has no existence, except in the mind of its author, or in the papers in which he, for his own convenience, may have

(a) *Jefferys* v. *Boosey*, 4 H. L. C. 815 ; 1 Jur. (N.S) 615 ; 24 L. J. (Ex.) 81 ; *Low* v. *Routledge*, 10 Jur. (N.S.) 922 ; 10 L. T. (N.S.) 838 ; 11 Jur. (N.S.) 989 ; *Routledge* v. *Low*, Law Rep. 3 H. L. 100 ; 37 L. J. (Ch.) 454 ; 18 L. T. (N.S.) 874.

CAP. III. embodied it. Copyright, defined to mean the exclusive
right of multiplying copies, commences at the instant of
publication ; and if the author is at that time in England,
and while here he first prints and publishes his work, he
is, I apprehend, an author within the meaning of the
statute, even though he should have come here solely
with a view to the publication. The law does not require
or permit any investigation on a subject which would
obviously, for the most part, baffle all inquiry, namely, how
far the actual composition of the work itself had, in the
mind of its author, taken place here or abroad. If he
comes here with his ideas already reduced into form in his
own mind, still, if he first publishes after his arrival in
this country, he must be treated as an author in this
country. If publication, which is (so to say) the overt act
establishing authorship, takes place here, the author is
then a British subject, wherever he may, in fact, have composed his work. But if at the time when copyright commences by publication, the foreign author is not in this
country, he is not, in my opinion, a person whose interests
the statute meant to protect."

Extension of
copyright by
the Act of
1842.

Copyright under the statute of Anne was confined to
Great Britain. The case of *Jefferys* v. *Boosey* decided
that this statute gave the copyright in a work only to
British subjects or to foreign authors who at the time of
the first publication were in this country. But by the
29th section of the 5 & 6 Vict. c. 45, it is enacted " that the
Act shall extend to the United Kingdom of Great Britain
and Ireland, and to every part of the British dominions."
This section of the Act requires for its full effect, that the
area over which the copyright prevails should be limited,
only by the extent of the British dominions. And then it
follows that the term "author" must have a similar
extension. For in the case of *Jefferys* v. *Boosey* it was
not doubted that the term "author," though intended to
express a British subject, would apply to a foreigner
taking up residence within the limits to which copyright
extended under the 8 Anne, and those limits being now

enlarged by the 5 & 6 Vict., the residence which confers the rights of a British subject, as to copyright, upon a foreigner, may be in any part of the Queen's dominions.

It must be remembered that the case of *Jefferys* v. *Boosey* was decided under the old Copyright Act of Queen Anne, and not under the present Copyright Act, and though Lord Cranworth in a late case (a) said he could see no difference between the two statutes so far as relates to the subject of the residence of foreign authors; yet in the same case Lord Cairns was inclined to a different opinion, and in the opinion of Lord Westbury the case of *Boosey* v. *Jefferys* was a decision attached to and dependent on the particular statute of which it was the exponent; and that statute having been repealed, and replaced by another Act, with different enactments expressed in different language, could not be considered a binding authority on the exposition of this latter statute. "The Act," said his Lordship, "secures a special benefit to British subjects by promoting the advancement of learning in this country, which the Act contemplates as the result of encouraging all authors to resort to the United Kingdom for the first publication of their works. The benefit of the foreign author is incidental only to the benefit of the British public. Certainly the obligation lies on those who would give the term 'author' a restricted signification to find in the statute the reasons for so doing." "The Act," he remarks in another place, "appears to have been dictated by a wise and liberal spirit, and in the same spirit it should be interpreted, adhering of course to the settled rules of legal construction. The preamble is, in my opinion, quite inconsistent with the conclusion that the protection given by the statute was intended to be confined to the works of British authors. On the contrary, it seems to contain an invitation to men of learning in every country to make the United Kingdom the place of first publication of their works, and an extended term of copyright throughout the

(a) *Routledge* v. *Low*, L. R. 3 H. L. 114; and Lord Chelmsford was of the same opinion.

the whole of the British dominions is the reward of their so doing. So interpreted and applied, the Act is auxiliary to the advancement of learning in this country. The real condition of obtaining its advantages is the first publication by the author of his work in the United Kingdom. Nothing renders necessary his bodily presence here at the time, and I find it impossible to discover any reason why it should be required, or what it can add to the merit of the first publication. It was asked, in *Jefferys* v. *Boosey*, why should the Act (meaning the statute of Anne) be supposed to have been passed for the benefit of foreign authors? But if the like question be repeated with reference to the present Act the answer is, in the language of the preamble, that the Act is intended ' to afford greater encouragement to the production of literary works of lasting benefit to.the world; ' a purpose which has no limitation of person or place . . . . If the intrinsic merits of the reasoning on which *Jefferys* v. *Boosey* was decided be considered (and which we are at liberty to do, for it does not apply to this case as a binding authority), I must frankly admit that it by no means commands my assent."

Necessity for alien to be in the British dominions, and to publish in United Kingdom, to obtain copyright. It was admitted in *Jefferys* v. *Boosey* and expressly held in *Routledge* v. *Low* that an alien author may acquire copyright by first publishing in the United Kingdom, provided he be within the British dominions at the time of publication. It matters not where he has composed the work, nor whether he goes into the realm with the sole purpose of being there at the time of publication, and leaves when publication has taken place. The presence of the author is not necessary for any definite period, it is only necessary that he be on British soil at the time of publication (a). The author must be there in person—the presence of his assignee, publisher or agent is not sufficient. "Every alien coming into a British colony," said Turner, L.J. (b), "becomes temporarily a subject of the Crown—bound by, subject to, and entitled

(a) Suppose he went on board a British vessel?
(b) *Low* v. *Routledge*, L. R. 1 Ch. Ap. 42, 47.

to the benefit of the laws which affect all British subjects. He has obligations and rights both within and beyond the colony into which he comes. As to his rights within the colony he may well be bound by its laws, but as to his rights beyond the colony he cannot be affected by those laws; for the laws of a colony cannot extend beyond its territorial limits." And on appeal in the case last cited to the House of Lords (a), two of the greatest law lords on the Bench—Lord Cairns and Lord Westbury—were of opinion that the Act of Parliament gives a copyright to every author who first publishes his book in the United Kingdom, no matter where he lives, or under what dynasty he serves. "Protection," said the former learned judge, "is given to every author who publishes in the United Kingdom, wheresoever that author may be resident, or of whatever state he may be the subject. The intention of the Act is to obtain a benefit for the people of this country by the publication to them of works of learning, of utility, of amusement. The benefit is obtained, in the opinion of the legislature, by offering a certain amount of protection to the author, thereby inducing him to publish his work here. This is, or may be, a benefit to the author, but it is a benefit given, not for the sake of the author of the work, but for the sake of those to whom the work is communicated. The aim of the legislature is to increase the common stock of the literature of the country; and if that stock can be increased by the publication for the first time here of a new and valuable work, composed by an alien, who never has been in the country, I see nothing in the wording of the Act which prevents, nothing in the policy of the Act which should prevent, and everything in the professed object of the Act, and in its wide and general provisions, which should entitle such a person to the protection of the Act, in return and compensation for the addition he has made to the literature of the country. I

Cap. III.

Lord Cairns' and Lord Westbury's opinions on the interpretation of the Copyright Act.

(a) *Routledge* v. *Low*, L. R. 3 H. L. 100; 37 L. J. (Ch.) 454; 18 L. T. (N.S.) 874.

am glad to be able to entertain no doubt that a construction of the Act so consistent with a wise and liberal
policy is . the proper construction to be placed upon it."
To this view, however, Lord Cranworth objected, and
Lord Chelmsford doubted whether it was good in law.

In this same case it was unanimously held by Lords
Cairns, Chelmsford, Cranworth, Westbury, and Colonsay,
that to acquire a copyright under the 5 & 6 Vict. c. 45,
the work must be first published in the *United Kingdom*.
The law now, therefore, is, that if a literary or musical
work be first published in the *United Kingdom*, it may be
protected from infringement in any part of the *British
dominions;* provided that at the time of such publication, in the case of an alien friend, he is residing, however
temporarily, in any part of the British dominions ; and this
is so, although the temporary residence is in a British colony
with an independent legislature, under the laws of which
he would not be entitled to copyright; but if, on the other
hand, any such work be first published in India, Canada,
Jamaica, or any other British possession, not included in
the *United Kingdom*, no copyright can be acquired in that
work, excepting only such (if any) as the local laws of the
colony, &c., where it is first published, may afford (a).

Such portion of a work as is first pub-lished in this country will be protected. If only a portion of a work be first published in this
country, or within the scope of the British Copyright Act,
it will be protected. A., a citizen of the United States,
published a work of which he was the author, in monthly
parts between January and December, 1867, of a magazine
published in the United States. In October, 1867, A.
went to reside in Canada for the purpose of acquiring a
British copyright, and during such residence, when the
work wanted six chapters for completion in the magazine,
an edition of the whole was published in London under an

(a) The 2nd section of the Naturalization Act, 1870 (33 Vict. c. 14),
enacts that "real and personal property of *every description* may be taken,
acquired, held, and disposed of by an alien in the same manner in all
respects as a natural-born British subject; and a title to real and personal
property of every description may be derived through, from, or in succession
to an alien, in the same manner in all respects as through, from, or in
succession to a natural-born British subject."

agreement between A. and the plaintiff, an English
publisher. A cheap reprint taken from the pages of the
'American Magazine' having been subsequently published in this country by the defendant, it was held that
the copyright was divisible and could be claimed for a
portion of the book only; and accordingly the publication
by the defendant of the last six chapters of the work was
restrained by injunction (a).

(a) *Low* v. *Ward*, L. R. 6 Eq. 415; 37 L. J. (Ch.) 841; but see *Routledge* v. *Low*, 37 L. J. (Ch.) 454; 18 L. T. (N.S.) 874; L. R. 3 H. L. 100.

On the subject-matter of these cases, the Royal Commissioners on Copyright report as follows:—" We recommend, generally, that where a work
has been first published in any one of your Majesty's possessions, the proprietor of such work shall be entitled to the same copyright, and to the
same benefits, remedies, and privileges in respect of such work as he
would have been entitled to under the existing Imperial Act, if the work ·
had been first published in the United Kingdom.

" With regard to publication in foreign states, the law now is that,
except under treaty, no copyright can be obtained if a book has been
published in any foreign country before being published in the United
Kingdom, but it is doubtful whether contemporaneous publication in this
and a foreign country would prevent the acquisition of copyright here.

" It is a grave question whether it is desirable that the condition
requiring first publication in this country should continue, and whether
the reason advanced for this condition, namely, that it is advantageous to
this country that works should be first published here, outweighs the
hardship that may be inflicted upon British authors by preventing them
from availing themselves of arrangements which they might otherwise
make with foreign or colonial publishers.

" We have come to the conclusion that a British author who publishes
a work out of the British dominions should not be prevented thereby from
obtaining copyright within them by a subsequent publication therein.
Yet we think that such republication ought to take place within three
years of the first publication, and we may add that we think the law
should be the same with reference to dramatic pieces and musical compositions first performed out of your Majesty's dominions, even though
they are not printed and published—in other words, that first performance
in a foreign country should not injure the dramatic right in this country.
It has been decided under the 19th section of the International Copyright
Act, that the writer of a drama loses his exclusive right to the performance of his drama here in England, if it has been first performed abroad;
that is to say, representation has been held to be a publication. We see
no reason why the rule which may be finally determined upon in reference
to first publication of books should not apply to first representation of
dramatic pieces. The evidence shews how hardly the present law presses
upon British dramatic authors.

" As to aliens, although we would give them the same rights as British   Suggestion as
subjects if they first publish their works in the British dominions, it is   to aliens.
obvious that the same reason does not exist for giving them copyright if
they do not bring their books first to our market: and we therefore
recommend that aliens, unless domiciled in your Majesty's dominions,
should only be entitled to copyright for works first published in those
dominions. It is to be borne in mind that, even though aliens may be
deprived of British copyright by first publication abroad, they may still
obtain it in many cases by means of treaties.

" With regard to the persons who are capable of obtaining imperial

There may be copyright in part of a work.

"There are numerous cases," says Sir G. M. Giffard, V.C., " shewing that where the parts of a work can be separated, there may be a copyright in any distinct part of it. I may instance the cases of the last canto of Lord Byron's 'Childe Harold,' Croker's Notes to 'Boswell's Life of Johnson,' and of particular articles in cyclopædias. There is no analogy in this respect between a patent and the case of copyright, as it matters not whether the copyright is for the entire work or for a part only . . . . I see nothing to deprive plaintiffs of their right to an injunction as to the last six chapters of the work."

The Government may own a copyright.

A manuscript or a copyright may be owned by the government or a corporation as well as by an individual, and the rights of the government or corporation are governed by the same principles as those of an individual owner (a). So statutes, judicial decisions, public documents, official reports, and productions which are the direct results of official labour, become the property of the government which pays for such services. But the government can have no proper claim to the literary property in a work produced by an officer independently of his official duties.

Copyright in work written for another, in the employer.

It is a well-known rule, that if a person be employed to produce anything for another, whether by writing or not, it is to be inferred (in the absence of any circumstances shewing the contrary) that the writing or thing produced

---

Suggestions as to persons capable of holding copyright.

copyright in your Majesty's dominions, as distinguished from international copyright under treaty, we find that, according to the existing law the author in order to obtain copyright must be either—

" (a) A natural-born or naturalized subject of your Majesty, in which case the place of residence at the time of publication of the book is immaterial; or

" (b) A person who, at the time of the publication of the book in which copyright is to be obtained, owes local or temporary allegiance to your Majesty, by residing at that time in some part of your Majesty's dominions.

" Besides these, it is probable, but not certain, that an alien friend who first publishes a book in the United Kingdom, even though resident out of your Majesty's dominions, acquires copyright therein. We think this doubt should be set at rest, and that, subject to our previous recommendation as to place of publication by aliens not domiciled in your Majesty's dominions, the benefit of the copyright laws should extend to all British subjects and aliens alike." Par. 58–64.

(a) *Marzials* v. *Gibbons*. L. R. 9 Ch. 518.

by the person so employed is produced upon the terms that it shall be the property of the employer (*a*).

Transactions of this kind between publishers and authors resemble contracts for so much work and labour towards a general undertaking—so many bricks towards the erection of an edifice—and are different from the sale of a copyright. When delivered by the author, his contribution appears to be the property of the owner of the general work, more especially as the several articles are wrought into their appropriate form by the literary agent of the proprietor. In this manner contributions seem after leaving the hands of their authors to lose their separate identity (*b*).

In *Shepherd* v. *Conquest* (*c*) the Court of Common Pleas questioned whether *under any circumstances* the copyright in a literary work, or the right of representation of a dramatic one, could become vested *ab initio* in an employer other than the person who has actually composed or adapted the work; and they decided that no such effect could be produced where the employers merely suggest the subject and have no share or design in the execution of the work, the whole of which, so far as any character of originality belongs to it, flows from the mind of the person employed; for it would be an abuse of terms to say that in such a case the employers were the authors of a work, to which their minds had not contributed an idea.

Where, however, the employers do more than suggest the subject, and have a share in or solely design the execution of the work, the case is different. Thus in *Barfield* v. *Nicholson* (*d*) Sir John Leach said, " I am

Not so, however, if employer merely suggest the subject.

(*a*) *Sweet* v. *Benning*, 24 L. J. (C.P.) 175 ; 16 C. B. 459 ; *Cox* v. *Cox*, 11 Hare, 118 ; see *Hatton* v. *Kean*, 29 L. J. (C.P.) 20, *post*, and 2 Hill, ' Torts.'

(*b*) Maugham on ' Copyright,' 171.

(*c*) 17 C. B. 427, see 25 L. J. (N.S.) C.P. 127 ; 2 Jur. (N.S.) 236. See *Pierpont* v. *Fowle*, 2 Wood & Min. (Amer.) 23 ; *Atwill* v. *Ferrett*, 2 Blatch. *ibid.* 36 ; *De Witt* v. *Brooks*, M.S. Nelson, J., N. Y. 1861 ; *Binns* v. *Woodruff*, Wash. (Amer.) 53.

(*d*) 2 Sim. & Stu. 1 ; S. C. 2 L. J. (Ch.) 90 ; *Heine* v. *Appleton*, 4 Blatch. (Amer.) 125 ; *Siebert's Case*, 7 Opin. 656—Cushing, Attorn.-Gen. (Amer.) 1856.

of opinion that, under the statute (8 Anne, c. 19), the person who forms the plan, and who embarks in the speculation of a work, and who employs various persons to compose different parts of it, adapted to their own peculiar acquirements, that he, the person who so forms the plan and scheme of the work, and pays different artists of his own selection, who, upon certain conditions contribute to it, is the author and proprietor of the work, if not within the literal expression, at least within the equitable meaning of the statute of Anne, which, being a remedial law, is to be construed liberally."

On this principle was determined the case of *Hatton* v. *Kean* (a), where the defendant, with the aid of scenery, dresses, and music, adapted one of Shakespear's plays to the stage, and found the general design of the representation. He employed the plaintiff, a well-known musician named Hatton, for reward, to compose, and he did compose, as part. of the representation, and as accessory to the dramatic piece, a musical composition, which formed part of the dramatic piece, on the terms that the defendant should have the liberty of representing and permitting to be represented the said musical composition with the dramatic piece as part thereof. And it was held that the defendant had the sole right of representing the entire dramatic piece, including the plaintiff's musical composition, and that he violated no right of the plaintiff within the 3 & 4 Will. 4, c. 15 (b), and the 5 & 6 Vict. c. 45, by representing, without the plaintiff's consent in writing, the entire dramatic piece, including the plaintiff's musical composition. The reason assigned was that, though the plaintiff was the author of the musical composition, it appeared that the defendant was the author and designer of the entire dramatic work, and with respect to a part, accessary to that whole (that whole consisting of some-

(a) 8 W. R. 7; see *Hazlitt* v. *Templeman*, 13 L. T. (N.S.) 593; *Stannard* v. *Harrison*, 24 L. T. (N.S.) 570; *Little* v. *Gould*, 2 Blatch. (Amer.) 165; *Lawrence* v. *Dana*, 2 Am. L. T. R. (N.S.) 402; *Commonwealth* v. *Desilver*, 3 Phila (Pa.), Amer. 31.
(b) *Vide post.*

thing produced by the skill of the defendant in its entirety), he employed the plaintiff. The production by the plaintiff would be a part of the whole, and the defendant would have the sole right of performing and representing the entire piece in conjunction with the music.

In this case there was an agreement to the effect that the music should be the property of the employer, but in a later case the Court, on the supposed authority of *Hatton* v. *Kean,* went much further. Matthews, the manager of the St. James's Theatre, had employed Wallenstein to furnish music for that theatre. The latter engaged and paid the musicians, supplied the instruments and compositions, and conducted the orchestra. Besides playing general orchestral music for the theatre, it was his duty to provide incidental music for dramas, when necessary; and such music he might either select or compose. In performance of this duty he composed incidental music for 'Lady Audley's Secret,' a drama brought out by Matthews, but of which the latter was not the author, and at that time was not even the owner. In composing the music the plaintiff had received no assistance from the manager, and had himself found the paper on which the music was written, and employed a person to copy the various orchestral parts from the original score. These parts the composer kept in his own possession, nor did the theatre have a library of music. When the engagement between Matthews and Wallenstein had ended, the former obtained from the latter a duplicate copy of the music, with permission to use it "on a provincial tour." Afterwards, when the defendant, Miss Herbert, had succeeded Matthews in the management of the St. James's Theatre, and Wallenstein had ceased to be the musical director, she obtained permission from Matthews to represent 'Lady Audley's Secret,' of which play he was then the owner, and received from him the duplicate copy of the music which Wallenstein had made for him. The original score was

K

still in the possession of the composer, who had given no consent either to Matthews or to Miss Herbert to use the music in London.

The Court held that the controlling facts in the case were not different from those in *Hatton* v. *Kean ;* that the music became an inseparable part of the drama, and was not an independent composition ; that Matthews, by virtue of the contract of employment, had acquired an unlimited right to use the music ; and that the defendant, as the licensee of Matthews, was also entitled to use it (*a*).

It is submitted that this case was not rightly decided. He who arranges music for any instrument is the author of such arrangement, though he may not be the composer of the music.

As to joint authorship.   The question may occasionally arise as to whether persons agreeing to arrange a piece together, become joint authors in the production, and frequently much difficulty is experienced in deciding what constitutes joint authorship. If there be a joint co-operation in carrying out the same design, it is not essential that the execution of the design should be equally divided. Having agreed to a general design and structure they may divide their parts, and work separately. The pith of the joint authorship consists in the co-operation in a common design, and whether this co-operation takes place subsequently to the formation of the design by the one, and is varied in conformity with the suggestions or views of the other, it has equally the effect of creating a joint authorship as if the original design had been their joint conception. But where there are merely some additions or improvements made to a complete piece, intended to render it more acceptable and attractive, the person making such additions or improvements does not thereby become joint author. The subject was fully debated in the late case of *Levy* v. *Rutley* (*b*). It appeared

---

(*a*) *Wallenstein* v. *Herbert.* 15 L. T. (N.S.) 364, on app. 16 Id. 453.
(*b*) L. R. 6 C. P. 523; *Maclean* v. *Moody*, 20 Sc. Sess. Cas. 2nd Ser. 1154.

from the evidence that in 1837 the plaintiff, who was then proprietor of the Victoria Theatre, employed a Mr. T. E. Wilks, author of about fifty other dramas, to write a play to suit the company employed at his theatre, for which Wilks was to be paid twenty guineas. 'The King's Wager' was accordingly composed by Wilks, and delivered to the plaintiff in October of that year. Before it was acted, upon the complaint of his stage manager, plaintiff requested Wilks to come to the theatre to make some alterations. Wilks promised to come, but never appeared, and certain alterations were made by the plaintiff and the stage manager, after which the play was acted with considerable success, and was continued at the Victoria for six weeks. When Wilks demanded his £21 as agreed, the plaintiff refused to pay the whole amount, on the ground that he had been obliged to make so many alterations before the play could be acted that Wilks could not be considered to have carried out his part of the agreement. Plaintiff offered ten guineas, which Wilks refused to accept, and eventually it was arranged by a Mr. Noel, plaintiff's then attorney, that Wilks should receive fifteen guineas and assign his copyright in the play to plaintiff: £4 15s. was paid by the plaintiff on account, for which the following receipt was produced :

"Received the 30th January, 1838, of Mr. L. Levy, the sum of £4 15s. on account of fifteen guineas, for my share, title, and interest as co-author with him in the drama entitled 'The King's Wager,' balance being paid me on assigning my share to him as soon as assignment prepared."

£4 15s.   T. E. Wilks,
Witness, John Noel.   Royal Victoria Theatre."

Afterwards Wilks refused to execute the assignment which was prepared, and he never received the balance of the fifteen guineas. Wilks died in the year 1854. The play was afterwards published as altered by the plaintiff, and the defendant had caused it to be represented at the theatre of which he was the lessee. It was shewn that the plot of the piece as designed by Wilks was not in any way altered by the plaintiff; his additions and variations

K 2

consisted only of improvements of the parts of some of the subordinate characters, and a new scene, together with some changes in words and directions.

The Court of Common Pleas were of opinion that joint authorship consisted in the co-operation of two or more authors in a common design, and not the alteration by one author of the work of another, without the latter's consent or ratification: that the admission of co-authorship in the receipt did not alter the facts, and that a mere receipt for money on account was no assignment. As to the joint authorship Mr. Justice Byles said : " It is admitted that Wilks wrote most of the play, and that plaintiff made only a series of small alterations; the plaintiff, therefore, cannot be said to have been the sole author, even if the declaration had been framed so as to enable him to make his claim on that ground. If there were an execution by two or more persons of one common design for a dramatic piece, it might constitute joint authorship, although one person had contributed a very small amount of work to the execution ; there is nothing here to shew any common design between Wilks and the plaintiff, and on these short grounds I am of opinion that the verdict should be entered for the defendant." And in this opinion both Mr. Justice Keating and Mr. Justice Smith coincided, the latter adding : "Although one of the persons engaged should actually write a much greater part of the work than the other, still they might possibly be joint authors. Here Wilks was employed to write as an author, and he did write a complete play ; Levy considered the play might be improved, and wrote a new scene, and made various alterations. The question for us is whether that constituted him joint author with Wilks, the original author. What is the scope of these alterations ? The main plot is the same now as in the original play, and it is only alleged that Levy merely improved and touched up some parts. There seems to have been no agreement between the two, or intention on Wilks' part that they should have been joint authors originally.

I suppose there are few instances in which alterations have not been made by managers after plays are written and before they are acted, and if in this case after the piece was first brought to Levy, there had been a joint remodelling of the play by Levy and Wilks together, they might have become joint authors; but the evidence fails to establish any such proceeding. Reliance was placed upon the words of Wilks' receipt of the money paid him on account ' for my share, title, and interest, as co-author with ' Levy; as we are in this case judges of fact, we may consider the circumstances under which this receipt was given. It might be evidence that they considered themselves to be co-authors at that time, but that statement of itself did not make them so, it was not an admission binding upon third persons, and, as I think, was not warranted by the facts " (a).

Abandonment of copyright.

It has been said that an author may by his conduct or by his express desire *abandon* his copyright, and give to the public a right to publish his work before the time when his copyright would expire (b). There is no authority on the point, and it is difficult to say what amount of evidence the court would require as to the fact of a dedication of a copyright to the public.

Abandonment of copyright not presumed from book being out of print.

But it is clear that a proprietor of a copyright does not lose his right of publication, by permitting his book to remain out of print and obsolete for any number of years (c). The copies may have been all sold, but he may exercise the right he has of republication at such periods as he thinks likely to answer his purpose and when he would

(a) 24 L. T. Rep. (N.S.) C. P. 621; L. R. 6 C. P. 523, to which report of the case is appended a note in which it is stated that the question of joint authorship of a dramatic piece came under consideration in a case of *Shelley* v. *Ross*, tried before Hannen, J., in the Bail Court, without a jury, on the 7th of June, 1871. The circumstances of that case were very similar to those of the principal case; and the learned judge distinctly laid it down that alterations in a dramatic piece, for the purpose of rendering it more attractive or better adapted for stage representation, did not constitute the person making them a "joint author."

(b) 4 Burr. 2346, 2367, 2466; and see 2 Stark. N. P. C. 382; 4 Camp. N. P. C. 8, n.; *Platt* v. *Button*, 19 Ves. 447; *Folsom* v. *Marsh*, 2 Story's R. (Amer.) 109; *Rundell* v. *Murray*, Jac. Rep. 311–316; see *Bartlett* v. *Crittenden*, 4 McLean (Amer.) 303; 5 *ib.* 41.

(c) *Weldon* v. *Dicks*, 10 Ch. Div. 247.

find purchasers. It is a matter on which he has a right to exercise his own judgment.

Nor does the proprietor of a copyright lose his right to prevent an infringement by reason of his not having proceeded against a prior infringement of which he had no knowledge. In one case it was argued that by reason of certain prior infringements having been passed by unrestrained, therefore the proprietor had lost his right to prevent any subsequent infringement, but the plaintiff stating that he was not aware of the prior infringement the court would not entertain the argument. There can only be acquiescence where there is knowledge, and the court will not assume that there is acquiescence where there is no knowledge, though it is true that knowledge and acquiescence are in many cases fatal to the parties.

Effect of un-limited right to publish. In a case (a) where the plaintiff gave her manuscript to a publisher, with a parol licence to publish it at his own risk and expense, and disclaimed any intention to receive any emolument from it, and the defendant published it for fourteen years (the first term under the statute then in force) and continued to publish and sell it afterwards, and the plaintiff then applied for an injunction to restrain its further publication by the defendant: Lord Eldon refused the injunction, upon the ground that the defendant had been licensed to publish without any limitation of time. The question, however, was left undecided whether the right to publish did not remain in the plaintiff concurrently with the defendant, or whether the defendant had acquired any right as against the public. The defendant's counsel expressly disclaimed any title to the copyright, admitting that there was no legal assignment of it. The case therefore proceeded upon the effect of a parol licence to publish, and shews that such licence conveys no copyright to the exclusion of the author.

(a) *Rundell* v. *Murray*, Jac. Rep. 311.

CHAPTER IV.

REGISTRATION OF COPYRIGHT.

A BOOK OF REGISTRY is kept by the Company of Sta- The Book of tioners, and the object of the entries therein is clearly Registry. shewn by the 2nd section of the Statute of Anne. The entry is deemed equivalent to notice of the existence of the copyright in the particular book or article registered. Unless such entry had been provided, many, through ignorance, would have offended (*a*). By the Statute of Anne it was enacted that no person should be subjected to the forfeitures or penalties therein mentioned in cases of infringement of copyright, unless the title to the copy of such book should, before publication, be entered in the register book of the Stationers' Company (*b*).

The Statute of Anne was, however, repealed and incorporated in that of the 5 & 6 Vict. c. 45, the 11th section of which provides that a book of registry, wherein may be registered the proprietorship in the copyright of books, and assignments thereof, and in dramatic and musical pieces, whether in manuscript or otherwise, and licences affecting such copyright, shall be kept at the hall of the Stationers' Company by the officer appointed by the said company for the purposes of the Act, which shall at all convenient times be open to inspection on payment of 1*s.* for every entry which shall be searched for or inspected in the same book; and that such officer shall, whenever

---

(*a*) Sect. 2 of the 8 Anne, c. 19.
(*b*) *Ibid.*, and see Malins, V.C., in *Cox* v. *The Land and Water Co.*, 18 W. R. 206; see *ante*, p. 81.

reasonably required, give a copy of any entry, certified under his hand, and impressed with the stamp of the said company, to any person requiring the same on payment to him of the sum of 5s. (a); and such copies shall be received in evidence in all courts, and in all summary proceedings, and shall be *primâ facie* proof of the proprietorship or assignment of copyright or licence as therein expressed, but subject to be rebutted by other evidence, and in the case of dramatic or musical pieces shall be *primâ facie* proof of the right of representation or performance, subject to be rebutted as aforesaid; and that making a false entry in the book of registry, or wilfully producing or causing to be tendered in evidence any paper falsely purporting to be a copy of any entry in the said book, shall be deemed an indictable misdemeanour, and punished accordingly. It provides, further, that it shall be lawful for the proprietor of the copyright in any book to make entry in the said registry book of the title of such book, the time of the first publication, the name and place of abode of the publisher, and the name and place of abode of the proprietor, in a form given in the schedule annexed to the Act, upon payment of 5s. to the officers of the said company; and that it shall be lawful for every such registered proprietor to assign his interest or any portion of his interest therein, by making entry in the said book of registry of such assignment, and of the name and place of abode of the assignees thereof, in the manner, and for the sum aforesaid. And such assignment shall have the same force and effect as if made by deed, without being subject to any stamp duty.

Neglect to register on the part of the official at Stationers' Hall prevents the author having the benefit of the statute as against the public (b).

Entry must be correct to support action for penalties. It is essential that the name of the author or composer be correctly stated in the register, and where B. adapted

(a) Under the present Stamp Act, the Stamp Act of 1870, a stamp of 1s. is required to be impressed upon a certified copy of the entry, because it is an entry on a public register.

(b) See *Cassell* v. *Stiff*, 2 K. & J. 279.

the music of N. so as to make it an independent composition, it was held that it was insufficient to describe the
work as that of N. (a). So the insertion in the register of
the wrong day of publication, or an inaccurate statement
of the names of the publishers, or their firm, renders the
entry on the registry invalid. A proprietor of copyright
in a book, registered his book by making an entry, purporting to be pursuant to the Act, but in such entry
the exact date of first publication was not stated, the day
of the month being omitted, and the month and year only
inserted; on his filing a bill to restrain a party from
infringing his copyright, the court held, that the suit
could not be maintained, as the entry was defective, there
being no entry of the date of first publication as required
by the statute, unless, in addition to the month and year,
the day of the month is also stated (b).

And where the entry in the registry of the name of the Full name of
publishers was "Sampson Low, Son, & Marston," whereas set out.
the name of the firm was "Sampson Low, Son, & Co., the
variance being the addition of the third name of the partner
in the firm, instead of the term "Company," the entry was
held invalid. "One almost regrets," said Kindersley, V.C.,
in the case in which these two last points were decided (c),
"to be obliged to come to the consideration of points
which are so very technical as these which I am obliged
to consider; but at the same time they are points not only
which a defendant or plaintiff has a right to take, but
which are of importance with reference to the carrying
out of the clearly expressed intention of the legislature
which has thought fit to require, in order to produce
certain effects, that certain strict particulars shall be complied with. . . . Now though it is probably optional either
to enter the name of the firm of publishers, or the names

(a) *Wood* v. *Boosey*, L. R. 2 Q. B. 340; affirmed in Exch. Ch. L. R. 3
Q. B. 223.
(b) *Mathieson* v. *Harrod*, L. R. 7 Eq. 270; 38 L. J. (Ch.) 139; 19 L. T.
(N.S) 629; 17 W. R. 99; *Wood* v. *Boosey*, *supra*; *Collette* v. *Goode*, 7 Ch.
Div. 842; *Low* v. *Routledge*, 33 L. J. (N.S.) Ch. 717.
(c) *Low* v. *Routledge*, *supra*.

CAP. IV. ___ of the individuals composing that firm, if you·profess to
enter the real name of the firm you must do so. And
looking again at the statement in the bill, I find in
express terms, that the name of the firm is not 'Sampson
Low, Son, & Marston,' but 'Sampson Low, Son, & Co.' I·
am almost ashamed to descend to these minute particulars,
but it must be done, and it is sufficient for me to say
that in my opinion either of these inaccuracies (that of
the date of assignment, and name of publishers) is quite
sufficient to lead me to hold that the entry of the
proprietorship is insufficient, and, upon that ground,
that there is no valid assignment effected by the subsequent entry which immediately follows that of the assignment."

Sufficient to
enter first
publication
under name of
firm.

But in registering it is sufficient to enter the first
publisher under the trade name of the firm, and the
actual proprietor of the copyright at the time of registration, without stating who the first proprietor
was, or how the copyright devolved upon the present
proprietor.

So where an author registered his work in 1877, it
having been published in 1854, by entering the name of
the publishers and place of abode as "Newby & Co.,
Welbeck Street, Cavendish Square, London," and the
name and place of abode of the proprietor of the copyright as Christopher Edward Weldon, and the date of the
first publication as "July 16, 1854," and it was objected
that the name of the original proprietor should have
appeared, Vice-Chancellor Malins held the registration
to be sufficient. He considered it clear that the "name
and place of abode of the proprietor of the copyright,"
meant not the original proprietor, but the person who is
the proprietor at the time the registration takes place.
" What difference," said he, " can it make to anybody
who the original proprietor was ? It may be material to
know who the original publisher is, the object being that
a person registering may not pass off a fraudulent entry,
but that he shall give the public an opportunity of

inquiring of the publisher whether it was a genuine CAP. IV.
transaction, or whether the date has been fictitiously
inserted, and therefore it is required that the name of the
original publisher should be given, but it does not mean
that the original proprietor, but that the present proprietor should be given " (a).

L. & Sons registered a cricketing scoring-sheet, dating First date of
it 1851, and, dissolving partnership, again registered it in publication
must be
L.'s own name, dating it 1863. P. having published the stated.
same thing, L. threatened an action. P. continued to publish, and, on L. becoming bankrupt, purchased it of the
assignees for £20. W., who had bid £10, purchased the
sheet of P. for some time, but ultimately printed and published the left-hand half, containing the totals of runs, but
not an analysis of bowling, which was on the right-hand
half. On a bill filed to restrain the alleged infringement of the copyright, it was determined that the second
registration was fatal, not shewing the real first date of
publication (b).

In *Lover* v. *Davidson* (c) the plaintiff, who was residing As to the place
in New York at the time the entry was made, gave the of residence.
address of his English publishers in the entry under the
above provision, and Cresswell, J., was of opinion that
Mr. Lover, the plaintiff, having at that time no other
place of abode in England, had very properly described
himself as of a place where he might be communicated
with.

The provision with reference to the place of abode of As to the
the assignee would seem not to apply to the case of an abode of the
assignee.
assignee to whom the proprietorship has been assigned,
not according to the statutory mode, but by an independent
method. As soon as the copyright is established in the
original proprietor, there is nothing to prevent him from
assigning by any other method, although the statute provides one more convenient and less expensive than the

(a) *Weldon* v. *Dicks*, 10 Ch. Div. 247; "Trial and Triumph."
(b) *Page* v. *Wisden*, 20 L. T. (N.S.) 435; 17 W. R. 483.
(c) 1 C. B. (N.S.) 182.

CAP. IV. ordinary mode of assurance by deed. If the statute is resorted to, the terms of it must be complied with. Unfortunately, there is a discrepancy between the enactment in the 13th section, and the schedule No. 5, to which that section expressly refers. The section requires that there shall be an entry " of such assignment, and of the name and place of abode of the assignee thereof, in the form given in that behalf in the said schedule," but when we turn to the schedule there is no reference to the place of abode of the assignee. In *Wood* v. *Boosey* (a) the question arose, whether section 24 (which enacts that no proprietor of copyright shall maintain an action for infringement of it, unless he shall have caused an entry to be made in the book of registry pursuant to the Act) applies to an assignee. Cockburn, C.J., without directly deciding the point, said : " I observe a distinction in the earlier sections between the term ' proprietor ' (as applied to the person by whom the work is originally published and in whom the property is vested), and any person who takes by assignment from him ; and there is no provision in the statute which gives the assignee a right to have his name inserted in the book of registry as the new proprietor. The only case in which the change of the name of the proprietor is to be made, is where the statutory form of assignment is resorted to, and even in that case it is only the assignor who can insist on the change being made in the book of registry. Taking all this into account, it seems to me that to hold that section 24 applies to an assignee, who has no power under the statute, either through this court or by any other means, to enforce registration of himself as ' proprietor,' would work considerable injustice."

Expunging or varying entry. By the 14th section it is provided, That if any person shall deem himself aggrieved (b) by any entry made under colour of this Act in the said book of registry, it shall be lawful for such person to apply by motion to the courts of

(a) 7 B. & S. 869, 897 ; L. R. 2 Q. B. 340 ; affirmed in Ex. Ch. L. R. 3 Q. B. 223.
(b) *Graves' Case*, L. R. 4 Q. B. 721–724, and the case of ' The Roll-Call,' *Publishers' Circular*, Feb. 16, 1876.

law in term time, or to apply by summons to any judge of such courts in vacation, for an order that such entry may be expunged or varied ; and that, upon any such application by motion or summons, the court or judge, as the case may be, shall make such order for expunging, varying, or confirming such entry, either with or without costs, and the officer appointed by the Stationers' Company for the purposes of this Act shall, on the production to him of any such order for expunging or varying any such entry, expunge or vary the same according to the requisitions of such order (*a*).

It seems that the court will not exercise its power under the above section to expunge any entry of proprietorship of copyright in the registry book, unless it be clearly and unequivocally shewn that it is false; or vary it, unless satisfied by affidavit that in doing so it would make a true entry (*b*). To induce the court to interfere it must be satisfied that there is something unfair in the entry, by reason of the misconduct of the person who made it, or some right of the applicant which has been injuriously affected thereby.

It is not every one who disputes the plaintiff's title, who has a right to call upon the court to expunge the entry; for it would seem that there is no power to restore the entry, if once struck out; and that the Court ought not, therefore, to take such a step, unless it be clear that the plaintiff has no right to use the entry at the trial, and this is a point which ought to be settled, not on affidavits, but by an issue. And in one case (*c*), where an additional entry had been made at Stationers' Hall concerning the

(*a*) See *Ex parte Bastow*, 11 C. B. 631.
(*b*) *Ex parte Davidson* (1856), 18 C. B. 297; S. C. 25 L. J. (C.P.) 237; 2 Jur. (N.S) 1024.
(*c*) "Persons aggrieved" are those whose title conflicts with that of the person registered: *Chappell* v. *Purday*, 12 M. & W. 303. As to who is a party aggrieved under the 14th section see further *Ex parte Davidson, supra*. But a person convicted of infringing the copyright in certain paintings and photographs of the registered proprietor, and who sets up no title in himself or adduces no evidence to rebut the *primâ facie* evidence of proprietorship afforded by the book of registry, is not a person "aggrieved" within the meaning of the above section: *Re Walker* v. *Graves*, 20 L. T. (N.S.) 877.

copyright of Auber's opera, 'Fra Diavolo,' subsequent to the commencement of disputes, and an application was made under section 14 to have the entries expunged, the court refused to expunge the entry, but ordered an issue to be tried to determine the question of copyright, on the trial of which the entry was (by consent) not to be used, and stayed proceedings in the action in the meantime.

In *Ex parte Davidson* (a) Cocks brought an action against Davidson for publishing three pieces of music alleged to be the copyright of Cocks. Before the action three entries had been made in the registry. These entries as they stood would afford *primâ facie* evidence of Cocks' copyright in the three pieces. Davidson obtained a rule nisi to expunge or vary these entries. It was obtained on an affidavit by which it appeared that Davidson claimed no copyright in the airs himself, but that his case was that they were old pieces, and that the persons who on the entries professed to be the authors were not really the authors ; and the affidavits deposed to information and belief as to the facts, which, if true, proved the pieces were older than the supposed authors. The counsel for Cocks refused to consent not to use these entries on the trial. The court declined to expunge the entries, but made an order, without consent, that the rule should be enlarged till the trial of an issue to determine the question of copyright, in which Cocks should be plaintiff, and on the trial of which the entries should not be used ; and that in the meantime proceedings in the action should be stayed.

No copyright acquired by registration beforepublication.

No copyright is acquired under 5 & 6 Vict. c. 45, by the registration of a book before its actual publication (b),

(a) 2 Ellis & B. 577 (1853).
(b) "It is inconsistent with the whole scheme of the Copyright Act," said Vice-Chancellor Wood, "that you should be able to register a book not published ; as the Act gives a right merely from the date of the first publication, and it must therefore be idle to register a book, as it were, in embryo." *Correspondent Newspaper Co.* v. *Saunders,* 11 Jur. (N.S.) 540 ; 13 W. R. 804 ; 12 L. T. (N.S.) 540 ; *Maxwell* v. *Hogg, Hogg* v. *Maxwell,* L. R. 2 Ch. 307 ; *Henderson* v. *Maxwell,* 5 Ch. Div. 89 ; *Cassell* v. *Stiff,* 2 Kay & J. 279 ; see also *Murray* v. *Bogue,* 1 Drew. 353.

and the mere registration of the name of a proposed CAP. IV.
periodical will not give copyright in that name or the Registration
right to use it as a trade-mark. In *Hogg* v. *Maxwell* (a), of name of of intended
it was contended, that as by sections 2 and 13 of 5 & 6 Vict. periodical will
c. 45, every "part" of a book may be registered, and a not give copy-right.
right to restrain the piracy of it thereby acquired, the
registration of the title 'Belgravia' by the Messrs. Hogg
in October, 1863, three years before the publication of a
magazine bearing that name, gave them a copyright in
that title. To this Lord Cairns replied: "It is said
that the word 'Belgravia' being used upon the title-
page of the magazine, was part of a volume. But at the
time of making the entry in the registry of Stationers'
Hall there was no volume, no part of a volume, no sheet,
no separate portion of a publication of any kind or
description. There was nothing in existence except that
very entry itself, and the entry of the name of a future
publication. It is quite absurd to suppose that the
legislature, in providing for the registration of that which
was to be the *indicium* of something outside the registry,
in the shape of a volume, or part of a volume, meant that
by the registration of one word, copyright in that one word
could be obtained, even although that one word should be
registered as what was to be the title of a book or of a
magazine. . . . I apprehend that if it were necessary to
decide the point it must be held that there cannot be
what is termed copyright in a single word, although the
word should be used as a fitting title for a book. The
copyright contemplated by the Act must be not in a single
word, but in some words in the shape of a volume, or part
of a volume, which is communicated to the public, by
which the public are benefited, and in return for which a
certain protection is given to the author of the work."

The statute contemplates two things, first, that the Condition of
person who makes the entry shall be the proprietor of work to secure
the copyright; and, secondly, that the book to which the registration.
entry relates shall be a published book. Until the thing is

(a) L. R. 2 Ch. Ap. 316; 36 L. J. (Ch.) 433; 16 L T. (N. S.) 133.

CAP. IV. published and given to the world it is not within the statute.

The entry requires the date of publication to be given, and the form in the schedule to the statute makes this clear, and this obviously cannot be given if the book be not already published.

Registration of periodicals. Registration under the 24th section is only necessary in order to secure the copyright in books under the 3rd section and not that of periodicals under the 18th section (a).

In the case of any encyclopædia, review, magazine, periodical work, or other work published in a series of books or parts, it is enough to register the title of the work, the date of the publication of the first volume, number or part, and the name and place of abode of the owner and the publisher. When the first volume, number, or part has been registered, all following numbers of the same work or series will be protected, without the necessity of any additional registration. As registration of the first number of a periodical applies to future issues, it extends to, and protects matter not published at the time of registration. But the copyright cannot vest in any number of the periodical until that number is published (b).

A newspaper need not be registered. It is now considered not necessary to register a newspaper. The Act which provided a special registry for them was repealed but lately by the 32 & 33 Vict. c. 24. It must not be inferred from this that there is no copyright in newspapers, for they are obviously covered by the phrase "periodical works" in the 18th section, and the proprietor would therefore have a copyright under that section in all compositions for which he had paid (c). He would also, by general law, have a right to prohibit others from appropriating the fruits of his own labour (d).

(a) *Cox* v. *The Land and Water Co.*, 18 W. R. 206; *Browne* v. *Cooke*. 16 L. J. (N.S.) Ch. 140; 11 Jur. 77; *Sweet* v. *Benning*, 3 W. R. 519; 16 C. B. 459; S. C. 24 L. J. (C.P.) 175; *Mayhew* v. *Maxwell*, 9 W. R. 118; 1 J. & H. 312.
(b) *Chappell* v. *Purday*, 12 M. & W. 303.
(c) *Strahan* v. *Graham*, 15 W. R. 487; see *Prowett* v. *Mortimer*, 4 W. R. 519.
(d) Per Malins, V.C., in *Cox* v. *The Land and Water Co.*, 18 W. R. 207.

The registration of the first number of a periodical publication is, as we have seen, sufficient to protect the whole (a). So also the registration of the first number of a periodical or magazine will enable the proprietor to prevent the publication in a separate form of a serial published in successive numbers of the periodical, although neither the serial nor the first number containing it has been separately registered (b). Thus where the proprietor of a magazine called 'The Orb,' employed a person to write a serial called 'The Verger's Daughter,' for publication in successive numbers, upon the usual terms that the copyright should belong to, and be paid for, by the plaintiff; and after it had been published in 'The Orb' the defendant published for the author the same work under the title of 'Dangerous Connections;' it appearing that the first number of 'The Orb' had been duly registered under section 19, the Master of the Rolls granted an injunction, saying : "Here the proprietor of the copyright of a periodical seeks to restrain a separate publication of an article which is part of that periodical; but I am told that he cannot maintain the action until he has registered that article or the first number of the serial, and the date. That is out of the question. A periodical is a book within the meaning of the Act, but the article or serial would be only part of the book, and it is unnecessary that it should be separately registered."

The law, as it existed previous to the 5 & 6 Vict., did not require registration as a condition precedent to the title to sue. The neglect to register did not affect the copyright (c), it merely prevented the recovery of the penalties imposed by the Acts in existence, until such entry had been made.

Registration a condition precedent to the title to sue under 5 & 6 Vict. c. 45.

Subsequent to the Act, however, although the author has copyright in his work still unregistered (d), yet he

(a) *Henderson* v. *Maxwell*, 4 Ch. Div. 163; but the entry must be after and not before publication: *Henderson* v. *Maxwell*, 5 Ch. Div. 892.
(b) *Henderson* v. *Maxwell*, 4 Ch. Div. 163.
(c) *Tonson* v. *Clifton*, 1 Wm. Bl. 330; *The University of Cambridge* v. *Bryer*, 16 East, 317 ; *Beckford* v. *Hood*, 7 T. R. 620.
(d) See *Chappell* v. *Davidson*, 25 L. J. (C.P.) 225; 18 C. B. 194.

cannot protect himself against infringement, unless he has duly registered in accordance with the Act (a). For, by the 24th section, it is declared that no proprietor of copyright in any book which shall be first published after the passing of the Act shall maintain any action or suit at law or in equity, or any summary proceeding, in respect of any infringement of such copyright, unless he shall, before commencing such action, suit, or proceeding, have caused an entry to be made in the book of registry of the Stationers' Company of such book, pursuant to the Act. Though the infringements have been made before registration, yet upon registration being effected an action can be maintained (b). It is worthy of note, that a different system is adopted in regard to fine arts copyright, the Act of 1862 not permitting actions or proceedings to be taken in respect to anything done before the registration is effected under section 4. This appears a fairer principle (c). If the process of registration is to be considered as useful as an authentic notice of the copyright, it would seem that it ought in all conscience to be effected at a date prior to that on which the infringement of the right takes place in order to operate on it, for, otherwise, the infringer cannot reasonably be affected by notice, when such notice is subsequent to the commission of the act for which he is called upon to make amends, by the legal process issued out against him.

The prohibition imposed by section 24 on the proprietor of copyright from suing before registration, applies only to books, and the exceptions of the section in favour of

(a) *Murray* v. *Bogue*, 1 Drew. 353; 17 Jur. 219; 22 L. J. (Ch.) 457. This applies only to books first published after the Act; it does not affect any book published prior.

(b) *Goubard* v. *Wallace*, W. N. (1877) 130.

(c) The Royal Commissioners in their recent report on copyright recommended that proprietors of copyright should not be entitled to maintain any proceedings in respect of anything made or done before registration, nor in respect of any dealings subsequent to registration with things so made or done before registration. But as this provision they considered might in some cases operate harshly, they thought it should not apply if registration were effected within a limited time, say one month after publication. Par. 154.

the sole representation of a dramatic piece is extended to the performance of a musical composition (a).

Where the first edition of a work of compilation was published before the 5 & 6 Vict. c. 45, and several editions were published after the Act but were not registered, it was held that, as to so much of the matter contained in the original as was contained in the subsequent editions, the proprietor of the copyright might sue, although such subsequent editions were not registered; but as to the new matter the subsequent editions were books which ought to have been registered, and the owner could not sue for infringement on that point (b).

It is not absolutely necessary to register a map, chart, or plan under the Literary Copyright Act, yet it is generally advisable—the point arose in *Stannard* v. *Lee* (c). The object of the bill was to restrain an alleged infringement by the defendant of the plaintiffs' copyright in a map or plan of the recent German-French War, which the plaintiffs by their bill described at ' No. 1 Stannard & Son's Panoramic Bird's-eye View of France and Prussia, and the surrounding countries likely to be involved in the war, with the railway and strategic positions of each army, and the great fortresses of the Rhine Provinces.' This map or plan was published by the plaintiffs, but it was never entered at Stationers' Hall. Subsequently to the publication of their map the defendant published a similar work, which he entitled ' Thomas W. Lee's Panoramic Bird's-eye View of the Seat of War, from special drawings by French and German artists, shewing the Rhine, France, Prussia, Belgium, and surrounding countries, rivers, roads, and railways, fortresses, and strategic positions of each army, &c.'

The bill charged that the publication of the defendant's map was contrary to the copyright statutes, and was an infringement of the plaintiffs' copyright.

Immediately on filing the bill the plaintiffs obtained

(a) *Russell* v. *Smith*, 12 Q. B. 217, 238.
(b) *Murray* v. *Bogue*, 1 Drew. 353.
(c) 24 L. T. (N.S.) 459.

L 2

ex parte, an injunction restraining the defendant from
continuing the publication of, and from selling his map.
A motion was made to dissolve this injunction, but was
refused, on the ground that the plaintiffs' work did not
require registration—and the defendant having subsequently pleaded this omission of registration, the plea
was for the same reasons overruled, hence the appeal.
It was contended in support of the two orders that the
copyright in maps, charts, or plans was still governed by
the 8 Geo. 2, c. 13, and the 7 Geo. 3, c. 38; that this
was the fact, although the preamble of the Act of 5 & 6
Vict. c. 45, mentioned and repealed the Acts 8 Anne, c. 19,
41 Geo. 3, c. 107, and 54 Geo. 3, c. 156, which all related
to books, there was no reference to the above two Acts,
which protected maps, engravings, &c. Those Acts required
no registration ; and their operation was extended to prints
taken by lithography or other mechanical process.   Lord
Justice James, however, remarking that if the latter
argument were to prevail, it would tend to one or other of
two results; either that there would be two kinds of
maps in respect of which there would be two distinct laws
or copyright, or else that with regard to every map
existing there would be now in this country two distinct
and separate laws of copyright; one, a law giving a
conditional right of property with an unconditional right
of action or suit ; the other, giving an unconditional right
of property, with a conditional right of action or suit, said :
" Such a result would be strangely inconvenient, and my
Lord Coke has observed that the *argumentum ab incon-
venienti* is always of great force, particularly where we
are asked to construe an Act of Parliament, not according
to its letter, but contrary to its letter, for the very purpose
of producing these inconveniences, because the Act of
Parliament which we have before us is in its letter very
plain and very simple.   It says that the word ' book '
shall mean ' a map, chart or plan separately published.'
This is a map separately published.   In another part of
the Act, after expressly excepting from its operation

anything affecting the right of property under this or any other Act of Parliament, it proceeds to say that 'no proprietor of copyright in any book' (that is to say, in any map, chart, or plan) 'which shall be first published after the passing of this Act, shall maintain any action or suit at law or in equity, or any summary proceeding in respect of any infringement of such copyright, unless he shall, before commencing such action, suit, or other proceeding, have caused an entry to be made in the Book of Registry of the Stationers' Company of such book pursuant to this Act.' That is no very heavy duty to impose upon a man, and no very difficult step for him to take before commencing his proceedings. Those words are plain and simple; it seems to me that there is no ground for saying that they do not express the intention of the Legislature, and, in truth, when one considers it, the object of the Legislature seems very reasonable.

"And there would be, as I have pointed out, clearly great inconvenience in having two laws of copyright as to two sets of maps, or as to the same set of maps. There being really no inconvenience in giving the ordinary and natural meaning to the words themselves, I am of opinion that this plea is well pleaded, and that the plaintiff has not entitled himself to commence his suit. Of course it is open to him to register the map whenever he pleases. He might have registered it on the day before he filed his bill for this injunction."

And Lord Justice Mellish, in concurring in this view, said: "It is impossible to read the 2nd section of the 5 & 6 Vict. c. 45, without seeing that, for some purposes at any rate, maps are now to be considered as books, and are brought into the Acts relating to copyright as to books. Therefore, beyond all question, the 5 & 6 Vict. c. 45, has made an alteration in the law respecting maps, and therefore that Act must to some extent have affected the Acts of 8 Geo. 2, c. 13, and 7 Geo. 3, c. 38, although these two Acts of Parliament are not recited in the preamble of the present Act."

This decision is very apt to deceive. It was decided upon principles which will not probably be extended in future cases, and its precise scope may best be exemplified by a commentary thereon made by Vice Chancellor Bacon in the subsequent case of *Stannard* v. *Harrison* (a): "Although in the case of *Stannard* v. *Lee* before the Lords Justices it was held that the design there was not protected for want of registration, that was because the plaintiff had alleged in his bill that he had invented a design and published 'a map,' and the defendant there pleads, relying on the large interpretation of the word 'book,' in the last Act, that the statute prohibited the institution of any suit before registration had been performed. Both the Lords Justices were of that opinion, but the Lords Justices have said nothing in any part of their judgment about the other two statutes except this: The plaintiff's counsel, desiring to save himself by reference to the earlier statutes, they said, 'You cannot do that now you are here; the plea has been filed to your bill, and the plea meets every thing that you allege in your bill; the plea must either be allowed or over-ruled.' The statutes were the thing relied upon. Every word of the Lords Justices' judgment proceeds upon that ground, and they never considered anything but that. The judgment of Mellish, L.J., puts that in the plainest light. He, as it were, congratulates them on having by a mere trick, or accident, the good fortune of placing a technical difficulty in the plaintiff's way, so as to get the plea allowed; but there is not a word about any meritorious elements in the case on the part of the defendant; there is not any doubt expressed that the plaintiff's claim in morals and in truth was a perfectly good and just claim. That this was so is seen in another part of the judgment, where the Lord Justice, answering Mr. Cotton, who desired to amend his bill so as to raise that question, as to its being an historical engraving, says: 'You ought to file a new bill; you have yourself put it into the category of maps.' " And in this

(a) 24 L. T. (N.S.) 573.

case from which we have just quoted it was held that a bird's-eye view of a locality is a landscape within the meaning of the 7 Geo. 3, c. 38, and as such does not require to be registered at Stationers' Hall pursuant to the provisions of the 5 & 6 Vict. c. 45, to entitle the designer to the protection afforded by the first Act.

A copy of every book (a), published since the 5 & 6 Vict. c. 45, together with all maps, prints, or other engravings belonging thereto, finished and coloured in the same manner as the best copies of the same shall be published, and also of any subsequent edition, whether the first edition of such book shall have been published before or after the passing of the Act, and also of any second or subsequent edition of every book of which the first or some preceding edition shall not have been delivered for the use of the British Museum, bound, sewed, or stitched together, and upon the best paper on which the same shall be printed, shall, within one calendar month after the day on which such book shall first be published within the bills of mortality, or within three months if the same shall first be published in any other part of the United Kingdom, or within twelve months after the same shall first be published in any other part of the British dominions, be delivered, on behalf of the publisher thereof, at the British Museum.

Copies are likewise to be delivered for the benefit of the Bodleian Library at Oxford, the Public Library at Cambridge, the Faculty of Advocates at Edinburgh, and Trinity College, Dublin, on demand at the place of abode of the publishers thereof, at any time within a month after demand, during the period of twelve months from the publication thereof.

According to these provisions, the main distinctions between a presentation to the British Museum, and a presentation to any of the other four libraries, are these: first, that the delivery to the Museum is to be made without demand on the part of that institution; whereas

Cap. IV.

Copy of every book to be delivered to the British Museum.

Copies for the use of university libraries.

Distinction between a delivery to the British Museum and the other libraries.

(a) *Routledge* v. *Low*, Law Rep. 3 H. L. 100; 37 L. J. (Ch.) 454.

delivery to any of the other libraries need not be made at all, unless there be a written demand within twelve months after publication; and secondly, that the copy presented to the Museum must be one from the best copies of the work, while that for any of the other libraries need be only a copy from the set the most numerous. Thus, if a publisher produce a superior and an inferior edition at the same time (as in cases of quarto and octavo editions, so frequent in illustrated works), he must give a copy of the more valuable impression to the Museum; whereas he need only make presentations to the other libraries from the set of lesser cost, provided that set exceed the other by even a single copy (a).

Penalty for default. The 10th section of the same statute enacts, that if the publisher of a book, or of a second or subsequent edition of a book, neglect to deliver a copy of it pursuant to this Act, he shall for every default forfeit, besides the value of the copy he ought to have delivered, a sum not exceeding £5, to be recovered by the librarian or other authorized officer of the library for whose use the copy should have been delivered; either summarily, on conviction before two magistrates for the county or place where the publisher making default resides, or by action of debt or similar proceeding at the suit of such librarian or other officer in any court of record in the United Kingdom, in which action, if the plaintiff obtain a verdict, he shall recover his costs reasonably incurred, or taxed as between attorney and client (b).

Delivery of copies to the various libraries—origin of claim. The first enactment extant, encouraging the establishment of libraries for the use of the learned bodies, is in the reign of Charles II., when two copies of every work were ordered to be delivered by the publisher for the two English universities, and one copy for the king's library, 13 & 14 Car. 2, c. 33, s. 17, continued by 16 Car. 2, c. 18; 17 Car. 2, c. 4; 1 Jac. 2, c. 17, s. 15, &c ., but expired in 1679. The clauses of the 17 Car. 2, appear to be perpetual, as far as they relate to the three copies,

(a) Burke's Sup. to Godson's Pat. and Copy. p. 97.
(b) *Ibid. British Museum* v. *Payne*, 4 Bing. 548.

although it seems it was not so considered, from their not being adverted to in the statute of Anne. The first foundation for the claim by any public library to a gratuitous delivery of new publications is in a deed of 1610, by which the Company of Stationers in London, at Sir Thomas Bodley's request, engaged to deliver a copy of every book printed by the company, and not before printed, to the University of Oxford. The next provision is to be found in the 8th Anne, c. 19, which extended the number of copies demandable to nine, viz., one for the royal library, two for the Universities of Oxford and Cambridge, four for the libraries of the four Scotch Universities, the library of Sion College in London, and the library of the Faculty of Advocates in Edinburgh. This provision was afterwards enforced in 1775 (15 Geo. 3, c. 53, s. 6), by an express enactment that no person should be subject to the penalties of those Acts for pirating books, unless the whole title to the copyright of the book was entered at Stationers' Hall, and the nine copies delivered there for the use of the libraries. Two additional copies were given to Trinity College and the society of King's Inn in Dublin by 41 Geo. 3. The 54 Geo. 3, c. 156, s. 1, repealed so much of the 8 Anne, c. 19, s. 5, and the 41 Geo. 3, c. 107, s. 6, as required that any copy or copies of every book printed should be delivered to the warehouse-keeper of the Stationers' Company for the use of the libraries mentioned, or by him for their use, or which imposes any penalty on such printer or warehouse-keeper for not delivering the copies; and provided that eleven copies should be delivered for the use of the British Museum, Sion College, the Bodleian Library at Oxford, the Public Library at Cambridge, the library of the Faculty of Advocates at Edinburgh, the libraries of the four Universities of Scotland, Trinity College Library, and that of the King's Inn at Dublin (a).

(a) In the United States, the law establishing the Smithsonian Institute (Act of Congress, August, 1846, c. 178), directs, without any penalty, that a copy of every book, of which the copyright shall be secured, shall be sent to the library of that institution and one to the library of congress. Repealed by s. 6 of the Act of 1859, c. 22. In 1865, the owner was

The Royal Commissioners in their recent report on Copyright came to this conclusion, that so much of the existing law relative to gratuitous presentation of books to libraries, as requires copies of books to be given to libraries other than that of the British Museum, should be repealed. In making that recommendation they stated that they had taken into consideration the facts that the bodies to whom the libraries belong were possessed of considerable means, and were well able to purchase any books which they might require : and also that the repeal of the clause giving the privilege would not deprive the libraries of any property already acquired but merely of a right to obtain property hereinafter to be created.

They added that the importance of securing a national collection of every literary work had been recognised in most of the countries where there are copyright laws ; and with a view to make the collection in this country more perfect, they were disposed to think that it would be desirable to require the deposit at the British Museum of a copy of every newspaper published in the United Kingdom.

On the general subject of registration the commissioners were of opinion that in order to provide an improved system of registration in substitution for that now in use, the two acts of registration and deposit of the copy of a book at or for the British Museum should be combined : or in other words, that, so far as the author is concerned, registration should be complete on the deposit of the copy and on obtaining an official receipt. One advantage of this would be a diminution of labour and expense, and the British Museum would probably receive all copyright books without the labour of hunting for them in booksellers' catalogues and advertisements, as the officials are obliged to do under the present system. Another advan-

---

again required to transmit within one month after publication, a copy of every book to the library of congress; and in 1867 a penalty of twenty-five dollars was imposed for failure to make such delivery. See further the Act of 1870 in the Appendix.

tage would be that the fees to be paid for registration might be materially diminished.

The principle of registration the commissioners intended to apply, with one exception, to dramatic pieces and musical compositions which are publicly performed but are not printed and published. Their suggestion that the acts of registration and deposit of a copy of a book should be combined manifestly could not conveniently be effected where the work had not been printed, therefore they proposed, in these cases, that it should be sufficient if the title of every drama or musical composition with the name of the author or composer and the date and place of its first public performance were registered.

CHAPTER V.

ASSIGNMENT OF COPYRIGHT.

Copyright personal property.
COPYRIGHT is personal property, and may be assigned. It must, however, be in existence to be assigned at law (*a*).

A local right.
It is after publication a local right only, embracing Great Britain and Ireland, the islands of Jersey and Guernsey, the British dominions in the East and West Indies, and the colonies, settlements, and possessions of the British Crown, acquired on or since the 1st day of July, 1842, or which hereafter may be acquired (*b*).

Its distinctive features.
It may be the subject of a bequest, and on the death of the person to whom it belongs, without any such bequest, will devolve on his personal representatives (*c*). The printer of a newspaper (the 'Bath Chronicle,') bequeathed to his widow the benefit of his trade, subject to the trust of maintaining and educating her family. The foreman, by her assistance in giving him the use of the letter-press, etc., on the premises, set up a paper bearing the same name. An injunction was granted, at the request of the executors, to restrain him from carrying it on (*d*). As

(*a*) *Sweet* v. *Shaw*, 8 L. J. (N.S.) Ch. 216 ; 3 Jur. 217 ; *Colburn* v. *Duncombe*, 9 Sim. 151.
(*b*) 5 & 6 Vict. c. 45, s. 3.
(*c*) See *Thompson* v. *Stanhope*, Amb. 737 ; *Burnett* v. *Chetwood*, 2 Mer. 441, n. As to the right of executors to publish, see *Dodsley* v. *M'Farquhar*, Mor. Dict. of Dec. 19 & 20 App. pt. 1, p. 1 ; and as to their right to receive the payment of the stipulated price of a portion of a work, although the author died before completing the other portion, see *Constable and Co.* v. *Robinson's Trustees*, 1 June, 1808 ; Mor. Dict. of Dec. No. 5, App., Mut. Contract.
(*d*) *Keene* v. *Harris*, cited 17 Ves. 338, and see *Cruttwell* v. *Lye*, 17 Ves. 335, and 8 Ves. 217.

the copyright in a work is entirely distinct from the property in the stereotype plates from which it may have been printed; a sale of these does not carry the right to print and publish, unless the vendor is the owner of the copyright and such is the intention of the parties. So, if an execution against a stereotype founder were levied on plates which he had made for an author and not delivered, the title to these plates would be passed by the execution sale, and the purchaser might sell them, but clearly he could not print and publish the book for which they were made (a). Trustees in bankruptcy are not entitled to the manuscripts of an author, although the copyright of a book which has been printed and published will legally pass for the benefit of the creditors (b), and the price paid by the bookseller is as completely open to the diligence of creditors as the price of any other commodity or piece of merchandise. The reason assigned for this distinction is, that the author's right of withholding the publication continues till the very moment his book is actually given out to the public. Even the printer of the book would not be entitled to sell it for payment of the costs of printing, although there is not the smallest doubt that he has a complete lien over it, till delivery, to prevent the author or his creditors from taking advantage of the publication, till he shall have been paid (c).

In *Mawman* v. *Tegg* (d), where it appeared that the author, who was one of the original owners and publishers of a work, had gone into bankruptcy, and his copyright had passed to assignees, from whom it was bought by the plaintiffs, Lord Eldon said: "Whatever question there

---

(a) *Stevens* v. *Cady,* 14 How. (Amer.) 528; *Stevens* v. *Gladding,* 17 How. 447; *Carter* v. *Bailey,* 64 Me. (Amer.) 458.

(b) *Longman* v. *Tripp,* 2 Bos. & Pull. New. 67 : see 4 Burr. 2311 ; Amb. 695 ; *Stevens* v. *Cady,* 14 How. (Amer.) 528 ; *Stevens* v. *Gladding,* 17 How. (Amer.) 447; *Cooper* v. *Gunn,* 4 B. Mon. (Amer.) 594, 596 ; see *Atcherley* v. *Vernon,* 10 Mod. 518.

(c) 1 Bell's Com. 68.

(d) 2 Russ. 392. *In re Curry,* the Irish Commissioner in Bankruptcy expressed the opinion that copyright would pass to the bankrupt's assignee without a writing ; 12 Ir. Eq. 391.

CAP. V. may be in some cases, whether an interest in copyright does or does not pass without writing, it would, I apprehend, be difficult to maintain that there must be an instrument in writing between the bankrupt and his assignees."

Assignment of manuscript. The property in an unpublished work is personalty, and is subject to the same general rules which govern personal property. Therefore it may pass by sale and delivery. Sales may be absolute or conditional, and they may be with or without qualifications, limitations, and restrictions; and the rules of law applicable in such cases to other personal property must be applied in determining the real character of a sale of literary property. Thus the right of first publication is vested in the author, but he may sell and assign the entire property to another; or may sell the manuscript on the condition that the same shall not be published, or be published only in a particular manner. An author who has not parted with the property in his production, or has not written it to the order of some other person, may secure the copyright to himself, and at any time afterwards may transfer it to an assignee; and when the author before publication transfers his unpublished production to another, then the assignee may register under the Act as the "proprietor" (a).

The Act defines the word "assigns" to mean and include every person in whom the interest of an author in copyright shall be vested, whether derived from such author before or after the publication of any book, and whether acquired by sale, gift, bequest, or by operation of law or otherwise" (b). Statutory copyright cannot exist until after publication, therefore what passes under any assignment before publication, must be the common law property in the manuscript: i.e. the right to publish with or without securing the copyright, and the right to withhold from publication.

It has been held that though statutory copyright must

(a) *Lover* v. *Davidson*, 1 C. B. (N.S.) 182.
(b) 5 & 6 Vict. c. 45, s. 2.

be in existence before it can be assigned in law (*a*);
yet an agreement may be made to assign at a future
time (*b*), in which case an equitable title may vest in
the assignee (*c*).

A transfer of the right will not be presumed, unless the An assign-
intention is manifest; such, for instance, as the acceptance ment not to be
of a receipt in writing for the price paid for the copyright (*d*); and evidence that the plaintiff, in an action for
printing a musical work, acquiesced in the defendant's
publication of it for six years, did not raise the presumption
that the plaintiff had transferred his interest in the copyright. But where a copyright was not asserted for *fifteen
years*, the Court of Chancery refused an injunction, until
the right should be established at law; the Lord Chancellor
saying: " I admit this to be the subject of copyright; but
the plaintiff has permitted several people to publish these
dances, some of them for fifteen years; thus encouraging
others to do so. That, it is true, is *not a justification;* but
under these circumstances a court of equity will not interfere in the first instance. If, as is represented, some of
them were published only last year, and one two months
ago, the bill ought to have been confined to those. You
may bring your action, and then apply for an injunction " (*e*).

Questions have arisen as to whether it is necessary to As to whether
the validity of an assignment of copyright that it should assignment
be in writing. Much confusion has existed by reason of writing.
the mixing up of rights which are essentially different.
The right of an author in his unpublished production is
obviously of a different nature to that which he may
secure in his published work under the Copyright Act.
The Copyright Act does not affect the rights of an author
in his composition before publication, and it does not

(*a*) *Colburn* v. *Duncombe*, 9 Sim. 151; *Sweet* v. *Shaw*, 3 Jur. 217; *Pulte* v.
Derby, 5 McLean (Amer.) 328; *Lawrence* v. *Dana*, 2 Am. L. T. R. (N.S.)
402, 414.
(*b*) *Leader* v. *Purday*, 7 C. B. 4; *Gould* v. *Banks*, 8 Wend. (N.Y.) 562.
(*c*) *Sims* v. *Marryat*, 17 Q.B. 281; *Lawrence* v. *Dana*, *supra*.
(*d*) Otherwise held previous to 5 & 6 Vict. c. 45; see *Latour* v. *Bland*,
2 Stark. 382.   (*e*) *Platt* v. *Button*, 19 Ves. 447; Coop. Ch. Cas. 303.

follow that that which may, by the express words of the Act, or by its implied effect, relate to the assignment of copyright as secured by the Act would apply to the author's rights, which exist independent of the Act. The author's right in his unpublished work exists only by common law, and the mode of its transfer must be governed by the only law applicable—the common law—and a parol assignment would seem to be sufficient at common law. If the transfer be made before the vesting of the statutory copyright and is made in England and is good by the common law, or if made in a foreign country, and is valid by the law of that land, the buyer becomes the owner of the property and is an assignee recognised by the statute.

This view has been partly recognised by the courts.

In *Cocks* v. *Purday* (a) it appeared that the plaintiff had bought from Hoffmann, of Bohemia, the exclusive right of publishing in Great Britain a musical composition which at the time of purchase had not been published anywhere. Hoffmann had bought the composition from the author, Labitzky. No writing appears to have passed between these two persons; but by the Austrian law, which prevailed in Bohemia, a parol transfer of copyright was valid. The sale by Hoffmann to Cocks was made by letter, and no formal assignment was executed until nearly a year after the latter had published and registered the work in England. The defendant argued that the plaintiff's title was not good, because it had not been derived by a written assignment. The Court, after quoting the definition of assigns in sect. 2 of 5 & 6 Vict., c. 45, said: " There being then a sale in this case valid by the law of Austria, where it was made, the interest of the author became vested in the plaintiff before publication, so as to make him an assignee within the meaning of the third section; and he, therefore, had a good derivative title."

(a) 5 C. B. 860 ; see as this case *post ; Jeffreys* v. *Kyle*, 18 Sc. Sess. Cas., 2nd Ser. 906 ; 3 Macq. 611 ; *Hazlitt* v. *Templeman*, 13 L. T. (N.S.) 593.

An assignment of the copyright of a work, under the Statute of Anne, must have been in *writing*, and attested by two witnesses, in order to entitle the assignee to maintain an action for pirating it (*a*). True, this was not expressly demanded, but as the statute required that there should be two witnesses to a consent to a publication, it was naturally inferred that an assignment, which was of a higher nature than a mere consent, must have at least the same solemnity (*b*). The 41 Geo. 3, c. 107, required the consent to be in writing, and to be signed in the presence of two or more credible witnesses. The 54 Geo. 3, c. 156, reciting the former enactments, generally extended the copyright, and spoke of the consent in writing, but said nothing about the two witnesses. Opinions differed upon this subject. It was contended by some that as it was only by implication from two witnesses being required to the consent, it was held that two witnesses were required to an assignment, therefore, when the latter Act, the 54 Geo. 3, c. 156, no longer required two witnesses to a consent, the reason failed for requiring, by implication, two witnesses to an assignment. Lord St. Leonards, however, was of opinion that it was properly decided that the assignment ought to be attested by two witnesses; that, he said, was decided upon the Act of Anne as it stood originally and as it was originally construed. "If, by a later Act," said he, "you take away that which was, no doubt, the ground of the decision, viz., the necessity for two witnesses to a consent, does it follow, that you therefore repeal that which was the proper construction of the law applicable to the higher instrument, viz., that the

(*a*) *Power* v. *Walker*, 4 Camp. 8; S. C. 3 M. & S. 7; *Morris* v. *Kelly*, 1 Jac. & W. 481; *Clementi* v. *Walker*, 2 B. & C. 861; *Davidson* v. *Bohn*, 6 C. B. 456; 12 Jur. 922; 18 L. J. (C.P.) 14; *Leader* v. *Purday*, 7 C. B. 4; *Jefferys* v. *Boosey*, 4 H. L. C. 815; *Cumberland* v. *Copeland*, 31 L. J. (Exch.) 19, 353, *post*, p. 162.

(*b*) Lord Ellenborough, in *Power* v. *Walker, supra ;* as to the distinction between a licence to publish and an assignment, see 27 L. J. (Ch.) 254, and the principle on which was decided the late case of *Lacy* v. *Toole*, 15 L. T. (N.S.) 512. The distinction between an assignment and a license is that by the former the ownership of the copyright is vested in the assignee, while by the latter the licensee acquires the privilege of publishing but no proprietary rights in the copyright.

M

assignment also required two witnesses? It would rather seem, after such a tenor of determination, after the law had been so settled, that the legislature, by being silent with regard to the assignment, meant that to remain, although it alters the law with respect to the consent." " The Act of Anne and the Act of the 54 Geo. 3 may well stand together; the latter one does not repeal the former expressly, and there is no reason why it should do so by intendment; and with respect to the assignment, the Act of Anne, being referred to generally by the 54 Geo. 3, must be considered to be referred to as bearing the construction put upon it by the authorities."

In *Cumberland* v. *Copeland* (a), the farce of the ' Happiest Day of my Life,' with seven other plays, were assigned by the author, Mr. Buckstone, to the plaintiff in 1835, which assignment was attested by one witness only. The majority of the Court of Exchequer held this to be fatal to the validity of the transfer, the assignment having been made previous to the 5 & 6 Vict. c. 45; but the Exchequer Chamber overruled this judgment, on the ground that, after the passing of the 54 Geo. 3, c. 158, s. 4, in an action for piracy, the consent in writing of the author became a good defence. That being so, the Court thought that an assignment in writing, without the attestation of witnesses, was sufficient, and reversed the previous ruling. Erle, C.J., in delivering judgment said: " The reasoning upon which that is founded is derived from the statute of 8 Anne, c. 19, which was passed to protect authors, and contains stringent provisions against what are called piracies, by those who infringe copyrights, and declares that when an author has established that his copyright has been infringed, the defence of the pirate, that the defendant has done what has been complained of by the consent of the author, should not be allowed in proof except by a writing attested by two witnesses. And so, therefore, the law was clearly established that the proprietor of a copyright could not give a consent

(a) 7 H. & N. 118; *Shepherd* v. *Conquest*, 17 C. B. 427.

to the publication except by writing attested by two witnesses; and the question having arisen in *Power* v. *Walker* (a), in 1814, whether a copyright itself could be assigned without writing (and that was the only point before the Court) the Court of King's Bench held that an assignment was in the nature of a perpetual licence—was greater than a licence—and if a licence required writing and two witnesses, an assignment certainly ought to be in writing; whether attested by two witnesses or not was not the question before the Court, and I may say here, that in *Davidson* v. *Bohn* (b), the question was considered as if it had arisen before the statute, 54 Geo. 3, c. 156, and the same minute reasoning was carried out: if the assignment must be in writing because the licence must be in writing, the assignment must be attested by two witnesses, because the licence must be attested by two witnesses; that is the line of reasoning followed out in the two cases. However, the 54 Geo. 3, c. 156, passed, enacting that from and after that statute the consent must be in writing, and that a consent in writing would be a defence against a suit for infringing the copyright; and an express enactment that a consent in writing should be valid is, to my mind, by implication, an enactment that a consent in writing may be valid without being attested by two witnesses. The former statute required a consent in writing attested by two witnesses; the latter requires a consent in writing only. It is clear to my mind, after the Act of 54 Geo. 3, c. 156, the plaintiff could not without infringing the express words of that statute, say a consent in writing was not valid without two witnesses, because there was an enactment to that effect in the statute of Anne. The two statutes are inconsistent. After that time if a consent in writing is valid without two witnesses, it seems to me, as a matter of reasoning, to follow, that an unattested assignment is also valid: for if, as it was argued prior to the statute, because a consent in writing is not

(a) 3 M. & S. 7.
(b) 6 C. B. 456; S.C. 18 L. J. (N.S.) C. P. 14.

valid without two witnesses, so neither is an assignment: as a consent is now valid without two witnesses, so, also, is an assignment valid without two witnesses." And, referring to Lord St. Leonards' opinion in *Jefferys* v. *Boosey* (a), to the contrary, he continues: "I cannot but think myself, though with great deference to Lord St. Leonards' reasoning powers, which are of the highest order, and the conflict of authority on one side and the other, that in the nature of things, the result of the legislation is very worthy of the attention of the Court. And it seems to me that to put a construction on a statute that would enable the vendor of a thing to take the price of it and defeat the sale, if the instrument of sale has not complied with a technical formality, would be a species of legislation that, to my mind, is bad."

Assignment under the 5 & 6 Vict. c. 45. Under the 5 & 6 Vict. c. 45, s. 13, the proprietor of a copyright in a composition, if he desire to sell and transfer his right, must make an entry in the register of the Stationers' Company of such work, the time of the first publication thereof, and the name and place of abode of the publisher and proprietor of the copyright; and every such registered proprietor may assign his interest, or any portion thereof, by making an entry in the register of the assignment and of the name and place of abode of the assignee (b); and the assignment so entered is expressly exempted from stamp duty, and is of the same force and effect as if it had been made by deed (c).

The entry is made on the application of the assignor, and sets forth the date of entry, title of the book, name of the assignor, and name and place of abode of the assignee. The statute makes a certified copy of the entry *primâ facie*

(a) 4 H. L. C. 915.
(b) *Ante*, p. 139.
(c) The proposition that an assignment in writing, since the 5 & 6 Vict. c. 45, need not be attested (4 H. L. C. 855, 881, 891, 931, 943), has been ably disputed in the 8th volume of the Jurist (N.S.) pt. ii. p. 148. And see *Power* v. *Walker*, 3 M. & S. 8. Lord Ivory, in *Jeffreys* v. *Kyle*, 18 Ct. of Sess. 2nd Ser. p. 911; see 21 Ct. of Sess. 2nd Ser. p. 8, and others, have thought that both *Power* v. *Walker* and *Davidson* v. *Bohn* were wrongly decided, see 3 H. L. C. 671, and *Cumberland* v. *Copeland*, on appeal, 31 L. J. (Ex. Ch.) 353.

proof of assignment "but subject to be rebutted by other CAP. V.
evidence."

As assignment of copyright after publication since the Assignment
passing of the 5 & 6 Vict. c. 45, must, unless made by must be in
writing, but
entry at Stationers' Hall, be in writing, but need not be need not be
attested.
attested, and an assignment not in writing is not suf-
ficient. So where a song was, in the year 1868, published
by the defendant under a verbal agreement with the author,
Suchet Champion, but no instrument of assignment
of the copyright was executed by him to the defendant;
and by an assignment in writing in 1874 Champion
assigned to the plaintiff the entire copyright of the
words and music of the said song in consideration of a
royalty on each copy sold, which assignment the plaintiff
made an entry of at Stationers' Hall, it was held that the
title of the plaintiff must prevail, and that he could sustain
an action to restrain the defendant from infringing his
copyright (a).

It will depend upon circumstances how far a receipt
for the purchase-money will operate as an assignment of
the copyright (b).

A sale made by letter may be a valid transfer. In Assignment
Lacy v. *Toole*, which was an action against the defendant may be made
by letter.
for representing a play written by the plaintiff, the de-
fence was that the latter was not the owner of the piece.
A letter was produced in which the plaintiff, in reply to a
letter from a third person, had written to the latter, " I
accept the offer you therein make me, and agree to the
conditions you propose for cancelling my debt to you;
viz., to let you have my drama of 'Doing for the Best,' in
discharge of £10 of the sum due." The Court expressed
the opinion that this letter was a valid assignment, but
left it to the jury to find whether the agreement was

(a) *Leyland* v. *Stewart*, 4 Ch. D. 419; so an assignment or license of
any design under the Designs Act, 1842, must be in writing; see *Jowitt* v.
Eckhardt, 8 Ch. Div. 404.

(b) See *Howitt* v. *Hall*, 6 L. T. (N.S.) 348; *Strahan* v. *Graham*, 16
L. T. (N.S.) 87; *Colburn* v. *Duncombe*, 9 Sim. 151; *Sims* v. *Marryat*, 17
Q. B. 281; *Levi* v. *Rutley*, L. R. 6 C. B. 523; *Cocks* v. *Purday*, 5 C. B. 860.

to transfer the property in the play, or simply to license its use. The verdict was in favour of the defendant, and the letter was accordingly held to amount to an assignment (a).

Questions have incidentally come before the Courts as to whether copyright is divisible. At present there are no express decisions on the point. It would seem, however, that it is in some instances divisible as to locality, and also as to time. *First*, as to locality. It is clear that it cannot be divided among independent owners so that each may have the exclusive right of sale for a distinct part of the same country, nor probably among different countries over which one copyright law extends. For instance it is clear that the owner of an English copyright could not make an assignment to one person in Lancashire and to another person in Middlesex, and doubtful whether he could make an assignment of copyright to one person in Canada and another in India. But where a person can secure a copyright in two countries governed by two distinct copyright laws, there would seem to be no valid objection to his assigning his rights in one country to another, securing his rights in the other country to himself. For instance, suppose an author to be able to secure a copyright for himself both in France and in this country, he might make a valid assignment of his French copyright to one person, and his English to another. But this could not be regarded, strictly speaking, as a division of copyright, the rights being distinct—the one conferred by one country, the other by another.

The question arose in *Jefferys* v. *Boosey*, where it appeared that Ricordi, the assignee of Bellini, being resident in Milan, assigned the copyright in 'La Sonnambula' to Boosey for publication in the United Kingdom only. Lord St. Leonards, in passing judgment, observed : "The exercise of the right is confined in that assignment to the United Kingdom. Now, by the 41 Geo. 3, c. 107, copy-

Divisibility of copyright as to locality.

(a) 15 L. T. (N.S.) 512; see *Kyle* v. *Jeffreys*, 21 Scotch Sess. Cas. (N.S.) 8.

right is extended to any part of the British dominions in Europe; and by the 54 Geo. 3, c. 156, it was further extended to every other part of the British dominions. It is quite clear, therefore, that if, in this case, there was a copyright under the law of this country, it was a copyright which extended to every part of the British dominions; even considering the right in England, if I may so call it, as being capable of being secured from any foreign right, it would consequently be a partial assignment; and, as a partial assignment, I should venture to recommend your Lordships to decide that it was wholly void, and therefore gave no right at all.

"There is also, let me observe, this particularity: that as the assignment from Ricordi is confined to the United Kingdom, Ricordi himself might, without any breach of his contract, have published this composition in any other part of the British dominions; he might, also by his Milanese right, have published it the very next day in Milan, without infringing on the right of Boosey under the assignment. The more, therefore, the question is considered, the more, I apprehend, will it appear clear that the assignment in question was void because it was limited to the United Kingdom, and did not extend to the whole of the British dominions." This also was the opinion of Lord Chief Baron Pollock and Baron Parke, but a majority of the Judges who advised the House of Lords were of opinion, that the owner might assign the exclusive right of publication in Great Britain, and reserve to himself the Austrian copyright (a).

Secondly, as to time. The proprietor of the copyright may assign his copyright for any period less than the period during which his copyright will continue. But in such case the question has been raised as to whether such limited transferee should be regarded as a limited assign or a licensee only, and, further, could the limited transferee register for a limited period. No provision is made by the

Divisibility of copyright as to time.

(a) 4 H. L. C. 815; see *D'Almaine* v. *Boosey*, 1 Y. & C. Exch. 288; *Cocks* v. *Purday*, 5 C. B. 860; *Low* v. *Ward*, L. R. 6 Eq. 415; *Routledge* v. *Low*, L. R. 3 H. L. 100.

Act, and it has been doubted whether an absolute assignment would not have to be made so far as the registry is concerned, and a re-assignment be made on the expiration of the period during which the limited assignment was made. But the practice has been for many years for the registrar to enter assignments for a certain number of years, or for certain numbers of copies, or for a certain number of editions, and this practice certainly seems to be justified by the Act. The 13th section of the Act of 1842, provides that it shall be lawful for the proprietor of the copyright in any book to make entry in the registry book of the title of such book, the time of first publication thereof, the name and place of abode of the publisher thereof, and the name and place of abode of the proprietor of the said book, or of any portion of such copyright; and that it shall be lawful for every such registered proprietor to assign his interest, *or any portion of his interest therein*, by making entry in the book of registry of such assignment, and of the name and place of abode of the assignee thereof. If the proprietor has a copyright extending over a period of forty-two years, surely an assignment for ten years would be an assignment of a portion of his interest in the copyright within the meaning of the above section.

The statute gives to the owner of a dramatic composition the exclusive right to print it, and the sole liberty of performing it. Either of these rights may be absolutely assigned independently of the other.

Assignment by foreigner. 　An assignment made by an assignee of a foreigner, though his title be good by the law of the country in which the assignment is made, and to which law both assignee and foreigner are subject, yet (being a foreigner), he has not, by the English law, an interest in the copyright, such as he may assign to an Englishman for exclusive publication in England; nor would such an assignment hold good though made according to the law of this country.

This point was determined in *Jefferys* v. *Boosey*, to

which we have already referred. Bellini, a foreigner, while living at Milan composed a musical work, in which, by the laws there in force, he had a certain copyright. In February, 1831, he there, by an instrument in writing, valid by the law of Milan, assigned the copyright to S. Ricordi, who afterwards came to this country, and in June, 1831, by deed under his hand and seal, in the presence of, and attested by, two witnesses, assigned for a valuable consideration the copyright in the composition to Boosey, for publication in the United Kingdom only. Boosey then printed and published the work in this country, and Jefferys, without licence from Boosey, printed and published a portion of it in England. The case was carried eventually into the Upper House, and judgment given by Lords Cranworth, Brougham, and St. Leonards. The last-named learned judge was of opinion that copyright by the law of Milan could have no effect in this country ; that the law of Milan, which gave to Bellini this copyright, could of course give him no right in this country. The first question was, how could a right exist in Bellini, as a foreigner, to copyright in this country ? He had it by the law of Milan, because he was a native-born subject, or a subject, at all events, by residence, and the law of that country gave it to him; but the moment he stepped out of that country he could have no other right than was involved in the mere possession of the subject-matter in his hands, except so far as the law of any country to which he resorted might give him such a right. Then, in order to obtain copyright here, he must come and perform the conditions annexed to the enjoyment of that right; and he (Lord St. Leonards) held it to be perfectly clear that that condition is, that he must reside in this country. Then, if that were so, as Bellini did not perform the condition, he never had the right to assign, and he could not assign that which never existed. Remaining abroad, he could not have the right, for the common law of this country gave him no such right, Neither did the statute law of this country give him any

CAP. V.

such right. Therefore, whilst at Milan he had a Milanese copyright; but he had not, and could not acquire, a British copyright; and if he had no right in this country he could assign none. And in this view he was supported by the other learned judges.

Cocks v. Pur-
day overruled.

This case completely overruled that of *Cocks* v. *Purday* (a). It had been held in that case that, where by the law of Austria (which prevailed where A., the author of a musical composition, and B., his assignee, were respectively domiciled) A. assigned his right to B., and B., before the publication of the work, sold his copyright to C., an Englishman, there being a sale valid by the law of Austria, the country in which the sale took place, the interest of the author became vested in C. before publication, so as to make him an assignee within the meaning of the 5 & 6 Vict. c. 45, s. 3, and to confer upon him a good derivative title.

The absence of an assignment in writing must be specially pleaded at law (b), but where one of the plaintiff's witnesses stated that he had heard the plaintiff declare, that he had parted with all his interest in the copyright, although he did not mention in what manner the transfer had been made, the plaintiff was immediately non-suited (c).

Right of
assignor to sell
stock on hand
after assign-
ment.

It has lately been determined that, in the absence of a special contract to the contrary, the assignor of a copyright is entitled, after the assignment, to continue selling copies of the work printed by him before the assignment and remaining in his possession (d).

In *Howitt* v. *Hall* (e), it appeared that the defendants,

(a) 5 C. B. 860; 12 Jur. 677; 17 L. J. (C.P.) 273; and that of *Boosey* v. *Davidson*, 13 Q. B. 257; 13 Jur. 678; 18 L. J. (Q.B.) 174; and *Boosey* v. *Jefferys* (in error), 6 Ex. 580; 15 Jur. 540; 20 L. J. (Ex.) 354; overruled by *Jefferys* v. *Boosey*, 4 H. L. C. 815; 24 L. J. (Ex.) 81; 1 Jur. (N.S.) 615.
(b) *Barnett* v. *Glossop*, 1 Bing. N. C. 633; but see *Johnson* v. *Dodgson*, 2 M. & W. 657; and *Buttermere* v. *Hayes*, 5 M. & W. 456; *De Pinna* v. *Polhill*, 8 C. & P. 78; *Cocks* v. *Purday*, 5 C. B. 860.
(c) *Moore* v. *Walker*, 4 Camp. 9, n.
(d) *Taylor* v. *Pillow*, Law Rep. 7 Eq. 418.
(e) 6 L. T. (N.S.) 348.

having bought the copyright for four years in a book of which the plaintiff was the author, were still continuing, several years after the end of that term, to sell copies which they had printed during the four years. The court in refusing an injunction to restrain such sales, held that the purchase of the copyright carried the right of printing; and that, while this right reverted to the author at the end of four years, the publishers were entitled to sell, after the expiration of that term, all copies which had been printed in good faith during the term. "The Copyright Acts," said Vice-Chancellor Wood, "were directed against unlawful printing; and when, as in this case, the defendant had acquired the right of lawfully printing the work, he was at liberty to sell at any time what he had so printed."

The two last cited cases must be taken as defining the law on the subject, but they are open to grave objections.

The Court of Chancery will disregard a permission from the author to infringe the copyright, given after he has parted with his equitable title for valuable consideration, and it has appeared upon the title page of his work that it was printed for the equitable assignee of the copyright (a). And when an author has parted with his copyright in a work, he is not at liberty to reproduce substantially the same matter in another publication (b).

A licence to publish is not an assignment of the copyright (c). A licence not an assignment.

An assignment may be made of a share in the copyright, either a third or other proportion, and it is the practice at Stationers' Hall to enter such assignments in the register when tendered at the office, though this does not seem to be generally known. Assignment of share in copyright by entry at Stationers' Hall.

(a) *Hodges* v. *Welsh*, 2 Ir. Eq. Rep. 266.
(b) *Rooney* v. *Kelly*, 14 Ir. Law Rep. (N.S.) 158; *Colburn* v. *Simms*, 2 Hare, 543.
(c) *Reade* v. *Bentley*, 4 K. & J. 656.

CHAPTER VI.

INFRINGEMENT OF COPYRIGHT.

" O imitatores, servum pecus !"

" Quid nos dura refugimus
Ætas? quid intactum nefasti
Liquimus ?"

HORACE.

Infringement
of copyright.

THE question must obviously arise somewhat frequently,
what is, and what is not, a piracy. In many cases the
line of demarcation is so loosely and indifferently drawn,
that arrival at a just conclusion is a matter of difficulty.
So entirely must each case be governed and regulated by
the particular circumstances attending it, that any general
rules on the subject must be received with extreme caution.
Regard must be had to the value of the work, and the
value of the extent of the infringements; for while, on
the one hand, the policy of the law allows a man to profit
by all antecedent literature, yet, on the other, the use
made of such antecedent literature may not be so extensive
as to injure the sale of the original work, even though
made with no intention to invade the previous author's
right (a); for the copyright having been violated, the
penalty must be paid (b).

The result, in such cases, is the true test of the act.

(a) *Roworth* v. *Wilkes,* 1 Camp. 94; *Emerson* v. *Davies.* 3 Story (Amer.)
768; *Campbell* v. *Scott,* 11 Sim. 31; 11 L. J. (N.S.) Ch. 166; 6 Jur. 186;
Clement v. *Maddick,* 1 Giff. (Ch.) 98: 5 Jur. (N.S.) 592; *vide* Kindersley,
V.C., in *Murray* v. *Bogue.* 1 Drew. 353; Wood, V.C. in *Reade* v. *Lacy,* 1
J. & H. 524; and Story, J., in *Folsom* v. *Marsh,* 2 Story (Amer.) 115; see
Gambart v *Sumner.* 5 H. & N. 5.

(b) *Millett* v. *Snowdon,* 1 West. L. J. (Amer.) 240; *Parker* v. *Hulme,* 7
ibid. 426: *Webb* v. *Powers,* 2 Wood & M. (Amer.) 497.

Full acknowledgment of the original, and the absence of CAP. VI. any dishonest intention, will not excuse the appropriator when the effect of his appropriation is, of necessity, to injure and supersede the sale of the original work; for a man must be presumed to intend all that the publication of his work effects (a).

In some of the cases it will be observed that stress is laid on the existence of the *animus furandi* (b). But the question of piracy cannot properly depend upon the intention of the pirate. The main point must always be what effect will the extracts have upon the original work—how far will they supply its place or injure its sale. If the extracts are such as to render the protected work less valuable, by superseding its use in any degree, the right of the author is infringed, and it can be of no importance to inquire with what intent this was done.

Plagiarism does not necessarily amount to an invasion of copyright, and the author of a published book has no monopoly in the theories and speculations, or even in the results of observations therein contained; but no one, whether with or without acknowledgment, can be permitted to take a material and substantial portion of the published work of another author, for the purpose of making or improving a rival publication (c). Plagiarism not necessarily an invasion of copyright.

La Bruyère declares that we are come into the world too late to produce anything new, that nature and life are preoccupied, and that description and sentiment have been long exhausted. However this may be, it is apparent that some similarities, and a use, to a certain extent, of prior Want of originality in modern works.

(a) Wood, V.C., in *Scott* v. *Stanford*, Law Rep. 3 Eq. 723; *Clement* v. *Maddick*, 1 Giff. 98; *Millett* v. *Snowden*, 1 West. L. J. (Amer.) 240; *Nichols* v. *Ruggles*, 3 Day (*ibid.*) 158; *Story* v. *Holcombe*, 4 McLean (*ibid.*) 306; McLean, J., Ohio, 1847.

(b) *Cary* v. *Kearsley*, 4 Esp. 170. The *animus furandi* will be taken into consideration in those cases where it is difficult to ascertain the extent of the copying, in order to determine whether the use made of a protected work by a subsequent author is fair or lawful : *Spiers* v. *Brown*, 31 L. T. (N.S.) 18 : 6 W. R. 352.

(c) *Pike* v. *Nicholas*, 38 L. J. (Ch.) 529 ; 20 L. T. (N.S.) 906 ; reversed, L. R. 5 Ch. 251; 18 W. R. 321 : 39 L. J. (Ch.) 435, but not in opposition to the principle above laid down.

works, even to the copying of small parts, must be tolerated in the case of such works as dictionaries, gazetteers, grammars, maps, arithmetics, almanacs, concordances, encyclopædias, itineraries, guide books, and similar productions, if the main design and execution are in reality novel and improved, and not a mere cover for important piracies (a).

All definitions of the same thing must be nearly the same, and descriptions, which are definitions of a more lax and fanciful kind, must always have in some degree that resemblance to each other which they all have to their object. Consequently, in compiling such works, the materials, to a considerable extent, must be nearly identical, and the prior compiler cannot monopolize what did not originate with himself, nor a subsequent compiler employ a prior arrangement and materials to such an extent as to be a substantial invasion of the anterior compilation.

Encyclopædias may not outstrip the limits of fair quotation.

Thus, where it appeared that 75 out of 118 pages of a work on fencing had been transcribed into an encyclopædia, the court held that a piracy had been committed; for though it is true that an encyclopædia may be allowed to embrace all the information contained in the newest works on the subject, yet definite limits must be set to its extracts. The same rule holds good in respect of works under review; the reviewer may fairly make extracts, and may comment on those portions, but it would be unfair if he were allowed to exhibit the substance of the work he chose to review. Sufficient may be taken to form a correct idea of the whole, but no one is allowed to review in such a manner as to make the review serve as a substitute for the work reviewed (b).

The latter, to be a piracy, need not serve as a substitute for the former work.

And yet to be a piracy it is not necessary that the latter work should be a substitute for the original composition. It can seldom be the criterion. Vice-Chancellor Shadwell,

(a) *Webb* v. *Powers*, 2 Wood & M. (Amer.) 497–512; *vide* 2 Hilliards on Torts, 49.

(b) 1 Camp. 97; 4 Esp. 168; 17 Ves. 422; Eden on Injunc. 281; see *Murray* v. *M'Fargilhar*, June 25, 1785, Mor. Dic. of Dec. 8309.

on one occasion, put the case in a simple aspect: "We all know that there has been a very valuable Greek lexicon published by Mr. Liddell and another friend of his at Oxford; no person who published this lexicon, omitting three or four words at the end of each letter of the alphabet, could have done a work of which it could be said, that it might be taken as a substitute, for nobody would take it as a substitute. But can it be doubted that it might have a very material effect in diminishing the price of the first book? For, though nobody would take it as a substitute, many people might not care about so much, and might take it cheaply for what it really did contain, which might be more than ninety-nine hundredths of the whole, and yet it would in no manner be a substitute; and, therefore, the language is not generally correct, so as to be capable of application to every case."

Where a work entitled 'A Practical Treatise on the Law Relative to the Sale and Conveyance of Real Property, &c.,' contained piratical extracts from an earlier standard work, which was entitled 'A Practical Treatise on the Law of Vendors and Purchasers of Estates,' the Vice-Chancellor Shadwell observed, "In cases of this nature, if the pirated matter is not considerable, that is, where the passages, which are neither numerous nor long, have been taken from different parts of the original work, this court will not interfere to restrain the publication of the work complained of, but will leave the plaintiff to seek his remedy at law. But in this case it is plain that the passages which have been pointed out have been taken from the plaintiff's book, and they are so considerable, both in number and length, as to make it right that this court should interfere (a)."

The inquiry in most cases, is not, whether the defendant has used the thoughts, conceptions, information, and discoveries promulgated by the original, but whether his composition may be considered a *new work*, requiring invention, learning, and judgment, or only a mere tran-

Principles by which a piracy is judged.

(a) *Sweet* v. *Cater*, 11 Sim. 580. See *Kelly* v. *Hooper*, 4 Jur. 21.

script of the whole or parts of the original, with mere colourable variations (a).

In *Scott* v. *Stanford* (b), the plaintiff had published statistical returns of all coal imported into London, and the defendant, in giving the universal statistics of the United Kingdom, had copied from the plaintiff's work to the extent of one-third of the whole of the defendant's work, at the same time acknowledging the source from which his information was derived. Vice-Chancellor Wood decided, that having regard to the quantity and matter of the information which had been republished without the exercise of any independent thought and labour, and the prejudice to the plaintiff in having the sale of his work superseded by this republication, the plaintiff was entitled to an injunction. If the defendant, after collecting the information for himself, had checked his results by the plaintiff's tables, that would have been a widely different thing from the wholesale extraction of the vital part of his work. But no man is entitled to avail himself of the previous labours of another for the purpose of conveying to the public the same information, although he may append additional information to that already published. This is consonant to the law as laid down in *Kelly* v. *Morris* (c), which was in the following terms: In the case of a dictionary, map, guide-book, or directory, where there are certain common objects of information which must, if described correctly, be described in the same words, a subsequent compiler is bound to set about doing for himself that which the first compiler has done. In the case of a road-book, he must count the milestones for himself, ... and the only use that he can legitimately make of a previous publication is to verify his own calculations and results when obtained.

(a) *Stowe* v. *Thomas*, 9 Wall. C. Ct. (Amer.) 547 ; S.C. 2 Amer. L. Reg. 231.
(b) L. R. 3 Eq. 718; *Morris* v. *Ashbee*, 19 L. T. (N.S.) 550 ; L. R. 7 Eq. 34; *Mawman* v. *Tegg*, 2 Russ. 398; *Jarrold* v. *Houlston*, 3 K. & J. 708 ; *Cox* v. *The Land and Water Co.*, 18 W. R. 206.
(c) L. R. 1 Eq. 697.

From these observations it is not to be inferred that in Cap. VI. compiling a directory the compiler may not look into the previous directory of another for the purpose of ascertaining where a particular person lives, and for the purpose of ascertaining from that book whether or not it is worth his while to call upon that person (a); they imply no further than that he may not take a passage from the directory, and go and see whether it happens to be accurate, and if it be accurate, bodily copy it into his directory.

This latter is precisely what was done in *Morris* v. *Ashbee* (b). The defendant copied the plaintiff's book, and then sent out canvassers to see if the information so copied was correct. If the canvasser did not find the occupier of the house at home, or could get no answer from him, then the information copied from the plaintiff's book was repeated bodily, as if it were a question for the occupier of the house merely, and not for the compiler of the previous directory. The copying was as direct in the case of *Kelly* v. *Morris*, to which we have already referred. Not only were the slips for the purpose of canvassing copied, but the course pursued really was, that when a slip was presented to the person who was canvassed, and his permission received for the insertion of the particular entry, the slip was forthwith copied into the book. "Now it is plain," observed Lord Justice Giffard, "that it could not be lawful for the defendants simply to cut the slips, which they have cut from the plaintiff's directory, and insert them in theirs. Can it then be lawful to do so, because, in addition to doing this, they sent persons with the slips to ascertain their correctness? I say, clearly not..... In *Pike* v. *Nicholas* (c) we had this: Two rival books were published with reference to the same subject matter, and we thought certainly that the defendant had been guided

(a) *Morris* v. *Wright*, 22 L. T. (N.S.) 78; 18 W. R. 327; L. R. 5 Ch. 279; *Scott* v. *Stanford*, L. R. 3 Eq. 718; *Cox* v. *Land and Water Journal Co.*, 9 Id. 324; *Pike* v. *Nicholas*, L. R. 5 Ch. 251; *Hogg* v. *Scott*, L. R. 18 Eq. 444.
(b) 19 L. T. (N.S.) 550; L. R. 7 Eq. 34.
(c) 38 L. J. (Ch.) 529.

CAP. VI.   by the plaintiff's book, more or less, to the authorities which the plaintiff had cited ; but it was a perfectly legitimate course for the defendant to refer to the plaintiff's book, and if he did, taking that book as his guide, himself go to the original authorities, and compile his book from the original authorities, he made no unfair or improper use of the plaintiff's book" (a).

How far prior literature may be used.   The question as to how far advantage may be reaped from the work of another, and what use may be legitimately made of it, is difficult of solution. Perhaps the strongest case in favour of the adoption by a subsequent compiler of the work of a preceding one, is that of *Cary* v. *Kearsley* (b), where Lord Ellenborough thought that the former might fairly adopt part of the work of the latter, and might so make use of his labours for the promotion of science and the benefit of the public ; but having done so, he was of opinion that the question would be, was the matter so taken used fairly with that view, and without what he might term the *animus furandi ?* For while he considered himself bound to secure every man in the enjoyment of his copyright, he was fearful of putting manacles upon science.

Sale of a sheet almauac printed from a directory restrained.   Where the defendant published a sheet almanac containing matter pirated from a distinct part of a directory published by the plaintiff, affording information with respect to the post office, compiled from public documents, and the matter pirated formed an exceedingly small portion of the plaintiff's work, though they bore a great proportion to the other matters in the defendant's work ; the court granted and continued an injunction against him (c).

In *Jarrold* v. *Houlston* (d), the publishers of Dr. Brewer's

---

(a) " The true principle in all these cases," said Vice-Chancellor Hall, in *Hogg* v. *Scott*, L. R. 18 Eq. 458, " is that the defendant is not at liberty to use or avail himself of the labour which the plaintiff has been at for the purpose of producing his work ; that is, in fact, merely to take away the result of another man's labour, or, in other words, his property."

(b) 4 Esp. 168.

(c) *Kelly* v *Hooper*, 4 Jur. 2.

(d) 3 K. & J. 708 ; 3 Jur. (N.S.) 1051.

'Guide to Science' obtained an injunction against the publication of the 'Reason Why.' The works in controversy
were written on the same plan, and presented, in the
form of question and answer, popular information on
a variety of scientific subjects. The earlier book, Dr.
Brewer's 'Guide to Science,' had evidently been used to
a considerable extent in the preparation of the later
one, although copying was denied. The judge said: "The
question I really have to try is, whether the use that in
this case has been made of the plaintiffs' book has gone
beyond a fair use. Now, for trying that question, several
tests have been laid down. One, which was originally
expressed, I think, by a common law judge, and was
adopted by Lord Langdale in *Lewis* v. *Fullarton*, is,
whether you find on the part of the defendant an *animus
furandi*—an intention to take for the purpose of saving
himself labour. I take the illegitimate use, as opposed
to the legitimate use of another man's works on subject
matters of this description to be this : if, knowing that
a person whose work is protected by copyright has, with
considerable labour, compiled from various sources a work
in itself not original, but which he has digested and
arranged, you, being minded to compile a work of a like
description, instead of taking the pains of searching into all
the common sources, and obtaining your subject matter
from them, avail yourself of the labour of your predecessor,
adopt his arrangements, adopt, moreover, the very questions he has asked, or adopt them with but a slight
degree of colourable variation, and thus save yourself
pains and labour by availing yourself of the pains and
labour which he has employed, that I take to be an illegitimate use." But where the same plaintiffs filed a bill
against the publishers of a work called 'Class Book of
Modern Science ;' compiled by Messrs. Thomas and Francis
Bullock, for a piracy of their ' Dr. Brewer's Guide,' and
it was admitted by the defendant that he had referred
to the plaintiffs' book in the course of compiling the
' Class Book ;' but he insisted that every fact or illustra-

tion referred to in the 'Class Book,' was verified by the labour and research of the authors themselves, by means of actual observation, inquiry, or experiment where such was possible, and by reference to scientific authorities and standard works of which the plaintiffs' book did not affect to be one ; it was held by Vice-Chancellor James, that though if any part of a work complained of was a transcript of another work, or with only colourable additions and variations, and prepared without any real independent literary labour, such portion of the work complained of was piratical, yet it was impossible to establish a charge of piracy where it was necessary to track mere passages and lines through hundreds of pages, or where the authors of a work challenged as piratical had honestly applied their labours to various sources of information. The learned Vice-Chancellor saying, " The whole of the part about sound, fogs, winds, dew, and hoar-frost in the defendants' work has a striking similarity, almost identity of appearance, with parts of the plaintiffs' work. The defendants' authors, however, have both of them sworn positively that they did not copy from the plaintiffs' work, although that work was known to them, and had been used in tuition, in common with nearly fifty other books of the same character, and on the same topics. These authors have not been cross-examined. The defendants' counsel have gone through the works in question passage by passage, and have shewn that in nearly all the instances of alleged piracy, the defendant's production had been, in fact, taken from other works which were antecedent to both plaintiffs' and defendant's books. The plaintiff said, that the difference of language between the two, was part of the defendant's authors' fraud and artful disguise of what they had done. But the language thus complained of, is conclusively traced to other books. This fact recoils destructively on the plaintiffs' case, for it goes far to shew that the defendant's writers honestly applied their labours to various sources of information. I do not consider that the imitation of the questions in the plaintiffs' book is a piracy, so long as the defendants' writers have gone to independent sources in the preparation of their answers." (a)

Cap. VI.

The rule appears now to be settled, that the compiler of a work in which absolute originality is of necessity excluded, is entitled, without exposing himself to a charge of piracy, to make use of preceding works upon the subject, where he bestows such mental labour upon what he has taken, and subjects it to such revision and correction as *to produce an original result*, provided that he does not deny the use made of such preceding works, and the alterations are not merely colourable (b)

A compiler must produce an original result.

So in the case of a descriptive catalogue of fruit and trees, the court was of opinion that the later compiler might use the work of his predecessor as a guide or instructor; but might not copy the descriptions from it, although he should verify and correct them from specimens of fruit before him. Though he could not be prevented from getting much aid in the way of information, suggestions, etc., from the protected work open before him, he must write his own descriptions from actual specimens, or common sources of information (c).

To further illustrate the principle, take the case of a dictionary. There may be a certain degree of skill exhibited as to order and arrangement, and there may be a good deal of ingenuity exhibited in the selection of phrases and illustrations, which are the best exponents of the sense in which the word is to be used: and there may also be great labour in the logical deduction and arrangement of the word in its different senses, when the sense of the word departs from its primary signification; but there cannot be copyright in much of the information contained in the numerous dictionaries published, each necessarily having a large number of words identically similar. The great point to decide in such cases is, as we have already

The case of a dictionary analyzed.

(a) *Jarrold* v. *Heywood*, 18 W. R. 279.
(b) *Spiers* v. *Brown*, 6 W. R. 352; *Reade* v. *Lacy*, 1 J. & H. 524; and in the case of a catalogue, *Hotten* v. *Arthur*, 1 H. & M. 603; 32 L. J. (Ch.) 771; 11 W. R. 934; 9 L. T. (N.S.) 199.
(c) *Hogg* v. *Scott*, L. R. 18 Eq. 444.

CAP. VI.

stated, whether in the particular case the work is a legitimate use of the plaintiff's publication in the fair exercise of a mental operation deserving the character of an original work (*a*).

The case of *Spiers* v. *Brown*.

Lord Hatherley, while Vice-Chancellor, in the case of *Spiers* v. *Brown* (*b*), thus summed-up the law in his peculiarly lucid style : All cases of copyright were very simple when a work of an entirely original character was concerned, being a work of imagination or invention on the part of the author, or original in respect of its being a work treating of a subject common to mankind, such as history, or other branches of knowledge varying much in their mode of treatment, and in which the hand of the artist would be readily discerned. But the difficulty that arose in cases of the class then before him was, that they not only related to a subject common to all mankind, but that the mode of expression and language was necessarily so common that two persons must, to a very great extent, express themselves in identical terms in conveying the instruction or information to society which they were anxious to communicate. The most obvious case was that of figures, such as the table of logarithms—the case before Sir John Leach—where it would be impossible to deviate in the calculations, or to vary the order, and the result must be identical. The same might be said of directories, calendars, court guides, and works of that description. Those were cases in which the only mode of arriving at the amount of labour bestowed was by the common test resorted to of discovering the copy of errors and misprints, indicating a servile copying. Copyright was considered, for the highest purposes of society in every country, as necessary to be secured to those who contributed to the civilization, refinement, or instruction of mankind, and extended, in this country, if not elsewhere, to every description of work, however humble it might be, even to

(*a*) *Vide Wilkins* v. *Aikin*, 17 Ves. 422 ; *Bramwell* v. *Halcomb*, 3 My. & Cr. 737 ; *Cornish* v. *Upton*, 4 L. T. (N.S.) 863.

(*b*) 6 W. R. 352.

the mere collection of the abodes of persons, and to streets and places; and labour having been employed upon subjects even of that class, no one had a right to avail himself of it. . . . The real question was, how far the Courts had decided that a certain amount of use of preceding works was legitimate in carrying out a second work of a similar description, calculated to afford instruction by means of a dictionary, vocabulary, or the like. In the case of *Cary* v. *Kearsley* (a), Lord Ellenborough laid down the law in a manner which had not been questioned. He said: "That part of the work of one author found in another is not of itself piracy, or sufficient to support an action. A man may fairly adopt part of the work of another; he may so make use of another's labour for the promotion of science and the benefit of the public; but, having done so, the question will be, was the matter so taken used fairly with that view, and without what I may term the *animus furandi?* Look through the book, and find any part that is a transcript of the other; if there is none such, if the subject of the book is that which is subject to every man's observation, such as the names of the places and their distances from each other, the places being the same, the distances being the same, if they are correct, one book must be a transcript of the other; but when in the defendant's book there are additional observations, and in some parts of the book I find corrections of misprintings, while I shall think myself bound to secure every man in the enjoyment of his copyright, one must not put manacles on science." Then there was the case of *Longman* v. *Winchester* (b), in which Lord Eldon said, "Take the instance of a map describing a particular county, and a map of the same county afterwards published by another person; if the description is accurate in both they must be pretty much the same, but it is clear that the latter publisher cannot, on that account, be

(a) 4 Esp. 168.
(b) 16 Ves. 269; *Cary* v. *Longman,* 1 East, 358; *Matthewson* v. *Stockdale,* 12 Ves. 270; *Bailey* v. *Taylor,* 3 L. J. (Ch.) 66; *Kelly* v. *Hooper,* 4 Jur. 21; *M'Neill* v. *Williams,* 11 Id. 344; *Murray* v. *Bogue,* 1 Drew. 353.

justified in sparing himself the labour and expense of actual survey, by copying the map previously published by another. So, as to Paterson's 'Road Book,' it is certainly competent to any other man to publish a book of roads, and if the same skill, intelligence, and diligence are applied in the second instance, the public would receive nearly the same information from both works; but there is no doubt that this court would interpose to prevent a mere republication of a work which the labour and skill of another person had supplied to the world. So, in the instance mentioned by Sir Samuel Romilly, a work consisting of a selection from various authors, two men perhaps might make the same selection, but that must be by resorting to the original authors, not by taking advantage of the selection already made by another." And again: "The question before me is, whether it is not perfectly clear that in a vast proportion of the work of these defendants no other labour has been applied than copying the plaintiff's work. From the identity of the inaccuracies it is impossible to deny that the one was copied from the other *verbatim et literatim* (a). To the extent, therefore, in which the defendant's publication has been supplied from the other work the injunction must go; but I have said nothing that has a tendency to prevent any person from giving to the public a work of this kind if it is the fair

(a) This is one of the surest tests of copying, see *Kelly* v. *Morris*, L. R. 1 Eq. 697; *Pike* v. *Nicholas*, L. R. 5 Ch. 251; *Cox* v. *Land and Water Journal Co.*, L. R. 9 Eq. 324. In *Murray* v. *Bogue*, 1 Drew. 353, 366, where instances were stated in the bill and at the bar in which the defendant had the plaintiff's errors, Vice-Chancellor Kindersley said, "Now the use of shewing the same errors in both is, that where the defendant says he has got his information, not from the plaintiff, but from other sources, if the evidence is unsatisfactory on the question whether the defendant did use the plaintiff's work or not, to shew the same errors in the subsequent work that are contained in the original, is a strong argument to shew copying." It will be in the defendant's favour if he shews that the matter in his own book is free from many of the errors in the plaintiff's; but still the errors may have been corrected in copying. In *M'Neill* v. *Williams*, 11 Jur. 344, it appeared that seven errors in the plaintiff's mathematical tables were also found in those of the defendant. The latter declared that this was accidental, and that the plaintiff's book contained seventy errors not to be found in his own. It does not appear what importance the Court attached to this circumstance; but the injunction was refused.

fruit of original labour, the subject being open to all the world." Another case—which seemed to condense into one point the view taken by the courts in cases where actual use is avowed and the only question is, whether it is a fair use (a),—where Lord Eldon says this: "Upon inspection of the different works, I observe a considerable proportion taken from the plaintiff's that is acknowledged, but also much that is not; and in determining whether the former is within the doctrine upon this subject the case must be considered as also presenting the latter circumstance. The question upon the whole is, whether this is a legitimate use of the plaintiff's publication in the fair exercise of a mental operation deserving the character of an original work." These were the words which had been relied on by Lord Cottenham in *Bramwell* v. *Halcomb* (b), and it was with the view thus taken by those learned judges that he (the Vice-Chancellor) had gone through a very laborious investigation of the works then in question, there being, as it seemed to him, a considerable portion of the defendant's work which came within the doctrine of its being a legitimate use and a fair exercise of mental operation, and (adding the negative used by Lord Ellenborough) not being done colourably. . . . His Honour said, that the real issue which the court was called on to decide was one of the most difficult ever presented to him, namely, as to how far this very considerable use of the work of another might be taken to be legitimate. There was no concealment of some use having been made; no colourable alteration proved, nor anything tending to shew a fraudulent design to make an unfair use of the work of another. The present case went as far as any previous, though not perhaps further than *Mawman* v. *Tegg* (c), where a very large and considerable portion of the plaintiff's work had been taken without any alteration or addition. Though a good deal had been taken from the plaintiff, yet a good deal of labour had been bestowed upon what had been taken.. . . . Upon the whole, he could not think that the defendant had gone beyond

(a) *Wilkins* v. *Aikin*, 17 Ves. 422.　　(b) 3 My. & Cr. 737.
(c) 2 Russ. 385.

CAP. VI.

Modes in
which copy-
right may be
infringed.

what the court would allow, having produced that which
in the result was, in fact, a different work from that of the
plaintiff.

Copyright may be invaded in several ways:—

    1st. By reprinting the whole work *verbatim*.

    2nd. By reprinting *verbatim* a part of it.

    3rd. By imitating the whole or a part, or by repro-
        ducing the whole or a part with colourable
        alterations.

    4th. By reproducing the whole or a part under an
        abridged form.

    5th. By reproducing the whole or a part under the
        form of a translation.

1. By reprint-
ing the whole
verbatim.

Piracies of the nature of the first division are seldom
committed, on account of the ease with which they could
be detected and punished.

2. By reprint-
ing *verbatim* a
part.

Piracies of the nature of the second division are far
more frequent and more difficult of detection. The quantity of matter subtracted cannot in all cases be a true
criterion of the extent of the piracy, for a work may be
a piracy upon another, though the passages copied are
stated to be quotations, and are not so extensive as to
render the piratical work a substitution for the original
work.

In questions as to the extent of appropriation which is
necessary to establish an infringement, extreme difficulty
is usually experienced, for the quality of the piracy is
frequently more important than the proportion which the
borrowed passages might bear to the whole work (a).

If so much is taken that the value of the original is
sensibly diminished, or the labours of the original author
are substantially, to an injurious extent, appropriated by
another, that is sufficient, in point of law, to constitute a
piracy *pro tanto*. The entirety of the copyright is the
property of the author; and it is no defence that another
person has appropriated a part and not the whole of such
property.

    (a) Vice-Chancellor in *Tinsley* v. *Lacy*, 1 H. & M. 747; 32 L. J. (Ch.)
535.

Lord Cottenham, in the cases of *Bramwell* v. *Halcomb* (a), and *Saunders* v. *Smith* (b), adverting to this point, said: Quantity but " When it comes to a question of quantity, it must be slight criterion very vague. One writer might take all the vital part of of piracy. another's book, though it might be but a small proportion of the book in quantity. It is not only quantity, but value, that is always looked to. It is useless to refer to any particular cases as to quantity." In short, we must often, in deciding questions of this sort, look to the nature and objects of the selections made, the quantity and value of the materials used, and the degree in which the use may prejudice the sale, or diminish the profits, or supersede the objects of the original work. Many mixed ingredients enter into the discussion of such questions. In some cases a considerable portion of the materials of the original work may be fused into another work, so as to be distinguishable in the mass of the latter, which has other professed and obvious objects, and cannot fairly be treated as a piracy ; or they may be inserted as a sort of distinct and mosaic work into the general texture of the second work, and constitute the peculiar excellence thereof, and then it may be a clear piracy. If a person should, under colour of publishing ' elegant extracts ' of poetry, include all the best pieces at large of a favourite poet, whose volume was secured by copyright, it would be difficult to say why it was not an invasion of that right, since it might constitute the entire value of the volume. The case of *Mawman* v. *Tegg* (c), is to this purpose. There was no pretence in that case that all the articles of the encyclopædia of the plaintiffs had been copied into that of the defendants ; but large portions of the materials of the plaintiff's work had been copied. Lord Eldon, upon that occasion, held that there might be a piracy of a part of a work, which would entitle the plaintiffs to a full remedy and relief in equity. In prior cases he had affirmed the like doctrine. In *Wilkins* v. *Aikin* (d) he said, " There is no doubt that

(a) 3 My. & Cr. 737.　　　　　(c) 2 Russ. 385.
(b) 3 My. & Cr. 711.　　　　　(d) 17 Ves. 422.

a man cannot, under the pretence of quotation, publish either the whole or a part of another's book, although he may use, what in all cases it is difficult to define, fair quotation."

Selections from various writers. Selections from various writers are frequently made and issued in one volume. Where the selections are made from works in which copyright subsists, questions have arisen as to whether the limits of lawful quotation have been exceeded. And in one case where it appeared to the court that the chief value of the compilation consisted in the selections, and not in the original matter, it held the work to be piratical. In the case referred to the defendant had published a 'Book of the Poets,' with the object of illustrating the characteristics of various poets, and the progress of English poetry during the nineteenth century. He had made 425 selections and extracts, from forty-three poets, and they were employed to illustrate an original essay of thirty-four pages on English poetry of the period covered, twenty-three biographical sketches of one page each, and twenty shorter notices of authors. Besides extracts, six poems were taken in their entirety from Campbell's works. "If," said Vice-Chancellor Shadwell (a),; "there were critical notes appended to each separate passage, or to several of the passages in succession which might illustrate them, and shew from whence Mr. Campbell had borrowed an idea, or what idea he had communicated to others, I could understand that to be a fair criticism. But there is, first of all, a general essay; then there follows a mass of pirated matters, which in fact constitutes the value of the volume."

"The Man of his Time," to illustrate career of person. In the case of *Bradbury* v. *Hotten* (b), the publication complained of was "The Man of his Time," the object of which was to illustrate the career of Napoleon III. by caricatures taken from leading English and foreign illustrated papers. Nine caricatures, with their original headings and references, but much reduced in size, were copied from nine numbers of 'Punch,' comprised within

(a) 11 Sim. 31. !   (b) L. R. 8 Exch. 1.

the period extending from 1849 to 1867. It was declared that·the selections had been taken for the sole purpose of illustrating the career of Napoleon. While admitting that limited extracts might be taken from copyright works for a fair purpose of this kind, the court found that the defendant had republished the caricatures in 'Punch' for the same purpose as they were originally published, namely, to excite the amusement of his readers. It was held that the defendant had gone beyond the privilege of fair quotation, and therefore a case of piracy was made out (a).

(a) Kelly, C.B., said, "The questions raised are of interest and importance, but it is difficult to lay down any fixed principle with regard to them. No doubt the matter is, to a great extent, one of degree. It may well be that an author might copy into his book a portion of some books previously published, and yet that a jury might be justified in finding there had been no infringement of copyright; whilst on the other hand, the copying might take place under such circumstances as clearly to amount to an infringement. . . Nine of these pictures the defendant has copied, in some instances alone, in others with the addition of the printed words underneath them. If they have been so copied as to amount to a copy of a material part of the plaintiffs' publication, and the defendant has thus obtained a profit which would or might otherwise have been the plaintiffs', then there has been a piracy, for which the defendant is responsible. It is said that to copy a single picture, at all events, could not be an infringement of the plaintiffs' copyright; but it is impossible to lay that down as a general rule. I can easily conceive a case where such an act would not be piracy. For example, where a picture is reproduced amongst a large collection, published for an entirely different object from that which the first publisher had in view. We must consider in such a case the intent of the copyist and the nature of his work. To turn for a moment from pictures to printed matter, the illustration put during the argument by my Brother Bramwell will explain my meaning.

"A traveller publishes a book of travels about some distant country like China. Amongst other things, he describes some mode of preparing food in use there. Then the compiler of a cookery book re-publishes the description. No one would say that that was piracy. So again, an author publishes a history illustrated with woodcuts of the heads of kings, and another person, writing another history of some other country, finds occasion to copy one of these woodcuts. That, again, would not be a piracy. Yet, on the other hand, the copying of a single picture may, under some circumstances, be an infringement. For example, take the case of a work illustrated by one engraving of the likeness of some distinguished man, where no other likeness is extant. No one would have a right to copy that into a book upon any subject whatever, and a jury would in such a case rightly find that there had been an infringement of the copyright.

"To return to the facts of the present case: the defendant has introduced nine pictures of the plaintiffs into what I may call his comic life of Napoleon III. Is he by so doing applying to his own use and for his own profit what otherwise the plaintiffs might have turned, and possibly still may turn, to a profitable account? The pictures are of great merit, and no doubt were largely paid for, and by inserting these copies the defendant has unquestionably added to the value of his publication. Why should

A similar case to the last cited was that concerning the book entitled 'Thackerayana, Notes and Anecdotes, illustrated by nearly Six Hundred Sketches, by William Makepeace Thackeray.' It purported to be a kind of biography of Thackeray, based on the assumption that his own experiences were narrated in certain of his novels. Besides some previously unpublished sketches and caricatures by Thackeray, the work contained extensive selections from his published works, the copyright of which belonged to the plaintiff. The extracts were prepared by, and interspersed with original comments by the compiler. The court found that the effect of the book was to supersede to a damaging extent the works

---

this not be an infringement? It was said by my brother Parry, in his able argument, that the plaintiffs will never make such a use of these pictures as the defendant has made. But suppose, as my brother Pigott suggested, that after the catastrophe which ended in the fall of Napoleon III., the proprietors of 'Punch' had chosen to re-publish all their caricatures of him, or that even now they should choose to do so. One cannot help seeing that the defendant's publication might cause many who would otherwise have bought to refrain from buying such a work. I need not refer at length to the authorities cited. The principle of them is, that where one man for his own profit puts into his work an essential part of another man's work, from which that other may still derive profit, or from which but for the act of the first he might have derived profit, there is evidence of a piracy upon which a jury should act."

Bramwell, B., said: "I am of the same opinion, though not without some doubt—doubt which it is natural to feel in a case like this, which is on the borderland between piracy and no piracy. But I think the plaintiffs are entitled to succeed. They are the proprietors of a sheet of letterpress within the meaning of the Act of Parliament. Now it is quite true that when a man publishes anything, he professes to add to the common stock of knowledge, and everybody may avail himself of what is published. This may be illustrated by the case put, of the compiler of a cookery-book taking from some traveller's account of his travels a receipt for a new dish. But, applying that principle here, it does not exonerate the defendant. If he had said, 'I propose to illustrate my history by extracts from the satirists of the day,' and had then gone on to quote to a reasonable extent the opinions, or even the very words of satirical writers, no one would call that piracy. Suppose, for instance, he had said, 'At this period of his career Napoleon was unpopular and the subject of ridicule in England. This may be seen by examining the sort of pictures of him which appeared in 'Punch.' Later on he became more popular, and the pictures published represented him more favourably.' That could not have been complained of. Then the defendant would simply have been using the knowledge acquired from 'Punch' for his benefit, as he would have a right to do. But here he has done more. He has not availed himself of the knowledge acquired from 'Punch,' but he has actually reproduced the very pictures published in 'Punch,' and for the same purpose as they were originally published, namely, to excite the amusement of his readers."

from which the selections had been made, and accordingly held it to be a case of piracy (a).

Many cases of extracts for criticism have come before the court. It is obvious that quotations to some extent must in such cases be made from the work reviewed, and this abstract right of the reviewer has never been impeached. To deny this privilege would be, as Lord Kinloch once said, " to sentence to death all our reviews, and the greater part of our works in philosophy." The reviewer may make extracts sufficient to shew the merits or demerits of the work, but not to such an extent as that the review may serve as a substitute for the book reviewed. Sufficient may be taken to give a correct view of the whole, but the privilege of making extracts is limited to these objects, and no person will be allowed to republish in the form of quotations a valuable part of the protected work and thus to an injurious extent to supersede the original (b).

Whether the limits of lawful quotation have been exceeded is a question to be governed by the particular circumstances of each case.

In a case in which the work alleged to be pirated was a play extending over forty pages, and the defendant had published a journal of theatrical criticism in which, as illustrative of his critical remarks, he had introduced broken and detached fragments of the piece in question, amounting in the whole to six or seven pages, some weight appears to have been allowed by the court to the fact of the extent of the extracts being so inconsiderable, as affording ground for doubt whether the defendant had transgressed the limits of fair quotation (c).

(a) *Smith* v. *Chatto*, 31 L. T. (N.S.) 775.
(b) *Roworth* v. *Wilkes*, 1 Camp. 94 ; *Mawman* v. *Tegg*, 2 Russ. 385 ; *Campbell* v. *Scott*, 11 Sim. 31 ; *Bohn* v. *Bogue*, 10 Jur. 420 ; *Black* v. *Murray*, 9 Sc. Sess. Cas. 3rd ser. 341 ; *Smith* v. *Chatto, supra* ; *Lawrence* v. *Dana*, 2 Am. L. T. R. (N.S.) 402.
(c) *Whittingham* v. *Wooler*, 2 Swans. 428. In *Cobbett* v. *Woodward* L. R. 14 Eq. 407, the Court was willing to grant an injunction against about eight lines copied from the plaintiff's publication. In *Sweet* v. *Benning*, 16 C. B. 459, copied matter forming about one-twentieth part of defendant's work was held to amount to piracy. See *Bradbury* v. *Hotten*, L. R. 8 Exch. 1 ; *Chatterton* v. *Cave*, L. R. 10 C. B. 572 ; 1st app. 2 C. P. D. 42 ; 2nd app. 3 App. Cas. 483 ; *Gray* v. *Russell*, 1 Story (Amer.) 20 ; *Tinsley* v. *Lacy*, 1 H. & M. 752.

In *Bell* v. *Whitehead* (a) the plaintiffs had published in the 'Monthly Chronicle' an article entitled 'The Great Western Railway Inquiry,' occupying nineteen pages; the defendant had extracted four pages and a half from this, and published it in the 'Railway Times,' a weekly paper, with animadversions. Lord Cottenham, C., in dissolving an injunction which had been obtained, made these observations: "It is difficult to prescribe the legitimate mode of extracting what is published in other publications, and to lay down the rule of quantity; but it is necessary for a party to be able to substantiate the value of the matter extracted before he comes for an injunction. It appears to me that the subject of the injunction comes within all the rules which are prescribed for trying what is a fair extract or not. The first is, that they are allowed for the purposes of criticism. Now, it is well known that there is a controversy going on as to the principles upon which a railway should be constructed, and on one side is Mr. Brunel, and on the other Dr. Lardner, and what they each contend for is found stated in the reports of the railway company. The 'Railway Times' is the medium of intelligence, and contributes information on the subject of railways; and in publishing the reports of the railway company it is admitted that they have done that which they had a right to do; but they take the side contrary to Dr. Lardner. They then print so much of the article from the 'Monthly Chronicle' as is complained of, and call it Dr. Lardner's further report, and they comment on the controversy between Mr. Brunel and Dr. Lardner. The controversy is also taken up by the editor. They say that they intended to give the whole of the article; but they state that they are unable to do so, and mean to give the remainder in the ensuing number; and there is an advertisement, saying, the next number will contain the whole. It is certainly not a report, but an article on the controversy which the respective engineers had engaged in. In the number of the 8th of January,

(a) 17 L. J. (Ch.) 141; 3 Jur. 68.

they state that Dr. Lardner was to superintend Mr. Wood's experiments, and that they should only extract that portion of the article which relates to the 'opposition of the air to railway trains at high velocities,' and they say they do not mean to publish the whole. . . . On Tuesday they state that they have given the substance of the report. It is not holding out a threat that they will publish more. They make uncourteous observations upon Dr. Lardner; and it is a pity that scientific gentlemen cannot discuss questions of science with more temper. It is fair that no strictures should be made on a work contrary to the spirit of prior decisions; but it would be injurious to the public to limit the right of discussing questions of this kind, and for that purpose to make necessary extracts. And the question is, whether this was inserted for purposes of criticism, and for the purpose of supporting such observations as the editor thinks proper to make. This was the ground proceeded on in *Whittingham* v. *Wooler*, and is acted on in such publications as the 'Edinburgh' and 'Quarterly' Reviews, and when fairly acted on, the result most probably is, that the sale is extended by the notice, when not given for the purpose of superseding the work itself. And, if I were to entertain this application, how could I exclude the similar application of one newspaper seeking to restrain the sale of an article taken from another. It is impossible to say there is any value in the nature of property in what is here inserted. The question is too minute, as a question of property or value, how far, in point of value, it interferes with the sale of the 'Monthly Chronicle.' The injunction is not to depend altogether on a question of account; but to what value the question, in point of utility, is to be carried. If no other danger were to arise from granting this application than what would be consequent in encouraging the litigation of such minute inquiries, it would be a sufficient ground to refuse it, that the court should not be so occupied to the exclusion of other matters which press upon it. The injunction is dissolved, each party paying their own costs."

O

But where, in a recent case (a), the publisher, Mr. Maxwell, applied for an injunction against the proprietor of the 'Bristol Mercury' restraining him from publishing two stories, 'A Troubled Life,' and 'How I Lost the County,' which he had taken *verbatim* from 'Belgravia' and the 'Belgravian Annual'; and it appeared that the magazines were sent to the defendants for review, and that it was the custom, and had been so for many years, to extract short stories in the way defendants had done, Vice-Chancellor Bacon decided that the defendants had no right to publish articles from publications sent to them for criticism; but in granting the injunction asked, made no order as to costs, being of opinion that the defendants had acted unwittingly in making use of the articles in question.

It is manifest, also, from what fell from Lord Chancellor Cottenham in *Saunders* v. *Smith* (b), that he entertained no doubt (although he did not decide the point) that there might be a violation of the copyright of volumes of reports, by copying *verbatim* a part only of the cases reported. It is questionable, how far and to what extent certain cases in Law Reports may be reprinted at length in a treatise on the particular subject to which they relate; but it is clearly piracy to collect together, and reprint from the reports all the cases upon a particular subject, though the collection and classification may be new, and the publication be adorned with the addition of several unpublished decisions and notes (c). In the case last cited, however, the substance and value of the book consisted mainly of the cases pirated; and a case presenting greater difficulty was that of the well-known book entitled 'Smith's Leading Cases,' where the annotations really form the substance and essence of the work. In regard to the legal right in the last-mentioned case (d) Lord Cottenham said: "In this case I find the publication complained of to be of a character which, whether

(a) *Maxwell* v. *Somerton*, 30 L. T. (N.S.) 11; 22 W. R. 313.
(b) 3 My. & Cr. 711; see *Hodges* v. *Welsh*, 2 Ir. Eq. Rep. 266.
(c) *Hodges* v. *Welsh*, *supra*.
(d) *Saunders* v. *Smith*, 3 My. & Cr. 711, 728.

it be or be not an infringement of the copyright of the plaintiffs, is a course of proceeding which has been pretty largely admitted, and pretty generally adopted. Several cases occurred to me, and several were mentioned to me at the bar, in which a gentleman at the bar, desirous of publishing a work upon a particular subject, has collected the cases upon that subject, and has taken these cases, generally speaking *verbatim*, from reports which are covered by copyright. No instance has been represented to me in which those entitled to the copyright have interfered; no judgment, therefore, has been pronounced upon that subject. I am not stating whether the owner of the copyright is entitled to interfere in such a case, or whether the use of published reports is or is not to be permitted. That is a question of legal right upon which I find at present no reason for coming to an adjudication." But in a subsequent case, where eleven cases only had been copied *verbatim*, and a considerable number of what were called abridged cases were mere copies of the plaintiff's with slight variation, Sir L. Shadwell, V.C., granted an injunction (a). He distinguished the case from *Saunders* v. *Smith*. "In that case," said he, "there was no question but some parts of the plaintiff's work had been copied in the defendant's work. But there the publication of the defendant appeared to me to be altogether distinguished from that in which the cases originally appeared, and one which could never be substituted for the other. In this case, from the class of persons who are held out as likely to be purchasers of the defendant's publication, I think it may be materially injurious to the sale of the plaintiff's work." This was the true criterion of the infringement, and it may be said generally that in cases where the work in which the copying or extract is introduced, is a new and distinct work, and not a work with merely colourable variations, the test which the court will apply is the capability of the new work being taken as a substitute

(a) *Sweet* v. *Shaw*, 3 Jur. 217; 8 L. J. (N.S.) Ch. 216; see *Wheaton* v. *Peters*, 8 Peters (Amer.) 591.

CAP. VI.

for the old work. In *Lewis* v. *Fullarton* (a), the case of a typographical dictionary, Lord Langdale held that largely copying from a work, in another book having a similar object, was a violation of that copyright, although the same information might have been (but, in fact, was not) obtained from common sources, open to all persons; and accordingly in that case he granted an injunction as to the parts pirated, notwithstanding the fact that there was much which was original in the new work (b).

The custom of the trade no excuse.

The copying into a newspaper whole articles taken from another periodical—as a monthly magazine—professedly for the purpose of reviewing, is an unlawful use for reviewing, and a Court of Equity will restrain the publication of the work containing these articles, notwithstanding an allegation that it is the custom of the trade (c).

3. By imitating the whole or part by reproduction with colourable alterations.

Distinction between a copy and an imitation.

3rd. Copyright may be infringed by imitating the whole or a part, or by reproducing the whole or a part with colourable alterations.

A copy is one thing, an imitation or resemblance another. It is indeed certain, that whoever attempts any common topic will find unexpected coincidences of his thoughts with those of other writers; nor can the nicest judgment always distinguish accidental similitude from artful imitation. "There is likewise," says Dr. Johnson, "a common stock of images, a settled mode of arrangement, and a beaten track of transition, which all authors suppose themselves at liberty to use, and which produce the resemblance generally observable among contemporaries. So that in books which best deserve the name of originals there is little new beyond the disposition of materials already provided; the same ideas and combinations of ideas have been long in the possession of other hands; and by restoring to every man his own, as

(a) 2 Beav. 6.
(b) See *Cox* v. *The Land and Water Co.*, 18 W. R. 206.
(c) *Maxwell* v. *Somerton*, 30 L. T. (N.S.) 11 ; 22 W. R. 313.

the Romans must have returned to their cots from the possession of the world, so the most inventive and fertile genius would reduce his folios to a few pages. Yet the author who imitates his predecessors only by furnishing himself with thoughts and elegancies out of the same general magazine of literature, can with little more propriety be reproached as a plagiary, than the architect can be censured as a mean copier of Angelo or Wren because he digs his marble from the same quarry, squares his stones by the same art, and unites them to columns of the same order."

There are many imitations of Homer in the '*Æneid*'; but no one would say that the one was a copy of the other. So also can similar passages be found in Virgil and Horace :

> " *Hæ tibi erunt artes—*
> *Parcere subjectis, et debellare superbos.*"
> VIRGIL.

> " *Imperet, bellante prior, jacentem*
> *Lenis in hostem.*"
> HORACE.

And Cicero observes of Achilles, that had not Homer written, his valour had been without praise : *Nisi Ilias illa extitisset, idem tumulus qui corpus ejus contexerat, nomen ejus obruisset;* while Horace remarks that there were brave men before the wars of Troy, but they were lost in oblivion for the want of a poet :

> " *Vixere fortes ante Agamemnona*
> *Multi ; sed omnes illacrymabiles*
> *Urgentur, ignotique longâ*
> *Nocte, carent quia vate sacro.*"

There may be a strong likeness without an identity. The question is, therefore, in many cases a very delicate one : what degree of imitation constitutes an infringement of the copyright in a particular composition ? Certainly not such a similitude as the instances from the classics given above.

It is very evident that any use of materials, whether they are figures or drawings, or other things which are

CAP. VI. well known and in common use, is not the subject of a
copyright, unless there be some new arrangement thereof.
Still, even here, it may not always follow that any person
has a right to copy the figures, drawings or other things,
made by another, availing himself solely of his skill and
industry, without any resort to such common source.   In
all cases the question of fact to come to the jury is,
whether the alterations be colourable or not.   There
must be a similitude, so as to make it probable and reasonable to suppose that one is a transcript of the other,
and nothing more than a transcript ; so with regard to
charts, there is no monopoly in that subject ; but upon
a question of the above nature the jury must decide
whether the latter work be a servile imitation of the
former or not.

In *Trusler* v. *Murray* (a) Lord Kenyon put the point
in the same light, and said, "The main question here is,
whether, in substance, the one work is a copy and imitation
of the other; for undoubtedly, in a chronological work
(such was the character of the work before the court) the
same facts must be related."   And Mr. Justice Story, in
his elaborate and learned judgment in *Emerson* v.
Davies (b), laid it down as the clear result of the authorities in cases of this nature, that the true test of piracy or
not, is to ascertain whether the defendant has, in fact,
used the plan, arrangements, and illustrations of the
plaintiff as the model of his own book, with colourable
alterations and variations only to disguise the use thereof:
or whether his work is the result of his own labour, skill,
and use of common materials and common sources of
knowledge, open to all men, and the resemblances are
either accidental or arising from the nature of the subject.
In other words, whether the defendant's book is, *quoad
hoc,* a servile or evasive imitation of the plaintiff's work,
or a *bonâ fide* original compilation from other common or
independent sources.

An American court, in speaking of a case in which

(a) 1 East, 363, note.   (b) 3 Story (Amer.), 768, 793.

the defendant had pirated a portion of an arithmetic belonging to the plaintiff, observed that the real question on the point was not whether certain resemblances existed, but whether these resemblances were purely accidental and undesigned, and unborrowed, because arising from common sources accessible to both the authors, and the use of materials equally open to both—whether, in fact, the defendant used the plaintiff's work as his model, and imitated or copied that, and did not draw from such common sources or common materials. Then again, it had been said that, to amount to piracy, the work must be a copy and not an imitation. This, as a general proposition, could not be admitted. It was true the imitation might be very slight and shadowy. But, on the other hand, it might be very close, and so close as to be a mere evasion of the copyright, although not an exact and literal copy. "It falls within that class of cases," said Mr. Justice Story, " where the differences between different works are of such a nature, that one is somewhat at a loss to say whether the differences are formal or substantial; whether they indicate a resort to the same common sources to compile and compose them, or one is (as it were) *uno flatu* borrowed from the other, without the employment of any research or skill, with the disguised but still apparent intention to appropriate to one what in truth belongs exclusively to the other, and with no other labour than that of mere transcription, with some omissions or additions as may serve merely to veil the piracy. It is like the case of patented inventions in art or machinery, where the resemblances or diversities between the known and the unknown, and between invention and imitation, are so various or complicated, or minute or shadowy, that it is exceedingly difficult to say what is new or not, or what has been pirated and what is substantially different. The approaches on either side may be almost infinitely varied, and the identity or diversity sometimes becomes almost evanescent. In many cases, the mere inspection of a work may at once betray the fact that it is borrowed from another author, with merely formal or colourable omissions or alterations. In others, again, we cannot affirm that identity in the appearance or use of the materials is a sufficient and conclusive test of piracy, or that the one has been fraudulently or designedly borrowed from the other. Take the case, for example, of two maps of a city, a county or a country. We cannot predicate that the one is a piracy from the other, simply because their external appearance is in nearly all respects the same, with or without some additions or alterations or omissions. Take the case of two engravings copied from the same picture, or two pictures of natural objects by different artists; it would not be practicable, in many cases, from the mere inspection of them and their apparent identity, to say, that the one was a transcript of the other. It would be necessary to resort to auxiliary and supplementary evidence to establish the fact either way (a)."

One test, substantial identity. Cases such as those referred to, namely, those where there is a resemblance between the substance and the general scheme of the two works in question, while at the same time the language of each is by no means similar, occasion great difficulty. The inquiry usually resolves itself into a matter of fact which rests with the court to determine—Is there such a resemblance between the two works in controversy as to constitute an infringement of copyright.

The most general test is that of substantial identity. Is the similarity between the two works such as to make the one substantially identical with the other? Has the second author produced what is substantially an independent work, or has he appropriated merely the fruits of another's labour? (b) Each case must depend on its own

(a) *Emerson* v. *Davies et al.*, 3 Story (Amer.), 768–784.
(b) *Wilkins* v. *Aikin*, 17 Ves. 422; *Mawman* v. *Tegg*, 2 Russ. 385; *Bramwell* v. *Halcomb*, 3 My. & Cr. 737; *Lewis* v. *Fullarton*, 2 Beav. 6; *Kelly* v. *Hooper*, 4 Jur. 21; *Sweet* v. *Maugham*, 11 Sim. 51; *Sweet* v. *Cater*, *Ib.* 572; *Campbell* v. *Scott*, *Ib.* 31; *Stevens* v. *Wildy*, 19 L. J. (N.S.) Ch. 190; *Rooney* v. *Kelly*, 14 Ir. Law Rep. (N.S.) 158; *Tinsley* v. *Lacy*, 1 H. & M. 747; *Kelly* v. *Morris*, L. R. 1 Eq. 697; *Scott* v. *Stanford*, 3 Id. 718; *Jarrold* v. *Heywood*, 18 W. R. 279; *Cobbett* v. *Woodward*, L. R. 14 Eq. 407.

peculiar circumstances, and different judges may upon the Cap. VI.
very same evidence arrive at different conclusions.

"As not every instance of similitude," observes Dr. John- Not every imitation a proof of plagiarism.
son, "can be considered as a proof of imitation, so not
every imitation ought to be stigmatized as plagiarism.
The adoption of a noble sentiment, or the insertion of a
borrowed ornament, may sometimes display so much judgment as will almost compensate for invention; and an
inferior genius may, without any imputation of servility,
pursue the path of the ancients, provided he declines to
tread in their footsteps."

4th. Copyright may be infringed by reproducing the 4. By repro-
duction under
an abridged
form.
whole or a part under an abridged form.

A fair abridgment, when the understanding is employed
in retrenching unnecessary circumstances, is not a piracy
of the original work. Such an abridgment is allowable,
and is regarded in the light of a new work. The law with
reference to abridgments might, we think, with justice receive some modification (a). The decisions on the subject
are somewhat inconsistent. The fundamental principle
on which is based the protection afforded to authors from
piracies, appears to be the injury or damage caused to
them by the depreciation in the value of their original
works. It seems a very unsatisfactory answer to an
author, who has been injured by an abridgment, to say,
that because the wrongful taker has exhibited talent and
ingenuity, both in the taking and in the use which he has
made of it, the original author has no remedy, "The form,"
says Mr. Curtis (b), "under which the original matter
reappears should be treated as a disguise; and the extent
of the transformation shews only the extent to which the
disguise has been carried, as long as anything remains
which the original author can shew to be justly and exclusively his own."

Now, few abridgments do not affect in some way the
original work. By the selection of all the important pas-

(a) See the suggestions of the Copyright Commissioners on the subject,
ante, p. 62, note (a).
(b) 'Copyright,' 272.

sages in a comparatively moderate space, the quintessence of a work may be piratically extracted, so as to leave a mere *caput mortuum*. These considerations have been relied upon by the judges in coming to a determination upon the subject, and the proposition, that an abridgment is not a piracy of the original copyright, must be received with many qualifications.

To constitute a proper abridgment, the arrangement of the book abridged must be preserved, the ideas must also be taken, and expressed in language not copied but condensed. To copy certain passages and omit others, so as to reduce the volume in bulk, is not such an abridging as the court would recognise as sufficiently original to protect the author. The judgment of the abridger must be called into play in condensing the views of the author. There is a clear distinction between an abridgment and a compilation. As an American judge (a) well observed: "A compilation consists of selected extracts from different authors; an abridgment is a condensation of the views of the author. The former cannot be extended so as to convey the same knowledge as the original work; the latter contains an epitome of the work abridged, and consequently conveys substantially the same knowledge. The former cannot adopt the arrangements of the works cited; the latter must adopt the arrangement of the work abridged. The former infringes the copyright, if matter transcribed, when published, shall impair the value of the original book; a fair abridgment though it may injure the original is lawful."

The first case is that of *Dodsley* v. *Kinnersley* (b), where

(a) Leavitt, in *Story's Executors* v. *Holcombe*, 4 McLean (Amer.), 314.
(b) Amb. 403. *Read* v. *Hodges*, 2 Atk. 141. See *Pinnock* v. *Rose*, 2 Bro. C. C. 85, note. Mr. Curtis, the learned author of an American work on copyright, thus states, in his lucid style, the injustice of the law respecting abridgments: "When the author of a book," says he, "of whatever kind, possessing the legal attributes of originality, has secured his copyright according to the prevailing law of his country, he has secured the exclusive right to print and publish his own book. In the jurisprudence with which we are concerned, this right includes the whole book and every part of it; for we have seen that there may be a piratical taking of extracts and passages, and that the quantity thus taken may be immaterial. It includes also, or may include, the style, or language and

an injunction was applied for, to restrain the publication of an abridgment of Dr. Johnson's 'Rasselas.' It appeared that not one-tenth part of the first volume had been abstracted, and that the injury alleged to have been sustained by the author arose from the abridgment containing the narrative

expression ; the learning, the facts, or the narrative ; the sentiment and ideas, as far as their identity can be traced ; and the form, arrangement, and combination which the author has given to his materials. These are, or may be, all distinct objects of the right of property ; and in every work of originality, likely to be abridged or capable of being abridged, they are all important objects of that right. However imperfectly the subject may have been regarded in former times, it is now, I think, to be regarded as settled, that whatever is metaphysically part or parcel of the intellectual contents of a book, if in a just sense original, is protected and included under the right of property vested by law in the author ; and it is very material to observe, that the arrangement, the method, the plan, the course of reasoning, or course of narrative, the exhibition of the subject, or the learning of the book, may be, according to its character, as much objects of the right of property as the language and the ideas.

"What then does the maker of an abridgment print, publish, and sell, after he has made it ? He has been employed, according to the definition above quoted, ' in retrenching unnecessary and uninteresting circumstances, which rather deaden the narration ;' that is to say, he has rejected what *in his judgment* are redundancies. Does this make him the author or proprietor of what remains ? If the work be a history, did he, the person abridging it, compile the materials into their present shape, and describe the course of events, and embody the whole of what constitutes the intellectual contents of the book, or are these things the product of another's labour, research and faculty of writing ? If it be a fictitious narrative, whose genius created the characters, and animated them with the sentiments which they utter, and invented the pleasing incidents of their mock existences, and wove the whole into the novel or the poem ; which exists as an intellectual whole, after as well as before the process by which ' the unnecessary and uninteresting circumstances' are ' retrenched' ? Or, if it be a work of science, or a treatise in any branch of knowledge, whose are the ideas, the course of reasoning and illustration, the plan and analysis of the subject, and the collection and arrangement of materials which constitute the identity of the book ? These questions can have but one answer ; and if the abridgment, in any given case, consists solely in the reduction of the bulk of the volume by the rejection of redundancies, it is a mere republication of a connected series of extracts, in a different juxtaposition from the original author's to which the party had no title whatever. On the other hand, if the abridgment not only rejects redundancies, but also clothes the sentiments and ideas which may be left, in different phraseology, then it falls under the predicament of a colourable alteration, which cannot escape the censure of justice." And in a note he takes the above case of Dr. Johnson's 'Rasselas,' and adds, " The moral reflections are left out, the narrative goes into the ' Gentleman's Magazine.' Whose genius produced that stately and immortal fiction ? Who described and created the characters of Imlac, and the Princess, and the Prince of Abyssinia, and placed them in the Happy Valley, and sent them forth in a series of gentle trials and pleasing and sad perplexities, in the world beyond its walls ? Who wrote that narrative ? Not, certainly, the Grub Street hack, who was employed to ' leave out the reflections.' What he took and his employers published, was the literary property of another, the profits of which the law had not vested in them."—Page 273.

of the tale, and not the moral reflections. The Master of the Rolls, Sir Thomas Clarke, refused the injunction, saying, "I cannot enter into the goodness or badness of the abstract. It may serve the end of an advertisement (a). In general it tends to the advantage of an author, if the composition be good; if it be not, it cannot be libelled. What I materially rely upon is, that it could not tend to prejudice the plaintiffs, when they had before published an abstract of the work in the 'London Chronicle.' If I were to determine this to be elusory, I must hold every abridgment to be so." Chancellor Kent, in referring to this case, says, "This latitudinarian right of abridgment is liable to abuse, and to trench upon the copyright of the author. The question as to a *bonâ fide* abridgment may turn, not so much upon the quantity as the value of the selected materials" (b).

But an injunction will be granted where the facts and the *terms* in which the facts are related are merely the same in both books. Thus where an injunction was moved for to restrain the publication of a book entitled 'Memoirs of the Life of Mrs. Bellamy,' which was alleged to have been pirated from a book called 'An Apology for the Life of George Anne Bellamy,' and it appeared in evidence that Mrs. Bellamy was author of the latter work; and that she sold the copyright to the plaintiff, who printed it in five volumes at a selling price of fifteen shillings; and that the work against which the injunction was prayed was in one volume, which sold for two shillings and sixpence; upon passages being read from each to shew that the *facts*, and even the *terms* in which they were related in the latter work, were frequently taken *verbatim* from the original one, an injunction was immediately granted (c).

The question as to how far an abridger may go without

(a) It is no defence to say that the pirated work is not offered for sale itself, but merely used to promote the sale of the books mentioned in it: *Hotten* v. *Arthur*, 1 H. & M. 603; 32 L. J. (Ch.) 771; 11 W. R. 934; 9 L. T. (N.S.) 199.

(b) 2 Kent's Com. 382, note; *Gyles* v. *Wilcox*, 2 Atk. 141. See Campbell's 'Lives of the Chancellors,' vol. v. p. 56; 2 Story, Eq. Jur. s. 939.

(c) *Bell* v. *Walker*, 1 Bro. C. C. 451.

infringing the rights of the author was exhaustively CAP. VI. considered in an American case which arose respecting Mr. Story's ' Commentaries on Equity Jurisprudence.'

It appeared that the chapters and the subjects were the same in Mr. Story's work and the work complained of; the former book contained 1,856 octavo pages, including notes, the latter 348 octavo pages, including notes; a page in the latter contained a little more than one in the former; reduced to the same sized page, the ratio in the amount of matter in the latter book to that in the former was about two to nine. In the entire work of Story there were 226 pages, constituting nearly an eighth part, on which there was some matter which had been extracted in the same language, or very nearly so, into the defendant's book, this matter comprising 879 lines, or about 24 pages of his book, and 30 pages of Story, which made one fifteenth part of the defendant's book and one-sixtieth of Story; this matter being found in scattered paragraphs in the first third of the defendant's book; all the other portions of Story's book were abridged without any transcription of his common language, the part so abridged comprising two-thirds of the defendant's book. The defence was set up that the defendant's book was a *bonâ fide* abridgment of the plaintiff's. The Master reported that Story's work had been fairly abridged, and hence that there was no infringement. Against this conclusion, the court found that the first third of the defendant's book, including one hundred pages, was not a fair abridgment, and granted an injunction against that part. The rest was regarded as an abridgment, and its publication was not enjoined. Mr. Justice McLean thus states the principles upon which the decision was arrived at: "This controversy has caused me great anxiety and embarrassment. On the subject of copyright, there is a painful uncertainty in the authorities; and indeed, there is an inconsistency in some of them. That the complainants are entitled to the copyright which they assert in their bill is not controverted by the defendants. The decision must turn on the question of abridgment. If this were an open question, I should feel little difficulty in determining it. An abridgment should contain an epitome of the work abridged—the principles, in a condensed form, of the original book. Now it would be difficult to maintain that such a work did not affect the sale of the book abridged. The argument that the abridgment is suited to a different class of readers, by its cheapness, and will be purchased on that account by persons unable and unwilling to purchase the work at large, is not satisfactory. This, to some extent, may be true; but are there not many who are able to buy the original work, that will be satisfied with the abridgment? What law library does not contain abridgments and digests, from Viner's and Comyn's down to the latest publications? The multiplication of law reports and elementary treatises creates a demand for abridgments and digests: and these being obtained, if they do not generally they do frequently, prevent the purchase of the works at large. The reasoning on which the right to abridge is founded, therefore seems to me to be false in fact. It does, to some extent in all cases, and not unfrequently to a great extent, impair the rights of the author, a right secured by law.

"The same rule of decision should be applied to a copyright as to a patent for a machine. The construction of any other machine which acts upon the same principle, however its structure may be varied, is an infringement on the patent. The second machine may be recommended by its simplicity and cheapness; still, if it act upon the same principle of the first patented, the patent is violated. Now, an abridgment, if fairly made, contains the principle of the original work; and this constitutes its value. Why, then, in reason and justice, should not the same principle be applied in a case of copyright as in that of a patented machine? With the assent of the patentee, a machine acting upon the same principle, but of less expensive structure than the one patented, may be built; and so a book may be abridged by the author, or with his consent, should a cheaper work be wanted by the public. This, in my judgment, is the ground on which the rights of the author should be considered.

" But a contrary doctrine has long been established in England, under the Statute of Anne, which in this respect is similar to our own statute ; and in this country the same doctrine has prevailed. I am therefore bound by precedent, and I yield to it in this instance more as a principle of law, than a rule of reason or justice" (a).

In *Dickens* v. *Lee* (b), the plaintiff's work was an imaginative tale; the defendant had taken the fable, the characters, the incidents, the names, and even the style of language. It is to be gathered from the report, that thus using all the plaintiff's materials, he had told the story in a shorter manner, and he relied upon abridgment as his defence; but the court held that such an abridgment was not an exercise of mental labour deserving the character of an original work, and granted an injunction, putting the plaintiff to establish his right at law, if the defendant desired it. In this case, Vice-Chancellor Knight Bruce is reported to have said, that he was not aware that one man had the right to abridge the works of another; on the other hand, he did not mean to say that there might not be an abridgment which might be lawful, which might be protected; but, to say that one man had the right to abridge, and so publish in an abridged form, the work of another, without more, was going much beyond his notion of what the law of this country was.

In the case of *Butterworth* v. *Robinson* (c), a motion was made upon certificate of the bill, for an injunction to restrain the defendant from selling a work, entitled, ' An Abridgment of Cases argued and determined in the Courts of Law, &c.,' until answer or further order. A copy of the work was handed to the Lord Chancellor. In support of the motion it was stated, that this work was by no means a

(a) *Story's Executors* v. *Holcombe*, 4 McLean (Amer.), 308.
(b) 8 Jur. 183.
(c) 5 Ves. 709.

CAP. VI.   fair abridgment; that, except in colourably leaving out
some parts of the cases, such as the arguments of counsel,
it was a mere copy *verbatim* of several of the reports of
cases in the courts of law, and among them of the ' Term
Reports,' of which the plaintiff was proprietor; comprising
not a few cases only, but all the cases published in that
work; the chronological order of the original work being
artfully changed to an alphabetical arrangement under
heads and titles, to give it the appearance of a new work.
In support of the motion, *Bell* v. *Walker* (a) was cited.
The Lord Chancellor said, " I have looked at one or two
cases, with which I am pretty well acquainted, and it
appears to me an extremely illiberal publication. Take
the injunction upon the certificate of the bill filed, to give
them an opportunity of stating what they can upon it."

Piracy by way   The leading case on the subject of piracy, by way of
of digest.
digest, is that of *Sweet* v. *Benning* (b), where it was held
by a majority of the judges that parties who take *verbatim*
portions of reports (as the head-notes), the copyright of
which belongs to others, and put them together, merely
arranged in a different manner (as in an alphabetical
order), so as to form a different work, of which they make
any considerable proportion, will be guilty of piracy. The
court were divided, and accordingly the judges delivered
their judgments *seriatim*. Jervis, C.J., on the question of
piracy, said : " The head-notes of the ' Jurist ' reports may
indeed be considered, perhaps, as in themselves a species
of brief and condensed reports, the reporter furnishing in
each case two reports, in one of which he gives the facts,
the arguments, and the judgments at length, and in the
other an abstract of the decision, conveying the principle
upon which it is founded, and the pith and substance of
the case. The defendants have, for the purposes of their
digest, copied *verbatim* the head-notes, the shorter species
of reports. But if they were allowed to take the head-
note, it is plain that they might equally have taken the

(a) 1 Bro. C. C. 451.
(b) 16 C. B. 459 ; Com. Law Rep. vol. ii. pt. ii. 1452.

report. And if they might take either, they might take both, and might republish the entire of the reports, merely altering their arrangement by putting them in alphabetical order. The question is, whether, by this arrangement of matter, which is taken *verbatim* from the plaintiffs' periodical, they acquire a right so to use it. I think not. I admit that a digest'may be made from a copyright work without piracy upon it, but that is a work in which a man applies his mind to the labour of extracting the principles of the original work, and by his labour really produces a new work. It is not so where he merely reduces extracts or passages of another man's work to an alphabetical order, which is a work a clerk might accomplish, and requires neither learning nor study, but may be little more than a merely mechanical operation of cutting out and classifying under certain letters of the alphabet. In one of the cases cited, the 'Term Reports' were so dealt with, and it was held to be a piracy. I think that case is decisive of the present, and therefore that the plaintiffs are entitled to our judgment."

Lord Hatherley, when Vice-Chancellor, in the case of *Tinsley* v. *Lacy* (a), spoke very unfavourably in regard to the rights of an abridger; he said: He must confess that did not agree in the reasons for upholding such a work given by some learned judges, viz: that an abridger was a benefactor. He should have himself regarded him rather as a sort of jackal to the public, to point out the beauties of authors.

In *D'Almaine* v. *Boosey* (b) the question arose as to what imitation or use of a musical composition constituted a piracy. In this case the plaintiffs published, first, the overture to Auber's opera of '*Lestocq*,' and then a number of airs, and all the melodies. It was admitted that the defendant had published portions of the opera containing the melodious parts of it; that he had also published

What use of former musical composition constitutes a piracy.

(a) 1 H. & M. 747; 11 W. R. 877; see *Story's Executors* v. *Holcombe*, 4 McLean (Amer.), 308.
(b) 1 Y. & C. 288.

P

entire airs; and that in one of his waltzes he had introduced seventeen bars in succession, containing the whole
of the original air, although he had added fifteen other bars
which were not to be found in it. It was nevertheless
contended that this was not a piracy, because the whole of
the air had not been taken; and because the latter publication was adapted for dancing only, and that some degree
of art was needed for the purpose of so adapting the
piece; and, moreover, but a small part of the merit
belonged to the original composer. Lord Lyndhurst, then
Lord Chief Baron, observed that it was a nice question,
what should be deemed such a modification of an original
work as should absorb the merit of the original in the
new composition. " No doubt," said he, " such a modification may be allowed in some cases, as in that of an
abridgment or a digest. Such publications are in their
nature original. Their compiler intends to make of them a
new use; not that which the author proposed to make.
Digests are of great use to practical men, though not so,
comparatively speaking, to students. The same may be
said of an abridgment of any study; but it must be a
boná fide abridgment, because if it contains many chapters
of the original work, or such as made that work most
saleable, the maker of the abridgment commits a piracy.
Now it will be said that one author may treat the same
subject very differently from another who wrote before
him. That observation is true in many cases. A man
may write upon morals in a manner quite distinct from
that of others who preceded him; but the subject of
music is to be regarded upon very different principles. It
is the air or melody which is the invention of the author,
and which may in such case be the subject of piracy;
and you commit a piracy if, by taking, not a single bar,
but several, you incorporate in the new work that in which
the whole meritorious part of the invention consists.

" I remember, in a case of copyright, at *nisi prius*, a
question arising as to how many bars were necessary for
the constitution of a subject or phrase. Sir George Smart,

who was a witness in the case, said, that a mere bar did not constitute a phrase, though three or four bars might do so. Now it appears to me that if you take from the composition of an author all those bars consecutively which form the entire air or melody, without any material alteration, it is a piracy; though, on the other hand, you might take them in a different order, or broken by the intersection of others, like words, in such a manner as should not be a piracy. It must depend on whether the air taken is substantially the same with the original. Now the most unlettered in music can distinguish one song from another, and the mere adaptation of the air, either by changing it to a dance, or by transferring it from one instrument to another, does not, even to common apprehensions, alter the original subject. The ear tells you that it is the same. The original air requires the aid of genius for its construction, but a mere mechanic in music can make the adaptation or accompaniment. Substantially, the piracy is, where the appropriated music, though adapted to a different purpose from that of the original, may still be recognised by the ear. The adding variations makes no difference in the principle."

Where only eight consecutive bars, taken from an opera, were inserted in a song and constituted but a small proportion of the eleven pages of the song, the court on application to dissolve would not continue the injunction.

5th. Copyright may be infringed by reproducing the 5. By translawhole or part under the form of a translation. Transla- tion. tions are protected in this country, and an unauthorized copy of a translation, though the original be not entitled to copyright here, but is open to any number of persons to translate, is a piracy.

Though it does not appear, if the original work be a foreign work, not entitled to protection in this country, and a translation of it be made and published first by A., and a translation be subsequently made and published by B., that this latter would be necessarily a piracy of A.'s translation or an infringement of his right; yet, a retranslation without the consent of the author of the original work is a piracy whenever that original work is entitled to copyright.

Translation of protected work a piracy.
It is clear that an unauthorized translation of a protected work is a violation of the copyright therein, for a translation cannot be made without appropriating the entire substance of the protected composition. It has been argued that the translator by his own labour and skill reproduces in a new and useful form what is practically a new work, and that having exercised independent labour in its production he is entitled to publish. But the same reasoning would lead to the conclusion that a person might republish any protected work, if he did so with notes which required the exercise of independent labour. A translation of an unprotected work is certainly a work deserving of copyright, and in respect of which copyright may be obtained, but the allowing of a translation to be issued of a protected work without the consent of the author is a very different thing.

Principle on which this rests.
The principle on which the position rests, that an unauthorized translation of a protected work is piratical, is that the property of the author consists not in the language alone; but in the matter of which the language is but the expression and means of communication. It is in the substance of the composition and not in the form only. And the matter is as much taken possession of by the translation into a different language, as it would be by a transcript of its language only.

The point has only once come before the court, and then the case was decided on other grounds. The case referred to came before Lord Chancellor Macclesfield 160 years ago, when he granted an injunction against an English translation of Thomas Burnett's 'Archæologia Philosophica,' a work which had been published in Latin and registered by the author. The unauthorized publication of the book in England was enjoined, on the ground that it "contained strange notions, intended by the author to be concealed from the vulgar in the Latin language, in which language it

could not do much harm." The Chancellor there remarks Cap. VI.
that "a translation might not be the same with the
original, on account that the translator has bestowed his
care and pains upon it, and so not within the prohibition
of the Act" (a).

In *Murray* v. *Bogue* (b), a case respecting an alleged Translation of
infringement of the copyright in a guidebook, the question a foreign work
of translations was again considered. The plaintiff com- protected
plained that his 'Handbook for Travellers in Switzerland' work.
had been infringed by a guidebook published by the
defendant. The latter had been made up from various
sources, and in part was an abridged translation of
Baedeker's German work, the copyright of which appears
not to have been secured in this country. It was claimed,
however, on this point that Baedeker's book was a translation of Murray's, and that its retranslation into English
by Bogue was a violation of Murray's copyright. The
Vice-Chancellor put the following case: If Baedeker's
were a translation of Murray's into German, and the other
defendant had retranslated Baedeker's work into English,
even if he did not know that Baedeker's was taken from
Murray, the plaintiff's book could not be thus indirectly
pirated. But it was found that Baedeker's was substantially an original work, and not a reproduction in German
of Murray's: and therefore its translation in English could
not infringe the copyright in Murray's book (c).

Notwithstanding what has been already said, it must Opinion of
be admitted that there are many who are of the opinion some that
that any work, whether the copyright therein be subsisting committed by
or not, may be translated with impunity, and indeed this has translation of
been held in America to be the law. The book in question work.
was Mrs. Stowe's celebrated 'Uncle Tom's Cabin.' She
first published it in America and secured the copyright
there, subsequently causing it to be translated into German
and securing copyright for such translation. Afterwards

(a) *Burnett* v. *Chetwood*, 2 Meriv. 441; *Wyatt* v. *Barnard*, 3 Ves. &
B. 77.
(b) 1 Drew. 353, 368.
(c) See the argument in *Jarrold* v. *Heywood*, 18 W. R. 279.

the defendant Thomas made a translation into German,
and this was the piracy complained of. Mr. Justice
Grier decided that Mrs. Stowe was not entitled to the
protection sought. He considered that by the publication
of her book, the creations of the genius and imagination
of the author had become as much public property as those
of Homer or Cervantes. That Uncle Tom and Topsy
were as much *publici juris* as Don Quixote and Sancho
Panza. That all her conceptions and inventions might be
used and abused by imitators, playwrights, and poetasters.
They were no longer her own ; those who had purchased
her book might clothe them in English doggerel, in German or Chinese prose. Her absolute dominion and property in the creations of her genius and imagination had
been voluntarily relinquished, and all that remained was
the copyright of her book, the exclusive right to print,
reprint, and vend it; and those only could be called
infringers of her rights or pirates of her property who
were guilty of printing, publishing, importing or vending
without her license " copies of her book." In tropical but
not very precise phraseology, a translation might be called
a transcript or copy of her thoughts or conceptions, but in
no correct sense could it be called a copy of her book (*a*).

This is a decision the principle of which we trust will
never be followed in this country, but that, when the
question shall come before the court, it will find itself, as
it is practically at present, unfettered by precedent, and
able to take that view which will at once afford protection
to literary men and be in accord with the spirit of the
copyright laws.

By the International Copyright Act, translations, entitled under that Act to protection in this country, are
prohibited (*b*).

Compiling
for various
objects.
It will be seen from what has been already said that
there is nothing to prevent a person from copying common
materials from an existing compilation, and arranging and

(*a*) *Stowe* v. *Thomas*, 2 Am. Law Reg. 231.
(*b*) See *post*, chapter on International Copyright.

combining them in a new form, or using them for a different purpose.

The first compiler had no copyright in the common materials, but only in his own arrangement of those materials, and if this be not infringed, though the subsequent compiler may have considerably profited by his compilation, yet there would be no remedy. There would be a difference, however, if the first compiler had so worked upon the common materials, whether by translation, paraphrase, or abridgment, as to have practically elaborated a new work. Thus would he have placed the stamp of authorship upon the same, and have acquired a title thereto accordingly.

Where the arrangement or general plan has been copied, Copying general arrangement. there may or may not be an infringement of the rights of the first compiler. The principle would seem to be this: that where the arrangement or general plan only is copied, the materials used being different, there is no infringement, but that where the arrangement or general plan and also the materials (though they may be taken directly from the original sources) are copied, then the rights of the first compiler are infringed. The first compiler's rights consisted not in the materials, for they were common to all, and not in the arrangement apart from the materials, for in such, copyright could not exist, but in the combined result of the common materials as arranged; and if the arrangement and materials together were taken, then the second compilation would be substantially the same work, it would be practically identical.

Though there has been no express decision on the above point, yet the principle has been frequently admitted. Thus, in the case of *Black* v. *Murray*, where Lockhart's annotated edition of Scott's ' Minstrelsy of the Scottish Border' was in question, and it appeared that of the two hundred notes added by the editor, all but fifteen were quotations from common sources, and the ballads themselves were common property, Lord Kinloch said: " To a considerable extent the notes borrowed (to use a euphe-

CAP. VI.   mism) from Messrs. Black's edition consist of quotations
from various authors, employed by Mr. Lockhart to
illustrate ballads in the 'Minstrelsy.' It was perhaps
thought that to repeat quotations from well-known
authors was not piracy. If so, I think a great mistake
was committed. In the adaptation of the quotation to the
ballad which it illustrates, the literary research which
discovered it, the critical skill which applied it, there
was, I think, an act of authorship performed, of which no
one was entitled to take the benefit for his own publication and thereby to save the labour, the learning, and the
expenditure necessary even for this part of the annotation " (a).

Dramatizing copyright work.   The unauthorized dramatization of a work for public
performance is not an infringement of the author's rights
in that work, nor in a drama adapted from it made by
the author himself after publication of the original work;
but when the author's drama has preceded the publication
of the novel, the latter cannot be dramatized without
violating the author's rights in his play, except with his
consent (b).

This subject is more fully dealt with under the head
Dramatic Copyright.

Gratuitous distribution of copies an infringement of author's rights.   The gratuitous distribution of copies of a copyright
work of another is an infringement. And an injunction
will be granted to restrain the publication of lithographic
copies of music intended for private use and not for sale
or exportation. The members of the Liverpool Philhar-
monic Society, who perform gratuitously, made impressions of a musical composition called 'Benedict's part
song, The Wreath,' and distributed them solely among
themselves; this was held to be an infringement of the
author's " sole and exclusive right and liberty of printing,
or otherwise multiplying copies," of any subject to which
the word " copyright " is applied (c).

(a) 9 Sc. Sess. Cas. 3rd Ser. 355.
(b) *Reade* v. *Conquest,* 9 C. B. (N.S.) 755; 11 Id. 479; *Toole* v. *Young,*
L. R. 9 Q. B. 523.
(c) *Novello* v. *Ludlow,* 12 C. B. 177; 21 L. J. (C.P.) 169.

The same view has been taken by the Scotch Court of CAP. VI. Session in the case of a gratuitous circulation (a).

Copyright may also be infringed by the importation for Infringement sale or hire into any part of the British dominions of by importation. copies printed abroad.

The 17th section of the Copyright Act provides that after the passing of the Act it shall not be lawful for any person not being the proprietor of the copyright, or some person authorized by him, to import into any part of the United Kingdom, or into any other part of the British dominions, for sale or hire, any printed book first composed or written or printed and published in any part of the United Kingdom, wherein there shall be copyright, and reprinted in any country or place whatsoever out of the British dominions; and if any person, not being such proprietor or person authorized as aforesaid, shall import or bring, or cause to be imported or brought, for sale or hire, any such printed book into any part of the British dominions, contrary to the true intent and meaning of the Act, or shall knowingly sell, publish, or expose to sale, or let to hire, or have in his possession for sale or hire any such book, then every such book shall be forfeited, and shall be seized by any officer of customs or excise, and the same shall be destroyed by such officer: and every person so offending, being duly convicted thereof before two justices of the peace for the county or place in which such book shall be found, shall also for every such offence forfeit the sum of ten pounds, and double the value of every copy of such book which he shall so import or cause to be imported into any part of the British dominions, or shall knowingly sell, publish, or expose to sale or let to hire, or shall cause to be sold, published, or exposed to sale, or let to hire, or shall have in his possession for sale or hire, contrary to the true intent and meaning of the Act, five pounds to the use of such officer of customs or excise, and the remainder of the

(a) *Alexander* v. *Mackenzie*, 9 Sc. Sess. Cas. 2nd Ser. 748.

penalty to the use of the proprietor of the copyright in
such book (a).

Offence committed though
no copy sold
or let out on
hire.

It is under this section an offence to import copyright
matter for sale or hire, and the defendant who has imported
such matter must pay the costs of an action, even if he
has not done so knowingly, and though he may not have
sold or let out on hire a single copy (b).

In Scotland it was held by Lord Gifford (c), that where
a bookseller had sold copies of a copyright work which
had been pirated and printed in America, an action of
damages lay against him at the instance of the proprietors
of the copyright in this country, though no such remedy
is prescribed in sect. 17 of the Copyright Amendment
Act, his Lordship being of opinion that copyright is not
the mere creature of a statute, but a natural and civil
right, entitled to protection at common law.

The pursuer A. Tennyson, D.C.L., who is the proprietor
of the copyright of the whole of his poetical works, had conveyed to the other pursuers, A. Strahan & Co., publishers,
London and Edinburgh, the exclusive right to print and
publish his poetical works within the British dominions for
five years, from and after 1 January, 1869. Messrs. S. & Co.
alleged that defender, who is a bookseller at Glasgow,
sold, published, exposed for sale, or had in his possession for
sale, reprints of Mr. Tennyson's works printed or published
in the United States of America, and that within the
period referred to and without their consent. They
accordingly raised a suspension and interdict against
defender, and on 20th April, 1870, that interdict was
declared perpetual. Messrs. Strahan & Co. then raised
the present action for damages averred by them to have
been incurred in consequence of the sale of said copies.
Damages laid at £500.

(a) This section would exclude books reprinted out of the British
Dominions only, and not books reprinted in a colony ; but see the 39 & 40
Vict. c. 36, s. 42, post.
(b) Cooper v. Whittingham, 28 W. R. 720.
(c) Tennyson v. Forrester, 43 Scottish Jurist, 278.

' The Lord Ordinary refused to give effect to the defender's argument for the following reason: He thought that the right of copyright, although protected and favoured, and regulated by statute, was not the mere creature of statute, and that offences against copyright were not to be viewed as mere statutory offences for which the statutory remedy or punishment was alone applicable. On the contrary, he thought that the right of the author and his assigns in his work was a natural and civil right which the statute had defined and protected but had not created, and infringements of copyright were violations of this civil right and not mere statute-made offences.

The 42nd section of the 39 & 40 Vict. c. 36 (The Customs Consolidated Act, 1876) gives a list of " goods, &c. absolutely prohibited to be imported, and which shall be forfeited, and shall be destroyed or otherwise disposed of as the Commissioners of Customs may direct." In this list will be found enumerated " Books wherein the copyright shall be first subsisting, first composed, or written, or printed in the United Kingdom, and printed or reprinted in any other country, as to which the proprietor of such copyright or his agent shall have given to the Commissioners of Customs a notice in writing that such copyright subsists, such notice also stating when such copyright will expire.

This section is much wider than the corresponding section in the 5 & 6 Vict. c. 45; it not only does away with the limitation of the restriction to books printed for sale or hire, but it prohibits books printed or reprinted in any other country.

The Copyright Act, 5 & 6 Vict. c. 45, especially prohibits books reprinted out of her Majesty's dominions; the Customs Act especially prohibits books reprinted in any other country. It is by no means clear whether in the latter Act the words " any other country " mean and include the colonies.

· The Commissioners of Customs are to have printed lists of all such books in respect of which they shall have

[Margin notes:] Cap. VI.

By Customs Act copies of books protected may not be imported.

received such notices, and to expose the same at the several ports in the United Kingdom and in Her Majesty's possessions abroad.

In the lists so to be printed and posted up a statement is to appear as to when the copyright will expire.

By the 152nd section of the same Act any book wherein the copyright may be subsisting, first composed, or written or printed in the United Kingdom, and printed or re-printed in any other country, are absolutely prohibited to be imported into the British possessions abroad. But it is provided that no such books shall be prohibited to be imported as aforesaid unless the proprietor of such copyright or his agent shall have given notice in writing to the Commissioners of Customs that such copyright subsists, and in such notice shall have stated when the copyright will expire. And it is further provided that the Commissioners shall cause to be made and to be publicly exposed at the several ports in the British possessions abroad, from time to time, printed lists of books respecting which such notice shall have been duly given, and all books imported contrary thereto shall be forfeited: but nothing contained in the Act shall be taken to prevent Her Majesty from exercising the powers vested in her by the 10 & 11 Vict. c. 95, intituled " An Act to amend the Law relating to the Protection in the Colonies of Works entitled to Copyright in the United Kingdom," to suspend in certain cases such prohibition.

The 45th section of the Act gives leave to any person complaining of the insertion of any books in the lists required by the above sections, to apply to any judge at chambers for a summons calling upon the person upon whose notice such book shall have been so inserted, to appear before such judge to shew cause why such book shall not be expunged from such list, and such judge is at the time appointed in the summons to hear and determine upon the matter and make his order thereon in writing: And it is provided that upon service of such order or a certified copy upon the Commissioners of Customs or their secretary, the said Commissioners shall expunge such book from the list, or retain the same therein, according to the tenor of such order.

It is further provided that if at the time appointed in any such summons the person summoned shall not appear before such judge, then upon proof by affidavit that such summons or a true copy thereof has been personally served upon or left at the last known or usual place of abode of the person so summoned, or in case the person to whom such summons was directed and his place of abode cannot be found, that due diligence has been used to ascertain the same, such judge shall be at liberty to proceed *ex parte* to hear and determine the matter.

In the event of either party being dissatisfied with the order of the judge, he may apply to the superior court of which such judge is a member to revise such order and make such further order thereon as such court may see fit.

CHAPTER VII.

REMEDY AT LAW IN CASES OF INFRINGEMENT OF COPYRIGHT.

Three reme-
dies for
infringement
of copyright.

THERE are three remedies in cases of infringement of copyright—an action at law, or in equity, and in some instances by summary proceeding before justices of the peace.

Since the Judicature Act has come into operation, Courts of Law and Equity are, at any rate in theory, no longer separate tribunals, but it must be remembered that though the rules of Law and Equity are assimilated and a uniformity of procedure established, yet suitors are not deprived of any of their existing rights or remedies. The nature of the relief granted in each particular case will, as heretofore, depend on the form of the action or proceeding in which the relief is sought; according as the plaintiff seeks to avail himself of his legal or his equitable remedy. It is therefore still advisable to consider separately what are the rights and remedies of the parties whose copyright is infringed both at law, and in equity. We propose to deal, in the first place, with the remedy provided by the 5 & 6 Vict. c. 45.

Actions at law may be divided into two classes, first, under the statute for penalties and forfeiture; and, secondly, independent of the statute, for damages. In other words, where the statute has imposed penalties and forfeiture for the violation of copyright, these may be sued for, but where the statute confers a right but provides no specific remedy, then an action for damages lies.

Of course a common law action for damages will not lie CAP. VII. where no right is conferred by the statute, but where the right exists and the statutory remedies are either not complete nor adequate for the protection of the right conferred, the common law remedies may be made available (a).

By the 15th section of the Act, it is provided, that if any person in any part of the British dominions shall print or cause to be printed, either for sale or exportation, any book in which there shall be subsisting copyright, without the consent in writing of the proprietor, or import for sale or hire any such book unlawfully printed from parts beyond the sea, or knowing such book to have been so unlawfully printed or imported, shall sell, publish, or expose for sale or hire, or cause to be sold, published, or exposed for sale or hire, or shall have in his possession for sale or hire, any such book without the consent of the proprietor, such offender shall be liable to a special action on the case, at the suit of the proprietor of the copyright, to be brought in any court of record in that part of the British dominions in which the offence shall be committed: Provided always, that in Scotland such offender shall be liable to an action in the Court of Session, there to be brought and prosecuted in the same manner as any other action of damages to the like amount (b). No person except the proprietor of the copyright, or some one authorized by him, may import into the United Kingdom, or other parts of the British dominions, for sale or hire, any printed book first composed or written, or printed and published, in the United Kingdom, wherein there is copyright, and reprinted in any country or place out of

Remedy for piracy by action on the case.

(a) Thus, by the 15th section of the Act of 1842, the printer is made liable to an action for damages only when the printing is for "sale or exportation," and the importer only when copies are imported for "sale or hire." No remedy is given against any person who prints or imports for gratuitous distribution, or who gratuitously distributes copies printed or imported without authority. But in *Novello* v. *Ludlow* (12 C. B. 177) it was held that an action for damages would lie under the statute for the gratuitous distribution among the members of a singing society of lithographic copies of a musical composition. See too *Rooney* v. *Kelly*, 14 Ir. L. R. (N.S.) 158.

(b) 5 & 6 Vict. c. 45, s. 15.

the British dominions; and if any person, not the proprietor or party authorized by him, shall import or bring or cause to be imported or brought, for sale or hire, any such printed book into the British dominions, or shall knowingly sell, publish, or expose for sale, or let to ·hire, or have in his ·possession for sale or hire, any such book, then every such book shall be forfeited and be seized and destroyed by any officer of the customs or excise, and every person so offending shall, on conviction, forfeit the sum of ten pounds, and double the value of every such book so unlawfully imported, sold, published, or exposed for sale, or let to hire; five pounds to the use of such officer of customs or excise, and the remainder of the penalty to the use of the proprietor of the copyright in such book (a).

By the customs laws, as we have already seen, it is absolutely prohibited to import into the United Kingdom books wherein the copyright shall be subsisting (first composed, or written, or printed in the United Kingdom, and printed or reprinted in any other country), as to which the proprietor of such copyright or his agent shall have given to the Commissioners of Customs a notice in writing that such copyright subsists, such notice also stating when such copyright will expire (b).

(a) 5 & 6 Vict. c. 45, s. 17. As to separate penalties upon each separate violation of the Act on the same day, see 12 Geo. 2, c. 36, and *Brooke* v. *Milliken*, 3 T. R. 509. A publisher of a piratical work will not be liable at law for the infringement, unless guilty knowledge can be brought home to him; such knowledge will not be presumed from the mere fact of his selling piratical works in print: *Leader* v. *Strange*, 2 Car. & Kir. 1010.

(b) The Consolidated Act, 39 & 40 Vict. c. 36, prohibits the importing of certain enumerated articles, and declares that they shall be forfeited and may be destroyed or otherwise disposed of as the Commissioners of Customs may direct. Among the things thus enumerated are "books wherein the copyright shall be first subsisting, first composed, or written or printed in the United Kingdom, and printed or reprinted in any other country, as to which the proprietor of such copyright or his agent shall have given to the Commissioners of Customs a notice in writing duly declared, that such copyright subsists, such notice also stating when such copyright will expire."

Section 44 enacts that "the Commissioners of Customs shall cause to be made and to be publicly exposed at the custom houses in the several ports of the United Kingdom, lists of all books wherein the copyright shall be subsisting, and as to which the proprietor of such copyright or his agent shall have given notice in writing to the Commissioners that such copy-

Neither the printer nor the importer can successfully Cap. VII. plead that he did not intentionally violate the copyright Ignorance of of another; but the publisher or the seller is not liable wrong no excuse for unless he knows that the book was unlawfully printed or printer or imported (a). Of course, if the publisher is also the importer. printer or the importer, ignorance of wrong cannot be any excuse.

All copies of any book wherein there may be copyright, Action for and of which entry shall have been made in the registry recovery of pirated copies. book, and which shall have been unlawfully printed or imported without the consent of the registered proprietor of such copyright, shall be deemed to be the property of the proprietor of such copyright; and such proprietor shall, after demand thereof in writing, be entitled to sue for and recover the same, or damages for the detention thereof, in an action of detinue, from any party who shall detain the same, or to sue for and recover damages for the conversion thereof in an action of trover (b).

The owner of the copyright may therefore sue for the recovery of the copies found in the possession of the wrongdoer, and for the value of those he may have unlawfully disposed of.

There is no common law right in the author or proprietor of a book which is pirated to the delivery up of the copies of the illegal work: and therefore, in a case under the 54 Geo. 3, c. 156, s. 4, it was held that the proprietor of a book who was entitled to an injunction to restrain the printing and sale of the unlawful work,

---

right exists, stating in such notice when such copyright expires, accompanied by a declaration made and subscribed before a collector of customs or a justice of the peace, that the contents of such notice are true."

Section 45 provides that persons complaining of the prohibition of books in the copyright lists may appeal to a judge in chambers.

Section 152 prohibits the importation into the British possessions abroad of foreign reprints of English copyright books, but provides that nothing shall be taken to prevent her Majesty from exercising the powers vested in her by the 10 & 11 Vict. c. 95, intituled "An Act to amend the Law relating to the Protection in the Colonies of Works entitled to Copyright in the United Kingdom," to suspend in certain cases such prohibition.

(a) Colburn v. Simms, 2 Hare, 543, 557; Leader v. Strange, 2 Car. & Kir. 1010.

(b) 5 & 6 Vict. c. 45, s. 23.

Q

CAP. VII.   nevertheless was not entitled to an order for the delivery
up of the illegal copies, if the book, the copyright of
which had been infringed, was not composed and entered
according to the statutes in force at the time the illegal
copies were printed (a). In a case, however, under the
Designs Act, Lord Justice Knight Bruce made an order
for the delivery up to the plaintiff, for the purpose of
being destroyed, of the drawings and cards used by the
defendant in applying the plaintiff's design, and also the
articles manufactured by the defendants to which the
plaintiff's design had been applied (b).

Notice of
objection to
plaintiff's title
to be given.

The 16th section of the Copyright Act, 1842, enacts
that in actions for piracy the defendant shall give notice
of the objections to the plaintiff's title on which he
intends to rely ; and if the nature of his defence be that
the plaintiff in such action was not the author or first
publisher of the book in which he shall by such action
claim copyright, or is not the proprietor of the copyright
therein, or that some other person than the plaintiff was
the author or first publisher of such book, or is the
proprietor of the copyright therein, then the defendant
shall specify in such notice the name of the person whom
he alleges to have been the author or first publisher of
such book, or the proprietor of the copyright therein,
together with the title of such book, and the time when
and the place where such book was first published ; otherwise the defendant in such action shall not, at the trial or
hearing of such action, be allowed to give any evidence
that the plaintiff in such action was not the author or
first publisher of the book in which he claims such copyright as aforesaid, or that he was not the proprietor of the
copyright therein ; and at such trial or hearing no other
objection shall be allowed to be made on behalf of such
defendant than the objections stated in such notice, or
that any other person was the author or first publisher of

(a) *Colburn* v. *Simms*, 2 Hare, 643 ; 12 L. J. (N.S.) Ch. 388 ; 7 Jur.
1104 ; and see *Delfe* v. *Delamotte*, 3 K. & J. 581.
(b) *McRae* v. *Holdsworth*, 2 De G. & Sm. 497. See *post*.

such book, or the proprietor of the copyright therein, than the person specified in such notice, or give in evidence in support of his defence any other book than one substantially corresponding in title, time, and place of publication, with the title, time, and place specified in such notice.

In *Leader* v. *Purday* (a) a gentleman named Bellamy adapted words to an old air called 'Pestal,' and procured a friend of the name of Horne to write an accompaniment. The defendant, in an action for piracy of the same, gave notice of the following objections, among others: "That the plaintiffs were not the owners of the copyright; that there was no subsisting copyright in the musical publication." It was held that evidence could not be given by the defendant, *that the copyright of the air was in Horne, and not assigned by writing to Bellamy,* Horne's name not being mentioned in the objections, as required by the above section. This was decided, although the objection appeared upon the plaintiff's case.

The notice of objection is sufficient, if it allege a *When sufficient.* definite publication of the disputed work at some particular place, by some definite party, either before, or simultaneously with, the publication by the plaintiff, or with a publication in another place (b).

And on application by the plaintiff to have the notice *Amending notice of objection.* of objections delivered with the defendant's pleas under this same section, amended, it was held that the alleged first publication having occurred abroad, and so far back as the year 1831, it was sufficient for the defendant to state the year of the first publication, and that it was not necessary that he should be bound to specify the day or month; but that he was bound to state the name of the

(a) 7 C. B. 4.
(b) *Boosey* v. *Purday,* 10 Jur. 1038; see *Boosey* v. *Davidson,* 4 D. & L. 147; *Leader* v. *Purday,* 7 C. B. 4; 1 D. & L. 408; *Sweet* v. *Benning,* 16 C. B. 451; Bullen and Leake's 'Pleadings,' 298, 720; and see *Neilson* v. *Harford,* 8 M. & W. 806. For form of particulars of objections, *Cocks* v. *Purday,* 5 C. B. 862.

party whom he alleged to be the proprietor or first publisher, the title of the work, the place where and the time when the first publication took place (*a*).

In *Chappell* v. *Purday* (*b*), however, the defendant was allowed to plead that the plaintiff was not the proprietor of the copyright at the time of commencing the grievance; and also that he was not the proprietor of the copyright when the books were printed. If no notice of objection, according to the statute, be given by the defendant, he will be precluded from giving any evidence in support of his case, or putting the plaintiff to the proof of his (*c*).

In any action the defendant may plead the general issue and give special matter in evidence. The 26th section of the Act enacts that if any action or suit be commenced or brought against any person for doing or causing to be done anything in pursuance of the Act, the defendant may plead the general issue and give the special matter in evidence; and if upon such action a verdict be given for the defendant, or the plaintiff become non-suited, or discontinue his action, then the defendant shall have and recover his full costs, for which he shall have the same remedy as a defendant has by law in any case.

Construction of the words "in pursuance of this Act." According to numerous decisions, the words, *in pursuance of this Act*, do not only refer to those who have kept within the strict line of their duty, but also to those who intended to do so, but have by mistake gone beyond it. The general rule seems to be settled, that persons who *bonâ fide* and honestly believe that they are acting in the execution of the powers conferred on them by such a statute as the above, are within its privilege, although, in fact, they may have mistaken the extent of their power and have exceeded it, or failed to comply with the directions of the enactment (*d*).

All actions to be commenced within twelve months All actions, suits, bills, indictments, or informations for.

(*a*)*Boosey* v. *Davidson*, 4 D. & L. 147.
(*b*) 1 D. & L. 458; 12 M. & W. 303.
(*c*) *Haycock* v. *The North of England Co-operative Printing Society* County Court, Manchester, 13 October, 1874, J. Russell, Q.C.
(*d*) *Smith* v. *Shaw*, 10 Barn. & Cres. 277; cited Burke's Sup. to Godson's Copy. 99; *Gaby* v. *The Wilts and Berks Canal Co.*, 3 M. & Selw. 580; *Theobald* v. *Crichmore*, 1 B. & Ald. 227; *Parton* v. *Williams*, 3 *ibid.* 330; *Smith* v. *Wiltshire*, 2 B. & B 619; *Cook* v. *Leonard*, 6 B. & C. 351.

any offence committed against the Act, must be commenced within twelve calendar months after the commission
of the offence ; but this limitation does not extend to
any actions, suits, or proceedings commenced under the
Act in respect of copies of books required to be delivered
to the British Museum and the four other libraries (a) ;
nor to suits in equity, nor to actions at common law for
infringement (b). Since the last edition of this work,
there has been an express decision in accordance with the
above view.

In *Hogg* v. *Scott* (c) it appeared that in 1868 the defendant had published the first edition of a work, and issued
a second edition in 1872. The work contained matter
pirated from the plaintiff's works. He also intended to
publish a third edition. In August, 1873, the plaintiff
applied for an injunction to restrain the defendant from
further publishing or selling any copies of such piratical
work. One of the defences set up was that the statutory
limitation applied to all actions and suits, whether for the
penalties, or damages, or injunctions, and hence that the
plaintiff's suit was barred by lapse of time. Vice-Chancellor Hall, however, expressed the opinion that the word
" offence " was not used in the above section in the same
sense as in section 15, which gives an action on the case
for damages ; that the limitation prescribed was intended
to apply only in cases of penalties and forfeitures, that it
could not operate to destroy the property secured ; and
that an action for damages, or a suit for an injunction
might be maintained, although more than a year had
passed since the wrong was done. But, however, this
might be, he had no doubt that the defendant could not
go on committing new wrongs or offences by continually
publishing and selling the piratical work, in violation of

(a) 5 & 6 Vict. c. 45, s. 26.
(b) See the principle on which were decided the cases of *Clark* v. *Bell*,
29 Feb. 1804 ; Mor. Dict. of Dec. No. 3, App., Lit. Prop. ; and *Stewart* v.
Black, 9 Sess. Cas., 2nd Ser. 1026 ; *Hogg* v. *Scott*, L. R. 18 Eq. 444.
(c) L. R. 18 Eq. 444. The offence is committed every time a copy is
sold : James, V.C., in *Jarrold* v. *Heywood*, 18 W. R. 281.

CAP. VII.   the plaintiff's right of property. The injunction was therefore granted.

The statutes of 31 Eliz. c. 5, s. 2, and 21 James 1, c. 4, s. 2, requiring that in actions on penal statutes, the venue shall be laid in the county where the offence was committed, do not apply to actions for debt, brought by a party aggrieved to recover a penalty expressly given to him, but has reference only to proceedings by informers. So in *Planché* v. *Hooper*, where the defendant sued for ten penalties of forty shillings each under the 3 & 4 Will. 4, c. 15, for representing a dramatic piece called the 'White Cat.' The representation constituting the breach took place at Bath, and the case was tried at Westminster, and the Court held that the venue was rightly laid in Middlesex, thus distinguishing between actions brought simply for penalties, and actions brought under penal statutes to recover compensation for injuries.

Matters of evidence.   For the plaintiff it must of course be proved, if the action be brought by him, that he is the author or proprietor of the work. It will next be necessary to produce a copy of the work complained of, and prove the injury sustained according to the specific allegations in the pleadings ; whether by printing and publishing, or by exposing to sale or hire or importing. Proof is often given that parts of the first work were used in the printing of the second, and that the alterations supplied in the MSS. were merely colourable. The prevalence of errors in the second work identical with those in the first is likewise good evidence of piracy, since it can scarcely have happened that two persons would fall into precisely the same mistakes in repeated instances. For the defendant the evidence will of course vary according to the nature of his defence.

In an action for infringing copyright airs in an opera, the defendant, to prove publication abroad, cannot ask a witness skilled in music to whom a piece of music had been shewn, whether he had seen printed copies of it at Milan, without accounting for the non-production of the original prints (*a*). Nor is a statement of the same witness that he had heard the music, produced in court, sung by persons in private society with printed music before them, as if singing therefrom, evidence to prove that the music so printed was the same as the music in court (*b*).

In an action for damages for infringement of copyright, the proprietor of a copyright need not aver that the defendant published the plaintiff's book (*c*). And where the *locus* of the infringement was not specified, yet the plaintiff was allowed to amend his statement on payment of expenses incurred since the closing of the record (*d*).

The Act 2 & 3 Vict. c. 12, imposes a penalty of 5*l.* per copy for every omission to print the name and place of abode of the printer, on the first or the last leaf of every paper or book. It is no answer, however, to an action for infringing the copyright of the work, that it was printed and published without the name and residence as required by this Act (*e*).

The evidence of an offer to compromise an action for a certain amount cannot be accepted as conclusive, or even as suggestive that such amount was the extent only to which the party so offering to compromise has been damaged or has suffered injury. So where a person had offered to take 160*l.* as the price of his right, and therefore had (it was argued) shewn that he did not consider the probable harm that would be done to him as irremediable, and consequently had no right to ask for an injunction, it was said by Sir William Page Wood, then Vice-Chancellor, that that argument would not go far with the court. A person might be willing to forego his rights, and so avoid litigation; but after the litigation, which he had shewn himself anxious to avoid, had begun,

Cap. VII.

Effect of evidence of offer to compromise.

(*a*) *Boosey* v. *Davidson*, 13 Q. B. 257.
(*b*) *Ibid.*
(*c*) *Rooney* v. *Kelly*, 14 Ir. C. L. R. 158, Q. B.
(*d*) *Graves & Co.* v. *Logan*, 7 Sc. Sess. Cas. 3rd Ser. 204.
(*e*) *Chappell* v. *Davidson*, 18 C. B. 194.

the circumstances were altered, and he surely should be
allowed to insist on his right to the utmost (a).

The court will not entertain an application for security
for costs, where there has been delay on the part of the
applicants in making the application (b); nor will it,
when a defendant has simply denied that a work was
duly registered, permit him to prove that the name of the
publisher has been untruly stated; nor even give him
leave to amend the statement of defence, so as to raise
the latter point (c).

(a) *Ainsworth* v. *Bentley*, 14 W. R. 632.
(b) *In re Musical Compositions called 'Kathleen Mavourneen' and
'Dermot Astore,' Ex parte Hutchins & Romer*, W. N. (1879) 99.
(c) *Collette* v. *Goode*, 7 Ch. Div. 842; 47 L. J. (Ch.) 370; 38 L. T. 504;
'What an Afternoon!'

CHAPTER VIII.

REMEDY IN EQUITY IN CASES OF INFRINGEMENT OF COPYRIGHT.

IN equity is to be found the most usual and expeditious Remedy by injunction. means of obtaining redress from piracy, and for preventing the continuance of the injury. "*Melius est in tempore occurrere, quam post causam vulneratam remedium quærere*" (a). Here, by the preliminary process of injunction, justice is more readily administered than in a court of law —the property in question protected from, perhaps, irreparable damage pending the trial of the right; and the wrong is not permitted to continue until the final decision of the court, at which time, frequently, from the circumstances of the case, the mischief may be irremediable (b).

Where formerly the question of legal injury was referred to a court of law under the sanction of a court of equity, an injunction was granted to restrain the evil complained of until the merits of the case could be finally heard, when, if the opinion of the court of law were in favour of the plaintiff, it granted its final preventive relief, which, by way of distinction from the temporary process just mentioned, was termed a perpetual injunction.

An injunction may be described as a prohibitory writ, Definition of an injunction. restraining the defendant from using some right, the exercise of which would be contrary to equity and good conscience; or from doing some act inconsistent with the admitted or probable legal rights of the complainant, and

(a) 2 Inst. 299.
(b) *Vide* 2 Story, Eq. Jur. 926 ; 1 Fonbl. Eq. 34, *notis* ; Kerr on Injunc. 439 ; *Saunders* v. *Smith*, 3 My. & Cr. 728 ; *Platt* v. *Button*, 19 Ves. 447.

CAP. VIII. with the due perservation of the property affected by the act sought to be restrained (a).

Formerly, courts of equity would not interfere by way of injunction, to protect copyrights any more than patent rights, until the title had been established at law (b). Thus, in an anonymous case reported in Vernon (c), upon a motion by the king's patentees for an injunction to stay the sale of English Bibles printed beyond the sea, Lord Keeper King refused the application until the validity of the patent had been established at law. The same judge again refused, in a subsequent case (d), to grant an injunction against printing Bibles, until the plaintiffs had brought their action in the King's Bench.

Lord Mansfield's opinion upon the issuing of injunctions.

In the general discussion of the common-law right of literary property, in *Millar* v. *Taylor* (e), great stress was laid upon the different injunctions which had been granted by courts of equity in favour of such right. Lord Mansfield (who had had very great experience in the Court of Chancery) said, that he looked at the injunctions which had been granted or continued before hearing, as equal to any final decree; for, such injunction never was granted upon motion, unless the legal property of the plaintiff was made out, or continued after answer, unless it remained clear. The Court of Chancery never granted injunctions in cases of this kind, when there was any doubt. Sir Joseph Yates, on the contrary, in combating the general common-law right, expressed his opinion that the injunction, being temporary only, decided nothing at all. Lord Camden, in his speech in *Donaldson* v. *Becket*, already referred to, expressed himself upon this part of the argument as follows: "All the injunction cases have been

(a) Drewry on Injunc. Intro. 5.
(b) 2 Story, Eq. Jur. chap. 23, s. 935; *Hill* v. *University of Oxford*, 1 Vern. 275; *Baskett* v. *Cunningham*, 2 Eden, 137; *East India Co.* v. *Sandys*, 1 Vern. 127; *Jeffreys* v. *Baldwin*, Amb. 164; *Bateman* v. *Johnson*, Fitz-Gib. 106; *Blanchard* v. *Hill*, 2 Atk. 485. See *Redfield* v. *Myddleton*, 7 Bosw. (Amer.) 649.
(c) 1 Vern. 120.
(d) *Hill* v. *University of Oxford*, 1 Vern. 275. See *Baskett* v. *Cunningham, supra; Grierson* v. *Jackson*, 2 Ridg. Irish T. R. 304.
(e) 1 Burr. 2303.

ably given; though I shall only add, in general terms, that they can prove nothing if a thousand injunctions had been granted, unless the Chancellor, at the time he granted them, had pronounced a solemn opinion, that they were grounded upon the common law. Lord Hardwicke, after twenty years' experience, in the last case of the kind that came before him, declared that the point had never yet been determined. Lord Northington granted them on the idea of a doubtful title (a). I continued the practice on the same foundation, so did the present Lord Chancellor. Where then is the Chancellor who had declared, *ex cathedrâ*, that he decided upon the common-law right? Let the decision be produced in direct terms " (b).

The modern practice of granting injunctions is somewhat different; for now, in cases where the circumstances warrant it, the party will be entitled to an injunction, not only to the hearing, but, upon proper application, a perpetual injunction will issue.

The jurisdiction will be exercised in all cases where there is a clear colour of title founded upon long possession and assertion of right (c). Lord Eldon distinctly lays down this doctrine, he says (d): " It is said in cases of this sort the universal rule is, that if the title is not clear at law, the court will not grant or sustain an injunction until it is made clear at law. With all deference to Lord Mansfield, I cannot concede to that proposition so unqualified. There are many instances in my own memory in which this court has granted or continued an injunction to the hearing under such circumstances. In the case of patent rights, if the party gets his patent, and

---

(a) But see *Osborne* v. *Donaldson; Miller* v. *Donaldson*, 2 Eden, 327.

(b) Cited from Evan's 'Statutes,' vol. ii. p. 26. *Vide Bruce* v. *Bruce*, cited 13 Ves. 505; *Harmer* v. *Plane*, 14 Ves. 130; *Hogg* v. *Kirby*, 8 Ves. 215, 224; and Lord Erskine, in *Gurney* v. *Longman*, 13 Ves. 493, 505.

(c) *Universities of Oxford and Cambridge* v. *Richardson*, 6 Ves. 689; *Mawman* v. *Tegg*, 2 Russ. 385, 391; *Sheriff* v. *Coates*, 1 Russ. & My. 159, 167; *Shaw* v. *Shaw*, 3 Jur. 217; *Colburn* v. *Duncombe*, 9 Sim. 151; *Chappell* v. *Purday*, 4 Y. & C. 485; *Bohn* v. *Bogue*, 10 Jur. 420; *Tonson* v. *Walker*, 3 Swanst. 679; Jeremy on Eq. Jur. bk. 3, ch. 2, s. 1; Eden on Injun. ch. 13, p. 284; Story on Eq. § 935.

(d) *Universities of Oxford and Cambridge* v. *Richardson*, 6 Ves. 707.

puts his invention in execution, and has proceeded to a sale, that may be called possession under it, however doubtful it may be whether the patent can be sustained. This court has lately said, possession under a colour of title is ground enough to enjoin and to continue the injunction until it shall be proved at law that it is only colour, and not real title." An injunction *pendente lite* should not be granted on light grounds, nor in doubtful cases, but should await the full proof upon the final hearing (*a*). Even an equitable interest limited in point of time or extent is sufficient (*b*). An equitable title, which will support an application for an injunction, occurs where the legal right has not been vested, but from the dealings between the actual owner and the party applying for the injunction such party has acquired a limited equitable right in the copyright, to the extent of being entitled to be one of the publishers, or the sole publisher of the work, for a given or an indefinite time.

Equitable title will support injunction.

"This court" said the Vice-Chancellor of England in *Bohn* v. *Bogue* (*c*), always takes notice of the equitable interest: and if the equitable right to the copyright is complete, this court will take care that the real question shall be tried, notwithstanding there may be a defect in respect of the legal property." As to what amounts to an equitable interest sufficient to maintain an action, must depend upon circumstances, but it is clear that where there is no material interest in the work for which protection is claimed, no action can be maintained. An injunction will not be granted until the work has been registered, but the court will interfere by injunction to protect the copyright of the assignee of the author, though it appear that at the time of the alleged piracy there was not an assignment in writing (*d*). But a mere agent to sell has not such a real interest in a work as will entitle him to relief (*e*).

(*a*) *Redfield* v. *Myddleton*, 7 Bosw. (Amer.) 649.
(*b*) *Sweet* v. *Cater*, 11 Sim. 572; *Chappell* v. *Purday*, 4 Y. & C. 485; *Sims* v. *Marryat*, 17 Q. B. 281.
(*c*) 10 Jur. 421.
(*d*) *Hodges* v. *Welsh*, 2 Ir. Eq. 266.
(*e*) *Nicol* v. *Stockdale*, 3 Swans. 687.

Nor will the court interfere where a *primâ facie* title is not Cap. VIII.
shewn, as in *Platt* v. *Button* (a), where the plaintiff claimed *Primâ facie*
protection for the music of certain dances which he had title must be shewn.'
permitted several persons to publish. Where the plaintiff
states circumstances shewing a good equitable title, the
court will, for the purpose of determining the fact of piracy,
order the defendant to admit the legal title of the plaintiff (b). Judge Story remarks: "In some cases a court of
equity will take upon itself the task of inspection and comparison of books alleged to be piracies; but the usual
practice is, to refer the subject to a master, who then reports
whether the books differ, and in what respects; and upon
such a report the court usually acts in making its interlocutory, as well as its final decree" (c). And Mr. Curtis,
on the same head, says: "In general, if the court sees strong
ground for supposing that the defendant's work is a
violation of the plaintiff's copyright, the course is to grant
an injunction *ex parte*, until answer or further order.
Then, in order to ascertain the fact of piracy or no piracy,
it is referred to a master to examine into the originality
of the new book, or the court takes upon itself the inspection of both works. Where the works are long and
of a complex character, containing original matter mixed
with much that is common property, they will be referred
to a master; but where they are of a class affording
facility for the detection of piracy by immediate inspection, the court will examine them" (d). At the present
day the court usually takes upon itself the inspection of
the book (e).

In all cases of injunctions in aid of legal rights, whether Injunction auxiliary to legal right.

(a) 19 Ves. 447.
(b) Kerr, on Injunc. 439, citing *Dickens* v. *Lee*, 8 Jur. 183; *Bohn* v.
Bogue, 10 Jur. 421; *Sweet* v. *Shaw*, 8 L. J. (N.S.) Ch. 216; *Sweet* v. *Cater*,
11 Sim. 572; 5 Jur. 68.
(c) 2 Story, Eq. Jur. 124, s. 941; Eden on Injunc. chap. 13, 289; *Carnan*
v. *Bowles*, 2 Bro. C. C. 80; —— v. *Leadbetter*, 4 Ves. 681; *Cary* v. *Faden*,
5 Ves. 24; *Jeffrey* v. *Bowles*, 1 Dick. 429; *Trusler* v. *Comyns*, cited Id.
(d) Curtis on Copy. 325.
(e) *Murray* v. *Bogue*, 1 Drew. 368; *Spiers* v. *Brown*, 6 W. R. 352;
Jarrold v. *Houlston*, 3 K. & J. 708; *Hotten* v. *Arthur*, 1 H. & M. 603; *Pike*
v. *Nicholas*, 38 L. J. (Ch.) 529; L. R. 5 Ch. Ap. 251.

CAP. VIII. it be copyright, patent right, or some other description of legal right which comes before the court, the office of the court is consequent upon the legal right; and it generally happens, that the only question the court has to consider is, whether the case is so clear and so free from objection upon the grounds of equitable consideration, that the court ought to interfere by injunction without a previous trial at law, or whether it ought to wait till the legal title has been established. This distinction depends upon a great variety of circumstances, and it is utterly impossible to lay down any general rule upon the subject, by which the discretion of the court ought in all cases to be regulated (a).

The court will exercise its discretion in following that course which appears to be most conducive to justice to both parties. Although the matter may not be wholly free from doubt, yet if the plaintiff makes out a *primâ facie* case, and the court is reasonably satisfied that a piracy has been committed, a temporary injunction will usually be granted.

In what cases it will be granted. If irreparable damage would be caused to the property of the plaintiff by the refusal of the court to interfere, the injunction will be immediately granted (b). If, however, an injunction would cause a severer injury to the defendant than that occasioned the plaintiff by reason of his being required, in the first instance, to establish his legal right, the other alternative will be adopted (c), and the court is disposed rather to restrict than increase the

(a) *Per* Lord Cottenham, in *Saunders* v. *Smith*, 3 My. & Cr. 728.
(b) *Sweet* v. *Shaw*, 8 L. J. Ch. (N.S.) 216; *Dickens* v. *Lee*, 8 Jur. 183.
(c) *Saunders* v. *Smith, supra; Bramwell* v. *Halcomb*, 3 My. & Cr. 737; *Spottiswoode* v. *Clarke*, 2 Ph. 154, 157; *M'Neil* v. *Williams*, 11 Jur. 344; *Smith* v. *Chatto*, 31 L. T. (N.S.) 775. "No doubt," said Hall, V.C., in this last case, "this question might be left to be decided at the hearing, but I think it better to decide it at once, particularly considering how difficult it would otherwise be to assess the plaintiff's damages, if he should ultimately prove to be in the right. But in granting the injunction for which the plaintiff asks I do not lose sight of the fact that compensation may have to be made to the defendants, if at the hearing I decide in their favour. The amount of such compensation can, however, be more easily fixed than if it had to be made to the plaintiff, and if given will have to be substantial. . . The plaintiff must undertake to abide by such damages, if any, as the Court may at the hearing think fit to award."

number of cases in which it interferes by injunction before the establishment of the legal title (a), and it will give great weight to the consideration of the questions, which side is more likely to suffer by an erroneous or hasty judgment, and the prejudicial effect the injunction may have on the trial of the action (b). In a case (c), where the defendant was a vendor of a literary work published in weekly numbers, and in one of the numbers of which was contained the commencement of a work of fiction, which, with the exception of a few colourable alterations, was in all respects similar to a prior work of which the plaintiff was the author and publisher; on a bill by the plaintiff, praying that the defendant might be restrained from publishing, selling, or otherwise disposing of the number containing the commencement of such work of fiction, or any continuation or other part thereof, and from copying "or imitating," the whole or any part of the plaintiff's book, the court granted an injunction as prayed, except as to the words "or imitating," but directed the plaintiff to bring an action within ten days against the defendant for the invasion of his alleged copyright.

Though the author or his assignee may enjoy a *primâ facie* legal title sufficient to support an application for an injunction, yet the subject of his title may be such that, for reasons of morality or public policy, no action at law could be maintained upon it (d). The doctrine of equity in reference to works of such a nature is, that if an author can maintain an action he may, at least with some exceptions, come into equity to have his remedy made more effectual. But if the action could not be maintained in the former court, nothing can be done in equity, which is

Equitable remedy refused in cases of a certain description.

(a) See *Bacon* v. *Jones*, 2 My. & Cr. 433; *Stevens* v. *Keating*, 1 Mac. & G. 659; *Norton* v. *Nicholls*, 6 W. R. 764.

(b) *McNeill* v. *Williams*, 11 Jur. 344.

(c) *Dickens* v. *Lee*, 8 Jur. 183; see also *Ingram* v. *Stiff*, 5 Jur. (N.S.) 947; 33 L. T. (N.S.) 195.

(d) *Vide* 2 Mer. 439; *Hime* v. *Dale*, 2 Camp. 31, *notis, per* Lord Ellenborough.

CAP. VIII.   only auxiliary to the law, and therefore gives not relief, except where the law gives damages (a).

Consequently an injunction will not be issued to restrain the publication of a literary composition, on the ground that it is injurious to the reputation or hurtful to the feelings of the person seeking relief. Nor on the ground that it is libellous or blasphemous, immoral or mischievous (b).

And where there is a fair doubt whether damages could be recovered at law, a court of equity will not maintain an injunction granted *ex parte*, but will leave the plaintiff to establish his legal right before it interferes in his behalf (c).

So also where evidence as to the plaintiff's right is contradicted by the defendant's evidence, no injunction will be granted until the right of the plaintiff be established at law. Thus where the copyright of a work had been assigned by the author to the plaintiff, and the plaintiff and author swore that A. (a stranger to the suit) had only a qualified interest in the work, but A., in an affidavit filed by the defendant, swore that, under a bargain between him and the author, he had the entire copyright of the work, but did not state any deed of assignment, the plaintiff was held not entitled to an injunction till he had established his right at law (d).

Scotch law on this subject.   In Scotland the question is disposed of otherwise; the principle adopted in English practice is not sanctioned. Even if property in the work be the sole ground of interdict, the proof of ownership alone (undistracted by any inquiry into the nature or value or subject of it) in that country guides judicial interference. For the use or abuse of that property the law provides another remedy,

(a) *Walcot* v. *Walker*, 7 Ves. 1; *Lawrence* v. *Smith*, 1 Jac. 471; *Murray* v. *Benbow*, 1 Jac. 474, *notis*; *Southey* v. *Sherwood*, 2 Mer. 435.

(b) *Southey* v. *Sherwood*. 2 Mer. 435; *Hime* v. *Dale*, 2 Camp. 27, note *b*; *Seeley* v. *Fisher*, 11 Sim. 581; *Clark* v. *Freeman*, 11 Beav. 112; *Walcot* v. *Walker*, *supra*.

(c) *Byron (Lord)* v. *Dugdale*, 1 L. J. (Ch.) 239.

(d) *Lowndes* v. *Duncombe*, 1 L. J. (Ch.) 51.

in administering which, that particular use forms the true CAP. VIII. point of inquiry.

In trifling cases an injunction has been denied. Thus, in a periodical work of theatrical criticism, the defendant inserted a few pages of scattered passages from a farce of the plaintiff's, forty pages in length. The profits did not amount to 3*l.*, and the court dismissed the bill for an injunction (*a*). So, an injunction was refused against the copying of tables of calculations, which could be cast anew for less than 8*l.*, and in a short time (*b*).

Where in 1830, A., a foreigner resident in Paris, made a legal assignment of his copyright in an opera ('*Fra Diavolo*') to L., a resident in England, and L., in the same year, sold his interest to C., without executing any written memorandum, and C. died in 1834, and in 1836 C.'s executrix obtained a legal assignment, and in the meantime copies of the full score had been imported into England, and sold in London by several tradesmen, and in 1841 P. published and sold the overture of the opera in London; the court held, that C.'s executrix could not maintain an injunction against P. for piracy, on the ground that the question being whether a party who, before the copyright had been actually parted with to him (because at the time there was no conveyance), had permitted the books to be imported here and sold without interference, was afterwards to be at liberty to come forward and say that no party should do the like again, and that it was an important question, and the court thought it sufficiently doubtful to prevent any interference by injunction until it was decided (*c*).

It is frequently a matter of difficulty to decide whether As to the the injunction should be continued, or whether it should continuation of the injunc- be dissolved until hearing (*d*). An injunction should in tion, or its dissolution. general be granted and maintained in the interim, if

(*a*) *Whittingham* v. *Wooler*, 2 Swans. 428; see *Bell* v. *Whitehead*, 8 L. J. (N.S.) Ch. 141; 3 Jur. 68. (*b*) *Baily* v. *Taylor*, 1 Russ. & My. 73.
(*c*) *Chappell* v. *Purday*, 4 Y. & C. 485.
(*d*) *Bramwell* v. *Halcomb*, 3 My. & Cr. 737; *Universities of Oxford and Cambridge* v. *Richardson*, 6 Ves. 689.

R

the defendant's publication is prejudicial to the plaintiff, although the plaintiff's right admits of a fair doubt: but in cases of works the sole or the chief value of which arises from a temporary demand, the court acts upon the opposite principle, and if there be a doubt as to the legal right, does not grant the injunction before the establishment of that right at law (a).

Thus, in *Spottiswoode* v. *Clarke* (b), the Lord Chancellor laid down the principles which ought to govern the discretion of the court, as follows: " I have often expressed my opinion, that unless a case depending upon a legal right is very clear, it is the duty of the court to take care that the right be ascertained before it exercises its jurisdiction by injunction. The first question to be determined is as to the legal right, and if the court doubts about that, it may commit great injustice by interfering until that question has been decided. One objection to that course is, that it compels future litigation, for it orders the plaintiff to bring an action ; whereas, by adopting the alternative course—suspending the injunction, with liberty to the plaintiff to bring an action,—it enables him to pause a little and consider whether it is worth his while to embark in such a course of litigation as will be necessary to establish the right on which he insists. A second objection is, that the court in granting the injunction is expressing a strong opinion upon the legal question, before that question is discussed in the proper tribunal. It is much better, if the legal right is to be litigated, that this court should abstain from expressing any opinion upon it in the meantime."

Where a portion only of the work is piratical. When the part which has been copied from the plaintiff's work can be separated from that which has not been copied, an injunction will be granted only against the objectionable part or parts, but even where a very large proportion of a work of a piratical nature is unquestionably original, but the parts which have been copied cannot be separated from those which are original without de-

(a) Curtis on Copy. 317.   (b) 2 Phillips' Ch. Rep. 154.

stroying the use and value of the original matter, he who CAP. VIII.
has made an improper use of that which did not belong
to him must suffer the consequences of so doing, for an
injunction will be issued against the whole.

In cases of this nature the court has first to decide
whether there ought to be an injunction; and if there is
to be one, it has next to determine whether the injunction
should be issued against the entire work, or only against a
portion of it. The extent to which the injunction ought
to go, must, in each case, depend on the particular circumstances attending it.

The opinion of Lord Hardwicke (a) appears to have To what
been that an injunction might be granted against the extent the
whole, although only a portion was pirated; and in the to go.
instance of Milton's 'Paradise Lost,' with Dr. Newton's
notes, there being nothing new in that work except
the notes, he granted an injunction against the entire
book. There is the record of a case tried before Lord
Kenyon (b), in which he states that the question whether
an injunction could be issued against the whole of a book
on account of the piratical quality of a part, came before
Lord Bathurst; and Lord Bathurst seems to have held it
could not, unless the part pirated was such, that granting
an injunction against such part necessarily destroyed the
whole. Lord Kenyon, who possessed great information on
this subject, states himself to have been perfectly satisfied
with the opinion of Lord Bathurst, as bearing upon the
judgment of Lord Hardwicke and the other cases. In the
case referred to before Lord Kenyon the declaration at
law contained a count for publishing the whole work, and
another for publishing a part; and Lord Kenyon's direction to the jury seems to have been to find damages for
publishing the part only.

" As to the hard consequences which would follow from

<hr/>

(a) 4 Burr. 2326. See *Campbell* v. *Scott*, 11 Sim. 31; *Kelly* v. *Hooper*,
4 Jur. 21; *Whittingham* v. *Wooler*, 2 Swans. 428; *Cobbett* v. *Woodward*,
L. R. 14 Eq. 407; see *Story's Executors* v. *Holcombe*, 4 McLean (Amer.),
306, 315.

(b) *Vide Cary* v. *Longman*, 1 East, 360; *Trusler* v. *Murray*, 1 East, 363.

granting an injunction," said Lord Eldon, in *Mawman v·
Tegg, (a) "when a very large proportion of the work is
unquestionably original, I can only say, that, if the parts
which have been copied cannot be separated from those
which are original, without destroying the use and value
of the original matter, he who has made an improper use
of that which did not belong to him must suffer the consequences of so doing. If a man mixes what belongs to
him with what belongs to me, and the mixture be forbidden
by law, he must again separate them, and he must bear
all the mischief and loss which the separation may occasion. If an individual chooses in any work to mix my
literary matter with his own, he must be restrained from
publishing the literary matter which belongs to me ; and if
the parts of the work cannot be separated, and if by that
means the injunction, which restrained the publication of
my literary matter, prevents also the publication of his
own literary matter, he has only himself to blame."

"In the cases which have come before me," continued
the Lord Chancellor, in the case from which we have
already quoted, " my language has been, that there must
be an injunction against such part as has been pirated ;
but in those cases the part of the work which was affected
with the character of piracy was so very considerable, that
if it were taken away there would have been nothing left
to publish except a few broken sentences. Now, the
difficulty here is this : whether I have before me sufficient
grounds to authorize me to say, how far the matter which
is proved (if I may use the word) to have been copied, is
sufficient to enable me to decide how much I may enjoin
against ; and if I can be thus authorized to say how much
I can enjoin against, then the question is, what will be the
effect if that injunction applied to so much of the work, in
the state of uncertainty in which we now are ? Or whether,
on the other hand, as the matter cannot be tried by the
eye of the judge, I must not pursue a course which has
been adopted in cases of a similar nature, namely, refer it

(a)   Russ. 385, 391.

to the Master (a) to report to what extent the one book is a copy of the other, upon the comparison of all the numbers [the works were periodicals] that have been published?

"Another way of ascertaining the facts of the case is to send it to a jury; and, in either of those ways of disposing of it, the court will order the defendant to keep an account of the profits in the meantime. But one difficulty in all these cases is that, though keeping an account of the profits may prevent the defendant from deriving any profit, as he may ultimately be obliged to account to the plaintiff for all his gains, yet, if the work, which the defendant is publishing in the meantime, really affects the sale of the work which the plaintiff seeks to protect, the consequence is, that the rendering the profits of the former work to the complaining party may not be a satisfaction to him for what he might have been enabled to have made of his own work, if it had been the only one published; for he would argue, that the profits of the defendant, as compared with the profits which he, the plaintiff, has been improperly prevented from making, could only be in the proportion of 8s., the price of a copy of the one book, to one guinea, the price of a copy of the other. If the principle upon which the court acts, is, that satisfaction is to be made to the plaintiff, I cannot see, though I never knew it done, why, if a party succeeds at law in proving the piracy, the court could not give him leave to go on to ascertain, if he can, his damages at law; or if, after applying the profits which are handed over to him by the defendants, he can shew that they were not a satisfaction for the injury done to him, I cannot see why the court might not in such a case direct an issue to try what further damnification the plaintiff had sustained."

Where the court, availing itself of the evidence read pending the motion, was led to conclude, that if the

(a) *Carnan* v. *Bowles*, 1 Cox, 283; S. C., 2 Bro. C. C. 85; *Jeffrey* v. *Bowles*, 1 Dick. 429; *Nicol* v. *Stockdale*, 12 Ves. 277; —— v. *Leadbetter*, 4 Ves. 681. In America, in *Smith* v. *Johnson*, 4 Blatch. (Amer.) 252.

CAP. VIII.   parts affected with the character of piracy were taken away, there would be left an imperfect work which could not, to any useful extent, serve the purpose intended by the publication, the injunction to restrain the publication of any parts pirated from the plaintiff's work was granted, without waiting till all the parts pirated could be distinctly marked (a).

Similarity of appearance.   An injunction may be obtained to restrain the publication of a book whose external appearance so nearly resembles that of a work wherein copyright exists as to have the effect of deceiving the public, by leading them to believe it to be the same or a continuation thereof (b).

Thus in one case the defendant was restrained from publishing, selling, or offering for sale the defendant's work, in or with its present form, title-page, or cover; or any other form, title-page, or cover, calculated to deceive persons into the belief that it was the plaintiff's work (c).

And in another case (d) Lord Romilly, M.R., said: "The defendants must be restrained from the publication of this work, and they are not entitled to publish a work with such a title, or in such a form as to binding or general appearance as to be a colourable imitation of that of the plaintiff."

The true criterion in such cases must be the effect upon the public, whether the similarity of the one publication to the other is so great as to mislead the public—is such as that an intending purchaser of the one might be misled into purchasing the other. And where such a similarity does not exist the court will not interfere. Thus where there was a well-known comic paper called 'Punch,' and another called 'Judy,' and the defendant issued a publication with the title, 'Punch and Judy,'

(a) *Lewis* v. *Fullarton*, 2 Beav. 6; *Kelly* v. *Morris*, L. R. 1 Eq. 697; *Stevens* v. *Wildy*, 19 L. J. (N.S.) Ch. 190.
(b) *Spottiswoode* v. *Clarke*, 2 Phillips, 154; *Chappell* v. *Davidson*, 2 K. & J. 123.
(c) *Metzler* v. *Wood*, 8 Ch. D. 609.
(d) *Mack* v. *Petter*, L. R. 14 Eq. 431.

the court held that though the defendant would not be at liberty to use either 'Punch' or 'Judy' singly as a title, yet there was no reason why he should not use the two combined, for in such combination the title was not such as to deceive persons of ordinary intelligence. The Vice-Chancellor considered that the defendants clearly had no right to use a name which was calculated to mislead or deceive the public in purchasing, and he intimated that if he had thought on the whole that their journal was calculated to mislead persons of ordinary intelligence (for those were the persons he had to consider) he would have granted the injunction. 'Punch,' said he, "is well known both in name and appearance. And its price is threepence. Could any one be misled into buying this other paper instead, which has the words 'Punch and Judy' printed on it in distinct letters, with a different frontispiece and its price a penny? I am clearly of opinion that the mass of mankind would not be so misled" (a).

An injunction may be obtained to restrain the publication of a literary composition falsely represented to be the production of the plaintiff (b); and also of manuscripts obtained surreptitiously (c); or about to be published in breach of some contract whereof the plaintiff has the benefit (d). *Publication falsely represented to be the production of another.*

The well-known composer, Gounod, in 1872 took proceedings against the publishers, Messrs. J. B. Cramer & Co., and Messrs. Hutchings, to restrain them from the publication of songs stated on the title-page to have been "composed by Gounod." In the first suit the two songs in question were called 'Good Night, Heaven bless you!' and 'Hero and Leander.' They were neither written nor composed by Gounod, nor published by his authority,

(a) *Bradbury* v. *Beeton*, 18 W. R. 33.
(b) *Byron* v. *Johnston*, 2 Meriv. 29; *Seeley* v. *Fisher*, 11 Sim. 581; see *Wright* v. *Tallis*, 1 C. B. 893; *Gounod* v. *Wood; Gounod* v. *Hutchings*, 'Times,' Nov. 22, 1872.
(c) *Tipping* v. *Clarke*, 2 Hare, 383; *Prince Albert* v. *Strange*, 2 De G. & Sm. 652; 1 M. & Gor. 25.
(d) *Colburn* v. *Simms*, 2 Hare, 543; *Ward* v. *Beeton*, L. R. 19 Eq. 207; *Kemble* v. *Kean*, 6 Sim. 333; see *Brooke* v. *Chitty*, 2 Coop. (*temp.* Cottenham), 216.

the music of the first being taken from a short chorus for soprano voices, written by the plaintiff, and entitled ' *Bon Soir*,' to which an accompaniment full of musical faults had been added ; and the music of the second being taken from a duet composed by the plaintiff for one of his early operas entitled ' *La Reine de Saba*,' with the music altered and the end changed.

These songs, the plaintiff alleged, were of a low order of merit, and calculated to injure his musical reputation. The defendants submitted to a perpetual injunction and paid the costs of the suit. In the second case, which was in respect of seven songs and three duets, the defendants stated that they had acted only in accordance with the custom of the trade in selling arrangements of music, but they offered to refrain from selling any of the works complained of with their present title-pages, and to undertake not to sell any arrangement of M. Gounod's music without expressing on the title-page that the music was arranged from music by him. And these terms were agreed to (a).

Due diligence to be observed in obtaining an injunction. A person who solicits the assistance of the court for the protection of his copyright from violation must evince due assiduity and diligence in coming to the court. Delay or acquiescence will be fatal to the success of the application unless it can be satisfactorily accounted for (b).

If a party is guilty of laches or unreasonable delay in the enforcement of his rights, he thereby forfeits his claim to equitable relief,—more especially where being cognizant of his rights, he does not take those steps to assert them which are open to him, but lies by and suffers other parties to incur expenses. The court looks most minutely to the time during which the parties have permitted the matter to proceed, and will not allow them to

---

(a) *Gounod* v. *Wood; Gounod* v. *Hutchings*, ' Times,' 22 Nov. 1872.

(b) *Mawman* v. *Tegg*, 2 Russ. 385, 393 ; *Baily* v. *Taylor*, Taml. 295 ; 1 Russ. & My. 73 ; *Campbell* v. *Scott*, 11 Sim. 31 ; 11 L. J. (N.S.) Ch. 166 ; 6 Jur. 186 ; *Buxton* v. *James*, 5 De G. & Sm. 80 ; *Tinsley* v. *Lacy*, 1 H. & M. 747 ; *Lewis* v. *Chapman*, 3 Beav. 133 ; *Crossley* v. *Derby Gas-Lights Co.*, 4 L. J. (N.S.) Ch. 25 ; 1 Webs. 119, 120 ; *Parrott* v. *Palmer*, 3 M. & K. 643 ; *Harrison* v. *Taylor*, 11 Jur. N.S. 408 ; see *Bagot* v. *Bagot*, 32 Beav. 509 ; *Tinsley* v. *Lacy*, 1 Hem. & M. 752.

obtain an injunction in the absence of the other party, when they have themselves, for some time, acquiesced (a). Acquiescence, although not conferring a right on the opposite party, deprives the complainant of his right to the interference of a court of equity, for unless the applicant has acted promptly, he is held to have impliedly authorized what he eventually objects to.

In *Mawman* v. *Tegg* five months' delay was adequately explained by the necessity of comparing the whole of the two works for the purpose of discovering the extent of the piracy (b).

And where the copyright of a work of an alien had been sold to a British subject, who published it in this country in 1844, and the copyright was infringed in 1849, but the state of the law then rendered it very doubtful whether the copyright was protected, and the purchaser merely protested against the infringement, but in 1851, within a reasonable time after the decision of a case in the Exchequer Chamber had established, as was then supposed, the general question of copyright in an alien, he filed his bill, and moved to restrain the publication of the pirated work, the court held that there had been no such delay as to disentitle him to an injunction (c). But where the publication of which the plaintiff complained as a piracy was completed six years and a half before the bill was filed, and for more than a year before the bill was filed a complete copy of the defendant's work was in the possession of the plaintiffs; the court said that it was its duty, in the circumstances of the case, to impute to the plaintiffs such a knowledge of the contents of the defendant's work as made it their duty to apply for an injunction, if at all, at a much earlier period (d).

Margin note: What sufficient excuse for delay.

(a) *Per* Lord Langdale, M.R., in *Mexborough* v. *Bower*, 7 Beav. 130.
(b) *Vide Smith* v. *London and S. W. Railway Co.*, 1 K. 408, 412; *Lewis* v. *Chapman*, 3 Beav. 133, 135; *Bridson* v. *Benecke*, 12 Beav. 3; *Lewis* v. *Fullarton*, 2 Beav. 8; *Buxton* v. *James*, 5 De G. & Sm. 80; 16 Jur. 15; *Wintle* v. *Bristol and S. Wales Union Railway Co.*, 6 L. T. (N.S.) 20; *Bacon* v. *Jones*, 4 My. & Cr. 433.
(c) *Buxton* v. *James, supra.*
(d) *Lewis* v. *Chapman, supra.*

The tendency of modern times is towards the doctrine
that a person does not lose his rights in equity by mere
delay, and the recent decision of Vice-Chancellor Hall in
Hogg v. *Scott* (a) is in favour of such view.   In that case
it appeared that the defendant had published in 1868 the
first edition of a work called 'The Orchardist,' and in the
latter part of 1872 the second edition, the book containing matter pirated from the plaintiff's works.   He also
intended to publish a third edition.   In August, 1873, the
plaintiff applied for an injunction to restrain the defendant
from further publishing or selling any copies of such
piratical work.   In defence it was urged that the plaintiff
had knowledge in 1869 of the piracy, and was therefore
barred by delay from sustaining his suit; that the defendant was entitled to re-issue in his third edition anything which had appeared in the earlier ones.   The court
held that, even if the plaintiff had been aware of the
piratical nature of the defendant's book for four years
before commencing the suit, he was not thereby deprived
of his remedies in equity.   "The omission to take any
proceedings at law or in equity for a time," said the Vice-
Chancellor, "does not in itself appear to me an encouragement to the defendant amounting to an equitable bar in
this court.   It is not enough to shew that the legal right
is not to be protected here."

One of the defences in this case was, that the statutory
limitation applied to all actions and suits, whether for the
penalties or damages or injunctions, and hence that the
plaintiff's suit was barred by lapse of time.   But to this
the Vice-Chancellor replied : "I cannot allow the objection taken to the plaintiff's right to sue, because more
than twelve months elapsed before he filed a bill in this
court.   By the 3rd section of the statute a property is
created in an author's work which *primâ facie* is to endure
for a term certain, and that property will remain in the
author or his representatives, as owners of it, till it be
taken away from him or them.   The argument that, if a

(a) L. R. 18 Eq. 444.

case arises for a suit in respect of the author's right to his
property, and the author does not commence his suit
within twelve months, that therefore his property is gone,
I do not agree with. I do not find that clearly expressed
in the statute, and I cannot put such a construction upon
the 26th section. The 15th section gives to an owner of
copyright a special action on the case in respect of any
piracy. The remedy so provided is apparently a cumulative one ; and, whether it be so or not, is not very
important. The remedy is given against the person who
is called the 'offender,' and the act spoken of as the
'offence' is the printing for sale or exportation of any book
in which there shall be subsisting copyright. Mr. Morgan,
in his argument, contended that the court ought to put
upon the word 'offence' in the 26th section the same
construction as it bears in the 15th section of the statute.
If that were a reasonable construction, it might be adopted ;
but looking at the other sections in the statute which refer
to penalties, I do not think it would be reasonable. There
is nothing to be found in them about any 'offence,' in the
sense contended for on the part of the defendant. If the
book which has been improperly published by the defendant contains property belonging to the plaintiff, the
owner of the copyright, I do not see how it can be successfully contended that he is suing in respect of an offence in
the sense urged on the part of the defendant. The
plaintiff is suing in respect of his copyright ; that is his
property. The 20th section is, no doubt, not very happily
framed : but I am of opinion that, on the true construction of that and the other sections of the statute, the
'offence' contemplated by it must be the doing, in contravention of its provisions, of something expressly
prohibited by them.

"The real question is, what is the 'offence' intended
by the statute ? It is the printing for sale or exportation
of any work, or part of a work, by a person who is not the
owner of the copyright of that work, and without the
consent of the owner. The non-suing by the owner of

the copyright in respect of a particular edition, or part of
an edition, of the defendant's work is one thing; and even
if it could be said that so far the owner's remedy was
barred by his own neglect, still I find nothing in the
statute which states that the person who has already
published the edition or part of the edition complained of,
may go on doing so, and that if he does, the owner has
then no remedy for such further ' offence.' . . . The
right of the owner of the copyright to his property in it, is
not to cease because one copy of the work, which without
his sanction contains the piracies, has been sold and
disposed of without any complaint on his part. He is not
on that account to lose all his property in his copyright;
therefore I hold, in accordance with the decisions referred
to, and on the construction of the statute, that the plaintiff
has not lost his right to sue."

If the conduct of the party complaining has conduced
to the condition of affairs that occasions the application,
or has been such as to lead to the supposition that the
publication would not be objected to, he cannot have
relief (a).

Injunctions
not granted
generally
where there
has been
acquiescence.
In *Rundell* v. *Murray* (b), where it appeared that the
plaintiff had given a manuscript to the defendant and
permitted him to publish it as his own for fourteen years,
at the end of which period she claimed the exclusive
property in it, and sought to restrain the defendant from
further publishing it, Lord Eldon, in refusing to grant the
injunction sought, said: "There has often been great
difficulty about granting injunctions, where the plaintiff
has previously by acquiescing, permitted many others to
publish the work; where ten have been allowed to publish
the court will not restrain the eleventh. A court of
equity frequently refuses an injunction where it acknow-

(a) *Rundell* v. *Murray*, Jac. 311; *Saunders* v. *Smith*, 3 My. & Cr. 711;
7 L. J. (N.S.) Ch. 227; 2 Jur. 491, 536. See also *Lewis* v. *Chapman*, 3
Beav. 135; *Platt* v. *Button*, 19 Ves. 447; S. C. nom. *Platts* v. *Button*,
Coop. 303; *Campbell* v. *Scott*, 11 Sim. 31; 11 L. J. (N.S.) Ch. 166;
6 Jur. 186.

(b) Jac. 311.

ledges a right, when the conduct of the party complaining has led to the state of things that occasions the application, and therefore, without saying with whom the right is, whether it is in this lady, or whether it is concurrently in both, I think it is a case in which strict law ought to govern."

On somewhat similar grounds to this, yet, under the circumstances of the case pressing the doctrine still further, Lord Cottenham acted in *Saunders* v. *Smith*, where he refused to restrain the publication of the second volume of 'Smith's Leading Cases' before trial at law, for the reason that he found "in the dealings of the plaintiff in this case what amounts to that species of conduct which prevents, in this stage of the cause at least, the interposition of this court." And he continued, referring to the case of *Rundell* v. *Murray*, "Lord Eldon there lays it down that not only conduct with the party with whom the contest exists, but conduct with others, may influence the court in the exercise of its equitable jurisdiction by injunction. Now here I find permission, whether express or implied, given to others" (a).

The view taken in this case by Lord Cottenham does not seem to have met with unqualified approval in later times, and in a recent case (b) where it was stated in defence by one of the defendants that the plaintiff had said to him that it would not be unlawful for any one to copy certain parts from the plaintiff's or any other directory, the Vice-Chancellor said: "A copyright is not lost by the mere expression of an opinion." "In order that the defence should prevail, it must be made out that there is proof of, at least, one of three propositions: viz., either that the plaintiff authorized what was done by the defendants; or that his conduct conduced to what was done by them; or that there is enough to displace the *primâ facie* proof of the plaintiff's copyright."

No custom of the trade can be pleaded as a justification Custom of trade no

(a) 3 My. & Cr. 729.
(b) *Morris* v. *Ashbee*, L. R. 7 Eq. 34.

for infringement of the copyright. Thus in a case (a)
where the publisher of the "Belgravia Magazine" and the
'Belgravia Annual' was plaintiff, it appeared that the
periodical had been sent for about eight years to the defendants, who had been in the habit of selecting therefrom
extracts, and occasionally entire stories, and reprinting them
in the 'Bristol Mercury.' The 'Mercury' was a weekly
paper, and copies of the same were sent to the plaintiff, he
thus being acquainted with the defendants' general custom.
In 1873, the defendants received the 'Belgravia Annual'
with a request to notice it in their paper. This they did, and
reprinted one entire story.   The following month to this
they reprinted another story from the magazine, in each
case the sources from which the tale emanated being
acknowledged. Without any notice to the defendants the
plaintiffs moved to restrain the further publication or
sale of any copies of the paper containing either of the
stories.   In defence the custom of the trade was relied on,
but V.-C. Bacon held that any such alleged custom was
no defence, and that the defendants could not thus be
justified in reprinting, as they had done, entire stories,
and the injunction sought for was accordingly granted.

If the court is satisfied that the alleged title is good,
and that there has been a piracy, it may interfere at once
and restrain the piracy *simpliciter* by injunction; but if
the title is not clear, or the fact of violation is denied,
the course the court usually adopts is either to grant
an *ex parte* injunction, with an undertaking by the plaintiff
as to damages, or to direct the motion to stand over until
hearing, on the terms of the defendant keeping an account
of the number of copies sold, in order that justice may
ultimately be done between the parties (b).

Formerly when an injunction was granted for the protection of a legal right, and a question was raised as to
the existence of the right, the court made the continuance

(a) *Maxwell* v. *Somerton*, 30 L. T. (N.S.) 11; *Campbell* v. *Scott*, 11
Sim. 31.
(b) Kerr on Injunc. chap. 20; *Walcot* v. *Walker*, 7 Ves. 1; *Wilkins* v.
Aiken, 17 Ves. 422.

of the injunction depend upon an action being brought to try the right, or it required the complainant first to establish his title at law, and suspended the grant of the injunction until the result of the legal investigation had been ascertained ; but the Chancery Amendment Act, 15 & 16 Vict. c. 86, s. 62, provided, that in cases where it was the practice of the court to decline to grant equitable relief until the legal title or right of the parties seeking such relief had been established in a proceeding at law, the court might itself determine such title or right without requiring the parties to proceed at law to establish the same : and the 21 & 22 Vict. c. 27, s. 3, provided for the trial of questions of fact arising in any suit or proceeding in Chancery, either before a common or special jury, or (s. 5) before the court itself without a jury (a). Where the trial takes place before a jury, the court has the same powers, jurisdiction, and authority, as any judge of any of the superior courts sitting at *nisi prius*. But this provision does not, by its reference to proceedings at law, impose limits upon the right of appeal previously existing upon questions both of law or fact, against any order made by the Court of Chancery (b). Nor does it give the defendant a right *ex debito justitiæ* to have his case tried by a jury, where a trial by the judge alone is preferable (c) ; and by 25 & 26 Vict. c. 42, s. 1, it is enacted, that in all cases in which any relief or remedy within the jurisdiction of the Court of Chancery is sought in any cause or matter instituted or pending in either of the said courts, and whether the title to such relief or remedy be, or be not, incident to, or dependent upon, a legal right, any question of law or fact cognizable in a court of common law, on the determination of which the title to such relief or remedy depends, *shall* be determined by or before the same courts (d). But whenever it shall appear that any question of fact may be more conveniently tried by a jury

(a) See *Simpson* v. *Holliday*, L. R. 1 Ch. Ap. 316.
(b) *Curtis* v. *Platt*, L. R. 1 Ch. Ap. 337.
(c) *Bovill* v. *Hitchcock*, L. R. 3 Ch. Ap. 417.
(d) *Fernie* v. *Young*, L. R. 1 Eng. & Ir. App. 63.

at the assizes, or at any sitting in London or Middlesex for the trial of issues, the court may, nevertheless, direct any issue to try the question at the assizes, or at a sitting for the trial of issues in London or Middlesex. All the provisions with reference to the trial of questions of fact by the Court of Chancery, contained in the Chancery Amendment Act, 1858 (21 & 22 Vict. c. 27), apply to the determination of questions of fact under this Act. But the court is not bound to grant relief in any matter respecting which a court of common law has concurrent jurisdiction, if it shall appear that such matter has been improperly brought into equity, and that the same ought to have been left to the sole determination of a court of common law (s. 4). It has been held that this section applies to cases where there has been some interference with the plaintiff's rights, but not sufficient to entitle the plaintiff to an injunction (a).

Under this Act therefore it was compulsory upon the Court of Chancery to decide the whole question brought forward, both as regards the legal title of the parties, and the claim to equitable relief (b). The above Act applies not only to rights, but to remedies given by a court of equity, and does away with the power of refusing or postponing remedies until the legal title has been established by an action at law (c). There is nothing, however, which authorizes the court to transfer to itself an action actually pending at law (d), or to take cognizance of wrongs and interfere by injunction, when the act complained of has been done, and the question whether the act is wrongful or not depends upon matters of fact and law, for the trial of which no tribunal is so fit as a jury having the assistance of a judge to direct them (e).

(a) *Darell* v. *Pritchard*, L. R. 1 Ch. Ap. 244.
(b) *Fernie* v. *Young*, L. R. 1 Eng. & Ir. App. 63.
(c) *In re Hooper*, 32 L. J. (Ch.) 55.
(d) *Curlewis* v. *Carter*, 33 L. J. (Ch.) 370.
(e) *Att.-Gen.* v. *United Kingdom Telegraph Co.*, 30 Beav. 287; 31 L. J. (Ch.) 329; *Dowling* v. *Betjemann*, 2 J. & H. 544.

But now, under the recent Judicature Acts (*a*), the CAP. VIII. Chancery and the Common Law Divisions of the High Court of Justice have equal jurisdiction in determining rights and redressing wrongs. Consequently the Courts of Equity now determine all questions relating to the validity of the copyright and the alleged piracy.

In a late case it was held that the court will hesitate to commit a defendant alleged to have violated an *interim* injunction, if he has endeavoured to set himself right with regard to the original charge against him, of infringing the plaintiff's copyright (*b*). In *McRea* v. *Holdsworth* (*c*) Vice-Chancellor Sir W. M. James said that the cases in which the Court of Chancery had given a decree not in accordance with a verdict were either cases in which the trial had taken place before it, and it had full cognizance of the matter, or cases in which it had directed an issue to be tried, the object of which was merely to inform the conscience of the court. When the court withheld granting relief until a right was established at law, it was bound by the decision at law. But the court is not bound by the amount of damages awarded by the jury, and the Vice-Chancellor directed an inquiry as to what damage the plaintiff had sustained by reason of the piracy of his design; the defendants to pay the costs of the suit.

It is here worthy of remark, that if the work be of such a character that the sale is temporary, the Court of Chancery is more cautious, inasmuch as an intermediate injunction in such a case may be of equal effect with a perpetual injunction (*d*). In instances where the publication is of a temporary character.

In refusing to restrain in December the sale of an almanac for the ensuing year, in a case where the rights of the parties were doubtful, Lord Cottenham said: "But the greatest of all objections is that the court runs the

---

(*a*) 36 & 37 Vict. c. 66; 38 & 39 Vict. c. 77; 39 & 40 Vict. c. 59; 40 & 41 Vict. c. 9 and c. 57.
(*b*) *Cornish* v. *Upton*, 4 L. T. (N.S.) 862.
(*c*) 18 W. R. 489.
(*d*) See *Gurney* v. *Longman*, 13 Ves. 493, *ante*, pp. 238, 242.

risk of doing the greatest injustice in case its opinion upon the legal right should turn out to be erroneous. Here is a publication, which, if not issued this month, will lose the greater part of its sale for the ensuing year. If you restrain the party from selling immediately, you probably make it impossible for him to sell at all. You take property out of his pocket, and give it to nobody. In such a case, if the plaintiff is right the court has some means at least of indemnifying him, by making the defendant keep an account; whereas, if the defendant be right, and he be restrained, it is utterly impossible to give him compensation for the loss he will have sustained. And the effect of the order in that event will be to commit a great and irremediable injury. Unless, therefore, the court is quite clear as to what are the legal rights of the parties, it is much the safest course to abstain from exercising its jurisdiction, till the legal right has been determined " (a).

Yet in some cases the ephemeral character of the work in question may be an additional reason for an interlocutory injunction being granted, especially when the publication complained of is sold, or intended to be sold, at a lower price than the original work from which it has been taken. It is obvious that in some such cases the remedies after sale of the plaintiff might be practically worthless. The principle was recognised by Lord Eldon in a case relating to an East India Calendar or Directory.

He considered there was a great difference between works of a permanent and of a transitory nature. The case upon the former might be brought to a hearing, but he effect was very different upon a work of a perishable kind—a work that would be good for nothing in a year's time. " I am bound," said he, " under these circumstances to continue this injunction to the hearing; for the defendant would merely have to account at the rate of 2s. 6d. for each book: and if his publication proceeds at that reduced price, it will be impossible for the plaintiffs,

(a) *Spottiswoode* v. *Clarke*, 2 Phillips, 157.

obliged by the expense they have been at, to charge a   C\P. VIII.
much higher price, to sell another copy (a).

Where indeed an intermediate injunction is granted it As to bringing
does not often happen that the cause is brought to a to hearing
hearing; for the merits of the case will probably have locutory
been discussed upon the motion (b), and therefore it rarely granted.
happens that a perpetual injunction is decreed (c). If,
however, the cause should be brought to a hearing, the
court will then, if the plaintiff's cause be relieved of all
doubt, grant a perpetual injunction (d), or it will dismiss
the plaintiff's bill (e). And the plaintiff has a right to
bring his cause to a hearing for the purpose of obtaining a
perpetual injunction, although he has obtained an interlocutory injunction, which has been acquiesced in by the
defendant (f), and though the general rule of the court is
not to grant perpetual injunctions except at the hearing
of the cause (g), yet by consent an injunction may be
made perpetual on an interlocutory motion (h).

It is not necessary to apply in the first instance on
interlocutory application, for a perpetual injunction may
be obtained without such application at the hearing (i);
but care should be taken in such case to bring the cause
to the hearing in a state such as to enable the court to
adjudicate upon it without delay; for it is a mere matter
of discretion how far the court will assist at the hearing if
this be neglected (k).

A necessary incident to an interlocutory injunction is Dissolving of
a liability to be terminated or *dissolved* before the termina- injunctions.

(a) *Matthewson* v. *Stockdale*, 12 Ves. 275; see *Johnson* v. *Egan*, Sol.
Journ. 29 May, 1880.
(b) 4 Burr. 2324, 2400; *Tonson* v. *Walker*, 3 Swans. 672; 2 Eden, 328.
(c) 2 Sw. 430. See *Whittingham* v. *Wooler*, 2 Swans. 428, ц.
(d) *Macklin* v. *Richardson*, Amb. 694.
(e) *Dodsley* v. *Kinnersley*, Amb. 403.
(f) *Beaufort* (*Duke of*) v. *Morris*, 6 Hare, 350; 2 Ph. 683; 12 Jur. 614.
(g) *Day* v. *Smee*, 3 V. & B. 171.
(h) *Morrell* v. *Pearson*, 12 Beav. 284.
(i) *Bacon* v. *Jones*, 4 M. & C. 436; *Collins & Co.* v. *Walker*, 7 W. R.
222; *Davies* v. *Marshall*, 1 Dr. & Sm. 557; *Gale* v. *Abbott*, 8 Jur.
(N.S.) 987.
(k) *Bacon* v. *Jones*, *supra*; *Ward* v. *Key*, 10 Jur. 792; *Rodgers* v. *Nowill*,
6 Hare, 331; *Norton* v. *Nicholls*, 4 K. & J. 475; *Patent Type Foundry
Co.* v. *Walter*, Johns. 721.

CAP. VIII.   tion of the suit in equity of which it was made a part.
Whether or not an injunction should be dissolved, rests in
the discretion of the court. If the answer or statement of
defence contains a sufficient defence to the case stated in
the bill, the injunction will be dissolved. So where a plea
is allowed, there is ordinarily an end of the injunction, but
not always; and the court has said that an injunction is
not absolutely dissolved upon the allowance of the plea,
but only *nisi*, because there may be some equity shewn
to continue it. Where a cross bill has been filed, if, when
the first has been answered, the second is not answered in
eight days, the injunction will be dissolved.

The usual method of obtaining a dissolution of injunctions has been by *answer*. And it has been held that an
order *nisi* for dissolution cannot be obtained on putting
in a *plea*. The Vice-Chancellor in the case referred to
said : " It cannot stand for a moment. The order *nisi*
begins with a recital that the defendant has put in a full
answer, and thereby denied the plaintiff's equity " (*a*).

An injunction may be continued to the hearing, though
the equity of the bill is fully answered by the defendant.
Where its dissolution would work a greater injury than
its continuance, the question of continuance must rest in
discretion, though controlled by rules. So, notwithstanding
a complete denial of the equity of the bill, the court may,
at the hearing, retain the injunction in so far as it finds
in the facts disclosed good reason for so doing.

If the plaintiff shew that his copyright has been infringed, the court will grant an injunction without proof
of actual damage (*b*).

Where copy-
right
infringed,
injunction
granted
without proof
of damage.

" Then the only question," said Vice-Chancellor Shadwell (*c*), " is whether there has been such a *damnum* as will
justify the party in applying to the Court; because *injuria*
there clearly has been.   What has been done is against
the right of the plaintiff.   Now, in my opinion, he is

(*a*) *Wroe* v. *Clayton*, 10 Sim. 185.
(*b*) *Smith* v. *Johnson*, 33 L. J. (Ch.) 137 ; 9 Jur. (N.S.) 1223.
(*c*) *Campbell* v. *Scott*, 11 Sim. 39 ; *Tinsley* v. *Lacy*, 38 L. J. (N.S.) Ch.
539 ; *Kelly* v. *Hooper*, 4 Jur. 21 ; *Sweet* v. *Maugham*, 11 Sim. 51.

the person best able to judge of that himself; and if the court does clearly see that there has been anything done which tends to an injury, I cannot but think that the safest rule is to follow the legal right and grant the injunction."

Where a plaintiff claiming a copyright in a work of a foreigner, obtained an injunction on giving an undertaking to abide by any order the court might make respecting damages, and the law was, pending the suit, finally settled against the existence of such a copyright, the Lords Justices held that the defendant was entitled to have the damages sustained by him ascertained as correctly as practicable and paid, and that a mere dismissal of a bill with costs was not a sufficient accurate assessment and award of damages (a).

As to the piratical copies which may have been sold, the registered proprietor is not entitled in equity to the gross produce of the sale, but only to the nett *profits* which the defendant may have made by the sale (b). Nor will a court of equity grant its assistance to the party seeking its relief, unless he waive the penalty or forfeiture imposed by the Acts of Parliament (c).

To recover the pirated copies he must proceed at law (d).

Direct invasions of copyright by several persons, cannot be restrained in one suit (e).

The right of an author against different booksellers selling the same spurious edition of his work is not joint but perfectly distinct, for there is no privity between them (f).

Cap. VIII.

Proprietor entitled to nett profits only.

Matters of procedure.

(a) *Novello* v. *James*, 5 De G. M. & G. 876.

(b) *Delf* v. *Delamotte*, 3 Jur. (N.S.) Ch. 933; 3 K. & J. 581. The defendant must account for every copy sold, as if it had been the plaintiff's, and pay the profits to him: *Pike* v. *Nicholas*, 38 L. J. (Ch.) 529; 20 L. T. (N.S.) 906; 17 W. R. 842.

(c) *Colburn* v. *Simms*, 2 Hare, 554; see *Geary* v. *Norton*, 1 De G. & Sm. 9; and *Stevens* v. *Gladding*, 17 How. (Amer.) 455; *Mason* v. *Murray*, cited 3 Bro. C. C. 38; *Brand* v. *Cumming*, 22 Vin. Abr. 315, pl. 4.

(d) *Delf* v. *Delamotte*, supra.

(e) *Dilly* v. *Doig*, 2 Ves. 486; and see *Hudson* v. *Maddison*, 12 Sim. 416; and *Midwinter* v. *Kincaid* (H.L.), 11 Feb. 1751, 1 Pat. App. 488; *Pollock* v. *Lester*, 11 Hare, 274; *Cowley* v. *Cowley*, 9 Sim. 299.

(f) *Dilly* v. *Doig*, supra; *Brinckerhoff* v. *Brown*, 6 John. Ch. (Amer.) 155.

But it would be otherwise of a right of fishery, or the custom of a mill : such bills prevent multiplicity of suits, and one general right being in the latter cases liable to invasion by all the world. But a plaintiff must not act oppressively and file an unnecessary number of bills : if he does, the court will order them to be consolidated or make some other equivalent order (a).

An injunction against the seller will not be refused on the ground that the plaintiff has not proceeded against the publisher.

The court will not restrain one of the several partners in a patent from publishing a book containing an account of the invention (b).

If the defendant transfers his interest in the publication to another person, it seems that the latter may be made a party to the suit. Where a joint proprietorship exists, either party may sue.

Formerly a bill of complaint was the formal document for the commencement of a suit, but now, under the new procedure, suits have become actions and are commenced by writ of summons. The writ is to specify the division of the High Court to which it is intended that the action should be assigned, and if assigned to the Chancery Division it must be marked with the name of such of the judges thereof as the plaintiff may think fit (c).

Every writ of summons is to be indorsed with a statement of the nature of the claim made, or of the relief or remedy required, in the action (d).—It is not essential in the indorsement to set forth the precise ground of complaint, or the precise remedy or relief to which the plaintiff considers himself entitled, but the general nature of the claim and relief sought must be clearly indicated, especially when different causes of action are joined, for the plaintiff will be limited to

(a) *Foxwell* v. *Webster*, 10 Jur. (N.S.) 137 ; 12 W. R. 186 ; 2 De G. & Sm. 250 ; 9 Jur. (N.S.) 1189 ; Daniel's Chan. Prac. 286, 1492, note (z).
(b) *Hawkins* v. *Blackford*, 1 L. J. (Ch.) 142.
(c) Jud. Act, 1873, s. 42.
(d) Ord. ii. r. 1.

the indorsement on the writ unless he obtains leave to
amend.

If the plaintiff has merely an equitable title, the person in possession of the legal title should be made a party (a).

It is not necessary to allege in a statement of claim under the Copyright of Designs Act, 5 & 6 Vict. c. 100, which provides that no person is to have the benefit of the Act *unless* every article has attached thereto the letters " Rd.," that that had been done, and it has been held that a bill was not on the ground of such omission alone, open to a demurrer (b).

Every application for an injunction before answer must be supported by an affidavit of merits verifying the material statements of the plaintiff (c); and where the plaintiff had forgotten a material fact when he made his application for the injunction, and so stated on oath in answer to a motion to dissolve, his defect of memory was held to be no excuse, otherwise the same excuse might prevail in every case.

There must be an affidavit of title, when the injunction is applied for *ex parte*, and the affidavit in support should always state the precise time at which the plaintiff, or those acting for him, became aware of the alleged injury (d). They must shew either that notice to the defendant would be mischievous, or that the mischief is so urgent that it would be done if notice were served on the defendant before the injunction could be obtained. If the affidavits fall short of this point, the motion will be ordered to stand over, and notice of it must be served on the defendant (e).

(a) *Colburn* v. *Duncombe*, 9 Sim. 151.
(b) *Suraxin* v. *Hamel* [No. 1], 32 Beav. 145.
(c) No affidavit as to the title of the author or proprietor will be received after the defendant's answer has been filed, though affidavits in opposition to the answer may be read as to the facts : *Platt* v. *Button*, 19 Ves. 447; and see *Norway* v. *Rowe, Id.* 143.
(d) An affidavit in which it was stated that the plaintiff had purchased or legally acquired the copyright, was considered to be bad, for not stating that he had purchased it from the author: *Gilliver* v. *Snaggs*, 4 Vin. Abr. 278.
(e) *Anon.* 1 L. J. (Ch.) 4.

Upon the hearing no reference was formerly allowed to the affidavit filed upon the application for the injunction (a): but under the 15 & 16 Vict. c. 86, such affidavits may be made evidence in the cause.

Not necessary to specify in statement parts of work said to be pirated. Neither the statement of claim nor affidavit need specify the parts of the work stated to have been pirated; though no copyright is claimed in all the identical passages, a general allegation that the defendant's work contains pirated passages, and a verification by affidavit of those passages, are sufficient. The Vice-Chancellor, in *Sweet* v. *Maugham* (b) said, "It has always been considered sufficient to allege, generally, that the defendant's work contains several passages which have been pirated from the plaintiff's work. Then, when the injunction has been moved for, the two works have been brought into court, and the counsel have pointed out to the court the passages which they rely upon as shewing the piracy."

But where A. applied for an injunction against the stereotyper, to prevent his selling copies printed by him from advance sheets, furnished him by A., of a work written by B., it was held that an allegation " That sheets were sent to him for the advantage of said B.," and of himself, was too vague to be made the foundation of an injunction on the ground of protecting B.'s rights (c).

In an American case (d), where a bill was filed against three defendants shewing title on its face in the plaintiff to a copyright, and shewing a wrongful and wilful violation of it by all the defendants, and serious injuries inflicted

---

(a) *Barfield* v. *Kelly*, 4 Russ. 359; and see *Dunstan* v. *Patterson*, 2 Ph. 341.

(b) 11 Sim. 51; 9 L. J. (N.S.) Ch. 323; 4 Jur. 456, 479; *Hotten* v. *Arthur*, 1 H. & M. 603; 32 L. J. (Ch.) 771; 11 W. R. 934; 9 L. T. (N.S.) 199. See other instances where generality of statement is permitted of those facts well known to the defendant: *Darthez* v. *Clemens*, 6 Beav. 164; *Williams* v. *Earl of Jersey*, Cr. & Ph. 91; *Smith* v. *Kay*, 7 H. of L. Ca. 764–766; *Baker* v. *Bradley*, 7 De G. M. & G. 597; Lewis on Eq. Pleading, 83, 84, 129.

(c) *Redfield* v. *Myddleton*, 7 Bosw. (Amer.) 649.

(d) *Atwill* v *Ferrett*, 2 Blatch. Cir. Ct. (Amer.) 39.

by, and apprehended from such violation, and praying
for an injunction against all the defendants, and for
discovery from all. On general demurrer it was held
that the relief by injunction was not dependent upon the
discovery prayed for, but rested on the equities set forth in
the bill, and might be refused or granted irrespective of the
discovery, although the bill was bad as a bill of discovery.

If the plaintiff claims as assignee, he must, by affidavit
or otherwise, shew that the assignment to him has been
in accordance with the provisions of the Act, or in what
other way; if, however, he claims as assignee of an assignee,
it will be sufficient for him to shew that the assignment to
himself was in writing, without tracing the title through
the *mesne* assignees from the original author; under such
circumstances the court will assume that the title is
regular, until the contrary is shewn (*a*); and if there has
been a complete assignment, the assignor should not be
made a party to the suit (*b*). Any one associated by the
proprietor of a copyright with himself in an entry in the
book of registry has *primâ facie* a title to sue jointly with
him in a court of equity (*c*). Thus where the bill stated
that one of the plaintiffs had composed a book, and that
all the plaintiffs had caused the book to be printed and
published for their joint benefit, and that the book had
been registered by the plaintiffs as proprietors of the
copyright thereof, and that the copyright had ever since
remained in the plaintiffs for their joint benefit, and
that the defendants had published a book in which
numerous passages were copied from the plaintiffs' book;
the court held, upon a motion for the injunction, that
under the Copyright Act, 5 & 6 Vict. c. 45, the plaintiffs

On claim by assignee what must be shewn.

(*a*) *Morris* v. *Kelly*, 1 Jac. & W. 481. An instance has occurred in
which the assignee of a copyright, to whom the assignment was made *by
parol*, obtained an injunction. The distinguishing feature of that case
was this, that some of the defendants had actually received the purchase-
money and had permitted the plaintiffs to print and publish the work:
Longman v. *Oxberry*, Nov. 1820, MSS. cited Godson on Patents, &c.,
314; see *Gilliver* v. *Snaggs*, 2 Eq. Abr. 522; 4 Vin. Abr. 278, A 4.

(*b*) *Sweet* v. *Maugham*, 11 Sim. 51; 9 L. J. (N.S.) Ch. 323; 4 Jur. 456;
Colburn v. *Simms*, 2 Hare, 560.

(*c*) *Stevens* v. *Wildy*, 19 L. J. (N.S.) Ch. 190.

CAP. VIII. had a joint right to sue: and upon comparison of the two books, that in the defendants' book there had been such copying from the plaintiffs' book as entitled them to an injunction (a).

Where the plaintiff has suffered persons to publish the subject of his copyright without interposition, the court will not interfere. But this acquiescence is no proof of assignment, even if a receipt be produced for money paid for copyright.

Nature of relief usually sought and obtained.

In the majority of cases, the statement of claim prays that an account may be taken of the books printed, and of the profits thereof, from the person who has pirated from the plaintiff's works, and moreover that an injunction may be issued to restrain the further sale (b).

The court may require the defendant to disclose the number of piratical copies which he has printed, imported, or sold, the number on hand, the proceeds of sale, &c. And the plaintiff has a right to a full and particular discovery as to the original sources from which the defendant alleges himself to have drawn his work (c), and this notwithstanding the defendant offers to submit to an injunction, and to pay the costs, and a motion by the defendant to stay proceedings after interrogatories had been filed, and before the defendant had answered,

(a) *Stevens* v. *Wildy,* 19 L. J. (N.S.) Ch. 190.

(b) Where in America an account only was sought for, and no injunction applied for, the Court held that the party must proceed at law for damages: *Monck* v *Harper,* 3 Edw. Ch. (Amer.) 109. Equity cannot relieve on the ground of a right which the party has failed to redress at law; but proper matters for the exercise of its jurisdiction must be set out and sustained: *Stevens* v. *Gladding,* 17 How. (Amer.) 447; *Stevens* v. *Cady,* 2 Curt. (Amer.) 200. If no benefit appears to be gained by proceedings in equity rather than at law, the bill will be dismissed without prejudice, in order that proceedings may be had at law. In this country, where the powers of law and equity are concurrent, equity may in its discretion proceed to act; but in the Circuit Court of the United States it is otherwise, under the Judiciary Act of 1789, if the remedy at law and in chancery is equally full and perfect; and the objection may sometimes be taken under the answer, and at the hearing as well as by demurrer. But where the title to the copyright under a contract of sale is also in dispute, this question may be settled in equity, in preference to sending the parties to the law side of the court. *Id.;* Hilliard on Injunctions, 2nd Ed. ch. xxv. s. 5, note (a).

(c) *Kelly* v. *Wyman,* 17 W. R. 399; see also *Tipping* v. *Clarke,* 2 Hare, 383.

was refused (a). And in a suit to restrain an infringement, CAP. VIII.
a plaintiff who, in opposition to the defendant's denial of
his title, has obtained an injunction, is entitled to an answer
from the defendant for the purpose of having his title
admitted (in case, by arrangement between the parties, the
title is not established at law), and also for the purpose of
having an account from the defendant of the profits made
by the sale of the spurious work. The plaintiff, therefore,
under such circumstances, is entitled to the costs of the
suit, including the answer; and if, by the refusal of the
defendant to pay those costs, the plaintiff is compelled to
bring his cause to a hearing, he will be entitled to the
whole costs of the suit as between party and party,
although at the hearing he may waive the account; and
the plaintiff's equity in this respect will not be affected
by his having offered to waive his right to an answer
with a view to obtain terms more beneficial to himself
than the court would, under any circumstances, accord to
him, as for instance, with a view to receive costs as
between solicitor and client (b).

The parts to be restrained from publication may be Form of
injunction.
specified in the order, or the defendant may be enjoined
from printing, publishing, selling, or otherwise disposing
of any copies of the book "containing any articles or
article, passages or passage copied, taken or colourably
altered from" the plaintiff's book (c); or, "from doing
any other act or thing in invasion of the plaintiff's copyright in the said" book (d). Or, the injunction may
be directed specially against the piratical parts, and
generally against any unlawful copying from the plaintiff's
work (e).

In *Dickens* v. *Lee* (f), where an injunction had been
granted enjoining the defendant from "copying or
imitating the whole or any part of the plaintiff's book,"

(a) *Stevens* v. *Brett*, 10 L. T. (N.S.) 231.
(b) *Kelly* v. *Hooper*, 1 Y. & C. Ch. 197.
(c) *Lewis* v. *Fullarton*, 2 Beav. 14; *Hogg* v. *Scott*, L. R. 18 Eq. 458.
(d) *Scott* v. *Stanford*, 36 L. J. (N.S.) Ch. 732.
(e) *Jarrold* v. *Houlston*, 3 K. & J. 723.
(f) 8 Jur. 185.

Knight Bruce, V.C., struck out " or imitating," saying there was no precedent for such words, but without expressing an opinion whether an injunction would properly go that length.　It is apprehended it could not, for it must be remembered that there may be imitations which are not piratical.

Right to account incident to other relief.　Should the cause be brought to a hearing, and a perpetual injunction be issued, the right to the account will invariably be decreed as incidental to the plaintiff's other relief (a).　The account is in practice generally waived; but where it is not, the court grants it upon the principles enumerated in *Colburn* v. *Simms* (b).　"It is true," said Sir James Wigram in that case, "that the court does not, by an account, accurately measure the damage sustained by the proprietor of an expensive work from the invasion of his copyright by the publication of a cheaper book.　It is impossible to know how many copies of the dearer book are excluded from sale by the interposition of the cheaper one.　The court, by the account, as the nearest approximation which it can make to justice, takes from the wrongdoer all the profits he has made by his piracy, and gives them to the party who has been wronged.　In doing this the court may often give the injured party more, in fact, than he is entitled to, for *non constat* that a single additional copy of the more expensive book would have been sold, if the injury by the sale of the cheaper book had not been committed.　The Court of Equity, however, does not give anything beyond the account."

Any party in a cause or matter may require the attendance of any witness before an examiner of the Court, or before an examiner specially appointed for the purpose, and may examine such witness orally, for the purpose of using his evidence upon any motion or other proceeding before the court; and any party having made an affidavit

---

(a) *Hogg* v. *Kirby,* 8 Ves. 215; *Baily* v. *Taylor,* 1 Russ. & My. 73; Taml. 295; *Sheriff* v. *Coates,* 1 R. & M. 159; *Kelly* v. *Hooper,* 1 Y. & Coll. 197; *Grierson* v. *Eyre,* 9 Ves. 341; *Universities of Oxford and Cambridge* v. *Richardson,* 6 Ves. 689; 2 Story's Eq. Jur. § 933.

(b) 2 Hare, 543, 560; 12 L. J. (N.S.) Ch. 388; 7 Jur. 1104.

to be used on any motion or other proceeding is bound, CAP. VIII.
on being served with a subpœna, to attend before an examiner for the purpose of being cross-examined (a). But
the court has a discretionary power of acting upon such
evidence as may be before it at the time of the application, and of making such interim order or otherwise as
may appear necessary to meet the justice of the case (b).
However, no weight is to be attached to an affidavit
where the opposite party has had no opportunity to cross-
examine the witness (c).

Though the general rule of the court is that he who Nature of
gives discovery at all must give full discovery, yet the discovery given.
court will take care that injury shall not be done to a
defendant by compelling him to make discovery in a case
where there is no real prospect of its being of material
service to the plaintiff at the hearing. Therefore in a
suit to restrain the alleged improper use by the defendants
of the plaintiffs' trade marks, where the defendants denied
the plaintiffs' right to the exclusive use of the marks in
question, it was held by the Lords Justices (reversing a
decision of Vice-Chancellor Wickens) that the defendants,
under an order for production of documents, were not
bound to disclose the names of their customers, nor the
prices at which they bought or sold the goods which they
exported; but it was held that they must state the names
of the places to which they exported goods, the name of
the writer of any letter addressed to them by a former
partner of their own, and, in any case in which they admitted that they used one of the marks claimed by the
plaintiffs, the other marks which they used in combination
therewith (d).

There can be no account if the case for the injunction Where no account allowed.

(a) 15 & 16 Vict. c. 86, s. 40 ; *Besemeres* v. *Besemeres*, Kay, App. xvii.;
Normanville v. *Stanning*, 10 Hare, App. xx.; *Clarke* v. *Law*, 2 K. & J. 28 ;
Lloyd v. *Whitty*, 19 Beav. 57 ; *Nicholls* v. *Ibbetson*, 7 W. R. 430 ; *Edwards* v.
Spraight, 2 J. & H. 617 ; *Singer Sewing Machine Co.* v. *Wilson*, 2 H. & M.
584; Dan. Ch. Pr. 4th ed. 822.
(b) 15 & 16 Vict. c. 86, s. 40.
(c) *Wightman* v. *Wheelton*, 23 Beav. 397; 3 Jur. (N.S.) 124.
(d) *Carter* v. *Pinto Leite*, 20 W. R. 134.

fails, or if at the hearing there is nothing on which an injunction can operate (a), or in respect of acts unattended with profits (b). The rule applies even although it may appear that since the notice for an interim injunction the defendant has sold articles which the court would, upon that application, have restrained him from selling, had the facts and the law been at that time sufficiently ascertained (c).

To what account limited.

It is not necessary specifically to ask for an account, for it may be ordered under the prayer for general relief. The accounts may have reference to past as well as future sales and may be ascertained from affidavits made by or on behalf of the defendants (d).

The account is limited to the nett profits actually made and the moneys actually received by the wrongdoer (e).

It was held in an American case (f) that commissions on the sale of a pirated work, received by a bookseller from the publisher of it, were profits which the bookseller must account for to the proprietor of the copyright, where a decree for an account had been made. Curtis, J., in the case referred to, said : "If the proprietor will waive his action for damages, he may have an account of profits, upon the ground that the defendant has, by dealing with his property made gains which equitably belong to the complainant, and I perceive no sound reason for restricting those gains to the difference between the cost and the sale price of the map or book, or limiting the right to an account to those persons who have sold the work solely on their own account. He who sells on commission does in truth sell on his own account, so far as he is entitled to a percentage on the amount of the sales. What he so

(a) *Baily* v. *Taylor*, 1 R. & M. 73; *Price's Patent Candle Co.* v. *Bauwen's Candle Co.*, 4 K. & J. 727; see *Garth* v. *Cotton*, 3 Atk. 751; 1 Ves. 524. 546.

(b) *Lee* v. *Alston*, 1 Ves. Jun. 78; 1 Bro. C. C. 194; 3 Bro. C. C. 37; *Colburn* v. *Simms*, 2 Hare, 560; *Powell* v. *Aikin*, 4 K. & J. 343, 351.

(c) *Price's Patent Candle Co.* v. *Bauwen's Candle Co.*, *supra*.

(d) *Pike* v. *Nicholas*, 20 L. T. (N.S.) 909; *Kelly* v. *Hodge*, 29 L. T. (N.S.) 387.

(e) *Delf* v. *Delamotte*, 3 K. & J. 581; 3 Jur. (N.S.) 933.

(f) *Stevens* v. *Gladding*, 2 Curt. (Amer.) 608.

receives is the gross profit coming to him from the proceeds of the sales, and what he so receives, diminishes the net profit of the one who employs him to sell. That part of the profits of the sales, being in the hands of the commission merchant, the consignor is not accountable for them. But why should not the commission merchant, who has them, account for them? He was liable to an action for damages for selling. That right is waived. I think he should pay over to the proprietor in lieu of damages, the gain he has made from the sales. It does not seem to me that the term 'profits' necessarily, or, when construed in reference to the subject matter, properly has so restricted a meaning as to exclude commissions received from the proceeds of sales of the property of the complainant."

If the account is small it is usually waived (a), and if the defendant submits, the suit does not proceed to the hearing, but a decretal order is made, giving effect to the agreement between the parties. The defendant must, if required to do so for the purpose of the account or the inquiry as to damages, set out the price and profit and names of the purchasers of the pirated articles (b); and the plaintiff is entitled to continue the suit, until the discovery is given (c).

If the account small, usually waived.

A person whose copyright has been infringed is not bound to rest satisfied with the promise of the defendant not to commit any further infringement, but he has a right to have an injunction (d), and is entitled to the costs of such injunction (e).

Points as to costs.

If the defendant do not offer to submit to the injunction and pay all the costs up to that time (f), or if,

---

(a) See *Fradella* v. *Weller*, 2 R. & M. 247.
(b) *Stevens* v. *Brett*, 12 W. R. 572; and with regard to patents, *Howe* v. *M'Kernan*, 30 Beav. 547; see *Delarue* v. *Dickenson*, 3 K. & J. 388.
(c) See *Colburn* v. *Simms*, 2 Hare, 543; *Kelly* v. *Hooper*, 1 Y. & C. C. C. 197.
(d) *Geary* v. *Norton*, 1 De G. & Sm. 9; *Losh* v. *Hague*, 1 Webs. 200; 2 Coo. C. C. 59, n.
(e) *Geary* v. *Norton*, *supra*.
(f) *Potts* v. *Levy*, 2 Drew. 272.

although he offer to submit to the injunction, he refuse
to pay the costs or to give the plaintiff any of the other
relief to which he is entitled, the plaintiff is entitled to
bring the suit to a hearing, and will have the costs of the
suit (a). But if the defendant offer to submit to the
injunction with costs, and to give the plaintiff all the other
relief to which he may be under the circumstances entitled, and no account is sought, or the account is waived,
the court, though it may give judgment in the plaintiff's
favour, will not give him the costs of the subsequent
prosecution of the suit up to the hearing (b).

The tender must include the costs of the suit up to the
time when the tender is made (c). If both parties are in
the wrong, the one claiming more than he is entitled to
claim, and the other offering less than he was bound to
offer, costs will not be given to either side (d).

A *bonâ fide* offer from the defendants before suit to give
the plaintiff all the relief to which he is entitled, and
which he ultimately obtains by the suit, may be a reason,
as we have seen, for depriving him of the costs of it (e);
but in *Edelsten* v. *Edelsten* (f), however, Lord Westbury
said he could not take notice of negotiations antecedent
to the suit, save in case of bad faith, unless they amounted
to a release or binding agreement with respect to the cause
of action. A man, however, whose legal right has been

(a) *Fradella* v. *Weller*, 2 R. & M. 247 ; *Geary* v. *Norton*, 1 De G. & Sm.
12 ; *Kelly* v. *Hooper*, 1 Y. & C. C. C. 197 ; *Colburn* v. *Simms*, 2 Hare, 561 ;
Jamieson v. *Teague*, 3 Jur. (N.S.) 1206 ; *Chappell* v. *Davidson*. 2 K. & J.
123 ; *Burgess* v. *Hill*, 26 Beav. 244 ; *Burgess* v. *Hately*, Ib. 249 ; *M'Andrew* v.
Bassett, 33 L. J. (Ch.) 561.

(b) *Millington* v. *Fox*, 3 M. & C. 352 ; *Colburn* v. *Simms, supra ; Nunn* v.
d'Albuquerque, 34 Beav. 595 ; *Harvey* v. *Ferguson*, 15 Ir. Ch. 277 ; *Hudson* v.
Bennett, 12 Jur. (N.S.) 519.

(c) *Fradella* v. *Weller, supra ; Geary* v. *Norton, supra ; Jamieson* v.
Teague, supra ; Burgess v. *Hill, supra ; Remnant* v. *Hood*, 27 Beav. 74 ;
Moet v. *Couston*, 33 Beav. 578.

(d) *Moet* v. *Couston, supra ;* see *Rochdale Canal Co.* v. *King*, 16 Beav.
630 ; *Pearce* v. *Wycombe Railway Co.*, 17 Jur. 660 ; *Ainsworth* v. *Walmerley*,
L. R. 1 Eq. 518.

(e) *Millington* v. *Fox, supra ; Colburn* v. *Simms, supra ; Chappell* v.
Davidson, supra ; Williams v. *Thomas*, 2 D. & Sm. 29, 37 ; see *Woodman* v.
Robinson, 2 Sim. (N.S) 204 ; *Nesbitt* v. *Berridge*, 32 Beav. 282.

(f) 1 D. J. & S. 185, 203.

invaded is under no obligation to make an application to the defendant before filing his bill for an injunction (a). The costs of the suit are often disposed of on an interlocutory application before judgment (b).

In a case where the plaintiff after the hearing, but before judgment was delivered, became bankrupt, the bill was dismissed, but on the defendant moving that the plaintiff might be ordered personally to pay the costs, Wood, V.C., refused to make any order, and his decision was upheld on appeal (c).

By the 21 & 22 Vict. c. 27, s. 2, the Court of Chancery was empowered to assess and award damages either in lieu of, or in addition to, an injunction (d), and it has this jurisdiction under the new judicial system.

The rule laid down for estimating the damages sustained by a plaintiff in a case of piracy was thus laid down by James, V.C., "The defendant is to account for every copy of his book sold, as if it had been a copy of the plaintiff's, and to pay the plaintiff the profit which he would have received from the sale of so many additional copies" (e).

We will conclude this subject with the words of Sir William D. Evans: "It is clear," says he, in the second volume of his 'Statutes' (f), "that the proceeding by injunction is the most ready and effectual remedy which can be resorted to on the part of the plaintiff, but that a great degree of caution in the application of that proceeding, in the first instance, is requisite for preventing injustice to the defendant, whose loss does not, from the nature of it, admit of reparation if the injunction should, upon further investigation, be found to have been erroneously applied; and the judges of courts of equity have in many cases expressed a strong sense of the importance of this principle."

(a) *Burgess* v. *Hill*, 26 Beav. 244; *Burgess* v. *Hateley*, *Ib.* 249.
(b) Morg. & Dav. on Costs, 47–62.
(c) *Boucicault* v. *Delafield*, 10 Jur. (N.S.) 1063.
(d) *Tinsley* v. *Lacy*, 1 H. & M. 747; *Johnson* v. *Wyatt*, 2 De G. J. & S. 18; *Pike* v. *Nicholas*, L. R. 5 Ch. 260; *Cox* v. *Land and Water Journal Co.*, L. R. 9 Eq. 324: *Smith* v. *Chatto*, 31 L. T. (N.S.) 775.
(e) *Pike* v. *Nicholas*, *supra*.   (f) Part iii. class 1, note 29.

T

CHAPTER IX.

CROWN COPYRIGHT.

Prerogative copyright.

THE prerogative copyrights of the Crown constitute a peculiar branch of literary property which has given rise to much controversy.

The sovereign's prerogative in granting letters patent for the privilege of printing prerogative copies, as they are called, is said to embrace the English translation of the Bible, the Book of Common Prayer, the statutes, almanacs, and the Latin grammar.

The validity of this privilege has been questioned on the ground that grants of this exclusive nature tend to a monopoly. They contribute forcibly to enhance the prices of books, to restrain free trade, to discourage industry, and by discountenancing competition they serve to render the patentees careless and remiss in their duty. Notwithstanding, it must be admitted that the sovereign has a peculiar prerogative in printing, which has been vindicated, allowed, and maintained ever since the introduction of printing.

Nature of the right.

The right is said to be founded on grounds of public policy. Lord Mansfield considered it as merely a modification of the general and common right of literary property ; and from the cases which had been decided in favour of the particular copies, he inferred, as a necessary consequence, the existence of the general right. They rested upon property arising from the king's right of original publication. The copy of the Hebrew Bible, of the Greek Testament, or of the Septuagint, did not belong to the king,—it was common ; but the English translation he bought, and therefore it was concluded to be his property.

Printing, on its first introduction, was considered, as well in England as in other countries, to be a matter of state. The quick and extensive circulation of sentiments and opinions which that invaluable art produced could not but fall under the grip of government, whose strength was to some extent based upon the ignorance of the people governed. The press was, therefore, wholly under the coercion of the Crown, and all printing, not only of public books, containing ordinances, religious or civil, but of every species of publication whatsoever, was regulated by the king's proclamations, prohibitions, charters of privilege, and, finally, by the decrees of the Star Chamber. After the demolition of that odious jurisdiction (a), the Long Parliament, on its rupture with Charles I., assumed the power which had previously existed solely in the Crown. After the Restoration, the same restrictions were re-enacted and re-annexed to the prerogative by the statute 13 & 14 Car. 2, and continued down, by subsequent Acts, until after the Revolution. The expiration of these disgraceful statutes, by the refusal of Parliament to continue them any longer, formed the great era of the liberty of the press in this country, and stripped the Crown of every prerogative over it, except that which, upon just and rational principles of government, must ever belong to the executive magistrate in all countries, namely, the exclusive right to publish religious or civil constitutions, in a word, to promulgate every ordinance by which the subject is to live and be governed. These always did belong, and from the very nature of civil government always ought to belong, to the sovereign, and hence have gained the title of "prerogative copies" (b).

(a) " Where change of fav'rites made no change of laws,
　　And senates heard before they judged a cause "(?)—JOHN.
(b) Lord Erskine's Speeches, vol. i. p. 40, by Ridgway.

The Bible and Book of Common Prayer (a).

The Bible and Common Prayer Book.　For two hundred years and more the kings have in England granted patents to their printers (b). From the time of Henry VIII. have different persons enjoyed, by letters patent, the privilege of printing prerogative copies to the exclusion of all other persons.

These patents have, from time to time, come under the consideration of the courts, and the judges have been invited to settle their limits. Many have given it as their opinion, that the prerogative is founded on the circumstance of the translation of the Bible having been actually paid for by King James, and its having thus become the property of the Crown (c). Others have referred it to the circumstance of the king of England being the supreme head of the Church of England, and have invested him with the prerogative in virtue of that character. This latter argument, Mr. Godson (d) contends, destroys the proposition it is adduced to support; for, if the sovereign *as head of the church*, has the exclusive right of printing *all books* of Divine service, why not, as head of the church have a right to print the principal book used in the Divine service—*the Bible*—and all kinds of Bibles, in whatever language they may be written? And yet the principle of *property* is resorted to for the right of printing the present edition of the Bible; and Lord Mansfield has declared that there is no prerogative right to the Bible in the original languages (e).

Others again have been of opinion that it is to be referred to another consideration, namely, to the character of the duty imposed upon the chief executive officers of

(a) See *Mayo* v. *Hill*, cited 2 Show. 260; *King's Printer* v. *Bell*, Mor. Dict. of Dec. 19–20, p. 8316; Chitty's Prerogative of the Crown, ch. xi. s. 3.

(b) The letters patent conferring the office of King's Printer (Scotland) bear that he shall have " solum et unicum privilegium imprimendi in Scotia Biblia Sacra, Nova Testamenta, Psalmorum libros, et libros Precum communium, Confessiones Fidei, Majores et Minores Catechismos, in lingua Anglicana."

(c) *Nullum tempus occurrit regi. Rex nunquam moritur.*

(d) ' Patents and Copyrights,' p. 437.

(e) 4 Burr. 2405, cited Godson's Pat. and Copy. 437.

.the government, to superintend the publication of the acts
of the legislature and acts of state of that description ; and
also of those works upon which the established doctrines
of our religion are founded, that it is a duty imposed upon
the first executive magistrate, carrying with it a corresponding prerogative.   That was the opinion of Lord
Camden as expressed in the case of *Donaldson* v. *Becket,* and
of Chief Baron Skinner in *Eyre and Strahan* v. *Carnan* (*a*).

No attempt has ever been made to prevent any person
from publishing a translation of one book, or of a part of
the Bible, from the original text, and enjoying a copyright
in his production.   And, with respect both to Acts of
Parliament and Bibles, any one is at liberty to print them
with notes.

Mr. Reeves, one of the royal patentees, and the writer
of several learned juridical publications, in the preface to
his edition of the Bible (divided into sections), observes,
that all the authorized Bibles published by the king's
printer and the universities are wholly without explanatory
notes.   These privileged persons have confined themselves
to printing the bare text, in which they have an exclusive
right, forbearing to publish it with notes, which it is
deemed may be done by any of the king's subjects as well
as themselves.   He subjoins to this passage a note in the
following terms : " I mean such notes as are *bonâ fide*
intended for annotations, not the pretence of notes which
I have seen in some editions of the Bible and Common
Prayer Book, placed there merely as a cover to the piracy of
printing upon the patentees, as if fraud could make legal
anything that was in itself illegal.   In some of these
editions the notes are placed purposely to be cut off by
the binder " (*b*).

In *Grierson* v. *Jackson* (*c*), upon an application for an View taken in
injunction against printing an edition of a Bible in numbers Ireland.
with prints and notes, Lord Clare, as Chancellor of Ireland,

(*a*) Exchequer, 1781, cited 6 Ves. 697, and reported at length in 6 Bac.
Abr., tit., Prerog. 509.
(*b*) 2 Evans' 'Statutes,' 2nd Ed. p. 19.
(*c*) Irish T. R. 304.

asked if the validity of the patent had ever been established at law, and said he did not know that the Crown had a right to grant a monopoly of that kind. In the course of the discussion he made the following observations: "I can conceive that the king, as head of the church, may say that there shall be but one man who shall print Bibles and Books of Common Prayer for the use of churches and other particular purposes, but I cannot conceive that the king has any prerogative to grant a monopoly as to Bibles for the instruction of mankind in the revealed religion; if he had, it would be in the power of the patentee to put what price he pleased upon the book, and thus prevent the instruction of men in the Christian religion. If ever there was a time which called aloud for the dissemination of religious knowledge, it is this, and therefore I should with great reluctance decide in favour of such a monopoly as this, which must necessarily confine the circulation of the book."

View taken in England. This has not been the view taken of the subject in England, for in the case of the *Universities of Oxford and Cambridge* v. *Richardson* (a), an injunction upon motion was granted against the king's printer in Scotland, who had a patent for the sale of Bibles, printing or selling them in England, upon the ground that possession, under colour of title, was sufficient to injoin and to continue the injunction till it was proved at law that it was only colour and not real title. In the course of the case it appeared that, in the year 1718, Sir Joseph Jekyll, as Master of the Rolls, had granted an injunction in a similar case, which was supported on appeal before the Lord Chancellor; and also, that a decree of the Court of Session had, in the year 1717, been reversed by the House of Lords in favour of the right of the king's printer in England, confining the right of the Scotch printer to Scotland. With respect to the precedent of the injunction, it is clear that there had been abundance of injunctions before upon private copyright, until the claim was finally put an end to by the decree of

(a) 6 Ves. 689. See *Manners* v. *Blair*, 3 Bli. R. (N.S.) 391.

the Lords; and questions between rival patentees were not the most probable method of bringing into fair discussion the general rights of the subject to resist the claim of prerogative, root and branch (a). The Lord Chancellor, in his judgment, said, " My opinion is, that the public interest may be looked to upon a subject, the communication of which to the public in an authentic shape, if a matter of right, is also a matter of duty in the Crown, which are commensurate. It is not accurate to say, these privileges are not granted for the sake of unlimited sale, and for the sake of the universities, &c. They are, to a certain degree, like all other offices, calculated for that sort of advantage which will secure to the public the due execution of the duty; upon this principle proceed all the branches of our constitution, (which does not adopt the wild theories that require the execution of a duty without a due compensation,) that the duty is well secured in one way by giving a responsibility, in point of means, to the person to execute it. The reasoning which affects to depreciate monopoly, will perhaps tend to create it." There certainly is no great risk that false copies of the Bible would get into general circulation by an unlimited right of printing them. We do not find it materially the case in other works; and there are very few persons indeed who would admit that the beneficial circulation of any commodity in general, or of these writings in particular, can be promoted by means of an exclusive monopoly; and the principal object, both of the right and the duty, with respect to the particular subject, appears to be the benefit arising to the privileged individuals (b).

The question was afterwards brought before the House of Lords, and the injunction against the Scotch printer continued.

The Universities of Oxford and Cambridge and the queen's printer long exercised this monopoly, under patents from the Crown, but the claim has not been very rigidly

(a) 2 Evans' 'Statutes,' 2nd ed. p. 17.
(b) 2 Evans' 'Statutes,' 2nd ed. p. 18.

enforced. The patent granted to the queen's printer expired a short time back, and it was recommended by a committee of the House of Commons that the exclusive privilege of publishing the sacred volume should not be renewed. The House, however, took no action on this recommendation, and the Crown renewed the patent during pleasure.

Acts of Parliament and Matters of State.

The right in state documents.

The exclusive right of printing Acts of Parliament has been regarded somewhat more favourably than the other branches of the royal prerogative in question. Upon what ground, however, it is in some degree difficult to discover. Lord Clare, while negativing the prerogative in the matter of the Bible, said he could well conceive that the king should have a power to grant a patent to print the statute books, because it was necessary that they should be correctly printed, and because the copy can only be had from the rolls of Parliament, which are within the authority of the Crown.

There was no king's printer by patent till the reign of Edward VI., who, in 1547, granted one to Grafton.

The right seemed to have been in effect recognised and established in the case of *Millar* v. *Taylor* (a), by the unanimous opinion of the judges, though they differed respecting the origin of it. This is certain respecting its origin, that it has ever been a trust reposed in the king, as executive magistrate, to promulgate to the people all those civil ordinances which are to be the rule of their civil obedience. There are traces of the ancient mode of promulgating the ordinances of the state yet remaining to us, suited to the gloominess of the times when few who heard them could have read them ; the king's officers transmitted authentic copies of them to the sheriffs, who caused them to be publicly read in their county court (b). When the

(a) 4 Burr. 2303.
(b) The statute itself was drawn with the aid of the judges and other grave and learned men, and was entered on a roll called the 'Statute Roll.' The tenor of it was afterwards transcribed into parchment, and annexed to the proclamation-writ, directed to the sheriff of every county in England,

demand for authentic copies began to increase, and when the introduction of printing facilitated the multiplication of copies, the people were supplied with them by the king's patentee. From such source they were far more likely to be correct and accurate than if obtained from those unable to resort to the fountain head; and our courts of justice appear to have so considered, when they established it as a rule of evidence, that Acts of Parliament printed by the king's printer should be deemed authentic, and received in evidence as such.

The patent was to print " all law books that concern the common or statute law." The first case on the subject arose between Atkyns, the law-patentee, and some members of the Stationers' Company. The plaintiff claimed under the letters patent. The defendants had printed ' Rolle's Abridgment.' The bill was brought for an injunction, and the Lord Chancellor issued one against every member of the company. The defendants appealed to the House of Lords, but the decree was affirmed.

It was argued that printing was a power of the Crown, acquired by Henry VI. by purchase, the first printer established in England having been brought to Oxford, by Archbishop Bourchier, at that king's expense! (a)

Perhaps the most important case on this head is that of *Roper* v. *Streater* (b), decided in 1672, the facts of which were these :—Roper bought of the executors of Justice Croke the third part of his reports, which he printed; Colonel Streater had a grant for years from the Crown for printing all law books, and he reprinted Roper's work without permission; on which Roper brought an action under the Licensing Act. Streater pleaded the king's grant, and on demurrer it was adjudged for the plaintiff against

---

and commandment given him, that he should not only proclaim it through his whole bailiwick, but see that it was firmly observed and kept; and the usage was, to proclaim it at his county court, and there to keep the transcript, that whoso would might read or take a copy of it.—Dwarris on Stat. p. 16; 4 Inst. cap. 1.

(a) *Atkyns's Case,* Carter, 89; 1 Bl. 113; 6 Bac. Abr. 507; 10 Mod. 105.
(b) Skin. 234. See 1 Mod. 257; 2 Show. 260; 10 Mod. 105.

the validity of the patent, on these grounds ; that the
patent tended to a monopoly ; that it was of a large extent ;
that printing was a handicraft trade, and no more to be
restrained than other trades; that it was difficult to
ascertain what should be called a law book ; that the words
in the patent "touching or concerning the common or
statute law," were loose and uncertain ; that if this were to
be considered as an office, the grant for years could not be
good, as it would go to executors and administrators : and
that there was no adequate remedy in the way of redress
in case of abuses by unskilfulness, selling dear, printing ill,
&c. This judgment, however, was reversed on a writ of
error in Parliament, for the following reasons : that the
invention of printing was new ; that this privilege had
been always allowed, which was a strong argument in its
favour, although it could not be said to amount to a prescription, as printing was introduced within time of
memory ; that it concerned the state, and was matter of
public care ; that it was in the nature of a proclamation,
which none but the king could make ; that the king had
the making of judges, serjeants, and officers of the law ;
that as to the uncertainty, these words in the patent were
to be taken *secundum subjectam materiam,* and not to be
extended to a book containing a quotation of law but
where the principal design was to treat on that subject ;
that as to its being an office, it was not so properly an
office as an employment, which may well enough be
managed by executors or administrators ; and that as to
abuses, these, like all others, were punishable at common
law, or the patent itself might be repealed by *sci. fac. (a).*

In the case of *Baskett* v. *The University of Cambridge (b)*
the prerogative right of printing Acts of Parliament was
sanctioned by a decision of the Court of King's Bench.
That case arose upon a bill filed by the plaintiffs for an
injunction to restrain the defendants from printing and

(a) 3 Mod. 77 ; 6 Bac. Abr. 507.
(b) 1 W. Bl. 105 ; 2 Burr. 661 ; see 2 Bla. Com. 416 ; and 5 Bac. Abr.
tit. Pre. F. 5.

selling a book entitled 'An Exact Abridgment of all the CAP. IX. Acts of Parliament relating to the Excise on Beer, &c.' Both parties claimed under letters patent from the Crown ; the plaintiffs as the king's printers. The court were of opinion that during the term granted by the letters patent to the plaintiffs, they were entitled to the right of printing Acts of Parliament and abridgments of Acts of Parliament, exclusive of all other persons not authorized to print the same by prior grants from the Crown; but they thought that by the letters patent granted to the university, it was entrusted with a concurrent authority to print Acts of Parliament and abridgments of Acts, within the university, upon the terms contained in those letters patent.

Soon after the Restoration an Act of Parliament having prohibited the printing of law books without the license of the lord chancellor, the two chief justices, and the chief baron, it became the practice to prefix such a licence to all reports published after that period, in which it was usual for the rest of the judges to concur, and to add to the *imprimatur* a testimonial of the great judgment and learning of the author. This Act was renewed from time to time, but finally expired in the reign of the third William. The form of licence and testimonial, however, was continued till the reign of George II., when the judges seemed to have arrived at the determination not to grant any more of them (*a*). Sir James Burrow offers an apology for publishing his reports without an *imprimatur* (*b*).

Though a court of justice appears to have the sole As to the publication of proceedings in courts of justice. power of authenticating the publication of its own proceedings, it does not necessarily follow that it has an exclusive right of publication.

Since the Year-Books, it seems that no judicial proceedings, with the exception of state trials, have been published under authoritative care and inspection, either by the House of Lords or by any court of judicature.

(*a*) Pref. to Dougl. R. (*b*) Burr. R. Pref. viii..

In *Sayer's Case* (a) the judges of the Court of Queen's Bench directed, and in part revised, a report of the trial. The trial of Lord Melville (b) was likewise published by order of the Lords; and the person appointed for that purpose by the Lord Chancellor obtained an injunction against a bookseller for publishing another report of the case. *Manley* v. *Owen* (c) recognises the exclusive right of the Lord Mayor of London, as head of the commission, to appoint a person to print the sessions papers of the Old Bailey. Formerly, it was held to be a contempt of court to publish any reports whatever, but the practical application of this doctrine was soon relaxed, and publication is now only treated as a contempt in those cases in which the report is published in opposition to an order of the court.

When publication during trial prohibited.

Publication during the course of a trial will be prohibited, when the publication would have a tendency to interfere with a fair and impartial decision; on this principle Lord Abbott, C.J., sitting at the Old Bailey, acted on the indictment of Thistlewood and others for high treason in the year 1820 (d). The prohibition was infringed by the proprietor of the 'Observer' newspaper, and the proprietor was fined 500l. for contempt of court. He appealed subsequently to the Queen's Bench, on which occasion Holroyd, J., in refusing to make absolute a rule *nisi* obtained, said: "This was an order made in a proceeding over which the court had judicial cognizance; the subject matter respecting which it was made was then in the course of judicature before them. The object for which it was made was already, as it appears to me, one within their jurisdiction, viz., the furtherance of justice in proceedings then pending before the court; and it was made to remain in force so long, and so long only, as those proceedings should be pending before them. Now, I take

(a) 16 How. St. Tr. 93; 8 Parl. Hist. 54.
(b) 29 How. St. Tr. 549. See *Bathurst* v. *Kearsley*, cited *Gurney* v. *Longman*, 13 Ves. 493, 509.
(c) Cited *Millar* v. *Taylor*, 4 Burr. 2329. See 13 Ves. 493; *Stockdale* v. *Hansard*, 9 Ad. & E. 1, 97.
(d) *Reg.* v. *Clement*, 4 Barn. & Ald. 218; see also *Tichborne* v. *Mostyn*, L. R. 7 Eq. 55, note.

it to be clear that a court of record has a right to make orders for regulating their proceedings and for the furtherance of justice in the proceedings before them, which are to continue in force during the time that such proceedings are pending. It appears to me, that the arguments as to a further power of continuing such orders in force for a longer period, do not apply. It is sufficient for the present case, that the court have that power during the pendency of the proceedings. This order was made to delay publication only so long as it was necessary for the purposes of justice, leaving every person at liberty to publish the report of the proceedings subsequently to their termination. I am therefore of opinion, that this was an order which the court had the power to make.'

A criminal information will lie for publishing an *ex parte* statement of the proceedings upon a coroner's inquest, accompanied with comments, although the statement be correct, and the party has no malicious motive in the publication. Mr. Justice Bayley on one occasion observed that it was a matter of great criminality ; for the inquest before the coroner leads to a second inquiry, in which the conduct of the accused is to be considered by persons who ought to have formed no previous judgment in the case. A jury who are afterwards to sit upon the trial ought not to have *ex parte* accounts previously laid before them ; they ought to decide solely upon the evidence which they hear upon the trial (*a*).

Publication of ex parte statements upon a coroner's inquest.

No prerogative claim to the exclusive publication of judicial proceedings has now been asserted for very many years, and in *Butterworth* v. *Robinson* (*b*), and *Saunders* v. *Smith* (*c*), individuals were treated as authors and proprietors of copyright in law reports (*d*).

(*a*) *Rex* v. *Fleet*, 1 Barn. & Ald. 379, 384. See *Tichborne* v. *Tichborne*, 15 W. R. 1072 ; 17 L. T. (N.S.) 5. As to staying reports of cases as libellous or unfair, see *Brooke* v. *Evans*, 6 Jur. (N.S.) 1025 ; *Coleman* v. *W. Hartlepool Railway*, 8 W. R. 734.

(*b*) 5 Ves. 709.

(*c*) 3 My. & Cr. 711, and *Vesey* v. *Sweet*, cited 5 Ves. 709, note 3.

(*d*) Phillips on Copy. 196. See *Wheaton* v. *Peters*, 8 Peters R. (Amer.) 591, 668, and remarks of Story, J., in *Gray* v. *Russell*, 1 Story, R. (Amer.) 4.

It is clear, however, that no individual can claim any copyright in the opinions or judgments of the judges, for though there is no express decision as to copyright in judicial decisions, yet it is obvious that the reporter who merely gives a copy of what he has taken down, probably *verbatim,* from the lips of the judge can claim no exclusive right to such decision.

It seems clear that if *bonâ fide* notes accompany statutes printed by others than those having the patent right, the copyright of the latter is not infringed, but the notes must be *bonâ fide,* and not merely colourable or collusive (*a*).

Almanacs.

As to the right in almanacs.   The origin of this absurd claim is put upon still more ridiculous grounds. Property in almanacs is said to be the king's: 1st, because derelict; 2nd, because they regulate the feasts of the church (*b*).

On the 8th of March, 1615, the king by letters patent granted to the Stationers' Company and their successors for ever (*inter alia*) exclusive power and licence to print, or cause to be printed, "all manner of almanacs and prognostications whatsoever in the English tongue, and all manner of books and pamphlets tending to the same purpose, and which are not be taken and construed other than almanacs or pronostications being allowed by the Archbishop of Canterbury and the Bishop of London, or one of them for the time being."

In an action of debt by the *Company of Stationers against Seymour* (*c*), for printing 'Gadbury's Almanac,' it was adjudged that the letters patent granted to the company for the sole printing of almanacs were valid: and though the jury found that the almanac so printed contained some additions, yet having likewise found that the said almanac had all the essential parts of the almanac

(*a*) *Baskett* v. *Cunningham,* 1 W. Bl. 370.
(*b*) 2 Show. 258; *Stationers' Co.* v. *Wright,* 2 Ch. Cas. 76.
(*c*) 1 Mod. 256.

that was printed before the Book of Common Prayer, the
additions were regarded as immaterial.

So also was an injunction granted against Lee (a), on
the application of the Stationers' Company, to restrain
him from selling "primers, psalters, *almanacs*, and
singing psalms, imported from Holland," the sole
privilege of printing these belonging to that company;
and that without any trial directed as to the validity of
the patent. Notwithstanding the above decisions, the
prerogative right to the printing of almanacs was strongly
protested against in the case of the *Stationers' Company* v.
Partridge (b). No judgment, indeed, was given in that
case, but it stood over that the company might see if they
could make it like the case of the Common Prayer Book,
—whether they could shew that the right of the Crown had
any foundation in property; and it was never referred
to again.

In a subsequent case, that of the *Stationers' Company* v.
Carnan (c), the right was successfully combated, and judgment given in favour of the defendant. An account of
these various phases of legal doubt and indecision is
succinctly given by Lord Erskine in *Gurney* v. *Longman* (d): "It appears in the case of *Millar* v. *Taylor* that
the Crown had been in the constant course of granting
the right of printing almanacs; and at last King
James II. granted that right by charter to the Stationers'
Company and the two universities, and for a century
they kept up that monopoly by the effect of prosecutions.
At length Carnan, an obstinate man, insisted upon printing them. An injunction was applied for in the Court of
Exchequer, and was granted to the hearing; but at the
hearing, the Court of Exchequer directed the question to
be put to the Court of Common Pleas, whether the king
had a right to grant the publication of almanacs, as not

(a) 2 Ch. Ca. 76, 93; 2 Show. 258; *Stationers' Co.* v. *Wright*, Skin. 234;
4 Burr. 2328.
(b) 10 Mod. 105, cited 2 Bro. P. C. 137.
(c) 2 Wm. Bl. 1004.
(d) 13 Ves. 508.

falling within the scope of the necessity or expediency, the foundation of prerogative copies. It was twice argued in the Court of Common Pleas; and the answer returned by that court to the Court of Exchequer was, that the charter was void, and almanacs were not prerogative copies. The injunction was accordingly dissolved, that usurpation having gone on for a century; and the House of Commons threw out a bill, brought in for the purpose of vesting that right in the Stationers' Company."

In consequence of this decision, an Act was passed, which, after reciting, that the power of granting a liberty to print almanacs and other books was theretofore supposed to be an inherent right in the Crown, and that the Crown had, by different charters under the great seal, granted to the universities of Oxford and Cambridge, among other things, the privilege of printing almanacs; and that the universities had demised to the Company of Stationers their privileges of printing and vending almanacs and calendars, and had received an annual sum of £1000 and upwards as a consideration for such privilege, and that the money so received by them had been laid out and expended in promoting different branches of literature and science, to the great increase of religion and learning and the general benefit and advantage of these realms; and that the privilege or right of printing almanacs had been, by a late decision at law, found to have been a common right, over which the Crown had no control, and consequently the universities no power to demise the same to any particular person or body of men, whereby the payments so made to them by the Company of Stationers had ceased and been discontinued, enacted that £500 a year should be paid to each of the universities, out of the moneys arising from the duties upon almanacs (a).

Any person may now make the calculations usually published in almanacs, and claim a copyright therein.

A power was given by Act of Parliament to certain

(a) 21 Geo. 3, c. 56, s. 10.

commissioners, to publish a 'Nautical Almanac, or Astro-
nomical Ephemeris,' and to *license* some one to print it.
Any other person printing, publishing, or vending it, subjects himself to a penalty. The 'Nautical Almanac' is
now, however, placed under the control of the Lords of the
Admiralty, and the penalty is increased to £20 with costs
of suit, to be paid and applied to the use of the Royal
Hospital for Seamen at Greenwich (*a*).

The claim to the prerogative right in 'Lilly's Latin
Grammar' was founded on an allegation that the work
had been originally written and composed at the king's
expense. Mr. Justice Yates observed in *Millar* v. *Taylor*
that the expense of printing prerogative books was " in
fact no private disbursement of the king, but done at the
public charge, and formed part of the expense of government." How, then, could they be his private property,
like private property claimed by an author in his own
compositions ? (*b*) The claim has long been abandoned.

(*a*) 9 Geo. 4, c. 66.
(*b*) See *Stationers' Co.* v. *Partridge,* 4 Burr. 2339, 2382, 2402; 10 Mod.
105; *Nicol* v. *Stockdale,* 3 Swans. 687.

CHAPTER X.

UNIVERSITY AND COLLEGE COPYRIGHT.

Copyright at the universities and colleges.

UPON the introduction of the art of printing into England by Henry VI. a press was set up at Oxford; and an important dominion over the publication of books was, for many years, very naturally assumed by that learned body. The sway was extended to the sister university, and increased in power by charters and grants conferred upon them by the liberality and bounty of several kings.

Immediately after, and in consequence of, the decision in *Donaldson* v. *Becket* (a), the universities hastened to Parliament, and in the same year obtained an Act (b) for enabling the two universities in England, the four universities in Scotland, and the several colleges of Eton, Westminster, and Winchester, to hold in perpetuity their copyright in books given or bequeathed to them for the advancement of useful learning and other purposes of education.

The right exists in all such books as had, before the year 1775, or have since, been given or bequeathed by the authors of the same, or their representatives, to or in trust for those universities, or any college or house of learning within them, or to or in trust for the colleges of Eton, Westminster, and Winchester, or any of them, for the beneficial purpose of education within them or any of them.

The exception in favour of the universities and colleges is to extend only to their own books, so long as they are

(a) 4 Burr. 2408.   (b) 15 Geo. 3, c. 53.

printed at the college press and for their sole benefit; and Cap. X.
any delegation of the right works a forfeiture, and the
privilege becomes of no effect.

A power is given to the universities to sell or dispose As to their
registration
and sale.
of the copyrights given or bequeathed to them, but if they
delegate, grant, lease, or sell the copyright of any book, or
allow any person to print it, their privilege ceases to exist.
The copyright of any work presented to the universities
must be registered at Stationers' Hall within two months
after any such gift shall come to the knowledge of the
officers of the universities.

The register book may be inspected without fee, and Registration.
the clerk is to give a certificate of any entry on payment
of a fee not exceeding sixpence.   If the clerk refuse to
make entry or give certificates of entries, the university or
college which owns the copyright (notice being first given
of such refusal by an advertisement in the *Gazette*), is to have
the like benefit as if such entry or certificates had been
duly made and given, and the clerk who refuses is for every
offence to forfeit 20*l*. to the proprietors of the copyright.

If any one prints, reprints, or imports, or causes to be Piracy.
printed, reprinted, or imported, any such book or books, or,
knowing the same to be so printed or reprinted, sells,
publishes, or exposes to sale, or causes to be sold, published, or exposed to sale, any such book or books, he is
to forfeit the books and every sheet of them, to the
proprietor of the copyright, and one penny for every sheet
found in his custody either printed, or printing, published,
or exposed to sale, contrary to the true intent and meaning of the Act, one half to go to the Crown, the other
half to the prosecutor (*a*).

By an Act passed in the forty-first year of Geo. 3,
c. 107, a similar copyright is given to Trinity College,
Dublin.   And by the 27th section of the 5 & 6 Vict.
c. 45, the rights of the respective universities and colleges
above enumerated are saved from the operation of the
Copyright Act.

(*a*) 15 Geo. 3, c. 53, s. 2.

CAP. X.

Copyrights
at present
possessed
by the
universities.

It appears that the University of Oxford possesses six copyrights, and the University of Cambridge has none. " This fact," say the Royal Commissioners in their recent Report on Copyright, " shews that the privilege, which is by no means of recent origin, is of very little real value, and as it is undesirable to continue any special and unusual kinds of copyright, we are of opinion that this exceptional privilege should be omitted from the future law. We do not, however, think it would be right to deprive the institutions above named of the copyrights they already possess, without their consent, but should they be retained, we suggest that the universities and other institutions should be placed upon the same footing as regards protection of their copyrights as other copyright owners, and that the exceptional penalties and remedies given by the Act which was passed in the 15th year of the reign of his late Majesty King George III. should be repealed."

CHAPTER XI.

MUSICAL AND DRAMATIC COPYRIGHT.

MUSICAL compositions, when in manuscript, are protected like other literary compositions; when printed and published they are books within the meaning of the Literary Copyright Act. Musical compositions within the Literary Copyright Act.

The point whether there could be copyright in a musical composition first came before Lord Mansfield in *Bach* v. *Longman* (a). It was a case sent out of Chancery for the opinion of the Court of King's Bench: "Whether, in a composition for the harpischord, called a *sonata*, the original composer had a copyright?" The opinion given was, that the same rules of law apply both to literary and musical compositions. It was said that the words of the Act of Parliament were very extensive: "Books, or other

(a) Cowp. 623. In *D'Almaine* v. *Boosey*, 1 Y. & C. Exch. 299, Lord Abinger said: "I spent three or four days at Stationers' Hall in order to ascertain what entries were made under the Act of Parliament, and I found not only that short publications on single sheets of paper were entered as books, but also a great deal of music. There is no doubt, therefore, that printed music, in whatever form it may be published, is to be considered in reference to proceedings of this nature, as a book." Music copyrights are sometimes of great value. At a recent sale of Messrs. Hopwood and Crewe, the copyrights of that firm fetched a total of £15,000— Coote's 'Burlesque Valse,' £175 10s.; the 'Sweetly Pretty Valse,' £215; the 'Cornflower Valse,' £132; and the 'Prince Imperial Galop,' £990, the largest sum ever obtained, it is believed, for a single piece of dance music; Hobson's 'Popular Favourites for the Pianoforte' sold for £412 10s.; Buckley's song, 'Come where the Moonbeams Linger,' £157 10s.; and H. Clifton's 'Very Suspicious,' £330. Mr. Coote purchased his own 'Snowdrift Galop' for £561.

The copyright of some comic songs often fetch high prices. It was given in evidence, in a case which came before the Common Pleas Division of the High Court of Justice a short time since, that they were worth sometimes from £1000 to £2000, the comic music publisher, Henry d'Alcorn, stating that he had sold as many as 90,000 copies of the music of 'Slap Bang! Here We Are Again!' and of another song he had sold 70,000 copies.

writings," and consequently they were not confined to language and letters only. Music is a science; it may be written, and the mode of conveying the ideas is by signs and marks. If the narrow interpretation contended for were to hold (*i.e.* confined to books only), it would apply equally to mathematics, algebra, arithmetic, or hieroglyphics. The case being one sent out of Chancery, the certificate of the judge was : that a musical composition is a writing within the statute of 8 Anne, c. 19, and that of course the plaintiff was entitled to the copyright given to the author by that Act.

In *Storace* v. *Longman* (a), a " certain musical air, tune, and writing," on one sheet, was protected, and in a later case (b) a single sheet of music was held to be a book within the meaning of the statute of Anne. And where copyright was claimed under 54 Geo. 3, c. 156, in a piece of instrumental music, Chief Justice Abbott, in delivering the judgment of the King's Bench, expressed the opinion that "any composition, whether large or small, is a book within the meaning of the Act of Parliament " (c).

Now, by the interpretation clause of the 5 & 6 Vict. c. 45, the word " book," in the construction of the Act, is to mean and include " every volume, part or division of a volume, pamphlet, sheet of letterpress, *sheet of music*, map, chart, or plan separately published."

Musical compositions intended for the stage come under the head of dramatic compositions.

The man who adapts words of his own to an old air, and adds thereto a prelude and accompaniment also his own, acquires a copyright in the combination.

The 20th section of the 5 & 6 Vict. c. 45, secures the sole liberty of performing musical compositions on the same conditions and for the same term as are prescribed in the case of dramatic compositions.

Instrumental music.   This provision would seem to include and indeed to be

(a) 2 Camp. 27, note a.
(b) *Clementi* v. *Golding*, 2 Camp. 32.
(c) *White* v. *Geroch*, 2 Barn. & Ald. 298 ; see *Clayton* v. *Stone*, 2 Paine (Amer.) 383.

specially aimed at the right of playing instrumental music, for *dramatic musical* compositions were already protected by the statute of 3 & 4 Will. 4, c. 15, and are included in the definition of dramatic pieces in the statute of Victoria.

Hence the owner of a purely instrumental piece, whether written for the orchestra, organ, piano, or other instrument, has not only the copyright therein, but also the exclusive right to the performance of, or the playing of it in public. And it may be here observed that both in the case of dramatic and musical compositions the right of representation and performance is secured to the authors thereof while yet in manuscript.

In an early case, it was declared that the acting a play was not a publication of it; and by analogy, it was subsequently held, at common law, that the mere *acting* a play which had been printed and published did not constitute a piracy or an infringement of the copyright (*a*).

In the former case, the plaintiff was the author of a farce called 'Love à la Mode,' consisting of two acts, which was performed, with his permission, several times at the different London theatres in successive years, but was never printed or published by him. When the farce was over, the plaintiff used to take the copy away from the prompter, and when it was played at the benefits of particular actors he made them pay a certain sum for the performance. The defendants, who were proprietors of a magazine, called 'The Court Miscellany, or Gentleman and Lady's Magazine,' employed a shorthand writer to take down the words of the play at the theatre, and thus published the first act, giving notice that they would publish the second act in their next number. An injunction, however, was obtained on the ground that acting a play was not a publication of it (*b*).

(*a*) In equity, injunctions have been granted to stop the performance of printed dramatic works at the request of the authors of them : *Morris* v. *Harris*, *Morris* v. *Kelly*, 1 Jac. & W. 481 ; cited Godson on ' Patents and Copyrights,' 390.

(*b*) *Macklin* v. *Richardson*, Amb. 694 ; but see 5 & 6 Vict. c. 45, s. 20.

The latter case was an action on the statute of Anne, for publishing an entertainment called 'The Agreeable Surprise.' The plaintiff had purchased the copyright from O'Keefe, the author, and the only evidence of the publication by the defendant was the representation of the piece upon his stage at Richmond. It was held that there was no publication; the statute for the protection of copyright only extending to prohibit the publication of the work itself by any other than the author (a).

American law on this subject. Though the law on this point has been altered as to the English law, the American law would appear to be in accordance with the above decision. In a late case before the Superior Court of New York (b), the facts were as follows. The action was brought to obtain an injunction restraining the printing and publishing by the defendant of a drama or comedy called 'Play,' and the complaint alleged that immediately prior to February, 1868, Mr. Robertson, of London, sold to the plaintiff his exclusive right of performing the drama upon the stage, and printing and publishing the same within and throughout the United States; that the first performance of it was at the Prince of Wales Theatre, in London, but that there had been no *publication* in any other way. The defendant, however, had obtained the words of the play, &c., from persons who had seen it acted in London, and he published it in the United States before the plaintiff. This the defendant justified on the ground that the tickets admitting the spectators to the performance in London contained no notice or prohibition against carrying the comedy away, by memory or otherwise, and using, printing or publishing the same; nor was any notice to that effect posted in any of the theatres in view of the spectators. The question was, whether the performance in London was such a publication as would deprive the owner of his

(a) *Coleman* v. *Wathen*, 5 T. R. 245. Sheridan's opera of the 'Duenna' (*The Proprietors of Covent Garden* v. *Vandermere and others*) was also represented on the stage without the permission of the proprietor on similar grounds; see, however, 5 & 6 Vict. c. 45, s. 40.
(b) *Palmer* v. *Dewett*, 23 L. T. Rep. (N.S.) 823.

common law right of property in it, and the court held that it was not. Mr. Justice Monell, in his judgment, after examining the case of *Keen* v. *Clark* (a), where it has been decided that it is not unlawful for a spectator to carry away in memory and give to the world an unpublished literary production, the performance of which he had witnessed, or to the recital of which he had listened, saying: "The question of what constitutes publication is not much enlightened by any of the adjudicated cases which have come under my observation. Most of the cases involve considerations arising from copyright laws, and do not undertake to determine when or in what manner an author may be said to surrender his property in his literary work. The case most relied on by the defendant, *Boucicault* v. *Delafield* (b), arose under the English statute of copyright. That statute provides that one public representation or performance of any dramatic piece shall be deemed sufficient, in the construction of the Act, to be a publication of the work. It was accordingly held, in an action to recover a penalty imposed by the statute, that public performance of the drama in the United States, before taking out a copyright in England, was a publication within the statute. Words used in a statute to define the meaning of particular parts of it, are never extended beyond the statute, and have, therefore, no controlling effect, except in the interpretation of the statute. They define the intent and meaning of the law makers, and are made to extend the statute to cases not otherwise recognised as coming within its purview. But the legislature cannot, by merely expressing the intent of the law in respect to a particular statute, affect the meaning of words used in other statutes, or deprive them of the significance which they receive from settled principles of the common law. The case therefore of *Boucicault* v. *Delafield* is not an authority upon any question of actual or constructive publication not arising under the English

(a) 5 Robt. (Amer.) 38.
(b) 33 L. J. (N.S.) 38 Ch.; 9 L. T. (N.S.),709.

copyright law. Nor is it entitled to any more weight than the statute itself, which is a mere legislative interpretation of what, for certain purposes, shall be deemed a publication of a dramatic piece.". . . " My conclusions upon the whole case are, that there was no such publication by the plaintiff, or by his assignor, of the play in question as to deprive the plaintiff of his common law right of property in it. That public representations of the play were not a publication of the play so as to take away the common law right. . . . . I am, therefore, of opinion that the plaintiff is entitled to a judgment restraining the defendant from further printing or publishing the play, and requiring him to deliver up to be destroyed such as are now in print " (a).

Performing play in an abridged form.

When the play is a fair abridgment or alteration of a former dramatic representation, it is doubtful whether an action can be maintained by the original author. Thus where Lord Byron's tragedy of ' Marino Faliero,' altered and abridged for the stage, was performed without the consent of the owner of the copyright, who applied for an injunction, it was laid down, that an action could not be maintained, " for publicly acting and representing the said tragedy, abridged in manner aforesaid " (b). As, however, in the case cited the plaintiff, apart from the question of abridgment, had no exclusive right, it is difficult to see what stress the court laid upon the fact of the alleged piracy being an abridgment.

Where the similarity between two pieces arises from the fact of their being taken from a source open to all, there is no piracy. As Lord Eldon said, " All human events are equally open to all who wish to add to or improve the materials already collected by others." There can be no plagiarism in dramatizing the same incidents. In *Seman* v. *Copeland*, where the action was for having caused to be represented the plaintiff's play, or a portion thereof, proof that the plot had been taken from the same source,

(a) 7 Rob. (N.Y.) 530 ; 2 Sweeny (N.Y.) 530 ; 47 N. Y. 532, 543.
(b) *Murray* v. *Elliston*, 5 Barn. & Ald. 657 ; and S. C. 1 Dowl. & Ryl. 299.

namely, that of a newspaper report of some stirring events which took place during the Indian Mutiny at Delhi, was a good defence. Here the narrative suggested the plot, and most of the characters, alike in the minds of both parties; but when a scene only from the play of another, mixed up with that which is not original, is infringed, the court will protect the author. Copyright, therefore, may be said to exist in the incidents of a play. Thus in *Boucicault* v. *Egan* an injunction was granted to restrain the representation of the water-cave scene in the plaintiff's drama of 'The Colleen Bawn.' The defendant had represented a play dramatized from Gerald Griffin's novel of 'The Collegians,' the parent of the plaintiff's play also; but the scene in question, of which the defendant's representation was a colourable imitation, was original, and the most important and effective in the plaintiff's piece, and not contained in the novel.

The many defects existing in the law of dramatic copyright led to the passing of the 3 & 4 Will. 4, c. 15 (*a*), which gave to the author, or his assignee, of any printed and unpublished tragedy, comedy, play, opera, farce, or other dramatic piece or entertainment (*b*), composed and not printed and published, the sole right of having it represented in any part of the British dominions; and to the author, or his assignee, of any such dramatic production which was printed or published the sole right of representation from the time of publication, for a period of twenty-eight years, and also if the author were living at the end of that time, for the remainder of the author's life. And further enacted, that if any person should represent, or cause to be represented, without the consent in writing of the author or other proprietor, at any place of dramatic entertainment, any such production, or any part thereof, every such offender should be liable for each and every such representation to the payment of an amount not less

(*a*) Commonly called Sir Edward Bulwer Lytton's Act.
(*b*) In *Lee* v. *Simpson*, 3 C. B. 871, 4 D. & L. 666, it was determined that a pantomime, or rather the introduction to one, which is the only written part of the entertainment, is protected from piracy under this Act.

than 40s. or to the full amount of the benefit or advantage arising from such representation, or the injury or loss sustained by the plaintiff therefrom, whichever should be the greater damages, to the author or other proprietor of such production so represented, to be recovered, together with double costs of suit.

Double costs were taken away in all cases by the 5 & 6 Vict. c. 97, s. 2. and the plaintiff can now only recover a full and reasonable indemnity as to all expenses incurred, to be taxed by the proper officer in that behalf.

Provisions of the 3 & 4 Will. 4, c. 15, extended to musical compositions, and representation made equivalent to publication.
The provisions of the 3 & 4 Will. 4, c. 15, are extended to musical compositions, and the term of copyright as provided by the 5 & 6 Vict. c. 45, applied to the liberty of representing dramatic pieces and musical compositions, by the 20th section of the latter Act, which enacts that the sole liberty of representing or performing, or causing (a) or permitting to be represented or performed, any dramatic piece or musical composition shall endure and be the property of the author thereof and his assigns for the term in the Act provided for the duration of copyright in books (b); and the provisions thereinbefore enacted in respect of the property of such copyright, and of registering the same, shall apply to the liberty of representing or performing any dramatic piece or musical composition, as if the same were therein expressly re-enacted and applied thereto (c), save and except that the first public representation or performance of any dramatic piece or musical composition shall be deemed equivalent, in the construction of the Act, to the first publication of any book: provided always, that in case of any dramatic piece or musical composition in manuscript, it shall be sufficient for the person having the sole liberty of representing or performing, or causing to be represented or

(a) See Parsons v. Chapman, 5 Car. & Payne, 33.
(b) Strictly, a copyright song cannot be publicly sung, or a tune publicly played, without the permission of the composer or his assigns.
(c) By virtue of this section the 5 & 6 Vict. c. 45, is retrospective as to the exclusive right to the performance of musical compositions published before the passing of the Act: Ex parte Hutchins and Romer, W. N. (1879) 114.

performed, the same, to register only the title thereof, the
name and place of abode of the author or composer thereof,
the name and place of abode of the proprietor thereof, and
the time and place of its first representation or performance.

The common law right to the exclusive representation Effect of re-
presentation
of manuscript
play.
of a manuscript play is lost by the public performance of
the piece, and since the passing of the statute the only
protection the author can claim is that conferred by the
statute. This evidently does not attach until the play has
been publicly represented.

It is doubtful whether, supposing a dramatic piece or
musical composition in manuscript to have been registered
so as to give protection to the right of representing it or
performing it, the subsequent printing and publication of
such piece or composition, if not followed by the deposit at
Stationers' Hall, can be held to take away that right (a).

The Act of 5 & 6 Vict. c. 45, in extending the term of The remedies
provided by
the Act of
Will. 4,
not affected
by the 5 & 6
Vict. c. 45.
copyright in dramatic pieces, and providing for their
registration and assignment, does not deprive the proprietor of the remedies given by the Act of Will. 4.

This was seen in a case which came before the Court of
Exchequer a few years since. The facts were briefly these :
The plaintiff purchased from a Mr. Elton all the property
in the copyright in the words of a comic song called ' Come
to Peckham Rye,' of which the latter was the author, the
sum given being £2. Mr. Clark was in the habit of
singing this song at the Oxford Music Hall, and similar
places of entertainment. In the course of his performance
the song attracted much attention, and he was offered by
a certain publisher ten guineas for his property in the
composition. The defendant Bishop, who was a publisher
in the East end of London, contrived to obtain a copy
of the song, which up to this moment remained in
manuscript, and published the same with some slight
alterations. The plaintiff, feeling himself aggrieved,
brought an action for damages against Bishop for the

(a) See *Boosey* v. *Fairlie*, 7 Ch. Div. 301.

infringement of his copyright. The case was tried before the common serjeant in the Lord Mayor's Court, when a verdict was returned against the defendant with £10 damages. A rule to set aside such verdict was, however, obtained on the ground that the plaintiff not having registered his copyright at Stationers' Hall, he had no right to sue for damages in respect of it. The point having been fully argued, the court decided that the 24th section of the Act applied only to books, and had no reference to such productions as that in question: and that the other sections relating to songs and dramatic representations connected with them, did not make it obligatory on the owners to register them in order to preserve them against any infringement of their copy-

Omission to register does not affect the copyright or the recovery of penalties.

right (a). Consequently it may be taken that the omission to register will not prejudice the remedies which the proprietor of the sole liberty of representing any dramatic piece has by virtue of the Act 5 & 6 Vict. c. 45, or of the 3 & 4 Will. 4, c. 15.

There are several points which we propose now to consider in the order in which they are enumerated in the sections before us.

Where the copyright in unpublished work dates from.

There is nothing in the Act to shew when the right in an unpublished play is to begin, and when it is to end.

As to the consent of the author.

The penalties are only incurred if the representation be without the *consent in writing of the author or other proprietor.* The consent may be given by the author's agent, and it has been decided that the Dramatic Authors' Society is agent to its members, for the purpose of authorizing managers of theatres to perform pieces composed by its members (b).

The plaintiff was a member of the Dramatic Authors' Society, which announced that leave might be obtained from the secretary to represent pieces belonging to the members at certain prices mentioned in a list, and that

(a) *Clark* v. *Bishop*, Exchequer, Jan. 11th, 1872; 25 L. T. (N.S.) 908.
(b) *Moreton* v. *Copeland*, 16 C. B. 517; S. C. 24 L. J. (C.P.) 169 *Fitzball* v. *Brooke*, 2 Dow. & Lown. 477; *Shepherd* v. *Conquest*, 25 L. J (C.P.) 127; 17 C. B. 427.

lists would be published from year to year containing the names of the new pieces. In 1849 the secretary of the society gave the defendant leave in writing, signed by himself, to play " dramas belonging to the authors form- ing the Dramatic Authors' Society, upon his punctual transmission of the monthly bills, and payment of the prices for the performance of such dramas." Three pieces were performed belonging to the society. It was held that the defendant was not liable to penalties; that the documents given by the secretary amounted, under the circumstances, to " a consent in writing of the author."

The consent may apply to works not in existence at the time it is given. It is not as it is under the Statute of Frauds, which expressly requires that the contract shall be signed by the party to be charged; and even that is satis- fied, if it is signed in his name by an agent duly authorized so to sign. It is very rarely the case that a document required by the law need be wholly in the handwriting of the party on whose behalf it is to be given. The present statute does not require signature, nor the *handwriting* of the author. All that it requires is that there should be his consent, and that it should appear in writing (a).

Where there are several owners of a copyright, consent must be obtained from all, one co-owner cannot grant a license in respect of that which really belongs to two. Thus in an action by the co-owners of a moiety of the copyright of an opera to restrain the defendant, who on the evidence in the case had only a license from the other co-owner, from representing it, and for damages, the Master of the Rolls held that the plaintiffs were entitled to sustain the action and to recover a moiety of the statutory penalty of £2 a night for each representa- tion (b).

Again, although by a former Act the performance which Performance is alleged to be an infringement of the original right must at a place of have taken place at some place of dramatic entertainment, entertainment.

(a) *Per* Maule, J., in *Moreton v. Copeland*, 16 C. B. 517.
(b) *Powell v. Head*, W. N. (1879) 86.

for the author to have maintained an action, yet the above provision does not appear to be so restrictive. It has never been judicially decided that an infringement which is not committed in a place of dramatic entertainment would be the subject of an action; but, from the general aspect of the above, we are inclined to think that it would. The question was raised in *Russell* v. *Smith* (a), but the judges did not express an opinion upon it, because the case was decided upon other grounds. Mr. Russell, who was the composer of a song called 'The Ship on Fire,' brought an action against a man of the name of Smith for singing the same song, among others, at an entertainment which he opened at Crosby Hall, Bishopsgate, and to which he gave admission by shilling and two-shilling tickets. The building called Crosby Hall belonged to a literary institution, and contained a large room in which elocution classes met periodically, but which, at other times, was let out for concerts and musical entertainments. It had been hired for recitations intermixed with songs, and for performances of ventriloquy; and a music licence had been taken out for it under statute 25 Geo. 2, c. 36. On the trial it was objected that Crosby Hall was not a "a place of dramatic entertainment" within the meaning of statute 3 & 4 Will. 4, c. 15, s. 1, referred to by statute 5 & 6 Vict. c. 45, s. 20. But Lord Denman held, that as Crosby Hall was used for the public representation for profit of a dramatic piece, it became a place of dramatic entertainment for the time being within the statutes in question. "The use for the time in question," added the learned chief justice, "and not for a former time, is the essential fact. As a regular theatre may be a lecture-room, dining-room, ball-room, and concert-room on successive days, so a room used ordinarily for either of those purposes would become for the time being a theatre, if used for the representation of a regular stage play (b).

(a) 12 Q. B. 217.
(b) In the same case Patteson, J., remarked that "the street where 'Punch' is performed is for the time being a place of dramatic entertainment."

In this sense, as 'The Ship on Fire' was a dramatic piece in our view, Crosby Hall, when used for the public representation and performance of it for profit, became a place of dramatic entertainment."

In an action for penalties brought under the 3 & 4 Will. 4, c. 15, the declaration stated that the plaintiff was the author of a certain dramatic piece or musical composition, &c., and that defendant caused the said piece to be represented at a certain place of dramatic entertainment, &c., whereby, &c. It was determined, first, that the introduction of a pantomime was a dramatic entertainment, within the meaning of the statute; secondly, that it was not necessary to allege in the declaration, or to prove at the trial, that the defendant knew that the plaintiff was the author; thirdly, that the allegation in the declaration, that the same was represented at a certain place of dramatic entertainment, was sufficient.

Though it was here decided that a person ignorant of the piratical nature of a representation may be an offender within the meaning of the Act, yet one cannot be considered a transgressor of the provisions of the statute, so as to subject himself to an action of the above nature, unless he himself, or his agent, actually takes part in the representation which is a violation of copyright. Were it to be otherwise held, all those who supply any of the means of representation to him who actually represents, would have to be considered as thereby constituting him their agent, and thus *causing* the representation, within the meaning of the Act; such a doctrine would embrace a class of persons not at all intended by the legislature (a).

A person, therefore, who lets for hire by the evening a place of dramatic entertainment for the public performance of songs and music, and provides the hirer, who performs songs and music which he has not liberty to perform, with lights, benches, &c., is not liable to pay damages to the author for causing or permitting to be

Punishment for infringement not to be visited on one not actually taking part in the performance.

(a) *Russell* v. *Briant*, 19 L. J. (C.P.) 33; 14 Jur. 201; 8 C. B. 836.

represented or performed a musical composition without the author's written consent (a).

This doctrine was followed in *Lyon* v. *Knowles* (b). The defendant, the proprietor of a theatre, allowed one Dillon to have the use of it for the purpose of dramatic entertainments. The defendant provided the band, the scene-shifters, the supernumeraries, the money-takers, and paid for printing and advertising. Dillon employed his own company of actors and actresses, and selected the pieces which were to be represented, free from control on the part of the defendant. It was arranged that the money taken at the doors should be divided equally between the defendant and Dillon. During the period of such occupation of the theatre by Dillon, certain pieces were performed which the plaintiff had the sole liberty of representing or causing to be represented; and it was held, in an action to recover the penalties imposed by the above sections, that the plaintiff could not recover, inasmuch as, under the circumstances, the defendant was not shewn to have represented, directly or indirectly, the said dramatic pieces. If the representation of the pieces could have been considered a joint act of the defendant and Dillon, the defendant would have been liable. The defendant had no right to interfere in the choice of the pieces to be represented; and in short, though the proprietor, he was not the manager. Neither was he a partner; for the receipt of the moneys at the door was a receipt of gross proceeds, not net profits, and was merely a mode of receiving and securing the rent. There was an agreement between them to divide the gross receipts in lieu of payment of a specific sum as rent. But this did not make them partners. The defendant, then, having no control over the performances, could not be said to have caused them to be represented, and was consequently not liable. The defendant, to have been made liable, must have been shewn to have been either the partner or

(a) *Russell* v. *Briant*, 19 L. J. (C.P.) 33; 14 Jur. 201; 8 C. B. 836.
(b) 11 W. R. 266; 32 L. J. (Q.B.) 71; 10 L. T. (N.S.) 876.

principal of Dillon, the person who actually directed the representation (a).

In the case last referred to Mr. Justice Blackburn said: "I do not think that, by furnishing servants to another, a man can be said to do all that is done by those servants while under the command of that other. A familiar example may be found in the case of a man letting a ready-furnished house, leaving an old servant in it. Suppose the tenant gave a dinner, which was cooked by that servant, who also attended on him at it, and for which the plates and furniture of the landlord were used, no one would say that, in any sense of the words, the landlord gave that dinner."

In another case (b) the defendant was the owner and manager of the Grecian Theatre, and for £30 he had let for one night to his son, who was the stage manager, the use of the theatre, company, and all persons employed. The son selected and brought out a play, for which representation the court held the defendant liable. The judgment was based on the fact that the defendant had the control and management of the theatre and the company during that performance. "I think," said Erle, C.J., "the defendant is responsible for that representation. He was the proprietor of the theatre, and had entire control over the establishment and all belonging to it; and what was done by his son was done by his permission. The case of *Lyon* v. *Knowles* seems to me to recognise that distinction. There the defendant merely let his theatre with the scenery, scene-shifters, bands, lights, &c., to Dillon, who brought his own company to represent pieces of his own selection, the plaintiff having no control whatever over any person employed in the representation. Here, however, the piece is performed by the defendant's own *corps dramatique,* his son being one of them; and the performance takes place for the defendant's profit to the extent

(a) *Lyon* v. *Knowles,* 11 W. R. 266; 3 B. & S. 556; affirmed on appeal 5 B. & S. 751; 12 W. R. 1083; 10 L. T. (N.S.) 876.
(b) *Marsh* v. *Conquest,* 17 C. B. (N.S.) 418. See *Parsons* v. *Chapman,* 5 C. & P. 33.

of £30. I think, therefore, it is impossible to say that the defendant did not cause the piece to be represented."

What amounts to a representation. Representing, within the meaning of the Act, is defined to be the bringing forward on a stage or place of public representation; and the question whether in any particular case the act done amounts to a representation, is a proper question for a jury.

If the words of one song only be taken from a musical or dramatic piece protected by the Act, or be sung on a stage or in any place of theatrical entertainment, without the permission of the proprietor, the representation will be actionable (a).

In *Planché* v. *Braham*, the defendant sang two or three songs of the plaintiff's libretto to an opera, and one in particular commencing with the words

"Ocean! thou mighty monster!"

And it was held that this was an infringement of the plaintiff's sole right of representation.

So, too, the playing in public the music, though other words than the original be used, would be an infringement.

What is a dramatic composition. The Act of William IV. gives to the authors of "any tragedy, comedy, play, opera, farce, or other dramatic piece or entertainment," the sole liberty of representing it. This right is affirmed by the statute of Victoria, which further declares that "the words 'dramatic piece' shall be construed to mean and include every tragedy, comedy, play, opera, farce, or other scenic, musical, or dramatic entertainment."

The above terms are not very distinct, and questions have arisen as to what is, or is not included in the "or other scenic, musical, or dramatic entertainment."

A work not intended for the stage may be in substance a drama, and may be easily adapted for representation. Is it excluded from the operation of the statute, because

---

(a) *Planché* v. *Braham*, 1 Jur. 823; 8 C. & P. 68; 4 Bing. (N.C.) 17: Two pounds may be exacted for each song, and if there is a performance in which 1000 people take part, as in a chorus, each would be liable for a separate penalty.

it is not in form and name a drama? Again, if fitness for public performance is the test of a dramatic composition, are songs within the purview of the statute? Though hardly dramatic compositions in the ordinary acceptation of the term, they seem to come within the words " musical entertainment." Whether a production is called a poem, or a tragedy, or novel, or a comedy, a history, or a drama, or whether its author did or did not intend it for public representation, is immaterial in ascertaining whether it is a dramatic composition. This question is determined by the character of the work, and not by what it is called, or the purpose for which the author has intended it. So also it is immaterial whether the words of a drama are spoken or sung; whether they are or are not accompanied with instrumental music. An opera, not less than a play without music, is a drama. The judicial construction given to "dramatic .piece," as used and defined in the statute, is broad enough to embrace every composition which is dramatic in character and is suitable to be performed, recited, read, or sung for the entertainment of an audience. Thus it has been decided that a song which related the burning of a ship at sea, and the escape of those on board, describing their feelings in vehement language, and sometimes expressing them in the supposed words of the suffering parties, is dramatic, and consequently within the meaning of the statute, even though it be sung by one person only, sitting at a piano, giving effect to the verses by the delivery, but not assisted by scenery or appropriate dress (a).

That the whole is expressed in music makes no difference. The early Greek drama was musical throughout; so in the modern Italian opera. Nor can any distinction arise from the want of scenery or appropriate dress: an oratorio has neither, yet it is often dramatic. Nor, again, is it material that no second person performs. No one would suggest that Mr. Mathews' representations, or the readings of Shakespeare by Mrs. Siddons or Mr. Charles

(a) *Russell* v. *Smith*, 12 Q. B. 217.

Kemble, were not dramatic. The character of Elijah is essentially a dramatic one, requiring, however, not dramatic action, but dramatic sentiment, in order to delineate it. Sometimes the wrath and gloom of such a character must be displayed, at other times the most pathetic tenderness. If the character of drama were denied to this species of entertainment, nothing short of requiring all the ingredients of a play would be admitted as a dramatic representation. If the interpretation clause of statute 5 & 6 Vict. c. 45, be referred to, it will be remarked that the 2nd section declares that "dramatic pieces" within that Act include "tragedy, comedy, play, opera, farce," or "other scenic, musical, or dramatic entertainment." These words comprehend any piece which can be called dramatic in its widest sense; any piece which, on being presented by any performer to an audience, will produce the emotions which are the purpose of the regular drama, and which constitute the entertainment of the audience (a).

In a recent case, the court held the song, 'Come to Peckham Rye,' which has little, if any, of the dramatic character, to be a dramatic piece (b). And though there is no express decision to the effect that all songs are entitled to protection, yet there can be little doubt that this is practically the effect of the judicial decisions.

The statute under consideration does not, however, protect a literary production which is not a musical or dramatic composition, and the author has no remedy against any person who publicly reads or recites such production. Of course this applies only to published works, for the unauthorized public reading of any unpublished production, whether a dramatic composition or not, would be a violation of the owner's common law rights in the manuscript.

Copyright in spectacular piece.

A spectacular piece is within the protection afforded by the statute. Thus in a case to be hereafter more fully considered, where it appeared that the defendant had

(a) Lord Denman, C.J., in *Russell* v. *Smith*, 12 Q. B. 217; 17 L. J. (Q.B.) 225.
(b) *Clark* v. *Bishop*, 25 L. T. (N.S.) 908.

taken from the plaintiff's play two scenes or situations, CAP. XI.
consisting more of scenic effects than of dialogue, Mr.
Justice Brett said : " Now, it was first said that the subject
matter of the action was not the subsequent matter of
copyright; that the Act gives a property in words, and
not in situations and scenic effects; but I think that
these latter are more peculiarly the subject of copyright
than the words themselves (a).

Copyright may be secured in the adaptation of a play Adaptation of
which is itself common property. Thus in *Hatton* v. old play.
Kean, where it appeared that the defendant had designed a
dramatic representation, consisting of one of Shakespeare's
plays, with certain alterations in the text, original music,
scenic effects, and other accessories, the court did not doubt
that the production, as a whole, was a proper subject of
copyright, although the play itself was, in its original
form, common property (b).

A translation of a foreign play not entitled to protection Translation of
in this country, will receive the same protection as an foreign drama.
original drama. Any number of persons may dramatize
or translate a work which is common property, or, with the
consent of the owner of the copyright, a work wherein
copyright exists, and whatever may be the similarity
between two dramatizations, adaptations, or translations,
each dramatist will have copyright in his own version.

Though the words in the Act 3 & 4 Will. 4 imposed Principal
the penalties there specified upon any who may pirate decisions on
questions of
any protected " production or any part thereof," yet it piracy under
the Act of
was not necessarily intended to prevent the copying and Will. IV.
reproduction of every and any part without regard to its
importance. At the same time it does not follow that
either the very language of the original drama, or a very
considerable portion of it, must be appropriated in order
to bring the case within the statute.

In considering and judging of what amount of copying or
imitation would constitute piracy, similar rules to those

(a) *Chatterton* v. *Cave*, 33 L. T. (N.S.) 256.
(b) 7 C. B. (N.S.) 268.

already laid down with reference to copyright in books may be applied to the authors and owners of dramatic productions, for it would seem to be a proper rule to apply the same principle of construction to statutes which aim at objects substantially the same. The question of materiality must depend upon a consideration of the quantity and value of the portion taken or use made, and must vary indefinitely in various circumstances. As Lord Chancellor Cottenham said in *Bramwell* v. *Halcomb* (a): "It is useless to refer to any particular cases as to quantity." The quantity taken may be great or small, but if it comprise a material portion of the book, it is taken illegally. The question is as to the substance of the thing, and if there be no abstraction of that which may be substantially appreciated, no penalty is incurred. In all cases, the matter is dealt with as one of degree. In all, quantity and value are both the subjects of consideration, and in none of them has an infringement been established without satisfactory evidence of an appropriation, possibly involving a substantial loss to one person, and a substantial gain to another.

The question in every case must be a question of fact, and therefore one for a jury.

The two principal cases under the 3 & 4 Will. 4, c. 15, are the cases of *Planché* v. *Braham* (b), and *Chatterton* v. *Cave* (c). In the first of these cases the defendant used the words of two or three songs of the plaintiff's as the vehicle of some airs in an English version of Weber's opera of 'Oberon,' and the action was brought under the above Act. The rest of the version had been written by another person. There was no question as to appropriation of the music; and Lord Chief Justice Tindal left it to the jury to say whether there had been a representation of a part of the plaintiff's dramatic production. The jury found that there had been; and gave a verdict accordingly for the statutory penalty. Serjeant Wilde moved to set aside the verdict on the ground that as there had been

(a) 3 My. & Cr. 738.   (b) 4 Bing. N. C. 17.
(c) L. R. 10 C. P. 572; 2 C. P. D. 42; 3 App. Cas. 483.

no representation of a part of the plaintiff's piece,—the
words of the songs adapted to the music being immaterial
to the development of the drama,—the defendant was
entitled to a judgment. But the court affirmed the
the verdict, holding that the question before it must in all
cases be determined by a jury. " It is difficult," said the
Chief Justice, " to say what is or is not a representation of
a part of a dramatic production, ... and it must be left
to a jury to determine the fact."

The second case was an action against the defendant
in respect of his having committed an infringement of the
copyright of the plaintiffs in a drama founded on the
novel by Eugène Sue called 'The Wandering Jew.'
There had been a drama in French founded on the same
novel, and the version claimed by the plaintiffs, prepared
by Mr. Lewis and assigned by him to them, was an
adaptation from the French. The defendant had since
brought out another adaptation, which it was alleged was,
in part, an imitation of the former, and had thereby
committed an infringement of the plaintiffs' copyright.
When the case came on for trial, it was agreed to discharge the jury, Lord Coleridge undertaking to read the
plays, to receive such evidence as he might deem material,
and to find whether there had been any copying so as to
bring the case within the statute. He found there had
been two "scenes or points" of the plaintiffs' drama
taken by the defendant without recourse either to the
French novel or to the drama constructed from it, and
he directed the verdict to be entered for the defendant.
The finding was as follows:—" I find in this case that
two scenes or points of the drama of the defendant
have been taken direct from the drama of which Mr.
Lewis was the author and the plaintiffs the assignees,
without recourse to either the French novel or the
French drama, originals common to the dramas of both
the plaintiffs and defendant. I find this, first, in respect
of the final scene of the defendant's drama ; and secondly,
of the appearance of the Wandering Jew, and the stage

business connected with that appearance, which are to be found in the second scene of the second act of the defendant's drama, and in the fourth scene of the first act of the plaintiffs' drama. I find that the drama of the defendant is not, except in these respects, a copy from or a colourable imitation of, the drama of the plaintiffs'. I direct the verdict to be entered for the defendant. I assess the damages at 40s. if upon argument, as provided by the terms agreed to at the trial, the court should be of opinion that the verdict ought to be entered for the plaintiffs." The case was argued upon a rule obtained to enter the verdict for the plaintiffs. This rule was discharged (a), and on appeal this decision was affirmed (b). The plaintiffs appealed to the House of Lords, and it was argued that the scenes, or points, as they were called, were material, valuable, and striking points, and affected considerably the attractiveness of the drama, and no one doubted that they had been copied from the plaintiffs' production, but the House affirmed the decisions of the courts below, Lord Hatherley saying: " There is indeed one obvious difference between the copyright in books and that in dramatic performances. Books are published with an expectation, if not a desire, that they will be criticised in reviews, and if deemed valuable, that parts of them will be used as affording illustrations by way of quotation or the like, and if the quantity taken be neither substantial nor material, if, as it had been expressed by some Judges, 'a fair use' only be made of the publication, no wrong is done and no action can be brought. It is not, perhaps, exactly the same with dramatic performances. They are not intended to be repeated by others, or to be used in such a way as a book may be used, but still the principle *de minimis non curat lex* applies to a supposed wrong in taking a part of dramatic works, as well as in reproducing a part of a book. The minimum of damages, to be awarded when the fact of damage and the right to damages have been once established, was no doubt fixed because of the difficulty of

(a) L. R. 10 C. P. 572.   (b) 2 C. P. D. 42.

proving with definiteness what amount of actual damage had been sustained, by perhaps a single performance at a provincial theatre of a work belonging to a plaintiff, whilst at the same time his work might be seriously depreciated if he did not establish his right as against all those who infringed upon it. . . . I think, my lords, regard being had to the whole of the case, to the finding of the Lord Chief Justice that the parts which were so taken were neither substantial nor material parts, and the impossibility of damage being held to have accrued to the plaintiff from such taking, and the concurrence of the other Judges before whom the case was brought, that this appeal should be dismissed, and dismissed with costs " (a).

It is worthy of note here that when the question was raised in the Common Pleas, Lord Coleridge set out fully the reasons which had dictated his direction, and it then appeared that though the finding had no explicit allegation as to the character of the "scenes " or "points " which it finds to have been taken, their immateriality was meant to be conveyed. "These points so copied," said he, "were not parts of the dialogue or composition of the plaintiffs' drama, but were in the nature of dramatic situations or scenic effects. It appeared to me that, looking to the general character of the two dramas respectively, the extent to which the one was taken from the other was so slight, and the effect upon the total composition was so small, that there was no substantial and material taking of any one portion of the defendant's drama from any portion of the plaintiffs'. Therefore, though I felt bound to find that there was a taking of these two small points, I decided to enter the verdict for the defendant."

The court will not protect any person in the exclusive Immoral play. right of representing an immoral play (b).

The proprietor of a drama whether published or un- Licences.

(a) 3 App. Cas. 483, 492, 493.
(b) The Lord Chamberlain recently ('The Happy Land' at the Court Theatre) interposed to prevent certain high personages being represented in ludicrous positions upon the stage; see the powers of the Lord Chamberlain, 6 & 7 Vict. c. 68, Appendix.

published, may license one or more persons to perform it anywhere, without giving to any one the exclusive right of representation. But in such case the owner of the copyright only could maintain an action in respect of unlicensed performances. The owner may grant the exclusive right of representation for any named part of the country, or any town, city, or county, and within such limits, no one without the consent of the licensee has the right to perform the play.

Assignment of the right of representation

By the 22nd section of the 5 & 6 Vict. c. 45, it is enacted that no assignment of the copyright of any book consisting of or containing a dramatic piece or musical composition, shall be holden to convey to the assignee the right of representing or performing such dramatic piece or musical composition, unless an entry in the registry book, to which reference has already been made (a), shall be made of such assignment, wherein shall be expressed the intention of the parties that such right should pass by such assignment. Under an assignment of " all present and future vested and contingent copyright in a musical composition," together with " all property" therein, the exclusive right of performance passes (b).

It is competent for an assignee of the sole right of representing a dramatic piece to sue for penalties under 3 & 4 Will. 4, c. 15, notwithstanding the assignment is not made by deed, or registered under 5 & 6 Vict. c. 45 (c).

The administrator of an author of a dramatic piece first acted in 1843, by deed dated the 14th of April, 1859, in consideration of £100, assigned to the plaintiff the copyright and right of representation in all dramatic pieces written by the author; no entry of the assignment to the plaintiff had been made in the registry book in pursuance of the section under consideration; but it was held that the plaintiff might maintain an action for penalties under statute 3 & 4 Will. 4, c. 15, against the defendant, for

(a) *Ante*, p. 135.
(b) *Ex parte Hutchins and Romer*, W. N. (1879) 114.
(c) *Marsh* v. *Conquest*, 17 C. B. (N.S.) 418 ; 10 L. T. (N.S.) 717.

representing the piece without his license within twenty-eight years of its publication, the period for which the sole liberty of representation is given by that statute, although the deed was not registered under statute 5 & 6 Vict. c. 45, s. 22.

That section in terms applies only to the effect of an assignment of the copyright, limiting its operation as such, and was intended to correct what had probably been an omission in previous legislation; for upon the construction of statute 3 & 4 Will. 4, c. 15, s. 1, the Court of Queen's Bench in *Cumberland* v. *Planché* (a) had held that the assignment of the copyright of a dramatic piece carried with it, incidentally, the exclusive right of representation. Section 22 of statute 5 & 6 Vict. c. 45, was intended to meet that decision by enacting that no assignment of the copyright of a dramatic piece or musical composition should be holden to convey the right of representing or performing it, unless an entry was made in the registry book that it was the intention of the parties that such right should pass by the assignment. That enactment does not apply to a case in which there is an express assignment of the *right of representing or performing*. In the case of *Lacy* v. *Rhys*, there was an assignment of the right of acting, as well as of the copyright; and it was held, that it did not follow that, because section 24 required registration of an assignment of the copyright, and there was such an assignment there, therefore the assignment of the *right to represent* was in any way affected: *Utile per inutile non vitiatur.* When a person professes to convey two things, one of which he has a right to convey and the other he has not, the instrument operates to pass the property in that which he has a right to convey, and the rest is surplusage (b).

It is clear, therefore, that an assignment merely of the right of representation needs not to be registered under

Assignment of the right of representation need not be registered.

(a) 1 Ad. & E. 580.
(b) *Per* Cockburn, C.J., in *Lacy* v. *Rhys*, 4 B. & S. 873, 883; 12 W. R. 309; 33 L. J. (Q.B.) 157; 10 Jur. (N.S.) 612. See *Marsh* v. *Conquest*, 10 L. T. (N.S.) 717; 17 C. B. (N.S.) 418.

the 22nd section; nor indeed need it be in writing according to some authorities. The provision of this section applies only to cases where the copyright in a dramatic or musical composition is assigned without any mention of the right of representation, and where consequently it may be doubtful whether the latter right was intended to be passed (*a*).

The legal assignment must be in writing. The legal assignment either of the right to represent a dramatic piece or perform a musical composition must be in writing (*b*), but need not be attested (*c*) or sealed (*d*). This was decided in *Shepherd* v. *Conquest* (*e*), where it appeared that the plaintiffs, being proprietors of the Surrey Theatre, verbally agreed with one Courtney that the latter should go to Paris for the purpose of adapting a piece there in vogue for representation on the English stage ; that the plaintiffs should pay all Courtney's expenses, and should have the sole right of representing the piece in London, Courtney retaining the right of representation in the provinces. Courtney accordingly proceeded to Paris, produced a piece called 'Old Joe and Young Joe,' and was paid by the plaintiffs as agreed. The piece was brought out at the Surrey Theatre by the plaintiffs, and afterwards at the Grecian Saloon by the defendant, who had obtained an assignment from Courtney. The representations by the defendant at the Grecian Saloon were the infringements of the plaintiffs' right complained of. The defendant objected that, as there was no assignment in writing from Courtney to the plaintiffs, the action was not maintainable. The plaintiffs contended that no assignment was necessary, for that, by virtue of Courtney's employment by them, they were the proprietors of the piece in question from the first moment

(*a*) See *Wood* v. *Boosey*, 7 B. & S. 869; L. R. 10 Q. B. 347.
b) See *ante*, pp. 164, 165, as to what is an assignment, see *Leader* v. *Purday*, 7 C. B 4 ; *Lacy* v. *Toole*, 15 L. T. (N.S.) 512.
(*c*) *Cumberland* v. *Copeland*, 1 Hurl. & C. 194.
(*d*) *Marsh* v. *Conquest*, 17 C. B. (N.S.) 418; 10 L. T. (N.S.) 717.
(*e*) 17 C. B. 427 ; 25 L. J. (C.P.) 127. When A. agrees with B. to "let B. have" a particular drama in discharge of £10 due from A. to B. this is a complete assignment of A.'s whole property in the drama: *Lacy* v. *Toole*, *supra*.

of its composition, or that at least they were entitled to the sole right of representation in London. The Court of Common Pleas were of opinion that though Courtney made the adaptation at the suggestion of the plaintiffs, he acquired for himself, as the author of the adaptation, and as far as that adaptation gave any new character to the work, the statutory right of representing it; and that, inasmuch as the plaintiffs had no assignment in writing of that right, they could not sue for an infringement of it.

In the course of the delivery of the judgment, Jervis, C.J., doubted whether, under any circumstances, the copyright in a literary work, or the right of representation of a dramatic one, could become invested *ab initio* in an employer other than the person who had actually composed or adapted the work. But he was clearly of opinion that no such effect could be produced when the employers merely suggested the subject, and had no share in the design or execution of the work, the whole of which, so far as any character of originality belonged to it, flowed from the mind of the person employed. It appeared to him to be an abuse of terms to say that, in such a case, the employers were the authors of a work to which their minds had not contributed an idea; and it was upon the author, in the first instance, that the right was conferred by the statute which created it. Literary property stood upon a different and higher ground from that occupied by mechanical invention. The intention of the legislature in the enactments relating to copyright was to elevate and protect literary men; such an intention could only be effectuated by holding that the actual composer of the work was the author and proprietor of the copyright, and that no relation existing between him and an employer, who himself took no intellectual part in the production of the work, could, without an assignment in writing, vest the proprietorship of it in the latter (a).

This case must be distinguished from those in which *No assignment necessary where work executed for another.* one person forms the original and general design of a

(a) *Ante*, pp. 126–130.

piece, and another merely carries out that design, as in *Hatton* v. *Kean*, already referred to (a), where the defendant verbally employed the plaintiff to compose music as part of the representation of one of Shakespeare's plays, adapted to the stage by the defendant, with the aid of scenery, dresses, music, and other accompaniments, the general design of which was formed by the defendant. There it was held that, as between the parties, the defendant had the sole liberty of performance without assignment or consent in writing from the plaintiff. Nor is there any conflict with the principle laid down by Sir John Leach in *Barfield* v. *Nicholson* (b): " That the person who forms the plans and who embarks in the speculation of a work, and who employs various persons to compose different parts of it, adapted to their own peculiar acquirements, that he, the person who so forms the plan and scheme of the work, and pays different artists of his own selection, who, upon certain conditions, contribute to it, is the author and proprietor of the work, if not within the literal expression, at least within the equitable meaning of the statute of Anne, which, being a remedial law, is to be construed liberally."

The enactments upon which literary property and patents for inventions are respectively founded differ widely in their origin and in their details. In order to shew that the position and rights of an author within the former Acts are not to be measured by those of an inventor within the latter, it is only necessary to bear in mind that, whilst on the one hand a person who imports from abroad the invention of another, previously unknown here, without further originality or merit in himself, is an inventor entitled to a patent; on the other hand, a person who merely reprints for the first time in this country a valuable foreign work, without bestowing on it any intellectual labour of his own, as by translation (which, to some extent, must impress a new character), cannot thereby acquire the title of an author within the

(a) 29 L. J. (C.P.) 20.   (b) 2 Sim. & Stu. 1.

statutes relating to copyright (*a*).   In *Morris* v. *Kelly* (*b*)   CAP. XI.
an injunction was granted to restrain the performance of
a comedy, the copyright of which had been sold by the
author and had been afterwards assigned by writing to
the plaintiffs, although it did not appear whether the
original assignment was in writing, that fact being presumed till the contrary was shewn.

The making mere alterations, additions, or improve-   What con-
ments, whether with or without the consent of the author,   stitutes joint
does not constitute a joint authorship.   In the late case
of *Levy* v. *Rutley* (*c*), the plaintiff, Mr. L. Levy, proprietor of the Victoria Theatre, employed a Mr. Wilks to
write for him a piece called ' The King's Wager, or the
Camp, the Cottage, and the Court,' and himself suggested
the subject.   Mr. Wilks having completed the play, the
plaintiff and some members of his company introduced
various alterations in the incidents and in the dialogue,
to make it the more attractive, and one of them wrote an
additional scene.   Under these circumstances it was held
that there was no joint authorship.   It was admitted that
it was not necessary that each should contribute the
same amount of labour, yet to constitute joint authorship
there must be a joint labouring in furtherance of a
common design.   " All that the plaintiff has done," said
Mr. Justice Keating in giving judgment, " is this: Wilks
having written a dramatic piece complete, the plaintiff
thinks it might be made more attractive, and accordingly
he, without any co-operation with Wilks, introduces a
new scene, and makes various alterations and additions to
the dialogue.   Could the additions so made, constitute him
a joint author with Wilks of the whole piece?   There
may, no doubt, be a plurality of authors: the statute, in
s. 1, dealing with the duration of copyright, speaks of ' the
author or authors, or the survivor of the authors.'   But
I fail to discover any evidence that there was any co-
operation of the two in the design of this piece, or in its

(*a*) Jervis, C.J., in *Shepherd* v. *Conquest*, 25 L. J. (N.S.) Ch. 127.
(*b*) 1 Jac. & W. 481.
(*c*) Law Rep. 6 C. P. 523; *Shelley* v. *Ross*, L. R. 6 C. P. 531 note (1).

execution, or in any improvements either in the plot or
the general structure. All the plaintiff claims to have
done is to vary some of the dialogue, so as to make it
more suitable for his company or for his audience. If
the plaintiff and the author had agreed together to
re-arrange the plot, and so to produce a more attractive
piece out of the original materials, possibly that might have
made them joint authors of the whole. So, if two persons
undertake jointly to write a play, agreeing in the general
outline and design, and sharing the labour of working it
out, each would be contributing to the whole production,
and they might be said to be joint authors of it. But to
constitute joint authorship, there must be a joint common
design. Nothing of the sort appears here. The plaintiff
made mere additions to a complete piece, which did not
in themselves amount to a dramatic piece, but were
intended only to make the play more attractive to the
audience."

The composer's interest is not affected by shewing that
the song was composed to be sung by a particular performer at the Opera, and that by the regulations of that
establishment such compositions become the property of
the house (a).

The right of
representation
in MS. plays. It will be observed that copyright is secured in
manuscript dramatic compositions, the right of exclusive
representation is under certain conditions vested in the
author, while at the same time copyright is conferred in
dramatic works printed and published, and the right of
exclusive representation is likewise conferred on the
author.

It is obvious that here many questions of difficulty
may arise.

Some of the general principles seem clear, but there
are very nice distinctions on which little light is
obtainable from the reported cases. When the right of
representation has once been secured, it will be unaffected
by any subsequent representation of the piece. There-

(a) *Storace* v. *Longman*, 2 Camp. 27.

fore, if first published in Great Britain and the copyright in the piece duly secured, the first representation of the play afterwards in a foreign country would not affect the copyright.

But a previous publication of the play in print in a foreign country would defeat the claim to copyright in this, and the right of representation could not be secured in this country, even though the first representation of the play were to take place here.

It is said that the duration of the copyright is governed not by the representation, but by the publication, and that as the copyright dates from publication, it cannot be defeated or affected by any public performance of the play, no matter when or where made.

But this must be accepted with caution, for it would make the right of representation begin with and depend upon the first publication in print. And if such were the case a dramatist might have enjoyed the exclusive right of representing a manuscript play under the 2nd section of the Copyright Act for nearly forty-two years, and then publish it in print and secure the copyright in the publication for another period of forty-two years. For the copyright in the piece itself would commence to run from the date of publication in print, but in such case it is doubtful whether the author would have the exclusive right of representation during this second period also. For, it must be remembered that the 20th section expressly provides that the sole right of representation is to be secured to the author of a dramatic piece in manuscript by entering on the register, amongst other things, "the time and place of the first representation or performance;" and that "the first public representation or performance of any dramatic piece shall be deemed equivalent in the construction of the Act to the first publication of any book."

It therefore seems more likely that, should the question arise, it would be held that the right of exclusive representation would run from the date of the first representation of the play in manuscript, and not from the date of the publication of the same play in print. No limit is fixed for the duration of the exclusive right of representation of the play while yet in manuscript; and therefore if not perpetual, the right would seem to last for 42 years or for the life of the author, and seven years after his death, whichever may be the longer period.

Where the right to the exclusive representation of a piece in manuscript has been lost by first representing the same in a foreign country, it cannot be recovered afterwards by printing and publishing the piece; for though the copyright in the printed piece might be thus secured, the right of representation having become common property, could not thus be regained.

It has been thought that the right of representation, secured by registration in accordance with the Act, of a piece in manuscript may be lost by such a publication in print as will amount to an abandonment of the copyright. It is argued that the right of representing a manuscript play rests on the condition that the composition is not published in print,—after it has been so published it passes from the class of manuscript to that of printed plays, and becomes subject to the conditions on which the right of exclusive representation will vest in published plays:—that this right then becomes subordinate to the copyright, and the validity of the former is dependent on that of the latter right; that an abandonment of the copyright, which is the greater right, involves an abandonment of the lesser right of representation; and that when the title to copyright is forfeited, the work becomes public property as far as printing copies is concerned; and this would make it public property as far as representing it is concerned (a).

In this view, however, we are unable entirely to concur.

(a) Drone's 'Law of Copyright and Playright,' (Amer.) 607. The point was raised, but not decided, in the recent case of *Boosey* v. *Fairlie*, 7 Ch. Div. 316.

As to dramatic pieces and musical compositions, the Cap. XI.
Royal Commissioners in their recent report said: " While
in books there is only one copyright, in musical and dramatic works there are two, namely, the right of printed
publication and the right of public performance.

" These rights are essentially different and distinct, and
we find that many plays and musical pieces are publicly
performed without being published in the form of books,
and thus the acting or dramatic copyright is in force, while
as to literary copyright, such plays and pieces retain the
character of unpublished manuscripts.   Music printed
and published becomes a book for the purpose of the
literary copyright, and so, we presume, does a play ; but
it is a question what becomes of the performing copyright
on the publication of the work as a book ; and there is a
further question, whether the performing copyright can
be gained at all, if the piece is printed and published as a
book before being publicly performed.

" With regard to the duration of copyright in dramatic
pieces and musical compositions, we recommend that both
the performing right and the literary right should be the
same as for books.

" We further propose, in order to avoid the disunion
between the literary and the performing rights in
musical compositions and dramatic pieces, that the
printed publication of such works should give dramatic
or performing rights, and that public performance should
give literary copyright.   For a similar reason it would be
desirable that the author of the words of songs, as
distinguished from the music, should have no copyright
in representation or publication with the music, except by
special agreement (a)."

In order that the performance be an infringement of Private
the rights of the proprietors, it is necessary that it takes performance.
place in public, a strictly private performance not being
within the prohibition of the statute.

But a representation may be regarded as a public one,

Marginal notes:
Suggestions of the Copyright Commissioners as to musical and dramatic copyright.

(a) Par. 72-75.

though the privilege of admission be denied to the general public and be extended only to certain persons. And though the fact that no charge is made for admission is no doubt one ingredient in determining whether the performance be public or private, yet it cannot in all cases be taken as conclusive. For as the object of the law is to protect the proprietor of the copyright from injury, a performance nominally private, but in reality public, whether a charge be made for admission or not, would be restrained, on the ground that it might be as injurious to the proprietor as if the representation had been public. " Private theatricals " are sometimes given by amateur performers in a place of public amusement to which a charge is made for admission. This undoubtedly would be regarded as a representation in public, although only invited persons or members of a certain society were privileged to buy tickets of admission.

So too if amateurs forming a society or a club subscribe among themselves to get up a dramatic entertainment, they are liable to pay the fees for the authorship as if they received money at the doors.

What is piracy of a dramatic piece. In considering what amounts to an infringement of the right of exclusive representation, the same general principles that govern infringement of copyright generally are applicable. An unauthorized performance of parts— such parts being material parts of a dramatic composition— will amount to piracy; and it is a question of fact and common sense whether the parts taken are of such a substance and value, or used in such a way, as to amount to an infringement (a). Unless a material part has been taken there is no infringement, but substantial identity is sufficient to constitute piracy (b).

As to what amounts to substantial identity is well

(a) See *Planché* v. *Braham*, 8 C. & P. 68 ; on app. 4 Bing. N. C. 17; *Reade* v. *Conquest*, 11 C. B. (N.S) 479 ; *Boosey* v. *Fairlie*, 7 Ch. D. 301; *Chatterton* v. *Cave*, L. R. 10 C. P. 572; on app. 2 C. P. D. 42; 3 App. Cas. 483.

(b) *Reade* v. *Conquest*, *supra* ; *Boosey* v. *Fairlie*, *supra*.

illustrated by a recent American case (a). The matter
alleged to have been pirated was the " railroad scene " in
Daly's play ' Under the Gaslight.' In this scene is
represented a surface railroad and a signal-station shed,
in which a woman, at her own request, is locked by the
signalman, who then disappears. Next are seen two
men, one of whom binds the other with a rope, fastens
him to the railroad track, and leaves him to be killed
by an expected train. From a window in the shed
the woman sees what is done, hears the noise of the
approaching train, breaks open the door with an axe,
and frees the intended victim an instant before the train
rushes by.

This scene was reproduced, but with variations, by
Mr. Boucicault in his drama entitled ' After Dark.' In
that play he makes one of the characters, from a wine
vault where he had been thrown, see, through a door into
an adjoining vault, two persons pass through a hole in the
wall the body of a man who had been made unconscious
by drugs. With an iron bar he enlarges an orifice in
the wall of the vault, which opens on an underground
railway, and sees lying insensible on the track the
person whose body had just been put there by the two
men in the adjoining vault. Hearing the noise of a
coming locomotive, he quickly makes his way through
the opening in the wall and moves the body from the
track, just in time to prevent it from being run over by
the passing train.

In Daly's drama this incident occupies the third scene
of the fourth act, and during its progress, there is considerable conversation between the several characters on
the stage. In Boucicault's drama, it is represented in
three scenes of the third act, chiefly by action, but partly
by monologue spoken by one of the characters after he
has seen the body on the track. In laying down the law
applicable to these facts, Mr. Justice Blatchford said :—

(a) *Daly* v. *Palmer*, 6 Blatch. (Amer.) 256; see *Boucicault* v. *Wood*,
2 Biss. (Amer.) 34 ; *Martinetti* v. *Maguire*, 1 Deady (Amer.) 216.

"The series of events so represented, and communicated by movement and gesture alone to the intelligence of the spectator, according to the directions contained in parentheses, in the two plays in question here, embraces the confinement of A. in a receptacle from which there seems to be no feasible means of egress: a railroad track, with the body of B. placed across it in such a manner as to involve the apparent certain destruction of his life by a passing train; the appearance of A. at an opening in the receptacle, from which A. can see the body of B., audible indications that the train is approaching, successful efforts by A. from within the receptacle, by means of an implement found within it, to obtain egress from it upon the track; and the moving of the body of B. by A., from the impending danger, a moment before the train rushes by. In both of the plays the idea is conveyed that B. is placed intentionally on the track, with the purpose of having him killed. Such idea is, in the plaintiff's play, conveyed by the joint medium of language uttered, and of movements which are the result of prescribed directions, while in Boucicault's play it is conveyed solely by language uttered. The action, the narrative, the dramatic effect and impression, and the series of events in the two scenes, are identical. Both are dramatic compositions, designed or suited for public representation. It is true that in one A. is a woman, and in the other A. is a man; that in one A. is confined in a surface railroad station-shed, and in the other A. is confined in a cellar abutting on the track; that in one A. uses an axe, and in the other A. uses an iron bar; that in one A. breaks down a door, and in the other A. enlarges a circular hole; that in one B. is conscious, and is fastened to the rails by a rope, and in the other B. is insensible, and is not fastened; and that in one there is a good deal of dialogue during the scene, and in the other only a soliloquy by A. and no dialogue. But the two scenes are identical in substance, as written dramatic compositions, in the particulars in which the plaintiff alleges that what he has invented, and set in order, in the scene, has been appropriated by Boucicault.

"All that is substantial and material in the plaintiff's railroad scene has been used by Boucicault, in the same order and sequence of events, and in a manner to convey the same sensations and impressions to those who see it represented, as in the plaintiff's play. Boucicault has, indeed, adapted the plaintiff's series of events to the story of his play, and, in doing so, has evinced skill and art; but the same use is made in both plays of the same series of events, to excite, by representation, the same emotions, in the same sequence. There is no new use, in the sense of the law, in Boucicault's play, of what is found in the plaintiff's railroad scene. The railroad scene in Boucicault's play contains everything which makes the railroad scene in the plaintiff's play attractive as a representation on the stage. As, in the case of the musical composition, the air is the invention of the author, and a piracy is committed if that in which the whole meritorious part of the invention consists is incorporated in another work, without any material alteration in sequence of bars; so in the case of the dramatic composition, designed or suited for representation, the series of events directed in writing by the author, in any particular scene, is his invention, and a piracy is committed if that in which the whole merit of the scene consists is incorporated in another work, without any material alteration in the constituent parts of the series of events, or in the sequence of the events in the series.

"The adaptation of such series of events to different characters who use different language from the characters and language in the first play is like the adaptation of the musical air to a different instrument, or the addition to it of variations or of an accompaniment. The original subject of invention, that which required genius to construct it and set it in order, remains the same in the adaptation. A mere mechanic in dramatic composition can make such adaptation, and it is a piracy, if the appropriated series of events, when represented on the stage, although per-formed by new and different characters using different language, is recognised by the spectator, through any of the senses to which the representation is addressed, as conveying substantially the same impressions to, and exciting the same emotions in the mind, in the same sequence or order. Tested by these principles, the rail-road scene in Boucicault's play is, undoubtedly, when acted, performed, or represented on a stage or public place, an invasion and infringement of the copyright of the plaintiff in the railroad scene in his play."

Infringement of the copy-right in a musical composition. As to what amounts to an infringement of the copyright in a musical composition (a), it has been decided that to publish, in the form of quadrilles and waltzes, the airs of an opera in which there exists an exclusive copyright, amounts to such. In *D'Almaine* v. *Boosey* (b), the plain-tiff published, first the overture, and then a number of airs, and all the melodies. It was admitted that the defendant had published portions of the opera containing the melodious parts of it; that he had also published entire airs; and that, in one of his waltzes, he had introduced seventeen bars in succession containing the whole of the original air, although he added fifteen other bars which were not to be found in it. This, it was contended, was not a piracy: first, because the whole of each air had not been taken; and secondly, because what the plaintiff had purchased of the original author was the entire opera, and the opera consisted, not merely of certain airs and melodies, but of the whole score. Lord Lyndhurst, Chief Baron, however, held, as to the first argument, that piracy might be of part of an air as well as of the whole; and with reference to the second, that, admitting that the opera consisted of the whole score, yet if the plaintiff was entitled to the work, *à fortiori* he was entitled to publish the melodies which formed a part. The Lord Chief Baron regarded the subject of music on a

(a) Assumption of the name and description of a song, see *Chappell* v. *Sheard*, 2 K. & J. 117.

(b) 1 Y. & C. 288. See *Chappell* v. *Sheard*, 1 Jur. (N.S.) 996.

different principle to that which he regarded other literary works; for he would not admit that the adapting for dancing, or otherwise, from the original composition, in which some degree of art is needed, could be deemed such a modification of an original work as should absorb the merit of the original in the new composition. It is the air or melody which is the invention of the author, and which may, in such case, be the subject of piracy; and a piracy is committed if, by taking, not a single bar, but several, that in which the whole meritorious part of the invention consists is incorporated in the new work.

"If," said Lord Lyndhurst, "you take from the composition of an author all those bars consecutively which form the entire air or melody, without any material alteration, it is a piracy; though, on the other hand, you might take them, in a different order, or broken by the intersection of others, like words, in such a manner as should not be a piracy. It must depend on whether the air taken is substantially the same with the original. Now, the most unlettered in music can distinguish one song from another, and the mere adaptation of the air, either by changing it to a dance or by transferring it from one instrument to another, does not, even to common apprehensions, alter the original subject. The ear tells you that it is the same. The original air requires the aid of genius for its construction, but a mere mechanic in music can make the adaptation or accompaniment. Substantially, the piracy is, when the appropriated music, though adapted to a different purpose from that of the original, may still be recognised by the ear. The adding variations makes no difference in the principle."

The author of a dramatic work which has been first represented in a foreign country (such country not being a country with which a convention has been entered into) is not entitled to any exclusive right of representation in this country, the representation of a dramatic work being a publication of it within the meaning of the statute 7 Vict. c. 12, s. 19. This section provides that no author or composer of any dramatic piece or musical composition which shall, after the passing of the Act, be first published out of Her Majesty's dominions, shall have any copyright therein, or any exclusive right to the public representation or performance thereof, otherwise than such (if any) as he may become entitled to under that Act.

The only question which seems to have arisen upon this section has been as to the meaning to be attached to the word "published." In 1863 the point came before Vice-Chancellor Wood with reference to the piece known as 'The Colleen Bawn.' Mr. Boucicault filed his bill against Mr. Delafield, the proprietor of a theatre in the provinces, to restrain his performing this play. It appeared that 'The Colleen Bawn' had been performed in New York, and the Vice-Chancellor decided that the public performance in New York was a publication, and that having published it in that way, Mr. Boucicault was, under the 19th section of the 7 Vict. c. 12, absolutely deprived of the exclusive right in this country (a). After referring to the 19th section the Vice-Chancellor says: "If Mr. Boucicault had first represented his piece in this country, he would have been entitled to the copyright given by the earlier statutes. So, also, if he had given his first representation in any country with which a convention had been made under the International Copyright Act, he would have been entitled under that Act to all the same privileges. But in no case is a person to enjoy any rights conferred by the old Acts concurrently with those created by the International Copyright Act. This is the effect of the 19th section. . . . . The plain purpose of the statute is to secure for this country the benefit of the first publication of new works, and certain conditions are made without which works first published abroad are not to be entitled to copyright. These conditions have not been complied with. The plaintiff, therefore, fails in his demand, and the bill must be dismissed."

The point was again raised by the same plaintiff in a subsequent case (b).

(a) *Boucicault* v. *Delafield*, 1 H. & M. 597.
(b) *Boucicault* v. *Chatterton*, 5 Ch. Div. 267.

Mr. Boucicault applied for an injunction to restrain
Mr. Chatterton, who was the lessee of the Adelphi Theatre,
from representing the drama called 'The Shaughraun,'
the copyright in, and the sole right of representing or
performing which, he claimed. 'The Shaughraun' was
written by the plaintiff in 1874, and was first performed
in New York in November of that year. It was registered
at Stationers' Hall in 1874, as a book under the Copyright Act, 1842, but there being an inaccuracy in the form
of the registration, the drama was again registered in
November, 1876, in the name of Mr. Boucicault as the
proprietor of the copyright. In September, 1875, the
play was produced at Drury Lane under an arrangement
between the plaintiff and defendant, and it was there
performed till the month of December, after which it was
transferred to the Adelphi, and played till January, 1876.
Mr. Boucicault then went to America, where he had been
naturalized. After this a correspondence took place
between the plaintiff and the defendant, in which the
defendant expressed his desire to reproduce the drama
at the Adelphi Theatre, but the plaintiff declined the
defendant's proposals, and refused to permit the performance. The defendant thereupon advertised the performance, and the plaintiff commenced an action. He
claimed under the Act 3 & 4 Will. 4, c. 15, and contended
that his rights under this Act were unaffected by the
7 Vict. c. 12. It was argued that the play had not been
published abroad, as representation did not amount to publication; that the statute 7 Vict. c. 12, only took away the
right conferred by the 3 & 4 Will. 4, c. 15, and preserved
by the 5 & 6 Vict. c. 45, as far as regards plays *published
abroad* by printing. Vice-Chancellor Malins considered
himself bound by the decision in *Boucicault* v. *Delafield*,
and held that the acting of the play in New York was a
publication within the meaning of 7 Vict. c. 12, s. 19,
and that by that publication Mr. Boucicault had lost his
exclusive right of performance.

On appeal this view was confirmed, Lord Justice James

saying : " The 19th section of the International Copyright
Act has a limited purpose only, expressed in terms
shewing the meaning of the word ' published,' which must
express something that can be predicated of a book, of a
dramatic piece, of a musical composition, of a print or
article of sculpture, or any other work of art ; that is to
say, its being made public by those means which are
appropriated to the particular thing.   A book is published
by being printed and issued to the public, a dramatic piece
or a musical composition is published by being publicly
performed, a piece of sculpture or other work of art by
being multiplied by casts or other copies.   That, as it
appears to me, is the natural meaning of the word
' published ' in that section, and that is the meaning
attributed to it by the Vice-Chancellor." And Brett, J.A.,
saying : " A dramatic composition differs from many compositions in this, that it can be made use of in two different
ways.   It may be made use of by printing it, and dis-
tributing it as a written composition or a book.   It may
also be used by having it acted on the stage of a theatre.
If the author be an Englishman, no doubt he has certain
rights given to him by the statute 3 & 4 Will. 4, c. 15,
but a foreign author has no rights at all under that
statute.   If, therefore, a foreign author's play was first
acted abroad, he could not afterwards claim any protection
in England.   He would by acting it abroad have made it
publici juris in England, and, therefore, anybody in England
might act it here.   It is said that an English author,
although he allows his compositions to be acted abroad,
does not come under the same difficulty, because he is
protected by the statute of 3 & 4 Will. 4, c. 15.   That
may be, and although I have some doubts whether the
limitation of the meaning of the word ' published ' which
has been contended for applies even to that statute, I will
assume that it does, and that an Englishman, although
his piece was first acted abroad, could claim the protection
given by the statute of 3 & 4 Will. 4, c. 15.   A foreigner,
however, certainly could not claim that protection.   Then, if

that be the state of things before the statute 7 Vict. c. 12, Cap. XI. we have two sets of people to deal with as regards dramatic compositions, that is, foreign authors who had no protection in England, and English authors who might first of all have their pieces acted abroad, and yet have protection under 3 & 4 Will. 4, c. 15. The statute of Victoria begins by giving the Queen power to give protection to foreign authors and dramatic composers, and that is done under section 5, which has regard to their protection against performances. Their protection against publication by printing is given to them under other sections. The 5th section provides that where the authors of dramatic pieces have first publicly represented or performed them in any foreign country, the Queen shall have the power of giving them sole liberty of representing. or performing the same in any part of Her Majesty's dominions. The statute is dealing with several kinds of things to be protected, which may be published in different ways, and with different persons, with foreigners, and, as we shall presently see, with Englishmen. Then the 19th section provides in perfectly general words, 'That the author of no dramatic piece or musical composition which shall after the passing of this Act be first published out of Her Majesty's dominions shall have any copyright therein respectively, or any exclusive right to the representation or performance thereof, otherwise than such (if any) as he may become entitled to under this Act. Now, it is said that the word 'published' ought to be restricted to the meaning which is said to have been affixed to it in the statute 3 & 4 Will. 4, c. 15. If so, the word 'published,' when applied to English authors, must have one meaning, and another when applied to foreign authors under precisely similar circumstances. That seems to me to be contrary to the common canon of the construction of statutes, for it requires us to introduce into the statute the proviso that in the case of English authors representation out of Her Majesty's dominions shall not be considered a publication. That would be to introduce words which we have no right to introduce, unless there be something in the nature of the case which makes it obvious that such must have been the object of the legislature. It is endeavoured to make out this to have been the object by saying that it is unjust to take away the right of an English author. I see nothing contrary to reason or justice in saying that if an English author chooses to go abroad and there represent, or allow to be represented, his composition for the first time, he shall be in the same position as a foreigner who has done the same thing. If that be so, the word 'published' must have its natural construction, whether it is applied to the compositions of Englishmen or foreigners. That ordinary meaning is 'made public,' and a dramatic composition is made public the moment it is represented or acted. If Englishmen have their plays first represented abroad, they are by this statute placed on the same footing as foreigners; if they have them first represented in England they do not come under this statute at all; but their rights will be governed by 3 & 4 Will. 4, c. 15, and 5 & 6 Vict. c. 45."

A novel may be dramatized without infringement. Though no person may, without the author's written consent, represent the incidents of his published dramatic piece, however indirectly taken, yet no action will lie, at the suit of the author of a novel, against a person who dramatizes it and causes it to be acted on the stage (a).

This was decided in *Reade* v. *Conquest* (b). The second count of the declaration alleged that the plaintiff was the duly registered proprietor of the copyright in a certain registered book, namely, a tale or novel or story entitled 'It is Never too Late to Mend,' and complained that the defendant, without the plaintiff's consent, dramatized the said novel, and caused it to be publicly represented and performed as a drama at the Grecian Theatre for profit, and thereby the sale of the book was injured, &c. To this count there was a demurrer; and it was insisted, on the part of the defendant, that representing the incidents

(a) *Reade* v. *Conquest*, 9 C. B. (N.S.) 755; S. C. 30 L. J. (N.S.) (C.P.) 209; 9 W. R. 434; 7 Jur. (N.S.) 265.   (b) *Ibid.*

of a published novel in a dramatic form upon the stage, CAP. XI. although done publicly and for profit, is not an infringement of the plaintiff's copyright therein; and the Court of Common Pleas was of opinion that the defendant was right (a).

Neither the 3 & 4 Will. 4, c. 15, nor the 5 & 6 Vict. c. 45, contemplated the conversion of a book into a dramatic piece, and the definition of copyright in the second section of the latter Act, "the sole and exclusive liberty of printing or otherwise multiplying copies of any subject to which the said word is herein applied," evidently did not include the claim of the plaintiff in the above case.

All that was here decided was, that the defendant had a right to act, that is to say, to speak and *represent the drama* which was constructed out of the plaintiff's novel; it was not held that the defendant had a right to *print it*.

But the drama may not be printed.

In a subsequent case, in 1862 (b), Lush, as counsel for the defendant, submitted that he had a right to print and publish such a drama, with the exception of any passages which were mere copies of the novel; but the circumstances of the case did not render it necessary that the point should be decided. " If that question should arise," said Erle, C.J., " it would then be time to decide whether the defendant could find any defence; but it is clear he could not in that case defend himself on the ground that he was the author of the parts which he copied."

The question, however, has since arisen in the case of *Tinsley* v. *Lacy* (c). A bill was filed by the publishers and owners of the copyright in two novels, called ' Aurora

---

(a) In a French case cited in Le Blanc on ' Piracy,' p. 233, under the name of *Lefranc* v. *Paul de Brusset,* a different principle was followed. The defendant there had dramatized a tale written by the plaintiff, and represented it upon the stage for profit; the plaintiff claimed to be entitled, as *collaborateur,* to a portion of the profits, and the court decided that, although he could not claim it in that capacity, inasmuch as the adaptation of the tale to the stage was without his knowledge or consent, still he had a good claim for damages against the defendant for the piracy, and it mulcted the defendant in damages and costs.

(b) *Reade* v. *Conquest,* 31 L. J. (C.P.) 153; 8 Jur. (N.S.) 764; 11 C. B. (N.S) 479.

(c) 32 L. J. (Ch.) 535; 11 W. R. 876; 1 Hem. & Mill. 747.

Floyd' and 'Lady Audley's Secret,' written by Miss Braddon. The novels had been dramatized by a Mr. Suter,
and performed at the Queen's Theatre. The defendant,
Mr. Lacy, had *published* the two plays as they were performed. It was proved that a large portion of the dramas,
including the most striking incidents and much of the
actual language of the novels, had been taken bodily
from the novels. Vice-Chancellor Wood, in passing
judgment, admitted that the defendant was entitled to
dramatize the novels for the purpose of a mere acting
drama; but held that he was not so entitled for the
purpose of printing or selling his compilation. "He has
taken," said the Vice-Chancellor, " to use the language of
Lord Cottenham in *Bramwell* v. *Halcomb*, the vital portion
of the novels, the leading incidents of the plot, and in
many instances the very language of the novel itself. He
reprints in his books (and I confine myself to what appears
in the books, and say nothing as to the represented drama),
the very words of the most stirring passages of the novels.
It is no answer to say that similar infringements have often
been committed. Although Sir Walter Scott' and other
authors did not choose to assert any claim of this kind,
this does not affect the rights of the plaintiff; and it is to
be observed, moreover, that there has been a considerable
alteration of the law since the time referred to by the
extension of copyright to dramatic performances. . . .
The question of the extent of appropriation which is necessary to establish an infringement of copyright, is often one
of extreme difficulty; but, in cases of this description, the
quality of the piracy is more important than the proportion which the borrowed passages may bear to the whole
work. Here it is enough to say, that the defendant
admits that one-fourth of the dramas is composed of matter
taken from the novels. In *Campbell* v. *Scott* (a), which
has a strong bearing on this point, the defendants had
published a work containing biographies and selections
from the works of a large number of modern poets, and

(a) 11 Sim. 31; 11 L. J. (N.S.) Ch. 166; 6 Jur. 186.

among others, six short poems, and extracts from larger poems written by the plaintiff. The defence was, that the poems were *bonâ fide* selections, forming a very small proportion of the writings of the plaintiff; that such compilations were cautiously made by the most respectable publishers; that the price of the compilation was £1 1s., while the plaintiff's entire works were published at 2s. 6d.; and that the plaintiff would be rather benefited than injured by the defendants' work, which contained 10,000 lines, of which only a few hundreds were taken from the plaintiff's poems." The Vice-Chancellor, after observing that in the case of the '*Encyclopædia Londinensis*' the jury found for the plaintiff, though the matter taken formed but a very small proportion of the work into which it was introduced, adds, that it is not necessary to consider whether the selections were the cream and essence of all that Mr. Campbell ever wrote. There is no doubt that in this case, as in that of Campbell's poems, the passages taken were the striking passages, and these have been taken by the author of the defendant's publications for the express purpose of using Miss Braddon's property for his own benefit. So long as he confined himself to dramatic representations he could not be interfered with; but when he printed his plays he brought himself within the letter of the law."

The author of a play who makes use of its plot and dialogue in the composition of a novel, does not thereby forfeit his right to restrain infringement of his copyright in the play, although such infringement takes place through the medium of the novel, by a person who was ignorant of the existence of the original play. The indirect appropriation, then, of any portion of the novel taken from the play, is an infringement of the copyright in the play. The plaintiff in *Reade* v. *Lacy* (a), wrote a play called 'Gold,' which he afterwards adapted as a novel, embodied a portion of the dialogue, and called it, 'Never too Late to Mend.' The novel was dramatized by

(a) 1 J. & H. 524.

CAP. XI.   another person, and, in doing so, portions of the original play were copied word for word, and in that form published by the defendant. It was held that ignorance would not justify the infringement of a right in one case more than in another, and that the publication of the play was an infringement of the copyright in 'Gold,' although the existence of that play was not known to the author, who took his materials from the novel (a).

Author cannot protect his novel by dramatizing it after publication.   But, according to the authority of *Toole* v. *Young* (b), an author cannot protect his novel from dramatization by dramatizing it after its publication, it must be effected before publication of the novel. In the case referred to John Hollingshead had published in 1863, in the magazine called 'Good Words,' a story entitled 'Not Above his Business,' which he had written in dramatic form, that it might, with slight alterations, be performed on the stage. Soon after, the author adapted the piece for representation and called the play 'Shop,' which was substantially the same as the published story. In 1865, the play was bought from the author by the comedian Toole; and, when the action was brought, it had not been published or acted. In 1870, Grattan dramatized the story, which had appeared in 'Good Words,' and afterwards sold the play to the defendant, by whom it was repeatedly performed on the stage under the name of 'Glory.' It was admitted that the plays were substantially the same, and that the defendant's had been obtained from the story, and not from the plaintiff's 'Shop.' The judgment of the court was that no rights, either in the work dramatized or in the plaintiff's play, had been invaded by the defendant's dramatization; but, by first publishing his composition as a book, an author forfeits the exclusive right to dramatize and to represent it on the stage; and though he should

---

(a) So in *Lee* v. *Simpson*, 3 C. B. 871; 4 D. & L. 666, where the defendant had purchased the piece which he represented and believed he had a right to, but on proof by the plaintiff that he, the plaintiff, had the right, the judgment was against the defendant. If the plaintiff had been bound to shew the defendant's knowledge, the protection conceded by the statute would be illusory.

(b) L. R. 9 Q. B. 523.

afterwards dramatize his own published composition, he cannot thereby bar others from exercising the same privilege.

It seems doubtful how far the distinction drawn by the court between the publication of the novelist's drama preceding the novel and succeeding the same is sound.

·The only way, therefore, according to the authorities, in which it appears possible for an author to prevent other persons from reciting or representing as a dramatic performance the whole or any portion of a work of his composition, is himself to publish his work in the form of a drama, before publishing the novel and thus bring himself within the scope of the dramatic copyright clauses (a).

(a) As to the dramatization of novels, the Royal Commissioners on Copyright in their recent report say : " With reference to the drama, our attention has been directed to a practice, now very common, of taking a novel and turning its contents into a play for stage purposes, without the consent of the author or owner of the copyright. The same thing may be done with works of other kinds if adapted for the purpose, but inasmuch as novels are more suitable for this practice than other works, the practice has acquired the designation of dramatization of novels. The extent to which novels may be used for this purpose varies. Stories have been written in a form adapted to stage representation almost without change. Sometimes certain parts and passages of novels are put bodily into the play, while the bulk of the play is original matter ; and at other times the plot of the novel is taken as the basis of a play, the dialogue being altogether original.

" Whatever may be the precise form of the dramatization, the practice has given rise to much complaint, and considerable loss, both in money and reputation, is alleged to have been inflicted upon novelists. The author's pecuniary injury consists in his failing to obtain the profit he might receive if dramatization could not take place without his consent. He may be injured in reputation if an erroneous impression is given of his book.

" In addition to these complaints, it has been pressed upon us that it is only just that an author should be entitled to the full amount of profit which he can derive from his own creation ; that the product of a man's brain ought to be his own for all purposes; and that it is unjust, when he has expended his invention and labour in the composition of a story, that another man should be able to reap part of the harvest.

" On the other hand, it has been argued that the principle of copyright does not prevent the free use of the ideas contained in the original work, though it protects the special form in which those ideas are embodied ; that a change in the existing law would lead to endless litigation ; and that it would work to the disadvantage both of the author and the public. Upon these grounds, or some of them, a bill introduced by Lord Lyttleton in 1866 and supported by Lord Stanhope was defeated.

" We have fully considered all these points, and have come to the conclusion that the right of dramatizing a novel or other work should be reserved to the author. This change would assimilate our law to that of France and the United States, where the author's right in this respect is fully protected.

" Were this recommendation adopted, a further question would arise

Not only an original composition, but any substantially new arrangement or adaptation of an old piece of music is a proper subject of copyright (a).

The pianoforte score of an already existing opera, whether arranged by the composer himself or by another person, is the subject of copyright; and as such is entitled to protection, provided the arranger had a right so to use the original. The arrangement of the opera score for the pianoforte involves labour as well as intelligence and skill, which constitutes it a new work (b). In Renouard's 'Traité des Droits d'Auteurs,' tome ii. p. 190, pt. iv. ch. 2, p. 78, it is said: "Des arrangemens, variations, valses, contredanses, etc., composés sur un thème, un air, un motif même, appartenant au domaine public ; des pots-pourris, sorte de compilation musicale, disposés dans un certain ordre et avec certaines liaisons ou transitions, sont-ils des objets de privilège ? Je n'hésite pas à croire que la solution affirmative résulte des principes généraux sur la matière, exposés au commencement de ce chapitre. Il résulte des mêmes principes que ces compositions ne conféreront un privilège qu'autant qu'elles supposeront de l'art, du travail, un effort d'intelligence ; qu'elles seront, en un mot, une production de l'esprit."

And in deciding the point in the last cited case Sir A.

---

as to the time during which this right should be vested in the author, and, in the event of his not choosing to dramatize his novel, whether other persons should be debarred from making use of the story he has given to the world. We are disposed to think that the right of dramatization should be co-extensive with the copyright. It has been suggested in the interest of the public, that a term, say of three or five years, or even more, should be allowed to the author, within which he should have the sole right to dramatize his novel, and that it should be then open to any one to dramatize it. The benefit, however, to the public in having a story represented on the stage does not appear to us to be sufficient to outweigh the convenience of making the right of dramatizing uniform in its incidents with other copyright." Par. 76–81.

(a) So also the arrangement for the piano of quadrilles, waltzes, etc., selected from an opera, is entitled to protection : Atwill v. Ferrett, 2 Blatch. (Amer.) 39. So copyright has been held to vest in a song consisting of new words and a new accompaniment written to an old air : Leader v. Purday, 7 C. B. 4.

(b) Wood v. Boosey, L. R. 2 Q. B. 340; 7 B. & S. 869; 36 L. J. (Q.B.) 103; 15 W. R. 309 ; 15 L. T. (N.S.) 530 ; affirmed 9 B. & S. 175; L. R. 3 Q. B. 223; 37 L. J. (Q.B.) 84 ; 16 W. R. 485; 18 L. T. (N.S.) 105 ; Boosey v. Fairlie, 7 Ch. Div. 301.

Cockburn, C.J., said : " It seems impossible to believe that any musician, however great his talent, whether as a composer or an executant, from the mere circumstance of having the opera in its entirety before him, that is to say, with all the score for all the instruments, which neither eye nor mind could take in at the same time, could be able to play the accompaniment while singing the music of the opera at the piano. It requires time, reflection, skill, and mind so to condense the opera score as to com- pose the pianoforte accompaniment. . . . . I cannot, there- fore, bring myself to think that the pianoforte arrangement of the music of an opera, which originally consisted of vocal music and instrumentation to be executed by some half- hundred instruments, can be said to be anything else than a specific, separate, and distinct work from the opera itself. And it seems to me to hold otherwise would lead to very serious consequences. Operas are very frequently ar- ranged, sometimes by the composer of the opera himself, sometimes by other persons, with the consent or without the consent of the original composer. It may be, if the arrangement be made without the consent of the composer of the opera, such an adaptation would be an infringement of his copyright, which would subject the adapter to an action. It is not necessary to decide that. But it may be that, after the copyright has expired, an arrangement for the pianoforte may be made in the first instance, or some musical composer, thinking that an arrangement that already existed of some well-known and popular opera is not as good as it can be made, might apply his hand to the work and make a new arrangement. Can it be said that such an arrangement, useful as regards the musical world, shall not be the subject of protection under the Copyright Acts ? "

And on appeal Sir Fitzroy Kelly, C.B. (a), in affirming the decision of the Queen's Bench, clearly pointed out the difference between the pianoforte score and the original score, and the fact that each might be the subject of copy-

(a) L. R. 3 Q. B. 223, 229 ; 15 L. T. (N.S.) 530.

right. " The opera " said he, " is composed and is published in score, and contains in each line of what is called
the entire score, the music for some one particular instrument, these instruments being some twenty in number.
Now let us come to what the arrangement is for the
pianoforte. Undoubtedly there are portions of it which
are identical, as in the case before the Exchequer, and
might subject, as I have already observed, the author of
the adaptation to an action if it had been published
without the authority of the author of the opera. But
what is the pianoforte arrangement? It is an arrangement of the whole of the music of this opera for the
pianoforte, a part of which is the ordinary pianoforte
accompaniment, the bass and the treble, played with both
hands, and which is independent of the melody. There
may be, as it appears, the line of music for one voice, or
two or three voices, as the case may be; and there are
separate and distinct lines for the accompaniment for the
pianoforte; and no doubt, here and there throughout this
accompaniment, and by going line by line through the
score of the original opera, there may be found the same
notes; but there are other parts of the accompaniment
which are merely the pianoforte accompaniment, the notes
forming which are nowhere to be found in the score at
all. The accompaniment for the pianoforte is a work of
greater or less skill. In some cases, perhaps in many
cases—it may be in this for aught I know—the operation of
adaptation is little more than mechanical, and what any
one acquainted with the science of music, any composer of
experience, might have been able to do without difficulty;
but it may be, and often is, as in the case of the six operas
of Mozart's, by Mazzinghi, a work—I would hardly use
the term of great genius, but a work—of great merit and
skill of that eminent composer and pianist, Mazzinghi.
If such a work be published as the adaptation to the
pianoforte by a composer, other than the composer of the
original opera, no doubt it is a piracy of the opera, and
the composer may maintain an action against the adapter

or the publisher of the adaptation: but, whenever the copyright in the original opera has expired, if after that, and for the first time, another composer composes another adaptation of that opera to the pianoforte, it is a new substantive work, in respect of which he is just as much entitled to the benefit of the copyright in this country, as the original composer of the opera; and if any one had by an adaptation pirated that arrangement, he would be liable to an action for that piracy. I consider that an infallible test to shew the difference between the one work and the other—between the original opera and the arrangement of it for the pianoforte. It is perfectly clear, therefore, that in point of fact—for it is rather a matter of fact than anything else—the adaptation to the pianoforte, or the arrangement for the pianoforte, of an opera already published, is itself a new and separate work, and is not one and the same with the original opera (a)."

So also with reference to a piece of music called ' Pestal,' which had been played by the military bands in the style of a Russian Polonaise. The plaintiff, in an action for infringement, had got possession of the score, it did not transpire how—set it to words, concocted a thrilling introductory anecdote, and sold the copyright to a music-seller who published it with success. Other publishers arranged new versions of song and verses, for which the proprietor recovered damages. The coincidence between the harmonies and accompaniments in such a case, must be relied on as forming the part alone in which copyright exists. The original composition, if not claimed by any one, becomes public property; and one person has as much right to publish it as another (b).

(a) In this same case Bramwell, B., said: "It has been said that there is nothing inventive on the part of the person who makes the arrangement. In one sense, there is not—that is to say, he neither invents the tune nor the harmony ; but there is invention in another sense, or rather there is composition in the adaptation to the particular instrument. Of that, the adapter is the author, and it is perfectly certain that the man who wanted to arrange this opera for a pianoforte would find it a great deal easier to copy what Brissler had done than to take the score and do it over again."

(b) *Leader* v. *Purday*, 7 C. B. 4.

In *Leader* v. *Cocks*, it was held that one who adapts words to an old air, and procures a friend to compose an accompaniment thereto, acquires a copyright in both words and accompaniment, and his assignee in declaring for an infringement, may describe himself proprietor of the copyright in the whole composition. So in *Chappell* v. *Sheard* (a), where new words had been adapted to an old American melody known as ' Lillie Dale,' in which there was no copyright, to which was added a symphony and accompaniments, and a cadence at the close, and entitled, ' Minnie,' with a portrait of Madame Anna Thillon ; and the defendant published a song to the same air, and called it ' Minnie Dale,' with a similar portrait, but different words, and represented it as having been sung by the same lady, whereas in truth this song had never been sung by her, it was held that the plaintiff had obtained a right of property in the name and description of his song, which a Court of Equity, as in the case of dramatic representations and literature, would restrain any person from infringing ; and that the publication of the defendant's song was a palpable attempt to induce the public to believe that the song so published was the same as that of the first publisher. In another suit (b), where the facts were nearly similar, and the title ' Minnie, dear Minnie,' it was held to be an obvious attempt to pass off the defendant's publication for that of the plaintiff which had obtained the public favour. Neither could the defendant escape his liability by cautioning his shopmen to explain to purchasers that his song was not the same as the plaintiff's ; because he could not secure that retail dealers purchasing from him would give the same information to their customers (c). But the court refused to extend the injunction to restrain the piracy of two bars of music which had been added by the plaintiff to the original air, until the fact had been established by a trial at law. The principle here expressed appears to be that where a

(a) 2 K. & J. 117.   (b) 2 K. & J. 123.
(c) See *Sykes* v. *Sykes*, 3 B. & C. 441.

great resemblance exists between a spurious article and the genuine, although the articles may not be exactly alike, yet if there be that which conveys the idea that the article is genuine, whereby the public is deceived, it is a colourable representation of the original, and a piracy of the author's copyright.

As each of two or more independent dramas from a common original is entitled to protection, one is not a piracy of another, unless there has been unlawful copying.

The 3 & 4 Will 4, c. 15, secures no other right and prohibits no other act than that of representation. The right secured by this statute is re-affirmed, its duration enlarged, and its application extended to musical compositions by the 20th section of the Act of 1842; but the remedies prescribed by the latter statute for the unlawful publication of a book do not apply, and are not extended to the unlicensed representation of a play. For the latter wrong, the penalties given by the statute of William are re-enacted by the 21st section of the 5 & 6 Vict. c. 45. This section gives to the proprietors of the right of dramatic or musical representation or performance, during the term of their interest, all the remedies provided by the 3 & 4 Will. 4, c. 15. By the second section of this latter Act it is enacted, that if any person, during the continuance of the exclusive right of representing a dramatic piece, cause to be represented, without the author's or the proprietor's previous written consent, such production at any place of dramatic entertainment within the British dominions, every such offender shall, for each representation, be liable to the payment of not less than 40s., or of the full amount of the advantage arising from the representation, or of the loss sustained by the plaintiff, whichever shall be the greater damages. These penalties are recoverable by the author or proprietor in any court having jurisdiction in such cases in that part of the British dominions where the offence is committed.

CAP. XI.   When the part taken is material, the plaintiff is not
bound to prove actual damage (a). "The positive enactment," said Tindal, C.J., in the last cited case, "that every
offender shall be liable to an amount not less than 40s.,
or to the full amount of the benefit derived or loss sustained,
shews that damage to the plaintiff is not the test of the
defendant's liability, but that 40s., is to be paid, even if
there be no actual damage." In a recent case (b), however, Lord Hatherley seems to have thought it necessary
to prove damage in order to subject the defendant to the
statutory penalty. "The minimum of damages," said he,
"to be awarded when the fact of damage and the right to
damages have been once established, was no doubt fixed
because of the difficulty of proving with definiteness what
amount of actual damage had been sustained, by perhaps
a single performance at a provincial theatre of a work belonging to a plaintiff, whilst at the same time his work
might be seriously depreciated if he did not establish his
right as against all those who infringed upon it."

The Copyright   The Royal Commissioners in their recent report on
Commis-   Copyright say (c):—"This provision for the 40s. penalty
sioners' sug-
gestions.   has lately been much abused. Copyright in favourite
songs from operas and in other works has been bought,
and powers of attorney have been obtained to act apparently for the owners of the copyright in such works,
and to claim immediate payment of £2 for the performance
of each song. These songs are frequently selected by
ladies and others for singing at penny readings and village
or charitable entertainments, and they sing them, not for
their own gain, but for benevolent objects. In such cases
there is manifestly no intention to infringe the rights of
any person; the performers are unconscious that they are
infringing such rights, and no injury whatever can be inflicted on the proprietors of the copyrights. In many
cases of this kind, and under a threat of legal proceedings,

(a) Planché v. Braham, 4 Bing. N. C. 19; and see Chatterton v. Cave,
3 App. Cas. 498.
(b) Chatterton v. Cave, 3 App. Cas. 492.
(c) Pars. 169, 171, 172.

in default of payment, the penalty has been demanded, and we have reason to believe that the money so demanded has been generally paid. Many instances of this proceeding have been brought to our notice from various parts of the country. . . . The amendment in the law which we propose as most likely to preserve control for the composers, and at the same time to check the existing abuse, is that every musical composition should bear on its title-page a note stating whether the right of public performance is reserved, and the name and address of the person to whom application for permission to perform is to be made. The owner of such composition should only be entitled to recover damages for public performance when such a statement has been made ; and instead of the minimum penalty of not less than 40s. at present recoverable for any infringement of musical copyright by representation, the court should have power to award compensation according to the damage sustained."

It did not seem to them that the abuse above referred to had arisen in the case of dramatic copyright, nor did it seem to them likely to arise so long as the present law of licensing places of dramatic performance exists, and therefore they did not suggest any alteration in the law so far as it applies to that copyright.

The third section of the 3 & 4 Will. 4, c. 15, provides that all proceedings for any offence or injury under that Act shall be brought within twelve months from the committing of the offence, or else the same shall be void and of no effect. This limitation seems to apply only to proceedings for penalties under the Act and not to actions for damages or in equity. ^{Actions to be brought within in twelve months.}

It is sufficient in an action upon this statute to describe the offence in the words of the Act ; and it is not necessary, in order to constitute the offence, to shew that the defendant knowingly invaded the plaintiff's right (a). The object of the legislature was to protect authors

(a) *Lee* v. *Simpson*, 4 D. & L. 666 ; 3 C. B. 871 ; *Reade* v. *Lacy*, 1 J. & H. 524.

against the piratical invasion of their rights, and in construing the law the Judges have given it the fullest interpretation. Therefore in an action of debt to recover penalties under the 3 & 4 Will. 4, c. 15, s. 2, for representing a pantomime, of which the plaintiff was the author, without his license, at a place of dramatic entertainment, upon *nil debet* by statute pleaded, it was held that the plaintiff's undertaking to give material evidence in Middlesex was fulfilled by proof of an offer to sell the pantomime in Middlesex by the plaintiff's agent, acting under his direction (*a*).

Where the plaintiff, as the author of a dramatic work, assigned the " London right " of it to A., the judge at the trial having found that " London right " meant the whole right of representation in London, and that the assignment was to A. and his assigns, it was held that the plaintiff could not bring an action for penalties under the 3 & 4 Will. 4, c. 15, in respect of representations in London, except as trustee for A. and his assigns (*b*).

(*a*) *Lee* v. *Simpson*, 4 D. & L. 666; 3 C. B. 871.
(*b*) *Taylor* v. *Neville*, 47 L. J. Q. B. 254; 26 W. R. 299; 38 L. T. 50.

CHAPTER XII.

COPYRIGHT IN ENGRAVINGS, PRINTS, AND LITHOGRAPHS.

STRANGE yet true it is, that an art of so much importance Nature and
—one which has exercised such an influence on the origin of the right. refinement of the people, and tended so apparently, yet indirectly, to the formation of the polished character of civilized Europe—should have remained for years without any protection whatever from the legislature.

In England, protection was not afforded to the artist until that great engraver and designer, Hogarth, arose like a giant from the most elevated of his associates in the art, and without the aid of his keen and penetrating intellect discovered, that, toil and labour how much soever he might, the product of his intellectual genius was by no means regarded as solely his, nor he deemed to have acquired a more permanent property in it, than the purchaser or imitator of one of his numerous works of art.

Engravings resemble literary works as regards the incorporeal right in them accruing to the author by the exertion of his mental powers in their production; but differ, as they also require a considerable amount of his manual skill and labour; they are, therefore, his property upon the same general principles as any other manufacture.

In handling the present state of the law on this branch of the fine arts we may properly investigate, under one view, the various Acts of Parliament which are particularly appurtenant to the collective arts of designing, engraving, and etching, inasmuch as they, unlike those respecting literary copyright, have not yet been con-

CAP. XII. solidated. A bill, however, to effectuate this, and to consolidate the whole of the law of copyright in works of fine arts, is certainly now before the House, but when it will become law, if at all, is a matter difficult to determine.

Engravings are works having a commercial value, and as such have a double claim upon the protection of the legislature. On the one hand, the artist claims that the productions of his genius may be protected, and injury to his fame and reputation, by the circulation of inferior imitations, prevened or guarded against; and on the other hand, security in the possession of the money value of the creation of his own mind.

Fine arts encouraged by the Stuarts. During the reign of the Stuarts the fine arts received more or less patronage, and engraving and other productive arts began to flourish accordingly. George I. knighted the engraver of the Cartoons. Line engraving, however, had been most cultivated, and the amount of skill required to imitate a plate must have nearly equalled that of its first production; every stroke of the graver would have to be repeated, so that the pirate could hardly undersell the original; and from the costliness of this style and its refinement few could afford to purchase, and perhaps, fewer could appreciate. As so much talent had to be spent by the engraver in transferring the forms to a new medium, from the canvas to the copper-plate, the value of the right of engraving to the owner of the picture was small; and the picture itself, whether a portrait or work of imagination, was executed solely as an individual work of art. Gradually, however, it became the practice to publish small prints, not for the profit on them, but to assist in spreading the reputation of the painter, and this was done in the case of portraits of public men. Of course the name of the artist was not omitted; it was attached to the corner, to secure, not, as now, the property in the print, but the fame of the picture. The diffusion of some new mechanic or chemic arts of engraving or etching facilitated this (a).

(a) Turner on 'Copyright in Designs,' p. 13.

The first Act recognising engraving as an art, and
extending towards its professors the protection they so
unquestionably deserved, was that of the 8 Geo. 2, c. 13,
entitled "An Act for the Encouragement of the Arts of
designing, engraving, and etching historical and other
Prints, by vesting the Properties thereof in the Inventors
and Engravers during the time therein mentioned."
After reciting that "divers persons had, by their genius,
industry, pains, and expense, invented and engraved, or
worked, in mezzotinto or chiaro-oscuro, sets of historical
and other prints, in hopes to have reaped the sole benefit
of their labours, and that printsellers and other persons
had of late, without the consent of the inventors, designers, or proprietors of such prints, frequently taken the
liberty of copying, engraving, and publishing, or causing
to be copied, engraved, and published, base (a) copies of
such works, designs, and prints, to the very great prejudice
and detriment of the inventors, designers, and proprietors
thereof," it enacted, that from and after the 24th of June,
1735, every person who should invent and design, engrave,
etch, or work in mezzotinto or chiaro-oscuro any historical
or other print or prints, should have the sole right and
liberty of printing and representing the same for the term
of fourteen years, to commence from the day of the first
publishing thereof, which should be truly engraved with the
name of the proprietor on each plate, and printed on every
such print or prints. And the Act inflicted on other persons
pirating the same "without the consent of the proprietor
thereof first had and obtained in writing," the penalty of forfeiting the plate, the sheets on which the prints were copied,
together with 5s. for every print so pirated, the one moiety
to the king, and the other to any person who should sue for
the same. And it further provided, that it should be lawful
for any person who should thereafter purchase any plate for
printing from the original proprietor, to print and reprint
from the said plates without incurring any penalty.
Under this Act Lord Hardwicke refused relief to a

(a) See *Graves v. Ashford*, L. R. 2 C. P. 419

person complaining of the piracy of a drawing or design which he had only procured to be made ; "for," said he, "the case was not within the statute, which was made for the encouragement of genius and art ; if it was, any person who employs a printer or engraver would be so too. The statute is, in this respect, like the statute of new inventions, from which it is taken " (a).

In *Blackwell* v. *Harper* (b) it was held that this Act was not confined to works of invention only, but included the designing or engraving anything already in nature, and that a print published of any building, house or garden fell within its scope.

No provision, it will be seen, is in this Act made for the protection of any work of which the engraver is not also the designer ; and this has been accounted for by the fact that Hogarth, by whose influence the Act was introduced, was invariably the designer as well as the engraver of his celebrated works.

The second Act. The 7 Geo. 3, c. 38, was made to remedy this oversight, and protection consequently extended to any person making an engraving from the original work of another. Its title is, " An Act to amend and render more effectual an Act made in the 8 Geo. 2, for Encouragement of the Arts of designing, engraving, and etching historical and other Prints, and for vesting in and securing to Jane Hogarth, widow, the Property in certain Prints." The first section recites that the former Act had been found ineffectual for the purposes thereby intended, and enacts that all and every person and persons who shall invent *or* design, engrave, etch, or work in mezzotinto or chiaro-oscuro, any historical print or prints, or any other print or prints of any portrait, conversation, landscape, or architecture, map, chart, or plan, or any other print or prints whatsoever, shall have the benefit and protection of the said Act and this Act, under the restrictions and limitation thereinafter

---

(a) *Jefferys* v. *Baldwin*, Ambl. 164 ; see *Pierpont* v. *Fowle*, 2 Wood. & Min. (Amer.) 46 ; *Binns* v. *Woodruff*, 4 Wash. (Amer.) 53.
(b) 2 Atk. 93.

mentioned. The second section enacts that all and every person and persons who shall engrave, etch, or work in mezzotinto or chiaro-oscuro, or cause to be engraved, etched, or worked, any print taken from any picture, drawing, model, or sculpture, either ancient or modern, shall have the benefit and protection of the said Act and this Act for the term thereinafter mentioned (twenty-eight years), in like manner as if such print had been graved or drawn from the original design of such graver, etcher, or drafts-man; and, if any person shall engrave, print, and publish, or import for sale, any copy of any such print, contrary to the true intent and meaning of this Act and the said former Act, every such person shall be liable to the penalties contained in the said Act, to be recovered as in the said Acts mentioned (a).

By the next statute of 17 Geo. 3, c. 57, it was enacted, that if any person should within the times limited by the aforesaid Acts or either of them, engrave, etch, or work, or cause, or procure to be engraved, etched, or worked in mezzotinto, or chiaro-oscuro or otherwise, or in any other manner copy in the whole or in part, by varying, adding to, or diminishing from the main design, any copy or copies of any historical print or prints, or any print or prints of any portrait, conversation, landscape, or architecture, map, chart, or plan, or any other print or prints whatso-ever, which had been, or should be engraved, etched, drawn, or designed in any part of Great Britain, without the express consent of the proprietor or proprietors thereof, the proprietor should, by a special action on the case, recover damages against the person so offending.

The inventor of the subject of an artistic design, al-though himself unable to draw, may nevertheless have a copyright in the design in question, if he has employed another person to make the drawings for him, and communi-cated his ideas to that person (b). But the design must be the production of the party claiming the copyright, and

(a) For the defective working of this Act, see Mr. Corrie's remarks in *Reg.* v. *Powell,* the 'Times,' November 10, 1862.
(b) *Stannard* v. *Harrison,* 19 W. R. 811.

difficulties may occasionally arise as to what constitutes a design within the meaning of the statute. "If," says Mr. Curtis (a), "the party personally engraves the subject of his conceptions, then he is both the inventor and designer; since he has not only conceived the subject of the picture, but has represented it in a visible form. But if the engraving is made by another under his direction, it must be made from his 'design;' and the question is, whether this term means only the intellectual conception, or work of the imagination, before it is reduced to some visible form, or whether it implies a drawing or other visible representation of the invention, by the hand of its author. Under the American Act of 29 April, 1802, ch. 36, which contained a similar provision, it was held by Mr. Justice Washington, that the party must not only have invented but he must have designed or represented the subject in some visible form, from which the engraver who executes it must have taken the picture (b). The term 'design,' therefore, means the visible form given to the conception of the mind, and must be done by the inventor himself."

In the case of *Stannard* v. *Harrison* (c) an engraver was examined. He proved that the plaintiff had brought to him his rough sketch or draft, a drawing of the same size as the stone upon which it was to be engraved, pointing out a rough sketch of the forts and towns to give the engraver an idea; he furnished him also with a large French map, and some maps published in the 'Times' and 'Daily Telegraph,' he also gave him notice daily of the earthworks that were made, and produced besides a picture published in the 'Illustrated London News.' The plaintiff could not draw himself—and the Vice-Chancellor said: "That the plaintiff cannot draw himself is a

(a) Copy. 145.
(b) *Binns* v. *Woodruff*, 4 Washington Rep. (Amer.) 48. The Act of 1802 was in these words: "Any person being a citizen of the United States, or a resident within the same, who shall invent and design, engrave, etch, or work, or from his own works and inventions shall cause to be designed and engraved, etched, or worked, any historical or other print, shall have the sole right," &c. *Ib.*
(c) 24 L. T. (N.S.) 570.

matter wholly unimportant if he has caused other persons to draw for him. He invents the subject of the design beyond all question. He prescribes the proportions and the contents of the design; he furnishes a part of the materials from which the drawing has to be made in the first instance, and afterwards collects daily from the proper sources, and even, if it be necessary to say so, from official sources, the decrees, the reports, the bulletins, and accounts contained in the newspapers of the different phases of the war, and especially of the places in which earthworks are thrown up. These he communicates to the man whom he has employed to make a drawing for him. . . . . Can there be anything more plainly within the words of the Act of Parliament than that Mr. Stannard did himself invent, that he did procure another person to design and draw for him, and do that which he himself could not do ? "

In order to vest the copyright of an engraving in the Provisions of designer or engraver of the same, no registration, such as Acts to be strictly is necessary in the case of literary copyright, is required ; complied with. the Acts above enumerated have merely to be strictly complied with. In the first place, it is therefore important that engravings should contain the date of publication and name of the publisher, in order to entitle the party to the penalties imposed by the statute Geo. 2. The reason assigned by the court in *Sayer* v. *Dicey* (a) being, " that any person may know when the proprietor's exclusive right ceases, and when, and against whom, he may be guilty of offending contrary to the statute." Lord Hardwicke, in an early case, doubted whether the clause on this subject in the Act ought to be construed as directory or descriptive, but he was of opinion that the property was vested absolutely in the engraver, although the *day* of publication was not mentioned, and compared it to the clause under the statute of Anne, which requires entry at Stationers' Hall, upon the construction of which it has been determined that the property vests although the direction has not been

(a) 3 Wils. 60.

CAP. XII. complied with (a). However, it has subsequently been taken for granted by the Court of King's Bench that both the name and date should appear; the *date*, Lord Kenyon observed, is of importance, that the public may know the period of the monopoly; the *name* should appear, in order that those who wish to copy it may know to whom to apply for consent (b).

As to the date. So in *Harrison* v. *Hogg* (c) Lord Alvanley differed from Lord Hardwicke, considering the insertion of the name and date essential to the plaintiff's right; that the correct date is a *sine quâ non* was expressly decided in *Bonner* v. *Field* (d). It was an action for pirating a print of the seal of the Countess of Talbot. The plaintiff had been employed by Lady Talbot to engrave this plate for her, which he executed on the 1st of June, 1778, when he took off some impressions for her use. On the *following day* she gave the plate to the plaintiff, who engraved on the bottom of it, "Drawn and engraved by J. Bonner; published on the 1st of June, 1778, as the Act directs." The declaration having stated that the plaintiff was the proprietor on the 1st of June, Lord Mansfield nonsuited the plaintiff on the ground that he had no title on the day when he claimed it.

The cases were fully reviewed and commented on in the leading case on the subject of *Newton* v. *Cowie* (e), and it was held that the proprietor's name and the date of publication must appear on the original print, but that it was not necessary that the designation "proprietor" should be

---

(a) *Blackwell* v. *Harper*, 2 Atk. 95 ; Barn. Ch. Rep 210. See *Jefferys* v. *Baldwin*, Amb. 164; *Roworth* v. *Wilkes*, 1 Camp. 94; *Harrison* v. *Hogg*, 2 Ves. Jun. 323 ; *Thompson* v. *Symonds*, 5 T. R. 41.

(b) *Thompson* v. *Symonds*, *supra*; *Mackmurdo* v. *Smith*, 7 T. R. 518; *Harrison* v. *Hogg*, *supra*.

(c) 2 Ves. Jun. 323 ; *Newton* v. *Cowie*, 4 Bing. 234 ; *Brooks* v. *Cock*, 3 Ad. & E. 138, 4 N. & M. 652; *Colnaghi* v. *Ward*, 12 L. J. (N.S.) (Q.B.) 1; 6 Jur. 969 ; *Bogue* v. *Houlston*, 5 De G. & Sm. 267; *Graves* v. *Ashford*, 15 W. R. 495; Kerr on Injunc. 465; *Kock* v. *Lazarus*, L. R. 15 Eq. 104; 27 L. T. (N.S.) 744. So the proprietor of a foreign print must print his name and the date of publication on the plate as required by 8 Geo. 2, c. 13, in order to claim copyright under the International Copyright Acts : *Avanzo* v. *Mudie*, 10 Exch. 203.

(d) Cited 5 T. R. 44.

(e) 4 Bing. 234

added to the name; and that the words on the print
"*Newton del.*, 1*st May*, 1826, *Gladwin sculp.*," was a
sufficient compliance with the provisions of the 8 Geo. 2,
c. 13. Best, C.J., on the occasion saying: " Looking at
the subject-matter of the law, at the language employed
by the legislature, and the practice which has uniformly
been followed by engravers, we cannot hesitate to determine that the proprietors of these prints are entitled to
the protection which is afforded by the statutes; a decision we have come to with satisfaction, seeing that
they exercise a branch of art eminently useful and which
in no slight degree *emollit mores, nec sinit esse feros.*
They contribute also by the same means to the circulation of a knowledge of mechanics so necessary to our
manufactures, and so useful to the best interests of the
country."

These essentials, in order to secure to the artist the Engravings or etchings when published with letter-press.
copyright in engravings or etchings when published sepa-
rately, are not requisite where the engravings form part
of a book in which there is copyright; for the Copyright
Act, 1842, gives a copyright in " every volume, part or
division of a volume, pamphlet, sheet of letter-press, sheet
of music, manuscript, map, plan, or chart, separately published," and this definition, though it would not, of course,
extend to prints or designs separately published, yet is
sufficiently comprehensive to include prints and designs
forming part of a book. The book is not less a book
because it contains prints or designs, or other illustrations
of the letter-press. A book must include every part of
the book; it must include every print, design, or engraving which forms part of the book, as well as the letter-
press therein, which is another part of it. A plaintiff
published a book containing letter-press, illustrated by
wood engravings, printed on the same paper at the same
time. The defendants published a similar book with different letter-press, but containing pirated copies of the
wood engravings. The plaintiff, upon motion for an injunction, proved that he had complied with the requisi-

CAP. XII.   tions of the Copyright Act, 1842, but had not complied with the Act for the protection of engravings (8 Geo. 2, c. 13), by printing the date of publication and the name of the proprietor on each copy. Vice-Chancellor Parker considered the plaintiff entitled to an injunction, for upon the construction of the 5 & 6 Vict. c. 45, where there are designs forming part of a book in which a person has copyright, such copyright extends to the illustrations and designs of the book, equally as to the letter-press (a).

Maps.   In regard to copyright in maps, there are two concurrent Acts relating to the same thing, the Literary Copyright Act, 1842 (5 & 6 Vict. c. 45), and the series of Acts, viz.: 8 Geo. 2, c. 13; 7 Geo. 3, c. 38; and 17 Geo. 3, c. 57.

Maps published together or in connection with letter-press, obviously come within the head "book," and as such are included in the former Act.

Maps, charts, or plans, separately published, are within the above Engraving Acts, as also within the 3rd section of the Literary Copyright Act. Viewed in the light of literary efforts they are entitled to copyright under the latter Act during the life of the author, and for seven years after his death, or for the term of forty-two years, as the case may be. Regarded as artistic works under the former statutes they are entitled to protection for an absolute term of twenty-eight years. Yet no action or suit in respect of an infringement of such copyright can be maintained under the 5 & 6 Vict. c. 45, until the author shall have previously registered in the manner prescribed by section 13 of the Act (b); nor under the Acts of Geo. 2 and Geo 3, unless the proprietor shall have printed his name and the day of publication on every copy (c).

This appears to be the law on the subject, notwithstanding the impression receivable from the unguarded decision in *Stannard* v. *Lee*; and the inference from that case to be

(a) *Bogue* v. *Houlston*, 5 De G. & Sm. 267; *Woods* v. *Highley*, 1866, before Vice-Chancellor Wood.

(b) *Stannard* v. *Lee*, 19 W. R. 615; L. R. 6 Eq. 346.

(c) *Bogue* v. *Houlston*, 5 De Gex & Sm. 267.

drawn would seem to be that if the proprietor wishes to
sue in respect of an infringement without having registered,
he must allege that it is an engraving, or otherwise bring
it within the Acts of Geo. 2 and Geo. 3, which do not
require registration, for in the event of his alleging he
has printed and published "a map," the plea that the map
has not been registered will meet the case; and this
under the rule that every allegation is to be taken most
strongly against the pleader, and therefore the defendant
is entitled to say that the thing which the plaintiff alleged
to be a map, was a map within 5 & 6 Vict. c. 45, and
consequently required to be registered (a).

In *Stannard* v. *Lee* (b), where the plaintiffs printed and
published on the 21st of July, 1870, a map described as
'No. 1, Stannard & Son's Panoramic Bird's-eye View of
France and Prussia, and the surrounding countries likely
to be involved in the war, with the railways and strategic
positions of each army, and the great fortresses of the
Rhine provinces,' and filed affidavits alleging in substance
that they had formed a design of publishing maps illustrating the seat of war, and had "designed a map," and
on the date above mentioned had "in accordance with the
Acts of Parliament in that behalf," printed and published
the said map by the above description, and that they were
proprietors of the map; it was held, that notwithstanding
that on the map itself it appeared that Messrs. Packer and
Griffin were the delineators and lithographers of the map,
there was a sufficient proof under the requirements of the
Acts of the plaintiffs' proprietorship, and a motion to
dismiss an *ex parte* injunction obtained against the defendant to restrain the infringement of the copyright
claimed by the plaintiffs, on the ground, "first, that the
plaintiffs were not registered as proprietors under the Act
of 5 & 6 Vict. c. 45; and, secondly, that it had not appeared on the map that they were the proprietors of the
copyright, was refused. "The Acts of Geo. 2 and Geo. 3,"

(a) See *Stannard* v. *Harrison*, 19 W. R. 811.
(b) 23 L. T. (N.S.) 306.

said Vice-Chancellor Bacon, "are not mentioned in the Act of 5 & 6 Vict. c. 45, and I do not construe that Act as interfering in any way with the previous Acts, and 15 Vict. c. 12, and the rights conferred thereby." The Lords Justices, however (a), were of opinion that the earlier Acts are virtually repealed by the 5 & 6 Vict. c. 45, and that registration is, therefore, a necessary preliminary to a suit for an infringement of copyright in the case of a map separately published. Lord Justice James said: "In this case, if the argument of Mr. Cotton were to prevail, it would lead at once to one of these two results; either there would be two kinds of maps,—maps published separately and maps forming part of a book, with respect to which there would be two distinct laws of copyright,— or else as to all maps there would be two distinct laws of copyright, one giving a conditional right of property with an unconditional right of action or suit, the other giving an unconditional right of property with a conditional right of action or suit. Either of these states of the law would be strangely inconvenient.

"Thus 5 & 6 Vict. c. 45, s. 2, says that a book shall mean and include every map, chart, or plan separately published; and in the 24th section it proceeds to say that no proprietor of copyright in any book, that is of a map, chart, or plan separately published, according to the definition given of a book, shall maintain an action or suit in respect of any infringement of such copyright unless he shall have previously registered such map, chart, or plan, in the way prescribed by the Act. No very heavy *onus* on the proprietor—no very difficult step to take before he commences his suit. The words are plain and simple, and there is no reason for saying that the intention of the legislature was different from that which is expressed by the words. The object of the enactment is very clear. Formerly maps have been considered artistic works: now they were to be brought into their proper place as literary works. And rightly so, in my opinion, for maps are

(a) *Stannard* v. *Lee*, 19 W. R. 615; L. R. 6 Ch. 346.

intended to give information in the same way as a book
does. A chart, for instance, gives similar information to
sailing rules; maps give instruction as to statistics and
history of the country portrayed; they point out the
amount of population, the places where battles were fought,
the dates when provinces were annexed, as in maps of
India, and give other geographical and historical details.
It was quite reasonable, therefore, to take them out of the
law of artistic works, and to give them greater protection
by bringing them under the law of copyright of literary
works. There is no inconvenience in giving the natural
meaning to the words of the statute, and there would be
great inconvenience in the contrary construction. I think,
therefore, the plea was well pleaded, and the plaintiffs
are not entitled to maintain their suit until they have
registered their maps."

Vice-Chancellor Bacon, however, evidently adhered to
his original decision, or rather to the exposition of the law
there given, and in the case of *Stannard* v. *Harrison* (a),
which was decided after the Lords Justices had reversed
his decision in *Stannard* v. *Lee*, he explained that they
held the map in question not to be protected "because
the plaintiff had alleged in his bill that he had invented
a design," and published a "map," and the defendants
there pleaded, relying on the large interpretation of the
word "book" in the last Act, that the statute prohibited
the institution of any suit before registration had been performed. But in the case then before him the facts were
different. The plaintiffs carried on the business of lithographers and publishers, and had acquired a reputation as
publishers of maps and lithographic views in the nature of
maps during the American War, giving bird's-eye views in
apparent relief of the seat of war. During the war between
France and Germany the plaintiffs published a series of
bird's-eye views or plans illustrating the seat of war, of
which they sold a great number of copies. On the 1st of
September, 1870, the plaintiffs published a bird's-eye view

(a) 19 W. R. 811; 24 L. T. (N.S.) 570.

CAP. XII.   of Paris and its fortifications under the following description : "No. 8, Stannard & Son's Perspective View of Paris
and its Environs, shewing all the fortifications and redoubts,
together with the lines of defence recently thrown up, and
the roads, rivers, and railways communicating with the
interior, compiled from the latest official sources by
Alfred Concanen." The plaintiffs alleged that this view
was duly designed, or caused to be designed and lithographed, and was duly printed and published by them in
accordance with the provisions of the several Acts of
Parliament made in that behalf, and that the lithographed copies of this view were prints within the
meaning of these Acts. The defendants were the proprietors of a weekly periodical called the 'Gentleman's
Journal and Youth's Miscellany,' and with the number of
that journal of the 1st of November, 1870, they published
a bird's-eye view of Paris and its fortifications, which the
plaintiffs alleged was an imitation of their view and an
infringement of their copyright. The plaintiffs accordingly filed their bill, and on the 19th of November, 1870,
a decree was made by consent, by which a perpetual injunction was granted restraining the defendants from
printing, publishing, or selling these views, directing an
inquiry as to damages, and ordering the defendants to pay
the plaintiffs' costs.

The defendants petitioned for a rehearing of the suit,
or for leave to file a bill of review on the grounds,
amongst others, that the plaintiffs had not registered their
alleged proprietorship of copyright in the bird's-eye view
in question at Stationers' Hall, pursuant to the 5 & 6 Vict.
c. 45, s. 13; that the facts in the case were substantially
the same as those in *Stannard* v. *Lee*; that on the
authority of that decision, as the plaintiffs had not before
the commencement of the suit registered their alleged
proprietorship of the copyright, they were debarred by
the 5 & 6 Vict. c. 45, from maintaining the suit, and that
that statute precluded the Vice-Chancellor from making
the decree, even with consent.

Bacon, V.C., dismissed the petition, refusing to re-open
the question, and in the course of his judgment said :—
"The case was formerly argued before me upon these
different statutes (the statutes of Geo. 2 and Geo. 3), and
Mr. Fooks in his argument insisted that the 5 & 6 Vict.
c. 45, containing that prohibition against commencing any
action or suit until registration had taken place, and
there being no evidence that that registration had been
made, he was entitled to use that as an objection to the
continuation of the injunction which had been granted.
I considered the point at the time. I have considered it
since, and more especially have I considered the judgment
of the Lords Justices, and I am of opinion that that
statute has nothing in the world to do with it. That
there is no prohibition in the first two statutes I have
mentioned is unquestionable ; and although in the case
of *Stannard* v. *Lee* before the Lords Justices it was held
that the design there was not protected for want of
registration, that was because the plaintiff had alleged
in his bill that he had invented a design and published
a map, and the defendant there pleads, relying on the
large interpretation of the word 'book' in the last Act,
that the statute prohibited the institution of any suit
before registration had been performed. Both the Lords
Justices were of that opinion, but the Lords Justices have
said nothing in any part of their judgment about the other
two statutes except this : The plaintiff's counsel, desiring
to save himself by reference to the earlier statutes, they
said 'You cannot do that now you are here ; the plea has
been filed to your bill, and the plea meets everything that
you allege in your bill ; the plea must be either allowed
or overruled.' The statutes were the thing relied upon.
Every word of the Lords Justices' judgment proceeds
upon that ground, and they never considered anything
but that. The judgment of Mellish, L.J., puts that in the
plainest light. He, as it were, congratulates them on
having, by a mere trick, or accident, the good fortune of
placing a technical difficulty in the plaintiff's way so as to

get the plea allowed; but there is not a word about any meritorious elements in the case on the part of the defendant; there is not any doubt expressed that the plaintiff's claim in morals and in truth was a perfectly good and just claim. That this was so is seen in another part of the judgment, where the Lord Justice, answering Mr. Cotton, who desired to amend his bill so as to raise that question as to its being an historical engraving, says: 'You ought to file a new bill; you have yourself put it in the category of maps.' Nothing could be further from my wish and desire, as nothing could be more opposed to the proper discharge of my duty, than to call in question, or to express any doubt, of the correctness of the judgment of the Lords Justices, or to decline to follow it. I am bound by whatever judgment they pronounce.

" Upon the question of the prohibition contained in the statute, I can see no application to this case, because there is no prohibition in the two statutes upon which alone the plaintiffs can rely. An argument was addressed to me upon the Shipping Acts; it is not necessary to pause long upon that in order to see that there is no kind of resemblance between the two things. It is for the public benefit, for the actual defence of the realm among other things, that certain restrictions should be placed upon dealings in ships, and therefore the legislature has thought fit to lay down certain conditions with respect to which there can be no doubt, and without which having been fulfilled there is no validity in any contract entered into. The court is bound to take notice of all those things there stated which are applicable to the matter. But there are many other statutes; there are statutes, for example, which require notice to be given before an action shall be brought against a magistrate. There has been a very notorious statute in force for a long time, 1 mean the Statute of Frauds, but unless the objection is raised, the court never pays any attention to it. The court does not attend to the Statute of Frauds unless it is pleaded in some way or other. That is a prohibition

of the same kind and degree as that which is contained CAP. XII.
in the Act of the 5 & 6 Vict. c. 45, and that is done in
order that every man who is dealing with this kind of
property, who is the owner of it, should have a place to
resort to, to satisfy any inquiries that he may choose to
make. There is nothing to induce us to call it a prohibition beyond what the necessities of the case require.
The new matter which has been discovered consists of the
judgment of the Lords Justices, and of facts which have
been extracted from Mr. Concanen in his examination,
which I do not think maintain the defendant's contention
in the slightest degree. All those things now before the
court, in my opinion, furnish no reason for a rehearing
of this case" (a).

As to Christmas cards, the mode in which the copyright Christmas
should be secured depends to a certain extent on their cards.
nature and general character. Some are of such a nature
as that protection may be found under the Engravings
Acts of Geo. 2 and Geo. 3; or the 25 & 26 Vict. c. 68,
if in the nature of a painting, drawing, or photograph;
others again may be registered under the Ornamental
Designs Act, 1842.

It matters not whether the person selling the pirated Ignorance no
engravings is aware of their being spurious or genuine; excuse.
for though the 8 Geo. 2, c. 13, imposed, first, a penalty
upon any person who should engrave, copy, or sell, or
cause to be copied or sold, in the whole or in part, by
varying, adding to, or diminishing from the main design;
and, secondly, upon persons selling the same, " *knowing the
same to be so printed or reprinted ;* " yet in the 17 Geo. 3,
c. 57, the words "knowing the same to be printed or
reprinted" are omitted; and it may, therefore, fairly be
inferred that the legislature intended to comprehend
even those who were not aware that they were selling base
copies (b).

(a) *Stannard* v. *Harrison*, 24 L. T. (N.S.) 570.
(b) *West* v, *Francis*, 5 Barn. & Ald. 737 ; 1 D. & R. 400 ; *Gambart* v.
Sumner. 1 L. T. (N.S.) 13 ; 5 Hurl. & Nor. 5 ; *Clement* v. *Maddick*, 1 Giff.
98 ; 5 Jur. (N.S.) 592.

The former part of the 17 Geo. 3, c. 57, s. 1, applies to persons who actually make the copy, and who therefore must know it to be a piracy. But the latter branch applies to all persons who import for sale, or sell, any copy of a piratical print.

As to what is an infringement.   What is an infringement is, in many cases, a difficult matter to solve. There can be no reason why a person should not be liable where he sells a copy with a mere collusive variation, for a copy is defined to be that which comes so near to the original as to give to every person seeing it the idea created by the original (a).

Great solicitude is requisite to guard against two extremes equally prejudicial : the one, that men of ability, who have employed their energies for the service of the community, may not be deprived of their just merits, and the reward of their ingenuity and labour ; the other, that the community may not be deprived of improvements, nor the progress of the arts retarded. The Act which secures copyright to authors, guards against the piracy of the words and sentiments, but it does not prohibit writing on the same subject. As in the case of histories and dictionaries : in the first, a man may give a relation of the same facts, and in the same order of time ; in the latter, an interpretation is given of the identical words. In all these cases the question of fact to come before a jury is, whether the alteration be colourable or not ? There must be such a similitude as to make it probable and reasonable to suppose that one is a transcript of the other, and nothing more than a mere transcript. So in the case of prints, no doubt different men may take engravings from the same picture. There is no monopoly of the subject here any more than in the other instances, but upon any question of this nature, the jury will have to decide whether it be a servile imitation or not (b).

The first engraver does not claim the monopoly of the use of the picture from which the engraving is made ; he

(a) West v. Francis, 5 Barn. & Ald. 737. See Roworth v. Wilkes, 1 Camp. 94 ; Moore v. Clark, 9 M. & W. 692.
(b) Sayre v. Moore, 1 East, 361, n.

says, Take the trouble of going to the picture yourself, but CAP. XII.
do not avail yourself of my labour, who have been to the
picture and have executed an engraving (*a*).

Where an engraving is made of an object in nature, as An engraver
of a particular flower or plant, the artist cannot restrain has no mono-
any one from executing a similar print of the same flower subject.
or plant; but no one is allowed to copy from the work of
another person, each must draw from nature. When it
was contended before Lord Hardwicke (*b*) that some
engravings of plants could not be protected, because every
herbal-book had prints of those plants in them, he
observed: "The defendant, to make out the case he aims
at, must shew me that these prints of medicinal plants
are in any book or herbal whatsoever, in the *same manner
and form* as they are represented here; for they are
represented in all their several gradations, the flower, the
flower-cup, the seed-vessel and the seed."

So on the same principle if two persons should *bonâ fide*
make engravings from a perusal of the same text,
although there might, and probably would be, a similarity
between them, yet each would acquire a copyright in the
engraving which he has made.

An engraver is invariably a copyist, and if engravings
from drawings were not to be deemed within the intention
of the legislature these Acts would afford no protection
to that most useful body of men, the engravers. The
engraver, although a copyist, produces the resemblance
he is desirous of obtaining by means very different from
those employed by the painter or draftsman from whom
he copies: means which require great labour and talent.
The engraver produces his effects by the management of
light and shade, or, as the term of his art expresses it,
the *chiaro-oscuro.* The due degrees of light and shade
are produced by different lines and dots; he who is the
engraver must decide on the choice of the different lines
or dots for himself, and on his choice depends the success

(*a*) *De Berenger* v. *Wheble*, 2 Stark. N. P. C. 548.
(*b*) *Blackwell* v. *Harper*, 2 Atk. 94; S. C. Barn. 210.

2 B

CAP. XII.   of his print. If he were to copy from another engraving, he might see how the person who engraved that had produced the desired effect, and so without skill or attention become a successful rival (a).

Engraving Acts extended to Ireland.   The Engraving Acts were extended to Ireland in 1837. By the 6 & 7 Will. 4, c. 59, it was enacted that, from and after the passing of that Act, if any engraver, etcher, printseller, or other person should, within the period limited for the protection of copyright in engravings, engrave, etch, or publish, or cause to be engraved, etched, or published, any engraving or print of any description whatsoever, either in whole or in part, which might have been or which should thereafter be published in any part of Great Britain or Ireland, without the express consent of the proprietor or proprietors thereof first had and obtained, in writing signed by him, her, or them respectively with his, her, or their own hand or hands in the presence of and attested by two or more credible witnesses, then every such proprietor might, by and in a separate action upon the case, to be brought against the person so offending in any court of law in Great Britain or Ireland, recover such damages as a jury on the trial of such action, or on the execution of a writ of inquiry thereon, should give or assess.

Engravings. Acts to include lithographs.   The 15 & 16 Vict. c. 12, s. 14, declares that the provisions of this Act and the Engraving Acts collectively are intended to include prints taken by lithography or any other mechanical process by which prints or impressions of drawings or designs are capable of being multiplied indefinitely, and the said Acts shall be construed accordingly.

The right in engravings may be infringed by photography.   It is therefore an infringement of the copyright given by the Engraving Acts to copy by photography, or sell a photographic copy of a print in which a copyright has been acquired under these Acts (b). The question arose not long since.

<hr/>

(a) *Newton* v. *Cowie, per* Best, C.J., 4 Bing. 246; *Martin* v. *Wright,* 6 Sim. 297.
(b) *Gambart* v. *Ball,* 14 C. B. (N.S.) 306; 9 Jur. (N.S.) 1059; 11 W. R. 699; 32 L. J. (C.P.) 166; *Graves* v. *Ashford,* 15 W. R. 495; L. R. 2 C. P. 410; 16 L. T. (N.S.) 98; 36 L. J. (C P.) 139.

It was in an action for the infringement by the defendant of the plaintiff's copyright in two engravings, the one from Rosa Bonheur's 'Horse Fair,' the other from Holman Hunt's 'Light of the World.' It was proved that the plaintiff was the proprietor of these two engravings, and that the defendant had copied them on a very reduced scale by means of photography, and sold a great number of copies. The point was argued before the Court of Common Pleas, and it was unanimously decided that all processes for the indefinite multiplication of copies, whether mechanical or otherwise, were within the Acts for the protection of artists and engravers ; and that when they declare mechanical processes of multiplying copies to be within them, no doubt they would have also thus declared the multiplication by means of photography, if the art of photography had then been known. If the object of the Acts of Parliament on the subject were, not simply to protect the reputation of the artist or the engraver, but to protect him against the invasion of his substantial commercial property in the work of his genius or of his industry, it is plain that he sustains an injury by another offering a photographic copy which is capable of exciting in the mind of the beholder the same or some- what similar pleasurable emotions as would be com- municated by a copy of the engraving itself. The value of the artist's property would be sensibly diminished were the multiplication of copies by means of photography held to be lawful. In the case above referred to, Chief Justice Erle, in passing judgment, said : " In the repre- sentation of ' The Horse Fair,' we feel the same degree of pleasure in looking at the forms and attitudes of the beautiful animals there portrayed, whether we see them in the size in which they are drawn in the original picture, or in the reduced size of the engraving, or in the still more diminished form in which they appear in the photo- graph. . . . The object of the statute, to my mind, was, not merely to prevent the reputation of the artist from being lessened in the eyes of the world, but to secure to him the commercial value of his property, to encourage the arts, by securing to the artist a monopoly in the sale of an object of attraction. . . . It seems to me that the making of copies in that way and selling them is within the words as well as the meaning of the Act " (a).

Though the language of the statute includes, as we have seen, copies made by mechanical or chemical process, and capable of being multiplied indefinitely, yet it has been doubted whether it would include copies made by hand or designs transferred to an article of manfacture.

At the date of the first edition of this work it had not been decided whether the words of the statute would include designs transferred to an article of manufacture (b).

The point however arose in the recent case of *Dicks* v. *Brooks* (c). Plaintiffs were the publishers and proprietors of a weekly periodical called 'Bow Bells.' Defendants were the proprietors by assignment of the copyright of a print called ' The Huguenot,' engraved from Millais' picture, and of a photograph taken from the print. The plaintiffs had published for their Christmas number of 1877 a chromo-printed pattern for wool-work, called ' The Huguenot,' taken, as they stated, from a Berlin wool pattern which had been imported by a German warehouse. The leading incident of Millais' picture, the farewell of two lovers of different creeds on the eve of the massacre of St. Bartholomew, was to be found in the Berlin wool pattern, but a different background had been introduced, and the colours were not the same as those of the picture. In December, 1877, the defendants issued a circular containing a warning against the sale of any copy of the subject, ' The Huguenot,' without the stamp or imprint of their firm, in whom the sole subsisting copyright existed, and that all such unstamped copies were imitations and unlawfully made. The plaintiffs, alleging that the publication of this circular was a false and malicious libel on

(a) This judgment was confirmed on appeal by the Court of Exchequer Chamber.

(b) See remarks of Byles, J., in *Gambart* v. *Ball*, 32 L. J. (N.S.) (C.P.) 166, 168.   (c) 15 Ch. Div. 22.

their print and pattern, which was not an imitation of any picture to the copyright of which the defendants were entitled, and that their sale of the publication had been greatly damaged by such circular, brought an action to restrain, and obtain damages for, this alleged libel and slander of title. The defendants by their statement of defence and counterclaim asserted their title to the engraving, averring that the plaintiffs had unlawfully copied it in whole or in part, and greatly damaged the defendants' property therein; and they claimed an injunction and the penalty of 5s. under the Act 8 Geo. 2, c. 13, for every copy sold by the plaintiffs, and damages.

Vice-Chancellor Bacon held that the defendants had the exclusive right of publishing the subject delineated in the print taken from Millais' picture. He considered that the plaintiffs' pattern was to all intents and purposes a direct copy of that print. Were they then entitled, said he, to despoil the defendants of their property, and foist upon the public a very coarse imitation of a very celebrated picture. Being mere pirates, they complained that their title was being slandered, and that they were injured by the circular issued by the defendants for the protection of their property. It was the old story of the wolf and the lamb. There was no pretence for the first action, which he accordingly dismissed with costs; and as the defendants had established the right set up by their counterclaim to restrain this piratical publication by the plaintiffs, he decided that they were entitled to the statutory penalty of 5s. for every copy sold by the plaintiffs. The court, however, on appeal held that a pattern for Berlin wool-work could not be regarded as a copy of an engraving within the meaning of the statutes, inasmuch as though there was a reproduction of the design, there was no reproduction of anything which constituted the work of the engraver. And they accordingly reversed the judgment of the Vice-Chancellor (a).

(a) 15 Ch. Div. 22. The judgment of the Lords Justices in this important case will be found in the Appendix.

And where the print or engraving differs materially
from the original in character, and is dealt with in a
different manner, the former cannot be considered a piracy
of the latter within these Acts. Thus in 1821, plaintiff, a
celebrated artist, composed and painted from sketches he
had designed a picture called ' Belshazzar's Feast,' which
he shortly afterwards sold. In 1826 he engraved and
published from the sketches a print of the same name,
having previously done all necessary acts for securing to
himself the copyright of the print. The defendant having
purchased one of the prints, had it copied on canvas in
colours on a very large scale, with dioramic effect; and
he publicly exhibited such dioramic copy at the Queen's
Bazaar in Oxford Street for money, describing it, in
his handbills and advertisements, as "Mr. Martin's grand
picture of ' Belshazzar's Feast,' painted with dioramic
effect." The plaintiff applied for an injunction, but the
Vice-Chancellor refused to grant one, on the ground that
exhibiting for profit was in no way analogous to selling a
copy of the plaintiff's print, but was dealing with it in a
very different manner. The Engravings Acts were not
intended to apply to a case where there was no intention
to print, sell, or publish, but to exhibit in a certain
manner. "If, however," added the Vice-Chancellor,
" Martin had exhibited his picture as a diorama, then he
might have been entitled to an injunction " (a).

The statutes do not apply to the sale of prints taken
from the original plate with the consent of the proprietor.
In *Murray* v. *Heath* (b) where the defendant, an engraver,
took a number of impressions from a plate engraved by
himself, but for the use of the plaintiff, he being permitted to retain certain copies, but not to sell them;
afterwards defendant became bankrupt, and his assignees
advertised the copies retained for sale. In an action for
damages, in which the assignees were co-defendants, the
defence was set up that the copies had not been unlawfully

(a) *Martin* v. *Wright*, 6 Sim. 297 ; *Page* v. *Townsend*, 5 Sim. 395.
(b) 1 Barn. & Adol. 804.

printed or imported, and therefore their sale was not piracy. The court held that the sale complained of, though a breach of contract, was not a violation of copyright, and consequently that no action was maintainable under the 17 Geo. 3, c. 57.

So, upon a similar principle, it was held in *Mayall* v. *Higbey* (a) that a person who lends photographs to another for a particular purpose, may prevent him from taking and selling copies, except in pursuance of the purpose for which they were lent, and this, although the photographs have been published, and irrespective of the question of copyright. The above was a case in which the plaintiff had lent photographs of eminent persons to Tallis, the proprietor of the 'Illustrated News of the World,' for the purpose of engraving them for that newspaper. Tallis became bankrupt, and his assignees sold the photographs to the defendant; and it was held that the plaintiff was not only entitled to the photographs but to the unsold copies, and to an injunction to restrain the further sale. The court said that there was no question of copyright, and compared it to the case of a valuable statue, which a friend to whom it is lent had no right to get copied.

No copyright can exist in any obscene, immoral, or libellous engraving (b); and were one to destroy such a print or engraving, he would merely be liable at law to pay the value of the paper and print (c). *In what class of engravings no copyright.*

An assignee may maintain an action for the piracy of an engraving, although the statute does not expressly give him that right (d): also it has been held in Scotland necessary to allege where the piracy has been committed (e).

(a) 1 H. & C. 148.
(b) See 5 Geo. 4, c. 83, s. 4; 1 & 2 Vict. c. 38, s. 2; 20 & 21 Vict. c. 83; *Fores* v. *Johnes*, 4 Esp. 97.
(c) *Du Bost* v. *Beresford*, 2 Camp. 511. In *The Emperor of Austria* v. *Day and Kossuth*, 7 Jur. (N.S) 641, Ch.; on appeal, 4 L. T. (N.S.) 494, the Lord Chancellor stated that the cases of *Burnett* v. *Chetwood* (2 Mer. 441, note) and *Du Bost* v. *Beresford*, *supra*, were wrongly decided. Compare the fact of the liability of the destroyer for the amount of the paper, with the maxim in Moor. 813: "*Inveniens libellum famosum et non corrumpens punitur*," and, *if possible*, reconcile the two.
(d) *Thompson* v. *Symonds*, 5 T. R. 41.
(e) *Graves* v. *Logan*, 7 Sc. Sess. Cas. 3rd Ser. 204.

CAP. XII.   By an Act of Parliament to amend the law relating to
International   international copyright (7 & 8 Vict. c. 12, ss. 2–4), Her
copyright.   Majesty is empowered by an order in council to grant the
privilege of copyright for such period as shall be defined
in such order (not exceeding the term allowed in this
country) to the authors, inventors, and makers of books,
prints, articles of sculpture, and other works of art, or
any particular class of them to be defined in such order,
which shall, after a future time to be specified in such
order, be first published in any foreign country, to be
named in such order.   But no such order in council shall
have any effect unless it shall be therein stated as the
ground for issuing the same that due protection has been
secured by the foreign power named in such order in
council for the benefit of parties interested in works first
published in the dominions of Her Majesty similar to those
comprised in such order.   And every such order in council
is to be published in the 'London Gazette' as soon as
may be after the making thereof, and from the time
of such publication shall have the same effect as if
every part thereof were included in the Act.   And no
copyright is allowed in any work of art first published
out of Her Majesty's dominions otherwise than under this
Act.

Penalty for   The penalty incurred by a pirate under the Engravings
piracy.   Acts is the forfeiture of the plates on which the prints are
copied, and every sheet on which the engraving has been
printed, to the proprietor of the original print, who must
forthwith destroy or damage them; and he must also
forfeit the sum of five shillings for every print found in his
custody.   The same penalties attach to one who has
published, exposed to sale, or disposed of, any pirated
engravings: 'one moiety passing to the Sovereign, and
the other being given to the informer.

Special action   By the 17 Geo. 3, c. 57, it is enacted that a special
on the case.   action on the case may be brought against the person
offending, to recover such damages as a jury on the trial
of such action, or on the execution of a writ of inquiry,

may give; and though all actions under the 8 Geo. 2, c..13, must have been brought within three months, and under the 7 Geo 3, c. 38, within six calendar months after *Limitation of* the offence, no limitation is mentioned in the 17 Geo. 3, *time as to* c. 57, as to the time in which this special action on the *actions.* case is to be brought (*a*).

In concluding, we will offer a few remarks on the *Summary pro-* remedy afforded by a late Act of Parliament for the *ceedings for* recovery of the penalties for infringement under the *of penalties.* Engravings Acts. The mode of recovery was much simplified by the 8th section of the 25 & 26 Vict. c. 68, commonly known as the Copyright (Works of Art) Act. By this clause all pecuniary penalties which shall be incurred, and all such unlawful copies, imitations, and all other effects and things as shall have been forfeited by offenders pursuant to any Act for the protection of copyright engravings, may be recovered by the person empowered to recover the same, and thereinafter called the complainant or the complainer, as follows:

In *England* and *Ireland,* either by action against the *In England* party offending, or by summary proceedings before any *and Ireland.* two justices having jurisdiction where the party offending resides (*b*);

In *Scotland,* by action before the Court of Session in *In Scotland.* ordinary form, or by summary action before the sheriff of the county where the offence may be committed or the offender resides, who, upon proof of the offence or offences, either by confession of the party offending or by the oath or affirmation of one or more credible witnesses, shall convict the offender, and find him liable to the penalty or penalties aforesaid, as also in expenses; and it shall be lawful for the sheriff, in pronouncing such judgment for

---

(*a*) See *Graves* v. *Mercer*, 16 W. R. 790.

(*b*) A magistrate sitting at a police court within the metropolitan police district, and every stipendiary magistrate appointed or to be appointed for any other city, town, liberty, borough, or place, or the lord mayor, or an alderman of London, sitting at the Mansion House, or Guildhall Justice Rooms, has power, when sitting alone, to exercise the jurisdiction given by this Act to two justices. 2 & 3 Vict. c. 71, s. 14; 11 & 12 Vict. c. 43, ss. 29, 33, 34; see also 21 & 22 Vict. c. 73.

the penalty or penalties and costs, to insert in such judgment a warrant, in the event of such penalty or penalties
and costs not being paid, to levy and recover the amount
of the same by pounding; provided always that it shall
be lawful to the sheriff, in the event of his dismissing
the action and assoilzieing the defender, to find the complainer liable in expenses; and any judgment so to be
pronounced by the sheriff in such summary application
shall be final and conclusive, and not subject to review by
advocation, suspension, reduction, or otherwise.

It will be observed here that though the procedure of
the 25 & 26 Vict. c. 68, is extended to the Engravings
Acts, yet the penalties recoverable are only those given
by the Engravings Acts.

Orders for inspection or account. Further, it is declared lawful for the superior courts of
record in which any action may be pending, or if the courts
be not then sitting, then for a judge of one of such courts,
on the application of either the plaintiff or defendant, to
make an order for an injunction, inspection, or account, as
to such court or judge may seem fit.

As pirated copies are made very much to resemble the
original in particular parts, and to be totally distinct in
other parts, care must be taken to draw the statement so as
to charge the defendant with *copying part*, as well as with
copying the whole (a).

Evidence on behalf of plaintiff. The evidence to be adduced at the trial on behalf of
the plaintiff is simply that he is the proprietor of the
print or engraving pirated; and it is sufficient that he
produce one of the prints taken from the original plate.
The production of the plate itself is not requisite.

It seems the best way to continue the name of the first
proprietor on the print: for it is doubtful whether a plate
with name of the assignee (although the date be correct)
is good evidence (b).

(a) 5 Barn. & Ald. 737; and 1 Dowl. & Ry. 400, cited Godson on
Patents, &c. 301.
(b) In *Bonner* v. *Field*, cited 5 T. R. 44, Lord Mansfield nonsuited a
plaintiff under similar circumstances, cited Godson on Patents, &c. 301.

CHAPTER XIII.

COPYRIGHT IN SCULPTURE AND BUSTS.

THE art of sculpture has never been particularly favoured The art of by the English nation. It is an art which ought cer- sculpture. tainly to be patronised more extensively, for it refines and improves the public mind and taste.

The erection of national monuments to the memory of individuals who by their works or their virtues have conferred lasting benefit or honour on mankind in general or their own country in particular, or in order to commemorate important public events, is a means by which the art produces the most influential moral effects.

These mementoes or memorials, though in the present age the unphilosophical and sciolistic spirit of some have led them to regard with contempt this method of honouring the illustrious great, excite a laudable admiration for the service or benefit to which they testify, and are living realities to perpetuate at once the respect entertained by the nation, both for the individual himself and the performance that has entitled him to their gratitude. When efficiently executed, they not only perpetuate the memory of the individual himself and record his good deeds, but appeal continuously to the national mind, and encourage and stimulate all posterity to follow in his footsteps. The person represented seems to be ever present. The deeds commemorated appear still in vivid force, and although we have not the actual presence of the departed, we retain his remembrance and preserve much of his influence.

"Public monuments, moreover," says Mr. Harris (a), "give a character to a nation and record the existence of what are in reality its noblest treasure,—the great men who have adorned it. They much influence the genius of a people, and in their turn exhibit the national feeling and genius. Indeed, the moral effect of these erections, both in ancient and modern times, has been made obvious. . . . . . The essential advantage in regard to civilization arising from the national veneration paid to heroes and great men, results from the stimulus which it excites to emulate their virtues, and to shun all those vices which are opposed to the latter, and by which lustre like theirs would be tarnished. The use of monuments in this respect is two-fold : first, to preserve the memory of those great men to whom they are erected, and of their virtues also; secondly, to testify the regard of the nation for those great men and for the virtues which they displayed. In both these respects, they are extensively and directly conducive to civilization, and are calculated to carry it to its highest point."

On these social grounds, therefore, it is incumbent upon the legislature to cherish and encourage an art yielding fruit such as this is capable of bearing.

Busts of private individuals are not likely to have much value as copyright, but busts of great men have a general interest and value. The demand for copies is so small that seldom is it that piracy takes place. The only case in which we remember the Sculpture Act being applied, is that of a bust of Fox.

The means of reproduction by a cast is very simple and merely mechanical (at least, after a single copy has been obtained), and this fact accounts for the limited application of the Act. Most of the ornamental casts in request are taken from foreign works of art, or from such as have been dedicated to the public by exposure or become public property ; seldom is the licence of the original designer required. There is little skill in the

(a) 'Civilization considered as a Science'

preparation of the type-mould, which corresponds to the plate of the engraver, unless, perhaps, where the scale is reduced (a).

The copyright in busts and sculptures mainly depends upon the 54 Geo. 3, c. 56. This Act amended and extended the provisions of the 38 Geo. 3, c. 71, which had been found ineffectual for the purposes thereby intended. So ineffectual had it proved that although avowedly passed for the preventing the piracy of busts and other figures made and published by statuaries, it was decided to be no offence to *sell* a pirated cast of the bust if the piracy had any addition to or diminution from the original; nor was it an offence to *make* a pirated cast if it were a perfect *fac-simile* of the original (b). Lord Ellenborough thought the statute had been passed with a view to defeat its own object, and taking advantage of the opportunity of making a joke, which the bar, as a matter of duty, had to imagine exceedingly good, advised artists when they applied to Parliament for further protection, not to *model* the new Act themselves as they appeared to have done the one in question.

The two statutes above referred to are commonly known as the Sculpture Copyright Acts, and the court will, in putting a construction upon either of them, give effect to the intention of the legislature by construing them collectively (c).

The 54 Geo. 3, c. 56 (18th of May, 1814), enacts that every person or persons who shall make or cause to be made any new and original sculpture, or model, or copy, or cast of the human figure or human figures, or of any bust or busts, or of any part or parts of the human figure, clothed in drapery or otherwise, or of any animal or animals or any part or parts of any animal, combined with the human figure, or otherwise, or of any subject being matter

(a) Turner on ' Copyright in Design.'
(b) *Gahagan* v. *Cooper*, 3 Camp. 111.
(c) *Newton* v. *Cowie*, 4 Bing. 245, and *Russell* v. *Smith*, 17 L. J. (Q.B.) 225, 229 ; the former with reference to the Engravings Acts, the latter to literary copyright.

of invention in sculpture, or of any alto- or basso-relievo representing any of the matters or things thereinbefore mentioned, or any cast from nature of the human figure, or of any part or parts of the human figure, or of any cast from nature of any animal, or of any part or parts of any animal, or of any such subject containing or representing any of the matters and things thereinbefore mentioned, whether separate or combined, shall have the sole right and property of all and in every such new and original sculpture, model, copy, and cast of the human figure and human figures, and of all and in every such bust or busts, and of all and in every such part or parts of the human figure, clothed in drapery or otherwise, and of all and in every such new and original sculpture, model, copy, and cast, representing any animal or animals, and of all and in every such work representing any part or parts of any animal combined with the human frame or otherwise, and of all and in every such new and original sculpture, model, copy, and cast of any subject being matter of invention in sculpture, and of all and in every such new and original sculpture, model, copy, and cast in alto- or basso-relievo, representing any of the matters or things thereinbefore mentioned, and of every such cast from nature, for the term of fourteen years from first putting forth or publishing the same ; provided in all and every case the proprietor or proprietors do cause his, her, or their name or names, with the date, to be put on all and every such new and original sculpture, model, copy, or cast, and on every such cast from nature, before the same shall be put forth or published.

After the expiration of this term of fourteen years the copyright shall return to the person who originally had the copyright, if he be then living, for the further term of fourteen years, excepting in the case where such person shall by sale or otherwise have divested himself of such right (a).

The copyright is to run from the "first putting forth

(a) Sect. 6. See *Grantham* v. *Hawley*, Hob. 132, cited *Lunn* v. *Thornton*, 1 C. B. 379; Vin. Abr. 'Grants,' M., *Carnan* v. *Bowles*, 2 Bro. C. C. 85.

or publishing the same." The property secured by the Act CAP. XIII.
seems to be comprehensive enough to embrace the right
of public exhibition. The opinion has . been judicially
expressed that, within the meaning of the statute, a work
may be published by being publicly exhibited (a). In
Turner v. *Robinson*, Lord Chancellor Brady said : "In the
statutes bestowing protection upon works of sculpture,
the terminus *a quo* from which the protection commences
is the publication of the work, that is, from the moment
the eye of the public is allowed to rest upon it. Many
large works in this branch of art, which decorate public
squares and other places, are of course so published, but
there are others not designed for such purposes which
could never be published in any other way than in exhibitions; therefore I apprehend that these works of
sculpture must be considered as published by exhibition
at such places as the Royal Academy and Manchester, so
as to entitle them to the protection of the statutes from
the date of publication " (b).

The conditions under which the copyright is acquired Conditions to
are almost identical with those required to be performed be complied with in order
in order to obtain a copyright under the Engravings Acts. to effectuate a
When a sculptor models a design for himself, and after- copyright.
wards executes from such model a finished bust for
another in marble or any other material, it is not sufficient
for the sculptor, in order to acquire the copyright therein,
to affix his name and the year when the finished copy
from the model was executed (as is frequently the case) ;
he must conform strictly to the letter of the Acts (c), and
therefore engrave on the *model*, as well as on every cast or
copy thereof, his name (d), and the day of the month

(a) *Turner* v. *Robinson*, 10 Ir. Ch. 516.
(b) The Royal Commissioners proposed that the term of copyright in all
works of fine art other than photographs should be the same as for books,
music, and the drama, namely, the life of the artist, and thirty years after
his death ; par. 95.
(c) As under the Designs Act, see *Pierce* v. *Worth*, 18 L. T. (N.S.)
710.
(d) The name need not necessarily be the baptismal and surname of the
proprietor, but such as he or his co-proprietors are commonly known by or
trade under.

and year when the model is first shewn or otherwise published in his studio, or elsewhere ; and such *date must never be altered.*

Assignment of the right. By the 54 Geo. 3, c. 56, it was further provided that no person who should thereafter purchase the right or property of any new and original sculpture, or model, or copy, or cast, or of any cast from nature, of the proprietor, expressed in a deed in writing signed by him in the presence of and attested by two or more witnesses, should be subject to any action for copying, or casting, or vending the same; and that all actions brought for pirating under this Act should be commenced within six calendar months next after the discovery of the offence (a).

Registration. Sculptures and models may now be registered under the Designs Act (13 & 14 Vict. c. 104, s. 6), which provides that the registrar of designs, upon application by or on behalf of the proprietor of any sculpture, model, copy, or cast within the protection of the Sculpture Copyright Acts, and upon being furnished with such copy, drawing, print, or description, in writing or in print, as in the judgment of the said registrar shall be sufficient to identify the particular sculpture, model, copy, or cast in respect of which registration is desired, and the name of the person claiming to be proprietor, together with his place of abode or business, or other place of address, or the name, style, or title of the firm under which he may be trading, shall register such sculpture, model, copy, or cast, in such manner and form as shall from time to time be prescribed or approved by the Board of Trade, for the whole or any part of the term during which copyright in such sculpture, model, copy, or cast may or shall exist under the Sculpture Copyright Acts ; and whenever any such registration shall be made, the said registrar shall certify under his hand and seal of office, in such form as the said board shall direct or approve, the fact of such registration and the date of the same, and the name of the registered proprietor, or the style or title of the firm under which such proprietor

(a) See form of assignment, Crabb's Prec.

may be trading, together with his place of abode or busi-   ness, or other place of address.

The application under this section need not necessarily be made by the author; it is to be made by the proprietor.

The 54 Geo. 3, c. 56, s. 3, gives an action for damages against any person who shall make or import or cause to be made or imported or exposed to sale or otherwise disposed of any pirated copy or pirated cast, whether it be produced by moulding or copying from or imitating in any way the original.

The 7th section of the 13 & 14 Vict. c. 104, provides *Infringement* that if any person shall, during the continuance of the copy- *of the right,* right in any sculpture, model, copy, or cast which shall *and penalties* *attached* have been so registered as aforesaid, make, import, or cause *thereto.* to be made, imported, exposed for sale, or otherwise disposed of, any pirated copy or pirated cast of any such sculpture, model, copy or cast, in such manner and under such circumstances as would entitle the proprietor to a special action on the case under the Sculpture Copyright Acts, the person so offending shall forfeit for every such offence a sum not less than £5 and not exceeding £30, to the proprietor of the sculpture, model, copy, or cast whereof the copyright shall have been infringed ; and for the recovery of any such penalty the proprietor of the sculpture, model, copy, or cast which shall have been so pirated shall have and be entitled to the same remedies as are provided for the recovery of penalties incurred under the Designs Act, 1842 : provided always, that the proprietor of any sculpture, model, copy, or cast which shall be registered under this Act shall not be entitled to the benefit of this Act unless every copy or cast of such sculpture, model, copy, or cast which shall be published by him after such registration, shall be marked with the word " registered " and with the date of registration.

This is a great improvement on the law as it stood prior to the year 1842, but why the provisions for registration should not have been extended to engravings, prints and photographs is a matter of surprise.

In conclusion, we must express a hope that protection will before long be afforded to the sculptor against drawings or engravings of any description, which may now be taken from his work with impunity. If the sculpture be a production of any merit and value, if well designed and engraved, it might be profitable to the author in various ways; while, on the contrary, if it be badly or carelessly executed, it may be alike annoying to him and injurious to his reputation and fame.

On this subject the Royal Commissioners in their report on Copyright, 1876, say :—" Upon the whole we are disposed to think that every form of copy, whether by sculpture, modelling, photography, drawing, engraving, or otherwise, should be included in the protection of copyright. It might be provided that the copying of a scene in which a piece of sculpture happened to form an object should not be deemed an infringement unless the sculpture should be the principal object, or unless the chief purpose of the picture should be to exhibit the sculpture.

" It was also suggested that copyists of antique works ought to be protected by copyright so far as their own copies are concerned. Many persons spend months in copying ancient statues, and the copies become as valuable to the sculptors as if they were original works. It may be doubted whether the case does not already fall within the Sculpture Act, but we recommend that such doubts should be removed, and that sculptors who copy from statues in which no copyright exists should have copyright in their own copies. Such copyright should not, of course, extend to prevent other persons making copies of the original work " (a).

(a) Pars. 99, 100.

CHAPTER XIV.

COPYRIGHT IN PAINTINGS, DRAWINGS, AND PHOTOGRAPHS.

OF all the branches of the fine arts this was the last The arts of painting and recognised as worthy of protection by the legislature. On drawing. what ground it is difficult to comprehend. Where is the difference in principle between a picture and a poem ?

The claims of the artist to a copyright in his works are quite as valid as those of the literary author in his; and if the principle were once admitted that a man should be protected in the enjoyment of his intellectual productions, and a certain period of exclusive possession allowed to the author for his benefit, before the public were in full and free enjoyment of the work, on what ground could Parliament so long withhold the same privilege from the artist as it had already granted to the author ?

It is a strange anomaly that while the law gave a property to that which was, in the ordinary way, the work of a man's hands, and allowed a copyright in inventions and designs, it should have afforded no protection to those productions which were more exclusively the creations of the mind. It was thought but an act of justice and right that a copyright should exist in literary productions, but when it was proposed, as late as 1862, to give a similar right in pictures, a cry was raised that it was derogatory on the part of jurisprudence to protect the works of those who contributed by their art to the honour of their country, the elevation of the national taste, and the amusement, instruction, and delight of the community at large.

With respect to the fine arts, two series of Acts had been passed, giving a copyright of a limited and special nature in sculptures and engravings; hence this unaccountable opposition to the bestowing a copyright in paintings appears the more extraordinary. For while an engraving enjoyed protection, the picture from which it was taken was without. A man might make any number of copies of the best work of the artist—sell them, and there was no remedy. Not unfrequently these copies were sold as originals, and even the name of the original artist forged upon them, but the injured party was without redress.

The evil was almost peculiar to this country. In most European countries the principle of copyright extended through the whole range of the fine arts, and, unlike our law, especially protected the work of painters.

At the present day, if one purchases the copyright of a picture he holds the picture free from any interference, and with the perfect right of dealing with it as he pleases. If, however, he buys the picture simply as a picture, he will then have the gratification and delight resulting from its contemplation—he cannot make copies or engravings from it, or use it for a different purpose from that for which the artist sold it (a). The same rule applies to authors. When a person buys a book he can read it, but cannot multiply copies of it unless he purchases the copyright. This appears but fair, especially if we bear in mind that the greater part of the artist's remuneration probably arises from the reproduction of his work (b).

The existence of copyright in painting is a protection also to the purchaser of a picture. It was formerly well known that after a person had purchased a picture the artist might have made a copy and multiplied it to any extent, although the purchaser might have been under the impression that he had bought a picture as being the single work of the artist. Of course such an action would not have become an honourable man, but still the right remained to the artist to act in such a manner had he

(a) Of course the purchaser of the picture is not bound to lend it to the artist or any other person for the purpose of engraving, and this is only here mentioned as there seems to be some such extraordinary idea prevalent among engravers.

(b) The painting of 'The Roll Call,' by Miss Thompson, was sold for £100, the right of engraving fetched £1200, see *post*, p. 397

thought proper. It is not a desirable thing to have a Cap. XIV. great work of art multiplied indefinitely, and hawked about for sale. It is well known that the frequent repetition of a work of art diminishes the worth of the original ; indeed, nothing detracts so much from its commercial value.

At length the wished-for day arrived, and the artists succeeded in obtaining for their protection an Act of Parliament.

The Act (25 & 26 Vict. c. 68) is entitled, ' An Act for amending the Law relating to Copyright in Works of the Fine Arts, and for repressing the commission of Fraud in the Production and Sale of such works.' It provides that the author, being a British subject or resident within the dominions of the Crown, of every original painting, drawing (a), and photograph which shall be or shall have been made, either in the British dominions or elsewhere, and which shall not have been sold or disposed of before the commencement of the Act, and his assigns, shall have the sole and exclusive right of copying, engraving, reproducing, and multiplying such painting or drawing and the design thereof, or such photograph and the negative thereof, by any means and of any size, for the term of the natural life of such author, and seven years after his death ; provided that when any painting or drawing or the negative of any photograph shall for the first time after the passing of this Act be sold or disposed of, or shall be made or executed for or on behalf of any person for a good or a valuable consideration, the person so selling or disposing of or making or executing the same shall not retain the copyright thereof unless it be expressly reserved to him by agreement in writing, signed at or before the time of such sale or disposition by the vendee or assignee of such painting or drawing or of such negative of a photograph, or by the person for or on whose behalf the same shall be so made or executed, but the copyright shall belong to the vendee or assignee of such painting or drawing or of such negative of a photograph, or to the person

Creation of copyright in works of art.

(a) An architectural design is protected under this word.

for or on whose behalf the same shall have been made or executed; nor shall the vendee or assignee thereof be entitled to any such copyright, unless at or before the time of such sale or disposition an agreement in writing, signed by the person so selling or disposing of the same, or by his agent duly authorized, shall have been made to that effect.

By whom it may be claimed.

It is important that the artist, at the sale, or at or before the time of delivery or the completion of the bargain, should obtain the signature of the vendee or assignee, or of the person for whom the work has been executed, to a written reservation of the copyright to himself, if he desires to retain it; or assign in writing the same to the purchaser at or before the completion of the transaction, otherwise the copyright will be irredeemably lost (a). If the vendee obtains not this agreement in writing, he will be unable to protect himself against piracy or repetition by the artist, as section 6 only protects pictures, &c., in which there is subsisting copyright. The copyright cannot, unless reserved in writing, vest in the vendor; it cannot, if not assigned in writing, vest in the vendee or assignee. It, however, would pass without a written agreement to the person for or on whose behalf a work is expressly executed, *as in commissions* (b).

(a) Forms of various kinds of agreements under this Act will be found in the Appendix. Agreements under the Act require a sixpenny stamp.

(b) The Royal Commissioners in their recent report on Copyright, were of opinion that it was clearly undesirable that copyrights, which are in many cases of great value, should be in this way left free to piracy, and that the law therefore should distinctly define to whom, in the absence of an agreement, the copyright should belong.

They also referred to the expediency of making a distinction between pictures painted on commission and others. They experienced a difficulty in defining what a commission was, and, looking to the evidence before them upon the point, they arrived at the conclusion that no distinction could practically be made.

The majority of the Commissioners came to the conclusion that in the absence of a written agreement to the contrary, the copyright in a picture should belong to the purchaser, or the person for whom it is painted, and follow the ownership of the picture. They mentioned that the final proviso in the 1st section of the Act of 1862 was apparently added to the Bill without sufficient consideration during its progress through Parliament.

As to whether an artist who has sold a picture should be at liberty without the consent of the owner to make replicas of it, or whether a distinction should be made between replicas made by the artist, and copies made by others than the artist, the Commissioners reported that they were not inclined to recognise any distinction.

The copyright given by the above section is qualified by the following one, to the extent that nothing shall prejudice the right of any person to copy or use any work in which there is no such copyright, or to represent any scene or object, notwithstanding that there may be copyright in some representation of such scene or object.

This must refer to and include all works of ancient and deceased masters, and all paintings of living artists sold before the passing of this Act, or since, without the statutory provisions having been complied with for the creation and transfer of copyright.

All formalities, such as are required under the Engraving or the Sculpture Copyright Acts, are unnecessary in the assignment and transfer under this Act; for copyright is declared to be personal property, and capable of being assigned by any note or memorandum in writing, signed by the proprietor of the copyright, or by his agent appointed for that purpose in writing.

Where S., the proprietor of a periodical called 'Good Assignment Words,' agreed verbally with G. to purchase the right to and registra-tion. engrave certain photographs to illustrate 'Good Words,' G. reserving the right to use them in any other publica-tion, and subsequently signed a receipt for "the use of photographs in 'Good Words' reserving all rights to issue the same in any other publication," and afterwards S. commenced publishing in a separate volume these articles, illustrated by engravings from the same photographs, and G. brought an action under the 25 & 26 Vict. c. 68, for damages and for a writ of injunction; and S. filed a bill for a declaration that under the verbal agreement he was entitled to republish the engravings taken from G.'s photo-graphs, for specific performance of an alleged verbal agreement to grant a licence to use the photographs for the purpose of engraving and publishing in 'Good Words,' or in any republication of the articles which they illus-trated, and that the action at law might be restrained; Vice-Chancellor Malins held, that the verbal agreement

CAP. XIV.   extended to the use of the photographs in 'Good Words' only, that there was no part performance by G. of a contract or licence by G. to publish in a separate form, and that S. had no equity, inasmuch as by the 25 & 26 Vict. c. 68, s. 3, every leave or licence for the publication of photographs must be in writing, and dismissed the bill with costs (a).

Assignment of the copyright when limited in effect.   And an assignment in terms of the copyright in a picture may be qualified by the obvious intention of the parties to a licence to copy it, or to an assignment for the limited purpose of producing an engraving or photograph.

Thus in a very recent case (b), an action was brought to restrain an alleged infringement by the defendant of the plaintiff's copyright in an oil painting called 'Going to Work,' and in an engraving made from it. The picture was painted by the artist for a Mr. Halford, who, on the 9th of November, 1870, wrote the following memorandum addressed to the plaintiff: "I assign to you for the purpose of producing an engraving of one size, the copyright of the picture painted by Mr. Eddis, entitled 'Going to Work,' and being a portrait of my daughter." The picture represented a little girl in a sea-side costume with bare feet walking on the sea-shore, carrying in one hand a spade over her shoulder, and in the other hand a bucket. The plaintiff, on the 12th November, 1870, registered himself under the 25 & 26 Vict. c. 68, as the proprietor of the copyright of the picture, and in July, 1871, he published an engraving of the picture, his name being engraved on the plate as the proprietor.

In 1879 the defendant published a chromo-lithograph which the plaintiff alleged to be an infringement of his copyright. This picture was called 'Holiday Time,' and it also represented a girl on the sea-shore, with bare feet, with a spade in one hand over her shoulder, and a bucket in the other hand. But her dress was different from that

(a) *Strahan* v. *Graham*, 16 L. T. (N.S.) 87; 17 L. T. (N.S.) 57; 15 W. R. 487.

(b) *Lucas* v. *Cooke*, 13 Ch. Div. 872.

of the girl in the picture, and she was standing still instead of walking. The evidence shewed that the chromo-lithograph was derived from a photograph published in New York, and that neither the defendant nor the artist whom he employed to produce the chromo-lithograph had, before its production, seen either the picture or the engraving. There was no evidence to shew how the photograph was produced, or whether the photographer had, before he produced it, seen either the picture or the engraving. The photograph was evidently taken from life.

Mr. Justice Fry held that the letter of the 9th November, 1870, amounted only to an assignment of the copyright of the picture or a licence to copy it, for the limited purpose of producing an engraving of one size, and that the right of producing copies in other ways and of other sizes remained in Halford, and could be assigned by him to any one else. And by sect. 11 of the 5 & 6 Vict. c. 45, the registration gave only a *primâ facie* title which could be rebutted, and here the assignment itself rebutted the *primâ facie* title. The result was that the plaintiff was only the proprietor of the engraving. It was very possible that the photograph might have been in substance copied from either the picture on the engraving, but there was no evidence on which the court was entitled to assume that it was copied from either. But, even if it was copied from one or the other, it might have been copied from the picture, in which the plaintiff had no right, just as well as from the engraving, and the court could not assume without evidence that it was copied from the latter. Before the plaintiff could succeed, he must shew that the photograph had been taken from the engraving, and this he had not done.

By the 4th section it is declared that a book of registry shall be kept at Stationers' Hall, entitled 'The Register of Proprietors of Copyright in Paintings, Drawings, and Photographs,' in which shall be entered a memorandum of every copyright to which any person shall be entitled

CAP. XIV. under this Act, and also of every subsequent assignment;
and that such memorandum shall contain a statement of
the date of the agreement or assignment, and of the name
and address of the person in whom such copyright shall
be vested, and also of the author of the work, together
with a short description of the subject of the work; and, if
the person registering shall so desire, a sketch, outline, or
photograph of the work.

It is not a valid objection that the registration does not
give such a description of the work as may enable a person
from it alone to ascertain whether he is about to sell the
copy of a registered work, for that knowledge may be
gained from other sources, and the object of the legislature,
as pointed out by the statute, is that there shall be such a
description of the picture as to enable a person who has it
before him to judge whether or not the registration applies
to the one he is about to copy. This was decided in 1868.
Mr. Henry Graves, being the proprietor of the copyright
in two paintings in oil and in a photograph, entered them
under this section, thus: "Painting in oil, 'Ordered on
Foreign Service;' painting in oil, 'My First Sermon;'
photograph, 'My Second Sermon.'" The first picture
represented an officer taking leave of a lady; the second,
a young child sitting in a pew, apparently listening with
her eyes wide open; the photograph represented the same
child asleep in a pew; and it was considered that the
nature and subject of the works were sufficiently described
under this section. "If we consider it as a question of
fact," observed Mr. Justice Blackburn, "there can be no
reasonable doubt that the description of each of the
pictures is sufficient. The picture, 'Ordered on Foreign
Service,' represents an officer who is ordered abroad,
taking leave of a lady, and no one can doubt that is the
picture intended. So again 'My First Sermon' describes
with sufficient exactness a child, impressed with the
novelty of her situation, sitting in a pew, and listening
with her eyes open; while the same child, fast asleep in
a pew, forms the subject of 'My Second Sermon.' Who

can doubt that in each of these cases the description is sufficient? There may be a few instances in which the mere registration of the name of the picture is not sufficient; for instance, Sir E. Landseer's picture of a Newfoundland dog might possibly be insufficiently registered under the description of 'A distinguished Member of the Humane Society.' Similarly, the well-known picture called 'A Piper and a Pair of Nutcrackers,' representing a bullfinch and a pair of squirrels, might not be accurately pointed out by its name. In either of those cases the names would scarcely be sufficient, and it would be advisable for a person proposing to register them to add a sketch or outline of the work. But when the subject is indicated, as it is here, it seems to be merely a question of fact whether the description affords enough information, and I cannot doubt that it does" (a).

It is further enacted by the 4th section that no proprietor of any copyright shall be entitled to the benefit of this Act until such registration, and no action shall be sustainable nor any penalty be recoverable in respect of anything done before registration (b).

Benefit of Act cannot be claimed until after registration.

This section, though it prevents an assignee from suing for penalties, before the assignment to him has been registered (c), does not render it necessary that all or any previous assignment should also be registered, or that the copyright of the original author should be registered (d). Registration of the proprietorship of the copyright is only *primâ faeie* evidence of title, and may be rebutted by the terms of the assignment of the copyright to the person who has made the registration (e).

The enactments of the 5 & 6 Vict. c. 45, in relation to the registry thereby prescribed, are applicable to the registry under the 25 & 26 Vict. c. 68, except that the

---

(a) *Ex parte Beal*, Law Rep. 3 Q. B. 387; 37 L. J. (Q.B.) 161; S. C. 18 L. T. (N.S.) 285.
(b) *Vide ante*, p. 146.
(c) *Dupuy v. Dilkes*, W. N. (1879) 145. 'The Young Cricketer.'
(d) *Re Walker & Graves*, 20 L. T. (N.S.) Q. B. 877; L. R. 4 Q. B. 715.
(e) *Lucas v. Cooke*, 13 Ch. Div. 872. 'Going to Work.'

forms of entry prescribed by the earlier Act may be varied under the latter to meet the circumstances of any case (a). Consequently, the making of false and fraudulent entries of proprietorship of copyright for any purpose, either to acquire property in such copyright or to improperly restrain the publication or copying of works in which no copyright lawfully exists, is a misdemeanour. And the person aggrieved may apply to the court or a judge to obtain an order for the cancellation or substitution of names so inserted (b).

Aggrieved person.

A person who has been convicted of infringing the copyright in certain paintings and photographs of the registered proprietor, but who sets up no title in himself or adduces any evidence to rebut the *primâ facie* evidence of proprietorship afforded by the book of registry, is not a person "aggrieved" within the meaning of this or the 14th section of the 5 & 6 Vict. c. 45.

"A person," said Hannen, J. (c), "to be 'aggrieved' within the meaning of the statute must shew that the entry is inconsistent with some right that he sets up in himself or in some other person, or that the entry would really interfere with some intended action on the part of the person making the application."

"It seems," said Blackburn, J., in the same case, "that to make a person aggrieved within the meaning of the statute, the applicant must have some substantial objection, and one going to the merits of the registered

(a) The Royal Commissioners in their recent report on Copyright recommended that registration of paintings and drawings should not be insisted on as long as the property in the picture and the copyright were vested in the same person, but that if the copyright were separated by agreement from the property in the picture, there should be compulsory registration, and that the register should shew—
    (a) The date of the agreement.
    (b) The names of the parties thereto.
    (c) The names and places of abode of the artist, and of the person in whom the copyright is vested.
    (d) A short description of the nature and subject of the work, and, if the person registering so desires, a sketch, outline, or photograph of the work in addition thereto.
As to engravings, prints, and photographs, however, they thought registration should be compulsory.
(b) *Chappell* v. *Purday*, 12 M. & W. 303.
(c) *Graves's case*, L. R. 4 Q. B. 724; 20 L. T. (N.S.) 877.

proprietor's title ; then the court may direct an issue, or Cap. XIV.
have the question otherwise disposed of, or, if they think
this the proper course, may set aside or expunge the
entry. But I do not think it is enough to entitle a
person to say that he is aggrieved, and that the entry
ought to be expunged, that, although the registered proprietor has a complete title in equity and in good sense,·
yet there is some slip either in the signing of the memorandum or in the spelling of a name ; this would be my
view if it were necessary to decide this question."

An application under the 14th section was made to the Expunging entry in register.
High Court of Justice, Queen's Bench Division, in
February, 1876, for an order to expunge from the register
the entry of the copyright of the well-known picture called
' The Roll Call,' painted by Miss Elizabeth Thompson, who,
by an agreement dated 11th of May, 1874, had sold the
copyright to Messrs. Dickinson & Co. for the sum of £1200.
It appeared that the copyright was not, in fact, vested in
Miss Thompson, and she had no right to assign it. She
had painted the picture on commission for a gentleman
named Galloway, who had paid her £100 in advance.
There was no contest as to the ownership of the copyright; it was conceded that Mr. Galloway held it. He
had parted with the picture to the Queen for the same
price he himself had paid for it, but as this did not carry
the copyright, it still remained in Mr. Galloway. Mr.
Galloway did not oppose the application, and an order to
expunge the entries so as not to affect the rights to the
copyright was made.

Invasion of the property is guarded against by the 6th Infringement of the right, and penalties attached thereto.
section, which provides that if the author, after having
sold or disposed of the copyright, or if any other person
not being the proprietor for the time being of the copyright, shall repeat, copy, colourably imitate, or otherwise
multiply for sale, hire, exhibition, or distribution, or cause
or procure to be repeated, copied, imitated, or otherwise
multiplied for sale, hire, exhibition, or distribution, any
such work or the design thereof, or knowing that any such

CAP. XIV. repetition (a), copy, or other imitation has been unlawfully
made, shall import into the United Kingdom, or sell,
publish, let to hire, exhibit or distribute, or offer for sale,
hire, exhibition, or distribution, or cause or procure to be
imported, sold, published, let to hire, distributed or offered
for sale, hire, exhibition, or distribution any repetition,
copy, or imitation of the said work, or of the design thereof,
such person, for every such offence, shall forfeit to the
proprietor of the copyright for the time being a sum not
exceeding £10 : and all such repetitions, copies, and
imitations, and all negatives of photographs made for the
purpose of obtaining such copies, shall be forfeited to the
proprietor of the copyright.

Under this clause, where the subject of a picture is
copied, it is of no consequence whether that is done
directly from the picture itself or through intervening
copies ; if, in result, that which is produced be an imitation
of the picture, then it is immaterial whether that be
arrived at directly or by intermediate steps. A copy,
therefore, from an intervening copy is a copy from the
original work, and within the prohibitory clauses of the
statute. Nor does the copying refer merely to the imitation of a painting by a painting, or drawing by a drawing,
or a photograph by a photograph, so that a photograph
of a drawing, or a drawing of a painting, protected by the
Act, would be a piracy. For, on inspecting the 1st
section, which is the key to the whole Act, it gives to the
author of every original painting, drawing, or photograph
the sole and exclusive right of copying, engraving, reproducing, and multiplying such painting or drawing and the
design thereof, or such photograph and the negative
thereof, by any means and of any size ; and the terms
used are so extensive that it is plain that a photograph of
a painting, of a drawing, or of another photograph made
without the consent of the owner, though of a different size,

(a) *Actus non facit reum, nisi mens sit rea* (*Reg.* v. *Sleap*, 8 Cox, C. C.
472 ; *Reg.* v. *Cohen, ibid.* 41 ; *Hearne* v. *Garton*, 28 L. J. (M.C.) 216) ; as
to the licence required to copy photographs, see *Strahan* v. *Graham*, 16
L. T. (N.S.) 87 ; 17 L. T. (N.S.) 457.

provided it be a reproduction of the design, is an infringement such as would subject the maker to the penalty.

Before the existence of statutory copyright in paintings, it was held by the Irish Chancery Court, that the
owner's common law rights in a painting were not prejudiced by his public exhibition of it. The case referred
to is *Turner* v. *Robinson* (a). The defendant was charged
with piracy in having made for sale copies of a painting
representing the death of Chatterton. He denied direct
copying, but admitted that he had seen the original while
on exhibition, and said that he had made his photograph
from an arrangement of figures, objects, and scenery
which he had prepared in his own gallery. He further
admitted that he had made the arrangement from his
recollection of the painting, and with a view of presenting
a stereoscopic photograph of the same representation as
that given by the painting. The court declared this to
be an unlawful use of the plaintiff's property.

" If there was no statute protecting copyright in literary
works," said the Master of the Rolls, " and Sir Walter
Scott had read out ' Waverley ' to a large party of friends, it
is idle to say that such would have amounted to a publication, so as to have deprived him of his common law
right; and the painter or the owner of a painting who
exhibits it at such exhibitions as those of London, Dublin,
and Manchester, and, having regard to the object of such
exhibitions, should be considered as allowing it to be
viewed by the public on a tacit understanding that an
improper advantage would not be taken of the privilege
thus granted ; and I am disposed to think, without
reference to the letters I have read, that such an exhibition would not be a publication so as to deprive a painter
or the owner of a painting of his common law right." And
upon the other point, upon appeal, the Lord Justice of
Appeal said : " The stereoscopic slides are not photographs
taken directly from the picture, in the ordinary mode of
copying ; but they are photographic pictures of a model

(a) 10 Ir. Ch. 121, 510.

itself copied from, and accurately imitating in its design and outline, the petitioner's painting. It is through this medium that the photograph has been made a perfect representation of the painting. Thus the object contrived and achieved, and the consequent injury, are the very same as if the copy had, in breach of confidence, been made on ,the view, and by the eye ; and no court of justice can admit that an act illegal in itself can be justified by a novel or circuitous mode of effecting it. If it is illegal, so must the contrivance be by means of which it was effected."

In a recent case (a) it was contended that a photograph of an engraving was not an original production within the meaning of the Act. In overruling this objection, Mr. Justice Blackburn said : "The distinction between an original painting and its copy is well understood, but it is difficult to say what is meant by an original photograph. All photographs are copies of some object, such as a painting or a statue, and it seems to me that a photograph taken from a picture is an original photograph, in so far that to copy it is an infringement of this statute. As I have already pointed out, by section 2, although it is unlawful to copy a photograph or the negative, it is permitted to copy the subject-matter of the photograph by taking another photograph."

The penalties cumulative.   The offending individual is liable to the penalty for every copy sold. Thus, where twenty-six copies were disposed of in two parcels of thirteen copies each, it was held that the penalty was properly imposed on every copy sold. "In the case of *Brooke* v. *Milliken* (b)," says Mr. Justice Blackburn, in *Beal's Case* (c), to which we have already referred, "the penalty was imposed by 12 Geo. 3, c. 36, for importing for sale any book first published in this kingdom and reprinted in any other place, and it enacted that the offender should forfeit £5, and double the value of every book sold. In that case

(a) *Graves's Case*, L. R. 4 Q. B. 723.
(b) 3 T. R. 509.
(c) Law Rep. 3 Q. B. 395.

there could be no doubt that the meaning of the statute Cap. XIV. was, the penalty should be cumulative, viz., double the value of each book. In the present case the words are, 'such person for every ?such offence shall forfeit to the proprietor of the copyright for the time being a sum not exceeding £10.' It is quite clear that this imposes a penalty for every copy sold ; a different construction would result in an absurdity, and defeat the intention of the legislature. The penalty is imposed also for importation, and it would be monstrous, that if a man had consigned from abroad a cargo of imitations, the utmost penalty that could be imposed on him would be the sum of £10. It would be well worth his while to run the risk of paying that small sum, and to import and distribute for sale elsewhere a quantity worth many thousands. The legislature were dealing with an offence which was likely to be committed wholesale, and they have used words meaning that the sale of every copy shall be an offence, and if ten copies be sold at one time, ten offences are committed, and the offender may be punished for each separately."

The provision as to forfeiture of piratical copies is almost Provisions as to forfeiture of piratical copies. nugatory, as the Act gives no power to enter a house and search for copies. One case was brought before the Royal Commissioners appointed to report on the subject of Copyright in 1876, where a conviction for selling piratical copies having been obtained, the magistrate had made an order that the copies should be delivered up, but it was found that the order could not be enforced.

The bill recently introduced into Parliament provides by the 64th section that where any copy of a subject of copyright is under the Act forfeited to the proprietor of the copyright, then, without prejudice to any other remedy, a court of summary jurisdiction may order any such copy to be delivered to the proprietor of the copyright. This bill also proposes to give power to seize piratical copies where they are seen, and when they might be taken, it being proved by experience that the power to proceed by summons is generally ineffectual where persons selling copies go round from house to house, and refuse to give either a name or address, and are altogether lost sight of before a summons could be procured. It therefore provides that if any person in any street or highway, or elsewhere than at his own house, shop, or place of business, hawks or offers or keeps for sale, hire, or distribution any such copy it may be seized by any constable under the orders of the proprietor of the copyright, or of any person authorized by him, and forthwith taken before a court of summary jurisdiction with a view of obtaining an order for its delivery to the proprietor of the copyright.

The Commissioners further suggested that these provisions should be extended to sculpture and other works of fine art.

Provisions for repressing the commission of fraud in the production and sale of works of art.

The 7th section imposes penalties on every person doing or causing to be done any of the following acts:

1st. If he shall fraudulently sign or otherwise affix, or cause to be signed or otherwise affixed, to any painting, drawing, or photograph, or the negative thereof, any name, initial, or monogram.

This clause was rendered necessary by the decision in the case of *The Queen* v. *Closs* (a). A picture had been painted by Mr. Linnell, who signed and sold it for £180. The prisoner was a picture dealer, and was indicted for fraudulently selling a copy of Linnell's picture as and for the genuine picture which he had painted. Mr. Linnell's name was likewise painted on such copy, which the prisoner sold for £130. The indictment contained three counts: the first charged the prisoner with obtaining money under false pretences, but upon this count he was acquitted; the second count charged him with a *cheat* at common law (b), by means of writing Linnell's name upon the copy; and the third count charged the prisoner with a *cheat* by means of a forgery of Linnell's name upon the copy. Upon these last two counts the prisoner was convicted; but his counsel objecting, that they disclosed no indictable offence

(a) 27 L. J. (M. C.) 54; 7 Cox, C. C. 494; 6 W. R. 109.
(b) *Albin's Case*, Tremaine, P. C. 109; *Worrall's Case*, *ibid.* 106; 2 East, P. C. 18, cited 2 Russell on Crimes, 282.

at common law, the judgment was respited in order that the opinion of the Criminal Court of Appeal might be taken upon the objection so raised. The case was afterwards argued before five judges, who formed such court of appeal, and they unanimously held that the conviction was *wrong;* that there was no forgery; that "forgery must be of some document or writing," and Linnell's name in this case must be looked at merely as in the nature of an arbitrary mark made by the master to identify his own work, and was no more than if the painter had put any other arbitrary mark made by him, as a recognition of the picture being his. As to the second count of the indictment, the court held that the conviction could not be sustained, because it did not sufficiently shew that the prisoner sold the copy by *means* of Linnell's signature being forged upon it.

2nd. If he shall fraudulently sell, publish, exhibit or dispose of the same, or offer it for sale, exhibition or distribution.

3rd. If he shall fraudulently sell any copy or colourable imitation of any painting, drawing, or photograph, or negative of a photograph, whether there shall be subsisting copyright therein or not, as having been executed by the author of the original work from which such copy or imitation shall have been made.

4th. If, where the author of any painting, drawing, or photograph, or negative of a photograph, shall have sold such work, any person shall afterwards make any alteration by addition or otherwise during the life of the author, without his consent, and shall knowingly sell (a) or publish such work, or any copies thereof so altered, or of any part thereof, as or for the unaltered work of such author.

This clause is intended to prevent the alterations so frequently made in the works of great artists for fraudulent purposes. Mr. Charles Landseer stated a most glaring case in his evidence before a committee appointed by the

(a) Unless the person selling were cognizant of the fact of alteration th·
Act would be an entirely innocent one. See *Reg.* v. *Sleap,* 8 Cox, C. C 472;
Reg. v. *Cohen, ibid.* 41; *Hearne* v. *Garton,* 28 L. J. (M.C.) 216.

CAP. XIV. Society of Arts. It appears that he painted a picture called the 'Eve of the Battle of Edgehill,' in which he introduced two dogs, which had been touched up by his brother Sir Edwin, and, as he himself admitted, greatly improved. The picture was sold to a dealer, who cut out the figures of the dogs and sold them as the work of Sir Edwin Landseer, and he then filled up the hole in the original picture with two dogs painted by an inferior artist, and sold the whole picture as the work of Mr. Charles Landseer.

Every offender under this section shall forfeit to the person aggrieved a sum not exceeding £10, or not exceeding double the full price at which all such copies or altered works shall have been sold or offered for sale; and they shall be forfeited to the person, or the assigns, or legal representatives of the person whose name, initials, or monogram shall have been fraudulently used; provided such person shall have been living at or within twenty years next before the time when the offence may have been committed.

It would seem that if the double price of the copies be less than £10, yet that amount may still be recovered, and that if the double value exceed £10, then any sum up to such double price may be recovered by the person aggrieved, as an inducement to him to proceed, he having to give up the spurious work to the true artist or his representatives, and receive from the person who has defrauded him the price he has paid and as much more.

The penalties imposed as a punishment for a criminal offence. Under these penal sections it has been determined that a person sentenced to pay a penalty cannot, by executing a deed of arrangement with his creditors, escape from the imprisonment consequent on a failure to pay (a). Mr. Graves, the well-known publisher of engravings,

(a) *Graves, Ex parte, In re Prince,* 19 L. T. (N.S.) 241; Law Rep. 3 Ch. 642; 16 W. R. 993; *Bancroft v. Mitchell,* Law Rep. 2 Q. B. 549. See, however, *Johnson, Ex parte, In re Johnson,* 15 W. R. 160; 15 L. T. (N.S.) 163; *Rex v. Stokes,* Cowp. 136; *Rex v. Wakefield,* 13 East, 190; *Rex v. Myers,* 1 T. R. 265. As to limitation of time of three months for action under the 8 Geo. 2, c. 13, not applying to an action on the case brought under 17 Geo. 3, c. 57, see *Graves v. Mercer,* 16 W. R. 790.

became the proprietor of the copyright in Frith's 'Railway Station' and other paintings, and the designs thereof, and also in the copyright in the engravings of such pictures. Photographic copies of these engravings were then fraudulently made, and sold for about one-twentieth of the price at which the copies of Mr. Graves's prints were sold. Such photographic copies were exact reproductions of the engravings and of a large size. Upon the 16th of May, 1868, a man named William Banks Prince was convicted by a magistrate at Lambeth of having sold no less than nineteen of the fraudulent photographic copies in question. He was adjudged to pay a penalty of £5 in respect of each of the copies sold ; and in default of payment the magistrate, under powers given him by the Small Penalties Act, 1865, sentenced Prince to fourteen days' imprisonment in respect of each of the nineteen offences he had committed by selling the photographic copies. While the magistrate was giving his judgment Prince executed a deed of composition with his creditors, which contained a release from them. That deed was assented to by certain creditors of Prince, and then registered in due form. Not having paid the penalties in which he was convicted he was taken into custody upon a magistrate's warrant, and imprisoned pursuant to his sentences. Thereupon he applied to the Bankruptcy Court for his discharge from custody, upon the ground that the penalties in which he had been convicted were *debts*, from the payment of which he had been released by the deed of composition executed between him and his creditors. The court held that Prince was entitled to his discharge.

From this decision Mr. Graves appealed to the Lords Justices, upon the ground that penalties recovered under the Copyright (Works of Art) Act, 1862, were in the nature of a punishment, and consequently were not released by the composition deed which had been executed between Prince and his creditors. On the contrary, it was argued for the respondent that, inasmuch as under the Copyright (Works of Art) Act the penalties were payable to Mr.

Graves, they amounted in the aggregate to nothing more than a debt, which would have been provable under bankruptcy, and was therefore released by the deed. But Lord Justice Page Wood held that what Prince had done in selling the photographic copies was throughout the Copyright (Works of Art) Act treated as an offence, as a *fraudulent* act, for which a punishment was to be inflicted. The penalty provided by the Act was not meant to be the measure of damage sustained by the proprietor of the copyright work which had been pirated, because he was expressly permitted to recover damages by action (in addition to the penalties) under the 11th section of the Act. The object of the Small Penalties Act was merely to provide a simple method of enforcing the payment of penalties not exceeding £5. The penalty given by the Copyright (Works of Art) Act was, in his Lordship's opinion, a punishment for what was in the nature of a criminal offence, and the debtor was therefore not entitled to his discharge from custody unless the penalties were paid. The Lord Justice Selwyn was also of opinion that whether the words or the spirit of the Copyright (Works of Art) Act, under which the penalties had been incurred, were looked at, the order in bankruptcy was wrong, and must therefore be dismissed with costs.

By section 10 of the Act, the importing of piratical copies is expressly prohibited, and by the 11th section, besides the penalties and forfeitures to which we have already referred, a remedy by action for damages is given to the injured owner of the copyright; no limitation as to time within which actions are to be brought is prescribed by the Act.

The provisions of the International Copyright Act, 7 & 8 Vict. c. 12, are extended to paintings, drawings and photographs, by section 12 of the Copyright (Works of Art) Act, 1862.

The Royal Commissioners in their Copyright report, 1876, felt some difficulty on the subject of photographs. They doubted whether the copyright should be assimilated to that in paintings and pass to a purchaser, or whether it should remain with the photographer. "When photographs," said they, "are taken with a view to copies being sold in large numbers, it is practically impossible that the copyright in the negative should pass to each purchaser of a copy, and it must remain with the photographer, or cease to exist. On the other hand, the same reasons exist for vesting the copyright of portraits in the purchaser or person for whom they are taken, as in the case of a painting.

"Indeed, considering the facility of multiplying copies, and the tendency among photographers to exhibit the portraits of distinguished persons in shop windows, it may be thought that there is even greater reason for giving the persons whose portraits are taken the control over the multiplication of copies than there is in the case of a painting. It therefore becomes a question whether it is not necessary to make that distinction between photographs that are portraits and those that are not, and between photographs taken on commission and those taken otherwise, which we have deprecated in the case of paintings. We suggest that the copyright in a photograph should belong to the proprietor of the negative, but in the case of photographs taken on commission, we recommend that no copies be sold or exhibited without the sanction of the person who ordered them."

The Commissioners further thought that the same questions arose in respect of engravings, lithographs, prints, and similar works, and were of opinion that, so far as regards the transfer and vesting of the copyright, these arts should be placed upon the same basis as photographs.

In concluding their general report upon the fine arts they referred to a matter as to which artists say the law is disadvantageous to them. Before the artist paints a picture, he frequently finds it necessary to make a number of sketches or studies, which, grouped together, make up the picture in its finished state. These works may be studies expressly made for the picture about to be painted, or

Artists' studies and sketches.

CAP. XIV. they may be sketches which have been made at various times, and kept as materials for future pictures. If after a picture is so composed, the copyright is sold, the artists are afraid that they are prevented from again using or selling the same studies and sketches, as they have been advised that such user or sale would be an infringement of the copyright they have sold (a).

The Commissioners doubted whether this fear was well-founded, but as the use of such studies and sketches as they had described could not, in their opinion, result in any real injury to the copyright owner, who has copies of them in his picture in a more or less altered shape, and combined with other independent work, they thought the doubt should be removed, and that the author of any work of fine art, even though he may have parted with the copyright therein, should be allowed to sell or use again his *bonâ fide* sketches and studies for such works and compositions, provided that he does not repeat or colourably imitate the design of the original work (b).

Replicas. Where an artist has painted a picture on commission, as the copyright is in the commissioner, he may not paint a *replica*, but where this is not the case, and there is no agreement as to the copyright within the 25 & 26 Vict. c. 68, the artist is at liberty so to do.

Copyright in photographs and property in negatives. As to photographs, the copyright in non-commissioned works belongs to the photographer, if reserved in writing, and in commissioned works the negative and the glass on which it is, is usually considered to belong to the photographer, while the copyright belongs to the person who gives the commission.

(a) The doubt exists by reason of the terms of the 6th section of the 25 & 26 Vict. c. 68.
(b) Par. 118–124.

CHAPTER XV.

COPYRIGHT IN DESIGNS.

CALICO-PRINTING, the art of dyeing woven fabrics of cotton with variegated figures and colours more or less permanent, has been practised from time immemorial in India. The art was known to the ancient Hindus and Egyptians. Pliny describes it with sufficient precision. "Robes and white veils are painted in Egypt," says he, " in a wonderful way ; being first imbued, not with dyes, but with dye-absorbing drugs, by which they appear to be unaltered, but when plunged for a little in a cauldron of the boiling dye-stuff they are found to be painted. Since there is only one colour in the cauldron, it is marvellous to see many colours imparted to the robe in consequence of the modifying agency of the excipient drug. Nor can the dye be washed out. Thus the cauldron, which would of itself undoubtedly confuse the colours of cloths previously dyed, is made to impart several dyes from a single one, painting while it boils " (a).

Anderson, in his 'History of Commerce,' places the origin of English calico-printing as far back as the year 1676; but Mr. Thomson, a better authority, assigns the year 1696 as the date of the commencement of the practice of this art in England, when a small print-ground was established on the banks of the Thames, at Richmond, by a Frenchman.

Linen was long ago, and silks and woollen fabrics also have recently been, made the subject of topical dyeing,

(a) Pliny, 'Natural History,' lib. xxxv. c. 2.

CAP. XV.   upon principles analogous to those of calico-printing, but
with certain peculiarities arising from the nature of their
textile materials.

The first Act   The first Act granting protection to the inventor of de-
for protection
of designs.   signs was passed in 1787 (the 27 Geo. 3, c. 38). This Act
was followed by the 29 Geo. 3, c. 19, and the 34 Geo. 3,
c. 23. But these Acts did not extend to Ireland, nor to
fabrics other than linen and cotton, and did not afford any
protection to designs on fabrics composed of animal pro-
ducts, as wool, silk, or hair, or mixtures of those materials
with flax and cotton. The printing on fabrics of animal
and vegetable substances, and on mixed fabrics, having
subsequently grown up into an important branch of manufacture, an Act of Parliament was introduced in 1839
(2 Vict. c. 13), by which the same protection was given
to designs printed on fabrics of animal substances, or
a mixture of animal and vegetable substances, as was
afforded to designs printed on fabrics of vegetable substances; and the provisions of the existing Acts were
extended to Ireland.

We followed the French in establishing any design
rights at all; and it would be well if we adopted their
simple, sensible arrangement for securing them.

In the early part of the last century the French entertained more correct notions of the rights of property in
designs than the British, and so convinced were they that
great benefits would flow from rejecting the claim of the
copyist to reap the original designer's profits, that, in 1737
and 1744, laws established a property in designs for the
manufacturers of Lyons, and in 1787 the benefits of legal
protection were fully established. The basis of the pre-
eminence of the French, and the means by which they have
attained their unrivalled position in *taste*, is *efficient protection*, and it is certainly singular that this fundamental
element and primary cause of superiority should have
been so long overlooked in this country.

Division of   We have in England two distinct rights, founded upon
the right.   different Acts of Parliament, in the application of designs

—copyright in the application of designs for ornamental CAP XV.
purposes, and copyright in the application of designs for
the shape and configuration of articles of utility.

The former, of which we shall first treat, is regulated
by the 5 & 6 Vict. c. 100, amended by 6 & 7 Vict. c. 65,
13 & 14 Vict. c. 104, 21 & 22 Vict. c. 70, and 24 & 25
Vict. c. 73.

The 5 & 6 Vict. c. 100, repeals all the previous Designs Copyright in designs for ornamental purposes.
Acts, and enacts that the proprietor of every new and
original design not previously published (a), whether such
design be applicable to the ornamenting of any article
of manufacture, or of any substance, artificial or natural,
or partly artificial and partly natural, and whether such
design be so applicable for the pattern or for the shape
or configuration, or for the ornament, or for any two or
more of such purposes, or by whatever means such design
may be so applicable, whether by printing or by painting
or by embroidery, or by weaving, or by sewing, or by
modelling, or by casting, or by embossing, or by engraving, or by staining, or by any other means whatsoever,
natural, mechanical, or chemical, separate or combined,
shall have the sole right of applying the same to any
article of manufacture or to any such substance as aforesaid during the respective terms thereinafter mentioned.

The statute does not mention " any article of manufacture" being a design, but considers the design to be
protected as applicable to the ornamenting of any article
of manufacture. The design is always considered different
from the "article of manufacture, or the substance to
which it is to be applied."

(a) As to what amounts to publication, see *Cornish* v. *Keene*, Webst.
Pat. Ca. 501, 508. See *Anon.* 1 Chitt. 24; *Carpenter* v. *Smith*, 9 M. &
W. 300; S. C. Webst. Pat. Ca. 530, 536; *Jones* v. *Berger*, *ibid*. 550; *The
Househill Co.* v. *Neilson*, *ibid*. 718, n.; *Stead* v. *Williams*, 7 Man. & Gran.
818. See *Prince Albert* v. *Strange*, 1 H. & Tw. 1; *Dalglish* v. *Jarvie*, 14
Jur. 945; S. C. 2 Mac. & G. 231; 2 H. & Tw. 437. In the last cited case
it was queried whether the nine months' copyright given by the Act in
any designs for ornamenting articles of manufacture dates from the
publication of the manufacture or from the publication of the design.

The terms are to be computed from the time of the design being registered.

Class

I. Articles of manufacture composed wholly or chiefly of any metal or mixed metals.	}	Five years.
II. Articles of manufacture composed wholly or chiefly of wood.		
III. Articles of manufacture composed wholly or chiefly of glass.		
IV. Articles of manufacture composed wholly or chiefly of earthenware, bone, papier-mache, and other solid substances.		
„ Articles of ivory not comprised above (a).		
V. Paper-hangings.		
VI. Carpets.		
„ Oil-cloths (b).		
VIII. Shawls to which the design is not applied solely by printing, or by any other process by which colours are or may be produced upon tissue or textile fabrics (c).	}	The period of three years.
XI. Woven fabrics composed of linen, cotton, wool, silk, or hair, or of any two or more of such materials, if the design be applied by printing, or by any other process by which the colours are or may hereafter be produced upon tissue or textile fabrics, such woven fabrics being or coming within the description technically called furnitures, and the repeat of the design whereof shall be more than twelve inches by eight inches.	}	
VII. Shawls, if the design be applied solely by printing, or by any other process by which colours are or may hereafter be produced upon tissue or textile fabrics.	}	The period of nine months.
IX. Yarn, thread, or warp, if the design be applied by printing, or by any other process by which colours are or may hereafter be produced.		
X. Woven fabrics composed of linen, cotton, wool, silk, or hair, or of any two or more of such materials, if the design be applied by printing, or by any other process by which colours are or may hereafter be produced upon tissue or textile fabrics, excepting the woven fabrics enumerated above (d).	}	The period of three years.
XII. Woven fabrics not comprised above (e).	{	The period of twelve calendar months.
XIII. Lace, and any article of manufacture or substance not comprised above.		

(a) By the 13 & 14 Vict. c. 104, s. 8.
(b) By the 6 & 7 Vict. c. 65, s. 5.
(c) *Norton* v. *Nicholls,* 5 Jur. (N.S.) 1203 ; 7 W. R. 420.
(d) *Vide Lowndes* v. *Browne,* 12 Ir. Law Rep. 293 ; time of protection extended by 21 & 22 Vict. c. 70.
(e) *Harrison* v. *Taylor,* 4 H. & N. 815 ; 5 Jur. (N.S.) 1219 ; 29 L. J. (Ex.) 3. Copyright in designs for damasks after the 5th of November, 1850, under the power conferred on the Board of Trade (now the Commissioners of Patents), by the 9th section for the period of two years, in addition to the term of one year given by the Act.

By the 13 & 14 Vict. c. 104, s. 9, as amended by the 38 & 39 Vict. c. 93, the Commissioners of Patents are empowered from time to time to order that the copyright of any class of designs or any particular design registered or which may be registered under the Designs Act, 1842, shall be extended for such term, not exceeding the additional term of three years, as the said Commissioners may think fit; and the said Commissioners have power to revoke or alter any order as may from time to time appear necessary. Whenever any order is made by the said Commissioners under this provision it must be registered in the office for the registration of designs; and during the extended term the protection and benefits conferred by the said Designs Acts are to continue as fully as if the original term had not expired.

No person is entitled to the benefit of the Act unless the design in respect of which he seeks protection has, previous to publication (a), been registered in accordance with the Act, and unless at the time of such registration such design has been registered in respect of the application thereof to some or one of the articles of manufacture or substances comprised in the above-mentioned classes, by specifying the number of the class in respect of which such registration is made, and unless the name of such person shall be registered according to the Act as the proprietor of such design (b), and unless after publication of such design every such article or substance to which the design is applied has thereon, at the end or edge

(a) In *Dalglish* v. *Jarvie*, 1 Sim. (N.S.) 336, it is *queried* whether the term "publication" here used is limited to publication after the design has been embodied and introduced into some fabric.

(b) The author of any new and original design is to be considered its proprietor, unless he has executed the work for another person for a good or a valuable consideration, in which case such person is to be considered the proprietor, and is entitled to be registered in place of the author. Every person acquiring for a good or a valuable consideration a new and original design or the right to apply the same to the above-mentioned articles or substances, either exclusively of any one else or otherwise, and every person upon whom the property in a design or the right to its application may devolve, shall be considered the proprietor of the design in the respect in and to the extent to which such property may have been acquired, but not otherwise (5 & 6 Vict. c. 100, s. 5).

thereof (a) or other convenient place, the letters " Rd.,'
together with such number or letter, and in such form as
shall correspond with the date of the registration of such
design according to the registry in that behalf; and such
marks may be put on any such article or substance, either
by making the same in or on the material itself, or by
attaching thereto a label containing such marks.

What suffi-
cient registra-
tion.
It was formerly held not sufficient registration under the
17th section, of an article comprised in class 8 of section 3,
to leave with the registrar an article manufactured according to the combinations relied upon, with an intimation
that it was to be applied to class 8, though it might be
sufficient as regards articles comprised in class 5.

Thus, in a case where the plaintiff had registered a
shawl, the component parts of the composition of which
were all old, but the combination itself new, by leaving
with the registrar one of his shawls, Lord Campbell said:
" Take the example of paper-hangings, class 5.   A section
of the paper having the design impressed upon it would
clearly disclose the claim of the inventor, and would fully
put the registrar in possession of all the information he
ought to have to enable him to perform the duties imposed
upon him.   But the plaintiff, by leaving one of his shawls
with the registrar, gives no information of the nature of
his claim, and cannot, we think, be said to have registered
his ' design ' " (b).

When the question came before Sir W. P. Wood (c) in
the previous year he was of opinion that the registration
was valid and that the provisions of the Act had been sufficiently complied with, but in referring to this judgment
in Norton v. Nicholls (d), Lord Campbell, C.J., said: " If the
facts before his Honour had been the same as those which
were proved at the trial, and upon which we have to

(a) *Heywood* v. *Potter*, 1 E. & B. 439; 22 L. J. (N.S.) Q. B. 133. And
see 21 & 22 Vict. c. 70, s. 4.
(b) *Norton* v. *Nicholls* 28 L. J. (Q.B.) 225, 227; 5 Jur. (N.S.) 1203;
7 W. R. 420.   But see 21 & 22 Vict. c. 70, s. 5.
(c) In *Norton* v. *Nicholls*, 4 K. & J. 475; *Norton* v. *Ford*, cited *Norton* v.
Nicholls, 5 Jur. (N.S.) 1203, 1205.   (d) 5 Jur. (N.S.) 1203, 1205.

adjudicate, we should have considered ourselves bound by his decision. But before him the five points seem to have been treated as all new, each being considered a design,' which might be applied to the shawl, the shawl being an article of manufacture. On this supposition there might probably be a design within the Act of Parliament; the deposit of the shawl with the registrar might possibly be a due registration; but when it appears that all the supposed designs to be applied to the article of manufacture were old, and that the old design contended for is a combination of all the parts of a manifold, complicated, and highly ornamental garment contrived to assume many different shapes; we felt bound, on all the questions submitted to us, to give judgment for the defendants."

With respect to copyright of design, no specification is required, as in the case of patents for inventions; but section 17 of the 5 & 6 Vict. c. 100, after empowering all the world to inspect the registered designs when the copyright has expired, gives a right under certain circumstances, before the copyright has expired, to an inspection of the registration, and requires the registrar, on the application of certain persons, to give to such persons "a certificate stating whether there be any copyright existing of particular designs, and if there be, in respect of what particular article of manufacture or substance such copyright exists." It is therefore essential that the registrar be provided with particulars sufficiently definite for him to be able to designate the individual parts in which protection is claimed.

Copies of a registered design published in a book for sale need no registration mark, nor is such publication a licence to the purchaser of the book to apply the designs to articles for sale (a).

A design may be registered in respect of one or more of the classes, according as it is intended to be employed in one or more species of manufacture, but a separate

(a) *Riego de la Brachardière* v. *Elvery*, 18 L. J. (Ex.) 381; 4 Ex. 380.

fee must be paid on account of each separate class, and all such registrations must be made at the same time.

The periods and prices of the classes vary, and it is the ultimate result that is looked to in selecting among them; thus in *Lowndes* v. *Browne* (a), a pattern first *printed* on the ground and then *worked* with a needle, was held to be well registered under class 10.

In *West's Case* a Mr. Barfourd had registered a design under class 2, for the application of an ornamental border of the Brazilian pine leaf to straw hats, which the defendant having, as the plaintiff alleged, pirated, he laid an information before justices against him, whereupon the defendant was convicted. It was subsequently contended that the conviction was bad, inasmuch as there had been no legal registration of the design, it being registered under a wrong class, namely, under class 2, and not 13, and there being a much shorter term of protection for the latter than for the former. The question, however, was not decided.

It might sometimes be worth while to register an ornamental design in more that one class to prevent vulgarization, such as the printing on calico a design registered for silks (b); but as publication in one class would be so in all, this must be done, as before mentioned, at the same time, or at least before any form of the pattern be in circulation.

By the 14th section of the 5 & 6 Vict. c. 100, as amended by the 38 & 39 Vict. c. 93, for the purpose of registering designs under that Act, the Commissioners of Patents were empowered to appoint a registrar, and if necessary a deputy-registrar, clerks, and other officers and servants, and, subject to the provision of the Act, were authorized to make rules for regulating the execution of the duties of the office.

(a) 12 Ir. L. R. 293.
(b) A registered pattern for a paper-hanging it will be competent for a carpet manufacturer to apply to carpets, unless the paper-stainer register for class 6, as well as class 5.

Accordingly, directions for registering and for facilitating searches have been issued (a).

CAP. XV.

Persons proposing to register a design for ornamenting an article of manufacture must deliver at the Designs Office : two exactly similar copies, drawings (or tracings), photographs, or prints thereof, with the proper fees : the name and address of the proprietor or proprietors, or the title of the firm under which he or they may be trading, together with their place of abode or place of carrying on business, distinctly written or printed ; and the number of the class in respect of which such registration is intended to be made, except it be for sculpture.

Mode of registration.

By the 21 & 22 Vict. c. 70 (a), it was declared that the registration of any *pattern* or *portion* of an article of manufacture to which a design is applied, instead or in lieu of a copy, drawing, print, specification, or description in writing, should be as valid and effectual to all intents and purposes as if such copy, drawing, print, specification, or description in writing had been furnished to the registrar under " The Copyright of Designs Acts."

Permissible to register by pattern.

The advisability of registering under this section by sample, or following the former mode of registration, will of course depend upon the nature of the design to be protected. There is a risk either way. There is a risk on the one hand of misdescription of the claim, for though the same nicety is not required in registering patterns or designs, as in describing inventions sought to be protected under the patent laws, yet it is necessary that the party should properly explain the nature of the design he is desirous of protecting, and on the other hand, where the party exercises the option of silence, and merely produces the pattern of his invention, he is exposed to this :— that as by the registration of the sample he has claimed protection in respect of the entirety of what is exhibited on the face of that pattern ; if only a part is used in a

When advisable to do so.

(a) These will be found in the Appendix.

2 E

Cap. XV. different combination, he is without the protection which
he would otherwise have had (a).

When not
advisable.

When a piece of manufacture with a design impressed
upon it is registered without any explanation or addition
in writing, and that design consists of several parts not
necessarily united in configuration, but capable of being
severed into independent integral parts, then the design
registered is the entire thing, exactly as it is described in
the pattern furnished to the registrar; and such registration is therefore not open to the objection of uncertainty,
but is valid according to the foregoing provision. The
designer, however, is, as we have already pointed out,
under this disadvantage, that when he registers a pattern
of material, there is no infringement unless it is exactly
copied. If the designer be content with putting a design,
which is composed of several parts placed together, but
capable of being severed and used in a separate form, upon
the register without limitation and without explanation,
he claims simply to be the inventor of the entire thing,
exactly as it is described in the drawing or pattern which
he has exhibited, and all that he can claim to protect
against imitation is, that thing in its exact form and relative
position and proportions as they appear upon his pattern.
Anything, therefore, which is a *fac-simile* of that drawing,
any other pattern which is a reproduction of that in its
integrity, becomes an infringement. But that which is
different in shape and form, or in the relative positions of
its several parts, which is not a reproduction of it, as a
replica or copy of a picture, would not be an infringement
of the thing specified (b).

When sample
of article
registered,
design not
infringed by
article pro-
duced on same
principle, if
different in
style.

Thus where a sample of an article had been registered
under the 21 & 22 Vict. c. 79, s. 5, Vice-Chancellor
Wickens was of opinion that the design so registered would
not be infringed by an article produced upon the same
principle, if different in style. In the case referred to (c),
two patterns, in respect of which the infringement was

(a) *Holdsworth* v. *M'Crea*, Law Rep. 2 H. L. 390.
(b) *Per* Lord Westbury in *Holdsworth* v. *M'Crea*, L. R. 2 H. L. 388.
(c) *Thom* v. *Syddall*, 20 W. R. 291.

claimed, were registered by the plaintiff by the registration of samples in accordance with the above provision, without any written description or specification. These patterns, similar in character, but differing slightly in the water-figure, or *moire*, consisted of a species of *moire* or water-pattern, formed by the intersection of two series of bands of lines, which left interstices in a constantly varying manner, through which the white calico was seen, which patterns could be printed in one colour, or in two colours, or in different shades of the same colour. By the crossing or intersection of the two series of bands variable white spaces were left, which formed a *moire*, or water-figure; whilst the dark lines of which the bands were composed on crossing one another formed another dark *moire*, or water-figure, and the whole formed a complete and constantly recurring pattern.

The designs of the defendants, the subject of the motion then before the court, which was for an injunction, were formed in a similar manner by the interlacing or inter-section of two series of bands of lines, leaving in places the white calico to be seen through, and by means of the interstices and of the darker parts of the bands, the double *moire* or water-pattern was produced, exactly in the same manner as in the plaintiff's patterns. The general appear-ance of the patterns of the plaintiff and defendants were similar as respects the method in which the white and dark spaces were left; but while the configuration of the water-figure in the designs of the plaintiff was wavy, the water-figure in the defendants' designs represented a succession of chevrons, or vandykes, thus forming a visible distinction.

For the defendants it was objected that, as the plaintiff had registered his patterns by sample only, without claiming by specification novelty for any particular part, the use of the same principle, producing a different style of design, was no infringement. The Vice-Chancellor thought that the registration of a pattern by registering a sample could not in any degree whatever give the person registering it a monopoly of the mode of producing a certain effect, and that plaintiff might have been in a different position if he had specified that the intersection of the bands of lines was the gist of his invention. After referring to the case of *M'Crea* v. *Holdsworth* he continued : " The precise question which was determined after. so much litigation, was that a design, however complex, might become private property by the registration of a sample. It was strongly urged that if a design consisting of various parts, new and old, is registered by sample, without anything to disclaim what is old and point out what is new, future designers are put to a most unfair and unreasonable disadvantage, since they cannot tell what is sought to be protected, and have thus the unfair onus thrown upon them of finding out what is really claimed, and avoiding that in future designs. To this all the courts successively seem to have given the same answer : ' It is not thrown upon you to find out what is or is not claimed ; all is claimed, not the separate parts, of which nine-tenths may be new or not, but the whole as one thing.' No exclusive right is claimed to any design which is not as one design substantially connected with that shewn by the sample registered. It seems to me, I confess, that the difficulties raised about the registration of a complex design could have been solved in no other way. After the application, which was to enter a verdict for the defendant, on the ground that the registration of such a complex design was bad in point of law, had failed before three courts, it was discovered that a very minute difference existed between the designs. What was claimed was the particular collocation of the shaded and bordered stars upon the ornamental chain surface. In the defendant's design the star was shifted or moved round, but so that the outward appearance remained exactly the same, and the two things were, for the purpose for which they were manufactured, identical. That the defendant's design was an infringement had been found by the jury without objection, or indeed contest, and the objection that there was no infringement in consequence of a small variation between the designs, was never raised till an equity suit, which had stood over to await the result of the proceedings at law, was brought to a hearing. It was then argued, but surely not hopefully, that the defence never insisted upon before through the very long proceedings to try the right, was to be treated at the very last stage as shewing that the plaintiff had no case from the beginning. Lord Justice James, then Vice-Chancellor, disregarded this, as might have been expected; and the Lord Chancellor on appeal took the same view without hesitation.

"But the Lord Chancellor in giving judgment proceeded to point out the futility of the contention if it had been then raiseable. He stated that the words of some of the noble lords who addressed the House on the appeal were to be taken with due reference to the question before them, not in the most literal strictness; but nothing whatever was said by him to throw doubt on the general proposition, common alike to the judgments of the Exchequer Chamber, and to the speeches of Lord Chelmsford and Lord Westbury in the House of Lords, that the whole design is claimed when the registration is by sample, and that when there is no reproduction of the whole design there is no infringement; but that there may be a reproduction of the whole design, notwithstanding small variations in particular parts of it.

"Supposing a design in stars, arranged in a complicated series of interlacing and recurring curves, so as to produce a striking and pleasing effect to the eye, and the design to be registered by a sample shewing the design in five pointed blue stars on a white ground, a design with six pointed stars in the same arrangement would probably be an infringement, a design with black stars instead of blue might perhaps be an infringement, but a design of rosebuds in the very same arrangement, or of mere circular rings in the very same arrangement, would, I am inclined to think, be no infringement (a).

(a) Compare the words in *italics* of the Lord Chancellor, pp. 424, 425.

"The proprietor of the registered design might say, 'The real merit, attraction, and novelty in my design is in the series of curves in which the elements of the design, whatever they may be, are arranged; everything else in my design is well known, obvious, and unattractive.' The answer would be: 'If you had claimed that you might possibly have protected it. But you have claimed a great deal more, and you cannot now disclaim the rest of it for the purpose of putting a subsequent design in the wrong.' I am now dealing with the motion only, and express no final or conclusive opinion, but I am bound to say that the designs complained of seem to me different as wholes from those of the plaintiff, substantially and not colourably different; so different, indeed, that I can fancy an un-biassed person considering them as very much prettier and more attractive than those of the plaintiff. It is said that the principle on which the defendants' effects are produced is precisely the same as that on which the plaintiff's are produced; that when the plaintiff's design was once known it required taste only, and not inventive-ness or original power of design, to develop it into the defendants'; that, in fact, the defendants finding the plain-tiff's design attractive determined to work on it, as a thing from which a design different but having analogous attractions, might be developed. Whether these conten-tions are or are not well-'ounded, I express no opinion, but I may take the fact almost as admitted, I mean to say by the defendants. with reference to their working on the plaintiff's design, but still they constitute in my opinion no case to shew that the plaintiff's patterns registered by sample only have been infringed by the defendants. The motion therefore fails, and but for the unfortunate and inconvenient rule (derived from another state of practice) that the plaintiff must make such a motion if he intends to ask a perpetual injunction at the hearing, I should dis-miss it: as it is, I can only order it to stand to the hearing."

Great care must be taken not to be misled by the above opinion expressed by the learned Vice-Chancellor. The latter part expresses more correctly the true ground of his decision, namely, that the designs complained of were different as wholes from those of the plaintiff, substantially and not colourably different; some expressions in the former part of the judgment apparently go beyond that which is warranted by the opinions of the law lords in *M'Crea* v. *Holdsworth*, and it is somewhat to be regretted that they even went so far. The true test of the infringement of a design registered by sample is stated by perhaps the highest living authority in the appeal from the decree of Vice-Chancellor James in *M'Crea* v. *Holdsworth* (a). "It is said that because you register a design of this kind for some useful purpose or other in connection with furniture, or whatever it may be, and instead of describing your design in words you choose to place your design, for which you seek protection, upon the register in the shape of a part of the article designed, that then you are tied down to that identical article so exhibited, and to the design so exhibited, and are not at liberty to complain of any person making a thing which shall be to all outward appearance exactly the same, and which shall for all purposes for which the thing is manufactured be identical, if the person who has determined to exhibit a design for all practical purposes identical with yours is astute enough to turn a star, or what is called a star in this case, of exactly the same number of foliages or points, in the opposite direction. On the other fabric it is apparently of exactly the same dimensions and effect to the eye, but if looked at by a microscope—which is not the way in which people regard furniture generally—or if looked at with a pair of spectacles very carefully, or looked at closely, not for the purpose of ascertaining its general effect, but so as to see how far a person might escape who was said to have pirated the design, it will be found that he has merely altered the position of the star by two hairs'-breadths. The thing seems to me to be perfectly idle, and it seemed to me once or twice during the course

(a) 23 L. T. (N.S.) 445.

of the argument, that Mr. Ince put the case as it ought
to be put, although he did not apparently do so for that
purpose. He said, twice or thrice, that it cannot be said
to be the same or to the same effect. 'The same effect'
is a very proper mode of describing it. . . . With the un-
erring judgment of their own eyes, the judge held and the
jury held that these two articles were manufactured of the
same stuff, manufactured of the same cloth, manufactured
with the star and the chain, in exactly the same situation,
as distinguished from position; that they were placed in
the same part of the pattern, between the two links of the
chain, as it were, the only difference being that the star
was a little turned round, so that the point of the link
would come between the intervals in the one case and
would come upon the spur or projecting part in the other.
That being the only difference, and that not being in the
least a difference of effect in what was intended to be
produced and used for the particular purposes for which it
was used, the two things were identical, and I do not
imagine that anything that was said by their lordships in
the House of Lords means that if a person simply makes
a thing which shall to the outward eye, and for every
purpose for which it is usable, be identical with the other,
that can possibly be protected. What was said, and very
reasonably said, if I may be allowed to say so with respect,
in the judgment of the House of Lords, was this : If you
choose to protect your chain and star, and the other things
which you have here, you must protect them just as they
are represented, and you can only protect your pattern as
representing exactly what is exhibited, and if there is the
least difference of effect in that which is produced by your
putting the star in a different situation, or putting it at
a wider distance, or the like, which may easily be done
with the identical pattern so as to produce an entirely
different effect, all that will be left to the jury, and the
jury will have to say whether or not the two things are
the same. *I do not think it was intended by their Lordships to say that you shall do that which shall have to every*

eye exactly the same effect as that produced in the one case by the plaintiff which may be produced by the defendant, as long as he can shew you by a very minute examination, such as is never usual nor desirable, nor in any way likely to be had with reference to those who are purchasing the articles, that you produce by an infinitesimal variation of that kind a difference of pattern which will allow you to escape from doing that which it is just and right to do, namely, assuming the pattern which has been exhibited to be another pattern. This seems to me simply an attempt to stretch these observations, thrown out as they were by Lord Chief Justice Erle in the first instance, and afterwards by several noble lords in the House of Lords, to a purpose totally and entirely distinct from any possible purpose to which they were meant to be applied. It seems to me all that was meant was, you are not bound, as you are in patent cases, to distinguish the new from the old. In this particular case you have part of the pattern, namely the chain, which is altogether old ; you have another part of it which is found by the jury, in combination with this chain pattern, to be new ; and you are allowed to have this new pattern without distinguishing what is new and what is old; but if you choose to put it in that way and present it to the public without distinguishing what is new and what is old, you cannot expect to be protected as against the public in case they choose to use the portion you use in any manner substantially differing from your use of it. If they are used in exactly the same manner, as I hold they are in this case, and have the same effect, or nearly the same effect, then of course the shifting or turning round the spurs of the stars in this particular case cannot be allowed to protect the defendant from the consequences of the piracy."

The appointment and duties of the registrar are set forth in the 5 & 6 Vict. c. 100, ss. 14, 15, and the 6 & 7 Vict. c. 65, ss. 7–9. Under this last section a discretionary power is conferred upon him of refusing to register under the latter Act if it should appear to him that the

The appointment and duties of the registrar.

CAP. XV. design brought to him for that purpose would more properly be registered under the former ; and further, he is at liberty to exercise his discretion in refusing to register any design which is not intended to be applied to any article of manufacture, but only to some label, wrapper, or other covering in which such article might be exposed for sale, or any design which is contrary to public morality or order ; subject, however, to an appeal to the Privy Council.

Power to dispense with drawings, &c., in certain cases.

If in any case in which the registration of a design is required to be made under either of the Designs Acts, it appears to the registrar that copies, drawings, or prints, as required by those Acts, cannot be printed, or that it is unreasonable or unnecessary to require them, he may dispense with such copies, drawings, or prints, and may allow in lieu thereof such specification or description, in writing or in print, as may be sufficient to identify and render intelligible the design in respect of which registration is desired. Whenever registration shall be so made in the absence of such copies, drawings, or prints, the registration is to be valid and effectual to all intents and purposes as if such copies, drawings, or prints had been furnished (a).

After the design has been registered, one of the two copies, drawings (or tracings), or prints, will be filed at the office, and the other returned to the proprietor with a certificate annexed, on which will appear the *mark to be placed* on each article of manufacture to which the design shall have been applied (b).

Certificate of registration.

This certificate, in the absence of evidence to the contrary, shall be sufficient proof of the design, and of the name of the proprietor therein mentioned, having been duly registered; of the commencement of the period of registry; of the person named therein as proprietor being the proprietor; of the originality of the design, and of the provisions of the Copyright Designs Act, and of any rule under which the certificate appears to be made having

(a) 13 & 14 Vict. c. 104, s. 11.   See 38 & 39 Vict. c. 93.
(b) 5 & 6 Vict. c. 100, ss. 15, 16.

been complied with. And such certificate may be received in evidence without proof of the handwriting of the signature thereof, or of the seal of the office affixed thereto, or of the person signing the same being the registrar or deputy registrar (a).

If the design is for an article registered under class 10, no mark is required, but there must be printed on such article, at each end of the original piece thereof, the name and address of the proprietor, and the word "Registered," together with the years for which the design is registered (b).

This alteration in the mode of marking the design for articles registered under class 10, was effected by the 4th section of the 21 & 22 Vict. c. 70.

If the design is for sculpture, no mark is required to be placed thereon after registration, but merely the word "Registered" and the date of registration.

If the design is for provisional registration, no mark is required to be placed thereon after registration, but merely the words "Provisionally registered" and the date.

Any person putting the registration mark on a design not registered, or after the copyright thereof has expired, or when the design has not been applied within the United Kingdom, is liable to forfeit for every offence £5 (c).

The provisions of the Copyright of Designs Act will be construed strictly, and should any copies of a registered design be sold without bearing the registration mark when necessary, and the name, address and date as provided by the Acts—protection will be lost. This case arose under the 6 & 7 Vict. c. 56, on a bill being filed by Mr. Pierce, described as the proprietor of a newly invented chair called "the registered royal step chair," against the defendants, who were furniture manufacturers, to restrain

---

(a) 5 & 6 Vict. c. 100, s. 16. See 13 & 14 Vict. c. 104, ss. 12–14, and 38 & 39 Vict. c. 93. And an action lies for false representation as to the registry of a design: *Barley* v. *Walford*, 9 Q. B. 197.

(b) *Harrison* v. *Taylor*, 3 H. & N. 301, reversed (Ex. Ch.) 4 H. & N. 815; 29 L. J. (Ex.) 3; 5 Jur. (N.S.) 1219.

(c) 5 & 6 Vict. c. 100, s. 11; *Barley* v. *Walford*, 9 Q. B. 197. See *Rodgers* v. *Nowell*, 5 C. B. 109. £10 by 21 & 22 Vict. c. 70, s. 7.

the sale of certain articles of furniture described as
improved combined chair and steps, used principally for
library purposes. The defendants, by their answer and
the evidence, contended that the article was not a new
invention, but that similar articles of furniture had been
made and sold by them and others in the trade long before
the registration of this particular article. In addition, they
said that the plaintiff had sold some of the articles
without having the word "registered" attached to them
with the date of registration. It was given in evidence
by a person who had been in the employ of the plaintiff,
that he was his foreman at the time of the registration of
the design, the 13th Nov. 1867. That, as such foreman,
he had forwarded on the 15th Nov. 1867, an order to a die-
cutter at Sheffield for a die to be made for stamping oval
metal plates which should have on them the words
"Alfred E. Pierce, 109 Hatton Garden, London," and
also the word "registered" and the date of the registration,
the "13 Nov. 1867," and also for the striking off and
stamping 2000 of such plates to be delivered to plaintiff
in London. That none of the said plates were delivered
to the plaintiff until the 31st January 1868, when a
packet containing 100 of such oval metal plates was
delivered to him. That before the delivery of the said
100 plates there were not on the business premises of
plaintiff any similar plates. That between the date of
the said plaintiff's registration of his said design and the
31st Jan. 1868, a large number of combined chairs and
steps made according to said plaintiff's said registered
design, and amounting to upwards of fifty, were sold by
plaintiff and delivered to various customers [the names
of several of such customers were set out], and that they
had not on them the word "registered" or the date of
registration, but that all the said combined chairs and
steps had on them an oval metal plate having on it the
words "Alfred E. Pierce, patentee, 109 Hatton Garden,
London," with the royal arms in the centre. The
question was whether, under the circumstances, the

plaintiff could obtain the relief prayed. For him it was contended that the spirit of the Act had been fully complied with, but the Vice-Chancellor Giffard said he considered the words of the 3rd section of the Act too clear for argument. It was a statute which must be rendered strictly; and therefore from the fact contained in the evidence, which was not denied, that plaintiff had sold many of these articles without the word " registered " or the date of registration attached to them, he must dismiss the plaintiff's bill with costs (a).

But although a bill to prevent an infringement did not allege that the requirements of the Acts had been complied with, yet the Master of the Rolls held, that the bill was not on that ground alone open to demurrer (b). And it has been held that the copyright of a registered design is lost if the proprietor (whether English or foreign) sells the registered article even *abroad* without the letters, " Rd." being attached thereto, as required by the 5 & 6 Vict. c. 100, s. 4, and 24 & 25 Vict. c. 73; and so the benefit of the Acts is forfeited unless the proper registration marks are attached to all articles and substances to which the design is applied, whether the same are sold abroad or in the British dominions (c).

All designs of which the copyright has expired may be inspected at the Designs Office (d) on the payment of the proper fee; but *no* design, the copyright of which is existing, is, in general, open to inspection. Any person, however, may, by application at the office, and on production of the registration mark of any particular design, be furnished with a certificate of search, stating whether the copyright be in existence, and in respect of what particular article of manufacture it exists; also the term of such copyright, the date of registration, and the name and address of the registered proprietor thereof (e).

The registration books open to inspection.

(a) *Pierce* v. *Worth*, 18 L. T. (N.S.) 710.
(b) *Sarazin* v. *Hamel*, 32 Beav. 145; 9 Jur. (N.S.) 192; 32 L. J. (Ch.) 378–380.
(c) *Sarazin* v. *Hamel*, 32 Beav. 151; 9 Jur. (N.S.) 192; 32 L. J. (Ch.) 380.
(d) No. 1 Whitehall, S.W.
(e) 5 & 6 Vict. c. 100, s. 17. *Et vide* 6 & 7 Vict. c. 65, s. 10.

Any person may also, on the production of a piece of the manufactured article with the pattern thereon, together with the registration mark, be informed whether such pattern, supposed to be registered, is really so or not.

As this mark is not applied to a provisional registered design, or to articles registered under class 10, certificates of search for such designs will be given on production of the design, or a copy or drawing thereof, or other necessary information, with the date of registration.

The transfer and authority to register same.
In case of transfer of a registered design, whether provisionally or completely, a copy of the certified copy thereof must be transmitted to the registrar, together with the form of application properly filled up and signed. The transfer will then be registered, and the certified copy returned.

The following may be the form of transfer and authority to register :—

"I, *A.B.*, author [*or proprietor*] of designs No.
having transferred my right thereto [*or, if such transfer be partial*], so far as regards the ornamenting of   [*describe the articles of manufacture or substances, or the locality, with respect to which the right is transferred*], to *B.C.*, of
, do hereby authorize you to insert his name on the register of designs accordingly " (*a*).

The following may be the form of request to the registrar :—

"I, *B.C.*, the person mentioned in the above transfer, do request you to register my name and property in the said design as entitled [*if to the entire use*] to the entire use of such design [*or, if to the partial use*], to the partial use of such design, as far as regards the application thereof [*describe the articles of manufacture, or the locality, in relation to which the right is transferred*]."

(*a*) The form of transfer may be varied at pleasure; no particular form is imperative.

The transfer of the copyright of a design must be in
writing, as must also any partial assignment or licence (a).
The 6th section of the Act provides that every person
purchasing or otherwise acquiring the right to the entire
or partial use of any design may enter his title in the
register, and any writing purporting to be a transfer of
of such design, and signed by the proprietor, shall operate
as an effectual transfer, and it is further provided that the
registrar shall on request and the production of such
writing, or in the case of acquiring such right by any other
mode than that of purchase, on the production of any
evidence to the satisfaction of the registrar, insert the
name of the new proprietor in the register.

Upon this section and the 3rd and 5th sections of the
Act it was that the Master of the Rolls, in the case of
Jewitt v. *Eckhardt* (a), decided that an assignment must be
in writing. " My reason," says Sir George Jessel, " is,
that when you come to look at the framing of the Act of
Parliament it stands in this way : the 3rd section provides
that the proprietor of a design shall have the sole right to
apply the same to any articles of manufacture for a
certain term of years. Then when you come to the 5th
section it makes the proprietor who is to have this sole
right not merely a sole proprietor but a limited proprietor including, as I read it, a licensee. The words are :
' Every person acquiring for a good or a valuable consideration a new and original design, or the right to apply
the same,' which is the same thing for the purpose of the
Act of Parliament, ' to any one or more of the articles
registered, or any one or more substances,'—you can
divide it in that way, and can give a right to apply it to
certain articles and not to others—' every person upon
whom the property in such design or such right to the
application thereof shall devolve '—it may devolve on an
executor and so on—' shall be considered the proprietor of
the design.' Therefore a licensee does acquire the right
to a design as well as an assignee, so that a partial assignee,
or a total assignee, or any person upon whom the right

(a) *Jewitt* v. *Eckhardt*, 8 Ch. Div. 404 ; 26 W. R. 415.

may devolve, whether executor or administrator, is also within the Act. Then it gives the person the right, not as proprietor according to the 3rd section, but to the extent to which his right may have been acquired, but not otherwise. It is a kind of supplement to, or interpretation of, the 3rd section. He shall have the sole limited right, or the limited sole right. It is not absolutely exclusive, but only to the extent of excluding other persons who have not any share of the right at all, and no further. But as I read the 6th section it provides that the person purchasing or otherwise acquiring the right to use any such design ' may enter his title in the register hereby provided, and any writing purporting to be a transfer of such design and signed by the proprietor thereof, shall operate as an effectual transfer; and the registrar shall, on request and the production of such writing, or in the case of acquiring such right by any other mode than that of purchase, on the production of any evidence '—that is, devolution, such as death or administration—' to the satisfaction of the registrar,' enter it on the register. Now what is the entering on the register?' 'I, A.B., author or proprietor of design No.   , having transferred my right thereto, &c.' That shews it is a design already registered. You cannot enter on the register a transfer of any design not registered, and that transfer must obviously be in writing, because the writing is produced to the registrar. So that whenever you get a partial assignment, or a licence, or a devolution by law after the registration, it obviously must be in writing."

No time should be allowed to elapse between a transfer and its registration; for, in case of the bankruptcy of the registered proprietor of a design, after the execution of a transfer and before registration of such transfer, the copyright of the design would probably be considered in the order and disposition of the bankrupt, and would therefore pass to his trustee (a).

An original combination a proper subject of registration.   A new combination of old patterns may be a new and

(a) See *Longman* v. *Tripp*, 2 Bos. & Pul. New R. 67 ; *Hesse* v. *Stevenson*, 3 Bos. & Pul. 565 ; *Re Dilworth*, 1 Dea. & Chitt. 411.

original design, and as such would be a proper subject of registration.

This was determined in the Exchequer Chamber, on appeal from the Court of Exchequer, in the case of *Harrison* v. *Taylor* (a). The plaintiff registered, under the 5 & 6 Vict. c. 100, a design for ornamenting woven fabrics. The design was applied to a fabric woven in cells, called " The Honeycomb Pattern," and it consisted of a combination of the large and small honeycomb, so as to form a large honeycomb stripe on a small honeycomb ground. Neither the large honeycomb nor the small honeycomb was new, but they had never been used in combination before the plaintiff registered his design. Other fabrics had been woven with a similar combination of a large and small pattern. In an action against the defendant for infringing the plaintiff's copyright it was held that the plaintiff's design was a "new and original design" within the meaning of the 5 & 6 Vict. c. 100.

But where four old designs were respectively applied to three ribbons and to a button, and the three ribbons were then united by the button so as to form a badge, it was held that such union did not amount to a new design within the above statute (b).

A. registered as " a design " within class 12, sect. 3, of the 5 & 6 Vict. c. 100, a pattern of a woven fabric. He gave no written description of his claim. The design consisted of six pointed stars on an Albert chain arranged in a particular manner, and shaded, and he claimed " the particular collocation of the shaded and borrowed stars upon the ornamental chain surface, as shewn in the registered pattern, thus forming together the ornamentation of the woven fabric." B. slightly altered the com-

(a) 3 H. & N. 301, reversed (Ex. Ch.) 4 H. & N. 815 ; 29 L. J. (Exch.) 3 ; 5 Jur. (N.S.) 1219.

(b) *Mulloney* v. *Stevens*, 10 L. T. (N.S.) 190. A claim to a monopoly in a design registered under the 6 & 7 Vict. c. 65, for the shape or configuration of the body of a four-wheel dog-cart was rejected, because the design consisted only of an arch in the fore part of the carriage, made a little higher than that in ordinary use, to permit the convenience of larger fore wheels : *Windover* v. *Smith*, 11 W. R. 323 ; 32 Beav. 200 ; 32 L. J. (Ch.) 561 ; 9 Jur. (N.S.) 397 ; 7 L. T. (N.S.) 776.

Cap. XV.   bination, but not so as to affect the general appearance of
the pattern, and it was adjudged that this was an infringement of the pattern registered (a).

But the com-   In the *Queen* v. *Firman* (b) it was decided that the result
bination must of simultaneously applying two old and known designs to
be one design
and not a   the ornamenting of a button might be a new and original
multiplicity. combination to be protected as a design; but the result
of the combination to be protected as a " design " must be
one design and not a multiplicity of designs (c).

Therefore where a claim was made in respect of a design
of a shawl, and it was contended that there were five points
in respect of which the shawl was new and entitled to
protection—first, a reversible cloth, with the two sides of
different texture and colours; secondly, a scollop pattern
in parts of the shawl; thirdly, a particular border round
the shawl; fourthly, a particular configuration of the
corners of the shawl; fifthly, a newly invented fringe to
surround the shawl; and the evidence clearly shewed that
all these five points, or " designs," had been in public use
and had been applied to shawls before the registration of
the plaintiff's shawl, but that the combination of them in
the plaintiff's shawl was new; the court held that such a
combination was not a " design " within the meaning of the
Act of Parliament. " The five points relied upon," said
Lord Campbell, C.J., " being all old, no distinction is to
be made between them and any other in the texture,
configuration, or ornaments of the shawl. Therefore the
combination supposed to constitute the design which the
plaintiff now seeks to protect comprehends all that is to
be discovered on both sides of the shawl, colour as well as
shape. . . . The design is always to be considered different
from the 'article of manufacture or the substance to which
it is to be applied.' This is particularly to be observed in
sect. 3, in which the articles of manufacture are enumerated
to which the design is to be applied. Among these

(a) *M'Crea* v. *Holdsworth*, 23 L. T. (N.S.) 444.
(b) Cited in *Harrison* v. *Taylor*, 3 H. & N. 304.
(c) *Norton* v. *Nicholls*, 5 Jur. (N.S.) 1202, 1205.

(classes 7 and 8) are 'shawls,' the 'shawl' is not the 'design,' but 'the article of manufacture to which the design is to be applied.' An ornament for a lady's gown may well be a 'design,' to be protected, although the ornament be the result of a new combination of lace and ribands; but the gown itself could hardly be such a 'design,' although it be granted that the component parts and ornaments, before well known separately, are arranged according to a fashion entirely new. Such an extension of the statute is quite unnecessary for the object which the legislature seems to have had in view, and we need not point out the great public inconvenience which would arise if we were to put such a construction upon it" (a).

The mere copy of a photograph of a well-known public character, which is common to all the world, is not "a new and original design" within the meaning of the Act. Thus where, in the case of *Adams* v. *Clementson* (b), the plaintiff, who was a manufacturer of earthenware, claimed an injunction to restrain the defendant, who was in the same line of business, from infringing his copyright in a design which he had registered under the 5 & 6 Vict. c. 100, and it appeared that the design consisted of a portrait of General Martinez de Campos, Captain General of Cuba, copied from a photograph which had been sent to the plaintiff from Cuba, and which had been applied by him to plates and other articles of earthenware which had been sent out to Cuba for sale; and that the defendant had received an order for a supply of earthenware and been furnished with a similar photograph of the General, an injunction was refused.

Copy of photograph of well-known public character not a new design.

The 7th section of the 5 & 6 Vict. c. 100, enacts, for preventing the piracy of registered designs, "that during the period of any such right to the entire or partial use of any such design, no person shall either do or cause to be done (c) any of the following acts, with regard to any articles

Remedies for piracy of the right in designs for ornamental purposes.

(a) *Norton* v. *Nicholls,* 5 Jur. (N.S.) 1203; 1 El. & E. 761; 7 W. R. 420.
(b) W. N. (1879) 32.
(c) *Mallet* v. *Howitt,* W. N. (1879) 107.

of manufacture or substance, in respect of which the copyright of such design shall be in force, without the licence or consent in writing of the registered proprietor thereof" (that is to say) :—

> No person is to apply any registered design, or any fraudulent imitation thereof, for the purpose of sale, to the ornamenting of any article. No person is to publish, sell, or expose for sale, any article to which a pirated design, or any fraudulent imitation of a registered design, shall have been applied, after the person has received verbally or in writing, or otherwise, from any source other than the proprietor, notice that his consent has not been given to such application, nor after the person has been served with or had left at his premises a written notice signed by the proprietor or his agent.

Under this section it has been held that a manufacturer of an article within the provisions of the Act is bound to inquire whether the design has been already registered.

In the case referred to (a) the defendant was not a manufacturer, but a lace merchant, who bought the undressed lace from manufacturers and then caused it to be dressed and completed ready for sale. He had received a pattern of lace sent him by letter of the plaintiff's registered design, which he had sent with other designs to the manufacturer. He had only sold one parcel of the lace complained of when he received notice that the same was registered, and stopped the sale. The court being of opinion that the defendant's design was an imitation of the plaintiff's, the only question was, whether what had been done by the defendant came within the section under consideration, and the Master of the Rolls held, that the defendant, though not the actual manufacturer, had " caused to be applied " the plaintiff's design within the meaning of the 7th section, and that this amounted to piracy.

(a) *Mallet* v. *Howitt*, W. N. (1879) 107.

The words of the old Act rendered it necessary that the proprietor should prove that the offending party exposed the pirated goods for sale, knowing that the proprietor had not given his consent; and the proof by the proprietor of this knowledge on the part of the offending party was more than the proprietor could, in general, adduce. The objectionable words are omitted in the above clause, and in their stead are substituted the words relative to notice.

A notice under this section is not sufficient unless it expressly state that the proprietor of the design has not given his consent to the application of the design; and whether he intends to sue either for the application of the design to an article of manufacture or for the sale of such article with the design applied. It should also specify the real claim intended to be made.

Thus where a notice was addressed to the defendants, both as manufacturers who had applied the design to articles of manufacture, and as retail dealers who had sold articles of manufacture to which the design had been applied by others, and stated, that if the defendants either applied the design to an article of manufacture, or sold an article of manufacture with the design applied to it, the plaintiff would sue them; it was held that a sufficient notice had not been given under this section, the court being of opinion that it was not tantamount to a notice that he had not given his consent to the application of his design to the manufactured article, and that such notice was perfectly consistent with the fact of his having actually given his consent, and could not be considered the performance of a condition introduced to save retail dealers from very serious liability (a).

In order to establish a case of piracy under these provisions, the plaintiff must prove that the alleged piracy is an application or a fraudulent imitation of his registered design.

In a late case (b), it was contended by the defendant

(a) *Norton* v. *Nicholls*, 5 Jur. (N.S.) 1203.
(b) *M'Crea* v. *Holdsworth*, 2 De G. & Sm. 496; 2 Jur. 820.

that this 7th section must be taken in conjunction with the 3rd section, and must be held to restrict the expression, "sole right to apply the same," to an application *for the purpose* of sale during the period of the protection afforded by the Act, and in answer to this contention on the part of the plaintiff it was argued that if the privilege were thus restricted, it would lose a great part of its value, inasmuch as the period during which protection is afforded by the Act might be employed in preparation for the purpose of selling piracies at the very moment when the period expired. The Vice-Chancellor, however, thought that the manufacture, although without the intention of selling within the period, was a piracy within the meaning of the Act. The 3rd section conferred the title. The 7th section must be read in conjunction with the 8th, which provided for the recovery of penalties in the cases specified. He did not consider the legislature intended the Act to be construed according to the argument of the defendant.

Ignorance of the registration of the design does not excuse the piracy.

The above section is extended by 6 & 7 Vict. c. 65, s. 2, to designs for articles of manufacture having reference *to some purposes of utility*, so far as the design shall be for the *shape* and *configuration* of such article.

As to what is a subject proper for registration under the Designs Act. Where the design was of a new ventilator, consisting of an oblong pane of glass fixed in a frame, which was inserted into an ordinary window-frame, and was hinged at the top, so as to open and admit the air, by means of a screw acted upon by cords passing over its head, and having a half-pane of glass fixed in the lower portion of the frame in which the ventilating frame ended, so as to prevent a downward draught, the claim of the inventor was said to be for the general configuration and combination of the parts, some of which were not original. This was held not to be a design for the shape and configuration of an article of manufacture within the 6 & 7 Vict. c. 65, and therefore not the subject of registration; and a conviction for the infringement of such a registered design was quashed for want of jurisdiction (a). Erle, J., in giving his opinion that the invention was not within the meaning of the statute, said: "It is a combination of means for the purpose of easily admitting air and avoiding a downward draught, and there is a skilful combination of means to produce this result. But the particular shape or configuration is accidental and wholly unimportant, and unconnected with the purpose to be attained. An oblique pane is of no particular use ; a square or circular pane, and a straight or curved screen, would produce the same result. If the prosecutor relies on the shape or configuration as producing a useful result, he fails in making out that the defendant has infringed his right, because there is no doubt that the shape of the defendant's invention varies materially from that registered by the prosecutor: in the one the pane being nearly square and in the other oblong, and the screw being straight in the one, and crooked in the other. The prosecutor intended to protect a combination of means producing a useful result, and that is within the law relating to patents, and not within statute 6 & 7 Vict. c. 65" (b).

Again, the design of a " protector label," which consisted in making in the label an eyelet-hole, and lining it with a ring of metallic substance, through which a string attaching the label to packages passed, was held not to be within the protection of this statute (c). But the design of a newly invented brick, the utility of which consisted in its being so shaped that when several bricks were laid together

---

(a) *Reg.* v. *Bessell*, 15 Jur. 773 ; 20 L. J. M. C. 177 ; 16 Q. B. 810.

(b) The contrary was held in *Heywood* v. *Potter*, 1 E. & B. 439 ; 17 Jur. 528 ; 22 L. J. (Q.B.) 133 ; but subsequently the 21 & 22 Vict. c. 70, s. 4, enacted that nothing in the 4th section of the 5 & 6 Vict. c. 100, should extend, or to be construed to extend, to deprive the proprietor of any new and original design applied to ornamenting any article of manufacture contained in the said 10th class of the benefits of the Copyright of Designs Act or of this Act ; provided there shall have been printed on such articles at each end of the original piece thereof the name and address of such proprietor, and the word " Registered," together with the year for which such design was registered.

(c) *Margetson* v. *Wright*, 2 De G. & Sm. 420.

in building a series of apertures were left in the wall through which the air might circulate, and a saving in the number of bricks effected, was held to form the proper subject of registration under this Act (a).

The inventor of a design for a " dog-cart phaeton " claimed four things as new and as conducive to the *utility* of the design, the specified purpose of utility being that "higher front wheels could be used, or closer coupling effected, and a saving in horse power." Three of the things claimed as new (the seat, the opera board, and the boot) were not new, and did not contribute to the utility. The fourth (the curved arch under which the wheels turned) did contribute to the utility, but it was not new. It was held that the design did not come within the protection of 6 & 7 Vict. c. 65. Neither was it protected under the 5 & 6 Vict. c. 100, as an *ornamental* design, not having been registered under that Act (b).

The subject of registration must not be an article of manufacture, but a design; that is, a combination of lines producing pattern, shape, or configuration, by whatever means such design may be applicable to the manufacture. The "design" is always considered different from the "article of manufacture, or the substance to which it is to be applied."

This is particularly to be observed in section 3 of the Act in course of examination, where the articles of manufacture are enumerated to which the design is to be applied. Among these are "shawls." The "shawl" is not the "design," but the article of manufacture to which the design is to be applied.

Mr. Carpmael, of the Repertory of Patent Inventions, Lincoln's Inn, has thus endeavoured to make the distinction clear : " In registering any new design for a table lamp, all which could be secured under such registration would be some peculiarity of form of an ornamental

(a) *Rogers* v. *Driver*, 20 L. J. (Q.B.) 31 ; 16 Q. B. 102. See *Millingen* v. *Picken*, 1 Com. Ben. Rep. 799 ; 14 L. J. (N.S.) (C.P.) 254 ; 9 Jur. 714.
(b) *Windover* v. *Smith*, 32 Beav. 200 ; 32 L. J. (Ch.) 561 ; 7 L. T. (N.S.) 776.

character in the stem or oil vessel, or in the glass shade, or some ornament applied thereto, if under the first mentioned statute, or some novelty in the shape or configuration, without reference to ornament, if under the second statute;—no new mode of supplying oil to the wick, nor any new mode of raising the wick, nor any new apparatus for supplying air to support combustion, could become the subject-matter of a registration. The simple configuration, or contour, or ornament of the lamp, or some particular part of the lamp, would be the only subject for registration; and any person might, without infringing the registration, make the same description of lamp, all parts acting mechanically in the same manner to produce the same end, so long as the outer configurations were not imitated. A patent, on the contrary, can scarcely ever be said to depend on shape; supposing a patent be taken for any improved construction of lamp—such, for instance, as an improved means of raising the oil from the stem or pillar of a table lamp,—the patent would be equally infringed whether the external figure or design be retained or not so long as the means of raising the oil were preserved."

There are several methods by which redress may be obtained in cases of infringement of copyright in designs.

It is provided by the 9th section of the 5 & 6 Vict. c. 100, that notwithstanding the remedies given by the Act for the recovery of penalties, it shall be lawful for the proprietor in respect of whose right such penalty shall have been incurred (if he shall elect to do so) to bring such action as he may be entitled to, for the recovery of any damages which he shall have sustained, either by the application of any such design or of a fraudulent imitation thereof, for the purpose of sale, to any article of manufacture or substance, or by the publication, sale, or exposure to sale as aforesaid, by any person, of any article or substance to which such design or any fraudulent imitation thereof shall have been so applied, such person knowing that the proprietor of such design had not given his consent to such application.

A remedy is given by the 8th section of the 5 & 6 Vict. c. 100, which provides that in cases of infringement the offender shall be liable to forfeit a sum of not less than £5, nor exceeding £30, to the proprietor of the design, who may recover such penalty as follows :—

In England, either by an action of debt or on the case against the party offending, or by summary proceeding before two justices having jurisdiction where the party offending resides.

If the proprietor proceed by summary proceeding, any justice of the peace acting for the county, riding, division, city, or borough where the party offending resides, and not being concerned either in the sale or manufacture of the article of manufacture, or in the design to which such summary proceeding relates, may issue a summons requiring such party to appear on a day, and at a time and place to be named in such summons, such time not being less than eight days from the date thereof; and every such summons shall be served on the party offending, either in person or at his usual place of abode ; and either upon the appearance or upon the default to appear of the party offending, any two or more of such justices may proceed to the hearing of the complaint, and upon proof of the offence, either by the confession of the party offending, or upon the oath or affirmation of one or more credible witnesses, may convict the offender in a penalty of not less than £5 or more than £30 for each offence, as to such justices may seem fit ; but the aggregate amount of penalties for offences in respect of any one design committed by any one person up to the time at which any of the proceedings shall be instituted, shall not exceed the sum of £100 ; and if the amount of such penalty or of such penalties, and the costs attending the conviction, so assessed by such justices, be not forthwith paid, the amount of the penalty or of the penalties and of the costs,

together with the costs of the distress and sale, shall be CAP. XV.
levied by distress and sale of the goods and chattels of
the offender wherever the same happen to be in England;
and the justices before whom the party has been convicted,
or on proof of the conviction, any two justices acting for
any county, riding, division, city, or borough in England,
where goods and chattels of the person offending happen
to be, may grant a warrant for such distress and sale; and
the overplus, if any, shall be returned to the owner of the
goods and chattels on demand.

Every information and conviction in any summary
proceedings before two justices under the Act may be in the
forms or to the effect given in the Act, *mutatis mutandis*
as the case may require.

In Scotland the proprietor may proceed by action before Scotland.
the Court of Session in ordinary form, or by summary
action before the sheriff of the county where the offence
may be committed, or the offender resides, who, upon proof
of the offence or offences, either by confession of the party
offending, or by the oath or affirmation of one or more
credible witnesses, shall convict the offender and find him
liable in the penalty or penalties aforesaid, as also in
expenses. And the sheriff in pronouncing judgment for
the penalty or penalties and costs, may insert in the
judgment a warrant in the event of such penalty or
penalties and costs not being paid, to levy and recover the
amount of the same by pounding.

And it is provided that in the event of the sheriff dismissing the action, and assoilzieing the defender, he may find
the complainer liable in expenses; and any judgment so to
be pronounced by the sheriff in such summary application
shall be final and conclusive, and not subject to review
by advocation, suspension, reduction, or otherwise.

In Ireland, the proprietor may proceed either by action Ireland.
in a superior court of law at Dublin, or by civil bill in the
civil bill court of the county or place where the offence
was committed.

It is provided that no action or other proceeding for

any offence or injury under the Act shall be brought after
the expiration of twelve calendar months from the commission of the offence ; and in every such action or other
proceeding the party who shall prevail shall recover his
full costs of suit, or of such other proceeding (a).

Limitation of actions.

This provision seems to apply as well to summary
proceedings as to actions for damages referred to in the
9th section.

Justices may order payment of costs in cases of summary proceedings.
In the case of summary proceedings before any two
justices in England, they may award payment of costs to
the party prevailing, and grant a warrant for enforcing payment thereof against the summonsing party, if
unsuccessful, in the like manner as provided by the
Act for recovering any penalty with costs against any
offender (b).

The above provisions to apply to useful designs.
By the 6th section of the 6 & 7 Vict. c. 65, the above
provisions as to the mode of recovering penalties, actions
for damages, limitation of actions, and awarding of costs
are made applicable to designs having reference to some
purpose of utility; and by the 15th section of the 13 & 14
Vict. c. 104, they are also extended to works provisionally
registered under that Act.

Proceedings may be taken in the county court.
By the 8th section of the 21 & 22 Vict. c. 70, proceedings for the recovery of damages for infringement
may be brought in the county court, provided in any such
proceeding the plaintiff shall deliver with his plaint a
statement of particulars as to the date and title or other
description of the registration whereof the copyright is
alleged to be pirated, and as to the alleged piracy ; and
the defendant, if he intends to rely as a defence on any
objection to such copyright, or to the title of the proprietor therein, shall give notice in the manner provided
in the 76th section of the 9 & 10 Vict. c. 95, of his intention to rely on such special defence, and shall state in
such notice the date of publication and other particulars of
any designs whereof prior publication is alleged, or of any
objection to such copyright, or to the title of the proprietor

(a) Sect. 12.   (b) Sect. 13.

to such copyright; and it shall be lawful for the judge of Cap. XV. the county court, at the instance of the defendant or plaintiff respectively, to require any statement or notice so delivered by the plaintiff or by the defendant respectively to be amended in such manner as the said judge may think fit.

And further, the proceedings in any plaint, and those in appeal and in writs of prohibition, provided by the 9 & 10 Vict. c. 95, and the 12 & 13 Vict. c. 100 (a), shall be applicable to any proceedings for piracy of copyright of designs under the Copyright of Designs Act.

In selecting the mode of proceeding the effect of Considerations as to the remedy to select. publicity in deterring others, the moral weight of the decision of the court in which the action or suit is brought, and the probability of the judge or magistrate going more or less into the minutiæ of the case, should be thoughtfully regarded. In some cases, either from the fact of the defendant being in such a position that the moral effect of so doing would be more effectual in preventing similar thefts for the future, or from the fact that the defendant may be a man of straw, it may be advisable to place him in the police court, while in others the more costly and efficient remedy provided by the Superior Courts of Judicature may be adopted.

There is no provision in the Designs Acts analogous to No provisions for delivery up of pirated designs. that of the 23rd section of the Literary Copyright Act, 1842, as to the delivery up of unsold copies of a pirated book to the proprietor of the copyright without his making any compensation for the cost of production and publication; but in the case of *M'Crea* v. *Holdsworth* (b), Lord Justice Knight Bruce made an order under the Designs Act for the delivery up to the plaintiff, " for the purpose of being destroyed, the drawing or drawings, point paper, and the several cards used in applying his design, and also of the articles manufactured by the defendants to which the plaintiff's design had been applied."

(a) So printed by the Queen's printers, but it is clearly a mistake. It is evidently intended for 12 & 13 Vict. c. 101, which amends the County Court Act, 9 & 10 Vict. c. 95.　　　　(b) 2 De Gex & Sm. 497.

Proceedings may also be taken in the Chancery Division of the High Court of Justice in all cases.

In a statement of claim under the Designs Act the following allegations should be inserted in their proper places ; first, that previously to publication of the design the plaintiff caused a proper entry thereof to be made in the registry ; and that he duly caused the letters Rd. &c., to be duly marked on each piece of the said fabrics, and duly complied in all respects with all the provisions of the statute and all the requisitions required by law in such cases ; secondly, there should also be special allegations that the design is new and original, and has not been previously published in the United Kingdom or elsewhere. It should also be shewn that the infringer had notice of the piracy when he disposed of the articles complained of, as if part of the articles were sold previously to a direct notice pursuant to the 7th section of 5 & 6 Vict. c. 100, the plaintiff would not be entitled to the costs of the suit, unless the defendant then had notice of the plaintiff's copyright by other means.

The articles alleged to be piracies should be produced to the court, in order that they may be compared with the original design and the articles to which it has been applied by the proprietor (a). But where the alleged piracies were proved to have been stolen out of the possession of the plaintiff, the uncontradicted testimony of a witness as to their nature has been held sufficient (b).

The court, or a jury, will then be able to pronounce, on the comparison, whether the registered design has been applied or not. But if what is complained of is a fraudulent imitation, and not an application of the exact design, it will be convenient, if possible, to shew by direct evidence that the defendant's design has been taken from the plaintiff's (c).

Copyright in designs of utility.
With regard to any new or original design for any

(a) *Sheriff* v. *Coates*, 1 Russ. & My. 159.
(b) *Fradella* v. *Weller*, 2 Russ. & My. 247.
(c) *Lowndes* v. *Browne*, 12 Ir. L. Rep. 293 ; cited Norman on 'Designs,' p. 51.

article of manufacture having reference to some purpose of utility, so far as such design shall be for the shape or configuration of such .article, and that, whether it be for the whole of such shape or configuration or only for a part thereof, it has been enacted by the 6 & 7 Vict. c. 65, that the proprietor of such design not previously published in the United Kingdom of Great Britain and Ireland, or elsewhere, shall have the sole right to apply such design to any article, or make or sell any article according to such design, for the term of three years, to be computed from the time of such design being registered according to the Act. But it is provided that this enactment shall not extend to such designs as are within the 5 & 6 Vict. c. 100, 38 Geo. 3, c. 71, or the 54 Geo. 3, c. 56.

It appears to be the received opinion that under this clause may be registered designs, the subjects of which could, in many cases, have obtained a patent (a).

To obtain the protection of the Act it is necessary :—

    1st. That the design should not have been published, either within the United Kingdom or elsewhere, previous to registration (b).

    2nd. That after registration every article of manufacture made according to such design, or to which such design is applied, should have upon it the word " Registered," with the date of registration.

Persons proposing to register a design for purposes of utility must furnish the registrar with two exactly similar drawings or tracings, photographs or prints of such design, made on a proper geometric scale on two separate sheets of paper or parchment not exceeding the size of twenty-four by fifteen inches, and with a blank space in front of each sheet six inches long, by four inches broad, upon which the certificate of registration

(a) 16 Q. B. 108 ; see 1 C. B. 812.
(b) 6 & 7 Vict. c. 65, s. 3.

will be placed (*a*). All registered designs must have a
title and be accompanied by such description in writing as
may be necessary to render the same intelligible, according
to the judgment of the registrar, together with the name
of every person claiming to be proprietor, or of the style
or title of the firm under which such proprietor may be
trading, with his place of abode, or place of carrying on
business, or other place of address (*b*). But by the 5th
section of the Copyright of Designs Act, 1858, it is
declared that the registration of any *pattern* or *portion* of
an article of manufacture to which a design is applied,
instead or in lieu of a copy, drawing, print, specification,
or description in writing, shall be valid and effectual to
all intents and purposes as if such copy, drawing, print,
specification, or description in writing had been furnished
to the registrar under the above Act.

Amending or
cancelling
registration.
The registration of any design, whether for purposes of
ornament or utility, may be amended or cancelled by
decree or order of a judge in equity, where it is made to
appear to him that the design has been registered in the
name of a wrong person.

Section 10 of the 5 & 6 Vict. c. 100, enacts, "that in any
suit in equity which may be instituted by the proprietor
of any design, or the person lawfully entitled thereto,
relative to such design, if it shall appear to the satisfaction
of the judge having cognizance of such suit, that the
design has been registered in the name of a person not
being the proprietor or lawfully entitled thereto, it shall
be competent for such judge, in his discretion, by a decree
or order in such suit, to direct either that such registration be cancelled (in which case the same shall thenceforth be wholly void), or that the name of the proprietor

(*a*) It is well when "provisional" registration is applied for, to leave an
additional blank space of six inches by four for the future complete
registration to be placed on, in order to save the additional expense of
having new drawings prepared for that purpose.

(*b*) The drawings are of course prepared at the expense of the person
registering, and vary according to their intricacy; they cost on an average
two guineas per sheet.

of such design, or other person lawfully entitled thereto, be substituted in the register for the name of such wrongful proprietor or claimant, in like manner as is hereinbefore directed in case of the transfer of a design, and to make such order respecting the costs of such cancellation or substitution, and of all proceedings to procure and effect the same, as he shall think fit; and the registrar is hereby authorized and required, upon being served with an official copy of such decree or order, and upon payment of the proper fee, to comply with the tenour of such decree or order, and either cancel such registration or substitute such new name as the case may be " (a).

As this Act affords protection only to the shape or configuration of articles of utility, and not to any mechanical action, principle, contrivance, application, or adaptation (except in so far as these may be dependent upon and inseparable from the shape or configuration), or to the material of which the article may be composed; no design will be registered the description of or statement respecting which shall contain any expressions suggestive of the registration being for any such mechanical action, principle, contrivance, application, or adaptation, or for the material of which the article may be composed (b).

Protection afforded only to shape or configuration.

A discretionary power is vested in the registrar, either to register any design under the 5 & 6 Vict. c. 100, or the 6 & 7 Vict. c. 65; and a further power is given him to reject such designs as are simply labels, wrappers, or other coverings in which any article of manufacture may be exposed for sale, or such designs as may appear to him to be contrary to public morality or order. From the exercise of this latter power there is an appeal to the Privy Council.

Discretionary power in registrar.

All the clauses and provisions contained in the 5 & 6 Vict. c. 100, with reference to the transfer of designs, to their piracy, to the mode of recovering penalties, to actions for damages, to cancelling and amending registrations, to

(a) See also 6 & 7 Vict. c. 65, s. 6.
(b) See *Millingen* v. *Picken*, 1 C. B. 799; 14 L. J. (N.S.) (C.P.) 254; 9 Jur. 714.

CAP. XV.   the limitation of actions, to the awarding of costs, to the
certificate of registration, to the fixing and application of
fees for registration, and to the penalty for extortion, are
extended and applied to this Act (a).

In addition to the penalties imposed by virtue of the in-
corporation of the penal clauses of the 5 & 6 Vict. c. 100,
is imposed a penalty of not more than £5 nor less than
£1, upon all persons marking, selling, or advertising for
sale any article as "registered," unless the design for
such article has been registered under one of the above-
mentioned Acts. This penalty may be recovered by any
person proceeding for the same (b).

Provisional registration of designs.   Provisional registration is permitted by the 13 & 14
Vict. c. 104, the 1st section of which provides that any
design registered in accordance with that Act shall be
deemed "Provisionally registered," and the registration
shall continue in force for the term of one year (which
may be further extended for six months by the Commissioners of Patents) from the time of such registration,
during which period the proprietor shall have the sole
right and property in such design, and be protected in
the enjoyment of this right by the penalties and provisions
enumerated in the Designs Act, 1842. During the term
for which protection is afforded by this provisional
registration, the proprietor of any design may sell or
transfer the right to apply the same to an article of manufacture, but should he sell, expose, or offer for sale, any
article to which the design has been applied until after
complete registration, the provisional registration shall be
deemed null and void (c).

Exhibition of design provisionally registered not to prevent future registration.   Neither the exhibition nor the exposure of any design
provisionally registered, or of any article to which such
design may have been applied, in any place, whether
public or private, in which articles are not sold, or exposed,
or exhibited for sale, and to which the public are not
admitted gratuitously, or in any place which shall have

(a) Sect. 6.   (b) Sect. 4.
(c) 13 & 14 Vict. c. 104, s. 4.

been previously certified by the Board of Trade to be a place of public exhibition within the meaning of the 13 & 14 Vict. c. 104, shall prevent the proprietor thereof from registering such design: provided that every article to which such design shall be applied and which shall be exhibited or exposed by or with the consent of the proprietor of such design, shall have thereon or attached thereto the words "Provisionally registered," with the date of the registration (a).

The government fee for the "provisional" registration Fees for of designs of utility, or for registering and certifying provisional registration. transfers, is ten shillings; and for the provisional registration of ornamental designs in all classes, one year, the sum of one shilling for each design, and for their transfer the sum of five shillings each.

By the 14 Vict. c. 8, provision was made for the protection of those exhibiting in the Exhibition of 1851, the 8th section of that Act declaring that, notwithstanding anything contained in the Designs Act, 1850, and those of 1842 and 1843, the protection intended to be by them extended to the proprietors of new and original designs should be extended to the proprietors of all new and original designs which should be provisionally registered and exhibited in such place of public exhibition as aforesaid, notwithstanding that such designs might have been previously published or applied elsewhere than in the United Kingdom of Great Britain and Ireland: provided such design or any article to which the same had been applied had not been publicly sold or exposed for sale previously to such exhibition thereof (b).

The 24 & 25 Vict. c. 73, declares that the various Acts on the subject of copyright of designs shall be construed as if the words "provided the same be done within the United Kingdom of Great Britain and Ireland" had not been contained in the said Acts; and that they shall apply to every design as therein referred to, whether the application thereof be within the United Kingdom or else-

(a) *Ibid.* s. 3.   (b) Since extended by 15 Vict. c. 6.

2 G 2

CAP. XV.   where, and whether the inventor or proprietor be or be not a subject of Her Majesty. And that the said Acts shall not be construed to apply to the subjects of Her Majesty only (a).

All powers by Designs Acts given to Board of Trade now vested in Commissioners of Patents.   By the Copyright of Designs Act, 1875 (b), all powers, duties, and authorities vested in, or to be exercised by the Board of Trade, are transferred to, vested in, and imposed on the Commissioners of Patents for Inventions. And it is provided that the Commissioners may from time to time make, revoke, and alter general rules for regulating registrations under the Designs Acts, and any discretion or power vested in the registrar under such Acts shall be subject to the control of the Commissioners and shall be exercised by him in such manner, and with such limitations and restrictions (if any) as may be prescribed by the general rules, and any provisions contained in the said Acts as to the copies, drawings, prints, descriptions, information, matters and particulars to be furnished to the registrar, and generally as to any act or thing to be done by the registrar, may be modified by such general rules, in such manner as the Commissioners may think expedient.

General rules are to be laid before Parliament within a limited time.

By the 4th section of the Copyright of Designs Act, 1875, it is provided that the office of registrar under the previous Acts shall cease to exist as a separate paid office, and the Commissioners may from time to time make arrangement as to the mode in which, and the person or persons by whom the duties of registrar, and other duties under the said Acts are to be performed, and may from time to time delegate to any such person or persons, all or any of the duties of the registrar, and any person or persons to whom such duties may be delegated shall, in so far as delegation extends, be deemed to be the registrar within the meaning of the said Acts.

(a) 24 & 25 Vict. c. 73, s. 2.
(b) 38 & 39 Vict. c. 93.

CHAPTER XVI.

NEWSPAPERS.

PAPERS for circulating news were first used in England in the reign of Queen Elizabeth (*a*). It was not until the reign of Queen Anne that any notice appears to have been taken of them by the legislature. Newspapers

The Acts of Parliament on the subject of the press are 36 Geo. 3, c. 8; 39 Geo. 3, c. 79; 51 Geo. 3, c. 65; 55 Geo. 3, c. 65; 55 Geo. 3. c. 101; 60 Geo. 3 & 1 Geo. 4, c. 9; 11 Geo. 4 & 1 Wm. 4, c. 73; 6 & 7 Wm. 4, c. 76; 2 & 3 Vict. c. 12; 5 & 6 Vict. c. 82; 9 & 10 Vict. c. 33; 16 & 17 Vict. c. 59. They were, with the exceptions hereafter enumerated, repealed by "The Newspapers, Printers, and Reading Rooms Repeal Act, 1869" (the 32 & 33 Vict. c. 24).

Every person printing any paper, except bills, bank notes, bonds, deeds, agreements, receipts, &c., or any paper printed by the authority of any public board or public office (*b*), for profit, must keep one copy at least of such paper, and write or print thereon the name (*c*) and abode of his employer, and, if required, produce and shew the same to any justice of the peace within six months next after the printing, on penalty, in case of neglect or refusal, of the sum of £20 (*d*). Name and abode of printer to appear.

(*a*) The oldest newspaper extant is dated July 23, 1588, 'The English Mercurie, published by authoritie for the prevention of false reports.' It is among the state papers in the British Museum: Godson on Patents, &c., 249.

(*b*) 51 Geo. 3, c. 65, s. 3.

(*c*) See *Bensley* v. *Bignold*, 5 B. & Ald. 335.

(*d*) 39 Geo. 3, c. 79, s. 29; 32 & 33 Vict. c. 24; 33 & 34 Vict. c. 99.

If any person file a bill for the discovery of the name of any person concerned as printer, publisher, or proprietor of any newspaper, or of any matters relative to the printing or publishing of any newspaper, in order the more effectually to bring or carry on any suit or action for damages alleged to have been sustained by reason of any slanderous or libellous matter contained in any such newspaper respecting such person, it is provided by the 19th section of the 6 & 7 Wm. 4, c. 76, that it shall not be lawful for the defendant to plead or demur to such bill. He may be compelled to make the discovery required, which discovery, however, cannot be used in any proceeding against the defendant except in that for which the discovery is made.

In the late case of *Dixon* v. *Enoch* (a), a general demurrer was filed to a bill for discovery brought under the provision of this section. The bill was filed against the printer and publishers of the 'Pall Mall Gazette' and 'Pall Mall Budget' for the purpose of obtaining discovery as to the names of the proprietors of these newspapers at the time when certain articles or paragraphs were inserted which, as the plaintiff alleged, contained libellous matter with reference to himself. It appeared that these articles or paragraphs occurred in some or one of these newspapers on the 18th May, 1870, and on the 7th and 9th and 12th of August, 1871, and it was alleged that the plaintiff had sustained great loss and damage by reason of them, but the bill did not set out the alleged libels, though the pages of the publications in which they had occurred, seemed to have been pointed out to the defendant's advisers, neither was it distinctly alleged that the plaintiff intended to bring an action of libel, or that he was ignorant of the proprietors' names. The bill charged that the plaintiff was entitled, under the circumstances, to a full discovery from the defendant of the names or name of the proprietors or proprietor of the papers on the days of the above mentioned issues and publications, containing the alleged

(a) 20 W. R. 359.

libellous matter, in order the more effectually to enable him to bring and carry on an action for the damages sustained by him therefrom, and it then prayed relief accordingly. It was contended in support of the demurrer that by the statute the legislature only intended to give the right of filing a bill of discovery subject to the ordinary rules of the court, and that such a bill as that could therefore only be maintained against a party to the record at law; the defendant in that case at the most would be only a witness in the action. Further it was argued that if the demurrer were not allowed, it must be considered that any person complaining of libellous matter in a newspaper may file a bill against any other person in the world, for the purpose of discovering the name of the proprietor, if the plaintiff should think that it might be accidentally known to such other person. Vice-Chancellor Wickens in overruling the demurrer said: " The statements in the bill shew that the plaintiff instructed his solicitor to bring an action for the libels complained of, against the proprietors or proprietor of the newspaper; that the plaintiff's solicitor applied to a person whom he supposed to be the proprietor, and was referred to a solicitor, who declined to state, or at least did not state when asked to do so, the name of the proprietor or proprietors, but suggested, as the usual and proper course, that the action should be brought against the publisher (the present defendant) on whose behalf he was willing to meet it. The bill does not set out the alleged libels, and, in fact, contains no more distinct allegation as to their nature or character than what I have already mentioned, though it appears incidentally, from the correspondence stated in it, that the pages of the publications in which the alleged libels occur have been pointed out to the defendant's advisers. There is also no distinct statement of the plaintiff's intention to bring an action, or of his ignorance of the proprietors' names. The deficiency of allegation in those respects was, however, not strongly insisted on at the hearing; probably because it would be obviated by amendments. The first of them might be of some general importance, as a matter of pleading, but for the anomalous and unusual nature of the suit. If the defence were the legitimate one, that the alleged libel is not a libel, the mode of pleading here adopted might place the defendant at considerable disadvantage. It is to be gathered, however, from the correspondence, that this is not the objection intended to be insisted on in this court, and as a matter of fact it was not pressed in the argument. Under these circumstances, and not without considerable hesitation, I hold that there are in the present case just sufficient allegations in the bill to save it from a general demurrer, if in substance the plaintiff has a right to the discovery he asks. The objection to his right, as I understand it, is thus put: It is said that when the legislature gave the right of filing a bill of discovery in certain cases, it must be taken to authorize a bill which shall be subject to the ordinary rules governing such bills, in this, the natural court for filing them, one of which is, that the bill can only be maintained against a person who is, or is to be, a party to the record at law, and not against a witness whose evidence may go to charge some third person. And it is said that any other construction would enable a person complaining of a libel in a newspaper to file a bill against any human being, whether connected with the newspaper or not, for the purpose of discovering the names of the proprietors if accidentally known to him. It seems to me that those objections cannot succeed. In the first place it is to be observed that this is a bill of discovery to be filed 'in any court'; when the clause was first enacted, the Court of Exchequer in Equity (in which, it may be observed, witnesses were, for some purposes, considered proper defendants to bills of discovery) was in existence as a general court of equity. But the expression, 'in any court,' can hardly be cut down to the Court of Chancery and Exchequer, since, when the clause was re-enacted, the latter was not a general court of equity. The legislature can, perhaps, have hardly intended to give a person com-

plaining of a libel a right to file a bill of discovery for the
purpose in question in courts having no practice, and no
machinery appliable to such bills.   Still, to read the
expression, 'bill of discovery,' as importing into the clause
the special rules of the Court of Chancery, would seem a
little unreasonable where the bill may be filed in any
court.   Moreover, the Act seems to presume that the bill
authorized by it would be pleadable or demurrable, if not
protected by the enactment, and in any case the very
object of it must have been to enable the plaintiff to
extract from the defendant the name or names of some
person or persons, other than himself, who might be sued
at law, though, according to the defendant's contention
here, not alone, or otherwise than in conjunction with the
defendant in equity.   The supposition that if the plaintiff
knows the name of one proprietor he can make him tell
the names of all the others, but that not knowing one
name he cannot get the information from the printer and
publisher, who is the agent of the proprietors, and is put
forth to stand between them and the public, is one that
does not commend itself to one's common sense, and is
not to be accepted without absolute necessity.   It is not
necessary to consider whether the enactment would cover
the case of a mere witness in the strictest sense of the
word ; that is, of a person accidentally knowing the names
of the proprietors, but wholly unconnected with the newspaper.   I merely decide that by force of this enactment a
person complaining of a libel in a newspaper may file a
bill against the printer and publisher to ascertain the
names of the proprietors, for the purpose of bringing his
action against the proprietors alone; and I do so, because
any other conclusion seems to me inconsistent with the
spirit and intention, as well as with the words, of the statute.
I therefore overrule the demurrer."

By the 2 & 3 Vict. c. 12, s. 2, it is provided that every
person who shall print any paper or book whatsoever
which shall be meant to be published or dispersed, and who
shall not print upon the front of every such paper, if the

same shall be printed on one side only, or upon the first or last leaf of every paper or book consisting of more than one leaf, in legible characters, his or her name and usual place of abode or business, and every person who shall publish or disperse, or assist in publishing or dispersing any printed paper or book on which the name and place of abode of the person printing the same shall not be printed as aforesaid, shall, for every copy of such paper so printed by him or her, forfeit a sum of not more than £5 (a).

In the case of books or papers printed at the University Press of Oxford or the Pitt Press of Cambridge, the printer, instead of printing his name thereon, is to print the following words: "Printed at the University Press, Oxford," or, "The Pitt Press, Cambridge," as the case may be (b).

These enactments do not extend to impressions of engravings, or the printing of the name and address or business or profession of any person, and the articles in which he deals, or to any papers for the sale of estates or goods by auction or otherwise (c).

Prosecutions to be commenced within three months. Prosecutions must be commenced within three months after the penalty is incurred; and where the penalty incurred does not exceed £20 it may be recovered before any justice of the peace for the county or place where the same may have been incurred, or where the offending party may happen to be (d); one moiety of such penalty to the informer and the other to Her Majesty.

All proceedings to be conducted in the name of the Attorney- or Solicitor-General. By the 4th section of the 2 & 3 Vict. c. 12, and 9 & 10 Vict. c. 33, s. 2, no action for penalties may be commenced except in the name of the Attorney- or Solicitor-General in England, or the Queen's Advocate in Scotland; and every action, bill, plaint, or information which may

(a) And a printer whose name does not thus appear cannot recover in an action for work and labour for printing it: *Marchant* v. *Evans* 2 B. Moore, 14.

(b) 2 & 3 Vict. c. 12, s. 3.

(c) 39 Geo. 3, c. 79, s. 31.

(d) 39 Geo. 3, c. 79, ss. 35, 36.

be commenced or prosecuted in the name or names of any other person or persons, and any proceeding thereon, are thereby declared null and void to all intents and purposes (*a*).

Whether copyright exists at all in the case of newspapers has been doubted by Lord Chelmsford (*b*), who referred to .the language of Knight Bruce, L.J., in *Ex parte Foss* (*c*), as seeming to imply a doubt in the mind of that learned judge also whether there was such a thing as copyright in a newspaper. There cannot, however, be much doubt as to the existence of the copyright.

In *Cox* v. *The Land and Water Company* (*d*) it was contended that newspapers being but ephemeral productions, seldom, if ever, reprinted, could not properly be the subject of copyright. But Vice-Chancellor Malins decided otherwise, remarking that the idea of there being no copyright at all in newspaper articles was repugnant to common sense and common honesty. At the same time the Vice-Chancellor decided that it was not necessary to register a newspaper under the 5 & 6 Vict. c. 45. The case is the only one on the subject, and the decision is somewhat remarkable. The learned Vice-Chancellor considered that the object of the 5 & 6 Vict. c. 45, in requiring registration was to let the public know when the copyright in a work would expire. Registration was clearly unnecessary for this purpose in the case of a newspaper, which, therefore, was not within the policy of the Act; neither was it within the words. By the 2nd section " book " was to include " every volume, part, or division of a volume, pamphlet, sheet of letter-press, sheet of music, map, chart, or plan separately published.' A newspaper, he considered, was not within any one of those words; it was a well-known species of publication, and would have been inserted by name if intended to be included (*e*).

Copyright in newspaper, though registration unnecessary.

(*a*) 32 & 33 Vict. c. 24.
(*b*) *Platt* v. *Walter*, 17 L. T. (N.S.) 159.
(*c*) 2 De G. & J. 230.
(*d*) 18 W. R. 206; L. R. 9 Eq. 324; 39 L. J. (Ch.) 152; 21 L. T. (N.S.) 548; *Kelly* v. *Hutton*, L. R. 3 Ch. App. 703.
(*e*) *Ibid.*

" For the purposes of the argument," says Malins, V.-C., " it must be assumed that the article complained of was a copy of the article of the plaintiff: and upon that ground the defendant takes the objection that there can be no copyright in any article published in this newspaper, because it is not registered under the Act 5 & 6 Vict. c. 45, commonly called the Copyright Act. Now suppose, for instance, the proprietor of a newspaper employs a correspondent abroad, and that correspondent being employed, and sent abroad at great expense, makes communications to a newspaper which are highly appreciated by the public, can it be said that another newspaper, published perhaps in the evening of the same day, may take and publish those communications *in extenso* with or without acknowledgment? If the contention of the defendants is right, the paper which copied might say : ' But they are common property. True it is, I admit, that you have paid for them. I admit you have given a great deal of money for them, and they are so very valuable that I desire to turn them to account by publishing them in my newspaper; but you have no property in them, although you pay for them ; you cannot sue for your newspaper as a book, for then the copyright must be registered, and as you have not registered the book, nothing in the newspaper is protected.' If that is the law, it is a monstrous state of law, repugnant to common sense and common honesty, because that there is a property in those articles there can be no shadow of doubt. Still, however clear the right of property may be, if the case falls within the Act of Parliament, I must follow the same course which I took in the ' Brighton Directory ' case (*Mathieson* v. *Harrod*) (a). That was clearly admitted to be a book within the Copyright Act, and it had been registered at Stationers' Hall, but instead of entering the day of publication, according to the requisition of the Act, the month only was entered ; and I considered, as other judges had done before, that the object of registration was to ascertain at what time

(a) L. R. 7 Eq. 270.

the publication took place, in order that the public might know when the copyright expired, and when they would be at liberty to publish it in a separate form; therefore though everything else was complied with except the statement of the day of the month, I held that the omission was fatal, and the bill was dismissed with costs. So, in this case, however clearly I am of opinion that this is a property that ought to be protected, if a newspaper is a book within the 2nd section of the Copyright Act, and it being admitted that the 'Field' was not registered, that would be equally fatal to the plaintiff's suit. Now I have put the case of letters from correspondents abroad. With foreign papers we all know it is the practice to publish novels, and in some English newspapers it is also done. Supposing a newspaper proprietor were to engage the first novelist of the day to write for him a novel to be published in his newspaper, part every day, and pay him highly, is the proprietor of such a newspaper to lose all property because the paper is not registered? What information would it give, if it were registered? Would the registration of a paper called the 'Field,' registered twenty years ago, give information as to when the copyright would commence and end? Not the slightest; and therefore it is not within the policy of the Act, and I am of opinion that it is not within the words of the Act. The question depends, first, upon the 2nd section of the Act. What is a book? because every book must, by the 24th section, be registered. We find that 'book' under the 2nd section 'shall be construed to mean and include every volume, part or division of a volume, pamphlet, sheet of letter-press, sheet of music, or dramatic piece,' and so forth. Now certainly a newspaper does not fall within any of those descriptions, and if it was intended that this Act should be applied to newspapers, it would have been inserted, as the word 'newspaper' is well understood; and that word not being inserted, I must take it as advisedly omitted, because it was not the intention of the legislature that newspapers should be

CAP. XVI. included within the Act. Then comes the section which prescribes what is to be done with regard to periodical publications. Section 19 provides: 'That the proprietor of the copyright in any encyclopædia, review, magazine, periodical work, or other work published in a series of books or parts, shall be entitled to all the benefits of the registration at Stationers' Hall, under this Act, of entering in the said book of registry the title of such encyclopædia, review, periodical work, or other work, published in a series of books or parts, the time of the first publication of the first volume, number, or part thereof, or of the first number or part thereof, or of the first number or volume first published after the passing of this Act, in any such work which shall have been published heretofore, and the name and place of abode of the proprietor thereof, and of the publisher thereof, when such publisher shall not also be the proprietor thereof.' That, again, does not mention newspapers, and I must come to the same conclusion, that a newspaper was not mentioned because it was not intended to be included. Then can a person have any copyright or property in that which is not registered under the Act? This depends, I apprehend, upon the construction of the 18th section, which enacts that when any publisher or other person shall . . . . have projected, conducted and carried on . . . . any encyclopædia, review, magazine, periodical, work, or work published in a series of books, or parts, or any book whatsoever, and shall have employed any person to compose the same, or any volumes, parts, essays, articles, or portions thereof, for publication or as part of the same, and such work, &c., shall be composed on the terms that the copyright shall belong to such proprietor, and be paid for by him, then the proprietor of such work shall be entitled to copyright (except that after the term of twenty-eight years the copyright shall revert to the author) and shall be entitled to sue upon registering the same at Stationers' Hall. Now must every right included in this section be registered according to the Act? The present Lord Chancellor decided that question in *Mayhew* v. *Maxwell* (a). Mr. Mayhew wrote a certain article or series of articles in a periodical called the ' Welcome Guest,' and the proprietor proceeded to publish them in a separate form. The plaintiff filed his bill to restrain him from publishing them in any other form than in that for which he wrote the work. The same point arose in *Strahan* v. *Graham*, where Mr. Graham had sold the right of publishing photographs of the Holy Land in a publication called ' Good Words,' in which Dr. McLeod was publishing a work with regard to the Holy Land, and the proprietors of ' Good Words' had given him permission to use the photographs, but Mr. Graham contended that Mr. Strahan had no right to give it to Dr. McLeod. I decided in that case, and my decision was confirmed by Lord Chancellor Chelmsford, that there was no right to publish in a separate form that which he had authority only to use in ' Good Words' and that Mr. Graham had a good right of action. But these cases are distinct authorities to shew that there is a property in a publication, although it is not registered. That is the ground upon which Vice-Chancellor Wood commented on the 24th section in *Mayhew* v. *Maxwell* (b). He says: 'The plaintiff has not registered under the 24th section, now I have been referred to the case of *Sweet* v. *Benning* (c), which was a case between Mr. Sweet, the proprietor of the ' Jurist,' and Mr. Benning, a bookseller. Sweet brings an action against Benning for copying the marginal notes of cases in a separate publication. This was the subject of the action. I suppose the ' Jurist' had been published before this Act of 5 & 6 Vict., and therefore it was not registered at all. If so, the question whether these reports published in the ' Jurist' were subject to the provisions of the Act did not arise. Now in deciding that case Jervis, C.J., said (d): ' I think that under the circumstances stated there is an implied

(a) 1 J. & H. 312.   (b) *Ibid.* 312, 314.   (c) 16 C. B. 459.
(d) 16 C. B. 480, 481.

condition, understanding or arrangement between the proprietors of the 'Jurist' and the gentlemen who furnished them with reports, that the former shall acquire a copyright in the articles so written.' Now, therefore, it appears to me that a 'newspaper,' which is the best possible and only definition of such a publication as the 'Field,' not being within any of the provisions of this Act, I must infer that it was not the intention of the legislature to apply the Act to newspapers (for it was absolutely impossible that it should have missed insertion in some of the sections), and that the circumstance of non-registration throws no difficulty in the way of the plaintiff maintaining his right in law or equity ; and though it is seldom worth the while of proprietors to assert the copyright in articles in a newspaper, I am of opinion that whether it be the letters of a correspondent abroad, or the publication of a tale, or a treatise, or the review of a book, or whatever else, he acquires—I will not say as copyright, but as property—such a property in every article for which he pays, under the 18th section of the Act, or by the general rules of property, as will entitle him, if he thinks it worth while, to prohibit any other person from publishing the same thing in any other newspaper, or in any other form."

Copyright in a newspaper included in the term "goods and chattels" in the Bankruptcy Act.

The copyright in a newspaper was held to be included in the words " goods and chattels," in the 125th section of the Bankruptcy Law Consolidation Act, 1849.

The registered proprietor of a newspaper mortgaged the copyright of the newspaper, and also the type and machinery used in printing it, to the petitioner. The proprietor remained in possession and no change was made in the registration. Afterwards the sheriff seized the type and machinery under a judgment obtained by a creditor. While he was in possession the proprietor filed a declaration of insolvency and was made bankrupt. It was held on a petition by the mortgagee to have the benefit of his security, that the type and machinery, having been seized by the sheriff, were not in the " order

and disposition" of the bankrupt at the time of the
bankruptcy, but that the copyright of the newspaper
could not be seized by the sheriff, and therefore remained
in the order and disposition of the bankrupt as registered
proprietor (a). In thus deciding Turner, L.J., said: " The
case in the argument before us was very properly divided
into two considerations—first, as it affects the newspapers,
and, secondly, as it affects the plant. As to the newspapers, it was, in the first place, contended that they are
not goods and chattels within the meaning of the 125th
section of the Bankrupt Act, which provides for goods
and chattels of which the bankrupt is reputed owner
passing to the assignee. It was said that the right in the
newspaper is a mere right to publish the paper under
that name, and that such a right could not be considered
as goods and chattels within the meaning of the Act.
But, to say nothing of the copyright in the newspapers,
which undoubtedly exists, the right to publish the newspapers is a right to which an interest is attached. It is
a right protected by courts of law and by courts of equity,
and therefore a proprietary right; and the statutes—the
very Newspaper Acts on which the argument before us
proceeds—treat the matter as a matter of property and as
being a proprietary right. I feel, therefore, that the
property in these newspapers must be considered as goods
and chattels within the meaning of the Bankrupt Act·
These words, 'goods and chattels,' are words of very
extensive signification, and undoubtedly comprise both
property tangible and property which is not tangible. If
there had been any doubt in my mind on that point, it
would have been removed by the case of *Longman* v.
Tripp (b), which seems to me to be a decisive authority
upon the subject, and to be well founded in point of law.
The case was argued further as to the question of the
copyrights on this ground—it was said that the News-

(a) *Ex parte Foss, Re Baldwin; Ex parte Baldwin, Re Baldwin.* 6
W. R. 417; *Longman* v. *Tripp*, 2 Bos. & Pul. (New R.) 67; see also
Kelly v. *Hutton*, L. R. 3 Ch. App. 703.
(b) 2 Bos. & P. N. R. 67.

2 H

CAP. XVI.

paper Acts were Acts that were merely passed for fiscal purposes; that they had nothing to do with the rights of property, and therefore could not be considered as at all affecting the question whether the property was in the nature of goods and chattels within the meaning of the Bankrupt Act. But the case of *Longman* v. *Tripp* governs that point also; and independently of the case of *Longman* v. *Tripp* I think that the argument derived from the newspaper statutes is not well founded: for whether these statutes are for fiscal purposes or not, they at all events furnish the means by which the ownership of the property may be made known to the world. The declarations which are made under the Newspaper Acts are *indicia* of the property, and where such *indicia* exist I apprehend they must be attended to for the purpose of taking the property out of the disposition of the bankrupt, and removing them out of the operation of the reputed ownership clauses. The declaration is evidence of the ownership, and what may be effectual to remove that evidence must be resorted to."

Mortgage of share of newspaper not assignment of copyright requiring registration.

A mortgage of a share in a newspaper and the copyright and right of publication thereof, and all profits arising therefrom, is not an assignment of copyright which requires registration at Stationers' Hall, but merely an assignment of a chattel interest in the publishing adventure, which derives no additional efficacy from the registration (*a*).

During the progress of a suit instituted by Mr. Beeton against Mr. Hutton in reference to the proprietorship of the 'Sporting Life,' in which it was ultimately decided that the parties were entitled in equal shares, Mr. Beeton assigned by way of mortgage his share in the newspaper "and the copyright and right of publication thereof and all profits arising therefrom," to Messrs Wrigley & Son, the assignment reciting certain chancery proceedings, and containing a power of sale.

(*a*) *Kelly* v. *Hutton*, L. R. 3 Ch. App. 703; 38 L. J. (Ch.) 917; 19 L. T. (N.S.) 228.

Mr. Beeton subsequently mortgaged his same share to his partner Mr Hutton, to secure two sums of £2000 and £512, with interest at 7½ per cent. ; the former sum being the amount Beeton had been overpaid in a settlement of accounts with Hutton, the latter being the balance of Beeton's purchase-money for his moiety of the newspaper. Messrs Wrigley & Son registered the assignment to them at Stationers' Hall, under the provisions of the Copyright Act, and subsequently sold the mortgaged share to the plaintiff Kelly, who filed a bill for a declaration that he was entitled to a moiety of the newspaper. Both Wrigley & Son and the plaintiff had permitted the newspaper to be carried on as formerly by Beeton and Hutton. It was held by the Lords Justices that the plaintiff could only take Beeton's share in the newspaper subject to the equities subsisting between the parties. "Many points have been raised before us," said Wood, L.J., "as regards the property which was the subject of the mortgage to Wrigley & Son. . . . . It appears to us that Beeton & Hutton were engaged in a joint adventure, namely, the publishing of the paper in question. Capital was required for the adventure, and the co-partners or co-adventurers possessed leasehold premises and type, and other chattels necessary for carrying it on. The mortgage to Wrigley & Son assigned to them Beeton's share in the newspaper, whatever it might be, and all profits belonging thereto or arising therefrom. In the habendum the deed speaks of the copyright of the newspaper, and the right of continuation and publication thereof. Now it appears to us that there is nothing analogous to copyright in the name of a newspaper, but that the proprietor has a right to prevent any other person from adopting the same name for any other similar publication; and that this right is a chattel interest capable of assignment was held in *Longman* v. *Tripp* (a), and *Ex parte Foss* (b). The mortgage, then, to Wrigley & Son was that of Beeton's share of a chattel, which formed the

(a) 2 Bos. & P. 67.　　　　(b) 2 De G. F. & J. 230.

principal subject of the co-adventure between Beeton and Hutton.   Considerable stress has been laid in argument, on the part of the appellants, on the necessity of notice being given of such an assignment, either by direct notice to Hutton, or by an entry at the Inland Revenue Office ; and much controversy has arisen in evidence as to whether Hutton had or had not in fact such notice previously to the 9th of March, 1866.   The entry of their mortgage by Wrigley & Son at Stationers' Hall was clearly futile ; but we do not pause to consider the question further, because it is clear on the face of their mortgage deed that Wrigley & Son were aware of the litigation between Beeton and Hutton.   They allowed the joint adventure to be worked jointly, whether with or without notice, and it is impossible that they can now take to themselves the subject of that adventure and the profits arising therefrom without being subject to every equity of the co-adventurer.   A judgment creditor in execution against one partner, his debtor, takes only the interest of the debtor, subject to his co-partner's equities ; and Wrigley & Son could not claim the asset without satisfying in the first place the lien of £512 for the unpaid purchase-money of Beeton's moiety, nor without satisfying the balance of accounts due from Beeton to his co-adventurer Hutton. The lien of Hutton as *quasi* partner in the adventure must be satisfied before the subject-matter of the adventure can be passed over to any person claiming under an assignment from Beeton ; and this lien must continue so long as Wrigley & Son, as the assigns of Beeton by way of mortgage, allow the business to be carried on in co-partnership by Beeton and Hutton.   Irrespective of the doctrine of notice, they cannot take the benefit of Hutton's capital in carrying on the concern (whether they have given him notice or not) and then ask to have the share of Beeton in the chattel, and still less in the profits of the concern, handed over to them without first satisfying the lien of the co-adventurer for what may be due to him on taking the accounts of the adventure.   The same reasoning applies to the plaintiff as purchaser. His letter of the 27th of December, 1866, to Hutton the elder, set out in the amended bill, shews that he, at least up to that time, acquiesced in the arrangement under which the newspaper was to be carried on. In fact, having acquired the interest of Beeton in the newspaper, his mortgagees allow Beeton to conduct the business, and he must be taken to act as their agent and on their behalf. They do not advance any capital, and ask no question as to how it is to be provided. They must therefore take the business as they found it, at least up to the time of the actual exclusion of the plaintiff by Hutton from the concern, and even after that time profits cannot be claimed without making all just allowances in respect of such moiety. Hutton, therefore, wholly irrespective of his mortgage of the 9th of October, 1866, would be entitled to a lien on Beeton's share in the newspaper for £512, the unpaid purchase-money. He would also, we think, be entitled to the balance on the account settled on the 9th of March, 1866, with Beeton (which account came down to the 30th of September, 1865), and to the £2000 due to Hutton as the result of that account and the arrangement subsequent on it. We think, also, that interest at the rate of $7\frac{1}{2}$ per cent. per annum must be allowed on those two sums: for Hutton was clearly entitled to decline carrying on the business, whether with or without the knowledge of Wrigley & Son's mortgagee, except in the terms of being allowed interest on his capital. It is in fact advanced to the plaintiff. . . . . As to the whole case, therefore, we conclude that the plaintiff has become entitled to the interest of Beeton in the newspaper. We see no reason why that interest should not be dealt with as on former occasions, by directing the defendants to concur in procuring the plaintiff's name to be registered at the office of Inland Revenue as such owner, subject to the lien before mentioned " (a).

(a) *Kelly* v. *Hutton*, L. R. 3 Ch. App. 703; 38 L. J. (Ch.) 917; 19 L. T. (N.S.) 228.

In a case which came before Lord Curriehill, in November, 1875, wherein Mr. Charles Reade brought an action against the 'Glasgow Herald' for damages for infringement of copyright by the publication of his sketch called 'A Hero and Martyr' which appeared originally in the 'Pall Mall Gazette,' and which the 'Herald' had transmitted daily from London by its special wire for the next day's paper; his Lordship, in giving judgment, so far as concerned the plea of irrelevancy set up by the defendants against the plaintiff's action, said : "The defenders maintain that as the London newspaper is not registered as copyright, they are entitled to copy and publish in their journal any thing which appears in it, and that even if its proprietor might have a title to sue for damages for such appropriation of matter published, the author, who has been paid by the proprietors for the right to publish such matter, has no action against the journal so appropriating. This raises a question of great importance both to authors and journalists. I am of opinion that the defence is not relevant, and that the counter-issues proposed by the defenders must be disallowed. I know of no principle or authority holding that the author loses his copyright by permitting third parties to print and publish his work. To hold such a doctrine would, I think, be analogous to holding that a patentee loses his monopoly on licensing a third party to manufacture his patented invention."

An injunction will be granted against assuming the name of a newspaper published by the plaintiff, for the purpose of deceiving the public and supplanting the goodwill of such paper (a), or against publishing a magazine in the name of one who no longer authorizes it (b).

(a) *Bell* v. *Locke*, 8 Paige (Amer.) 75. See *Snowden* v. *Noah*, Hopk. (Amer.) 347.   (b) *Hogg* v. *Kirby*, 8 Ves. 215.

CHAPTER XVII.

INTERNATIONAL COPYRIGHT.

Non erit alia lex Romæ, alia Athenis ; alia nunc alia posthac, sed et apud
omnes gentes et omnia tempora una eademque lex obtinebit.—CICERO.

INTERNATIONAL law is entirely the offspring of modern civilization, and is the latest important discovery in political science.

International copyright the offspring of modern civilization.

The origin and progress of international law is itself a remarkable step in the march of civilization. Nations now begin to acknowledge their subjection to laws in conformity with natural justice and reason, as in the very origin of society individuals acknowledged themselves so bound. And the development of international law will proceed amongst the civilized nations of the earth, until citizens can enjoy in foreign countries all the rights which they enjoy in their own. Commerce, the influence of which unites the human family by one of its strongest ties, the desire of supplying mutual wants, demands an international code for the civilized nations of the earth. Art demands that the property in its inventions should be secured by an international law of patents. Literature, that the property in its works should be secured by international copyright.

" The actual law of nations," observes Mr. Curtis (a), " knows no exclusive right of an author to the proceeds of his work, except that which is enforced by the municipal law of his own country, which can operate nowhere but in its own jurisdiction. As soon as a copy of a book is

(a) 'Copyright,' p. 22.

CAP. XVII. landed in any foreign country, all complaint of its republication is, in the absence of a treaty, fruitless, because
no means of redress exist, except under the law of the
author's own country. It becomes public property, not
because the justice of the case is changed by the passage
across the sea or a boundary, but because there are no
means of enforcing the private right."

International
copyright
regulated by
7 Vict. c. 12,
and 15 Vict.
c. 12.

International copyright is regulated by the 7 Vict. c. 12,
explained by the 15 Vict. c. 12.

The former repealed the 1 & 2 Vict. c. 59, which had
been found "insufficient to enable Her Majesty to confer
upon authors of books first published in foreign countries
copyright of the like duration, and with the like remedies
for the infringement thereof, which were conferred and provided by the said Copyright Amendment Act (5 & 6 Vict.
c. 45), with respect to authors of books first published in
the British dominions."

Formerly, if a book were written by a foreigner and
published abroad, a person who purchased the right to
publish here could not enjoy the right exclusively (a).

In the case of *Guichard* v. *Mori* (b), the defendant
published a piece of music called ' The Charms of Berlin,'
about a third of which consisted of a piece of music sold
by the composer in 1820 to the plaintiff. The music had
been published in France in 1814, six years before the
sale to the plaintiff. " The policy of our law," observed
Lord Lyndhurst, " recognises by statutes, express in their
wording, that the importation of foreign inventions shall
be encouraged in the same manner as the inventions made
in this country and by natives. This is founded as well
upon reason, sense, and justice, as it is upon policy. It
appears that this piece of music was published in France
by Kalkbrenner, or some one to whom he sold it, so long
ago as 1814, six years before the sale to the plaintiff.'
There can be no question, then, of the right of the
defendant, or any one else, to publish it in this country."

(a) *Guichard* v. *Mori*, 9 L. J. (Ch.) 227.
(b) 9 L. J. (Ch.) 237.

To remedy this, and to afford protection in this CAP. XVII. country to the authors of books first published in foreign countries, in cases where protection should be afforded in such foreign countries to the authors of books first published here, the International Copyright Act, 1837, was passed.

This Act, however, did not empower Her Majesty to confer any exclusive right of representing or performing dramatic pieces or musical compositions first published in foreign countries upon the authors thereof, nor to extend the privilege of copyright to prints and sculpture first published abroad ; it merely had reference to books.

The Act of 1837 has reference solely to books.

In order to confer such power an Act of Parliament was passed in 1844 to amend the law. By this Act (a) Her Majesty was empowered by any Order in Council to direct that as respects all or any particular class of the following works (namely) books, prints, articles of sculpture, and other works of art to be defined in such order, which should, after a future time to be specified in such order, be first published in any foreign country to be named in such order, the authors, inventors, designers, engravers, and makers thereof respectively, should have the privilege of copyright therein during such period as should be defined in such order, not exceeding, however, as to any of the above-mentioned works, the term of copyright which authors, inventors, designers, engravers, and makers of the like works respectively first published in the United Kingdom might be entitled to.

Enlargement of the power conferred on Her Majesty of concluding international copyright conventions.

If the order applied to books, the copyright law as to books first published in this country should apply to the books to which the order related, except so far as might be excepted in any order, and except as to the delivery of copies of books at the British Museum and the other libraries.

And if the order applied to prints, articles of sculpture, or to any such other work of art as aforesaid, the copy

<hr>

(a) 7 Vict. c. 12.

CAP. XVII. right law as to print, sculptures, and such other works of art first published in this country should apply to the prints, sculptures, and other works of art to which such order related, except as might be provided in any order.

The 5th section of the Act enacts that it shall be lawful for Her Majesty, by Order of Her Majesty in Council, to direct that the authors of dramatic pieces and musical compositions which shall after a future time, to be specified in such order, be first publicly represented or performed in any foreign country, to be named in such order, shall have the sole liberty of representing or performing in any part of the British dominions such dramatic pieces or musical compositions during such period as shall be defined in such order, not exceeding the period during which authors of dramatic pieces and musical compositions first publicly represented or performed in the United Kingdom may for the time be entitled by law to the sole liberty of representing and performing the same: and from and after the time so specified in any such last-mentioned order the enactments of the said Dramatic Literary Property Act and of the said Copyright Amendment Act, and of any other Act for the time being in force with relation to the liberty of publicly representing and performing dramatic pieces or musical compositions, shall, subject to such limitations as to the duration, of the right conferred by any such order as shall be therein contained, apply to and be in force in respect of the dramatic pieces and musical compositions to which such order shall extend, and which shall have been registered as thereinafter provided in such manner as if such dramatic pieces and musical compositions had been first publicly represented and performed in the British dominions, except such of the said enactments or such parts thereof as shall be excepted in such order.

Registration. The provisions in regard to registration under the International Copyright Act are contained in the 6th section, which requires that every author, to entitle himself to the protection thereby afforded, shall, within a time to be prescribed in each Order in Council made in pursuance of the Act, register the same at Stationers' Hall. It is necessary to register the title to the copy thereof, the name and place of abode of the author or composer thereof, the name and place of abode of the proprietor of the copyright, the time and place of the first publication, representation, or performance, as the case may be, in the foreign country. One printed copy of the whole of any book, and of any dramatic piece or musical composition, in the event of the same having been printed, and of every volume, shall be delivered to the officer of the Company of Stationers.

The copy delivered to Stationers' Hall must be on the best paper upon which the largest number or impression of the work has been printed for sale, and must contain all maps and prints. *Delivery of copies.*

The officer of the Stationers' Company to whom the delivery of a copy is made, is to give a receipt in writing for the same, and such delivery is to be to all intents and purposes a sufficient delivery under the provisions of the Act. As to editions, after the first, unless such subsequent editions contain additions or alterations, it is not necessary to deposit another copy.

If the dramatic piece or musical composition be in manuscript, all that is required is that the title, the name and place of abode of the author or composer, the name and place of abode of the proprietor of the right of performing or representing, and the time and place of the first representation or performance in the foreign country, shall be entered in the register. No copy is required to be deposited. *Dramatic piece or musical composition.*

As to engravings and prints, the title, the name, and place of abode of the inventor, designer, or engraver, the name of the proprietor of the copyright, and the time and place of the first publication in the foreign country, must be entered on the register, and a copy of such print upon the best paper upon which the largest number of *Engravings and prints.*

CAP. XVII.   impressions shall have been printed for sale, must be
delivered to the officer of the Company of Stationers.

Articles of   As to any article of sculpture or other work of art, the
sculpture.   register must contain a descriptive title thereof, the name
and place of abode of the maker of it, the name of the
proprietor of the copyright, and the time and place of its
first publication in the foreign country.

Mode of entry.   The task of making and also of construing the statutable entries is rendered somewhat difficult owing to the
circumstances, first, that the statute does not require, or
the book of registry in form provide for, any description of
the thing to be registered apart from its title; and,
secondly, that the register in its actual form is framed
with headings applicable only to the registration of a book
or other printed matter. In *Wood* v. *Boosey* (a), the
registration of the pianoforte arrangement of an opera
was held to be invalid, because the name of the composer
of the opera had been entered in the registry, instead of
the name of the person who had made the arrangement.
In the opinion of the court, the latter, and not the former
was the author of what was registered.

In *Boosey* v. *Fairlie* (b), the plaintiffs claimed the
exclusive right of representing a comic opera known as
' *Vert-vert*,' composed by Offenbach, of which a pianoforte
arrangement made by Soumis, but not the orchestral parts,
had been published in print. There had been entered in
the registry the title of the opera, the name and place of
abode of Offenbach as composer and owner, and the time
and place of the first representation of the opera, and the
time and place of the first publication of the pianoforte
arrangement. A copy of the pianoforte arrangement, but
not of the opera itself, had been delivered to the officer of
the Stationers' Company. Vice-Chancellor Bacon ruled
that the pianoforte arrangement, and not the opera itself,
was the thing registered, and that, as the name and place
of abode of Soumis, the author of the arrangement, had not

(a) L. R. 2 Q. B. 340; 3 Q. B. 223.
(b) 7 Ch. Div. 307.

been entered, the registration, according to *Wood* v. C<small>AP.</small> XVII.
Boosey, was not valid. The Court of Appeal, however,
held that all the facts required for the registration of the
opera itself had been duly entered, and that the additional
entry of the time and place of the first publication of the
pianoforte arrangement, and the delivery of a copy of it,
were superfluous acts, which did not affect the registration
of the original opera. There was, therefore, a good registration of the unpublished opera, but not of the pianoforte
arrangement.

The 7th section of the International Copyright Act pro- Registration
vides for the registration of books published anonymously, of books published
it being sufficient in such case to insert in the entry the anonymously.
name and place of abode of the first publisher, instead of
the name and place of abode of the author, together with
a declaration that such entry is made either on behalf of
the author, or on behalf of such first publisher, as the case
may require.

The provisions of the Copyright Amendment Act as Effect of
regards entries in the register book of the Company of registration.
Stationers, inspection, searches, false entries, expunging,
and varying entries, are made to apply to entries under
the International Copyright Act, except that the forms of
entry may be varied to meet the circumstances of the
case, and the sum to be demanded by the officer of the
Stationers' Company for making any entry shall be one
shilling only (*a*).

And it is further provided (*b*), that every entry made in As to ex-
pursuance of the Act of a first publication shall be *primâ* punging or varying entry
facie proof of a rightful first publication; but if there be a grounded in wrongful first
wrongful first publication, and any party have availed him- publication.
self thereof to obtain an entry of a spurious work, no order
for expunging or varying such entry shall be made unless
it be proved to the satisfaction of the court or of the judge
taking cognisance of the application for expunging or
varying such entry, first, with respect to a wrongful publication in a country to which the author or first publisher

(*a*) Sect. 8.   (*b*) Sect. 9.

CAP. XVII. does not belong, and in regard to which there does not subsist with this country any treaty of international copyright, that the party making the application was the author or first publisher as the case requires ; secondly, with respect to a wrongful first publication, either in the country where a rightful first publication has taken place, or in regard to which there subsists with this country a treaty of international copyright, that a court of competent jurisdiction in any such country where such wrongful first publication has taken place has given judgment in favour of the right of the party claiming to be the author or first publisher.

Order may specify different periods for different foreign countries and for different classes of works.

By the 13th section it is provided that the respective terms to be specified in any Order of Council for the continuance of the privilege to be granted in respect of works to be first published in foreign countries may be different for works first published in different foreign countries and for different classes of works : and that the times to be prescribed for the entries to be made in the register book of the Stationers' Company, and for the deliveries of the books and other articles to the said officer of the Stationers' Company as thereinbefore mentioned, may be different for different foreign countries, and for different classes of books or other articles.

No order to be of effect unless it states reciprocal protection secured.

No Order of Council is to have any effect unless it shall be therein stated as the ground for issuing the same that due protection has been secured by the foreign power so named in such order in council for the benefit of parties interested in works first published in the dominions of Her Majesty, similar to those comprised in such order (a).

Orders to be published in 'Gazette.'

Provision is made that every order made under the powers conferred by the Act should be published in the 'London Gazette' as soon as may be after the making thereof, and from the time of such publication shall have the same effect as if every part thereof were included in the Act.

Proposal of Copyright

The Royal Commissioners, in their recent report on Copyright, propose that registration of foreign works in

(a) Sect. 14.

this country should not be required for the purpose of Cap. XVII. securing copyright here, or the right of representation or performance of musical and dramatic works, and that the production of a copy of the foreign register, attested by a British diplomatic or consular officer, should in all legal proceedings be *primâ facie* evidence of title to the copyright of the foreign work, but they suggest that this should not apply to English translations of foreign works and adaptations of foreign plays to the British stage, if published in this country. They also propose that the obligation to deposit copies of foreign books and other works for which authors may desire to obtain copyright in the British dominions should be abandoned; foreign govern-ments being, of course, requested to give up their rights to the deposit of English books.

In order to meet the difficulty of how the people of one state are to know what works of the other are protected and what not, the Commissioners recommend that a presumption should be allowed that every book has copy-right and is protected in the country of production; but, in case of legal proceedings, if the copyright in the country of production is disputed, proof of copyright should be required, and, as already proposed, such proof should be supplied by the production of an attested copy of the foreign register.

The 18th section provided that nothing in the Act *Translations.* should be construed to prevent the printing, publication, or sale of any translation of any book the author whereof and his assigns might be entitled to the benefit of the Act.

But this section has been repealed by the 1st section of the 15 Vict. c. 12, so far as it is inconsistent with the provisions of that Act. And the 2nd section of that Act provides that Her Majesty may by Order in Council direct that the authors of books which are, after a future time to be specified in such order, published in any foreign country to be named in such order, their executors, administrators, and assigns, shall, subject to the provisions thereinafter contained or referred to, be empowered to prevent the publication in the British dominions of any translations of such books not authorized by them, for such time as may be specified in such order, not extending beyond the expiration of five years from the time at which the authorized translations of such books thereinafter mentioned are respectively first published, and, in the case of books published in parts, not extending as to each part beyond the expiration of five years from the time at which the authorized translation of such part is first published.

The 15 Vict. c. 12, further provides that, subject to any provisions or qualifications contained in such order, and to the provisions in the Act contained or referred to, the laws and enactments for the time being in force for the purpose of preventing the infringement of copyright in books published in the British dominions shall be applied for the purpose of preventing the publication of translations of the books to which such order extends which are not sanctioned by the authors of such books, except only such parts of the said enactments as relate to the delivery of copies of books for the use of the British Museum, and for the use of the other libraries (a).

Articles of political discussion.

But it is provided that nothing shall prevent any article of political discussion which has been published in any newspaper or periodical in a foreign country from being republished or translated in any newspaper or periodical in this country, if the source from which it is taken be acknowledged : and that any article relating to any other subject which has been so published as aforesaid may, if the source from which the same is taken be acknowledged, be republished or translated in like manner, unless the author has signified his intention of preserving the copyright therein, and the right of translating the same, in some conspicuous part of the newspaper, or periodical in which the same was first published, in which case the same shall, without the formalities required by the 8th section,

(a) Sect. 3.

receive the same protection as is by virtue of the Inter- Cap. XVII.
national Copyright Act or that Act extended to books (a).

By the 4th section of the 15 Vict. c. 12, power is given Dramatic
by Order in Council to grant a further right to the authors works.
of dramatic pieces first represented in a foreign country.
It is enacted that Her Majesty may by Order in Council
direct that authors of dramatic pieces which are, after a
future time to be specified in such order, first publicly
represented in any foreign country, to be named in such
order, their executors, administrators, and assigns, shall,
subject to the provisions thereinafter mentioned or referred to, be empowered to prevent the representation in
the British dominions of any translation of such dramatic
pieces not authorized by them for such time as may be
specified in such order, not extending beyond the expiration of five years from the time at which the authorized
translations of such dramatic pieces thereinafter mentioned
are first published or publicly represented. And further,
that thereupon the law for protecting the representation
of such pieces shall extend to prevent unauthorized
translation (b).

Then follows a short, but most important provision Fair imita-
that nothing in the Act shall be so construed as to prevent tions or
adaptations
fair imitations or adaptations to the English stage of any not prohibited.
dramatic piece or musical composition published in any
foreign countries (c).

The case of *Wood* v. *Chart* (d) thus illustrates principles
by which the court will be guided in questions respecting
translations and imitations of foreign works under the
above Act.

The provisions of the International Copyright Act, so
far as they came in question in this case, were these : the
authors of foreign plays (*i.e.*, plays first published abroad)
may prevent the representation in the British dominions
of any unauthorized translation, for a period not exceeding

(a) Sect. 7. (b) Sect. 5.
(c) Sect. 6, but see amending Act 38 & 39 Vict. c. 12, *post* p. 485.
(d) L. R. 10 Eq. 193; 18 W. R. 822; 22 L. T. (N.S.) 432; 39 L. J.
(N.S.) Ch. 641.

four years from the first publication or representation of an authorized translation, but nothing in that Act, as we have already seen, was to prevent "fair imitations or adaptations to the English stage" of a foreign play. The facts of the case were as follows :—' *Frou-frou*,' a French comedy, was registered in England ; an English version was made, published, and registered. Mr. Wood, the plaintiff, became assignee of all English rights, both of the authors and translators. An unauthorized version was made and publicly acted by the defendants. Thereupon the plaintiff filed a bill for an injunction and an account. The authorized English version of the plaintiff was entitled ' Like to Like,' the scene transferred to England, the names of the characters changed to English names, and certain alterations and omissions made in the dialogue, but the plot and the main incidents continued the same. The Vice-Chancellor dismissed the bill, holding that the requisitions to entitle the plaintiff to the benefit of the Act had not been complied with, for ' Like to Like ' was not a "translation" within the meaning of the Act, but rather "an imitation or adaptation to the English stage."

"With respect to the representation of the English play," said Sir W. M. James, when Vice-Chancellor, "the plaintiff has got to make out his title, which depends upon the convention, and upon the Act. Now the Act of Parliament for some reason or other—I suppose a sufficient reason, but I do not know what it may be—has required, in order to give an author, or the assignee of that author, the particular copyright in question, that the original work shall be deposited in the United Kingdom ; and then with regard to works other than dramatic works, it says, ' The translation sanctioned by the author, or part thereof, must be published in the British dominions not later than one year after the registration and deposit in the United Kingdom of the original work.' That is, the translation of part thereof ; and the whole of such translation must be published within three years of such registration and deposit. It contemplates and requires that the whole work shall be translated. But it would not be a compliance with that to translate a quarter, or half, or three-quarters of a work that is protected, and then say, 'That is all I want protected, that is my authorized translation; and I have published the whole of that part which I have thought right to have translated.' The whole work must be translated, and the translation must be published in this country. Then, for some other sufficient reason, it is provided that in the case of dramatic pieces the translation sanctioned by the author must be published within three calendar months of the registration of the original work. Now, I do not think it is possible to say that this means that anything which the author shall sanction as a translation must be published within three calendar months; but that the translation which has been authorized and sanctioned by the author must be published within that time. It appears to me that the plaintiff has gone out of his course to dig a pitfall for himself; for that which he says he has done is, the original thing being called 'Frou-frou,' he has published in England' a comedy called 'Like to Like' . . . he has introduced English characters; he has transferred the scene to England; he has made the alterations necessary for making it an English comedy and not a translation of a French comedy; and he has left out a great number of speeches and passages, especially in the first act, which would seem to imply at first he was merely making an imitation or adaptation, and afterwards was minded more completely to make a translation.

"The first two acts seem particularly to be what is referred to in the Act of Parliament itself as 'an imitation or adaptation.' Whether it be a fair adaptation is another question; but if one wanted to have an example of what is an imitation or adaptation to the English stage, I should have said that this is exactly the thing. This is an imitation and adaptation to the English stage; that is, you transfer the scene to England, you make the characters English, you introduce English manners, when our manners differ from French manners, and you leave out things which you say would not be suitable for representation on the English stage. But what the Act required for some sufficient reason, as I have said before, when it required that a translation should be made accessible to the English people, was that the English people should have the opportunity of knowing the French work as accurately as it was possible to know a French work by the medium of a version in English. That seems to me to be what was intended, and having come to the conclusion that this is not a translation, I am of opinion that the plaintiff has failed to comply with the condition precedent which the Act has imposed upon him to entitle him to sustain this suit. It is said that one ought to give a liberal interpretation, that one ought not to strain the meaning of the word ' translation ' or any other word, for the purpose of depriving a foreign author of the benefit of the Act. Of course not. Of course, one ought to take a liberal view, and one ought not to strain any word, but one must at the same time give a real and natural meaning to those words, and, according to my view of the case, there never would have been the slightest difficulty whatever in the plaintiff's obtaining the full benefit of his assignment, and putting himself in a position to prevent any representation of the French play, or of any English translation of it, if he had simply employed Mr. Sutherland Edwards to do what he could very well have done, namely, have made a translation. If he had said to him, ' Now make a translation of this ; do not be thinking of an adaptation to the English stage, but make me a translation,' he could have made a translation which could have been published in this country ; and then it would have been quite open to the author, or the person claiming under the author, to have represented that, with any excision, with any alteration, with any adaptation he might have thought fit for the purpose of making it more suitable for the English stage. I have no doubt whatever

if he had published a translation, he could then have Cap. XVII.
acted the thing which Mr. Sutherland Edwards has called
a version, and that nobody could have acted anything
like that—anything approaching to it, because (although
I say this is not a translation, but an imitation and
adaptation to the English stage) I have no hesitation in
saying that if the authors, or any other persons claiming
under them, had complied with the condition required by
the Act of Parliament, I should at once have restrained
the acting of this very thing as not being a fair imitation
or adaptation, but as being a piratical translation of the
original work. That would have been the proper thing
for me to have done in that case; but the plaintiff
having brought his suit, and not having a title, must fail,
with the usual consequences—he must pay the costs."

The scope of the 6th section of the International Copyright Act as to fair imitations or adaptations to the English
stage of any dramatic piece or musical composition published in any foreign country has been restricted since
the first edition of this work, the 38 & 39 Vict. c. 12,
providing that the Queen by Order in Council may direct
that the 6th section of the said Act shall not apply
to dramatic pieces to which protection is so extended;
and thereupon the said recited Act shall take effect with
respect to such dramatic pieces, and to the translations
thereof, as if the said 6th section of the said Act were
thereby repealed.

As to what is a translation some difficulty has arisen. What is a
Dryden reduces translations to three heads: first, that of translation?
metaphrase, or turning an author word by word, and line
by line, from one language into another. Thus, or near
this manner, was 'Horace, his Art of Poetry,' translated
by Ben Jonson. The second way is that of paraphrase,
or translation with latitude, where the author is kept in
view by the translator, so as never to be lost, but his
words are not so strictly followed as his sense; and that,
too, is admitted to be amplified, but not altered. Such is
Mr. Waller's translation of ' Virgil's fourth Æneid.' The

third way is that of imitation, where the translator (if now he has not lost that name) assumes the liberty, not only to vary from the words and sense, but to forsake them both as he sees occasion; and taking only some general hints from the original, to run divisions on the groundwork, as he pleases. Such is Mr. Cowley's practice in turning two odes of Pindar, and one of Horace, into English (a).

It is, however, clear that the meaning of what are called in the convention "piratical translations," are all translations not authorized by the foreign author. A version must be distinguished from a translation, as will be presently seen.

Requisites in order to obtain protection. The following are the requisites in order to entitle an author to the benefit of the Act or of any Order in Council as to any translation or dramatic piece :—

1. The original work from which the translation is to be made must be registered, and a copy thereof deposited in the United Kingdom in the manner required for original works by the International Copyright Act, within three calendar months of its first publication in the foreign country.

2. The author must notify on the title-page of the original work, or if it is published in parts, on the title-page of the first part, or if there is no title-page, on some conspicuous part of the work, that it is his intention to reserve the right of translating it.

3. The translation sanctioned by the author, or a part thereof, must be published, either in the country mentioned in the Order in Council by virtue of which it is to be protected, or in the British dominions, not later than one year after the registration and deposit in the United Kingdom of the original work, and the whole of such translation must be published within three years of such registration and deposit.

(a) Dryden's Works (Scott's Ed.) xii. 11.

4. Such translation must be registered and a copy thereof deposited in the United Kingdom within a time to be mentioned in that behalf in the order by which it is protected, and in the manner provided by the International Copyright Act for the registration and deposit of original works.

5. In the case of books published in parts, each part of the original work must be registered and deposited in this country in the manner required by the International Copyright Act within three months after the first publication thereof in the foreign country.

6. In the case of dramatic pieces the translation sanctioned by the author must be published within three calendar months of the registration of the original work.

7. The above requisitions shall apply to articles originally published in newspapers or periodicals if the same be afterwards published in a separate form, but shall not apply to such articles as originally published.

In pursuance of the powers conferred by the 7 Vict. c. 12, a convention was signed between this country and France at Paris the 3rd of November, 1851, and subsequently ratified by Act of Parliament (a). Convention between England and France.

In order to obtain protection in either country the work must be registered in the following manner :— Registration.

If the work first appear in France it must be registered at Stationers' Hall, London.

If it appear first in England, at the Bureau de la Libraire of the Ministry of the Interior at Paris, within three months after the first publication in England. As to works published in parts, they must be registered within three months after the publication of the last part; but in order to preserve the right of translation each part must be registered within three months after its publication. A copy

(a) 15 & 16 Vict. c. 12.

of the work must also be deposited within the same time as registration is to be made either at the British Museum in London, or in the National Library at Paris, as the case may be.

In *Cassell* v. *Stiff* (a), Sir W. P. Wood, V.C., held that a French newspaper published weekly, and not intended to be completed in any definite number of parts, must be registered within three months after its commencement, or if it had commenced before 1852, within three months after the date of the Order in Council (10th January, 1852); and, *semble*, the registration of a number of such a periodical, in 1855, long after its commencement, did not extend to the succeeding numbers the protection of the International Copyright Acts.

The charge for registration is in France one franc twenty-five centimes, and in England one shilling; and the further charge for a certificate of such registration must not exceed the sum of five shillings in England nor six francs twenty-five centimes in France; and the certified copy of the entry in either case is evidence of the exclusive right of publication in both countries, until the contrary is proved.

With regard to articles other than books, maps, prints, and musical compositions, in which protection may be claimed, any other mode of registration which may be applicable by law in one of the two countries to any work or article first published in such country for the purpose of affording protection to copyright in such article, is extended on equal terms to any similar article first published in the other country.

Little difference is discernible between the treaty and the Act, with the exception that the latter explains clearly one or two passages in the former that might otherwise have been disputed.

But as the convention had been concluded under the provisions of the 7 Vict. c. 12, the 15 Vict. c. 12, went on to provide that during the continuance of the convention,

(a) 2 K. & J. 279.

and so long as the Order in Council already made under the International Copyright Act remained in force, the provisions contained in the 15 Vict. c. 12, should apply to the said convention, and to translations of books and dramatic pieces which were after the passing of the 15 Vict. c. 12, published or represented in France, in the same manner as if Her Majesty had issued her Order in Council in pursuance of such Act for giving effect to such convention, and had therein directed that such translations should be protected as is mentioned in the 15 Vict. c. 12, for a period of five years from the date of the first publication or public representation thereof respectively, and as if a period of three months from the publication of such translation were the time mentioned in such order as the time within which the same must be registered, and a copy thereof deposited in the United Kingdom (a).

Authors of works in France claiming copyright in this country are not exempt from the conditions affecting authors of works in this country (b).

By analogy it follows that to obtain the benefit of the International Copyright Act, the proprietor of a foreign print must comply with the provisions of the Engravings Acts and the proprietor's name must be printed on it (c).

The 19th clause of the 7 Vict. c. 12, which enacts that no author of any book or dramatic piece, which shall be first published out of Her Majesty's dominions, shall have copyright therein, otherwise than under the provisions of that Act, applies to British subjects first publishing in a country with which no international convention exists.

It has been held that this section applies to native as well as to foreign authors, and to works first published in any foreign country, whether the provisions of the International Copyright Acts have or have not been

(a) 15 Vict. c. 12, s. 11.
(b) *Cassell* v. *Stiff*, 2 K. & J. 279.
(c) *Avanzo* v. *Mudie*, 10 Ex. 203.

extended to that country ; and accordingly that no author, whether a British subject or an alien, is entitled to any other protection for a work first published abroad than that which he may claim under the International Copyright Acts. Therefore where a British subject first produced for representation a dramatic piece of which he was the author, at New York, and he subsequently produced it in London, Vice-Chancellor Sir W. P. Wood held that as he had not complied with the provisions of the 7 Vict. c. 12, and there being no international treaty or arrangement (which was alluded to by the above section), he had not obtained the copyright to such piece in England (a), nor the exclusive right to the representation of his drama, though he could not, by any possibility, have complied with the provisions of the said Act, no regulation having been made according to the course pointed out by the Act as to International Copyright between the two countries.

It was contended by the plaintiff that this Act could not annihilate the privileges enjoyed by British subjects under the former Acts. That the word " author " must mean an author in a country affected by the Act, and that the simple performance of a piece in manuscript abroad was not contemplated by the term " publication."

However, the contention failed, the Vice-Chancellor saying :—

" The 19th clause says, in effect, that this Act having been made, if any person, whether a British subject or not, chooses to deprive this country of the advantage of the first representation of his work, then he may get the right, if he thinks fit, under the arrangements which may have been come to with that country he so favours with his representation, pursuant to the 7 & 8 Vict. c. 12. If, however, he does not get it, if he chooses to publish his performance in a country which has not entered into any treaty or made any arrangement for that purpose, he may

(a) *Boucicault* v. *Delafield*, 9 Jur. (N.S.) 1282; 33 L. J. (Ch.) 38; 12 W. R. 101; 1 H. & M. 597.

do so, but this country has nothing more to say to him, and he must be taken to have elected under which of the statutes, which have been made respecting similar subjects, he wishes to come, and by performing his work in one country instead of the other, he is thereby excluded from all advantage of publishing in the other. I cannot see anything to justify me in restraining the provision, or to say that it applies to foreigners, and does not apply to British subjects, because if I did so, I should be bound, by parity of reasoning, to say, that any foreigner publishing first in this country, and acquiring a right under the existing law, would have to be deprived of that right by this Act, whilst a British subject would not be deprived of the benefit. The object of the legislature seems to have been in these cases to secure, in this country, the benefit of the first publication, and to extend to any other country the same benefit, only on certain conditions, namely, that reciprocity shall be afforded, and that the representation shall take place for the first time in England, which may be published afterwards in another country."

The same plaintiff in a subsequent case again tried to restrain the performance of a play of his, which had been first introduced in New York, but failed to establish his claim (a).

The Royal Commissioners in their recent report on copyright made some important suggestions as to the right of translation, copyright in translations, and adaptation of foreign plays to the English stage. They thought that instead of simply extending the periods for partial and complete translation, as was suggested to them, the better course would be that an unconditional right of translation should be reserved to every foreign author belonging to any state with which this country had entered into a copyright convention, for three years after publication of the original work.

Under the treaty with France, the period for the right

Suggestions of Copyright Commission as to translations and adaptations of foreign plays.

(a) *Boucicault* v. *Chatterton*, 5 Ch. Div. 267.

CAP. XVII. of translation is at present five years, the Commissioners considered that this period must in many instances be insufficient to secure a fair remuneration for the labour and outlay attendant upon the publication of a translation, and they therefore proposed that if an author publish an English translation of his work in this country within the three years during which they had proposed to reserve the right of translation for him, his work should be protected against unauthorized translations for a period of ten years from the date of publication of such translation (a).

Suggestions as to dramatic pieces and right of performance.

As to the right of translation and adaptation of dramatic pieces, and the right of performance of translations and adaptations, they recommended that there should be no obligation to publish a literal translation in order to acquire these rights, but that, in countries with which international treaties exist, a right to translate and adapt to the English stage should be reserved to the foreign dramatist, for a period of three years from publication, or first public representation of the original work. And they further recommended that if an authorized translation or adaptation were published in this country within the three years, the dramatist's work should be protected against unauthorized translations, adaptations, and imitations, for a period of ten years from publication or first public representation in this country of the translation or adaptation (b).

They thought that translators, whether of plays or books, and adapters of dramatic works to the English stage, should have the same rights as authors of original works; and that the right of representation on the stage of a translation or adaptation should endure for the same term as if the translation or adaptation were an original work.

Importation of copies prohibited.

Copies of books wherein copyright is subsisting printed in foreign countries, other than those wherein the book was first published, are prohibited to be imported.

(a) Par. 279–283.   (b) Par. 290.

The 10th section of the 7 Vict. c. 12, provides that no CAP. XVII. copies of books wherein there shall be any subsisting copyright under or by virtue of that Act, or of any Order in Council made in pursuance thereof, printed or reprinted in any foreign country, except that in which such books were first published, shall be imported into any part of the British dominions, except by or with the consent of the registered proprietor of the copyright or his agent authorized in writing, and if imported contrary to such prohibition, the same and the importers thereof are made subject to the enactments in force relating to goods prohibited to be imported by any Act relating to the customs; and as respects any such copies so prohibited to be imported, and also as respects any copies unlawfully printed in any place whatsoever of any books wherein there shall be any subsisting copyright as aforesaid, any person who shall in any part of the British dominions import such prohibited or unlawfully printed copies, or, who knowing such copies to be so unlawfully imported or unlawfully printed, shall sell, publish, or expose to sale or hire, or shall cause to be sold, published, or exposed to sale or hire, or have in his possession for sale or hire, any such copies so unlawfully imported or unlawfully printed, such offender shall be liable to a special action on the case at the suit of the proprietor of such copyright, to be brought and prosecuted in the same courts and in the same manner, and with the like restrictions upon the proceedings of the defendant, as are respectively prescribed in the Copyright Amendment Act with relation to actions thereby authorized to be brought by proprietors of copyright against persons importing or selling books unlawfully printed in the British dominions.

And by the 9th section of the 15 Vict. c. 12, these provisions are extended, that section enacting that all copies of any works of literature or art wherein there is any subsisting copyright by virtue of the International Copyright Act and the 15 Vict. c. 12, or of any Order in Council made in pursuance of such Acts or

Extended to unauthorized translations.

either of them, and which are printed, reprinted, or made in any foreign country except that in which such work shall be first published, and all unauthorized translations of any book or dramatic piece, the publication or public representation in the British dominions of translations whereof not authorized as in the Act 15 Vict. c. 12, mentioned, shall for the time being be prevented under any Order in Council made in pursuance of such Act, shall be absolutely prohibited to be imported into any part of the British dominions, except by or with the consent of the registered proprietor of the copyright of such work, or of such book or piece, or his agent authorized in writing.

Provision of the 5 & 6 Vict. c. 45, as to forfeiture, &c., to extend to works prohibited to be imported under this Act.

And it is further provided that the provision of the 5 & 6 Vict. c. 45, for the forfeiture, seizure and destruction of any printed book first published in the United Kingdom wherein there shall be copyright, and reprinted in any country out of the British dominions, and imported into any part of the British dominions by any person not being the proprietor of the copyright, or a person authorized by such proprietor, shall extend and be applicable to all copies of any works of literature and art, and to all translations, the importation whereof into any part of the British dominions is prohibited under the 15 Vict. c. 12 (a).

INTERNATIONAL COPYRIGHT WITH AMERICA.

An English author or publisher has no right as against an American publisher who reprints and issues his work in America. Therefore, immediately on publication of a work in this country, it may be with impunity reproduced on the other side of the Atlantic; and there is no legal obligation on the part of the American reproducer to pay a single farthing in respect of the copyright. The British author or publisher has of course power to prevent the importation of these piratical copies into this country, but

(a) Sect. 9.

the real hardship (if so it may be called) is that by reason of the reproduction in America, by the American publisher, he loses that profit which would otherwise accrue from the sale of copies in which he had an interest to the American public., The American readers are infinitely more numerous than the English, and the English author frequently finds that, whereas in this country he has realised perhaps next to nothing, the American publisher, who has merely reproduced his work abroad, has made large profits thereby.

There appears to be a growing feeling, both in America and in this country, that something should be done for the protection of authors and publishers, and the eyes of the public are opening to the justice and policy of effecting a settlement of this question, which has recently been, and still is, so much discussed. However, there is no disguising the fact that there is a strong disinclination to an arrangement for international copyright on the part of certain publishing houses in the United States. Nor is this repugnance on their part unnatural. The United States have many advantages over this country from the absence of an international law of copyright, and the great disparity of interest which the two countries would respectively reap from such an arrangement is one of the greatest difficulties in the way of any arrangement and settlement of the question being come to. The works of American authors are, generally speaking, far less in demand in England than those of British writers in the United States; and in addition to this, the reproducer in America has a wider public to provide for than his rival in this country. The American publishers are themselves sufficiently protected by their custom in the publishing trade that the man who first re-issues any work of an English author retains a monopoly of future productions from the same pen. No other publisher will interfere with him, and the amount he pays as acknowledgment depends wholly upon his sense of honour. In the case of publishers of reputation perhaps no great evil results from this arrangement, yet the

CAP. XVII. English author is left completely at the mercy of the American publisher.

A bill was introduced in Congress by Mr. Cox, dated December 6, 1871, which would have required reciprocal action on the part of our Government; and another in the publishers' interest by Mr. Appleton, and a third was presented by the executive committee of the International Copyright Association of the United States, in the interest of the copyright owners (a). As a compromise between these interests of authors and publishers a fourth bill was presented on the 20th February, 1872, which was as follows :—

An Act to secure a Copyright to Foreign Authors and Artists.

Be it enacted by the Senate and House of Representatives of the United States of America, in Congress assembled :

Sect. 1. That any author and artist who is not a citizen of the United States may secure a copyright for his or her work, in accordance with the regulations of the United States Copyright Act, provided such author and artist shall manufacture and publish said works in the United States.

This seems only a fair protection to the American people generally, for otherwise they would be seriously affected. In the bills presented to Congress in the interest of the authors this provision was omitted, and

(a) The brevity of the bill admits of its introduction here :—

An Act to secure Authors the Right of Property in their Works.

Be it enacted by the Senate and House of Representatives of the United States in Congress assembled:

1. All rights of property secured to citizens of the United States of America by existing copyright laws of the United States are hereby secured to the citizens and subjects of every country the Government of which secures reciprocal rights to citizens of the United States.

2. This Act shall take effect two years from the date of its passage.

This bill was forwarded to Washington with the sanction of William Cullen Bryant, Henry W. Longfellow, Richard Grant White, Francis Lieber, Professor Barnard of Columbia College, and other literary men of distinction ; and of George P. Putman, and Henry Holt, publishers of high respectability.

it was always alleged by the American publishers that the treaty was sought primarily in the interests of the English publisher, and yet when the bill introduced by Mr. Appleton contained a similar provision, it was urged that if it were conceded that English publishers could in any way, direct or indirect, extend their copyrights to that country, it would be a matter of comparatively small importance to American publishers, who were not themselves manufacturers, whether the books were made there or in England, since in that case the protection of the English publisher, which would be in the copyright, would be absolute, and shield him from all competition.

Sect. 2.—That any author who is not a citizen of the United States may secure the right of translation of his or her work, whether the original work be published in a foreign country or in the United States, provided that upon the first publication of such original work, the author shall have announced on its title-page his intention of translating it, and the original work shall have been registered in the office of the librarian of the Congress of the United States, and a copy of it shall have been deposited in the library of Congress within one month after its first publication in a foreign country, for copyright in accordance with the regulations of the United States Copyright Act, and provided also that the author shall manufacture and publish the translation of his or her work in the United States.

Sect. 3.—This Act shall take effect from the date of its passage.

A report adverse to the bill was made to the Senate in February, 1873, by Mr Morrill from the joint committee on the library, to whom the subject had been referred, and thus the question has been shelved for the time. The report closed as follows :—" Your committee are satisfied that no form of international copyright can fairly be urged upon Congress, upon reasons of general equity or of constitutional law. That the adoption of any plan for the purpose which has been laid before us would be of very doubtful advantage to American authors as a class, and would be, not only an unquestionable and permanent injury to the manufacturing interests concerned in producing books, but a hindrance to the diffusion of knowledge among the people and to the cause of universal education ; that no plan for the protection of foreign authors has yet been devised which can unite the support of all, or nearly all, who profess to be favourable to the general object in view, and that, in the opinion of your committee, any project for an international copyright will be found upon mature deliberation to be inexpedient."

Colonial copyright.
By the 5 & 6 Vict. c. 45, the copyright of books, &c., printed in the United Kingdom is extended to all the British dominions ; the words " British dominions," meaning "all parts of the United Kingdom of Great Britain and Ireland, the islands of Jersey and Guernsey, all parts of the East and West Indies, and all the colonies, settlements, and possessions of the Crown which now are or hereafter may be acquired ;" and the 8 & 9 Vict. c. 93, concerning the trade of the colonies, absolutely prohibited these dependencies from importing pirated editions of copyright works. Practically, this last enactment was unavailing. Large quantities of cheap reprints of British copyright books continued to be imported from the United States into the British American possessions. Remonstrances against these irregularities at length led to some special legislation.

In 1847 the 10 & 11 Vict. c. 95, was passed for enabling Her Majesty by Order in Council to suspend the enactment contained in the Copyright Act, 1842, against the importation into any part of Her Majesty's colonies, &c., of " foreign reprints " of English copyright works.

The Act provides that in case the legislative authorities in any British possession shall be disposed to make due provision for securing or protecting the rights of British authors in such possession, and shall pass an Act to make an Ordinance for that purpose, and shall transmit the same in the proper manner to the Secretary of State, in

order that it may be submitted to Her Majesty, and CAP. XVII.
in case Her Majesty should be of opinion that such Act
or Ordinance is sufficient for the purpose of securing
to British authors reasonable protection within such
possession, it shall be lawful for Her Majesty, if she
think fit so to do, to express her royal approval of such
Act or Ordinance, and thereupon to issue an Order in
Council declaring that so long as the provisions of such
Act or Ordinance continue in force within such colony,
the prohibitions contained in the aforesaid Acts (*i.e.* the
Copyright Act, 1842, and a certain Customs Act) and
therein before recited, and any prohibitions contained in
the said Act, or in any other Acts, against the importing, selling, letting out to hire, exposing for sale or
hire, or possessing, foreign reprints of books first composed, written, printed or published in the United Kingdom, and entitled to copyright therein, shall be suspended so far as regards such colony; and thereupon
such Act or Ordinance shall come into operation, except
so far as may be otherwise directed by such Order in
Council. Every such Order in Council to be published in
the *London Gazette*, and Orders in Council and the
colonial Acts or Ordinances to be laid before Parliament
within a certain specified time. Accordingly, the
following colonies have placed themselves within its provisions, viz.: Canada, December 12, 1850; St. Vincent,
August 18, 1852; Jamaica, December 29 and June 25,
1857; Mauritius, April 1, 1853; Nevis, Grenada, Newfoundland, July 30, 1849; St. Christopher, November 6,
1849; St. Lucia, November 13, 1850; New Brunswick,
August 11, 1848; St. Kitts, British Guiana, October 23,
1851; Prince Edward's Island, October 31, 1848; Barba-
does, December 16, 1848; Bermuda, February 13, 1849;
the Bahamas, May 21, 1849; Cape of Good Hope, March
10, 1851; Nova Scotia, August 11, 1848; Antigua, June
19, 1850; and Natal, May 16, 1857. In fact, all the
important colonies with the exception of Australia. The
understood arrangement is, that English publishers shall

2 K 2

furnish catalogues of their copyrights to the custom-house authorities in the different colonies, as a guide for exacting what is termed the protective duties (amounting in Canada to 12½ per cent. *ad valorem*). These measures are next to inoperative, and the whole thing is little better than a delusion ; so little is collected, that British authors and publishers reap either nothing or some paltry and insignificant amount, and they have now (a) generally ceased to give themselves any concern in the matter. In Canada the evil is experienced to a greater extent than in other colonies. Its proximity to the United States need only be recalled to mind to suggest the quarter from which the unauthorized reproductions of British works chiefly proceed. In short, unauthorized cheap reprints of British copyright works may be said to be freely imported into and sold in Canada and the adjacent provinces, this kind of trade in itself tending to indispose the United States to enter into an international treaty with the United Kingdom.

These statements are confirmed by a letter dated the 11th of June, 1868, from Mr. John Lovell (a Montreal publisher) to Mr. Rose, which appears in the correspondence carried on between the Canadian Government and the Imperial authorities upon the subject of "Copyright Law in Canada," and lately published. Mr. Lovell says: "At present only a few hundred copies pay duty, but many thousands pass into the country without registration, and pay nothing at all ; thus having the effect of seriously injuring the publishers of Great Britain, to the consequent advantage of the United States. I may add that, on looking over the custom-house entries to-day, I have found that not a single entry of an American reprint of

(a) A ludicrous but significant illustration of the value of colonial copyright to English authors is furnished in a document sent in 1875 to Archbishop Trench from Her Majesty's Treasury. It announced that the sum of elevenpence was in the hands of the Paymaster-General, and would be paid to Dr. Trench on presentation of a signed receipt. It appears that the elevenpence represented the whole amount the colonial authorities in Canada had levied on the Archbishop's behalf during nearly as many years, that is, at the rate of a penny a year. Yet it is well known that Dr. Trench's books had there a large and constant sale.

an English copyright (except the reviews and one or two Cap. XVII. magazines) has been made since the 3rd day of April last, though it is notorious that an edition of 1000 of a popular work coming under this description has been received and sold within the last few days by one book-seller in this city."

The Royal Copyright Commissioners in their report in The Copy- June, 1878, referring to the operation of the Foreign right Com-
missioners on Reprints Act, say, "So far as British authors and owners the "Foreign
Reprints Act." of copyright are concerned, the Act has proved a complete failure. Foreign reprints of copyright works have been largely introduced into the colonies, and notably American reprints into.the Dominion of Canada; but no returns, or returns of an absurdly small amount, have been made to the authors and owners. It appears from official reports that during the ten years ending in 1876, the amount received from the whole of the nineteen colonies which have taken advantage of the Act, was only £1155 13s. 2½d., of which £1084 13s. 3½d. was received from Canada; and that, of these colonies, seven paid nothing whatever to the authors, while six now and then paid small sums amounting to a few shillings."

In 1875, the Dominion Parliament passed an Act giving The Canadian
Act of 1875. copyright for twenty-eight years to any person domiciled in Canada, or in any part of the British dominions, or being the citizen of any country having an international copyright treaty with Great Britain. To secure copy-right, the book must be published or republished in Canada. Section 15 of the Act provides that "works of which the copyright has been granted and is subsisting in the United Kingdom, and copyright of which is not secured or subsisting in Canada under any Canadian or Provincial Act, shall upon being printed and published, or reprinted and republished in Canada, be entitled to copyright under this Act; but nothing in this Act shall be held to prohibit the importation from the United Kingdom of copies of such works legally printed there."

By the 38 & 39 Vict. c. 53, the Queen was authorized

to assent to the Canada bill, and by the 4th section of this Act it was further provided that " where any book in which, at the time when the said reserved bill comes into operation, there is copyright in the United Kingdom, or any book in which thereafter there shall be such copyright becomes entitled to copyright in Canada, in pursuance of the provisions of the said reserved bill, it shall be unlawful for any person, not being the owner, in the United Kingdom, of the copyright in such book, or some person authorized by him, to import into the United Kingdom any copies of such book reprinted or republished in Canada."   By section 5, the Order in Council of 1868 is continued in force, " so far as relates to books which are not entitled to copyright for the time being, in pursuance of the said reserved bill."

Under this law it appears the Canadian publishers considered themselves free to republish English copyright books in Canada without any consideration whatever.   Accordingly, on the appearance of Mr. Samuel Smiles's ' Thrift ' in England at the end of 1875, Messrs. Belford of Montreal at once proceeded to reprint and republish the book without any communication with Mr. Smiles, the author, or Mr. Murray, the publisher of the book.   The Copyright Association, assuming this to be a test case, then proceeded to dispute the right of the Canadian publishers to print and publish English copyright books without permission.   The case of *Smiles* v. *Belford* was accordingly argued before Vice-Chancellor Proudfoot, upon which he gave his judgment, which was in favour of the plaintiff on all points.   Messrs. Belford then appealed to the Canadian publishers, and they raised among them a considerable subscription to enable the case to be tried before the highest Canadian Court.   The appeal was argued before the Chancellor, Mr. Justice Burton, Mr. Justice Paterson, and Mr. Justice Moys, and their decision was again in favour of the plaintiff, Messrs. Belford's appeal being unanimously dismissed with costs.

The suggestions of the Royal Copyright Commissioners Cap. XVII. on the subject of colonial copyright are numerous. They Suggestions of Copyright Commissioners as to colonial copyright. recommended that the difficulty of securing a supply of English literature at cheap prices for colonial readers should be met in two ways : first, by the introduction of a licensing system in the colonies ; and, secondly, by continuing, though with alterations, the provisions of the Foreign Reprints Act.

In proposing the introduction of a licensing system, they did not intend to interfere with the power now possessed by the colonial legislatures of dealing with the subject of copyright, so far as their own colonies are concerned. They recommended that in case the owner of a copyright work should not avail himself of the provisions of the copyright law (if any) in a colony, and in case no adequate provision be made by republication in the colony or otherwise, within a reasonable time after publication elsewhere, for a supply of the work sufficient for general sale and circulation in the colony, a licence might, upon an application, be granted to republish the work in the colony, subject to a royalty in favour of the copyright owner, of not less than a specified sum per cent. on the retail price, as might be settled by any local law. Effective provision for the due collection and transmission to the copyright owner of such royalty should be made by such law (a).

The Commissioners could not recommend the simple Not recommend repeal of Foreign Reprints Act. repeal of the Foreign Reprints Act. They believed that although the system of republication under a licence, might be well adapted to some of the larger colonies which have printing and publishing firms of their own, and which could reprint and republish for themselves with every prospect of fair remuneration, it would be practically inapplicable in the case of many of the smaller colonies. These latter at present depend almost wholly on foreign reprints for a supply of literature ; and to sweep away the Foreign Reprints Act without establishing some other system of supply would be to

(a) Par. 207.

deprive them in a great measure of English books (a). The Commissioners considered that it had been proved that the existing law in the different colonies had failed to secure remuneration to proprietors of copyright, and therefore they suggested that power should be given to Her Majesty to repeal the existing Orders in Council, and that no future Order in Council should be made under the Foreign Reprints Act until sufficient provision had been made by local law for better securing the payment of the duty upon foreign reprints to the owners of copyright works (b).

It appeared to the Commissioners that possibly some arrangement might be effected by which all foreign reprints should be sent to certain specified places in the colony, and should be there stamped with date of admission upon payment of the duty, which could then be transmitted here to the Treasury or Board of Trade for the author. All copies of foreign reprints not so stamped, they thought should be liable to seizure, and possibly some penalty might be also affixed to the dealing with unstamped copies.

And having regard to the power which they had contemplated, for authors to obtain colonial copyright by republication in the colonies, and to the licensing system which they had suggested, they recommended that when an Order in Council for the admission of foreign reprints has been made, such reprints should not, unless with the consent of the owner of the copyright, be imported into a colony—

1. Where the owner has availed himself of the local copyright law, if any.

2. Where an adequate provision, as pointed out above, has been made ; or,

3. After there has been a republication under the licensing system (c).

And, lastly, the Commissioners were of opinion that colonial reprints of copyright works first published in the United Kingdom should not be admitted into the United Kingdom without the consent of the copyright owner;

(a) Par. 211.   (b) Par. 213   (c) Par. 215, 216.

and conversely, that reprints in the United Kingdom of CAP. XVII.
copyright works first published in any colony, should not
be admitted into such colony without the consent of the
copyright owners (a).

In the late case of *Routledge* v. *Low,* Lords Cairns,
Cranworth, Chelmsford, Westbury, and Colonsay, unanimously held that to acquire a copyright under 5 & 6
Vict. c. 45, the work must be first published in the *United
Kingdom.* The law now, therefore, is, that if a literary or
musical work be first published in the *United Kingdom,* it
may be protected from infringement in any part of the
British dominions ; but if, on the other hand, any such
work be first published in India, Canada, Jamaica, or any
other British possession not included in the *United
Kingdom,* no copyright can be acquired in that work,
excepting only such (if any) as the local laws of the
colony, &c., where it is first published may afford.

This opinion has caused great and general dissatisfaction
in the colonies and India ; it has either destroyed all copyright property in the numerous works since 1842, which
have been first published there, or rendered such property
comparatively worthless ; and this hardship is increased
by the fact that, since 1842, it has been, and still is, compulsory upon all publishers in the British dominions,
gratuitously to send one copy of every book published by
them to the British Museum, and on application four to
the libraries of Oxford, Cambridge, &c. (b).

The German Diet introduced a convention on the subject International
of international copyright between the different members copyright
conventions.
of the Confederation in 1837. Austria and Prussia gave
in their adherence on behalf of those portions of their
territories which did not belong to the Confederation.
Austria and Sardinia had a convention in 1840, to which
the other states of Italy, and one of the cantons, adhered.
In 1837, Prussia passed a law of reciprocity in this matter
with all foreign states.

(a) Par. 225, 226.
(b) See an able article in the *Athenæum,* Nov. 1820, 69.

Cap. XVII.

The following conventions have been entered into by Great Britain:

Prussia	.	. May 13, 1846.	Anhalt	.	. Feb. 8, 1853.
Saxony	.	. Aug. 24, 1846.	Hamburg	.	. Aug. 16, 1853.
Brunswick	.	March 30, 1847.	Belgium	.	. Aug. 13, 1854.
Thuringian Union	July	1, 1847.	Prussia (additional)	June	14, 1855.
Hanover	.	. Aug. 4, 1847.	Spain (a)	.	. July 7, 1857.
Oldenburg	.	Dec. 28, 1847.	Sardinia	.	. Nov. 30, 1860.
French Republic	Nov.	3, 1851.			

Copyright in India.

An Act of the Legislative Council of India was passed on the subject of Copyright in the year 1847. After reciting that doubts might exist whether copyright could be enforced by the common law, or by virtue of the principles of equity, in the territories subject to the government of the East India Company, and whether the Act of 5 & 6 Vict. c. 45, had made provision for the enforcement of the right against persons not being British subjects, it enacts that copyright in every book published in India in the author's lifetime, after the 28th of August, 1833, shall endure for the natural life of the author, and seven years after, or for forty years if the seven years sooner expire: and copyright in any book published after the death of the author shall endure for forty-two years, and shall be the property of the proprietor of the author's manuscript.

The enactments are almost in every respect similar to those contained in the 5 & 6 Vict. c. 45. The book of registry is to be kept in the office of the Secretary to the Government of India for the Home Department, and may be inspected at any time on payment of eight annas for every entry searched for or inspected; and certified copies of entries may be obtained on payment of two rupees. A like sum must be paid on registering any work.

A like power to that vested in the Judicial Committee of the Privy Council by the 5th sect. of the 5 & 6 Vict. c. 45, is as to books in India vested in the Governor-General in Council.

(a) Notice has been given by the Spanish Government for the termination of the International Copyright Treaty, and it expired therefore on March 17, 1880.

CHAPTER XVIII.

COPYRIGHT IN FOREIGN COUNTRIES.

France.

THE infringement of copyright was formerly visited with far heavier penalties in France than in this country. The printing a work, the sole right to which belonged to another, was regarded as little better than theft; indeed, it was said that such conduct was worse than to enter a neighbour's house and steal his goods; for, in the latter case, negligence might be imputed to him for permitting the thief to enter, whereas in the former, it was stealing a thing confided to the public honour (*a*). *Copyright in France.*

The protection afforded by the various edicts of the French kings to the authors of literary works was, however, taken away by the famous decree of the National Assembly, by which all privileges of whatever kind were abolished (*b*).

Before entering into any details of the law of copyright under the different heads of literature, the drama, music and art, it will tend to make the subject clearer, and will be more useful for reference, first, to give an account of the principal laws on the subject in their order of date, and then touch upon the application of these laws.

The first decree on copyright is that of 13th to 19th January, 1791, concerning public performances (*spectacles*). *Decree of 13 Jan., 1791. The drama.*

Art. 1. Gives a right to all citizens to open a theatre.

(*a*) Lowndes on Copy.
(*b*) 4th of August, 1789; Lowndes on Copy., App. 116.

Art. 2. The works of authors dead five years or more before the date of this decree are public property, and may, notwithstanding all ancient privileges which are abolished, be represented in any theatre.

Art. 3. The works of living authors cannot be represented in any public theatre throughout France without the formal consent in writing of such author under penalty of confiscation of the gross receipts (*du produit total*) from such representations for the benefit of the authors.

Art. 4. The provision of article 3 applies to works already represented, whatever the former rule may have been ; nevertheless agreements which may have been made (*les actes qui auraient été passés*) between comedians and living authors or authors dead within five years before the date of this decree, shall be performed.

Art. 5. The heirs or assigns of authors shall be the proprietors of their works for the period of five years after the death of the author.

The drama. Decree, 19 July, 1791. Then follows a further decree on the same subject dated 19th July to 6th August, 1791.

Art. 1. Conformably to the provisions of articles 3 and 4 of the decree of 13th January last, concerning public performances (*spectacles*), the works of living authors, although represented before that date, whether engraved or printed or neither, cannot be represented in any public theatre throughout the kingdom without the formal written consent of the authors, or in the case of authors dead within five years before the 13th day of January, that of their heirs or assigns, under penalty of confiscation of the gross receipts from such representations for the benefit of the author, his heirs or assigns.

Art. 2. Agreements between authors and managers (*entrepreneurs de spectacles*) shall be perfectly free, and no municipal or other public functionaries may tax any play, nor diminish nor increase the price agreed upon; the remuneration of authors, agreed upon between them or their representatives and such managers, can neither

be seised nor held back (*arrêtée*) by the creditors of such Cap. XVIII.
manager.

Then follows the decree of the National Convention of Literary
19th to 24th July, 1793, relating to the right of property copyright.
of authors in works of literature (*écrits*) of all kinds, of Decree, 19
composers of music, of painters and designers (*des-* July, 1793.
sinateurs). This may be looked upon as the fundamental
law on copyright although the majority of its provisions
have been modified by subsequent legislation. They are
as follows :

Art. 1. The authors of writings (*écrits*) of all kinds,
composers of music, painters and designers, who engrave
pictures or drawings, shall enjoy during their whole life
the exclusive right to sell, cause to be sold, and distribute
their works within the territory of the Republic, and to
assign their property in such right in whole or in part.

Art. 2. Their heirs or assigns shall enjoy the same
right for the space of ten years after the death of the
author.

Art. 3. The magistrates (*officiers de paix*) shall be bound
to confiscate for the benefit of the authors, composers,
painters or designers and others, their heirs or assigns, all
copies of editions printed or engraved without the formal
permission in writing of the authors.

Art. 4. Every infringer (*contrefacteur*) shall be bound
to pay to the true proprietor a sum equivalent to the
price of 3000 copies of the original edition.

Art. 5. Every seller of a pirated edition, if not convicted of being the infringer, shall be bound to pay to
the true proprietor a sum equivalent to the price of 500
copies of the original edition.

Art. 6. Every citizen who produces a work whether of
literature or engraving (*gravure*) of whatever kind, must
deposit two copies, for which he will get a receipt duly
signed, failing which he can have no right of action against
an infringer.

Art. 7. The heirs of an author of a work of literature
or engraving, or of every other production of the in-

Cap. XVIII. tellect or genius which can be classed as a work of art, shall have the exclusive property of such work during ten years (a).

Posthumous works.
Proprietors by descent, or any other title, of posthumous, literary and dramatic works have the same rights as the author; and the provisions of the law concerning the exclusive property of authors and its duration are applicable to such proprietors (b).

Procedure and remedies.
The "Code Civil," articles 544, 1382, the *Code de Procédure Civile*, articles 59 and 1036, and the *Code d'instruction criminelle*, articles 637 and 638, define property in general, indicate the remedies and procedure of injured parties, and limit the time during which actions may be

(a) These provisions embrace "les auteurs d'écrits en tout genre," and upon this expression M Merlin has made the following commentary: "Mais il ne faut pas séparer, dans cet article, les mots *écrits en tout genre* de l'expression *auteurs*; et la propriété, dont cet article déclare que les *écrits en tout genre* sont susceptibles, ne peut évidemment être réclamée que par ceux qui en sont *auteurs*, dans la véritable acception de ce terme.

"Or, le mot *auteurs*, quel sens a-t-il en général? Quel sens a-t-il relativement aux écrits? Quel sens a-t-il dans la loi du 19 juillet 1793?

"En général, le mot *auteurs* désigne, suivant la définition qu'en donne le Dictionnaire de l'Académie française, celui qui est la première cause de quelque chose; et il est aussi, suivant la même définition, synonyme d'inventeur.

"Appliqué aux écrits, le mot *auteur* se dit (toujours suivant le même Dictionnaire) *de celui qui a composé un livre, qui a fait quelques ouvrages d'esprit en vers ou en prose*; et il est bien clair qu'en ce sens, le mot *auteur* est opposé à *copiste*.

"Enfin, la loi du 19 juillet 1793 ne permet pas de douter qu'elle n'exclue également les copistes de la dénomination d'auteurs. *Les héritiers de l'auteur d'un ouvrage de littérature ou de gravure*, dit-elle, art. 7, *ou de toute autre production de l'esprit ou du génie, qui appartient aux beaux-arts, en auront la propriété exclusive pendant dix années*. Ces termes, *ou de toute autre production de l'esprit ou du génie, qui appartient aux beaux-arts*, ne sont ni obscurs ni équivoques. Ils signifient clairement que les productions de l'esprit, ou du génie sont de deux sortes; que les unes consistent en ouvrages de littérature; que les autres appartiennent aux beaux-arts; mais que nul ne peut être réputé auteur soit d'un ouvrage de littérature, soit d'un ouvrage d'arts, si ce n'est pas à son esprit ou à son génie qu'en est due la production.

"Donc, les expressions d'*écrits* en tout genre ne sont employées, dans l'art. 1er de la même loi, que pour désigner tous les genres de compositions littéraires.

"Donc, elles n'y désignent pas les écrits qui ne seraient pas de compositions, mais de simples copies.

"Donc, celui qui ne fait que copier une composition littéraire ne peut jamais être réputé auteur de la copie de cette composition, ni par conséquent en avoir la *propriété*, dans le sens attaché à ce mot par la loi du 19 juillet 1793, et par le code pénal 1810." Merlin, Répertoire de Jurisprudence, titre 'Contrefaçon,' § xi.

(b) Decrees, 8 Dec., 1805, 8 June, 1806; see also decree of 15 Oct. 1812.

brought. These general provisions are also applicable CAP. XVIII.
to copyright.

The *Code Pénal* of March 1810, articles 425 to 429, Penal Code
makes piracy a misdemeanor (*délit*). These articles are as on piracy.
follows:

" *Toute édition d'écrits, de composition musicale, de
dessin, de peinture, ou de toute autre production, imprimée
ou gravée en entier ou en partie, au mépris des lois et
réglemens relatifs à la propriété des auteurs, est une contrefaçon ; et toute contrefaçon est un délit.*

" *Le débit d'ouvrages contrefaits, l'introduction sur le
territoire français d'ouvrages qui, après avoir été imprimés
en France, ont été contrefaits chez l'étranger, sont un délit
de la même espèce.*

" *La peine contre le contrefacteur, ou contre l'introducteur,
sera une amende de cent francs au moins et de deux mille
francs au plus ; et contre le débitant, une amende de vingt-
cinq francs au moins et de cinq cents francs au plus. La
confiscation de l'édition contrefaite sera prononcée tant
contre le contrefacteur que contre l'introducteur et le débitant.
Les planches, moules, ou matrices des objets contrefaits,
seront aussi confisqués.*

" *Tout directeur, tout entrepreneur de spectacle, tout association d'artistes, qui aura fait représenter sur son théâtre
des ouvrages dramatiques au mépris des lois et réglemens
relatifs à la propriété des auteurs, sera puni d'une amende
de cinquante francs au moins, de cinq cents francs au plus,
et de la confiscation des recettes.*

" *Dans les cas prévus par les quatre articles précédens
le produit des confiscations, ou les recettes confisquées, seront
remis au propriétaire, pour l'indemniser d'autant du pré-
judice qu'il aura souffert ; le surplus de son indemnité,
ou l'entière indemnité, s'il n'y a eu ni vente d'objets confisqués ni saisie de recettes, sera réglé par les voies ordi-
naires* " (*a*).

The law of 3rd August, 1844, provides that the widows The Drama.
and children of the authors of dramatic works shall have Law of 3 Aug.,
1844.

(*a*) *Code Pénal*, lib. iii. tit. ii. art. 425-429.

from that date the right during twenty years to authorize the representation and to confer the advantages arising from such works (*d'en conférer la jouissance*) in conformity with the provisions of articles 39 and 40 of the imperial decree of the 5th February, 1810.

Reciprocity. Decree, 28 March, 1852. By the decree of 28th March, 1852, it is made unlawful without the permission of the author to publish a work already published in a foreign country with which no copyright convention exists. The provisions of this decree are as follows :—

Art. 1. Piracy on French territory of works published abroad and comprised in article 425 of the Penal Code constitutes a misdemeanor (*délit*).

Art. 2. The same holds good with regard to the sale, export, and consignment of pirated works. The export and consignment of such works are offences of the same kind as the introduction into French territory of works, which after having been printed in France have been pirated abroad.

Art. 3. The offences defined by the preceding articles are punished in accordance with articles 427 and 429 of the Penal Code, and article 463 is also applicable.

Art. 4. Nevertheless a prosecution can only take place under the conditions imposed with respect to works published in France by article 6 of the law of 19th July, 1793, which relates to the formalities of deposit.

Copyright. Law, 8 April, 1854. By the law of 8th April, 1854, the twenty years term of copyright vested in the children of the author was extended to thirty years. This law contains only one article, which is to the following effect: "The widows of authors, composers, and artists shall enjoy during life, the rights guaranteed by the laws of 13th January, 1791, and 19th July, 1793, the decree of 5th February, 1810, the law of 3rd August, 1844, and all other laws and decrees relating to this subject. The duration of the benefit given to children by the same laws and decrees, is increased to thirty years, dating either from the death of such author, composer, or artist, or from the cessation of the rights of his widow.

Lastly, we have the law of the 14th July, 1866, by which protection of copyright is given to all heirs of an author for fifty years after his death. The provisions of this law are as follows: "The duration of the rights given by former laws to the heirs, irregular successors (*successeurs irréguliers*), donees, and legatees of authors, composers, or artists, is extended to fifty years from the death of the author.

"During this term of fifty years the widow of such author, whatever may be the provisions of the marriage contract (*le régime matrimonial*), and independently of her rights under the *régime de la communauté*, has a life interest in the rights which her deceased husband has not alienated by assignment during life, or by will.

"Nevertheless if the author leave *héritiers à réserve* such life interest is reduced in favour of such heirs in accordance with the provisions of articles 913 and 915 of the Civil Code (a).

"This interest is not given if at the time of the author's death there be a decree of separation (*séparation de corps*) in force against his widow : it ceases as soon as the widow remarries.

"The rights of *héritiers à réserve* and of other heirs or successors during this period of fifty years are in other respects regulated by the provisions of the Civil Code.

"When the succession falls to the state, the exclusive right is extinguished, without prejudice to the rights of creditors, and contracts for assignment which may have been entered into by the author or his representative."

The above laws for the most part deal with the duration of copyright and its mode of descent. In other respects the provisions are general and somewhat difficult

(a) "*Héritiers à réserve*" are those heirs of a man who, by articles 913–915 of the Civil Code, are entitled to a certain share of his property, and whom he cannot disinherit either by act *inter vivos* or by will. M. Fliniaux remarks on this article : "C'est par une erreur de droit qu'il a été déclaré réductible conformément aux articles 913 et 915 du Code Civil ; c'est l'article 1094 du même code, relatif au droit du conjoint, qu'il aurait fallu viser. (Fliniaux, Prop. industrielle et prop. litt. et art. en France et à l'étranger : Paris, 1879. An excellent work, of which free use has been made in this chapter.)

to apply in particular cases. Hence it will be advisable to refer to the cases which have been decided in the French Courts of Law for information on many points.

Literary Copyright.

Literary copyright.   The works of literature protected by the copyright laws are comprised in the terms "*écrits en tout genre*" which occur in the law of 19th July, 1793. The following are a few of the principal decisions on the meaning of this expression.

What protected.   A compilation effected by an author by means of analysis and classification, such as a descriptive catalogue, a nautical almanac, or a dictionary, and having a scientific or literary character, is entitled to protection.

A newspaper may reproduce news, whether telegraphic or not, received and published by another newspaper (a). But literary articles and romances in a newspaper remain the property of the author, provided it be duly registered (b). Public dissertations and lectures of professors cannot be published without the consent of the authors (c). The publication of private correspondence is not allowed without the consent of the writer or his heirs (d).

Manuscripts form a distinct category, and can only be published by the heirs or assigns, and not by the creditors of the author (e). A translation is the property of the translator and cannot be copied (f), but it cannot be made without the consent of the author of the original or his legal representatives (g).

Duration.   The duration of literary copyright is regulated by the law cited above of the 14th July, 1866. By this law the

Rights of author's widow.   surviving widow has a right of survivorship over the works left by her husband, even when by the marriage settlement and the law of succession she has no such right in respect of other property of her husband : if the

(a) Cass. 8 Aug., 1861, Havas.
(b) Cass. 29 Oct. 1830, Le Pirate.
(c) Paris, 18 June, 1840, Hérit. Cuvier ; Lyon, 17 July, 1845, Marie.
(d) Paris, 11 June, 1875, Gentil.
(e) Dijon, 18 Feb. 1870, de Chapuys.
(f) Cass. 25 July, 1824, Ladvocat.
(g) Paris, 17 July, 1847, Leclerc.

author have assigned his rights the widow has no right of CAP. XVIII.
survivorship over the purchase-money (a).

The widower of an authoress has the same rights in Rights of
respect of her literary works as the widow of an author. widower of an
authoress.

The proprietors of posthumous works who publish them Posthumous
have the same rights as authors, on condition that they works.
do not publish such works in a collection with the other
works of the author (b).

The state enjoys copyright in perpetuity over works The state.
published by its order or by its agents (c).

In order that an author may be fully protected, and Registration
have a right of action in cases of piracy, he must and deposit.
deposit two copies of his work at the Ministry of the
Interior at Paris, and at the Prefecture in the departments,
in conformity with the law of 19th July, 1793 (art. 6), the
decree of 3rd Feb. 1810 (art. 48), and the orders of 24th
Oct. 1814 (arts. 4, 8), and of 9th Jan. 1828 (art. 1). A
receipt is given as evidence.

The copyright of a MS., even of a play already performed, is protected without the deposit of copies, so long
as it has not been made public by printing. But once
printed, the author or publisher who neglects the formality
of deposit in accordance with the provisions of the law,
cannot prosecute infringers of his rights (d).

Assignment of literary copyright is regulated by the Assignment.
general law of assignment of property. Heirs can assign their
rights like an author, either in whole, or in part, for a consideration or not. An author who has assigned the right to
publish an edition of one of his works, is bound not to publish a fresh edition before the former one is exhausted (e).
The assignment without any reserve of a work to which
an author has put his name, does not give the person to
whom it is assigned the absolute disposal of it to such
an extent that he can alter it by changes or additions (f).

(a) Fliniaux, l. c. p. 98.   (b) Fliniaux, l. c. p. 98.
(c) Cass. 27 May, 1842, Gros; Paris, 5 May, 1877, Peigné.
(d) Prop. litt. et art.: Pouillet, Paris, 1879.
(e) Cass. 22 Feb. 1847, Laurent.
(f) Paris, 14 Aug. 1860. Peigné. Seine, Tr. Civ. 12 Jan. 1875, Vve.
Michelet.

CAP. XVIII.   In those cases where an alteration in the law extends
the term of copyright granted to the heirs of an author,
the extended term is considered to belong to the family
of the author in preference to his assigns, and the term
vested in the persons to whom it has been assigned, is that
existing at the date of the assignment in conformity with
the Civil Code, art. 1153. Hence the extension of the
term of copyright granted by the laws of 8th April, 1854,
and the 14th July, 1866, is for the benefit of the author's
heirs, and not of the publishers to whom he may have
assigned his works (a).

Piracy.   Piracy under the French law is the illegal reproduction
of the works of another, literary or musical, not yet
public property, and which reproduction is made publicly
with the intention to injure, whether by printing or public
representation. Piracy gives rise, as a misdemeanor, to an
" action correctionnelle " ; if the intention to injure be not
proved, the author of the work reproduced may bring a
civil or commercial action for compensation in respect of
the damage done to him. Piracy is committed although
the offender may not have completed the printing of the
work.

A literal copy (la copie servile) of about one-fourth of a
work constitutes the offence of partial piracy. Il y a
également contrefaçon, quelle que soit la matière de la reproduction ou la qualité de l'auteur ou du propriétaire de
l'ouvrage contrefait. Elle est indépendante des moyens
à l'aide desquels elle est produite (b).

The following are a few decisions on cases of piracy.
1. Piracy is committed from the moment there is a
violation of the absolute right of property given by law,
no matter what be the merit or importance of the work
pirated (c). 2. It is piracy to copy without authorization a
work even of small extent and to annex it to another work

(a) Paris, 12 July, 1852; Cass. Ch. Crim. 29 April, 1876, Pradier;
Cass. Ch. req. 20 Nov. 1877, Degorce—Cadot.
(b) Code du Théâtre, &c. C. Le Senne, Paris, 1878.
(c) Paris, 11 March, 1869, aff. Godchau.

of a different author (*a*). 3. The composers of airs or of musical works can prevent such airs from being inserted without their consent in other works, even though they may have tolerated such insertion for a longer or shorter period.

The law prohibits piracy whether total or partial. There is no doubt that the protection of the law is extended to every work in its entirety, and to all its parts. It therefore follows that partial piracy is an offence of the same order as total piracy. The law has taken care expressly to provide for this, as may be seen from the words, "*en entier ou en partie*," in art. 425 of the Code Pénal (*b*).

Piracy, whether whole or partial, forbidden.

M. Renouard is of opinion that unauthorized translation is not piracy, because, first, the law is silent on this point, and, secondly, "*La différence de forme extérieure du langage*," says the learned author, "*empêche qu'il ne s'établisse ni confusion, ni rivalité. Les lecteurs ne seront probablement pas les mêmes. Quiconque sera capable de comprendre l'original ne manquera pas de le préférer à une traduction plus ou moins imparfaite. La gloire de l'auteur et la propagation de ses idées, la popularité de ses productions et leurs chances de débit, ont tout à gagner par l'existence des traductions et n'ont rien à y perdre.*" But at the same time he thinks that the question is not without difficulty.

Unauthorized translation.

M. Renouard's views are strongly opposed by M. Pouillet (*c*), who says, "*La contrefaçon, en effet, est pour nous l'atteinte portée au droit privatif, l'usurpation de la propriété ; c'est le fait de s'emparer, de profiter du travail d'autrui, sans son autorisation. Il y a contrefaçon, toutes les fois qu'on prend une œuvre qu'on n'a point faite soi-même, et que, sans permission de l'auteur, on la fait tourner à son propre profit. Si cela est, n'est-il pas certain que la traduction est une contrefaçon ?*"

Owing to their generality the provisions of the law of

(*a*) Paris, 27 June, 1812, aff. St. Georges.
(*b*) Traité, Prop. litt. et art. : Pouillet, Paris, 1879.
(*c*) Prop. litt. et art. : Pouillet, Paris, 1879.

CAP. XVIII. 1793, apply to every sort of reproduction which infringes the right of property of another. The translation of a French book into a foreign tongue is such a reproduction (a).

The following points have also been decided :

Points of note which have been decided.   1. That it is piracy to borrow from a published work, its subject, general plan, and the development of its episodes (b); 2. That it is piracy to publish in the form of a pamphlet the analysis of a play, even when accompanied with critical remarks, if such publication would clearly interfere with the sale of the original work (c); 3. That it is piracy for a newspaper to give literally an analysis of all the chapters of a romance, even when accompanied by critical remarks, if it is clear that such reproduction will interfere with the sale of the original, by revealing the plan and most important details of the work (d); 4. That it is a piratical reproduction to publish and sell a faithful *résumé* of a play so as to injure its sale (e); 5. That it is piracy on the part of an author to give his work a title analogous to that of another work already published, when he follows the plan and borrows passages from it (f).

Dramatic and Musical Works.

Dramatic and musical copyright.   The publication of dramatic and musical works is regulated by the same laws as those relating to literary works.

Operas, &c.   A work which consists of words and music by different authors is the joint property of the two, and cannot become public property until the rights of the heirs of each have expired: the unexpired rights of the heirs of one of the authors prolongs the existence of the rights of the heirs of the other author (g).

(a) Paris, 17 July, 1847, aff. Lecointe.
(b) Paris, 20 Feb. 1872, aff. Sarlit.
(c) Nîmes, 25 Feb. 1864, aff. Offray.
(d) Paris, 13 July, 1830, aff. Dartheuay, Dall. 30, 2, 235.
(e) Paris, 12 March, 1845, aff. Durand.
(f) Cass. 26 Nov. 1853, Laurent de Villedenil, Roland de Villargues, art. 425, Code Pénal.
(g) Paris, 27 June, 1866, Gérard.

It is lawful to appropriate the plot of a novel for the CAP. XVIII. purposes of a drama, but the characters, situations and episodes, must be changed (a).

Published dramatic works must be deposited like other Registration literary works—and the same with regard to music with a and deposit. text. In the case of music without words there is no law compelling deposit, but in practice it is generally made.

The exclusive right of representation of dramatic and Representa. musical works is by the law of 14th July, 1866, secured to tion. the author for life, and to his heirs for fifty years after his death, exactly as in the publication of works of literature.

The right of representation is distinct from the right of publication, each being guaranteed by different enactments, the former by the law of 1791 and art. 428 of the Penal Code, the latter by the law of 1793 and art. 425 of the Penal Code.

Before being represented every dramatic work must be submitted to authorities for approval (*censure*).

Every work intended for public performance is protected, as plays, operas, and musical compositions, whether vocal or instrumental.

The right of representation comprises as regards the author merely the right to authorize the representation of his work: the right of publication comprises the right of reproduction (*le droit de copie*) properly so called, the right to reproduce the work by copies (*exemplaires*) printed, engraved, or written by hand for circulation from one person to another. Hence it follows that the granting of one of these rights does not include the granting of the other. Therefore the director of a theatre authorized to 'represent a dramatic work cannot contend that he is invested with the *right of publication*, and, consequently, with the right of copying it for the purpose of representing it (*et par conséquent du droit de la copier pour l'exécuter*) (b).

An author who publishes his dramatic work does not Right of lose thereby the exclusive right of representation, as the representa- tion not lost

(a) Paris, 20 Feb. 1872, Delagrave.
(b) Traité, Prop. litt. et art. : Pouillet, Paris, 1879.

CAP. XVIII.   law of July–August, 1791, provides that the works of
by publica-   living authors, whether engraved or printed or not, cannot
tiou.   be represented without their consent (a).

Musical   The publisher of the music of an opera is not im-
works.   plicitly authorized by his contract with the composer
alone, to print the words with the music (b).

The grant of the right to publish a work does not give
the grantee the right to represent or execute it. This
question was raised in regard to barrel organs. A law
has authorized the reproduction on these instruments of
pieces of music which are still private property(c).

Piracy.   As regards French plays not yet public property, their
plan, subject, characters, arrangement of scenes and action,
are of capital importance, independently of style, language,
and composition. It is therefore piracy to write a similar
work, even in a foreign language, without the sanction of
the author of the original, and any such imitation may be
confiscated and the performance stopped.

The right which belongs to the author of a dramatic
work of preventing the representation of an imitation of
his work in a foreign language, is distinct from and independent of the right to prosecute for piracy committed by
printing. Consequently, loss by prescription of the right of
action against the person committing piracy, does not involve
loss of the right to forbid the representation of such work (d).

Adaptations.   The following cases have been decided as to adaptations:
1. That it is piracy to adapt a romance for the theatre
without the consent of the author (e); 2. That the transformation of a dramatic work in prose into an opera is also an
act of piracy (f); 3. That it is piracy to modify a theatrical
piece, so as to adapt it for use as an opera libretto, if the plot
and arrangement of the scenes (la disposition des scènes et
la marche générale de l'ouvrage) have not been altered (g).

(a) Prop. litt. V. Cappellemans : Bruxelles et Paris, 1854.
(b) Trib. Corr. de la Seine, 2 August, 1826.
(c) Traité Prop. litt. et. art. : Pouillet, Paris, 1879.
(d) Code du Théâtre : C. Le Seune, Paris, 1878.
(e) Paris, 27 Jan. 1840, aff. de Musset ; Dall. V. Prop. litt. No. 187.
(f) Paris, 6 Nov. 1841, aff. Victor Hugo.
(g) Paris, 30 Jan. 1865, aff. Scribe.

This principle applies also to unpublished works, and CAP. XVIII. it has been decided that it is piracy to take down by short- Piracy of an hand during representation an unpublished play, for the unpublished purpose of having it printed (a). play.

When a piece has been printed or engraved without the Right of formality of deposit, it does not follow that the author representation loses his right to control the representation. He can of deposit. always prosecute those who in contravention of his rights represent his works, whether printed or engraved, although no deposit has taken place (b).

The combined effect of the laws of 13th of January and Combined 6th August, 1791—19th July and 1st September, 1793, of 1791 and is to guarantee to the authors of dramatic works the right 1793. of property in such works, and the right to dispose of them during their lives, either for the double purpose of publication by printing and representation, or separately for either of these purposes (c).

Every infringement of the right of public representation Penalties. is punishable by confiscation of the gross receipts for the benefit of the author. This principle is established by the law of July-August, 1791, and art. 428 of the Code Pénal (d).

Artistic Copyright.

The law of 19th July, 1793, puts " *les peintres et* Artistic copy-*dessinateurs .qui font graver des tableaux ou dessins* " right. on the same footing with " *les auteurs d'écrits en tous genres.*" In subsequent laws this equality has only been maintained in the case of engravers, no mention being made of sculptors or other descriptions of artists; but the law courts have decided that the law is by analogy equally applicable in all cases (e).

The duration of copyright in works of art is for the life Duration.

(a) Paris, 18 Feb. 1836, aff. Fréd. Lemaître, Dall. V. Prop. litt., No. 345.
(b) Code du Théâtre, &c : C. Le Seune, Paris, 1878.
(c) Etude sur la Prop. des Œuvres posthumes : E. Collett & C. Le Seune, Paris, 1879.
(d) Code du Théâtre, Lois, Règlements, Usages, Jurisprudence, par C. Le Seune, Paris, 1878.
(e) Fliniaux, l.c, p. 111

CAP. XVIII. of the artist and fifty years after his death, exactly as in works of literature.

What protected.
Artists have a latitude which is not allowed to others. They may utilise the ideas and works of other people on condition that their work is not a servile reproduction, and that it possesses a certain amount of originality.

It is not lawful to reproduce for sale an engraving or picture which belongs to another, by sculpture, drawing, painting on porcelain, or by needlework, even though in the case of a picture the colours be omitted (a).

Photographs.
A photograph is not necessarily a work of art, nevertheless it may have the character of such a work, and then is protected against piracy like any other work of art (b).

Works of art which have become public property may be photographed; but to photograph for sale any work of art in which copyright exists without the consent of the owner thereof is an act of piracy (c).

Right of engraving.
The proprietor of a work of art has the sole right of engraving it.

Registration and deposit.
By the laws of the 19th July, 1793, and 9th January, 1828, engravings, lithographs, and other printed works of art must be deposited at the national library; and those artists who omit this formality cannot prosecute any one for piracy (d). On the other hand, no such formality is required in the case of works of art executed on wood, marble, metal, and ivory (e).

Penalties for piracy.
Piracy of works of art is punishable in the same manner as literary piracy, and the pirated work is liable to seizure and confiscation.

Reciprocity in literary, dramatic, and artistic copyright.
The decree of 28th March, 1852, protects the works of all foreigners published out of France on the sole condition that the formality of deposit in France be duly complied with. It is not necessary that any reciprocity

(a) Fliniaux, l.c. p. 111.
(b) Fliniaux, l.c. p. 112.
(c) *Ibid.*
(d) Paris, 6 June, 1861, Gilles.
(e) Paris, 26 Feb., 1868, and Cass. 12 June, 1868, Mathias.

should exist between France and the country in which the foreign work is published. And any foreigner who publishes a work in France, or causes a dramatic work to be represented in France, is by the French law put entirely on the same footing as a French author with respect to copyright (a).

The French law of domicile confers on an author very

(a) A peculiarity of the combined operation of the French law and the Convention of 1852 already referred to (p. 487), has been pointed out by a writer in the 'Athenæum,' whose letter will be found reprinted, 1 Jur. (N.S.) pt. ii. 523, 5th Jan. 1856 :—"Another flaw, it is believed, has been found in the Copyright Act. If our courts of law shall rule according to the letter of the International Convention—and we do not see how they can avoid such ruling—a mode of evasion has been discovered which will enable Americans, as well as all other aliens, to secure a copyright for works in this country. An experiment, having for its object to unsettle the law once more, is being made in the case of an Italian, Signor Ruffini, author of 'Lorenzo Benoni' and 'Doctor Antonio,' two tales written in English and intended chiefly for circulation in England. Anticipating for 'Doctor Antonio,' which has just appeared, a popularity similar to that which attended 'Lorenzo Benoni,' Signor Ruffini's publishers, Messrs. Constable & Co. of Edinburgh, were led to look into the state of the law. They found, that though the English law alone offered no security, the French law of copyright, taken in connection with the international copyright convention between England and France, seemed to furnish it. Mr. Burke in his 'Analysis of the Copyright Laws,' says " According to the law of France, a French subject does not injure his copyright by publishing his work first in a foreign country. It matters not where that publication has taken place, the copyright forthwith accrues in France, and on the necessary deposit being effected, its infringement may be proceeded against in the French courts. Moreover, a foreigner publishing in France will enjoy the same copyright as a native, and this whether he has previously published in his own or any other country or not.' Then comes the pleasantry. By the first article of the International Convention of 1852, it is provided that 'the authors of works of literature and art, to whom the laws of either of the two countries do now, or may hereafter, give the right of property or copyright, shall be entitled to exercise that right in the territories of the other such countries for the same term and to the same extent as the authors of works of the same nature, if published in such other country, would therein be entitled to exercise such right; so that the republication or piracy in either country, of any work of literature or art published in the other, shall be dealt with in the same manner as the republication or piracy of a work of the same nature, first published in the other country.' Here the text is clear. Publication in France confers copyright in that country, and the holder of such copyright in France becomes, in virtue of the convention of 1852, entitled to copyright in England! Let Signor Ruffini or Mr. Prescott first publish in Paris. He may then come to London and offer Mr. Murray or Mr. Bentley a monopoly of his works. Such at least is now the reading of the law which has been acted on in Signor Ruffini's case. His 'Doctor Antonio' was published first in Paris, in English, by Galignani, all the formalities required by the French law being complied with, and thus it is supposed no copies of the work will be published in Great Britain, except those issued by the Edinburgh publishers. Of course the convention with France never contemplated the admission of Americans to its benefits, still an American holding a French copyright, which he can easily hold, becomes *quoad*

CAP. XVIII. peculiar rights. Thus, a Frenchman may publish a work in England, and yet, some years afterwards, he, or his children, or their assigns, may have the copyright of that work in France. The case of 'Clery's Journal' is an instance in point (a). Clery had published in London a work entitled 'Journal of what happened in the Tower of the Temple during the Captivity of Louis XVI. King of France.' In July, 1814, the two daughters-in-law and heirs of Clery assigned to Chaumerot, a bookseller in Paris, the property in the 'Journal' of their father-in-law. In September he reprinted it, and made the ordinary declaration then required by the law of France. In June, 1817, Michaud, another bookseller, published a work entitled, 'History of the Captivity of Louis XVI., and of the Royal Family, as well at the Tower of the Temple, as at the Conciergerie,' in which work was inserted, entire, the 'Journal,' which was the property of Chaumerot. A proceeding as for piracy was commenced by Chaumerot, and by the judgment of the Court of Cassation he succeeded in his suit (b).

Rights of foreign dramatic authors.

It is the opinion of MM. Paulmier and Lacan (tom. ii No. 677, pp. 234–236) that a play by a foreign author represented with his consent out of France, can only be represented in France with his formal written consent. They consider that the decree of 22nd March, 1852, has placed this beyond a doubt, and that this is the case notwithstanding that no express mention is made in such decree of the right of representation (c).

---

copyright a Frenchman, and is entitled on the above interpretation to the protection of the Convention. Here is another and most powerful argument in favour of a revision of the law of copyright, as well as of the convention to which it has given rise."

(a) Rénouard, Traité des Droits d'Auteurs (1839), Part 4, c. 3, s. 89, vol. ii. p. 205. "Does any privilege belong in France to a foreigner who there first publishes his work?" Under the law of 1793, which preserved silence on this matter, this question was discussed. It has been formally solved by art. 4 of the decree of the 5 Feb. 1810, which assimilates foreign to national authors.

(b) Merlin, Questions de Droit, Contrefaçon, s. vii.

(c) Prop. litt. V. Cappellmas, Bruxelles et Paris, 1854.

Belgium.

From 1791 to 1814 copyright in Belgium was the Literary same as in France, the two countries being united during copyright in that time, and the French laws of that period are still Belgium. in force. Then, until 1830, Belgium was united with Holland, but the only laws passed during this latter interval affecting copyright, appear to be those of the 23rd September, 1814, and the 25th January, 1817. The first Belgian law on the subject was the decree of 21st October, 1830.

At present the law as to copyright is shortly as follows: Duration. Literary works are protected for the life of the author and twenty years after his death (Decree of 5th February, 1810).

Piracy is defined and punished by articles 425–429 of Piracy and the French Penal Code of 1810: we have already given penalties. these articles in the section on French copyright (a). There seems to be no doubt that these articles, which were not repealed by the Belgian Penal Code of 1867, are still in force, and such is also the opinion of M. Nypels in his 'Commentaire du Code Pénal.'

Three copies of every edition must be deposited with Registration. the communal authorities at the locality where the author resides, signed by the printer and the publisher, in order to secure protection.

Only those works are entitled to protection which are What pro-printed and published in Belgium. tected.

The heirs of an author have the copyright of his posthumous works on condition of not joining them to other works which have already become public property.

Copyright can be alienated in whole or in part by the Assignment. author or his legal representatives.

With regard to publication of dramatic and musical Dramatic and works the rules are the same as for other literary works. musical works.

With regard to their representation the exclusive right Representa-belongs to the author during his life, but it does not tion.

(a) Page 511.

CAP. XVIII. descend to any one except his issue, or failing them his widow; to these the right of representation is given for ten years.

Artistic copyright. The French law of 19th July, 1793, and the Dutch-Belgian law of 25th June, 1817, regulate artistic copyright.

The heirs and assigns of an artist enjoy protection for twenty years against reproduction of his work by any process except sculpture. In the case of sculpture this protection only lasts for ten years.

Rights of foreigners. As regards the rights of foreigners in Belgium they are regulated by international treaties with the following countries: France, England, Holland, Spain, Italy, Russia, Germany, Portugal, and Switzerland (e). The 1st article of all these treaties (except that of France) is, "The authors of works of literature or art, over which the laws of one of the two countries give either now or at any future time the right of property or copyright, will be permitted to exercise such right in the territory of the other state, in the same manner and subject to the same limitations as the rights given to authors of works of the same nature published in such other country, are exercised."

By this article in each treaty it is evident that the inhabitants of all these countries enjoy the same author's rights in Belgium as the Belgians themselves.

The effect of the treaty with France is the same, although with regard to dramatic representation, the Belgian courts for a long time gave to French dramatic authors more limited rights than the Belgians themselves possessed. But by a recent decision at Brussels, in the case of *Verdi* v. *The Directors of Le Théâtre de la Monnaie,* the Belgian law has now put France on the same footing as all other countries (a).

Proposed law on copyright in literature and art in Belgium. (a) Such is the law at present. But on 9 February, 1878, a draft law on literary and artistic copyright was laid before the Belgian Chambers by the Minister of the Interior, which we had hopes would have been passed by this time. It has, however, been referred to M. Demeur, deputy of the Belgian Parliament, to be reported upon, and it is expected

Cap. XVIII.

Holland.

Previously to the French Revolution, Holland acknow- Copyright in
ledged the author's right as a perpetual one, capable of Holland.

---

that his report will very shortly be ready. It is not probable that it will
undergo many alterations, and it may possibly become law before the end
of the present year. It repeals all former laws, and consolidates them
into a systematic whole. We have therefore no hesitation in giving a
summary of its chief provisions; apart from the probability of its shortly
being promulgated, it is interesting as shewing the tendency of continental
legislation on the subject.

Protection is afforded for copyright in works of literature and art, What protected.
including lectures, sermons, and public addresses, pleadings, and speeches
in court, or in political and administrative assemblies, dramatic and
musical works, drawings, pictures, works of sculpture, architecture, and
other works of art, except such as are applied to industrial purposes; the
latter shall for such application, be bound by the laws which govern industrial models and designs.

The author of every work of literature or art, enjoys during his lifetime Persons pro-
the exclusive right of publication and reproduction. His heirs enjoy the tected, and
same for fifty years after his death. In the case of posthumous works, the duration.
heirs of the author enjoy from the date of publication the same rights,
and the same rights belong to the publisher of an anonymous work. If a
proprietor of a work brought out by joint authorship, die without heirs,
his rights accrue to the surviving joint author. The publisher of dictionaries, and of works compiled by several authors, enjoys the same rights,
with the exception of the right which the joint authors may reserve to
themselves, of reprinting those portions of the book which are their own
work. An artist who sells a work of art produced by himself retains
the exclusive right of reproducing such work, either by the same or a
different process, saving always a stipulation to the contrary. If a work
of art be acquired by the State or a public administrative body, they can
authorize its reproduction, save in the case of contrary stipulations, or
where the right of reproduction does not belong to the seller. On the Registration and
issue of each edition of a work of literature or art, published in Belgium deposit.;
by printing or any other analogous process, the author or publisher shall in
order to secure himself the copyright, deposit at the latest within the
year of publication at the Ministry of the Interior a copy bearing on the
title, first page, or in some other conspicuous position, declarations in
conformity with the model forms appended to this law, one signed
by the author or publisher, and the other by the printer. A receipt shall
be given for this deposit. In case of works in several volumes, or brought
out in numbers, each volume, or number, shall be deposited within the
period fixed above.

An author may cede his rights for the whole or a part of the term of Alienation of
copyright. In the latter case his legal representatives only enjoy the right copyright.
during the portion of the period not comprised in the cession. Whoever
shall in violation of the rights guaranteed by this law, publish, print, Piracy and
engrave, or reproduce, in whole, or in part, writings or works of any kind, infringement.
drawings, pictures, sculptures, engravings, musical compositions, or other
literary or artistic productions, shall be guilty of piracy, and any one who
shall knowingly announce, sell, expose for sale, or introduce upon
Belgian soil, pirated works, shall be guilty of the same crime (*délit*).
Newspapers and periodicals are allowed to reproduce articles and extracts
published in another newspaper or periodical, provided the source from
which they are obtained be indicated; this provision does not apply to

CAP. XVIII. transmission to heirs or assigns for ever. By the law of the 25th of January, 1817, literary copyright was limited to the author for his life, and to his heirs or representatives for twenty years after his death. The penalty inflicted for infringement of copyright was con. fiscation of all the unsold pirated copies in the kingdom; also a fine, equivalent in value to 2000 copies of the original edition, to the use of the proprietor; besides a fine of not more than 1000, nor less than 100 florins, to be given to the poor of the district where the offender resided; and in case of a second offence, the offender was to be disabled from the exercise of his trade of printer or bookseller, the whole without prejudice to the provisions and penalties imposed, or to be imposed, by the general laws respecting piratical printing (a). Both

---

articles or extracts, the reproduction of which is expressly reserved. Infringers of this law will be prosecuted by the public prosecutor, but in addition to this the author or party injured has a right to sue for damages in a civil action.

Penalties. The author or introducer of a pirated work is punished with a fine, varying from 50 to 2000 francs, and the edition or article will be confiscated. The usurpation of the name of an artist for a work of art, or the fraudulent imitation of his signature, shall be punished with imprisonment for a period varying from three months to two years, a fine ranging from 100 to 2000 francs, and the confiscation of the works forming the subject of the fraud, and the introduction of any such works shall receive the same

Nationality and reciprocity. punishment. The rights guaranteed by this law are assured alike to native and foreign authors, and to each only for the period of the duration of their rights in the country of the original publication of their works, and in no case can duration of protection exceed the period fixed by the present law.

REPRESENTATION OF DRAMATIC AND MUSICAL WORKS.

Representation of dramatic and musical works. The author of a dramatic or musical work shall enjoy during his life the right of causing it to be publicly represented or rendered. His heirs enjoy the same right for ten years from the death of the author; where the work is the joint production of several authors the consent of all is required to the representation, and the proprietors of posthumous or pseudonymous dramatic or musical works, have the exclusive right to cause them to be represented for ten years from the first representation.

Infringement. Any representation or rendering of a musical or dramatic work, whether partial or entire, without the author's consent, is an infringement of his rights. Nevertheless after the author's death, any person may, on paying an indemnity, publicly represent or render a dramatic or musical work already published, represented, or rendered. In case of disagreement as to the indemnity the person interested shall appeal to the president of the court of first instance. The above provisions also apply to translation of dramatic works.

(a) Lowndes on Copyright, App. 121.

works of literature and art (except sculptures) are now CAP. XVIII.
protected for the term mentioned in the above law.

Only such works are protected as are printed in the
country, and the publisher must also reside there, but the
name of a foreign publisher may be coupled with that of
the native one.

The deposit of three copies with the communal
authorities, and a declaration by a Dutch printer that
the work has been printed by him, is necessary to secure
protection. Dutch authors are protected against pirated
works being imported from abroad.

In 1877 a new draft law on copyright was laid before
the Dutch parliament, but it does not appear to have yet
become law. By this law it was proposed to confer
the right of protection upon the author for the period of
fifty years from the first publication, and in the event
of his surviving this period, then during the remainder of
his life.

The German Empire.

Copyright in works of literature and art, in all the Literary
states of the German Empire, is now regulated by the copyright
three laws of the 11th June, 1870, the 9th January, with German Empire.
1876, and the 10th January, 1876. There is also a law
protecting industrial designs and models dated the 11th
January, 1876. The first of these laws was enacted by the
Federal Council and Parliament of the North German
Confederation, before the establishment of the German
Empire, and came into operation on the 1st January,
1871. It did not, therefore, originally apply to Bavaria,
Baden, Hesse, and Würtemberg. But by the constitution of the empire, on 16th April, 1871, this law was
adopted by these four states also, and is now in force in
the whole of the German Empire. In Alsace-Lorraine,
it took effect from 23rd January, 1873. This law relates What works
to copyright in works of literature, technical drawings protected.

2 M

CAP. XVIII. and designs which are not mere works of art, musical compositions and dramatic works (a).

Under "works of literature" are comprised not only printed books but manuscripts. Under technical drawings and designs are comprised maps, plans, charts, geographical, topographical, also scientific, architectural, mechanical, and technical drawings, which are not merely works of art: works of art as such being protected by the law of 10th January 1876.

Duration.   Copyright lasts for the life of the author and thirty years after his death, provided the real name of the author appear on the title page or at the end of the dedication or preface.   The right passes to his heirs, but does not fall to the treasury or other authorities empowered to administer estates to which there are no heirs.

Translations without the consent of the author are forbidden (if he has reserved the right) for a period of five years from the publication of the original works, and an authorized translator enjoys copyright for a period of five years from the first appearance of his translation. The copyright of a joint work lasts thirty years from the death of the survivor. Articles in periodicals are protected against separate publication by their authors for two years, after which period the author is at liberty to reprint them without the consent of the publisher of the periodical.

Anonymous and pseudonymous works are protected for thirty years from date of publication ; but if within thirty years from that date the author or his legal representatives disclose their names and have them duly registered, the work is protected for the full term of life and thirty years.   Posthumous works are protected for thirty years from the death of the author. Academies, universities,

(a) Gesetz, betreffend das Urheberrecht an Schriftwerken, Abbildungen, musikalischen Compositionen und dramatischen Werken. Bundes Gesetz Blatt von 1870, No. 19, p. 339. In making the résumé of this and the following German laws, reference has been made to Volkmann's Deutsche Gesetze und Verträge zum Schutze des Urheberrechts, Leipzig, 1877, the Annuaire de Législation étrangère, Paris, 1877, and the Law Mag. and Rev. 4th Series, May, 1878.

&c., have their publications protected for thirty years CAP. XVIII. from first appearance. The remainder of the year of the death of the author, or of the publication of a work, or its translation, is not to be taken account of in computing the duration of copyright.

A register is kept by the Stadtrath of Leipzig, in which Registration. entries of the dates of commencing and terminating translations of works, and of the names of authors are to be entered. The entries are to be made without any proof being demanded of the correctness of the author's claim. All persons are allowed to inspect the register, and take extracts. The entries are also to be published in an official journal.

An author's copyright may be assigned *inter vivos*, or Assignment. bequeathed by will. Failing these, it passes to his heirs.

The right of reproducing a work belongs exclusively Infringement
and piracy. to the author of the same.

Every mechanical multiplication of all, or part, of a work without the consent of the author is piracy (*Nachdruck*) and is forbidden.

Copies made by hand, if intended to take the place of Piracy by
copies made
by hand. printed copies, are also piracy. The following are also considered as piracy:

(*a.*) Printing a MS. without the consent of the author; even the legal owner of a MS. may not have it printed without the author's consent.

(*b.*) The like printing of lectures.

(*c.*) A new impression of a work by an author or publisher, in violation of any agreement between them.

(*d.*) The preparation of a greater number of copies by a publisher than is allowed by his agreement with the author.

Translations made without the consent of an author Piratical
translations. are piracy in the following cases:

(*a.*) When the original is in a dead language.

2 M 2

CAP. XVIII. (*b.*) When the original appears simultaneously in
            several languages and an unauthorized translation
            is made into one of these languages.

(*c*). When the author reserves to himself the right of
      translation on the title page, and such translation
      is commenced within one year, and ended within
      three years. The year in which the original
      appears is not counted. But in the case of dramatic
      works such reserved translation must be fully
      completed within six months from the day of the
      appearance of the original. The date of the
      beginning and ending of such reserved transla-
      tions must be registered.

The translation without consent of an unprinted MS. or
lecture is piracy.

Translations enjoy protection against piracy like
original works.

Exceptions.   The following are not regarded as piracy :

(*a.*) Citation of passages, or portions of works, or even
      incorporation of the whole of a small work in a
      large one of different scope, provided the source
      be duly acknowledged.

(*b.*) The printing of isolated articles from periodicals
      and newspapers, but novels and scientific articles
      are excepted, and some others where reproduction
      is expressly forbidden at the head.

(*c.*) The printing of laws, decrees, &c.

(*d.*) Of speeches in court, in political and similar
      assemblies.

Piracy of   It is piracy without the consent of the composer thereof
music.   to elaborate and publish any musical composition, unless
an independent composition is thereby produced, and in
particular, it is forbidden to publish extracts or arrangements for one or more voices or instruments. But it is
not piracy to make use of an isolated passage from an
already published work on the art of music, or to embody
a small published composition in a scientific work, or in a

collection of the works of different composers for the use CAP. XVIII.
of schools, provided the sources be duly acknowledged.
It is not piracy to make use of a published work of
literature as the text to a musical composition provided
the text and music are not separate. The texts of oratorios
and operas are excepted.

The right to bring an action for piracy belongs to any Remedy of
one whose copyright has been infringed or endangered. authors.
The ordinary courts are competent to decide upon all
claims for damages, the amount of penalties, and confiscation
of pirated copies. Criminal proceedings are not commenced
officially, but on the initiative of the injured person.

The right to prosecute for piracy, or to bring an action Prescription.
for damages, is lost after a period of three years, beginning
with the day on which the pirated work was first put into
circulation. And so with the right to prosecute and
bring an action for circulating pirated copies, but the
period in this case begins with the day on which the
pirated work was *last* put in circulation.

Piracy and circulation of pirated copies shall go
unpunished if the person entitled to prosecute neglect
to take action within three months after the knowledge
of such piracy, and of the person committing it, has been
acquired by the injured party.

Confiscation of pirated copies and plant for preparing Confiscation
the same may be applied for to the court as long as any of pirated
such copies or plant exist. works.

Whoever designedly or negligently pirates a work with Penalties.
a view to circulate it either in or out of the German
Empire, or induces any one so to pirate a work, is bound
to compensate the author or his legal representatives, and
is besides liable to be fined up to 3000 marks; if the
fine cannot be obtained, imprisonment up to six months
is the alternative. Instead of the compensation above
mentioned, the injured party may demand the imposition
of a fine, to be paid to him, up to the amount of 6000
marks. In this case no further compensation can be
claimed. If the accused has acted in good faith the fine

is not imposed and he is only liable in damages for the amount of his profits.

In all cases the Court decides whether damage has been done, its amount, and the amount of the profits last received.

All stocks of pirated copies and the plant expressly intended for producing the same are subject to confisca. tion. After the order for confiscation, such copies will either be destroyed or returned to their owner after being altered so as to be no longer injurious to the rights of the author. Confiscation may take place whether the pirated copies have been produced *bonâ fide* or not, and the heirs of the offender are liable. The injured party is at liberty to take over the whole or part of the pirated copies towards payment of costs, so long as the rights of others are not affected.

The offence of piracy is committed so soon as a copy in violation of the provisions of this law has been produced, either in or out of Germany.

Sale of pirated works. Whoever sells, or otherwise circulates, pirated copies, is bound to compensate the author, and is liable to be fined just as a person who commits an act of piracy.

Nationality and reciprocity. This law is applicable to all works of native authors, whether the same have appeared in the country or abroad, or have even never been published; and also to the works of foreign authors which are issued by publishers whose place of business is in Germany. Works of foreign authors published within the limits of the former Germanic Confederation, but not included in the German Empire, are protected by this law, on condition that reciprocity exists between the state where such works appear and the German Empire; but such protection only endures as long as the law in such state affords it. The same applies to unpublished works of authors belonging to such states.

Dramatic and musical representations. The right to represent in public a dramatic, musical, or dramatic-musical work belongs exclusively to the author and his legal representatives. In the case of dramatic and dramatic-musical works the fact of their having been Cap. XVIII. published or not makes no difference. But musical works which have been published can be performed in public without the consent of the author, unless he has reserved this right on the title-page or head of the work. An authorized translator of a dramatic work has the same right in this respect as an author.

The public representation of an illegal translation or, with reference to music, of an arrangement (*Bearbeitung*) is forbidden. Where there are joint authors, the consent of each is necessary. But in a musical work with which a text is incorporated, the consent of the composer alone is necessary.

The duration of the exclusive right to public repre- Duration sentation is the same as for copyright, viz. the life of the author and thirty years.

Whoever gives an illegal representation of the above mentioned works is bound to compensate the author, and is also liable to the same fines as in the case of piracy mentioned above of works of literature.

Whoever induces another to give an illegal representation, is punishable in the same way as one who induces another to commit an act of piracy.

The compensation payable to the author in all these cases consists of the entire gross receipts of each performance. If the work which has been illegally represented, has been performed along with others, a proportionate part of the receipts must be paid to the author as such compensation.

If the receipts cannot be ascertained, the amount of compensation may be fixed by the judge.

If the person who gave the illegal representation acted *bonâ fide,* he is liable for the amount of his profits only.

The remedies of the author, procedure, and registration, are the same as in ordinary works of literature.

The law of 9th January, 1876, concerns copyright in Artistic works of art. It is retrospective in its effect, and repeals copyright. all previous legislation on the subject. It took effect from 1st July, 1876, and its chief provisions are as follows:

What is protected.   It is not applicable to architecture, nor does it protect an artist who permits his works to be imitated in the productions of manufacturing and similar industries. His copyright in such manufactured articles is protected by the law of 11th January, 1876, given below.

Persons protected.   The right to reproduce a work of art in whole or in part belongs exclusively to the artist, and passes to his heirs, unless alienated previously; but does not pass to the Treasury or other authorities empowered to administer estates to which there are no heirs.

    Any one imitating a work of art with due authorization, but by a different art process, enjoys the same protection for his imitation as an original artist, even though the original be already public property (b).

Duration.   Copyright given by this law lasts for the life of the author and thirty years after his death. This protection is subject to the condition that the author's true name appears in full or by some unmistakable sign on the work.

    Anonymous and pseudonymous works are protected for thirty years from publication. If within this period the author's real name shall have been registered by the author or his authorized representatives, in accordance with art. 39 of the law of 11th June, 1870, the work is protected for the full period of life and thirty years after.

    When artistic works are published in volumes or parts, at intervals, the commencement of the period of protection of each part is the same as in the case of works of literature.

    Posthumous works are protected for thirty years from the death of the author.

    Works of art appearing in periodicals, can after the lapse of two years from publication, unless stipulated to the contrary, be reproduced elsewhere without the consent of the editor or publisher of such periodical.

    (a) Gesetz betreffend das Urheberrecht an Werken der bildenden Künste, vom 9. Januar 1876. (Reichs Gesetz Blatt,' No. 2).
    (b) Is said to be specially intended to apply to engravings.

The rules with regard to registration and the keeping
of registers are the same as in literary copyright.

An artist may alienate his copyright by contract or by will.

If an artist alienate his work, the alienation of his copyright is not necessarily included ; but in the case of portraits and busts, the copyright belongs to those who order them.

The owner of a work of art is not bound to place it at the disposal of the artist for reproduction.

Every reproduction for purposes of public circulation of a work of art without the consent of the person entitled to the copyright is forbidden.

The following acts are considered piratical :

(*a*). Obtaining the reproduction by a different process from that by which the original was produced.

(*b*). Indirect reproduction not from the original work but from a copy of it.

(*c*). The reproduction of a work of art in a work of architecture, industry, or manufacture.

(*d*). Reproduction by either author or publisher contrary to the contract binding them.

(*e*). Production by the publisher of a greater number of copies than he has a right to publish either by law or by contract.

It is not considered piracy :

(*a.*) Freely to make use of a work of art to produce a new one.

(*b.*) To copy by hand a work of art if the copy is not intended for sale, but it is forbidden to introduce in any way on the copy the name or monogram of the artist of the work under penalty of a maximum fine of 500 marks.

(*c.*) To reproduce by the plastic art a painting or a drawing and *vice versâ*.

(*d*) To reproduce works of art which are permanently exposed to view in the streets and public places. But such reproduction must not be in the same form (*in derselben Kunstform*).

(*e.*) The reproduction of a work of art in a work of

CAP. XVIII.

literature, provided such reproduction be subsidiary to and serves only to illustrate the text. But the source must be acknowledged under penalty of a maximum fine of sixty marks.

Remedies and penalties.

The remedies of the artist and penalties for infringement are in corresponding cases the same as those in literary copyright, as given in the law of 11th June, 1870.

Nationality and reciprocity.

The provisions as to nationality and reciprocity are also the same as in the law of 11th June, 1870.

Copyright in photographs.

The law of 10th January, 1876 (a), relates to the protection of photographs against unauthorized reproduction; it came into force on 1st July, 1876. It is not retrospective, but existing photographs, which up to this date were locally protected by law, continue to enjoy such protection.

What protected.

The provisions of this law apply to works produced by any process analogous to photography (durch ein der Photographie ähnliches Verfahren) but do not apply to photographs of works protected by law against unauthorized reproduction.

Any copy of a photograph produced by drawing, painting, or sculpture, is protected by the law on art copyright (art. 7) of 9th January, 1876.

Who protected.

The right to reproduce a photograph in whole or in part by mechanical means belongs exclusively to the photographer, and passes to his heirs.

Duration.

By this law photographs are protected against reproduction for five years. This period commences to run from the end of the year in which the first impressions from the original photograph appeared, and if no impressions are taken, then from the date of making such original photograph. In the case of photographs published in volumes, the beginning of the period of protection is determined in the same manner as in works of literature and art.

Every lawful photographic or other mechanical reproduction of an original photograph must bear, either on

(a) Gesetz betreffend den Schutz der Photographien gegen unbefugte Nachbildung, vom 10. Januar 1876. (Reichs Gesetz Blatt, No. 2.)

the picture itself or the mounting, (1), the name or firm CAP. XVIII. of the photographer or publisher; (2) his address; and (3), the year in which such reproduction first appeared.

Unless these conditions are complied with, no protection is afforded.

The producer of a photograph or his heirs can alienate his copyright, either by contract or by will, in whole or in part. But in the case of portraits the copyright vests in the person ordering them. *Alienation of copyright.*

It is not piracy to make free use of a photograph to originate a new work. *Piracy.*

The mechanical reproduction of a photograph without consent of the owner of the copyright, with a view to its public circulation (*in der Absicht dieselbe zu verbreiten*) is forbidden.

It is not piracy to copy a photograph for use in a work of industry, handicraft, or manufacture.

The provisions of the law of the 11th June, 1870, as to author's remedies, procedure, and penalties, apply in the corresponding cases to photographic copyright. *Remedies, penalties.*

The present law is applicable to all works of native photographers, whether such works have been published, in or out of Germany, or not at all. *Nationality.*

No provisions as to reciprocity are inserted in this law.

The law of 11th January, 1876 (*a*), relates to copyright in industrial designs and models. It came into force on 1st April, 1876, and is not retrospective. *Copyright in industrial designs and models.*

Designs and models within the meaning of this law are only such as are of a new and original character. *What protected.*

The right to reproduce an industrial design or model belongs exclusively to the author of the same. *Who protected.*

The proprietor of any industrial establishment in which designs and models are produced by persons in his employ is to be regarded as the author of such designs and models.

The right of the author passes to his heirs. It can be

(*a*) Gesetz betreffend das Urheberrecht an Mustern und Modellen.

CAP. XVIII.   alienated either in whole or in part, and either by act *inter vivos* or by will.

Duration.   The protection of this law against reproduction of industrial designs and models is given to the author for a period which lasts from one to three years, according to his wish, from the date of registration. On payment of a fixed sum this period may be extended to fifteen years as a maximum, and such extension must be registered.

Registration.   All designs and models in order to obtain protection must be registered, and a duplicate or copy deposited with the registrar, and such registration and deposit must take place before any goods manufactured from such designs or models have been circulated. The person registering a design is not obliged to prove beforehand his claim to be considered the author. The register is open to public inspection, and certified extracts can be obtained. A person who has registered a design or model is considered the author until the contrary is proved.

Piracy.   It is not piracy (*Nachbildung*) to make free use of different parts of a design or model for the production of a new design or model.

Every reproduction without the consent of the author of a design or model made with a view to its circulation is forbidden; as also (*a*) when such reproduction takes place by a different process from that by which the original was produced, or when it is intended to be used in a different branch of industry; (*b*) when it differs from the original in size and colour only, or can only be distinguished from the original by close observation; and (*c*) when it has been reproduced indirectly from a copy of the original instead of from the original itself.

What is not piracy.   It is not piracy (*verbotene Nachbildung*) (*a*) to make single copies of designs or models without the intention to use them for industrial purposes, or to derive profit from them; (*b*) to reproduce a surface design in the form of a plastic one, and *vice versâ*; (*c*) to incorporate reproductions of designs and models in a work of literature.

Nationality and   The provisions as to the remedies of the author,

procedure, and nationality, correspond to those in the Cap. XVIII.
three previous laws. The rights of foreign authors are reciprocity.
regulated in accordance with existing treaties.

Austria and Hungary.

Literary copyright lasts for the life of the author and Duration of
for thirty years after his death. In the case of posthu- copyright.
mous, anonymous, or pseudonymous works the right lasts
for thirty years from the year of their first publication.
Academies, universities, and other scientific or artistic
societies under state control, enjoy copyright in their
publications for fifty years; all other companies or
societies are only protected for thirty years. If a work be
published in several volumes, and not more than three
years elapse between the appearance of each volume, the
term of copyright begins to run from the date of publication of the last volume.

Unpublished manuscripts cannot be copied without the What works
permission of the author. Lectures and speeches whose protected.
aim is merely instruction or amusement are protected
against reproduction. Translations are protected against
reproduction in the same way as an original work, but any
one can make a fresh translation for himself of the original
work.

If the author of an original work duly reserve the right
of translation on the title page no one can translate such
work without his sanction, but the author's translation
must appear before the expiration of a year.

Periodicals and similar works which are the joint product of several authors, belong to the publisher; but it is
lawful to make extracts from such works to the extent of
one page on condition that the source be acknowledged.

There are no regulations regarding registration or Registration.
deposit of copies.

An author who has granted the right to publish an Assignment.
edition of his work must wait until such edition is
exhausted before he can publish a further edition.

Every illegal reproduction of a work is prohibited as piracy.

The sale of pirated copies in the country or abroad is prohibited as piracy.

Remedy of the author and penalties.
An action for piracy can only be brought by the party injured, and the offender is liable to a fine varying from 25 to 1000 florins, or in case of non-payment, to a term of imprisonment varying from eight days to three months. Damages may also be given to the plaintiff, in which case he is at liberty to take the pirated copies in part payment. If he should not so take them they must be destroyed, together with all implements used in producing the pirated copies. If the offender be unable to pay the damages he is liable to further imprisonment.

The same protection is ʃafforded to the authors and publishers of musical works as in the case of literary works.

Dramatic and musical representations.
The right toʹ authorize the representation or execution in public of a dramatic or musical work belongs exclusively to the author for his life: and after his death this right passes to his heirs or legal representatives for a term of ten years. In the case of an anonymous or posthumous work, such term begins from the date of the first publication.

The unauthorized representation of a dramatic or musical work is punishable by fines varying from 10 to 200 florins, or by imprisonment in case of non-payment; the author is also entitled to damages amounting at least to the gross receipts arising from the illegal representations, and all copies and parts are to be confiscated.

Artistic copyright.
The legislation on artistic copyright is the same as for literary, and the duration of the term is the same. But there are two conditions attached to the artist's exclusive right of reproduction: (1) he must expressly reserve this right at the time of publication of the work; and (2), he must exercise this right within two years after.

It is not illegal to make use of a work of art as a

model for an article of manufacture or handicraft, nor to Cap. XVIII. reproduce a picture by sculpture, or a sculpture by a picture.

Norway.

The law of copyright in this country was for a long time very incomplete, the enactments on the subject being numerous, fragmentary, and passed at various dates between the years 1839 and 1875. The law of 8th June, 1876 (a) and the two laws of the 12th May, 1877 (b), consolidate the whole. The principal provisions of the law of 8th June 1876, are as follows, taking force from the 1st January, 1877.

It is retrospective, subject to existing rights, and repeals all those provisions of previous laws which are at variance with it.

This law relates to copyright in works of literature, Works of the drama and musical compositions : geographical, topo- literature, graphical, technical and scientific maps, drawings, and tected. figures which have not the character of mere works of art. wⁱat pro-

The exclusive right of reproducing a work protected Persons by this law belongs to the author. The publisher of a protected. periodical, or other work, to which several authors contribute, has the right of an author, but the author of each article, unless prevented by express stipulation, may publish such article elsewhere, at any time after the lapse of one year from the date of its first publication in such periodical. Scientific institutes and societies also enjoy author's rights in respect of their publications subject to the same conditions.

The translator of a work written in a foreign language, Translators. enjoys the rights of an author in his translation, provided such translation do not infringe any provision of the law.

The exclusive right of publication lasts for the life of Duration. the author and fifty years after his death.

(a) Lov om Beskyttelse af den saakaldse Skrifteiendomsret, as given in the Annuaire de Législation étrangère, 6me année, Paris 1877.

(b) Lov om Beskyttelse af kunstnerisk Eiendomsret, Ann. de Législation étrangère, 7me ann. Paris 1878, and Lov om Beskyttelse af fotografiske Billeder, l. c.

CAP. XVIII.   Public bodies enjoy protection for fifty years from first publication, and the same with regard to anonymous and pseudonymous works, but the author on making himself known by announcement in the journal appointed for that purpose acquires protection for the full term of life and fifty years. Posthumous works are protected for fifty years from date of first publication.

Registration.   There are no provisions in this law as to registration.

Alienation.   Copyright can be alienated in whole or in part by deed or will, and in default of alienation after the author's death it descends first to his widow and then according to the law of succession in Norway.

Piracy and infringement.   Every infringement of the rights established by this law is punishable as piracy. The reproduction of a work with omissions, additions, and other alterations, which are not sufficiently extensive to change the character of the work, is also an act of piracy; and in musical compositions, unauthorized arrangements for other instruments or voices, and analogous alterations, are piratical; but not variations, studies, fantasies, &c., which can be considered as original productions.

The following are also piracy: (*a.*) The publication in the press or reproduction in any other way by mechanical means, without the consent of the author or his representatives, of MSS. sermons, speeches, lectures, and other oral communications of the same nature. (*b.*) The publication by author or publisher of a new edition in contravention of agreement. (*c*). The printing by the publisher of a greater number of copies of an edition than the agreement allows to him.

Piratical translations.   Translation without the consent of the author (*a*) of any work into a dialect of the language in which it is written (and for this purpose Norwegian, Swedish and Danish are all dialects of one language); or (*b*), of an unpublished work; or (*c*) of one that is written in a dead language into a living one or (*d*), of a work published simultaneously in several languages into one of such languages, is treated as piracy.

But it is no piracy (*a*) to quote passages from any work if the source be acknowledged, or (*b*) to incorporate extracts from the same or entire works in others of a different kind which are original, or (*c*) to employ poetry for the text of a musical composition, or (*d*) to make use of drawings (*dessins*) for purposes of illustration, or (*e*) to insert musical pieces in an original scientific work.

It is also no piracy for one newspaper or periodical to publish articles, &c., from another, unless the copyright be specially reserved. In any case the source must be acknowledged.

This law does not apply to publication in the press of debates in parliament or municipal assemblies, nor of proceedings in courts of law, public and political meetings, nor of laws, judgments, and public documents of all kinds.

When it has become impossible to obtain a copy of any work for five years, it is no piracy to print it: but the author or his legal representative in this case recovers his right if he bring out a new edition before any other person has done so, or has in the journal appointed for that purpose announced his intention so to do.

The offence of piracy is completed as soon as a copy is wholly printed: it is punishable by fine, varying from 10 to 1000 crowns, and the offender must also indemnify the injured party. The same applies to the person who knowingly sells or puts into circulation pirated copies.

Such illegal copies are also liable to confiscation for the benefit of the author, and all tools and plant will be destroyed, or otherwise rendered harmless.

The right to prosecute belongs to the party injured, and not to the government.

If two years be allowed to pass without prosecuting for an act of piracy, the right of action is lost; and if the injured party be aware of the offence, he must bring his action within twelve months from the date of his so becoming aware of it; but an action to compel confisca-

2 N

CAP. XVIII. tion, &c., of pirated copies can be brought so long as such copies exist.

Nationality and reciprocity.

The present law applies to the works of Norwegian authors and composers, and to works published by Norwegians, and on condition of reciprocity its provisions can be extended, in whole or in part, to works belonging to other countries protected by the laws of such other countries.

Representation of dramatic and musical works.

The exclusive right to represent dramatic and musical works belongs to the author and his legal representatives; and this right extends not only to the original piece, but to those translations of it which the author alone has the privilege of making. Again any person who, in accordance with this law, translates a play into Norwegian from another language, has the rights of an author in his translation. Composers of musical dramatic works have similar protection.

Representation within the meaning of this law.

Mere recitations without scenery are not representations within the meaning of this law.

Consent of joint authors.

If a work be the joint production of several authors or composers, the consent of each is necessary for its representation; but in the case of musical dramatic works the consent of the composer alone is sufficient, and in the case of dramatic works, in which detached pieces of music are incorporated, the consent of the author alone suffices.

Right of representation not assignable without author's consent.

Any one authorized by the author or composer may give as many representations of a piece as he likes, but may not transfer his right to another.

The author or composer may grant the right of representing a piece to as many persons as he likes, provided there be no agreement to the contrary, and even in the case of an exclusive grant he may grant the right to others if the person exclusively authorized have not given a representation for five years.

Duration of right of representation.

The author's exclusive right to represent such works lasts for his life and fifty years after—the remainder of

the year in which he dies not being reckoned in the fifty Cap. XVIII.
years.

The first law of the 12th May, 1877, relates to artistic Artistic copyright.
copyright: it is retrospective (subject to existing rights),
and repeals the law of 29th April, 1871, and other older
Acts. It came into force 1st January, 1878, and its
principal provisions are as follows:

This law does not apply to buildings, nor to utensils of What protected.
artistic design or decoration, but solely to works of art as
such, whether sculptures or pictures and similar works.

The exclusive right to reproduce isolated copies by Who is protected and duration.
hand for sale of an original work of art belongs to the
artist who has executed it for his life.

The artist has also the exclusive right to multiply his
work by engraving and other mechanical means, or by
photography and other analogous means which do not
require artistic labour. This exclusive right lasts for the
life of the artist and fifty years after his death.

Persons who reproduce in a lawful way and by an
artistic process, such as engraving, an original work of
art, enjoy the same rights over such reproductions as the
artists over the original works.

There are no provisions as to registration in this law. Registration.

An artist can alienate his rights by assignment, either Alienation.
with or without restrictions.

If he alienate the work itself, the right of reproduction
is not comprised in such alienation, except in the case of
busts and portraits made to order.

The alienation of the right to reproduce isolated copies
of a work by hand does not, unless agreed to the contrary,
exclude the artist himself from making such copies, and
from granting the same right to others.

If the artist have not alienated his right of reproduction during his life, it passes on his death first to the
person to whom he bequeaths it by will, and then to his
widow, and then according to the law of succession to his
heirs.

The testamentary, as well as every other heir, can

2 N 2

Cap. XVIII. dispose of this right *inter vivos,* and if there be no other heirs of the artist surviving, or the will authorize it, such heir can also dispose of the same right by his will.

Piracy.   All reproduction by hand, or multiplication by a mechanical process, in contravention of the provisions of this law, is forbidden as piracy.

And for the purposes of this provision it is not necessary to inquire whether the work has been reproduced in whole or in part, with additions, suppressions, or changes, so long as such reproduction is essentially a copy. Nor is it necessary to inquire (*a*) whether such reproduction is on another scale or of different materials; or (*b*) whether another technical process has been employed; or (*c*) whether the reproduction has been made directly or indirectly; or (*d*) whether it has been made for an insignificant purpose.

What is not piracy.   But, on the other hand, it is no piracy (*a*) if a painting, drawing, or engraving has been reproduced in the plastic form, or *vice versâ,* provided such reproduction has not been obtained by purely mechanical means, such as photography; or (*b*) if the original serve as a model for the fabrication or decoration of utensils; or (*c*) if a copy of a work of art be inserted in a work of literature for purposes of illustration.

Works of art in public places.   The above prohibitive provisions do not apply to works of art exposed in the streets or public places, or used for decorating the interior of public buildings. It is also lawful to take copies of works of art acquired for the public galleries.

Penalties, procedure, remedies.   The provisions as to penalties, compensation, destruction, and confiscation of unauthorized copies, procedure, and prescription, are the same as in the law of literary copyright of the 8th June, 1876, given above.

Nationality and reciprocity.   And the same with regard to nationality and reciprocity.

Photographic copyright.   The other law of 12th May, 1877, relates to photographs; it is very short, and may be given in an abridged form as follows:

Art. 1. The person who produces an original photograph CAP. XVIII.
from nature, or of a work of art which may lawfully be Who and
reproduced in such manner, has the exclusive right to what protected.
copy it by photography.

Art. 2. The word "*emberettiget*" (protected) must be Regulations.
inscribed on each copy, also the date when such copy
was first made, the name of the photographer, and,
if it be a reproduction of a work of art, the name of
the artist.

Art. 3. This right subsists for five years from the ex- Duration.
piration of the year in which the first copy was made,
but in all cases terminating with the life of the photographer.

A photographer is forbidden to make copies of photo- Commissioned photographs.
graphs executed to order, without the consent of the
person ordering them.

Art. 4. Penalties for infringement.   Penalties.

Art. 5. Destruction of illegal copies and negatives.

Art. 6. Prosecution for infringement is not undertaken Procedure.
by government.

Art. 7. Right of action is lost after a lapse of two Prescription.
years in any case, or after a year from infringement
becoming known to prosecutor. But the provisions of
art. 5 apply so long as the illegal photographs exist.

Art. 8. On condition of reciprocity the protection given Reciprocity.
by this law may be extended by royal decree to photographs of foreign origin. The king will determine
whether and what provisions of art. 2 shall apply to
such photographs.

Art. 9. This law will come into force on 1st January,
1878.

Sweden.

Copyright in this country was formerly perpetual (*a*). Literary copyright in Sweden.
Literary copyright is now protected by the law of 10th
August, 1877, which resembles in many points those of

(*a*) Amer. Juris. vol. x. 69, until 11 July, 1837.

CAP. XVIII. Norway and Denmark (a). This law applies to works already published before the date of its coming into force on 1st January, 1878, and repeals previous laws. Its principal provisions are as follows:

What protected.

For the purposes of this law the following are assimilated to works of literature, viz., musical compositions, drawings of natural history, marine charts, maps, architectural drawings, and all works of an analogous character which cannot be classed as mere works of art.

Persons protected.

The author has the exclusive right to reproduce his works by printing, whether already published or in manuscript.

Translators.

The translator of a work from a foreign language enjoys in his translation the same rights as the author of an original work, provided such translation do not infringe any provisions of the law, and subject to the right of any other person to translate the same original work.

Publishers of periodicals.

The publisher of a periodical or other work composed of distinct articles by different authors, is considered as an author, but has no right to reproduce such articles separately. One year after the publication of each article the author can reproduce the same (b).

Duration.

Copyright lasts for the life of the author and fifty years after his death. In a joint work, not consisting of several distinct articles, the fifty years begin to run from the death of the last surviving author.

The remainder of the year in which the author dies is not reckoned in the above fifty years.

Works published by learned societies or other associations, also works first published after the death of their author, are protected for fifty years from date of first publication; and the same with regard to anonymous and pseudonymous works, the authors of which, however, on making themselves known before the expira-

(a) Ann. de lég. étrang. vii. p. 658: Paris, 1878. Lag angående ganderätt till skrift.
(b) This is different from the corresponding provision in the Norwegian law of 8 June, 1876.

'tion of the fifty years, in the manner provided by the Cap. XVIII. law, acquire the full author's term of protection. The period of fifty years in all the above cases dates from the 1st January following the first publication.

There are no provisions as to registration in this Registration. law.

An author can transfer to others the rights given him Alienation of copyright. by this law with or without conditions or restrictions. Failing such transfer, the right passes to his heirs at his death.

The person to whom an author grants the right to publish a work may not publish more than one edition of it, nor more than 1000 copies in that edition.

It is forbidden as piracy, but subject to any provisions Piracy and infringement. to the contrary in this and in the law on liberty of the press, to print any work, in whole or in part, before the expiration of the term of copyright, without the consent of the owner of such copyright. Changes, abbreviations, or additions of no importance to a work, do not legalize such piracy.

The publication of a translation of an unprinted work, Piratical translations. without the consent of the author, or of a translation of his work from one dialect into another of the same language (and for the purposes of this provision, Swedish, Norwegian, and Danish, are all considered as different dialects of one language) is an act of piracy.

It is no piracy to reproduce passages from another What is not piracy. work in a new and original work, whether in full or abridged, for purposes of proof or illustration, provided the source be acknowledged. Neither is it piracy to reproduce in a periodical publication extracts from another periodical, provided the source be acknowledged. But scientific articles and *ouvrages d'esprit* of considerable extent are excepted, if the reservation of copyright be expressed at the head.

Whoever is guilty of the offence of piracy, is punishable Penalties. by a fine of from 20 to 1000 crowns. Moreover, the pirated edition is confiscated for the benefit of the plaintiff, and the value of the copies parted with (if any) are to be paid for by the offender.

All objects exclusively destined for the illicit printing of a work may be seized, and, subject to any agreement between the parties to the contrary, may be made so that they cannot be used again. The penal provisions of this law, are equally applicable to persons who expose for sale or import into Sweden for purposes of sale a work which they know to be pirated.

Actions for infringement of the provisions of this law can only be brought by the party injured.

Nationality and reciprocity. The present law applies to the works of Swedish citizens. Every anonymous or pseudonymous work is considered as emanating from a Swedish author until proof to the contrary.

The provisions of this law can be extended, in whole or in part, and on condition of reciprocity, to the works of foreign authors.

Representation of dramatic and musical works. No dramatic or musical dramatic work can be represented without the consent of the author or his representative. But the reading or public performance of a work is permitted if there be no scenic accompaniments.

The person authorized may give as many representations as he likes, but may not transfer his privilege to another.

The proprietor of such work may grant the same authorization to others if there be no agreement to the contrary. When a proprietor has granted the exclusive right of representation to another, and such grantee has failed to make use of his privilege for five consecutive years, the proprietor is again at liberty to grant the right of representation to others.

Duration. The above rights of the author or translator over representation last for his life and five years after his death, the remainder of the year in which he dies not being reckoned in the five years. If the author or translator has not made himself known the representation becomes Cap. XVIII. free to every one at the end of five years from the first representation or the first publication.

Whoever represents a work in violation of this law is Penalties. liable to a fine of from 20 to 1000 crowns; moreover, he will be compelled to hand over by way of compensation to the injured party the whole of his receipts, without deducting anything for costs, or for that part of such receipts which might be considered as arising from any piece represented at the same time.

All copies of a work destined to be illegally performed may be seized.

When there are several proprietors of a work the con- General sent of each is necessary for publication or representation. provisions. Moreover, in the case of a musical dramatic work the consent of the author suffices if the text forms the principal part, and of the composer if the music forms the principal part.

In the session of the Swedish parliament, 1876, two changes were made in the constitutional laws. One, which does not concern the subject of copyright. The other a modification in form, as follows : all provisions relative to literary property were expunged from these constitutional laws and remodelled into an ordinary law, so as to make it possible to amend or alter it, without the necessity of recurring to the procedure necessary to alter the constitution (*Annuaire de législation étrangère*, vi. p. 619, Paris, 1877). This remodelled law was replaced in the following year by the more complete one on literary copyright given above.

An additional law on literary property of 10th August Additional is as follows : law.

The provisions relating to literary copyright having Artistic been expunged from the constitutional law on liberty of copyright. the press, piracy of works of art by means of printing will in future be subject to the general rules of the law of 3rd May, 1867, on artistic works and the rights thereto belonging.

Denmark.

Literary
copyright.

The laws regulating literary copyright in Denmark are those of 29th December, 1857, 23rd February, 1865, and 21st February, 1868.

What pro-
tected.

Besides ordinary works of literature, protection is afforded to speeches, lectures, and sermons : but speeches at public political meetings are excepted.

An author's manuscripts are protected for thirty years after his death.

On condition of giving the author's name, it is lawful to make quotations and extract detached passages from any work for insertion in other works, but it is forbidden to reproduce a work by the free use of extracts.

Duration.

Copyright lasts for the life of the author and fifty years after his death.

In case of intestacy the copyright passes to the widow first, and then to the children and other heirs according to the Danish law of succession. If the author has bequeathed the copyright and the legatee die before the expiration of thirty years from the death of the author, such copyright passes to the widow of the author or other legatees, unless the author have made provision to the contrary: the widow or such legatees are not allowed to alienate the copyright if there be any heirs of the author to whom it can descend.

Works out of
print.

If it has not been possible to procure a copy of the last edition of any work during five successive years, the author loses his rights, but they may be recovered so long as a third person has not published or announced a new edition.

For anonymous and pseudonymous works copyright lasts for thirty years from the date of the last edition published within thirty years after the first edition, but the whole term from the date of the first edition cannot exceed fifty years.

The copyright of a work which consists of articles by different authors, belongs to the publishers, but any author,

unless agreed to the contrary, may publish separately Cᴀᴘ. XVIII.
his article after the lapse of one year.

No registration or deposit of copies is required. Registration.

All actions for piracy or infringement must be brought Remedies.
by the party injured within a year and a day from the
commission of the offence.

Pirated copies may be confiscated, and if the injured Penalties.
party do not wish to have them, they are to be destroyed.

With regard to the publication of musical and Dramatic and
dramatic works the rules are the same as for other works.
works of literature.

With regard to representation, the exclusive right to Representa-
authorize it belongs to the author and his representatives tion.
for thirty years. But it is no infringement of an author's
rights to represent a play without scenery, or to perform
at a concert overtures or extracts from musical works.

When an author gives permission for the representation
of his work, it does not confer the exclusive right of
representation, and he may therefore authorize a third
person to give representations. Where he has granted
the exclusive right the contract becomes void if no representation has been given for five years.

Artistic copyright is regulated by the law of 31st Artistic
March, 1864. copyright.

The reproduction of a work of art by any process is What
forbidden, unless sanctioned by the artist. Architectural protected.
designs are the property of the architect, unless he publish
them.

Works of art in public galleries and places are considered public property: any one who reproduces such
works enjoys the copyright of his work, but any other
person is at liberty to make a copy of the original by the
same process.

The exclusive right of reproduction belongs to the Duration.
artist for his life, and to his heirs or assigns for thirty
years after his death, on the same conditions as the copyright of works of literature.

Spain.

Literary
copyright.

Copyright in Spain has lately occupied the attention of
the legislature, and is now regulated by the new law on
intellectual property, the draft of which was reported on
to the Cortes on 4th January, 1877, and by previous laws
of 1834 and 10th June, 1847. The term of copyright
before the passing of the new law was for life of the author
and fifty years after his death.

What
protected.

The new law protects all scientific, literary, and artistic
works which are capable of being published by printing
or any similar process.

Persons
protected.

The persons protected are authors, translators, authorized
publishers, musical composers, painters and sculptors, and
the legal representatives of all these people.

The publishers of anonymous and pseudonymous works
have the rights of authors. But on proof of the identity
of the real author, such author shall regain his rights of
ownership.

Proprietors of newspapers may assimilate their publications to literary works, by annually presenting two complete files to the Registry of Intellectual Property.

The authors of works published in periodicals have the
right to publish such writings in a collected shape, unless
there be an agreement to the contrary. And the author
of various literary works may publish them in a collected
shape, even after he has sold one of them to a third party,
unless a stipulation to the contrary shall exist.

Duration.

Intellectual property lasts for life both in the case of
authors and translators, and of other persons to whom it
may pass by donation *inter vivos*. It then passes to their
heirs-at-law, or testamentary heirs, for a period of eighty
years from the death of the owner.

Registration.

A general registry of intellectual property is provided,
and a book is kept in every prefecture in which the works
protected by the present law are to be inscribed in order
of date. Copies of these entries are to be sent periodically

to the office of the Minister of Public Instruction, and two Cap. XVIII. copies of each work must be deposited.

Works must be registered within one year from their publication.

Every work published without indication of place, date, and selling firm, will be considered fraudulent, and cannot be inscribed on the register.

Every work not duly registered becomes public property.

The subjects of a foreign state, whose law recognises the Reciprocity. right of intellectual property, enjoy in Spain the rights recognised by the present law, on condition of observing its provisions.

Spain has treaties on copyright with England, France, Belgium, Italy, Portugal, and Holland.

The proprietor of a foreign work can exercise his right of property over it in accordance with the laws of his own country. He has the right of property in translations of such work, as long as he possesses the original work in the country where it was published, and for the time during which it is protected by the laws of such country.

A translation authorzied by the owner of a work, and printed abroad, is subject to the law of that country; if printed in Spain, it is governed by Spanish law.

No dramatic or musical work can be represented in Dramatic and whole or in part in any public place whatsoever, without musical previous consent of the author or his legal representative. works. The rate of remuneration must be fixed by the author at the time of giving such consent, otherwise he must accept the scale fixed by government.

No one may, without the author's permission, make a copy of an unprinted dramatic or musical work after representation in public, nor sell or hire out such copy. Joint authors of musical or dramatic works have equal shares, unless otherwise stipulated. In a musical dramatic work half the profits belong to the author of the libretto, and the other half to the author of the music. The consent of one of the authors shall suffice to authorize the representation. The author of the libretto and the

CAP. XVIII. composer of the music, have each the right of publish-ing separately their part of the work. The persons who give representations of such works may not change its title in announcing it, or make changes or additions without consent of the author. The fraudulent representation of a dramatic or musical work in any public place, is, independently of the penalties prescribed by the code, punished by the loss of the entire receipts, which must be handed over to the author of the work.

Duration. The duration of the right of representation is the same as that of copyright in works of literature.

Registration. When a work is represented before publication, registration and deposit of a manuscript copy are necessary.

Works of art. The law of copyright in works of art is the same as for literary property, but no deposit need accompany the registration.

Portugal.

Literary copyright. Literary copyright in Portugal is regulated by the law of the 8th July, 1851, and the penal code.

What protected. Under literary works are included public speeches, lectures, sermons, and translations; but speeches in parliament, courts of justice, and academies may be published in the reports of proceedings.

Quotations from a book or a newspaper are permitted, provided the source be acknowledged.

The publication of a work in a newspaper does not deprive the author of the right of separate publication.

Duration. Copyright lasts for the life of the author, and thirty years after his death.

Registration. Six copies of every book must be deposited at the Lisbon Library. Certificates are given on payment of a small fee.

Assignment. An author may alienate his rights during his lifetime or by testament.

Piracy. An author may obtain an injunction stopping the publication of a pirated work until the courts have decided the case.

The penalty of piracy is confiscation of the pirated Cap. XVIII. work, fine, and compensation to the injured party. Penalties.

The same rules apply to the publication of dramatic Dramatic and musical works. and musical works as to other works of literature, except that the six copies must be deposited at the " Conservatoire Royal."

The author's exclusive right of representation lasts for Representation. life, and for thirty years after his death. In the case of works published but not represented in the lifetime of the author, the term of thirty years commences with the first representation.

Any person representing a piece without the sanction Penalties. of the author is liable to the same penalties as a person who pirates a work of literature, and must pay, by way of compensation, the gross receipts resulting from such representation, and in addition the nett profits of one representation.

Artistic copyright is protected by the law of 1851 and Artistic copyright. the code of procedure of 3rd November, 1876.

The works protected are paintings, drawings, engravings, What protected. lithographs, and sculptures.

Six copies must be deposited at the Academy of Arts Registration. in Lisbon of every kind of drawing, but of works of sculpture, and others of a similar character, only two copies need be deposited.

An artist may alienate his right of reproduction without Assignment. parting with the work itself, but if he alienate the work, the copyright passes also, unless specially reserved.

All pirated works of art are liable to seizure and Piracy. confiscation.

Article 32 of the law of 1851 gives protection to Reciprocity. foreigners on condition of reciprocity.

Italy.

By the law of 25th June, 1865, article 8, copyright lasts Copyright in Italy. Duration. for the life of the author and forty years after his death. If the author die before the lapse of forty years from the first

CAP. XVIII. appearance of the work, his heirs or representatives enjoy the copyright for the remainder of that period: then begins a second period of forty years, during which the same work may, subject to certain regulations, be reproduced without the consent of the proprietors, but on condition of paying to them 5 per cent. on the published price of each copy, which price must be plainly printed on each.

Translations. By article 11 of the same law the author has the exclusive right of authorizing translations of his works for ten years from the date of their first publication. A translator has the same rights as an author.

Works of academies and public bodies. By article 10 copyright in works published by academies, universities, scientific and other societies, and government and public functionaries, is protected for twenty years from date of first appearance, and the author of any separate articles published in such works, can make free use of his contributions for publication, &c., provided he state the name of the collective work in which such contribution first appeared.

Registration. The author of every work must deposit three copies at the prefecture of his province, and make a declaration that he intends to reserve his rights.

Assignment. An author may alienate his rights, but a mere authorization to publish a work does not transfer the copyright.

After the death of an author, the state may on public grounds, and on payment of compensation to the parties entitled, declare any work to be the property of the state, or of any particular province or commune.

Piracy. Any person who publishes a work without the consent of the author, is guilty of illegal publication.

It is accounted piracy (1) to reproduce any work over which the author's rights shall still extend, or to sell such reproduction without his consent; (2), when a publisher produces and sells a greater number of copies than his agreement with the author allows; (3), to translate without consent any work during the ten years reserved to the anthor; (4), to publish a work during the second period of

forty years after the death of the author, without com- Cap. XVIII.
plying with the regulations laid down by the law.

Illegal publication and piracy are punishable by fine up Penalties.
to 5000 francs; confiscation of the illegal copies, and
implements for producing the same, follows in most cases,
and damages may be awarded to the author in addition.

A special law relating to dramatic and musical works, Dramatic and
and modifying the law of 25th June, 1865, was passed on musical works.
10th August, 1875. With regard to publication the term
of copyright is limited in the same manner as in the case
of ordinary works of literature, but if no deposit of the
work has been duly made within three months, either
from date of publication or first representation, the author
has no remedy against those who during such three
months, or before he has deposited the work, may have
reproduced his work or imported copies from abroad.
Copies of musical works must also be deposited, and in
all cases it is necessary to state whether the work has
been publicly represented before publication, and to give
the date of such representation.

By the law of 10th August, 1875, the duration of the Representa-
right of representation, is not as in the case of publication, tion.
divided into two periods of forty years after the death of
the author, but is simply limited to eighty years from the
date of the first publication, and is enjoyed by the author
and his heirs or legal representatives.

The composer of a musical work can prohibit any
extracts from or arrangements or variations of his work.

In works of art the duration of the artist's rights, is Artistic
the same as in works of literature, i.e. for the life of the copyright.
author and eighty years. Three copies of every work must
be deposited to secure copyright, and such copies may be
made by photography or any other method, so long as the
identity of the work be made certain. The work of an
artist cannot be copied or reproduced by any process
without his consent, during the ten years immediately
following the publication. After this period a picture may
be engraved or a statue drawn, these cases being put on

CAP. XVIII. the same footing as the translation of a work of literature.

Switzerland.

Copyright in Switzerland.

Works protected.

The law of copyright in Switzerland is laid down by a concordat entered into by fourteen separate cantons and approved 3rd December, 1856, by the Federal Council. Its provisions are as follows: authors and artists have the exclusive right of publishing or authorizing publication of their works. This right extends to all works of literature or art printed or published in any canton. Swiss citizens who publish works abroad may acquire the rights of an author in Switzerland, by sending a copy of the work to their government, and by declaring themselves as the authors (art. 1).

Duration. Copyright lasts for the life of the author, and if he die before the end of thirty years from the date of publication, then for the remainder of this period the copyright vests in his heirs or assigns. If no publication of the work took place during the life of the author, his heirs or legal representatives have the exclusive right of publishing the work during the ten years immediately following his death: if they avail themselves of this right the work is protected for thirty years dating from the death of the author (art. 2).

Piracy and infringement.

Reproductions which require intellectual work are not considered infringements of an author's rights: they are, on the contrary, equally protected with the original (art. 3).

It is not an infringement of copyright

(1.) To print the transactions and Acts of government and public authorities, unless they have previously been entrusted for publication to some person.

(2.) To print speeches made in public.

(3.) To reproduce newspaper articles.

(4.) To insert extracts from a work in a collection of passages from different authors (art. 4).

Penalties. The penalty for illegal publication of a work of literature or art, or for knowingly selling a pirated work is, by Çᴀᴘ. XVIII. fine up to 1000 francs, and the confiscation of the unsold copies for the benefit of the author (art. 5). The author is also entitled to damages (art. 6). Cases of piracy are tried in the courts of the canton in which such piracy takes place (art. 7).

The protection afforded to literary and artistic property Reciprocity. may be extended by treaty to the productions of foreign states who exercise reciprocity, and who by moderate duties on the productions of Swiss literature and art facilitate their sale ; but such treaties will only bind the separate cantons in so far as they agree to them (art. 8).

Turkey.

Before the year 1872 the copyright of authors was Former and protected by two decrees of January, 1850, and 19th April, present law. 1857. The first applied only to authors paid by government, the second was general. These measures were very imperfect, and merely made a publisher liable to damages for issuing more copies of a work than had been agreed upon between himself and the author. The right was also reserved to the state of publishing any work which it should think proper on payment of an indemnity, the amount to be fixed by the state itself, to the author. In the year 1872, however, a copyright law was sanctioned by the Sultan. The provisions of the new law are simple but comprehensive. The exclusive property in an original Duration. work, with the right of translation, is conferred on the author, his heirs or assigns, for forty years; for translations the privilege is to be for only half that period. All rights can be sold for the whole, or any part of the term. For publishing a translation of any work belonging to the government, permission must be obtained from the Ministry of Public Instruction. Piracy of copyright will Piracy. be punished under article 141 of the penal code, and every author or translator must conform to the press regulations.

CAP. XVIII.

Russia.

Literary copy-
right.

In Russia literary copyright is regulated by the penal code of 1832, and the ukases of 26th January, 1846, and of 7th May, 1857.

What
protected.

Speeches and lectures are comprised in works of literature. Translations are protected like original works, and an author cannot prevent another person from publishing a translation of his work, but an exception is made in favour of authors of scientific works involving research. They may reserve the right of translation but must make use of it within two years.

Private letters cannot be published without the mutual consent of the writer and receiver.

The copyright of musical compositions is the same as for literary works, and no musical composition can be arranged for or adapted to another instrument without the consent of the composer.

Duration.

Copyright lasts for the life of the author, and after his death is enjoyed by his heirs or assigns for fifty years. In the case of posthumous works this term only commences to run from the date of publication. Learned societies have the exclusive right of reproduction for fifty years from date of publication.

Registration.

Authors must register their works in order to secure the copyright, but no deposit of a copy is required. Every assignment of copyright must be in writing.

Assignment.

The assignment of a work to a publisher gives him the right to publish only one edition, unless a stipulation to the contrary be expressly made. Five years after the Censure Office has authorized the sale of this edition, the author or his heirs can publish a new one. The author can also publish a new edition before the expiration of these five years if he has made changes in or additions to his work equivalent to two-thirds of the whole. The author of articles in reviews and periodicals retains the right to publish them in a separate form

unless there be an agreement to the contrary. Manu- Cap. XVIII.
scripts cannot be seized by creditors.

No prosecution for piracy can take place except on the Remedies of
complaint of the injured party, and this complaint must the author
against
be formulated within two years from the commission of the piracy.
offence, or within four years if the plaintiff reside abroad.
The trial is held in the courts of the province in which
the defendant is domiciled.

Besides confiscation of pirated copies, damages may be Penalties.
awarded to the plaintiff in cases of piracy.

Any person guilty of the fraudulent publication in his
own name of the work of another, or of selling a manuscript, or the right of publishing it, to several persons, was,
by article 742 of the penal code of 1832, liable to
deprivation of his civil rights, to corporal punishment,
and to transportation into Siberia in addition to the
pecuniary penalties. But the penal code of 1857 does
not contain this provision.

There are no provisions regulating the right of repre- Dramatic and
sentation of dramatic and musical works. musical
works.

The same laws which regulate literary copyright apply Artistic
also to artistic copyright. Pictures, drawings, engrav- copyright.
ings, maps, statues and other works of art enjoy the same protected.
protection as works of literature. An architect's plans
are also his property, and it is not lawful to construct
a building on the lines of another designed by some one
else.

It is unlawful to reproduce a picture or any part of it Piracy.
by the same process without the artist's consent, or to
copy it by engraving or drawing.

A sculptor's work may not be reproduced by a cast,
nor in marble, nor in the form of a medallion, nor by an
engraving, so long as the reproduction is on the same
scale as the original. A sculptor is not allowed to copy
portions of the work of another sculptor in order to
introduce them in his own work.

In any case a piece of sculpture may be reproduced by
a painting, and *vice versá*.

CAP. XVIII.   Works of art belonging to the government may be reproduced without consent of the artist.

The free use of works of art for application to industrial purposes is allowed by the law of 11th July, 1864.

Portraits and family pictures cannot be reproduced, even by the artist without the consent of the owners.

Assignment.   All assignments of right of reproduction must be in writing; on the death of an artist the assignee or legatee of the right of reproduction must give notice to the heirs within a year, or, if he reside abroad, within two years.

When an artist assigns or bequeaths his artistic copyright in a work, or the work itself, the copyright passes completely to such assignee and his heirs: but if the work be of such a nature that it can be reproduced in a complete collection of the artist's works, the law reserves to him the right to insert it in such collection. Works of art may be sold to pay the artist's creditors, but in such case the copyright does not pass.

Registration.   An artist in order to secure his copyright must, before publication, duly register it in his district with a detailed description. The fact of registration is then gazetted by the Academy of Arts.

Greece.

Copyright in Greece.   Copyright of all kinds in Greece is regulated by the Penal Code of 1833. Its provisions are general, and make no distinction between literary, artistic, or industrial copyright.

Duration.   The term of copyright in this country lasts only for fifteen years from the date of first publication. But the king can grant an extension in particular cases. Inventions are also protected under this law.

Reciprocity.   Any foreigner is protected for fifteen years, provided the Greeks enjoy protection in the country of which he is a native.

Brazil.

There is copyright in works of literature for the life Brazil. of the author and for ten years after his death. Foreign works have no protection whatever (*a*).

Republic of Chili.

Literary and artistic copyright lasts for the life of the Chili. author and for five years after his death—and the right of representation of dramatic and musical works is protected for the same period—foreign works published out of Chili have no protection whatever (*b*).

Japan.

Literary copyright is secured to the author and his Japan. heirs for thirty years, which period may be extended to forty-five years in the case of works of great utility. Translators are put on the same footing as authors (*c*).

Mexico.

Literary copyright is perpetual, registration and deposit Mexico. of copies is obligatory. The right of representation of dramatic and musical works lasts for the life of the author, and for thirty years after his death. Artists are also protected against piratical reproductions of their works (*d*).

The United States of Venezuela.

Literary and artistic copyright lasts for the life of the Venezuela. author, and for fourteen years after his death. Deposit and registration are necessary (*e*).

(*a*) Fliniaux, l. c. p. 402.
(*b*) l. c. p. 405.
(*c*) l. c. p. 424.
(*d*) l. c. p. 385.
(*e*) l. c. p. 421.

CAP. XVIII.

Countries
with no copy-
right laws.

In the following countries there is no law on copyright:

1. The Argentine Republic.
2. Egypt.
3. The Republic of Paraguay.
4. The Republic of Peru.
5. The Republic of Uruguay.

United States.

Copyright and
its extent in
the United
States.

All statutes relating to copyright were repealed in 1870, and the entire law on the subject embodied in one Act. No change was made in the duration of copyright. To the subjects protected by previous statutes were added paintings, drawings, chromos, statues, statuary, and models or designs intended to be perfected as works of the fine arts.

In 1873–4 the copyright, with all other statutes of the United States, was revised.

Authors, inventors, designers, or proprietors of books, maps, charts, dramatic or musical compositions, engravings, cuts, prints, or photographs, or negatives thereof, or of any paintings, drawings, chromos, statues, statuaries, and of models or designs intended to be perfected as works of the fine arts, being citizens of the United States, or resident therein (a), and their executors, administrators, or assigns, are entitled to the exclusive right of printing, reprinting, publishing, completing, copying, finishing, and vending them, for the term of twenty-eight years from the time of recording the title thereof (b), and if the author, inventor, or designer, or any of them, where the work was originally composed and made by more than one person, be living, and a citizen of the United States, or resident therein, at the end of the term, or being dead

(a) *Keane* v. *Wheatley*, 9 Amer. Law Reg. 33, 45; *Boucicault* v. *Wood*, 16 Amer. Law Rep. 539.

(b) It seems that in the United States a title will not be protected under the copyright laws independent of the contents of the book. This was the decision of the United States Circuit Court in the recent Benn-Leclercq case.

shall have left a widow, or child, or children, either or all of them living, she or they are entitled to the same exclusive right for the further term of fourteen years, on complying with the terms prescribed by the Act of Congress within six months after the expiration of the first term. In order to acquire a copyright a person must be a resident in the country. A temporary residence there, even though with a declared intention of becoming a citizen, is not sufficient. Captain Marryat, the well-known novelist, a subject of Great Britain, and an officer under our Government, being temporarily in the United States, took the required oath of his intention to become a citizen, and then took out a copyright for one of his books and assigned the same to the plaintiff; but it was nevertheless held, that the author was not a "resident" within the meaning of the Act of 1831, so as to be entitled to a copyright in his book (*a*).

But where the intention of continuing in the United States existed at the time of publication, the courts have held the author to be a resident within the meaning of the Acts. Thus in *Boucicault* v. *Wood* (*b*), it appeared that the plaintiff, who was a native of Great Britain, had been in the United States from 1853 to 1861, when he returned to the former country. During this period he had registered certain plays which he had written and taken the usual steps to secure the copyright. The defence was, that the plaintiff, being a foreigner, was not entitled to copyright in this country. The jury was directed to find whether Boucicault, when he entered his copyright, intended to make the United States his home. It was found that such intention then existed in his mind, and accordingly the copyright was held to be valid. The law on this point was expounded by Mr. Justice Drummond as follows : " No person is entitled to the benefit of these Acts unless he be at the time publishing the title a

Cap. XVIII.

To acquire a copyright in the States a person must be a citizen.

(*a*) *Cory* v. *Collier*, 56 Niles Reg. 262; Betts, J. The assignee of the work composed by a non-resident alien cannot obtain a copyright in respect thereof.

(*b*) 2 Bliss. 38 ; 7 Am. Law Reg. N.S. 539, 545.

Cap. XVIII. citizen of the United States, or a resident therein. Residence ordinarily means domicile, or the continuance of a man in a place, having his home there. It is not necessary that he should be the occupant of his own house, he may be a boarder or a lodger in the house of another. The main question is the intention with which he is staying in a particular place. In order to constitute residence it is necessary that a man should go to a place, and take up his abode there with the intention of remaining, making it his home. If he does that, then he is a resident of that place. This question of residence is not to be determined by the length of time that the person may remain in a particular place. For example, a man goes into a place, and takes up his abode there with the intention of remaining, and if so, he becomes a resident there, although he may afterwards change his mind and within a short time remove. So if a person goes to a place with the intention of remaining for a limited time, although in point of fact he may remain for a year or more, still this does not constitute him a resident. So it is his intention accompanied with his acts, and not the lapse of time, which determines the question of residence. The plaintiff came to this country in 1853, and remained pursuing his profession as an actor and author till 1861; and if at the time of filing the title he had his abode in this country with the intention of remaining permanently he was a resident within the meaning of the law, even though he afterwards changed his mind and returned to England. If, however, he was a sojourner, or transient person, or at the time of the filing had the intention to return to England, he is not entitled to the protection of these laws."

Deposit of title and published copies.

No person is entitled to a copyright unless he has before publication delivered at the office of the Librarian of Congress, or deposited in the mail addressed to the Librarian of Congress at Washington, District of Columbia, a printed copy of the title of the book or other article, or a description of the painting, drawing, chromo,

statue, statuary, or a model or design for a work of fine Cap. XVIII.
art, for which he desires a copyright, nor unless he also,
within ten days from the publication, delivers at the office
above, or deposits in the mail addressed as aforesaid, two
copies of such copyright book or other article, or in
case of a painting, drawing, statue, statuary, model or
design for a work of the fine arts, a photograph of the
same (a).

The Librarian of Congress is to record the name of Book of entry
every copyright book or other article in a book to be copy.
kept for that purpose. And he is to give a copy of the
title or description, under the seal of the Librarian of
Congress, to the proprietor whenever he may require
it (b).

The proprietor of every copyright book or other article Copies of
is to deliver at the office of the Librarian of Congress, or works to be
send to him by post within ten days after its publication, furnished to
two complete printed copies thereof, of the best edition of Congress.
issued, or descriptions, or photographs of such article as
above required, and a copy of every subsequent edition
wherein any substantial changes may be made (c).

For every failure to deliver or send as above either the Penalty for
published copies, or description, or photograph, the pro- omission.
prietor of the copyright is liable to a penalty of twenty-
five dollars (d).

The resulting or contingent term secured to the author Assignment
in case he shall be living at the time of the expiration of of copyright.
the first term, or if he be then dead to his widow, child
or children if living, has been held not to pass under an
assignment of "the copyright of the book," and that the
word "copyright" embraces only the term then capable
of being secured, which at the time of the contract constituted the copyright of the book (e), and it is doubtful whether a general assignment by the author of all his

(a) Sect. 4956, Revised Statutes of the United States, being the Act of
July 8, 1870.
(b) Sect. 4957.
(c) Sect. 4959.
(d) Sect. 4960.
(e) *Pierpoint* v. *Fowle*, 2 Wood & Min. 23.

CAP. XVIII. interest in the copyright would deprive his widow and child or children living at that time in the event of the author's death (a).

It is not necessary that the assignee of an American copyright should be a citizen or a resident.

Publication of notice of entry for copyright prescribed.
It is provided that no person shall maintain an action for the infringement of his copyright unless he shall give notice thereof by inserting in the several copies of every edition published on the title-page or the page immediately following, if it be a book ; or if a map, chart, musical composition, print, cut, engraving, photograph, painting, drawing, chromo, statue, statuary, or model or design intended to be perfected and completed as a work of the fine arts, by inscribing upon some visible portion thereof, or of the substance on which the same shall be mounted, the following words, viz., " Entered according to Act of Congress, in the year ——, by A. B. in the office of the Librarian of Congress at Washington ; " or, at his option the word " Copyright," together with the year the copyright was entered, and the name of the party by whom it was taken out: thus: " Copyright, 18—, by A. B." (b).

Penalty for false publication of notice of entry.
A penalty of 100 dollars is imposed upon any person inserting or impressing such notice or words of the same purport in or upon any book, map, chart, musical composition, print, cut, engraving or photograph, or other article for which he has not obtained a copyright, half of such penalty to belong to the person suing for such penalty, and the other half to the use of the United States (c).

Damages and forfeiture for infringement.
The penalty for infringement of the copyright in a book is the forfeiture of every copy thereof to the proprietor, and the payment of such damages as he may recover in a civil action. The penalty for infringing

(a) See cases decided under a similar provision contained in the 8 Anne, c. 19 ; *Carnan* v. *Bowles*, 2 B. C. C. 80, and *Kennet* v. *Thompson*, there cited ; and *Rundell* v. *Murray*, Jacob, 315.
(b) Sect. 4962 und Act of 1874, s. 1.
(c) Sect. 4963.

the copyright in any map, chart, musical composition, CAP. XVIII. print, cut, engraving, or photograph, or chromo, or of the description of any painting, drawing, statue, statuary, or model or design intended to be perfected and executed as a work of the fine arts, is the forfeiture to the proprietor of the copyright of all plates on which the same shall be copied, and every sheet thereof either copied or printed, and of one dollar for every sheet of the same found in his possession, either printing, printed, copied, published, imported or exposed for sale; and in case of a painting, statue, or statuary the forfeiture of ten dollars for every copy of the same in his possession or by him sold or exposed for sale (a).

By the Act of Congress of the 18th of August, 1856, Dramatic s. 1, it was declared that any copyright thereafter granted, compositions. under the laws of the United States, to the author or proprietor of any dramatic composition, designed or suited for public representation, should be deemed to confer upon the author or proprietor, his heirs or assigns, along with the sole right to print and publish the said composition, the sole right also to act, perform, or represent the same, or cause it to be acted, performed, or represented, on any stage or public place, during the whole period for which the copyright was obtained. The above provisions are re-enacted in the Act of 1870.

The exclusive right to perform a drama can only be How to secure secured by first publication and registration as a literary exclusive composition. Copyright in a dramatic composition carries formance. with it the right of representation, which cannot be secured in respect of any play in manuscript only (b). No special conditions or requirements are prescribed for securing the right of representation. If the production be a "dramatic composition," it attaches simultaneously with the copyright in the same manner and on the same conditions.

(a) Sect. 4964–5.
(b) *Boucicault* v. *Hart*, 13 Blatchf. (Amer.) 47, practically overruling *Boucicault* v. *Wood*, 2 Biss. 34; *Roberts* v. *Myers*, 13 Monthly L. R. 396; *Boucicault* v. *Fox*, 5 Blatchf. 87; *Shook* v. *Rawkin*, 3 Cent. Law Jour. 210, 6 Biss. 477.

Both rights begin with publication in print and continue for the same term. Neither is affected by public performance of the play before its publication in print.

The Act of Congress of the 8th July, 1870, is declared not to extend to prohibit the printing, publishing, importation, or sale of any book, map, chart, dramatic or musical composition, print, cut, engraving, or photograph, written, composed, or made by any person not a citizen of the United States, nor resident therein. Authors may reserve the right to dramatize or to translate their own works.

Damages for printing or publishing manuscripts. A remedy is by the existing law (sect. 4967) provided for the unauthorized publication of a manuscript. It is declared that " every person who shall print or publish any manuscript whatever, without the consent of the author or proprietor first obtained, if such author or proprietor is a citizen of the United States or resident therein, shall be liable to the author or proprietor for all damages occasioned by such injury." This section is said to operate in favour of a resident assignee of a foreign author (a) ; but as copyright will not vest in a work written by a foreign author, and if section 4967, as is usually supposed, applies only to productions for which copyright may be obtained, it would appear that such section could give no redress for the unauthorized publication of a manuscript which a citizen or resident might have bought from a foreigner. The construction of the section is yet open for judicial determination.

(a) *Keene* v. *Wheatley* , 9 Amer. Law Rep. 45.

CHAPTER XIX.

ARRANGEMENTS BETWEEN AUTHORS AND PUBLISHERS.

A FEW remarks may, perhaps, be here advantageously offered on compacts, arrangements, and stipulations between authors and publishers, and we trust they may prove profitable both to the former and the latter.

In these days, when literature and commerce march in open array, and their pace is so rapid and great; when on the one hand a few authors write for fame, some for gain, and many for both; and on the other hand publishers regard their writings purely in a commercial point of view, estimating their worth (at least to them) by the amount of profit likely to accrue from the publication, two antagonistic parties frequently come in contact.

Authors who compose exclusively for fame are, on the assumption that they ever existed, rapidly becoming extinct, while those who write for gain are much on the increase. The spirit of the age is commerce, and almost every transaction of the present day is regarded in a commercial light (a).

Thus we have two parties in opposition: the one estimating the value of his work in proportion to his toil and labour in its composition, the other computing it in proportion as he conceives the public may become purchasers. The publisher could not undertake to requite or recompense the author according to the degree of exertion

Arrangements between authors and publishers.

(a) "Avarice," said Goldsmith, "is the passion of inferior natures; money, the pay of the common herd. The author who draws his quill merely to take a purse, no more deserves success than he who presents a pistol."—'An Inquiry into the Present State of Polite Learning,' chap. x.

employed by him; for what amount of drudgery and toil may not be expended upon a work which would not even cover the expenses of printing and publication? Publishers invariably act like merchants, whose principle is to risk as little capital as possible, and to replace *that* with profit as early as feasible.

The reward due to the author.

The reward due to an author is thus justly referred to by Mr. Serjeant Talfourd: " We cannot decide the abstract question between genius and money, because there exists no common properties by which they can be tested, if we were dispensing an arbitrary reward; but the question how much the author ought to receive is easily answered: so much as his readers are delighted to pay him. When we say that he has obtained immense wealth by his writing, what do we assert, but that he has multiplied the sources of enjoyment to countless readers, and lightened thousands of else sad, or weary, or dissolute hours? The two propositions are identical, the proof of the one at once establishing the other. Why, then, should we grudge it any more than we would reckon against the soldier, not the pension or the grant, but the very prize-money which attests the splendour of his victories, and in the amount of his gains proves the extent of ours? Complaints have been made by one in the foremost rank in the opposition to this bill [a bill for the extension of copyright], the pioneer of the noble army of publishers, booksellers, printers, and book-binders, who are arrayed against it, that in selecting the case of Sir Walter Scott as an instance in which the extension of copyright would be just, I had been singularly unfortunate, because that great writer received during the period of subsisting copyright an unprecedented revenue from the immediate sale of his works. But, sir, the question is not one of reward—it is one of justice. How would this gentleman approve of the application of a similar rule to his own honest gains? From small beginnings, this very publisher has, in the fair and honourable course of trade, I doubt not, acquired a splendid fortune, amassed by the sale of works, the property of the public—of works, whose authors have gone to their repose, from the fevers, the CAP. XIX. disappointments, and the jealousies which await a life of literary toil. Who grudges it to him? Who doubts his title to retain it? And yet this gentleman's fortune is all, every farthing of it, so much taken from the public, in the sense of the publishers' argument; it is all profits on books bought by that public, the accumulation of pence, which, if he had sold his books without profit, would have remained in the pockets of the buyers. On what principle is Mr. Tegg to retain what is denied to Sir Walter? Is it the claim of superior merit? Is it greater toil? Is it larger public service? His course, I doubt not, has been that of an honest, laborious tradesman; but what has been its anxieties compared to the stupendous labour, the sharp agonies, of him whose deadly alliance with those very trades whose members oppose me now, and whose noble resolution to combine the severest integrity with the loftiest genius, brought him to a premature grave,—a grave which, by the operation of the law, extends its chillness even to the results of those labours, and despoils them of the living efficacy to assist those whom he has left to mourn him? Let any man contemplate that heroic struggle, of which the affecting record has just been completed, and turn from the sad spectacle of one who had once rejoiced in the rapid creation of a thousand characters flowing from his brain and stamped with individuality, for ever straining the fibres of the mind till the exercise which was delight became torture, girding himself to the mighty task of achieving his deliverance from the load which pressed upon him, and with brave endeavour, but relaxing strength, returning to the toil, till his faculties give way, the pen falls from his hand on the unmarked paper, and the silent tears of half-conscious imbecility fall upon it—and to some prosperous bookseller in his counting-house, calculating the approach of the time (too swiftly accelerated) when he should be able to publish for his own gain, those works fatal to life; and then tell me, if we are to apportion the reward of the effort, where is the justice of the bookseller's claim? Had Sir Walter Scott been able to see, in the distance, an extension of his own right in his own productions, his estate and his heart had been set free ; and the publishers and printers, who are our opponents now, would have been grateful to him for a continuation of labour and rewards which would have impelled and augmented their own " (a).

Contracts between authors and publishers should be in writing.

Contracts between authors and publishers should be in writing—the Statute of Frauds applies to literary as well as other contracts (b). In *Sweet* v. *Lee* (c), it appeared that the agreement for the publication of a dictionary of legal practice was contained in a memorandum, which was signed with the initials of the publisher and of the author, and was to the effect that the latter should receive £80 a year for five years, and £60 a year for the rest of his life if he should live longer than five years. This was held to be void under the Statute of Frauds; because, being a memorandum of an agreement not to be performed within a year, no consideration was expressed on the face of it, and it was without any signature other than the initials of the parties. The plaintiff, therefore, was not entitled to damages claimed to have been sustained by the failure of the defendant to perform his agreement to prepare a new edition. Nor, although the contract was void, could the plaintiff, having paid for several years the sums mentioned in the memorandum, recover the money so paid on the ground of failure of consideration.

What necessary to satisfy the Statute of Frauds.

But the contract required to be in writing by the Statute of Frauds need not appear from one document,

(a) Speech in the Commons, April 25, 1838, 42 Parl. Deb. 560.

(b) But a contract by a printer to print, and find the paper for printing a number of copies of a work is not a contract for the sale of goods within the 17th section of the Statute of Frauds as extended by the 9 Geo. 4, c. 14, s. 7 ; and the printer consequently may recover the price in an action for work, labour, and materials, where the contract is a verbal one: *Clay* v. *Yates*, 1 H. & N. 73. And a printer who is employed to print certain numbers, but not all consecutive numbers, of an entire work has a lien upon the copies not delivered for his general balance due for printing the whole of those numbers: *Blake* v. *Nicholson*, 3 M. & S. 167. But it seems that by the custom of trade a printer cannot recover for the printing of a work before the whole is completed and delivered : *Gillett* v. *Mawman*, 1 Taunt. 137; see also *Adlard* v. *Booth*, 7 C. & P. 108.

(c) 3 Man. & Gr. 452.

it may be collected from any number of documents.
Thus, where a publisher proposed to publish by subscription an illustrated edition of Shakespeare, to appear in
numbers at the price of three guineas a number, two
guineas to be paid at the time of subscribing, and the
remaining guinea on the delivery of each successive
number; the prospectus stating "that one number at
least should be published annually," and that the proprietors were confident that they should be able to
"produce two numbers within the course of every year;"
and the defendant, wishing to become a subscriber, wrote
his name in a book kept for the purpose in the plaintiff's
shop, entitled 'Shakespearian subscribers, their signatures;'
printed copies of the prospectus lying at the same time in
the plaintiff's shop, but neither prospectus nor book of
subscribers containing any reference the one to the other,
it was held that the contract of the defendant was not one
to be performed within the space of a year from the
making thereof, and therefore that, in order to be enforceable by action, it must be writing. The defendant having
refused to continue to take in the numbers of the book, an
action was brought against him by the publisher; but it
was held that the action could not be maintained for
want of a written agreement or memorandum signed by
the party to be charged therewith, as required by the
4th section of the Statute of Frauds. The prospectus
contained the terms of the agreement, and if it could be
coupled with the book of subscribers in which the
defendant had signed his name, it would be a sufficient
memorandum of the agreement to satisfy the statute, but
as it contained no reference to the book, nor the book to
it, there was no connection in sense between them which
would enable the court to couple them together, and
treat them as one document; and parol evidence to
establish such a connection was inadmissible (a). "If,"
said Le Blanc, J. "there had been anything in the book
which had referred to the particular prospectus, that

(a) *Boydell* v. *Drummond*, 11 East, 142.

2 P 2

CAP. XIX. would have been sufficient; if the title to the book had been the same with that of the prospectus, it might, perhaps, have done; but as the signature now stands, without reference of any sort to the prospectus, there was nothing to prevent the plaintiff from substituting any prospectus, and saying that it was the prospectus exhibited in his shop at the time, to which the signature related; the case, therefore, falls directly within this branch of the Statute of Frauds."

An action maintainable for not supplying a work agreed to be furnished.

If an author agree in writing to supply a bookseller or publisher with a manuscript of a work to be printed by the latter, an action for damages can be maintained for refusing to furnish the same (a), provided the work be one which, if published, would not be libellous (b), or would not subject the author to punishment (c).

Should the work be stopped the author must be paid for work already done.

Where, however, the author was engaged for a certain sum to write an article to appear, among others, in a work called the 'The Juvenile Library,' and before he had completed his article, and before any portion of it had been published, the work in which it was to have appeared was discontinued, Lord Chief Justice Tindal held that the publishers were not entitled to claim the completion of the article in order that it might be published in a separate form for general readers, but were bound to pay the author a reasonable sum for the part which he had prepared (d).

Payment to author's representative for part of work finished.

Where a work called the 'Elements of Mechanical

(a) Gale v. Leckie, 2 Stark, N. P. C. 107; the Court of Chancery, however, could not compel him: Clarke v. Price, 2 Wills. C. C. 157.
(b) Lyne v. Sampson Low & Marston, 'Times,' 17th Feb., 1873.
(c) Gale v. Leckie, supra, and see Brook v. Wentworth, 3 Anstr. 881; Cowan v. Milburn, L. R. 2 Ex. 230; 36 L. J. (Ex.) 124; 16 L. T. (N.S) 290. A contract for the publication of a book which it is unlawful to publish is not valid. But where this defence is set up, and the work is not produced, and no evidence of its character is offered, the jury are not to pronounce that the book is obnoxious: Gale v. Leckie, supra. A printer cannot maintain an action against a publisher for money due for printing an obscene book: Poplett v. Stockdale, 1 Ryan & M. 337. But where a printer, after printing part of a book, received the manuscript of the other part and found it to be libellous, it was held that he was not bound to print the libellous part, and was entitled to recover for what he had printed: Clay v. Yates, 1 Hurl. & N. 73; Lyne v. Sampson Low & Marston, supra.
(d) Planché v. Colburn, 5 Car. & Pay. 58; on ap. 8 Bing. 14.

Philosophy' was published in parts, the agreement between CAP. XIX.
the author and publisher being that each part should be
paid for when issued, and after the publication of a
complete part the progress of the work was interrupted
by the death of the author, it was held that the representatives of the deceased author were entitled to payment
of the stipulated price of the published part (a).

A Court of Equity will not, however, decree specific No specific
performance of an agreement to write a book (b). It has performer of
agreement to
no power to go so far, and were it capable of such an write book.
order, there would be no means of enforcing it.

In the case of *Clarke* v. *Price* (c), the defendant, Mr.
Price, entered into an agreement with the plaintiffs, dated
the 27th of April, 1814, " to compose and write the cases
in the Court of Exchequer, commencing with Easter
Term, 1814, and to be published periodically," on the
terms of sharing the profits; and it was agreed that the
plaintiffs should be at liberty to relinquish the undertaking if they should think it advisable. As the first and
second volumes were published, the defendant, for certain
considerations, assigned the copyright in them to the
plaintiffs. Afterwards, in 1817, the terms of the arrangement were altered, and the following agreement was
executed :—" Memorandum, Mr. Price agrees with Messrs.
Clarke to receive for his interest in the agreement for the
Exchequer Reports, dated the 27th of April, 1814, commencing at the third volume, the sum of, &c. Mr. Price
agrees to give any further assignment of the copyright
and future interest to Messrs. Clarke at their expense."
The defendant having subsequently entered into an agreement with other publishers, who were made defendants,
to report the cases in the Exchequer; the bill was filed,

(a) *Constable* v. *Robinson's Trustees*, 14 Fac. Dec. 166, 1 June, 1868.
One judge, however, dissented, thinking the contract was one for the entire
work, and that the object of partial payment was the accommodation of
the author, and not any qualification of the original obligation.

(b) Specific performance of an agreement for the sale of copyright (even
though personal chattels, such as stereotype plates, printed sheets, &c.,
are included in the contract) will be decreed : *Thombleson* v. *Black*, 1 Jur.
198.

(c) 2 Wills. C. C. 157.

CAP. XIX.   praying to have a specific performance of the agreements
of 1814 and 1817, by permitting the plaintiffs to print and
publish the reports of cases in the Exchequer so long as he
should continue to compose and write them, upon the terms
of those agreements, and by executing an assignment of
the copyright ; and also praying an injunction. *Morris* v.
Colman (a), was relied upon. Lord Eldon, C., dissolved an
injunction which had been obtained *ex parte*, apparently
assuming that the agreement bore the construction contended for by the plaintiffs. His lordship said : " The case of
Morris v. *Colman* is essentially different from the present.
In that case Morris, Colman, and other persons were
engaged in a partnership in the Haymarket Theatre, which
was to have continued for a very long period, as long, indeed,
as the theatre should exist.   Colman had entered into an
agreement which I was very unwilling to enforce—not
that he would write for the Haymarket Theatre, but that he
would not write for any other theatre. The court could not
compel him to write for the Haymarket Theatre, but it
did the only thing in its power—it induced him indirectly
to do one thing by prohibiting him from doing another.
There was an express covenant on his part contained in the
articles of partnership.   But the terms of the prayer of
this bill do not solve the difficulty, for if this contract is
one which the court will not carry into execution, the
court cannot indirectly enforce it by restraining Mr. Price
from doing some other act.   This is an agreement which
expressly provides that Mr. Price shall write and compose
reports of cases to be published by the plaintiffs. In
Morris v. *Colman* there was a decree directing the
partnership to be carried on, it could not be put an end
to, and it was the duty of the parties to interfere.   But
I have no jurisdiction to compel Mr. Price to write
reports for the plaintiffs ; I cannot, as in the other case,
say that I will induce him to write for the plaintiffs by
preventing him from writing for any other person, for
that is not the nature of the agreement.   The only means

(a) 18 Ves. 437.

of enforcing the execution of this agreement would be to CAP. XIX. make an order compelling Mr. Price to write reports for the plaintiffs, which I have not the means of doing. If there be any remedy in this case, it is at law. If I cannot compel Mr. Price to remain in the Court of Exchequer for the purpose of taking notes, I can do nothing. I cannot indirectly, and for the purpose of compelling him to perform the agreement, compel him to do something which is merely incidental to the agreement. It is also quite clear that there is no mutuality in this agreement."

But an author may bind himself not to write upon a particular subject, or only for a particular person; for a bond or covenant to that effect would not resemble one in restraint of trade.

An author may bind himself not to write upon a particular subject.

Thus, in the case quoted in *Clarke* v. *Price*, where Colman had contracted with the proprietors of the Haymarket Theatre not to write dramatic pieces for any other theatre, the Lord Chancellor maintained that such a contract was not unreasonable upon either construction, whether it was that Mr. Colman should not write for any other theatre without the licence of the proprietors of the Haymarket Theatre, or whether it gave to those proprietors merely a right of pre-emption. If, said he, Mr. Garrick were now living, would it be unreasonable that he should contract with Mr. Colman to perform only at the Haymarket Theatre, and Mr. Colman with him to write for that theatre alone? Why should they not thus engage for the talents of each other? I cannot see anything unreasonable in this; on the contrary, it is a contract which all parties may consider as affording the most eligible, if not the only, means of making this theatre profitable to them at all as proprietors, authors, or in any other character which they are by the contract to hold (*a*).

(*a*) *Morris* v. *Colman*, 18 Ves. 437. In *Montague* v. *Flockton*, L. R. 16 Eq. 189, it was held that a contract between a manager of a theatre and an actor must be understood to be for the exclusive services of the latter during the period for which he had been engaged, though there was no express agreement that he should not act elsewhere.

CAP. XIX.

But in *Brooke* v. *Chitty* (a), where the defendant had

But court will not interfere until there be an actual publication.

undertaken not to write or edit any work upon the criminal law, except a work of which the plaintiff had purchased the copyright, and an advertisement of an edition of Burn's 'Justice of the Peace,' by the defendant, had appeared, Lord Brougham refused to grant an injunction, observing that the defendant was at liberty to write in his closet what he pleased, and that the court would not interfere until there was a violation of the alleged undertaking by actual printing and publication.

So, where an author sells the copyright of a work (b) published under his own name, and covenants with the purchaser not to publish any other work to prejudice the sale of it, it seems that another publisher, who has no notice of this covenant, may be restrained from publishing a work subsequently purchased by him from the same author, and published under his name, on the same subject, but under a different title, and though there be no piracy of the first book (c).

Independent of agreement to the contrary, author at liberty to publish a continuation of his work.

But where no such covenant had been entered into and the publisher had agreed with an author for an edition of a history to be written by the latter, in four volumes, and had obtained subscriptions for all that could fall within his edition, the court held that the author was at liberty to publish a continuation of the history which embraced part of the period and also much of the matter contained in the last of the four volumes (d).

'The Edinburgh Philosophical Journal.'

An arrangement was entered into between Dr. Brewster and Professor Jameson, on the one part, and an Edinburgh publishing firm on the other part, for the publication of a

(a) 2 Cooper's Cases, 216 ; see *Brook* v. *Wentworth,* 3 Anstr. 881.
(b) A contract for sale of a copyright is enforceable in equity : *Thombleson* v. *Black,* 1 Jur. 198.
(c) *Barfield* v. *Nicholson,* 2 Sim & Stu. 1 ; 2 L. J. (Ch.) 90. But where, in an action by several plaintiffs for piracy of copyright, it appeared that the defendant, the author, had published the work in question pursuant to the conditions of a *cognovit* given by him to one of the plaintiffs and another person, in an action for not performing an agreement to write the work in question, it was held that this was a sufficient defence : *Sweet et al.* v. *Archbold,* 10 Bing. R. 133 ; cited Curtis on Copy. 231.
(d) *Blackie & Co.* v. *Aikman,* May 26, 1827 ; 5 Ses. Cass. 719 (N.E.) 671.

work to be edited by the former, called 'The Edinburgh
Philosophical Journal,' the agreement to be binding for
five years, or till the termination of the twentieth number of
the journal. On the title-page the journal was stated to be
"conducted by Dr. Brewster and Professor Jameson." After
the twentieth number had appeared, Dr. Brewster, having
differed with the firm, published a prospectus of " No. 1 of
the 'New Series of the Edinburgh Journal,' conducted by
Dr. Brewster," whereupon the firm presented a bill of suspension and interdict of a work under this title, on the
ground that they were the proprietors of the original journal,
the publication of which they intended to continue, and
that the proposed work was an invasion of their property.
The Lord Ordinary, on the ground that the copyright of
the publication in question was the property of the com-
plainers, passed the bill, and granted the interdict. The
Court of Session recalled the interlocutor as deciding
the question to be discussed on the passed bill; but at
the same time remitted to pass the bill and continue the
interdict (a).

Where, in 1857, the defendant, being the proprietor of 'The London
a weekly publication, 'The London Journal,' the price of Journal.'
which was 1d., assigned his copyright and interest therein
to the plaintiff for £24,000, and entered into a covenant
with the plaintiff that he would not directly or indirectly,
alone or in partnership with any other person or persons,
engage himself or be concerned in bringing out or
publishing any weekly periodical of a nature similar to
'The London Journal,' selling at 1d. per copy, or commit any act or default which might tend to lessen or
diminish the sale or circulation of the said periodical,
or the profit to be derived by the plaintiff from the
future printing or publishing thereof, and in May, 1859,
the defendant issued an advertisement announcing the
publication by him, on the 1st of June following, of
a daily newspaper, to be called the 'The Daily London
Journal,' and to be sold at 1d., the plaintiff obtained an .

(a) *Constable* v. *Brewster*, 3 Scotch Ses. Cass. 215.

CAP. XIX. injunction. The injunction was appealed against, but
without effect. Sir J. L. Knight Bruce, L.J. (*dissentiente*
Sir G. J. Turner, L.J.), confirming the order, upon the
plaintiff undertaking to abide by any order the court
might make as to damages, and to bring an action against
the defendant within one week (*a*).

'London
Society.'
So also in the case of *Clowes* v. *Hogg* (*b*), an injunction was
applied for on behalf of Messrs. Clowes and Messrs. Wrigley,
the proprietors of a magazine called 'London Society,' to
restrain the defendant, Mr. James Hogg the younger,
from publishing a magazine under the name of 'English
Society,' or with a cover only colourably differing from
that used for the plaintiffs' magazine. It was only sought
to restrain the defendant from selling the Christmas
number of his intended magazine with a cover similar to
that used by the plaintiffs. 'London Society' was
brought out by the defendant in its present form in 1863,
but some time afterwards Messrs. Hogg, of whose firm
the defendant was a member, became indebted to Messrs.
Wrigley, paper makers, and a mortgage of the magazine
was executed as part of an arrangement to pay the debt,
the defendant at the same time entered into a covenant
not at any time to do, or cause to be done, anything
which might injure the said publication or decrease its
value. The copyright in the magazine was subsequently
assigned to the plaintiffs absolutely, subject to the before-
mentioned mortgage. The magazine continued to be
edited by the defendant, and was published at 217 Pic-
cadilly. In May, 1870, the plaintiffs, under the terms of
their agreement with the defendant, gave him three
months' notice of dismissal, and informed him that the
magazine, 'London Society,' would in future be published
by Messrs. Bentley, and would be edited by Mr. Blackburn. Upon this intimation the defendant proceeded to
make arrangements for bringing out another magazine,

(*a*) *Ingram* v. *Stiff*, 5 Jur. (N.S.) 947; 33 L. T. (N.S.) 195.
(*b*) W. N. (1870) V.-C. M. 268; see *Hogg* v. *Kirby*, 8 Ves. 115. And
see *Sedon* v. *Serrate*, cited 2 V. & B. 220.

entitled 'English Society,' and upon the termination of his notice of dismissal, he issued a circular in terms almost identical with the circular issued when the plaintiffs' magazine was first published, and which, it was alleged, contained expressions indicating that the defendant's magazine was a substitute for, or a continuation of, the plaintiffs' magazine ; and the defendant further threatened that he should endeavour to drive the rival publication out of the field. The defendant stated in his circular that he had ceased to be connected with ' London Society,' but proposed to carry into the new magazine whatever knowledge and spirit he had been able to impart into the old work, and announced that, with the aid of the well-known masters of the pen and pencil with whom he had so long been associated, he proposed "to continue all those sketches of London society and those studies of English life for which we have won some reputation." The covers of the two magazines had a general resemblance in colour, but the defendant's cover exhibited the picture of a lady in the place where a coat of arms appeared upon the plaintiffs' magazine. Vice-Chancellor Malins said, if the question had arisen between two independent publishers, he should have had some difficulty in deciding that the cover of the defendant's magazine was so close an imitation of that of the plaintiffs' as to entitle him to an injunction ; but as the defendant had entered into a covenant not to do anything to injure the magazine entitled ' London Society,' which covenant he thought was still in force so long as there was any money due upon the mortgage, and as the whole course of conduct pursued by the defendant evinced, in his opinion, an evident intention on the part of the defendant to injure the sale of the plaintiffs' magazine, and to lead the public to believe that his magazine was a continuation of, or a substitute for, the magazine of the plaintiffs', he had no hesitation in granting the injunction. But since there had been some amount of delay by the plaintiffs, in consequence of which the defendant had been induced, as he alleged, to expend a large sum of money in preparing the January number for publication, he thought it would be right to allow that number to appear in its intended form.

As to the alteration of an author's work by another. When a publisher is the absolute owner of the copyright, he is entitled, without the consent of the author, to publish successive editions of the work with additions and corrections; and, in bringing out new editions, may make such omissions and other changes in the original as will not injure the reputation of the author. But such revision when done by another, cannot lawfully be represented as having been made by the author of the original: and if the publisher issues a new edition under the author's name so incorrect as to be injurious to the author's reputation, he renders himself liable to an action for damages (a).

When, however, a portion of the work is written to be published under the name of another, the author would have no remedy in case of its alteration or variation (b). This was decided in *Cox* v. *Cox* (c). The defendant, a house agent, having prepared a book on the sale of estates, applied to the plaintiff, a barrister, to correct the work, and to supply the legal matter necessary to complete it, for which the plaintiff was to be paid a certain remuneration, according to the number of pages the work might contain. " No agreement," said the Vice-Chancellor in passing judgment, " was come to as to the name under which the work was to appear. The case, therefore, stood thus: The defendant said, ' I am going to write a work, which you shall correct and put into shape, and a part of which you shall supply for a certain remuneration.' If that be so, the plaintiff was evidently in the subordinate position of assisting in the production of a work which was to come

(a) See *Archbold* v. *Sweet*, 1 Moo. & Rob. 162 ; 5 Car. & Pay. 219.
(b) The name of the editor appearing upon the title-page forms no part of the title ; and the Master of the Rolls refused to restrain by injunction the proprietors of a journal from omitting the publication of the editor's name on the title-page, although the agreement between the proprietors and editor provided that the title of the journal should not be altered without mutual consent : *Crookes* v. *Petter*, 6 Jur. (N.S.) 1131.
(c) 11 Hare, 118.

out in the name and as the work of thé defendant. The
work would be partly the defendant's own composition,
and it would be partly the work of the plaintiff; but it was
to come out as one entire publication, and to be paid for at
one uniform rate. The bulk of the matter was apparently
to be supplied by the defendant. The plaintiff employed
himself in the preparation of a treatise on the law of vendor
and purchaser and landlord and tenant, the whole of which
the defendant desired to have compressed into one printed
sheet. The plaintiff, on the other hand, thought that no
information of value on the legal incidents of the property
treated of could be condensed within that compass, and he
extended this portion of the work to three sheets and a
half. The defendant then said : ' If you will reduce this
matter to one-half of its present magnitude, I am willing
to print it; if not, I decline to print it at all.' This was
an absolute rejection of the plaintiff's contribution, except
upon the terms of reducing it in quantity to the extent
which the defendant required. The plaintiff, on the other
hand, was resolved that the whole should be printed or
none. There was at this point of the transaction great
difficulty in the way of any arrangement. The defendant
said, ' I will have only one sheet and three-quarters of
legal matter.' The plaintiff insisted that he should have
three sheets and a half, or none. Then what followed ?
The plaintiff looked over the manuscript again, but did
not reduce it to the required dimensions ; and the defendant, although it had not been so reduced, took the manuscript in the state in which it had been left (which he could
only have been entitled to do under the contract), and he
began to print the work. The plaintiff proceeded to correct the proof sheets; but (as he states), when he began to
find that the legal portion of the work was introduced in a
mutilated form, he intimated his refusal to consent to any
alteration ; and in this state of things the application is
made for the injunction. I have stated what appears to
me to be the substance of the contract between the parties,
up to the time of the discussion as to the space which the

legal matter should occupy; and that contract the plaintiff has, by the fourteenth paragraph of the bill, treated as subsisting, for he thereby claims £60 as the unpaid part of the remuneration on the whole contract. On the other hand, the defendant, having taken the manuscript and used it, cannot, I think, dispute his liability to pay for it, according to the terms of the contract. But that would be a question for a court of law. Something was said with regard to the possible effect of the alteration of the plaintiff's portion of his work, as affecting his reputation; but, as it was held in Sir James Clarke's case (a), the possible effect on reputation, unless connected with property, is not a ground for coming to this court, though it may be an ingredient for the court to consider when the question of a right of property also arises. . . . . A serious question was then adverted to—but it is one which does not arise in this case—how far a party who had purchased a manuscript has a right to alter it, and produce it in a mutilated form?—how far, in a case in which the property has completely passed, it is to be assimilated to a case of goods sold and delivered, and thenceforward in the complete dominion of the purchaser? A qualified contract may be made; an essay may be supplied to a magazine or an encyclopædia, on the understanding that it is to be published entire; and it may be accepted by the editor, and paid for as what it purports to be. In the instance of an essay which had been accepted in that shape, the question might arise whether any curtailment could be allowed under that special contract. But here there is no such special contract. The contract is, that the plaintiff shall supply the defendant with the matter which is required, in such a form as to enable the defendant to publish it as his own. I can find no circumstances from which any such special contract as I have mentioned can be inferred. The plaintiff has, indeed, sought to make it a stipulation that his contribution of the legal materials shall not be published otherwise than entire; but this stipulation has no founda-

(a) *Clarke* v. *Freeman*, 11 Beav. 112.

tion in the original contract, upon which his case rests. Cap. XIX.
It may well be that this part of the work may suffer in
value from the alterations made by the defendant, but no
one will probably expect to find the law set forth with any
great amount of precision in a work issued by a house
agent for the guidance of his customers in dealings of a
simple character. If any such mistakes should occur in
the legal portion of the work, as the plaintiff apprehends,
he will have the remedy in his own hands, by correcting
the errors in a subsequent work, in which he may publish
his treatise in a distinct form."

The plaintiff would have had this right by analogy to
the principle that a publisher acquiring from an author
a right to publish a treatise in a particular work, such as
in the 'Encyclopædia Britannica,' would not be entitled
to make the publication in another work not embraced
in the contract, nor to publish generally beyond his
licence (a). But it must be borne in mind that the
opportunity of correcting the errors by separate publication could not have arrived until the expiration of twenty-
eight years from the first publication.

Where the agreement is for the exclusive publication
of a specified number of copies, that number only can be
printed and sold, and until their sale the author cannot
revoke the authority given to the publishers, or himself
publish the work.

An agreement that the publisher shall publish a second
edition, if demanded by the public, and print as many
copies as they can sell, gives them the right, when such
demand arises, to publish and sell as many copies as can
properly be considered to belong to that edition, and to
prevent the author or any other person from publishing
until such copies shall be sold (b).

The publisher is bound to observe the terms of the
contract between himself and the author as to the manner

Where agreement is for a specified number of copies.

Agreements as to style of publication.

(a) *Stewart* v. *Black*, 9 Sess. Cas. 2nd Series, 1026; cited Phillips on
Copy. 178. As to bookseller's lien on the copyright for his disbursements,
see *Brook* v. *Wentworth*, 3 Anstr. 881.
(b) *Pulte* v. *Derby*, 5 McLean (Amer.) 328.

and style of the publication, and the price at which it shall be issued to the public, but if the price at which the work is to be sold is not fixed by the agreement or otherwise arranged by the author and publisher, the latter is the proper person to determine the same. At the same time he would not be permitted to fix upon a style, or sell at a price, which would be clearly injurious either to the literary reputation or the pecuniary interests of the author without his consent.

When neither the time during which the publication is to last, nor the number of editions or copies to be published, is specified, the publisher is not bound to publish more than the first edition; and the author, by giving proper notice, may end the contract and prevent the publication of any further editions (a). But the publisher is at liberty to continue publishing successive editions on the terms of the contract until the receipt of such notice: and the author is not entitled to restrain the publication or sale of any edition on which the publisher has incurred expense before receiving notice to end the agreement (b).

After parting with copyright, author cannot reproduce matter in any other book. After an author has parted with the copyright in a book, he is not at liberty to reproduce substantially the same matter in another work. Even in the absence of any special agreement, the second publication would be an infringement of the copyright in the first (c).

A writer agreed with a publisher to edit a translation of Montaigne, adding notes and a biographical sketch of the author, for a particular sum, which was to be increased by other sums as further editions should be published. It was intended that the publisher should have the sole right of multiplying copies of the work, but there was no assignment to him of the copyright. After the publisher's death, his widow and executrix, with the author's

(a) *Reade* v. *Bentley*, 3 K. & J. 271; 4 Id. 656; *Warne* v. *Routledge*, L. R. 18 Eq. 497.
(b) *Reade* v. *Bentley, supra.*
(c) *Rooney* v. *Kelly*, 14 Ir. Law Rep. (N.S.) 158; *Colburn* v. *Simms*, 2 Hare, 543.

knowledge and assent, registered the copyright in her own Cap. XIX. name. On the publication of a fresh edition, the widow paid the author money, and gave him copies of the work on the same terms as were contained in the agreement made with her husband in his lifetime, and on three occasions, when the author claimed remuneration on those terms, she did not repudiate all liability, but disputed merely the amount. This was held to be evidence from which a jury might infer an agreement on the part of the widow to remunerate the author on the same scale as in the agreement with her husband, in consideration of the author assenting to her registering the copyright in her own name (a).

Where the executor and son of a deceased author, in reply to an offer from a publishing house relating to one of his father's works, replied that he would be happy to treat with them "respecting the copyright" in it; and, in another letter, said he had accepted their offer "for the exclusive right of publishing it," and gave a receipt for the money paid "for permission to publish the work so long as the copyright may endure; that right to be exclusively their own for ten years from this date," it was held that this amounted to an express warranty of title, and an equitable assignment of the copyright having, unknown to the executor, been previously made to another publisher, the executor was held liable to an action for breach of the warranty (b). *Warranty on sale of copyright.*

A person may be the proprietor of a copyright in the separate parts of a periodical simply by reason of his employment of the writers (c). It appears but reasonable, that where the proprietors of a periodical employ a gentleman to write a given article, or a series of articles or reports, expressly for the purpose of publication therein, to imply that the copyright of the articles so expressly written for such periodical, and paid for by the proprie- *Copyright of articles in the proprietor of periodicals.*

(a) *Hazlett* v. *Templemore*, 13 L. T. (N.S.) 593.
(b) *Sims* v. *Marryatt*, 17 Q. B. 281.
(c) But see Jervis, C.J., in *Shepherd* v. *Conquest*, 25 L. J. (C.P.) 127 17 C. B. 427.

CAP. XIX.   tors and publishers, shall be the property of such proprietors and publishers; otherwise the author the day after his article had been published by the persons for whom he contracted to write it, might republish it in a separate form, or in another serial, and there would be no correspondent benefit to the original publishers for the payment they had made (a).

How far proprietor of periodical can interfere with editor.   Without determining the extent to which the owners of the copyright in a journal are justified in interfering with the editor in his editorial capacity, where the remuneration of the editor depends upon the success of the journal, the court refused to restrain the proprietors from altering articles proposed to be inserted by the editor, or inserting others contrary to his wish, it being the province of a jury to determine the amount of damage, if any, which the editor sustained by reason of the conduct of the proprietors (b).

Where an editor and publishers have formed a partnership for the publication of a magazine of which they are joint owners, the editor, having taken steps to dissolve the partnership with the view of establishing another periodical, is not at liberty to advertise the discontinuance of the first magazine. The title of the latter and the right to publish it are partnership property, and may be sold for the benefit of the partners. But the editor may advertise its discontinuance by himself, or as far as he is concerned (c).

Construction of agreements between authors and publishers.   Should an author, in consideration of a sum of money paid to him, agree that certain persons shall have the sole power of printing, reprinting, and publishing a particular work for all time, that would be parting with the copyright; but if the agreement be that the publishers,

(a) Where publishers of a magazine employ and pay an editor, and the editor employs and pays persons for writing articles in the magazine,— Semble, the copyright in such articles is not vested in the publishers under 5 & 6 Vict. c. 45, s. 18; Brown v. Cooke, 11 Jur. 77; 16 L. J. (N.S) Ch. 140. Printers have a lien on undelivered copies of a work printed by them, for the balance due in respect of the whole work: Blake v. Nicholson, 3 M. & S. 167.
(b) Crookes v. Petter, 6 Jur. (N.S.) 1131; 3 L. T. (N.S.) 225.
(c) Bradbury v. Dickens, 27 Beav. 53; Hogg v. Kirby, 8 Ves. 215.

performing certain conditions on their part, should, so
long as they perform such conditions, have the right of
printing and publishing the book, that is a very different
agreement.

In the case of *Sweet* v. *Cater* (a) the agreement, after
reciting that the author had prepared a tenth edition of
his work, which the publisher was desirous of *purchasing*,
and that it had been agreed that a certain printer should
print a given number of copies, and the publisher should
pay to the author *for the said tenth edition* a certain sum,
went on to direct that the work should be in a given
number of volumes, and should *be sold* to the public for a
given price. It was objected that the plaintiff, the publisher, was not under this agreement the *proprietor of the
copyright* within the meaning of the statute (54 Geo. 3,
c. 156, s. 4), but a mere licensee to sell a given number of
copies. The court overruled the objection, holding that
the copyright was equitably vested in the publisher, on
the ground that the contract was obligatory on both parties, that the plaintiff was bound to sell, and therefore the
author was bound to abstain from doing anything which
would interfere with the sale. The court, moreover,
were of opinion that the equitable right to the copyright
endured until the number of copies fixed by the terms of
the agreement had been exhausted. It is to be regretted
that the court did not advert to the question whether the
words of purchase of the agreement—viz., that the publisher was to pay for *the edition*—gave him, independently
of the implied contract on the part of the author not to
do any act which might interfere with the sale, an equitable copyright in the work.

Where there was an agreement in writing between an
author and certain publishers, that they should print,
reprint, and publish his book, upon condition that the
author should prepare it all before a certain day, and
should correct the press, and that the publishers should
direct the mode of printing, and pay all the expenses and

Agreements
for division of
profits, per-
sonal.

(a) 5 Jur. 68; 11 Sim. 572.

take all risk of publishing, and out of the produce should first repay such expenses, and then divide the profits between themselves and the author equally; and that if all copies should be sold and a new edition should be required, the author should prepare the same, and the publishers should print and publish it on the same conditions: and that, if all the copies of any edition should not be sold in five years from the time of publication, the publishers might sell the remaining copies by auction or otherwise, in order to close the account; it was held to be a personal contract by the author, and not a contract for an assignment of the copyright; and, consequently, the benefit thereof could not be assigned by the publishers (a).

The benefit of right to publish not transferable by publisher.　　The case referred to is the leading case of *Stevens* v. *Benning*, in which the original contract was between Mr. William Forsyth and Messrs Saunders & Benning, for the publication of a treatise on the ' Law relating to Composition with Creditors.' After the issue of the second edition one of the parties became bankrupt, and there was an assignment by his assignees and a partner of the bankrupt to Messrs Stevens & Norton, who then endeavoured to restrain the issue of a third edition by William Granger Benning for the author.

" The principal question then is," said Vice-Chancellor Wood, " whether this agreement is a personal engagement or not. It would be difficult for me to say, that in a contract of this kind, the author is utterly indifferent into whose hands his interests under such an engagement are to be intrusted.

" It is not merely a question of his literary interests, but certain publishers undertaking to incur the expenses of bringing out the work, and fixing the price, the author is to have a share of the profits; and they are to decide in what shape the book is to come out, and at what price it is to be sold, and are to account with him. I must say,

---

(a) *Stevens* v. *Benning*, 1 K. & J. 168, affirmed, 6 D. M. & G. 223; 1 Jur. (N.S.) 74. See *Pulte* v. *Derby*, 5 McLean (Amer.) 332.

that, in my opinion, these are peculiarly personal consider- Cap. XIX.
ations; and that this contract bears the impress of being
a personal contract in all these respects. It could not be
a matter of indifference to Mr. Forsyth that the assignees
in bankruptcy of Mr. Benning should be at liberty to
transfer the future right of fixing the price of this and
subsequent editions, and the right to call upon him to
fulfil his duty of preparing a new edition, and the risk
which might be incurred in conducting it, and the other
benefits and obligations of the agreement, to any one
they might think proper; possibly to some one not even
carrying on the trade of a bookseller, as might happen in
case of an absolute sale to the best bidder. Regarding
the agreement as a contract for the purchase of a limited
right, according to the view of the Vice-Chancellor of
England in *Sweet* v. *Cater* (a), it is still impossible that it
should be indifferent to Mr. Forsyth that it should pass
from a respectable firm in London to booksellers residing
in a remote part of the country, or to other persons unable
to fulfil the engagements entered into with him. The
contract, therefore, is one which involves personal considerations; and framed as it is, I must regard it as a
special kind of agency, under which the agents were
bound to sell, and to take the risk of there being no
profits upon themselves" (b).

For similar reasons to those assigned above, a contract Nor whether
whereby the author is to receive a royalty on the copies author re-
ceives a
sold is not transferable by the publishers, but it seems royalty.
doubtful whether, where a definite sum has been agreed Otherwise
upon for the privilege of publication, the benefit of the where he
receives a
contract could not be assigned by the publisher, for though sum down.
the literary interests of the author might possibly be
affected to some extent, yet the change of publishers
could not, at least directly, cause him any pecuniary
injury.

This case of *Stevens* v. *Benning* was followed by Mr.

<hr>

(a) 11 Sim. 579.
(b) 1 Kay & J. 174; on appeal, 2 De G. M. & G. 223.

CAP. XIX. Justice Fry in the recent case of *Hole* v. *Bradbury* (a). The plaintiffs alleged themselves to be the owners of the copyright of a book called ' A Little Tour in Ireland,' and they brought the action to restrain the defendants, who were publishers, from publishing the book. The copyright had not been assigned to the defendants by writing or by entry at Stationers' Hall. The book was composed by two joint authors, one of whom was a plaintiff, the other was dead. The personal representative of the deceased joint author was the other plaintiff. The defendants alleged that before the first publication of the book, which was first published by a firm to whose business the defendants had succeeded, an arrangement had been made between that firm and the deceased joint author, acting on behalf of himself and his co-author, that the firm should engrave the illustrations and print and publish the book. If there were a loss from the publication, the firm were to bear the whole of it. If there were a profit they were to pay half of it to the plaintiff and the deceased joint author. The profits were to be ascertained after debiting the costs of the engraving, printing, and publication. The defendants alleged that this was an agreement for the sale of the copyright, and that they, as successors of the original firm, were entitled by assignment from them to the benefit of the agreement. No member of the original firm was a partner in the defendants' firm. The defendants had in their possession the blocks from which the illustrations to the first edition of the book had been printed, the drawings on the block having been made by the deceased joint author himself. It was held that the alleged agreement was a mere publishing agreement, and did not amount to a sale of the copyright, and that the benefit of the agreement was not assignable without the consent of the authors. Consequently, the defendants could derive no benefit from the agreement, and the injunction must be granted. And,

(a) 12 Ch. Div. 886.

as by the terms of the agreement, the cost of engraving
was to be paid out of the gross profits, the blocks were
not the property of the defendants, and must be delivered
up to the plaintiffs.

An agreement similar to that in *Stevens* v. *Benning*, and Agreement
without specifying a particular edition, constitutes a joint for division of profits a joint
adventure between the parties (*a*), which either party is adventure terminable
at liberty to terminate upon notice after the publication by notice.
of a given edition, if at the date of such notice no fresh
expense has been incurred by the party to whom such
notice be given.

By a memorandum of agreement made in November,
1852, between the plaintiff and the defendant, it was
agreed that the latter should publish, at his own expense
and risk, a work entitled 'Peg Woffington,' of which the
former was the author; and, after deducting from the
produce of the sale thereof the charges for printing, paper,
advertisements, embellishments (if any), and other incidental expenses, including the allowance of 10 per cent.
on the gross amount of the sale for commission and risk
of bad debts, the profits remaining of every edition that
should be printed of the work were to be divided into two
equal parts, one moiety to be paid to the plaintiff, and
the other to the defendant.

Subsequently the same parties entered into a similar
agreement relative to the publication of another work
entitled 'Christie Johnstone,' of which the plaintiff was
also the author; and they signed for that purpose a memorandum of agreement, which, except as to the date and
the title of the work, was in the same words as the former.
Two editions of the former work and four of the latter
having been published by the defendant, and no fresh
expenditure having been incurred by him since the publication of those editions, the plaintiff claimed a right to
terminate the joint adventure between them, and to pre-

(*a*) Joint owners of a copyright may make a contract between themselves
as to the printing and publishing of the work, and neither will be permitted to set up against the other his original rights as a joint owner in
violation of such contract: *Gould* v. *Banks*, 8 Wend. (Amer.) 568.

vent the defendant from publishing any further edition of either work.

The main question to determine was, what was the effect of the agreement which had been entered into between the plaintiff and the defendant?

It was contended by the plaintiff that the case was one of simple agency; that by the effect of the agreement the defendant became a mere agent of the plaintiff. "But," observed the Vice-Chancellor, " it is clear that he became more than that. A mere agent may be paid, as the defendant was to be paid, by a share of the profits; but a mere agent never embarks in the risk of the undertaking; and here the defendant took upon himself the whole expense and risk of bringing out the work. Clearly, therefore, the case is something more than one of simple agency."

Sir W. Page Wood, in passing judgment, made the following observations : " Agreements between authors and publishers assume a variety of forms. Some are so clear and explicit that no doubt can arise upon them. Thus, where an author assigns his copyright, the transaction is one which every person understands, and which leaves no room for uncertainty as to the rights of the parties. Again, where, as in *Sweet* v. *Cater* (a), the author assigns a particular edition, the rights of himself and the publisher are equally clear ; and although in that case the point did not require determination, the court observed, and justly observed, that, where an author has sold an edition of a given number of copies to one publisher, he is not at liberty, before they are sold, to publish the same work himself or through another publisher, in such a manner as to compete with the edition he has sold, but is bound to afford to the purchaser a full opportunity of realizing the benefit of his contract. The case before me, like that of *Stevens* v. *Benning* (b), is of an intermediate description. Here, as there, the author does not sell, or purport to sell, any

(a) 5 Jur. 68 ; 11 Sim. 572.
(b) 1 K. & J. 168 ; 6 D. M. & G. 223.

interest whatever in the copyright. It was contended, and very strongly, in *Stevens* v. *Benning*, that the author had done so ; but I held that he had not, and my view was affirmed by the Lords Justices. Here also, as there, the publisher was to publish at his own risk. Nevertheless, in *Stevens* v. *Benning*, the agreement contained other provisions, considerably more definite than any in this case. It pointed to a series of editions to be published for the author by the same publisher, as to every one of which the author himself stipulated, as part of the contract, that he would assist in the publication. Here the agreement is simply that the publisher shall publish the work at his own expense and risk, and, after deducting all the expenses specified in the memorandum, and an allowance of £10 per cent., the profits remaining of every edition that shall be printed of the work are to be divided into two equal parts, one of which is to be paid to the author, and the other to the publisher."

" It was contended for the defendant that if the effect of the agreement was not an assignment of the copyright (which it is now clearly decided that it could not be), it resulted in a joint adventure, in which the defendant was to have a licence to publish the work ; and that, from the nature of the case, and by the terms of the agreement, that licence was irrevocable. In *Stevens* v. *Benning* I considered the agreement must be regarded as creating, to a certain extent, a joint adventure, and Lord Justice Knight Bruce adopted the same view. He says, it must be observed, that such interest, if any, in the copyright of the author's work as the other parties to the agreement acquired under it, they acquired, not exclusively of the author, ' but by way of joint adventure with him, or of partnership with him, in respect and for the objects of which he undertook the fulfilment by himself personally of certain duties to them, and they undertook the fulfilment by themselves personally of certain duties to him ' (a). Community of risk does not appear to me to be by our law,

(a) 6 D. M. & G. 223, 229.

any more than it was by the civil law, essential to constitute
a partnership; one partner being at liberty to contract with
another that he will take all the losses of the concern upon
himself.   Lord Justice Turner looked upon the agreement
in *Stevens* v. *Benning* in the double light of a licence and
a partnership, speaking, however, less decidedly as to its
being a partnership. He says : ' Next if there was a partnership, then, if the agreement does not affect the copyright,
the partnership was not in the copyright, but in the copies
printed under the licence contained in the agreement ' (a)
—viewing it, therefore, as a licence for the publication of
the work, and then a joint adventure between the author
and publisher in the copies so to be published. If that were
the effect of the agreement in the present case, the question
would still remain, whether the licence be irrevocable.

" The plaintiff does not attempt to interfere with the
publication of an edition which the defendant had commenced, and incurred expense in preparing for publication, before he exercised the option of determining the
agreement.   His claim is limited to editions about which
no such expense had been incurred by the defendant;
and his argument is, that, unless he has a right to determine the agreement as to all such editions, the consequence will be, that, during the whole of the defendant's
life, he may be under an obligation to the defendant,
while the defendant will be under no reciprocal obligation
to him.   It is true that, according to *Stevens* v. *Benning*,
a licence like the present would, I apprehend, be restricted
to the defendant personally, and would not extend to his
executors, or to any future partner or assignee ; but if the
defendant's construction be correct, it follows that, so long
as he lives and is willing to continue publishing fresh
editions of the work, so long, according to the doctrine
in *Sweet* v. *Cater*, the plaintiff will be precluded from
asserting a right to publish any competing edition.   The
defendant could compel the plaintiff to abstain from publishing a single copy of the work, so long as he expressed

(a) 6 D. M. & G. 231.

his readiness to continue publishing. But the plaintiff Cap. XIX. has no reciprocal power. He could never compel the defendant to publish more than a single edition of the work. His powers are limited to what the contract gives him; and, according to the contract, when the defendant has published a single edition the contract on his part is fulfilled. That is a position of considerable hardship for an author, and one which ought to be clearly shewn, upon the face of a contract, to have been contemplated by the parties who entered into it . . . . In the present case, no new expense has been incurred by the defendant, either in printing, advertising, or otherwise, as regards 'Peg Woffington,' since the publication of the second edition, and, as regards ' Christie Johnstone,' since the publication of the fourth edition; and that being, as I have already intimated, the true test in construing the agreement, it appears to me, that, when those editions were published, the period had arrived at which the parties intended a division of profits to take place, and at which the plaintiff became entitled to terminate his agreement with the defendant. This is the only conclusion at which I can arrive, after a very careful consideration of the contracts. But it is much to be regretted that contracts should be framed with such uncertainty, when it would have been so easy to make them certain " (a).

The defendant, having printed a book, sold 300 copies Agreement not to sell under a certain price. of it to the plaintiff, a bookseller, at 40s. a copy, and agreed by letter " only to sell to others at 48s. in quires, and single copies at 50s. until the plaintiff's 300 copies were sold, or the plaintiff should consent." The letter also contained these words : " I do not expect you to sell under 48s. and 50s., but do as you like." The plaintiff, when he had sold part of the 300 copies, went into partnership with C. and transferred all his stock at the cost price; and also sold some copies at 45s. and 46s. An action being afterwards brought by him against the defendant for

(a) *Per* Wood, V.C., in *Reade* v. *Bentley*, 4 K. & J. 656, 669.

selling copies under the stipulated price, it was contended on behalf of the defendant, first, that the plaintiff was bound by implication not to sell the work himself under the price at which the defendant was to sell, and that his selling at 45s. and 46s. was an answer to the action, as being against the good faith and honour of the contract, inasmuch as it would tend to prevent the defendant from selling his copies at all; secondly, that the contract was put an end to by the plaintiff going into partnership with C., and transferring his interest to the firm at 40s. a copy, because the undertaking of the defendant was only to continue in force till the 300 copies were sold by the plaintiff, and his parting with them to a firm of which he was only a partner, was, in fact, a selling, just as much as it would be in the case of a joint stock company (a).

Denman, C.J., in summing up, said : " It seems that the defendant left the plaintiff at liberty to sell as he pleased, but bound himself down not to sell under the prices stated, and this is an answer to some part of the argument urged in favour of the defendant. You will have to say, first, whether the agreement was made ; of this, there does not seem any doubt ; and then, whether it was broken ; and if it was, you must spell out the damage as well as you can from the evidence. It is a very difficult thing to ascertain the amount of damage. I think, in considering that subject, you may reasonably consider, as damage must arise from the effect produced upon the price of the work in the market by the defendant's having sold copies at a sum lower than the stipulated price, whether the plaintiff's own selling at 45s. and 46s. might not have contributed to that depreciation. If you are satisfied that the agreement was broken, then you will have to say to what extent the plaintiff has been injured."

Ordinary
agreement
between
The ordinary agreement between authors and publishers to the effect that the owner shall contribute the manuscript, and the latter shall in the first place defray the

(a) *Benning* v. *Dove*, 5 Car. & P. 427.

cost of the bringing out of the work, and repay himself
out of the proceeds of the sale, and that the net profits
shall be divided, is not properly a partnership (a).

In all agreements between authors and publishers the
terms should be distinctly stated, and the respective rights
of the parties clearly defined. The number of copies of
which the edition is to consist should be declared, for
otherwise a publisher might, if so disposed, print 20,000
as one edition (b). But a person who has acquired the
right to publish one edition only of a work, cannot publish
another edition, without authority.

The meaning of the word "edition," and the construction to be placed upon it, were fully discussed in *Reade* v.
Bentley. It was argued that where a work had once been
stereotyped, the term "edition" was no longer applicable;
and that when a work is published in what are called
"thousands," 20,000 or 30,000 being circulated, each
thousand could not properly be called an "edition."
Wood, V.C., however, thought that not merely in point
of etymology, but having regard to what actually takes
place in the publication of any work, an "edition of a
work was the putting of it forth before the public, and if
this were done in batches at successive periods, each successive batch was a new edition; and the question whether
the individual copies had been printed by means of
movable type or by stereotype, did not seem to him to be
material. If movable type were used, the type having
been broken up, the new edition was prepared by setting-
up the type afresh, printing afresh, advertising afresh, and
repeating all the other necessary steps to obtain a new
circulation of the work. In that case the contemplated
break between the two editions was more complete,
because, until the type was again set up, nothing further

(a) See *Gardiner* v. *Childs*, 8 C. & P. 345 ; *Reade* v. *Bentley*, 3 K & J. 271,
and 4 *Ibid.* 656 ; *Wilson* v. *Whitehead*, 10 M. & W. 503 ; *Gale* v. *Leckie*,
2 Stark. 107 ; *Venables* v. *Wood*, 3 Ross, L. C. on Com. Law, 529, cited
Lindley on Partnership, 22.

(b) *Per* Wood, V.C., in *Reade* v. *Bentley*, 4 K. & J. 656, 669 ; 27 L. J. (Ch.)
254 ; *Sweet* v. *Cater*, 11 Sim. 572 ; 5 Jur. 68 ; *Stevens* v. *Benning*, 1 K. & J.
168 ; 6 D. M. & G. 223 ; *Benning* v. *Dove*, 5 C. & P. 427.

could be done. It made no substantial difference as
regards the meaning of the term "edition," whether the
new "thousand" had been printed by a resetting of movable type, or by stereotype, or whether they have been
printed at the same time with the former thousand or
subsequently. A new "edition" is published whenever,
having in his storehouse a certain number of copies, the
publisher issues a fresh batch of them to the public. This,
according to the practice of the trade, is done, as is well
known, periodically. And if, after printing 20,000 copies,
a publisher should think it expedient for the purpose of
keeping up the price of the work, to issue them in batches
of a thousand at a time, keeping the rest under lock and
key, each successive issue would be a new "edition" in
every sense of the word (a).

In many cases an advantage would accrue by a publisher so doing; for when an author sells the copyright
of a work to a publisher for a certain specified time, the
publisher has the right, after the expiration of that period,
of selling copies of the work he has printed before the
expiration of the time limited.

Right of the publisher to sell copies on hand prior to the expiration of his limited copyright. This was decided in the important case of *Howitt* v.
Hall (b). Mr. William Howitt applied for an injunction to
restrain the defendants Messrs. Hall & Virtue, the publishers, from selling or otherwise disposing of any copies of
an original work called 'A Boy's Adventures in the Wilds
of Australia,' of which Mr. Howitt was the author and
registered proprietor. It appeared by the affidavits that in
the year 1854, a negotiation was entered into with the
defendants by Mrs. Mary Howitt, the wife of the plaintiff,
who was then in Australia, for the sale to them of the

(a) Per Wood, V.C., in *Reade* v. *Bentley*, 4 K. & J. 656, 667. See *Blackwood* v. *Brewster*, 7 Dec. 1860; 23 Sess. Cas. 2nd Series, 142. In this case
it was held that an editor, under an agreement that he should prepare
every new edition of a work, and should receive a certain sum for his
services, is not entitled to superintend, or to claim payment for, the reprinting of a part of the work to replace copies destroyed by fire. The
copies reprinted under such circumstances do not form a new edition, but
go to replace the part of the edition destroyed.
(b) 10 W. R. 381; 6 L. T. (N.S.) 348.

copyright of the work in question for four years, for a sum of £250. This negotiation, after some discussion as to the precise date from which the contract was to commence, resulted in an agreement being entered into on behalf of the plaintiff, which was afterwards confirmed on his return from Australia by the following memorandum signed by him :—

"Gentlemen,—I confirm the agreement entered into with you by Mrs. Howitt on the 14th of March, 1854, for the publication of 'A Boy's Adventures in Australia,' being a copyright of four years from that date.

"WILLIAM HOWITT."

On the same day the defendants sent for the plaintiff's signature a receipt for the £250, "being the purchase-money, as agreed, for the copyright and sole right of sale for four years" of the work in question. In October, 1857, the work having then gone through two editions, the defendants contemplated issuing a third and cheap edition, and accordingly gave notice of their intention to Mr. Howitt, by whom it was revised previously to publication. No further copies had been printed, and the term of four years expired in March, 1858. In February of 1862, the plaintiff, being about to bring out a uniform edition of the juvenile works of Mrs. Howitt and himself, and having, as he stated, only then for the first time discovered that the defendants were continuing to sell the work and to advertise it for sale, wrote to them complaining of this as an infringement of his copyright and a breach of contract, and asking for compensation. In reply to this application, the defendants insisted on their legal right to sell the remaining stock, as their own *bonâ fide* property, when and as they pleased ; but at the same time they expressed their willingness to sell it by auction during the present month of March, so as not to stand in the way of the new edition. This suggestion, however, the plaintiff declined to accede to, and filed his bill pray-

CAP. XIX. | ing for an account of the profit made by the defendants since March, 1858, and for an injunction. Vice-Chancellor Wood said, that the purchase of the copyright carried with it the right of printing and publishing, and the defendant was entitled to continue selling after the expiration of the four years' term the stock printed by him under his purchase. "The Copyright Acts were directed against unlawful printing; and when, as in this case, the defendant had acquired the right of lawfully printing the work, he was at liberty to sell at any time what he had so printed. The words 'sole right of sale' might or might not have been superfluous; but after four years the right to print the work reverted to the author, who had taken care to secure himself in this respect. It had been suggested that the effect might be to destroy the copyright in the author altogether, as the publisher who had purchased the copyright for a limited period only might during that period print off copies enough to last for all time. A nice question might indeed arise as to the number of copies of which an edition might consist, but a publisher was not likely to incur the useless expense of printing copies enough to exhaust the demand for all time, and have them lying upon his hands unprofitably. Besides this, even if the effect of a sale for four years might operate in this way to deprive the author of all copyright in his work, the answer was that he had not guarded himself against such a contingency. If a manifest case of fraud upon the author were established, the court would know how to deal with it. But nothing of the sort was shewn. The defendants had acted quite *bonâ fide*, and were making a perfectly legitimate use of their contract, and the motion must be refused."

Assignor after assignment of copyright may sell copies remaining on hand. | So also it has been held that after he has assigned his copyright, the assignor is free to sell any copies of the book which he had printed before the assignment was made (a), but of course this was in the absence of any express agreement between the parties and of the

(a) *Taylor* v. *Pillow*, L. R. 7 Eq. 418.

existence of any circumstances from which any implied Cap. XIX.
agreement to the contrary might have been inferred.

The right of the publisher in the one case, and of the But the right
assignor in the other are not exclusive rights. Thus where is not an exclusive
the plaintiffs had orally agreed with Mrs. Cook to publish right.
at their own expense a book written by her and entitled
'How to Dress on £15 a Year as a Lady, by a Lady,' to
sell at a shilling a copy, and to pay her a penny for each
copy sold. Nothing was said as to how many copies, or
how long the plaintiffs should publish, or whether they
should be the sole publishers. When forty-four thousand
copies had been printed, and forty-two thousand sold, the
author notified to the plaintiffs the termination of the
agreement, and immediately authorized the defendants to
issue a new edition. The plaintiffs now sought to restrain
such publication until the copies printed by them under
the agreement should be sold. Sir George Jessel, M.R.,
held that the plaintiffs were entitled to be the exclusive
publishers while the agreement lasted; but that after its
termination, though they were at liberty to sell the copies
previously printed, they had no power to prevent the
author or any person claiming under her from publishing (a).

"Looking at the nature of the book," said the Master
of the Rolls, "and to the circumstance that it was a term
of the agreement that the publishers should publish at
their own risk, and pay the royalty, I think the contract,
so long as it existed, must be taken to be an exclusive
contract, that is to say, that so long as Messrs. Warne
& Co. were allowed to publish so long no one else
could publish—neither the lady herself, nor an assign
from her. That being established, what is the next right
it gives to either party? On the determination of the
partnership adventure, or whatever you choose to call it,
what right had Messrs. Warne & Co. in the book?
There is authority upon the subject, but I do not think it

(a) L. R. 18 Eq. 497.

2 R

wants authority. I think it is plain that no termination
of the agreement could deprive them of the right of selling
the copies which they have themselves printed under this
arrangement. Whether the arrangement was at will or
for a term, the publishers must retain the right of selling
for their own benefit (subject to the royalty) the copies
which they have printed at their own expense, in reliance
upon that agreement. So far I go with the plaintiffs; but
the plaintiffs then want me to import something else—not
only that the publishers should have the right to sell any
copies they might have printed before the disagreement,
but that the owner of the copyright should not have the
right to publish at all, so long as any copies remain unsold.
I cannot find that in the agreement, and it does not seem
to be reasonable to import it; because it would come to
this, that if the publishers printed a very large number of
copies it would deprive the authoress of the copyright
altogether. I cannot import such an unreasonable term
into the agreement.

"Then it is said, that, if you give the publisher no protection, the result may be that the author may publish
another edition a day or two after the publishing of the
first edition, and so destroy the value of the remaining
copies of the first edition remaining unsold. That may
be. And it is said that that is so unreasonable that you
must infer some stipulation to prevent it. Why? No
doubt partnerships at will have their inconveniences as
well as their conveniences. There is no reason why I
should make persons take up a totally different position
from that which they have agreed to take up, because it
might be convenient to one of the parties after the termination of the arrangement. If you do want that protection
for a term of years or for a definite term, you must contract for it. That is all. But I cannot import such a term
into the contract. If I did, I should make partnerships
at will involve consequences that the partners never
dreamt of."

This decision must be received with considerable caution. The Court held that so long as the arrange- ment between the parties held good the publishers , had the exclusive right of publication. They must have had this by reason of an implied agreement to that effect, there being nothing express on the subject in the contract. It was implied in consideration of the ex- pense incurred by the publishers, and must in reason be held to continue so long as there were any copies printed with the consent and concurrence of the author remaining unsold.

And of what value was the exclusive right of publication to the publisher, if this right was determinable at any moment by the author. In short the right existed so long as it was of no value, but the moment it might have had any value it ceased to exist.

In a case in the Irish Bankruptcy Court it appeared that Curry & Co. had published three novels by Charles Lever, under an agreement that they should bear the ex- pense of publication and pay to the author a specified sum for a certain number of copies, and should divide with him the nett profits on the copies sold beyond that number. While a large number of printed copies remained unsold, Curry became bankrupt, when Lever claimed to be entitled as partner to one half of the unsold stock, and to have a special lien on the other half, entitling him as a preferred creditor to be paid in full for whatever balance might be due to him. The commissioner held that if Lever were a partner in the unsold stock, he was a mere dormant and secret partner; and, as the whole of the stock had been in the possession and disposition of the bankrupt, it passed to the creditors under the Bankruptcy Act; and that, for the same reason, Lever had no special lien on it. The commissioner said that the question as to whom the copyright belonged was not within the jurisdic- of the Court; but he expressed the opinion that, as Curry had been permitted to advertise himself as the owner,

CAP. XIX. the copyright should be dealt with as his property in bankruptcy (a).

Accounts between authors and publishers.

As to accounts between authors and publishers, see *Barry* v. *Stevens* (b) aud *Stiff* v. *Cassell* (c).

(a) *In re Curry*, 12 Ir. Eq. 382. As to publisher's commission see case of *Gatty* v. *Pawson*, 'Times,' March 9, 1873.

(b) 31 Beav. 258.   (c) 2 Jur. (N.S.) 348.

APPENDIX (A).

8 ANNE, c. 19 (1709).

An Act for the Encouragement of Learning, by vesting the Copies of printed Books in the Authors or Purchasers of such Copies during the Time therein mentioned.

Repealed by 5 & 6 Vict. c. 45, § 1.

By 7 Geo 2, c. 24, the sole liberty of printing and publishing the Histories of Thuanus, with additions and improvements, during the time therein limited, is granted to Samuel Buckley.

---

8 GEO. II. c. 13 (1735).

An Act for the Encouragement of the Arts of designing, engraving, and etching historical and other Prints, by vesting the Properties thereof in the Inventors and Engravers during the Time therein mentioned.

WHEREAS divers persons have, by their own genius, industry, pains, and expense, invented and engraved, or worked in mezzotinto, or chiaro-oscuro, sets of historical and other prints, in hopes to have reaped the sole benefit of their labours: And whereas printsellers and other persons have of late, without the consent of the inventors, designers, and proprietors of such prints, frequently taken the liberty of copying, engraving, and publishing, or causing to be copied, engraved, and published base copies of such works, designs, and prints, to the very great prejudice and detriment of the inventors, designers, and proprietors thereof: For remedy thereof, and for preventing such practices for the future, may it please Your Majesty that it may be enacted, and be it enacted by the King's most excellent Majesty, by and with the advice and consent of the Lords spiritual and temporal, and Commons, in this present Parliament assembled, and by the

After 24th
June, 1735, the
prope'ty of his-
torical and
other prints
vested in the
inventor
for fourteen
years.
authority of the same, That from and after the twenty-fourth day
of June which shall be in the year of our Lord one thousand seven
hundred and thirty-five, every person who shall invent and design,
engrave, etch, or work, in mezzotinto or chiaro-oscuro, or from his
own works and invention shall cause to be designed and engraved,
etched, or worked, in mezzotinto or chiaro-oscuro, any historical
or other print or prints, shall have the sole right and liberty of
printing and reprinting the same for the term of fourteen years,
to commence from the day of the first publishing thereof, which

Proprietor's
name to be
affixed to each
print.
shall be truly engraved with the name of the proprietor on each
plate, and printed on every such print or prints; and that if any

printseller or other person whatsoever, from and after the said
twenty-fourth day of June one thousand seven hundred and thirty-
five, within the time limited by this Act, shall engrave, etch,
or work as aforesaid, or in any other manner copy and sell, or
cause to be engraved, etched, or copied and sold, in the whole or
in part, by varying, adding to, or diminishing from the main
design, or shall print, reprint, or import for sale, or cause to be
printed, reprinted, or imported for sale, any such print or
prints, or any parts thereof, without the consent of the proprietor
or proprietors thereof first had and obtained in writing signed
by him or them respectively in the presence of two or more
credible witnesses, or, knowing the same to be so printed or
reprinted without the consent of the proprietor or proprietors shall
publish, sell, or expose to sale, or otherwise or in any other
manner dispose of, or cause to be published, sold, or exposed to
sale, or otherwise or in any other manner disposed of, any such
print or prints, without such consent first had and obtained as
aforesaid, then such offender or offenders shall forfeit the plate or
plates on which such print or prints are or shall be copied, and all
and every sheet or sheets (being part of or whereon such print or
prints are or shall be so copied or printed), to the proprietor or
proprietors of such original print or prints, who shall forthwith
destroy and damask the same; and further, that every such
offender or offenders shall forfeit five shillings for every print
which shall be found in his, her, or their custody, either printed
or published, and exposed to sale or otherwise disposed of, contrary
to the true intent and meaning of this Act, the one moiety thereof
to the King's most excellent Majesty, his heirs and successors, and
the other moiety thereof to any person or persons that shall sue for
the same, to be recovered in any of His Majesty's Courts of Record
at Westminster, by action of debt, bill, plaint, or information, in
which no wager of law, essoign, privilege or protection, or more than
one imparlance, shall be allowed.

II. Provided nevertheless, That it shall and may be lawful for any person or persons who shall hereafter purchase any plate or plates for printing from the original proprietors thereof to print and reprint from the said plates without incurring any of the penalties in this Act mentioned. Not to extend to purchasers of plates from the original proprietors.

III. And be it further enacted by the authority aforesaid, That if any action or suit shall be commenced or brought against any person or persons whatsoever for doing or causing to be done anything in pursuance of this Act, the same shall be brought within the space of three months after so doing; and the defendant and defendants in such action or suit shall or may plead the general issue, and give the special matter in evidence; and if upon such action or suit a verdict shall be given for the defendant or defendants, or if the plaintiff or plaintiffs become nonsuited, or discontinue his, her, or their action or actions, then the defendant or defendants shall have and recover full costs, for the recovery whereof he shall have the same remedy as any other defendant or defendants in any other case hath or have by law. Limitations of actions for anything done in pursuance of Act. General issue.

IV. Provided always, and be it further enacted by the authority aforesaid, That if any action or suit shall be commenced or brought against any person or persons for any offence committed against this Act, the same shall be brought within the space of three months after the discovery of every such offence, and not afterwards, anything in this Act contained to the contrary notwithstanding. Limitation of actions for offences against this Act.

V. Repealed by 30 & 31 Vict. c. 59.

VI. And be it further enacted by the authority aforesaid, That this Act shall be deemed, adjudged, and taken to be a Public Act, and be judicially taken notice of as such by all judges, justices, and other persons whatsoever, without specially pleading the same. Public Act.

---

12 GEO. II. c. 36 (1739).

An Act for prohibiting the Importation of Books reprinted abroad, and first composed or written in and printed in Great Britain; and for repealing so much of an Act made in the Eighth Year of the Reign of her late Majesty Queen Anne as empowers the limiting the Prices of Books.

Repealed by 30 & 31 Vict. c. 59.

7 Geo. III. c. 38 (1766).

An Act to amend and render more effectual an Act made in the
Eighth Year of the Reign of King George the Second, for En-
couragement of the Arts of designing, engraving, and etching
historical and other Prints; and for vesting in, and securing to,
Jane Hogarth, Widow, the Property in certain Prints.

Preamble, re-
citing Act
8 G. 2.

Whereas an Act of Parliament passed in the eighth year of the
reign of His late Majesty King George the Second, intituled "An
Act for the Encouragement of the Arts of designing, engraving, and
etching historical and other Prints, by vesting the Properties
thereof in the Inventors and Engravers, during the Time therein
mentioned," has been found ineffectual for the purposes thereby
intended: Be it enacted by the King's most excellent Majesty, by
and with the advice and consent of the Lords spiritual and
temporal, and Commons, in this present Parliament assembled, and

The original
inventors, de-
signers, or en-
gravers, &c.,
of historical
and other
prints, and
such who shall
cause prints to
be done from
works, &c., of
their own
invention,

by the authority of the same, that from and after the first day of
January, one thousand seven hundred and sixty-seven, all and
every person and persons who shall invent or design, engrave, etch,
or work in mezzotinto or chiaro-oscuro, or, from his own work,
design, or invention, shall cause or procure to be designed, engraved,
etched, or worked in mezzotinto or chiaro-oscuro, any historical
print or prints, or any print or prints of any portrait, conversation,
landscape, or architecture, map, chart, or plan, or any other print
or prints whatsoever, shall have, and are hereby declared to have,
the benefit and protection of the said Act and this Act, under the
restrictions and limitations hereinafter mentioned.

and also such as
shall engrave,
&c., any print
taken from any
picture, draw-
ing, model, or
sculpture;
are entitled to
the benefit and
protection of
the recited and
present Act;

II. And be it further enacted by the authority aforesaid, That
from and after the said first day of January one thousand seven
hundred and sixty-seven, all and every person and persons who
shall engrave, etch, or work in mezzotinto or chiaro-oscuro, or
cause to be engraved, etched, or worked, any print, taken from
any picture, drawing, model, or sculpture, either ancient or modern,
shall have, and are hereby declared to have, the benefit and protection of the said Act and this Act, for the term hereinafter
mentioned, in like manner as if such print had been graved or
drawn from the original design of such graver, etcher, or drafts-

and those who
shall engrave
or import for
sale, copies of
such prints, are
liable to penal-
ties.

man; and if any person shall engrave, print and publish, or import
for sale, any copy of any such print, contrary to the true intent and
meaning of this and the said former Act, every such person shall
be liable to the penalties contained in the said Act, to be recovered
as therein and hereinafter is mentioned.

III. and IV. repealed by 30 & 31 Vict. c. 59.

V. And be it further enacted by the authority aforesaid, That all *Penalties may* and every the penalties and penalty inflicted by the said Act, and *be sued for as* extended, and meant to be extended, to the several cases comprised *by the recited* *Act is directed* in this Act shall and may be sued for and recovered in like manner, and under the like restrictions and limitations, as in and by the said Act is declared and appointed; and the plaintiff or common *and be re-* informer in every such action (in case such plaintiff or common in- *covered with* former shall recover any of the penalties incurred by this or the *full costs;* *provided the* said former Act) shall recover the same, together with his full costs *prosecution be* of suit. Provided also, that the party prosecuting shall commence *commenced* *within six* his prosecution within the space of six calendar months after the *months after* offence committed. *the fact.*

VI. And be it further enacted by the authority aforesaid, That *The right in-* the sole right and liberty of printing and reprinting intended to be *tended to be* *secured by this* secured and protected by the said former Act and this Act, shall *and the former* be extended, continued, and be vested in the respective proprietors, *Act, vested in* for the space of twenty-eight years, to commence from the day of *the proprietors* *for the term of* the first publishing of any of the works respectively hereinbefore *twenty-eight* and in the said former Act mentioned. *years from* *the first publi-*

VII. And be it further enacted by the authority aforesaid, That *cation.* if any action or suit shall be commenced or brought against any *Limitation of* person or persons whatsoever, for doing, or causing to be done, any- *actions.* thing in pursuance of this Act, the same shall be brought within the space of six calendar months after the fact committed; and the defendant or defendants in any such action or suit shall or may plead the general issue, and give the special matter in evidence; *General issue.* and if, upon such action or suit, a verdict shall be given for the defendant or defendants, or if the plaintiff or plaintiffs become non- suited, or discontinue his, her, or their action or actions, then the defendant or defendants shall have and recover full costs; for the *Full costs.* recovery whereof he shall have the same remedy as any other defendant or defendants, in any other case, hath or have by law.

15 Geo. III. c. 53 (1775).

An Act for enabling the two Universities in England, the four
Universities in Scotland, and the several Colleges of Eton,
*Westminster, and Winchester, to hold in perpetuity their Copy_*
right in Books, given or bequeathed to the said Universities and
Colleges for the Advancement of useful Learning and other
Purposes of Education ; and for amending so much of an Act of
the Eighth Year of the Reign of Queen Anne as relates to the
Delivery of Books to the Warehouse-keeper of the Stationers'
Company, for the Use of the several Libraries therein mentioned.

Preamble.   WHEREAS authors have heretofore bequeathed or given, and may
hereafter bequeath or give, the copies of books composed by them,
to or in trust for one of the two universities in that part of Great
Britain called England, or to or in trust for some of the colleges or
houses of learning within the same, or to or in trust for the four
universities in Scotland, or to or in trust for the several colleges of
Eton, Westminster, and Winchester, and in and by their several
wills or other instruments of donation, have directed or may direct,
that the profits arising from the printing and reprinting such books
shall be applied or appropriated as a fund for the advancement of
learning, and other beneficial purposes of education within the
said universities and colleges aforesaid : And whereas such useful
purposes will frequently be frustrated, unless the sole printing and
reprinting of such books, the copies of which have been or shall be
so bequeathed or given as aforesaid, be preserved and secured to
the said universities, colleges, and houses of learning respectively
in perpetuity : May it therefore please Your Majesty that it may
be enacted, and be it enacted by the King's most excellent Majesty,
by and with the advice and consent of the Lords spiritual and
temporal, and Commons, in this present Parliament assembled,

Universities, and by the authority of the same, That the said universities and
&c., in England colleges respectively shall, at their respective presses, have, for
and Scotland ever, the sole liberty of printing and reprinting all such books as
to have for
ever the sole shall at any time heretofore have been, or (having not been hereto-
right of print- fore published or assigned) shall at any time hereafter be being, &c., such queathed, or otherwise given by the author or authors of the same
books as have
been, or shall respectively, or the representatives of such author or authors, to or
be, bequeathed in trust for the said universities, or to or in trust for any college
to them,   or house of learning within the same, or to or in trust for the said
four universities in Scotland, or to or in trust for the said colleges
of Eton, Westminster, and Winchester, or any of them, for the
unless the same purposes aforesaid, unless the same shall have been bequeathed or

given, or shall hereafter be bequeathed or given, for any term of have been, or
years, or other limited term, any law or usage to the contrary shall be, given
hereof in anywise notwithstanding. for a limited time.

II. And it is hereby further enacted, That if any bookseller, After June 24,
printer, or other person whatsoever, from and after the twenty- 1775, persons
fourth day of June one thousand seven hundred and seventy-five, printing or selling such
shall print, reprint, or import, or cause to be printed, reprinted, or books shall
imported, any such book or books; or, knowing the same to be so forfeit the
printed or reprinted, shall sell, publish, or expose to sale, or cause same, and also
to be sold, published, or exposed to sale, any such book or books; 1d. for every
then such offender or offenders shall forfeit such book or books, and sheet;
all and every sheet or sheets, being part of such book or books, to
the university, college, or house of learning respectively, to whom
the copy of such book or books shall have been bequeathed or given
as aforesaid, who shall forthwith damask and make waste paper of
them; and further, that every such offender or offenders shall
forfeit one penny for every sheet which shall be found in his, her,
or their custody, either printed or printing, published or exposed
to sale, contrary to the true intent and meaning of this Act; the
one moiety thereof to the King's most excellent Majesty, his heirs one moiety to
and successors, and the other moiety thereof to any person or His Majesty,
persons who shall sue for the same; to be recovered in any of His and the other
Majesty's Courts of Record at Westminster, or in the Court of cutor.
Session in Scotland, by action of debt, bill, plaint, or information,
in which no wager of law, essoin, privilege, or protection, or more
than one imparlance, shall be allowed.

III. Provided nevertheless, That nothing in this Act shall extend Nothing in this
to grant any exclusive right otherwise than so long as the books or Act to extend
copies belonging to the said universities or colleges are printed only exclusive right
at their own printing presses within the said universities or colleges longer than
respectively, and for their sole benefit and advantage; and that if such books are
any university or college shall delegate, grant, lease, or sell their presses of the
copyrights, or exclusive rights of printing the books hereby granted, universities.
or any part thereof, or shall allow, permit, or authorise any person
or persons, or bodies corporate, to print or reprint the same, that
then the privileges hereby granted are to become void and of no
effect, in the same manner as if this Act had not been made; but
the said universities and colleges as aforesaid shall nevertheless Universities
have a right to sell such copies so bequeathed or given as aforesaid, may sell Copy-
in like manner as any author or authors now may do under the pro- rights in like
visions of the statute of the eighth year of Her Majesty Queen Anne. author.

IV. And whereas many persons may through ignorance offend No person sub-
against this Act, unless some provision be made whereby the ject to penalties
property of every such book as is intended by this Act to be for printing,
secured to the said universities, colleges, and houses of learning already be-

queathed, un-
less they be
entered before
June 24, 1775.

within the same, and to the said universities in Scotland, and to
the respective colleges of Eton, Westminster, and Winchester, may
be ascertained and known, be it therefore enacted by the authority
aforesaid, That nothing in this Act contained shall be construed to
extend to subject any bookseller, printer, or other person whatsoever, to the forfeitures or penalties herein mentioned, for or by
reason of the printing or reprinting, importing or exposing to sale,
any book or books, unless the title to the copy of such book or
books, which has or have been already bequeathed or given to any
of the said universities or .colleges aforesaid; be entered in the
register book of the Company of Stationers kept for that purpose,
in such manner as hath been usual, on or before the twenty-fourth

All books that
may hereafter
be bequeathed,
must be en-
tered within
two months
after such
bequest shall
be known.

day of June, one thousand seven hundred and seventy-five; and of
all and every such book or books as may or shall hereafter be bequeathed or given as aforesaid, be entered in such register within
the space of two months after any such bequest or gift shall have
come to the knowledge of the vice-chancellors of the said universities, or the heads of houses and colleges of learning, or of the
principal of any of the said four universities respectively; for every

6d. to be paid
for each entry
in the register
book, which
may be in
spected with-
out fee.

of which entries so to be made as aforesaid the sum of sixpence
shall be paid, and no more; which said register book shall and
may, at all seasonable and convenient times, be referred to and
inspected by any bookseller, printer, or other person, without any
fee or reward; and the clerk of the said company of Stationers shall,

Clerk to give
a certificate,
being paid 6d.

when and as often as thereunto required, give a certificate under
his hand of such entry or entries, and for every such certificate may
take a fee not exceeding sixpence.

V. And be it further enacted, That if the clerk of the said

If clerk refuse
or neglect to
make entry,
&c.

Company of Stationers for the time being shall refuse or neglect to
register or make such entry or entries, or to give such certificate,
being thereunto required by the agent of either of the said
universities or colleges aforesaid, lawfully authorised for that
purpose, then either of the said universities or colleges afore-

Proprietor of
such copyright
to have like
benefit as if
such entry
had been made,
and the clerk
shall forfeit
20l.

said, being the proprietor of such copyright or copyrights as
aforesaid (notice being first given of such refusal by an advertisement in the Gazette), shall have the like benefit as if such entry or
entries, certificate or certificates, had been duly made and given;
and the clerk so refusing shall for every such offence forfeit twenty
pounds to the proprietor or proprietors of every such copyright;
to be recovered in any of His Majesty's Courts of Record at
Westminster, or in the Court of Session in Scotland, by action
of debt, bill, plaint, or information, in which no wager of law,
essoin, privilege, protection, or more than one imparlance, shall be
allowed.

VI. and VII. repealed by 24 & 25 Vict. c. 101.

ᵥ III. And be it further enacted by the authority aforesaid, That Public Act this Act shall be adjudged, deemed, and taken to be a Public Act, and shall be judicially taken notice of as such, by all judges, justices, and other persons whatsoever, without specially pleading the same.

---

17 GEO. III. c. 57 (1777).

An Act for more effectually securing the Property of Prints to Inventors and Engravers, by enabling them to sue for and recover Penalties in certain Cases.

WHEREAS an Act of Parliament passed in the eighth year of the Recital of Acts reign of His late Majesty King George the Second, intituled "An 8 G. 2, and Act for the Encouragement of the Arts of designing, engraving, 7 G. 2. and etching historical and other Prints, by vesting the Properties thereof in the Inventors and Engravers, during the Time therein mentioned:" And whereas, by an Act of Parliament passed in the seventh year of the reign of His present Majesty, for amending and rendering more effectual the aforesaid Act, and for other purposes therein mentioned, it was (among other things) enacted, That from and after the first day of January one thousand seven hundred and sixty-seven, all and every person or persons who should engrave, etch, or work in mezzotinto or chiaro-oscuro, or cause to be engraved, etched, or worked any print taken from any picture, drawing, model, or sculpture, either ancient or modern, should have and were thereby declared to have the benefit and protection of the said former Act and that Act, for the term thereinafter mentioned, in like manner as if such print had been graved or drawn from the original design of such graver, etcher, or draughtsman; and whereas the said Acts have not effectually answered the purposes for which they were intended, and it is necessary for the encouragement of artists, and for securing to them the property of and in their works, and for the advancement and improvement of the aforesaid arts, that such further provisions should be made as are hereafter mentioned and contained: May it therefore please Your Majesty, that it may be enacted; and be it enacted by the King's most excellent Majesty, by and with the advice and consent of the Lords spiritual and temporal, and Commons, in this present Parliament assembled, and by the authority of the same, That from and after the twenty-fourth day of June, one thousand seven After June 24, hundred and seventy-seven, if any engraver, etcher, print-seller, or 1777, if any other person shall, within the time limited by the aforesaid Acts, or engraver. &c., either of them, engrave, etch, or work, or cause or procure to be shall, within the time

limited by the
afolesaid Acts,
engrave or
etch, &c., any
print without
the consent of
the proprietor,
he shall be
liable to
damages and
double costs.

engraved, etched, or worked, in mezzotinto or chiaro-oscuro, or otherwise, or in any other manner copy, in the whole or in part, by varying, adding to, or diminishing from the main design, or shall print, reprint, or import for sale, or cause or procure to be printed, reprinted, or imported for sale, or shall publish, sell, or otherwise dispose of, or cause or procure to be published, sold, or otherwise disposed of, any copy or copies of any historical print or prints, or any print or prints of any portrait, conversation, landscape, or architecture, map, chart, or plan, or any other print or prints whatsoever, which hath or have been, or shall be engraved, etched, drawn, or designed, in any part of Great Britain, without the express consent of the proprietor or proprietors thereof first had and obtained in writing, signed by him, her, or them respectively, with his, her, or their own hand or hands, in the presence of and attested by two or more credible witnesses, then every such proprietor or proprietors shall and may, by and in a special action upon the case, to be brought against the person or persons so offending, recover such damages as a jury on the trial of such action or on the execution of a writ of inquiry thereon, shall give or assess, together with double costs* of suit.

---

27 Geo. III. c. 38 (1787).

An Act for the Encouragement of the Arts of designing and printing Linens, Cottons, Calicoes, and Muslins, by vesting the Properties thereof in the Designers, Printers, and Proprietors for a limited Time.

Repealed by 5 & 6 Vict. c. 100, § 1.

---

29 Geo. III. c. 19 (1789).

An Act for continuing an Act for the Encouragement of the Arts of designing and printing Linens, Cottons, Calicoes, and Muslins, by vesting the Properties thereof in the Designers, Printers, and Proprietors for a limited Time.

Repealed by 5 & 6 Vict. c. 100, § 1.

---

* So much of this statute as relates to double costs is repealed by 24 & 25 Vict. c. 101.

34 GEO. III. c. 23 (1794).

An Act for amending and making perpetual an Act for the Encouragement of the Arts of designing and printing Linens, Cottons, Calicoes, and Muslins, by vesting the Properties thereof in the Designers, Printers, and Proprietors for a limited Period.

Repealed by 5 & 6 Vict. c. 100, § 1.

---

38 GEO. III. c. 71 (1798).

An Act for Encouraging the Art of making new Models and Casts of Busts, and other Things therein mentioned.

Repealed by 24 & 25 Vict. c. 101.

---

41 GEO. III. c. 107 (1801).

An Act for the further Encouragement of Learning, in the United Kingdom of Great Britain and Ireland, by securing the Copies and Copyright of printed Books to the Authors of such Books, or their Assigns, for the time therein mentioned.

Repealed by 5 & 6 Vict. c. 45, § 1.

---

54 GEO. III. c. 56.

An Act to amend and render more effectual an Act of His present Majesty, for encouraging the Art of making new Models and Casts of Busts, and other Things therein mentioned ; and for giving further Encouragement to such Arts.

[18th May, 1814.]

WHEREAS by an Act, passed in the thirty-eighth year of the reign of His present Majesty, intituled " An Act for encouraging 38 Geo. 3, c. 71. the Art of making new Models and Casts of Busts, and other Things therein mentioned," the sole right and property thereof were vested in the original proprietors, for a time therein specified : And whereas the provisions of the said Act having been found ineffectual for the purposes thereby intended, it is expedient to amend the same, and to make other provisions and regulations for the encouragement of artists, and to secure to them the profits of and in their works, and for the advancement of the said arts : May it therefore please your Majesty that it may be enacted, and be it enacted by the King's most excellent Majesty, by and with the advice and consent of the Lords spiritual and temporal, and Commons, in this present Parliament

The sole right and property of all new and original sculptures, models, copies, and casts, vested in the proprietors for fourteen years.

assembled, and by the authority of the same, That from and after the passing of this Act, every person or persons who shall make or cause to be made any new and original sculpture or model, or copy or cast, of the human figure, or human figures, or of any bust or busts, or of any part or parts of the human figure, clothed in drapery or otherwise, or of any animal or animals, or of any part or parts of any animal combined with the human figure or otherwise, or of any subject being matter of invention in sculpture, or of any alto or basso-relievo representing any of the matters or things hereinbefore mentioned, or any cast from nature of the human figure, or of any part or parts of the human figure, or of any cast from nature of any animal, or of any part or parts of any animal, or of any such subject containing or representing any of the matters and things hereinbefore mentioned, whether separate or combined, shall have the sole right and property of all and in every such new and original sculpture, model, copy, and cast of the human figure or human figures, and of all and in every such bust or busts, and of all and in every such part or parts of the human figure, clothed in drapery or otherwise, and of all and in every such new and original sculpture, model, copy, and cast, representing any animal or animals, and of all and in every such work representing any part or parts of any animal combined with the human figure or otherwise, and of all and in every such new, and original sculpture, model, copy, and cast of any subject, being matter of invention in sculpture, and of all and in every such new and original sculpture, model, copy, and cast in alto or basso-relievo, representing any of the matters or things hereinbefore mentioned, and of every such cast from nature, for the term of fourteen years from first putting forth or publishing the same : Provided, in all and in every case, the proprietor or proprietors do cause his, her, or their name or names, with the date, to be put on all and every such new and original sculpture, model, copy, or cast, and on every such cast from nature, before the same shall be put forth or published.

Works published under the recited Act, vested in the proprietors for fourteen years.

II. And be it further enacted, That the sole right and property of all works, which have been put forth or published under the protection of the said recited Act, shall be extended, continued to and vested in the respective proprietors thereof for the term of fourteen years, to commence from the date when such last mentioned works respectively were put forth or published.

Persons put-

III. And be it further enacted, That if any person or persons

shall, within such term of fourteen years, make or import, or cause ting forth
to be made or imported, or exposed for sale, or otherwise disposed pirated copies
of, any pirated copy or pirated cast of any such new and original or pirated
casts, may be
sculpture, or model or copy, or cast of the human figure or figures, prosecuted.
or of any such bust or busts, or of any such part or parts of the
human figure clothed in drapery or otherwise, or of any such work
of any animal or animals, or of any such part or parts of any
animal or animals combined with the human figure or otherwise,
or of any such subject being matter of invention in sculpture, or
of any such alto or basso-relievo representing any of the matters
or things hereinbefore mentioned, or of any such cast from nature
as aforesaid, whether such pirated copy or pirated cast be produced
by moulding or copying from, or imitating in any way, any of the
matters or things put forth or published under the protection of
this Act, or of any works which have been put forth or published
under the protection of the said recited Act, the right and property
whereof is and are secured, extended, and protected by this Act
in any of the cases as aforesaid, to the detriment, damage, or loss
of the original or respective proprietor or proprietors of any such
works so pirated ; then and in all such cases the said proprietor
or proprietors, or their assignee or assignees, shall and may, by
and in a special action upon the case to be brought against the
person or persons so offending, receive such damages as a jury on Damages and
a trial of such action shall give or assess, together with double double costs.
costs of suits.

IV. Provided nevertheless, That no person or persons who shall Purchasers of
or may hereafter purchase the right or property of any new and copyright se-
cured in the
original sculpture or model, or copy or cast, or of any cast from same.
nature, or of any of the matters and things published under or
protected by virtue of this Act, of the proprietor or proprietors,
expressed in a deed in writing signed by him, her, or them respectively, with his, her, or their own hand, or hands, in the presence
of and attested by two or more credible witnesses, shall be subject
to any action for copying, or casting, or vending the same, anything
contained in this Act to the contrary notwithstanding.

V. Provided always, and be it further enacted, That all actions Limitation of
to be brought as aforesaid, against any person or persons for any actions.
offence committed against this Act, shall be commenced within
six calendar months next after the discovery of every such offence
and not afterwards.

VI. Provided always, and be it further enacted, That from and An additional
immediately after the expiration of the said term of fourteen years, term of four-
teen years, in
the sole right of making and disposing of such new and original case the maker
sculpture, or model, or copy, or cast of any of the matters or things of the original
hereinbefore mentioned, shall return to the person or persons who sculpture, &c.,
shall be living.

2 s

originally made or caused to be made the same, if he or they shall
be then living, for the further term of fourteen years, excepting in
the case or cases where such person or persons shall by sale or
otherwise have divested himself, herself, or themselves, of such
right of making or disposing of any new and original sculpture,
model, or copy, or cast of any of the matters or things hereinbefore
mentioned, previous to the passing of this Act.

---

54 GEO. c. 156 (1814).

*An Act to amend the several Acts for the Encouragement of Learn-
ing, by securing the Copies and Copyright of printed Books to
the Authors of such Books or their Assigns.*

Repealed by 5 & 6 Vict. c. 45, § 1.

---

3 WILL. IV. c. 15.

*An Act to amend the Laws relating to dramatic literary
Property.*

[10th June, 1833.]

WHEREAS by an Act passed in the fifty-fourth year of the reign of
His late Majesty King George the Third, intituled "An Act to
amend the several Acts for the Encouragment of Learning, by
securing the Copies and Copyright of printed Books to the Authors
of such Books or their Assigns," it was amongst other things
provided and enacted, that from and after the passing of the said
Act the author of any book or books composed, and not printed
or published, or which should thereafter be composed and printed
and published, and his assignee or assigns, should have the sole
liberty of printing and reprinting such book or books for the full
term of twenty-eight years, to commence from the day of first
publishing the same, and also, if the author should be living at
the end of that period for the residue of his natural life: And
whereas it is expedient to extend the provisions of the said Act:
Be it therefore enacted by the King's most excellent Majesty, by
and with the advice and consent of the Lords spiritual and temporal, and Commons in this present Parliament assembled, and
by the authority of the same, That from and after the passing of
this Act the author of any tragedy, comedy, play, opera, farce or any
other dramatic piece or entertainment, composed, and not printed
and published by the author thereof or his assignee, or which
hereafter shall be composed, and not printed or published by the

Side notes:
54 G. 3, c. 156.

The author of
any dramatic
piece shall
have as his
property the
sole liberty of

author thereof or his assignee, or the assignee of such author, *representing it* shall have as his own property the sole liberty of representing, or *or causing it to be repre-* causing to be represented, at any place or places of dramatic *sented at any* entertainment whatsoever, in any part of the United Kingdom of *place of dra-* Great Britain and Ireland, in the Isles of Man, Jersey, and *matic enter-tainment.* Guernsey, or in any part of the British dominions, any such production as aforesaid, not printed and published by the author thereof or his assignee, and shall be deemed and taken to be the proprietor thereof; and that the author of any such production, printed and published within ten years before the passing of this Act by the author thereof or his assignee, or which shall hereafter be so printed and published, or the assignee of such author, shall from the time of passing this Act, or from the time of such publication respectively, until the end of twenty-eight years from the day of such first publication of the same, and also, if the author or authors, or the survivor of the authors, shall be living at the end of that period, during the residue of his natural life, have as his own property the sole liberty of representing, or causing to be represented, the same at any such place of dramatic entertainment as aforesaid, and shall be deemed and taken to be the proprietor thereof : Provided nevertheless, that nothing in this Act contained *Proviso as to* shall prejudice, alter, or affect the right or authority of any person *cases where,* to represent or cause to be represented, at any place or places of *previous to the passing of* dramatic entertainment whatsoever, any such production as afore- *this Act, a* said, in all cases in which the author thereof or his assignee shall, *consent has* previously to the passing of this Act, have given his consent to *been given.* or authorized such representation, but that such sole liberty of the author or his assignee shall be subject to such right or authority.

II. And be it further enacted, That if any person shall, during *Penalty on* the continuance of such sole liberty as aforesaid, contrary to the *persons per-* intent of this Act, or right of the author or his assignee, represent *forming pieces contrary to* or cause to be represented, without the consent in writing of the *this Act.* author or other proprietor first had and obtained at any place of dramatic entertainment within the limits aforesaid, any such production as aforesaid, or any part thereof, every such offender shall be liable for each and every such representation to the payment of an amount not less than forty shillings, or to the full amount of the benefit or advantage arising from such representation, or the injury or loss sustained by the plaintiff therefrom, whichever shall be the greater damages, to the author or other proprietor of such production so represented contrary to the true intent and meaning of this Act; to be recovered, together with double costs of suit, by such author or other proprietors, in any court having jurisdiction in such cases in that part of the said United Kingdom or of the British dominions in which the offence shall be committed ; and in every such proceeding where the sole liberty of such author or his assignee as aforesaid shall be subject to such right or authority as aforesaid, it shall be sufficient for the plaintiff to state that he has such sole liberty, without stating the same to be subject to such right or authority, or otherwise mentioning the same.

Limitation of actions.

III. Provided nevertheless, and be it further enacted, That all actions or proceedings for any offence or injury that shall be committed against this Act shall be brought, sued, and commenced within twelve calendar months next after such offence committed, or else the same shall be void and of no effect.

Explanation of words.

IV. And be it further enacted, That whenever authors, persons, offenders, or others are spoken of in this Act in the singular number or in the masculine gender, the same shall extend to any number of persons and to either sex.

---

5 & 6 WILL. IV. c. 65.

An Act for preventing the Publication of Lectures without Consent.

[9th September, 1835.]

WHEREAS printers, publishers, and other persons have frequently taken the liberty of printing and publishing lectures delivered upon divers subjects, without the consent of the authors of such lectures, or the persons delivering the same in public, to the great detriment of such authors and lecturers: Be it enacted by the King's most excellent Majesty, by and with the advice and consent of the Lords spiritual and temporal, and Commons, in this present Parliament assembled, and by the authority of the same, That from and after the first day of September one thousand eight hundred and thirty-five the author of any lecture or lectures, or the person to whom he hath sold or otherwise conveyed the copy thereof, in order to deliver the same in any school, seminary, institution, or other place, or for any other purpose, shall have the sole right and liberty of printing and publishing such lecture or lectures; and that if any person shall, by taking down the same in short-hand or otherwise in writing, or in any other way, obtain or make a copy of such lecture or lectures, and shall print or lithograph or otherwise copy and publish the same, or cause the same to be printed, lithographed, or otherwise copied and published, without leave of the author thereof, or of the person to whom the author thereof hath sold or otherwise conveyed the same, and every person who, knowing the same to have been printed or copied and published without such consent, shall sell, publish, or expose to sale, or cause to be sold, published, or exposed to sale, any such lecture or

Authors of lectures, or their assigns, to have the sole right of publishing them.

Penalty on other persons publishing, &c., lectures without leave.

lectures, shall forfeit such printed or otherwise copied lecture or lectures, or parts thereof, together with one penny for every sheet thereof which shall be found in his custody, either printed, lithographed, or copied, or printing, lithographing, or copying, published or exposed to sale, contrary to the true intent and meaning of this Act, the one moiety thereof to His Majesty, his heirs or successors, and the other moiety thereof to any person who shall sue for the same, to be recovered in any of His Majesty's Courts of Record in Westminster, by action of debt, bill, plaint, or information, in which no wager of law, essoign, privilege, or protection, or more than one imparlance, shall be allowed.

II. And be it further enacted, That any printer or publisher of any newspaper who shall, without such leave as aforesaid, print and publish in such newspaper any lecture or lectures, shall be deemed and taken to be a person printing and publishing without leave within the provisions of this Act, and liable to the aforesaid forfeitures and penalties in respect of such printing and publishing. *Penalty on printers or publishers of newspapers publishing lectures with out leave.*

III. And be it further enacted, That no person allowed for certain fee and reward, or otherwise, to attend and be present at any lecture delivered in any place, shall be deemed and taken to be licensed or to have leave to print, copy, and publish such lectures only because of having leave to attend such lecture or lectures. *Persons having leave to attend lectures not on that account licensed to publish them.*

IV. Provided always, That nothing in this Act shall extend to prohibit any person from printing, copying, and publishing any lecture or lectures which have or shall have been printed and published with leave of the authors thereof or their assignees, and whereof the time hath or shall have expired within which the sole right to print and publish the same is given by an Act passed in the eighth year of the reign of Queen Anne, intituled "An Act for the Encouragement of Learning, by vesting the Copies of printed Books in the Authors or Purchasers of such Copies during the Times therein mentioned," and by another Act passed in the fifty-fourth year of the reign of King George the Third, intituled "An Act to amend the several Acts for the Encouragement of Learning, by securing the Copies and Copyright of printed Books to the Authors of such Books, or their Assigns," or to any lectures which have been printed or published before the passing of this Act. *Act not to prohibit the publishing of lectures after expiration of the copyright.* *8 Ann. c. 19.* *54 G. 3, c. 156.*

V. Provided further, That nothing in this Act shall extend to any lecture or lectures, or the printing, copying, or publishing any lecture or lectures, or parts thereof, of the delivering of which notice in writing shall not have been given to two justices living within five miles from the place where such lecture or lectures shall be delivered two days at the least before delivering the same, or to any lecture or lectures delivered in any university or public school or college, or on any public foundation, or by any individual in *Act not to extend to lectures delivered in unlicensed places, &c.*

virtue of or according to any gift, endowment, or foundation; and that the law relating thereto shall remain the same as if this Act had not been passed.

---

6 & 7 WILL. IV. c. 59.

An Act to extend the Protection of Copyright in Prints and Engravings to Ireland.

[13th August, 1836.]

WHEREAS an Act was passed in the seventeenth year of the reign
17 G. 3, c. 57. of His late Majesty King George Third, intituled "An Act for more effectually securing the Property of Prints to Inventors and Engravers, by enabling them to sue for and recover Penalties in certain Cases:" And whereas it is desirable to extend the provisions of the said Act to Ireland: Be it therefore enacted by the King's most excellent Majesty, by and with the advice and consent of the Lords spiritual and temporal, and Commons, in this present
Provisions of Parliament assembled, and by the authority of the same, That from
recited Act extended to Ireland. and after the passing of this Act all the provisions contained in the said recited Act of the seventeenth year of the reign of His late Majesty King George the Third, and of all the other Acts therein recited, shall be and the same are hereby extended to the United Kingdom of Great Britain and Ireland.

Penalty on engraving or publishing any print without consent of proprietor. II. And be it further enacted, That from and after the passing of this Act, if any engraver, etcher, printseller, or other person shall within the time limited by the aforesaid recited Acts, engrave, etch, or publish, or cause to be engraved, etched, or published, any engraving or print of any description whatever, either in whole or in part, which may have been or which shall hereafter be published in any part of Great Britain or Ireland, without the express consent of the proprietor or proprietors thereof first had and obtained in writing, signed by him, her, or them respectively, with his, her, or their own hand or hands, in the presence of and attested by two or more credible witnesses, then every such proprietor shall and may, by and in a separate action upon the case, to be brought against the person so offending in any court of law in Great Britain or Ireland, recover such damages as a jury on the trial of such action or on the execution of a writ of inquiry thereon shall give or assess together with double costs of suit.

1 & 2 VICT. c. 59 (1838).

" The International Copyright Act."

Repealed by 7 Vict. c. 12.

---

2 VICT. c. 13 (1839.

*An Act for extending the Copyright of Designs for Calico-Printing
to Designs for Printing other woven Fabrics.*

Repealed by 5 & 6 Vict. c. 100, § 1.`

---

2 VICT. o. 17 (1839).

*An Act to secure to Proprietors of Designs for Articles of
Manufacture the Copyright of such Designs for a limited Time.*

Repealed by 5 & 6 Vict. c. 100, § 1.

---

5 & 6 VICT. o. 45.

An Act to amend the Law of Copyright.

[1st July, 1842.]

WHEREAS it is expedient to amend the law relating to copyright,
and to afford greater encouragement to the production of literary
works of lasting benefit to the world: Be it enacted by the Queen's
most excellent Majesty, by and with the advice and consent of the
Lords spiritual and temporal, and Commons, in this present
Parliament assembled, and by the authority of the same, That *Repeal of for-*
from the passing of this Act an Act passed in the eighth year *mer Acts:*
of Her Majesty Queen Anne, intituled "An Act for the Encourage- 8 Anne, c. 19.
ment of Learning, by vesting the Copies of printed Books in the
Authors or Purchasers of such Copies during the Time therein
mentioned;" and also an Act passed in the forty-first year of the
reign of His Majesty King George the Third, intituled "An Act 41 G. 3, c. 107.
for the further Encouragement of Learning in the United Kingdom
of Great Britain and Ireland, by securing the Copies and Copyright of printed Books to the Authors of such Books, or their
Assigns, for the Time therein mentioned;" and also an Act passed
in the fifty-fourth year of the reign of His Majesty King George
the Third, intituled "An Act to amend the several Acts for the 54 G. 3, c. 156.
Encouragement of Learning, by securing the Copies and Copyright

of printed Books to the Authors of such Books, or their Assigns,"
be and the same are hereby repealed, except so far as the
continuance of either of them may be necessary for carrying on or
giving effect to any proceeding at law or in equity pending at the
time of passing this Act, or for enforcing any cause of action or suit,
or any right or contract then subsisting.

Interpretation of Act.   II. And be it enacted, That in the construction of this Act the
word "book" shall be construed to mean and include every
volume, part or division of a volume, pamphlet, sheet of letter-
press, sheet of music, map, chart, or plan separately published:
that the words "dramatic piece" shall be construed to mean and
include every tragedy, comedy, play, opera, farce, or other scenic,
musical, or dramatic entertainment; that the word "copyright"
shall be construed to mean the sole and exclusive liberty of
printing or otherwise multiplying copies of any subject to which
the said word is herein applied; that the words "personal representative" shall be construed to mean and include every executor,
administrator, and next of kin entitled to administration; that the
word "assigns" shall be construed to mean and include every
person in whom the interest of an author in copyright shall be
vested, whether derived from such author before or after the
publication of any book, and whether acquired by sale, gift,
bequest, or by operation of law, or otherwise; that the words
"British Dominions" shall be construed to mean and include all
parts of the United Kingdom of Great Britain and Ireland, the
Islands of Jersey and Guernsey, all parts of the East and West
Indies, and all the colonies, settlements, and possessions of the
Crown which now are or hereafter may be acquired; and that
whenever in this Act, in describing any person, matter, or thing
the word importing the singular number or the masculine gender
only is used, the same shall be understood to include and to be
applied to several persons as well as one person, and females as well
as males, and several matters or things as well as one matter or
thing, respectively, unless there shall be something in the subject
or context repugnant to such construction.

Endurance of term of copy- right in any book hereafter to be published in the lifetime of the author;   II. And be it enacted, That the copyright in every book which
shall after the passing of this Act be published in the lifetime of
its author shall endure for the natural life of such author, and for
the further term of seven years, commencing at the time of his death,
and shall be the property of such author and his assigns: Provided
always, that if the said term of seven years shall expire before the
end of forty-two years from the first publication of such book, the
copyright shall in that case endure for such period of forty-two
years; and that the copyright in every book which shall be
published after the death of its author shall endure for the term

of forty-two years from the first publication thereof, and shall be the property of the proprietor of the author's manuscript from which such book shall be first published, and his assigns. ^{if published after the author's death.}

IV. And whereas it is just to extend the benefits of this Act to authors of books published before the passing thereof, and in which copyright still subsists, be it enacted, That the copyright which at the time of passing this Act shall subsist in any book theretofore published (except as herein-after mentioned) shall be extended and endure for the full term provided by this Act in cases of books thereafter published, and shall be the property of the person who at the time of passing of this Act shall be the proprietor of such copyright: Provided always, that in all cases in which such copyright shall belong in whole or in part to a publisher or other person who shall have acquired it for other consideration than that of natural love and affection, such copyright shall not be extended by this Act, but shall endure for the term which shall subsist therein at the time of passing of this Act, and no longer, unless the author of such book, if he shall be living, or the personal representative of such author, if he shall be dead, and the proprietor of such copyright, shall, before the expiration of such term, consent and agree to accept the benefits of this Act in respect of such book, and shall cause a minute of such consent in the form in that behalf given in the schedule to this Act annexed to be entered in the book of registry herein-after directed to be kept, in which case such copyright shall endure for the full term by this Act provided in cases of books to be published after the passing of this Act, and shall be the property of such person or persons as in such minute shall be expressed.

In cases of subsisting copyright, the term to be extended, except when it shall belong to an assignee for other consideration than natural love and affection ; in which case it shall cease at the expiration of the present term, unless its extension be agreed to between the proprietor and the author.

V. And whereas it is expedient to provide against the suppression of books of importance to the public, be it enacted, That it shall be lawful for the judicial committee of Her Majesty's Privy Council, on complaint made to them that the proprietor of the copyright in any book after the death of its author has refused to republish or to allow the republication of the same, and that by reason of such refusal such book may be withheld from the public, to grant a licence to such complainant to publish such book, in such manner and subject to such conditions as they may think fit, and that it shall be lawful for such complainant to publish such book according to such licence.

Judicial committee of the Privy Council to license the republication of books which the proprietor refuses to republish after death of the author.

VI. And be it enacted, That a printed copy of the whole of every book which shall be published after the passing of this Act, together with all maps, prints, or other engravings belonging thereto, finished and coloured in the same manner as the best copies of the same shall be published, and also of any second or subsequent edition which shall be so published with any additions

Copies of books published after the passing of this Act, and of all subsequent editions, to be delivered with-

in certain times or alterations, whether the same shall be in letter-press, or in the
at the British maps, prints, or other engravings belonging thereto, and whether
Museum. the first edition of such book shall have been published before or
after the passing of this Act, and also of any second or subsequent
edition of every book of which the first of some preceding edition
shall not have been delivered for the use of the British Museum,
bound, sewed, or stitched together, and upon the best paper on
which the same shall be printed, shall, within one calendar month
after the day on which any such book shall first be sold, published,
or offered for sale within the bills of mortality, or within three
calendar months if the same shall first be sold, published or offered
for sale in any other part of the United Kingdom, or within twelve
calendar months after the same shall first be sold, published, or
offered for sale in any other part of the British dominions, be
delivered, on behalf of the publisher thereof, at the British
Museum.

Mode of de-   VII. And be it enacted, That every copy of any book which
livering at the under the provisions of this Act ought to be delivered as aforesaid
British
Museum. shall be delivered at the British Museum between the hours of ten
in the forenoon and four in the afternoon on any day except Sunday,
Ash Wednesday, Good Friday, and Christmas Day, to one of the
officers of the said museum, or to some person authorized by the
trustees of the said museum to receive the same, and such officer
or other person receiving such copy is hereby required to give a
receipt in writing for the same, and such delivery, to all intents
and purposes, be deemed to be good and sufficient delivery under
the provisions of this Act.

A copy of every   VIII. And be it enacted, That a copy of the whole of every book,
book to be de- and of any second or subsequent edition of every book containing
livered within
a month after additions and alterations, together with all maps and prints
demand to the belonging thereto, which after the passing of this Act shall be
officer of the published, shall, on demand thereof in writing, left at the place of
Stationers'
Company, for abode of the publisher thereof, at any time within twelve months
the following next after the publication thereof, under the hand of the officer of
libraries : the the Company of Stationers who shall from time to time be appointed
Bodleian at
Oxford, the by the said company for the purposes of this Act, or under the
Public Library hand of any other persons thereto authorized by the persons or
at Cambridge, bodies politic and corporate, proprietors and managers of the
the Faculty of
Advocates at libraries following, (videlicet,) the Bodleian Library at Oxford, the
Edinburgh, and Public Library at Cambridge, the Library of the Faculty of
that of Trinity Advocates at Edinburgh, the Library of the College of the Holy
College, Dublin.
Undivided Trinity of Queen Elizabeth near Dublin, be delivered,
upon the paper of which the largest number of copies of such
book or edition shall be printed for sale, in the like condition as
the copies prepared for sale by the publisher thereof respectively

within one month after demand made thereof in writing as afore-said, to the said officer of the said Company of Stationers for the time being, which copies the said officer shall and he is hereby required to receive at the hall of the said company, for the use of the library for which such demand shall be made within such twelve months as aforesaid; and the said officer is hereby required to give a receipt in writing for the same, and within one month after any such book shall be so delivered to him as aforesaid to deliver the same for the use of such library.

IX. Provided also, and be it enacted, That if any publisher shall be desirous of delivering the copy of such book as shall be demanded on behalf of any of the said libraries at such library, it shall be lawful for him to deliver the same at such library, free of expense, to such librarian or other person authorized to receive the same (who is hereby required in such case to receive and give a receipt in writing for the same), and such delivery shall to all intents and purposes of this Act be held as equivalent to a delivery to the said officer of the Stationers' Company. *Publishers may deliver the copies to the libraries, instead of at the Stationers' Company.*

X. And be it enacted, That if any publisher of any such book, or of any second or subsequent edition of any such book, shall neglect to deliver the same pursuant to this Act, he shall for every such default forfeit, besides the value of such copy of such book or edition which he ought to have delivered, a sum not exceeding five pounds, to be recovered by the librarian or other officer (properly authorized) of the library for the use whereof such copy should have been delivered, in a summary way, on conviction before two justices of the peace for the county or place where the publisher making default shall reside, or by action of debt or other proceeding of the like nature, at the suit of such librarian or other officer, in any court of record in the United Kingdom, in which action, if the plaintiff shall obtain a verdict, he shall recover his costs reasonably incurred, to be taxed as between attorney and client. *Penalty for default in delivering copies for the use of the libraries.*

XI. And be it enacted, That a book of registry, wherein may be registered, as herein-after enacted, the proprietorship in the copy-right of books, and assignments thereof, and in dramatic and musical pieces, whether in manuscript or otherwise, and licences affecting such copyright, shall be kept at the hall of the Stationers' Company by the officer appointed by the said company for the purposes of this Act, and shall at all convenient times be open to the inspection of any person, on payment of one shilling for every entry which shall be searched for or inspected in the said book; and that such officer shall, whenever thereunto reasonably required, give a copy of any entry in such book, certified under his hand, and impressed with the stamp of the said company, to be provided by them for that purpose, and which they are hereby required to *Book of registry to be kept at Stationers' Hall.*

provide, to any person requiring the same, on payment to him of the sum of five shillings; and such copies so certified and impressed, shall be received in evidence in all courts, and in all summary proceedings, and shall be *primâ facie* proof of the proprietorship or assignment of copyright or licence as therein expressed, but subject to be rebutted by other evidence, and in the case of dramatic or musical pieces shall be *primâ facie* proof of the right of representation or performance, subject to be rebutted as aforesaid.

Making a false entry in the book of registry, a misdemeanor.

XII. And be it enacted, That if any person shall wilfully make or cause to be made any false entry in the registry book of the Stationers' Company, or shall wilfully produce or cause to be tendered in evidence any paper falsely purporting to be a copy of any entry in the said book, he shall be guilty of an indictable misdemeanor, and shall be punished accordingly.

Entries of copyright may be made in the book of registry.

XIII. And be it enacted, That after the passing of this Act, it shall be lawful for the proprietor of copyright in any book heretofore published, or in any book hereafter to be published, to make entry in the registry book of the Stationers' Company of the title of such book, the time of the first publication thereof, the name and place of abode of the publisher thereof, and the name and place of abode of the proprietor of the copyright of the said book, or of any portion of such copyright, in the form in that behalf given in the schedule to this Act annexed, upon payment of the sum of five shillings to the officer of the said company; and that it shall be lawful for every such registered proprietor to assign his interest, or any portion of his interest therein, by making entry in the said book of registry of such assignment, and of the name and place of abode of the assignee thereof, in the form given in that behalf in the said schedule, on payment of the like sum; and such assignment so entered shall be effectual in law to all intents and purposes whatsoever, without being subject to any stamp or duty, and shall be of the same force and effect as if such assignment had been made by deed.

Persons aggrieved by any entry in the book of registry may apply to a court of law in term, or judge in vacation, who may order such entry to be varied or expunged.

XIV. And be it enacted, That if any person shall deem himself aggrieved by any entry made under colour of this Act in the said book of registry, it shall be lawful for such person to apply by motion to the Court of Queen's Bench, Court of Common Pleas, or Court of Exchequer, in term time, or to apply by summons to any judge of either such courts in vacation, for an order that such entry may be expunged or varied; and that upon any such application by motion or summons to either of the said courts, or to a judge as aforesaid, such court or judge shall make such order for expunging, varying, or confirming such entry, either with or without costs, as to such court or judge shall seem just; and the officer appointed by the Stationers' Company for the purposes of this Act shall, on the production to him of any such order for expunging or varying any such entry, expunge or vary the same according to the requisitions of such order.

XV. And be it enacted, That if any person shall, in any part of the British dominions, after the passing of this Act, print or cause to be printed, either for sale or exportation, any book in which there shall be subsisting copyright, without the consent in writing of the proprietor thereof, or shall import for sale or hire any such book, so having been unlawfully printed, from parts beyond the sea, or, knowing such book to have been so unlawfully printed or imported, shall sell, publish, or expose to sale or hire, or cause to be sold, published, or exposed to sale or hire, or shall have in his possession, for sale or hire, any such book so unlawfully printed or imported, without such consent as aforesaid, such offender shall be liable to a special action on the case at the suit of the proprietor of such copyright, to be brought in any court of record in that part of the British dominions in which the offence shall be committed : Provided always, that in Scotland such offender shall be liable to an action in the Court of Session in Scotland which shall and may be brought and prosecuted in the same manner in which any other action of damages to the like amount may be brought and prosecuted there.

Remedy for the piracy of books by action on the case.

XVI. And be it enacted, That after the passing of this Act, in any action brought within the British dominions against any person for printing any such book for sale, hire, or exportation, or for importing, selling, publishing, or exposing to sale or hire, or causing to be imported, sold, published, or exposed to sale or hire, any such book, the defendant, on pleading thereto, shall give to the plaintiff a notice in writing of any objections on which he means to rely on the trial of such action; and if the nature of his defence be, that the plaintiff in such action was not the author or first publisher of the book in which he shall by such action claim copyright, or is not the proprietor of the copyright therein, or that some other person than the plaintiff was the author or first publisher of such book, or is the proprietor of the copyright therein, then the defendant shall specify in such notice the name of the person who he alleges to have been the author or first publisher of such book, or the proprietor of the copyright therein, together with the title of such book, and the time when and the place where such book was first published, otherwise the defendant in such action shall not at the trial or hearing of such action be allowed to give any evidence that the plaintiff in such action was not the author or first publisher of the book in which he claims such copyright as aforesaid, or that he was not the proprietor of the copyright therein; and at such trial or hearing no other

In actions for piracy the defendant to give notice of the objections to the plaintiff's title on which he means to rely.

objection shall be allowed to be made on behalf of such defendant
than the objection stated in such notice, or that any other person
was the author or first publisher of such book, or the proprietor
of the copyright therein, than the person specified in such notice,
or give in evidence in support of his defence any other book than
one substantially corresponding in title, time, and place of publication with the title, time, and place specified in such notice.

No person ex-
cept the pro-
prietor, &c.,
shall import
into the British
dominions for
sale or hire any
book first com-
posed, &c.,
within the
United King-
dom, and re-
printed else-
where, under
penalty of for-
feiture thereof,
and also of 10*l.*
and double the
value

XVII. And be it enacted, That after the passing of this Act
it shall not be lawful for any person, not being the proprietor
of the copyright, or some person authorized by him, to import
into any part of the United Kingdom, or into any other part of
the British dominions, for sale or hire, any printed book first
composed or written or printed and published in any part of the
said United Kingdom, wherein there shall be copyright, and
reprinted in any country or place whatsoever out of the British
dominions; and if any person, not being such proprietor or person
authorized as aforesaid, shall import or bring, or cause to be
imported or brought, for sale or hire, any such printed book, into
any part of the British dominions, contrary to the true intent and
meaning of this Act, or shall knowingly sell, publish, or expose
to sale or let to hire, or have in his possession for sale or hire, any
such book, then every such book shall be forfeited, and shall be
seized by any officer of customs or excise, and the same shall be
destroyed by such officer; and every person so offending, being
duly convicted thereof before two justices of the peace for the

Books may be
seized by offi-
cers of customs
or excise.

county or place in which such book shall be found, shall also for
every such offence forfeit the sum of ten pounds, and double the
value of every copy of such book which he shall so import or
cause to be imported into any part of the British dominions, or
shall knowingly sell, publish, or expose to sale, or let to hire, or
shall cause to be sold, published, or exposed to sale or let to hire,
or shall have in his possession for sale or hire, contrary to the true
intent and meaning of this Act; five pounds to the use of such
officer of customs or excise, and the remainder of the penalty to the
use of the proprietor of the copyright in such book.

As to the copy-
right in ency-
clopædias, peri-
odicals, and
works pub-
lished in a
series, reviews,
or magazines.

XVIII. And be it enacted, That when any publisher or other
person shall, before or at the time of the passing of this Act, have
projected, conducted, and carried on, or shall hereafter project,
conduct, and carry on, or be the proprietor of any encyclopædia,
review, magazine, periodical work, or work published in a series
of books or parts, or any book whatsoever, and shall have employed
or shall employ any persons to compose the same, or any volumes,
parts, essays, articles, or portions thereof, for publication in or as
part of the same, and such work, volumes, parts, essays, articles,
or portions shall have been or shall hereafter be composed under

such employment, on the terms that the copyright therein shall belong to such proprietor, projector, publisher, or conductor, and paid for by such proprietor, projector, publisher, or conductor, the copyright in every such encyclopædia, review, magazine, periodical work, and work published in a series of books or parts, and in every volume, part, essay, article, and portion so composed and paid for, shall be the property of such proprietor, projector, publisher, or other conductor, who shall enjoy the same rights as if he were the actual author thereof, and shall have such term of copyright therein as is given to the authors of books by this Act; except only that in the case of essays, articles, or portions forming part of and first published in reviews, magazines, or other periodical works of a like nature, after the term of twenty-eight years from the first publication thereof respectively the right of publishing the same in a separate form shall revert to the author for the remainder of the term given by this Act: Provided always, that during the term of twenty-eight years the said proprietor, projector, publisher, or conductor shall not publish any such essay, article, or portion separately or singly, without the consent previously obtained of the author thereof, or his assigns: Provided, *Proviso for* also, that nothing herein contained shall alter or affect the right *authors who* of any person who shall have been or who shall be so employed as *have reserved* aforesaid to publish any such his composition in a separate form *the right of* who by any contract, express or implied, may have reserved or *publishing* may hereafter reserve to himself such right; but every author *their articles* reserving, retaining, or having such right shall be entitled to the *form.* copyright in such composition when published in a separate form, according to this Act, without prejudice to the right of such proprietor, projector, publisher, or conductor as aforesaid.

XIX. And be it enacted, That the proprietor of the copyright *Proprietors of* in any encyclopædia, review, magazine, periodical work, or other *encyclopædias,* work published in a series of books or parts shall be entitled to *periodicals, and* all the benefits of the registration at Stationers' Hall under this *lished in a* Act, on entering in the said book of registry the title of such *series, may* encyclopædia, review, periodical work, or other work, published *enter at once at* in a series of books or parts, the time of the first publication of the *Hall, and* first volume, number, or part thereof, or of the first number or *thereon have* volume first published after the passing of this Act in any such *the benefit of* work which shall have been published heretofore, and the name *of the whole.* and place of abode of the proprietor thereof, and of the publisher thereof, when such publisher shall not also be the proprietor thereof.

XX. And whereas an Act was passed in the third year of the *The provisions* reign of His late Majesty, to amend the law relating to dramatic *of 3 & 4 W. 4,* literary property, and it is expedient to extend the term of the *to musical com-*

positions, and the term of copyright, as provided by this Act, applied to the liberty of representing dramatic pieces and musical compositions.

sole liberty of representing dramatic pieces given by that Act to the full time by this Act provided for the continuance of copyright: And whereas it is expedient to extend to musical compositions the benefits of that Act, and also of this Act, be it therefore enacted, That the provisions of the said Act of His late Majesty, and of this Act, shall apply to musical compositions, and that the sole liberty of representing or performing, or causing or permitting to be represented or performed, any dramatic piece or musical composition, shall endure and be the property of the author thereof, and his assigns, for the term in this Act provided for the duration of copyright in books: and the provisions herein-before enacted in respect of the property of such copyright, and of registering the same, shall apply to the liberty of representing or performing any dramatic piece or musical composition, as if the same were herein expressly re-enacted and applied thereto, save and except that the first public representation or performance of any dramatic piece or musical composition shall be deemed equivalent, in the construction of this Act, to the first publication of any book: Provided always, that in case of any dramatic piece, or musical composition in manuscript, it shall be sufficient for the person having the sole liberty of representing or performing, or causing to be represented or performed the same, to register only the title thereof, the name and place of abode of the author or composer thereof, the name and place of abode of the proprietor thereof, and the time and place of its first representation or performance.

Proprietors of right of dramatic representations shall have all the remedies given by 3 & 4 W. 4, c. 15

XXI. And be it enacted, That the person who shall at any time have the sole liberty of representing such dramatic piece or musical composition shall have and enjoy the remedies given and provided in the said Act of the third and fourth year of the reign of His late Majesty King William the Fourth passed to amend the laws relating to dramatic literary property, during the whole of his interest therein, as fully as if the same were re-enacted in this Act.

Assignment of copyright of a dramatic piece not to convey the right of representation.

XXII. And be it enacted, That no assignment of the copyright of any book consisting of or containing a dramatic piece or musical composition shall be holden to convey to the assignee the right of representing or performing such dramatic piece or musical composition, unless an entry in the said registry book shall be made of such assignment, wherein shall be expressed the intention of the parties that such right should pass by such assignment.

Books pirated shall become the property of the proprietor of the copyright, and may be recovered by action.

XXIII. And be it enacted, That all copies of any book wherein there shall be copyright, and of which entry shall have been made in the said registry book, and which shall have been unlawfully printed or imported without the consent of the registered proprietor of such copyright, in writing under his hand first obtained, shall be deemed to be the property of the proprietor of such copyright, and who shall be registered as such; and such registered proprietor shall, after demand thereof in writing, be entitled to sue for and recover the same, or damages for the detention thereof, in an action of detinue, from any party who shall detain the same, or to sue for and recover damages for the conversion thereof in an action of trover.

XXIV. And be it enacted, That no proprietor of copyright in any book which shall be first published after the passing of this Act shall maintain any action or suit, at law or in equity, or any summary proceeding, in respect of any infringement of such copyright, unless he shall, before commencing such action, suit, or proceeding, have caused an entry to be made, in the book of registry of the Stationers' Company, of such book, pursuant to this Act: Provided always, that the omission to make such entry shall not affect the copyright in any book, but only the right to sue or proceed in respect of the infringement thereof, as aforesaid: Provided also, that nothing herein contained shall prejudice the remedies which the proprietor of the sole liberty of representing any dramatic piece shall have by virtue of the Act passed in the third year of the reign of His late Majesty King William the Fourth, to amend the laws relating to dramatic literary property, or of this Act, although no entry shall be made in the book of registry aforesaid. *No proprietor of copyright commencing after this Act shall sue or proceed for any infringement before making entry in the book of registry.* *Proviso for dramatic pieces.*

XXV. And be it enacted, That all copyright shall be deemed personal property, and shall be transmissible by bequest, or, in case of intestacy, shall be subject to the same law of distribution as other personal property, and in Scotland shall be deemed to be personal and moveable estate. *Copyright shall be personal property.*

XXVI. And be it enacted, That if any action or suit shall be commenced or brought against any person or persons whomsoever for doing or causing to be done anything in pursuance of this Act, the defendant or defendants in such action may plead the general issue, and give the special matter in evidence; and if upon such action a verdict shall be given for the defendant, or the plaintiff shall become nonsuited, or discontinue his action, then the defendant shall have and recover his full costs, for which he shall have the same remedy as a defendant in any case by law hath; and that all actions, suits, bills, indictments, or informations for any offence that shall be committed against this Act shall be brought, sued, and commenced within twelve calendar months next after such offence committed, or else the same shall be void and of none effect; provided that such limitation of time shall not extend or be construed to extend to any actions, suits, or other proceedings which under the authority of this Act shall or may be brought, sued, or commenced for or in respect of any copies of books to be *General issue.* *Limitation of actions;* *not to extend to actions, &c., in respect of the delivery of books.*

2 T

delivered for the use of the British Museum, or of any one of the four libraries hereinbefore mentioned.

Saving the rights of the universities, and the colleges of Eton, Westminster, and Winchester.

XXVII. Provided always, and be it enacted, That nothing in this Act contained shall affect or alter the rights of the two universities of Oxford and Cambridge, the colleges or houses of learning within the same, the four universities in Scotland, the college of the Holy and Undivided Trinity of Queen Elizabeth near Dublin, and the several colleges of Eton, Westminster, and Winchester in any copyrights heretofore and now vested or hereafter to be vested in such universities and colleges respectively, anything to the contrary herein contained notwithstanding.

Saving all subsisting rights, contracts, and engagements.

XXVIII. Provided also, and be it enacted, That nothing in this Act contained shall affect, alter, or vary any right subsisting at the time of passing this Act, except as herein expressly enacted ; and all contracts, agreements, and obligations made and entered into before the passing of this Act, and all remedies relating thereto, shall remain in full force, anything herein contained to the contrary notwithstanding.

Extent of the Act.

XXIX. And be it enacted, That this Act shall extend to the United Kingdom of Great Britain and Ireland, and to every part of the British dominions.

Act may be amended this Session.

XXX. And be it enacted, That this Act may be amended or repealed by any Act to be passed in the present session of Parliament.

SCHEDULE to which the preceding Act refers.

No. 1.

FORM of MINUTE of CONSENT to be entered at Stationers' Hall.

We, the undersigned, *A.B.* of   the Author of a certain Book, intituled *Y.Z.* [*or* the personal Representative of the Author, *as the case may be*], and *C.D.* of   do hereby certify, That we have consented and agree to accept the Benefits of the Act passed in the Fifth Year (*a*) of

---

(*a*) Her Majesty's reign commenced on the 20th of June, 1837, and her royal consent was given to this Act on the 1st of July, 1842, consequently the Act was passed in the sixth year of the Queen, and should be so pleaded, or as having been passed " in the session held in the fifth and sixth years of her Majesty Queen Victoria :" *Rex* v. *Biers*, 3 Nev. & M. 475 ; *Gibbs* v. *Pike*, 8 Mee. & W. 223. The Schedule was drawn in the fifth year of the Queen, and has not been corrected. It will be advisable in the minute of consent to state the year, by a reference to the session, which will include the words of the schedule. The form is inaccurate in another part by confining the date of consent to the present century. Note by Sweet to Bythewood and Jarman's Conveyancing, vol. vii. p. 618.

the Reign of Her Majesty Queen Victoria, Cap.   , for the Extension of the Term of Copyright therein provided by the said Act, and hereby declare that such extended Term of Copyright therein is the Property of the said *A.B.* or *C.D.*

Dated this   day of   18   .

(Signed)   *A.B.*

Witness   *C.D.*

To the Registering Officer appointed by the Stationers' Company.

No. 2.

FORM of REQUIRING ENTRY of PROPRIETORSHIP.

I, *A.B.* of   do hereby certify, That I am the Proprietor of the Copyright of a Book, intituled *Y.Z.*, and I hereby require you to make entry in the Register Book of the Stationers' Company of my Proprietorship of such Copyright, according to the Particulars underwritten.

Title of Book.	Name of Publisher, and Place of Publication.	Name and Place of Abode of the Proprietor of the Copyright.	Date of First Publication.
Y.Z.		*A.B.*	

Dated this   day of   18   .

Witness, *C.D.*   (Signed)   *A.B.*

No. 3.

ORIGINAL ENTRY of PROPRIETORSHIP of COPYRIGHT of a BOOK.

Time of making the Entry.	Title of Book.	Name of the Publisher and Place of Publication.	Name and Place of Abode of the Proprietor of the Copyright.	Date of First Publication.
	Y.Z.	*A.B.*	*C.D.*	

No. 4.

FORM of CONCURRENCE of the PARTY assigning in any BOOK
previously registered.

I, *A.B.* of　　　　　　　being the assigner of the Copyright of the Book
hereunder described, do hereby require you to make entry of the Assignment of the Copyright therein.

Title of Book.	Assigner of the Copyright.	Assignee of Copyright.
Y.Z.	*A.B.*	*C.D.*

Dated this　　　　　day of　　18　．

(Signed)　　*A.B.*

No. 5.

FORM of ENTRY of ASSIGNMENT of COPYRIGHT in any BOOK previously
registered.

Date of Entry.	Title of Book.	Assigner of the Copyright.	Assignee of Copyright.
	[*Set out the Title of the Book, and refer to the Page of the Registry Book in which the original Entry of the Copyright thereof is made.*]	*A.B.*	*C.D.*

---

5 & 6 VICT. c. 47 (1842),

An Act to amend the Laws relating to the Customs.

Repealed by 7 & 8 Vict. c. 73.

5 & 6 VICT. C. 100.

An Act to consolidate and amend the Laws relating to the Copy-right of Designs for ornamenting Articles of Manufacture.

[10th August, 1842.]

WHEREAS by the several Acts mentioned in the Schedule (A.) to this Act annexed there was granted, in respect of the woven fabrics therein mentioned, the sole right to use any new and original pattern for printing the same during the period of three calendar months: And whereas by the Act mentioned in the Schedule (B.) to this Act annexed there was granted, in respect of all articles except lace, and except the articles within the meaning of the Acts hereinbefore referred to, the sole right of using any new and original design, for certain purposes, during the respective periods therein mentioned ; but forasmuch as the protection afforded by the said Acts in respect of the application of designs to certain articles of manufacture is insufficient, it is expedient to extend the same, but upon the conditions hereinafter expressed: Now for that purpose, and for the purpose of consolidating the provisions of the said Acts, be it enacted by the Queen's most excellent Majesty, by and with the advice and consent of the Lords spiritual and temporal, and Commons, in this present Parliament assembled, and by the authority of the same, That this Act shall come into operation on the first day of September one thousand eight hundred and forty-two, and that thereupon all the said Acts mentioned in the said Schedules (A.) and (B.) to this Act annexed shall be and they are hereby repealed. *Commencement of Act and repeal of former Acts.*

II. Provided always, and be it enacted, That notwithstanding such repeal of the said Acts every copyright in force under the same shall continue in force till the expiration of such copyright ; and with regard to all offences or injuries committed against any such copyright before this Act shall come into operation, every penalty imposed and every remedy given by the said Acts, in relation to any such offence or injury, shall be applicable as if such Acts had not been repealed ; but with regard to such offences or injuries committed against any such copyright after this Act shall come into operation, every penalty imposed and every remedy given by this Act in relation to any such offence or injury shall be applicable as if such copyright had been conferred by this Act. *Proviso as to existing copyrights.*

III. And with regard to any new and original design (except for sculpture and other things within the provisions of the several Acts mentioned in the Schedule (C.) to this Act annexed), whether such design be applicable to the ornamenting of any article of manufacture, or of any substance, artificial or natural, or partly artificial *Grant of copyright.*

and partly natural, and that whether such design be so applicable
for the pattern, or for the shape or configuration, or for the ornament thereof, or for any two or more of such purposes, and by
whatever means such design may be so applicable, whether by
printing or by painting, or by embroidery, or by weaving, or
by sewing, or by modelling, or by casting, or by embossing, or by
engraving, or by staining, or by any other means whatsoever,
manual, mechanical, or chemical, separate or combined, be it
enacted, That the proprietor of every such design, not previously
published, either within the United Kingdom of Great Britain and
Ireland or elsewhere, shall have the sole right to apply the same
to any articles of manufacture, or to any such substances as aforesaid, provided the same be done within the United Kingdom of
Great Britain and Ireland, for the respective terms hereinafter
mentioned, such respective terms to be computed from the time
of such design being registered according to this Act: (that is
to say,)

In respect of the application of any such design to ornamenting
any article of manufacture contained in the first, second, third,
fourth, fifth, sixth, eighth, or eleventh of the classes following,
for the term of three years:

In respect of the application of any such design to ornamenting
any article of manufacture contained in the seventh, ninth, or
tenth of the classes following, for the term of nine calendar
months:

In respect of the application of any such design to ornamenting
any article of manufacture or substance contained in the
twelfth or thirteenth of the classes following, for the term of
twelve calendar months:

Class 1.—Articles of manufacture composed wholly or chiefly
of any metal or mixed metals:

Class 2.—Articles of manufacture composed wholly or chiefly
of wood :

Class 3.—Articles of manufacture composed wholly or chiefly
of glass:

Class 4.—Articles of manufacture composed wholly or chiefly
of earthenware :

Class 5.—Paper-hangings:

Class 6.—Carpets:

Class 7.—Shawls, if the design be applied solely by printing,
or by any other process by which colours are or may hereafter be produced upon tissue or textile fabrics :

Class 8.—Shawls not comprised in class 7:

Class 9.—Yarn, thread, or warp, if the design be applied by

printing, or by any other process by which colours are or
may hereafter be produced:

Class 10.—Woven fabrics composed of linen, cotton, wool,
silk, or hair, or of any two or more of such materials, if
the design be applied by printing, or by any other process
by which colours are or may hereafter be produced upon
tissue or textile fabrics; excepting the articles included
in class 11:

Class 11.—Woven fabrics composed of linen, cotton, wool,
silk, or hair, or of any two or more of such materials, if
the design be applied by printing, or by any other process
by which colours are or may hereafter be produced upon
tissue or textile fabrics, such woven fabrics being or coming within the description technically called furniture, and
the repeat of the design whereof shall be more than twelve
inches by eight inches:

Class 12.—Woven fabrics not comprised in any preceding
class:

Class 13.—Lace, and any article of manufacture or substance
not comprised in any preceding class.

IV. Provided always, and be it enacted, That no person shall be Conditions of
entitled to the benefit of this Act, with regard to any design in copyright.
respect of the application thereof to ornamenting any article of
manufacture, or any such substance, unless such design have
before publication thereof been registered according to this Act,
and unless at the time of such registration such design have been Registration.
registered in respect of the application thereof to some or one of
the articles of manufacture or substances comprised in the above-
mentioned classes, by specifying the number of the class in respect
of which such registration is made, and unless the name of such
person shall be registered according to this Act as a proprietor of
such design, and unless after publication of such design every such
article of manufacture, or such substance to which the same shall
be so applied, published by him, hath thereon, if the article of
manufacture be a woven fabric for printing, at one end thereof, or
if of any other kind or such substance as aforesaid, at the end or
edge thereof, or other convenient place thereon, the letters " R^d," Marks denot-
together with such number or letter, or number and letter, and in ing a registered
such form as shall correspond with the date of the registration of design.
such design according to the registry of designs in that behalf;
and such marks may be put on any such article of manufacture or
such substance, either by making the same in or on the material
itself of which such article or such substance shall consist, or by
attaching thereto a label containing such marks.

V. And be it enacted, That the author of any such new and original design shall be considered the proprietor thereof, unless he have executed the work on behalf of another person for a good or a valuable consideration, in which case such person shall be considered the proprietor, and shall be entitled to be registered in the place of the author; and every person acquiring for a good or a valuable consideration a new and original design, or the right to apply the same to ornamenting any one or more articles of manufacture, or any one or more such substances as aforesaid, either exclusively of any other person or otherwise, and also every person upon whom the property in such design or such right to the application thereof shall devolve, shall be considered the proprietor of the design in respect of which the same may have been so acquired, and to that extent, but not otherwise.

VI. And be it enacted, That every person purchasing or otherwise acquiring the right to the entire or partial use of any such design may enter his title in the register hereby provided, and any writing purporting to be a transfer of such design, and signed by the proprietor thereof, shall operate as an effectual transfer; and the registrar shall, on request, and the production of such writing, or, in the case of acquiring such right by any other mode than that of purchase, on the production of any evidence to the satisfaction of the registrar, insert the name of the new proprietor in the register; and the following may be the form of such transfer, and of such request to the registrar:

Form of Transfer, and Authority to register.

" I, *A. B.*, author [*or proprietor*] of design, No.
having transferred my right thereto, [*or, if such transfer be partial,*] so far as regards the ornamenting of
[*describe the articles of manufacture or substances, or the locality with respect to which the right is transferred,*] to *B. C.* of
do hereby authorize you to insert his name on the register of designs accordingly."

Form of Request to register.

" I, *B. C.*, the person mentioned in the above transfer, do request you to register my name and property in the said design as entitled [*if to the entire use*] to the entire use of such design, [*or, if to the partial use,*] to the partial use of such design, so far as regards the application thereof [*describe the articles of manufacture or the locality in relation to which the right is transferred*]."

But if such request to register be made by any person to whom any such design shall devolve otherwise than by transfer, such request may be in the following form:

> "I, *C. D.*, in whom is vested by [*state bankruptcy or otherwise*] the design, No.   [*or, if such devolution be of a partial right*, so far as regards the application thereof] to [*describe the articles of manufacture or substance, or the locality in relation to which the right has devolved*]."

VII. And for preventing the piracy of registered designs, be it Piracy of de- enacted, That during the existence of any such right to the entire signs. or partial use of any such design no person shall either do or cause to be done any of the following acts with regard to any articles of manufacture, or substances, in respect of which the copyright of such design shall be in force, without the licence or consent in writing of the registered proprietor thereof; (that is to say,)

> No person shall apply any such design, or any fraudulent imitation thereof, for the purpose of sale, to the ornamenting of any article of manufacture, or any substance, artificial or natural, or partly artificial and partly natural:
>
> No person shall publish, sell, or expose for sale any article of manufacture, or any substance to which such design, or any fraudulent imitation thereof, shall have been so applied, after having received either verbally or in writing, or otherwise, from any source other than the proprietor of such design, knowledge that his consent has not been given to such application, or after having been served with or had left at his premises a written notice signed by such proprietor or his agent to the same effect.

VIII. And be it enacted, That if any person commit any such Recovery of act he shall for every offence forfeit a sum not less than five penalties for pounds and not exceeding thirty pounds to the proprietor of the piracy. design in respect of whose right such offence has been committed; and such proprietor may recover such penalty as follows:

> In England, either by an action of debt or on the case against the party offending, or by summary proceeding before two justices having jurisdiction where the party offending resides; and if such proprietor proceed by such summary proceeding, any justice of the peace acting for the county, riding, division, city, or borough where the party offending resides, and not being concerned either in the sale or manufacture of the

article of manufacture, or in the design, to which such summary proceeding relates, may issue a summons requiring such party to appear on a day and at a time and place to be named in such summons, such time not being less than eight days from the date thereof; and every such summons shall be served on the party offending, either in person or at his usual place of abode; and either upon the appearance or upon the default to appear of the party offending, any two or more of such justices may proceed to the hearing of the complaint, and upon proof of the offence, either by the confession of the party offending, or upon the oath or affirmation of one or more credible witnesses, which such justices are hereby authorized to administer, may convict the offender in a penalty of not less than five pounds or more than thirty pounds, as aforesaid, for each offence, as to such justices doth seem fit; but the aggregate amount of penalties for offences in respect of any one design, committed by any one person, up to the time at which any of the proceedings herein mentioned shall be instituted, shall not exceed the sum of one hundred pounds; and if the amount of such penalty or of such penalties, and the costs attending the conviction, so assessed by such justices, be not forthwith paid, the amount of the penalty or of the penalties, and of the costs, together with the costs of the distress and sale, shall be levied by distress and sale of the goods and chattels of the offender, wherever the same happen to be in England; and the justices before whom the party has been convicted, or, on proof of the conviction, any two justices acting for any county, riding, division, city, or borough in England, where goods and chattels of the person offending happen to be, may grant a warrant for such distress and sale; and the overplus, if any, shall be returned to the owner of the goods and chattels, on demand; and every information and conviction which shall be respectively laid or made in such summary proceeding before two justices under this Act may be drawn or made out in the following forms respectively, or to the effect thereof, *mutatis mutandis*, as the case may require:

Form of Information.

" Be it remembered, that on the   at
in the county of   A.B. of   in
the county of   [*or C.D.* of   in the
county of   at the instance and on the behalf of
A.B. of   in the county of   ] cometh
before us   and   two of Her

Majesty's justices of the peace in and for the county of
, and giveth us to understand that the said·*A.B.*
before and at the time when the offence hereinafter mentioned
was committed, was the proprietor of a new and original
design for [*here describe the design*], and that within twelve
calendar months last past, to wit, on the   at
in the county of   *E.F.* of   in the
county of   did [*here describe the offence*], contrary
to the form of the Act passed in the   year of the
reign of Her present Majesty, intituled ' An Act to consolidate
and amend the Laws relating to the Copyright of Designs for
ornamenting Articles of Manufacture.' "

Form of Conviction.

" BE it remembered, that on the   day of   in the
year of our Lord   at   in the county
of   *E.F.* of   in the county aforesaid is
convicted before us   and   two of Her
Majesty's justices of the peace for the said county, for that he
the said *E.F.* on the   day of   in the
year   at   in the county of
did [*here describe the offence*] contrary to the form of the statute
in that case made and provided; and we the said justices do
adjudge that the said *E.F.* for his offence aforesaid hath
forfeited the sum of   to the said *A.B.*"

In Scotland, by action before the Court of Session in ordinary
form, or by summary action before the sheriff of the county
where the offence may be committed or the offender resides,
who, upon proof of the offence or offences, either by confession
of the party offending or by the oath or affirmation of one or
more credible witnesses, shall convict the offender and find
him liable in the penalty or penalties aforesaid, as also in
expenses; and it shall be lawful for the sheriff, in pronouncing
such judgment for the penalty or penalties and costs, to insert
in such judgment a warrant, in the event of such penalty, or
penalties or costs not being paid, to levy and to recover the
amount of the same by poinding: Provided always, that it shall
be lawful to the sheriff, in the event of his dismissing the action,
and assoilzieing the defender, to find the complainer liable in
expenses; and any judgment so to be pronounced by the sheriff
in such summary application shall be final and conclusive,
and not subject to review by advocation, suspension, reduction
or otherwise:

In Ireland, either by action in a superior court of law at Dublin or by civil bill in the Civil Bill Court of the county or place where the offence was committed.

Proviso as to action for damages.

IX. Provided always, and be it enacted, That, notwithstanding the remedies hereby given for the recovery of any such penalty as aforesaid, it shall be lawful for the proprietor in respect of whose right such penalty shall have been incurred (if he shall elect to do so) to bring such action as he may be entitled to for the recovery of any damages which he shall have sustained, either by the application of any such design or of a fraudulent imitation thereof, for the purpose of sale, to any articles of manufacture or substances, or by the publication, sale, or exposure to sale, as aforesaid, by any person, of any article or substance to which such design or any fraudulent imitation thereof shall have been so applied, such person knowing that the proprietor of such design had not given his consent to such application.

Registration may in some cases be cancelled or amended.

X. And be it enacted, That in any suit in equity which may be instituted by the proprietor of any design or the person lawfully entitled thereto, relative to such design, if it shall appear to the satisfaction of the judge having cognisance of such suit that the design has been registered in the name of a person not being the proprietor or lawfully entitled thereto, it shall be competent for such judge in his discretion, by a decree or order in such suit, to direct either that such registration be cancelled (in which case the same shall thenceforth be wholly void), or that the name of the proprietor of such design, or other person lawfully entitled thereto, be substituted in the register for the name of such wrongful proprietor or claimant, in like manner as is hereinbefore directed in case of the transfer of a design, and to make such order respecting the cost of such cancellation or substitution, and of all proceedings to procure and effect the same, as he shall think fit; and the registrar is hereby authorized and required, upon being served with an official copy of such decree or order, and upon payment of the proper fee, to comply with the tenour of such decree or order, and either cancel such registration or substitute such new name, as the case may be.

Penalty for wrongfully using marks denoting a registered design.

XI. And be it enacted, That unless a design applied to ornamenting any article of manufacture or any such substance as aforesaid be so registered as aforesaid, and unless such design so registered shall have been applied to the ornamenting such article or substance within the United Kingdom of Great Britain and Ireland, and also after the copyright of such design in relation to such article or substance shall have expired, it shall be unlawful

to put on any such article or such substance, in the manner hereinbefore required with respect to articles or substances whereto shall
be applied a registered design, the marks hereinbefore required to be
so applied, or any marks corresponding therewith or similar thereto;
and if any person shall so unlawfully apply any such marks, or
shall publish, sell, or expose for sale any article of manufacture,
or any substance with any such marks so unlawfully applied,
knowing that any such marks have been unlawfully applied, he
shall forfeit for every such offence a sum not exceeding five pounds,
which may be recovered by any person proceeding for the same by
any of the ways hereinbefore directed with respect to penalties for
pirating any such design.

XII. And be it enacted, That no action or other proceeding for Limitation of
any offence or injury under this Act shall be brought after the actions.
expiration of twelve calendar months from the commission of the
offence; and in every such action or other proceeding the party
who shall prevail shall recover his full costs of suit or of such Costs.
other proceeding.

XIII. And be it enacted, That in the case of any summary Justices may
proceeding before any two justices in England, such justices are order payment
hereby authorized to award payment of costs to the party prevail- of costs in cases
ing, and to grant a warrant for enforcing payment thereof against proceeding.
the summoning party, if unsuccessful, in the like manner as is
hereinbefore provided for recovering any penalty with costs against
any offender under this Act.

XIV. And for the purpose of registering designs for articles of Registrar, &c.,
manufacture in order to obtain the protection of this Act, be it of designs to be
enacted, That the Lords of the Committee of Privy Council for appointed.
the consideration of all matters of trade and plantations may
appoint a person to be a registrar of designs for ornamenting
articles of manufacture, and, if the Lords of the said Committee
see fit, a deputy registrar, clerks, and other necessary officers and
servants; and such registrar, deputy registrar, clerks, officers, and
servants, shall hold their offices during the pleasure of the Lords
of the said Committee; and the Commissioners of the Treasury
may from time to time fix the salary or remuneration of such
registrar, deputy registrar, clerks, officers, and servants; and,
subject to the provisions of this Act, the Lords of the said Committee may make rules for regulating the execution of the duties
of the office of the said registrar; and such registrar shall have a
seal of office.

XV. And be it enacted, That the said registrar shall not register Registrar's
any design in respect of any application thereof to ornamenting duties.
any articles of manufacture or substances, unless he be furnished,

in respect of each such application, with two copies, drawings, or prints of such design, accompanied with the name of every person who shall claim to be proprietor, or of the style or title of the firm under which such proprietor may be trading, with his place of abode or place of carrying on his business, or other place of address, and the number of the class in respect of which such registration is made; and the registrar shall register all such copies, drawings, or prints, from time to time successively as they are received by him for that purpose; and on every such copy, drawing, or print, he shall affix a number corresponding to such succession; and he shall retain one copy, drawing, or print, which he shall file in his office, and the other he shall return to the person by whom the same has been forwarded to him; and in order to give ready access to the copies of designs so registered, he shall class such copies of designs, and keep a proper index of each class.

Certificate of registration of design.
XVI. And be it enacted, That upon every copy, drawing, or print of an original design so returned to the person registering as aforesaid, or attached thereto, and upon every copy, drawing, or print thereof received for the purpose of such registration, or of the transfer of such design being certified thereon or attached thereto, the registrar shall certify under his hand that the design has been so registered, the date of such registration, and the name of the registered proprietor, or the style or title of the firm under which such proprietor may be trading, with his place of abode or place of carrying on his business, or other place of address, and also the number of such design, together with such number or letter, or number and letter, and in such form as shall be employed by him to denote or correspond with the date of such registration; and such certificate made on every such original design, or on such copy thereof, and purporting to be signed by the registrar or deputy registrar, and purporting to have the seal of office of such registrar affixed thereto, shall, in the absence of evidence to the contrary, be sufficient proof, as follows:

Of the design, and of the name of the proprietor therein mentioned, having been duly registered; and

Of the commencement of the period of registry; and

Of the person named therein as proprietor being the proprietor; and

Of the originality of the design; and

Of the provisions of this Act, and of any rule under which the certificate appears to be made, having been complied with:

And any such writing purporting to be such certificate shall, in the absence of evidence to the contrary, be received as evidence, without proof of the handwriting of the signature thereto, or of the seal of office affixed thereto, or of the person signing the same being the registrar or deputy registrar.

XVII. And be it enacted, That every person shall be at liberty to inspect any design whereof the copyright shall have expired, paying only such fee as shall be appointed by virtue of this Act in that behalf; but with regard to designs whereof the copyright shall not have expired, no such design shall be open to inspection, except by a proprietor of such design, or by any person authorized by him in writing, or by any person specially authorized by the registrar, and then only in the presence of such registrar or in the presence of some person holding an appointment under this Act, and not so as to take a copy of any such design or of any part thereof, nor without paying for every such inspection such fee as aforesaid : Provided always, that it shall be lawful for the said registrar to give to any person applying to him, and producing a particular design, together with the registration mark thereof, or producing such registration mark only, a certificate stating whether of such design there be any copyright existing, and if there be, in respect to what particular article of manufacture or substance such copyright exists, and the term of such copyright, and the date of registration, and also the name and address of the registered proprietor thereof.

Inspection of registered designs.

XVIII. And be it enacted, That the Commissioners of the Treasury shall from time to time fix fees to be paid for the services to be performed by the registrar, as they shall deem requisite, to defray the expenses of the said office, and the salaries or other remuneration of the said registrar, and of any other person employed under him, with the sanction of the Commissioners of the Treasury, in the execution of this Act; and the balance, if any, shall be carried to the Consolidated Fund of the United Kingdom, and be paid accordingly into the receipt of Her Majesty's Exchequer at Westminster; and the Commissioners of the Treasury may regulate the manner in which such fees are to be received, and in which they are to be kept, and in which they are to be accounted for, and they may also remit or dispense with the payment of such fees in any cases where they may think it expedient so to do: Provided always, that the fee for registering a design to be applied to any woven fabric mentioned or comprised in classes 7, 9 or 10, shall not exceed the sum of one shilling; that the fee for registering a design to be applied to a paper-hanging shall not exceed the sum of ten shillings; and that the fee to be received by the registrar for giving a certificate relative to the existence or expiration of

Application of fees of registration.

any copyright in any design printed on any woven fabric, yarn, thread, or warp, or printed, embossed, or worked on any paper. hanging, to any person exhibiting a piece end of a registered pattern, with the registration mark thereon, shall not exceed the sum of two shillings and sixpence.

Penalty for extortion. XIX. And be it enacted, That if either the registrar or any person employed under him either demand or receive any gratuity or reward, whether in money or otherwise, except the salary or remuneration authorized by the Commissioners of the Treasury, he shall forfeit for every such offence fifty pounds to any person suing for the same by action of debt in the Court of Exchequer at Westminster; and he shall also be liable to be either suspended or dismissed from his office, and rendered incapable of holding any situation in the said office, as the Commissioners of the Treasury see fit.

Interpretation of Act. XX. And for the interpretation of this Act, be it enacted, That the following terms of expression, so far as they are not repugnant to the context of this Act, shall be construed as follows: (that is to say), the expression "Commissioners of the Treasury" shall mean the Lord High Treasurer for the time being, or the Commissioners of Her Majesty's Treasury for the time being, or any three or more of them; and the singular number shall include the plural as well as the singular number; and the masculine gender shall include the feminine gender as well as the masculine gender.

Alteration of Act. XXI. And be it enacted, That this Act may be amended or repealed by any Act to be passed in the present session of Parliament.

NOTE.—So much of this Act as relates to the appointment of a registrar of designs, and other officers, as well as the fixing of the salaries for the payment of the same, repealed by 6 & 7 Vict. c. 65, § 7.

[Schedules

SCHEDULES REFERRED TO BY THE FOREGOING ACT.

SCHEDULE (A).

DATE OF ACTS.	TITLE.
27 Geo. 3, c. 38. (1787.)	An Act for the Encouragement of the Arts of designing and printing Linens, Cottons, Calicoes, and Muslins, by vesting the Properties thereof in the Designers, Printers, and Proprietors for a limited Time.
29 Geo. 3, c. 19. (1789.)	An Act for continuing an Act for the Encouragement of the Arts of designing and printing Linens, Cottons, Calicoes, and Muslins, by vesting the Properties thereof in the Designers, Printers, and Proprietors for a limited Time.
34 Geo. 3, c. 23. (1794.)	An Act for amending and making perpetual an Act for the Encouragement of the Arts of designing and printing Linens, Cottons, Calicoes, and Muslins, by vesting the Properties thereof in the Designers, Printers, and Proprietors for a limited Time.
2 Vict. c. 13. (1839.)	An Act for extending the Copyright of Designs for Calico Printing to Designs for printing other woven Fabrics.

SCHEDULE (B).

DATE OF ACT.	TITLE.
2 Vict. c. 17. (1839.)	An Act to secure to Proprietors of Designs for Articles of Manufacture the Copyright of such Designs for a limited Time.

SCHEDULE (C).

DATE OF ACTS.	TITLE.
38 Geo. 3, c. 71. (1798.)	An Act for encouraging the Art of making new Models and Casts of Busts and other Things therein mentioned.
54 Geo. 3, c. 56. (1814.)	An Act to amend and render more effectual an Act for encouraging the Art of making new Models and Casts of Busts and other Things therein mentioned, and for giving further Encouragement to such Arts.

2 U

6 & 7 VICT. o. 65.

An Act to amend the Laws relating to the Copyright of Designs.

[22nd August, 1843.]

<table>
<tr><td>5 & 6 Vict.
c. 100.</td><td>WHEREAS by an Act passed in the fifth and sixth years of the reign of Her present Majesty, intituled " An Act to consolidate and amend the Laws relating to the Copyright of Designs for ornamenting Articles of Manufacture," there was granted to the proprietor of any new and original design, with the exceptions therein mentioned, the sole right to apply the same to the ornamenting of any article of manufacture or any such substance as therein described during the respective periods therein mentioned : And whereas it is expedient to extend the protection afforded by the said Act to such designs hereinafter mentioned, not being of an ornamental character, as are not included therein : Be it therefore enacted by the Queen's most excellent Majesty, by and with the advice and consent of the Lords spiritual and temporal, and Commons in this present Parliament assembled, and by the authority of the</td></tr>
</table>

Commencement of Act.   same, That this Act shall come into operation on the first day of September, One thousand eight hundred and forty-three.

Grant of copyright.   II. And with regard to any new or original design for any article of manufacture having reference to some purpose of utility, so far as such design shall be for the shape or configuration of such article, and that whether it be for the whole of such shape or configuration, or only for a part thereof, be it enacted, That the proprietor of such design not previously published within the United Kingdom of Great Britain and Ireland or elsewhere, shall have the sole right to apply such design to any article, or make or sell any article according to such design, for the term of three years, to be computed from the time of such design being registered according to this Act :

Proviso.   Provided always, that this enactment shall not extend to such designs as are within the provisions of the said Act, or of two other Acts passed respectively in the thirty-eighth and fifty-fourth years of the reign of His late Majesty King George the Third, and intituled

38 G. 3, c. 71.   respectively " An Act for encouraging the Art of making new models and Casts of Busts, and other things therein mentioned,"

54 G. 3, c. 56.   and " An Act to amend and render more effectual an Act for encouraging the Art of making new Models and casts of Busts, and other things therein mentioned."

Conditions of copyright.   III. Provided always, and be it enacted, that no person shall be entitled to the benefit of this Act unless such design have before publication thereof been registered according to this Act, and unless the name of such person shall be registered according to this Act as a proprietor of such design, and unless after publication of such design every article of manufacture made by him according to such design, or on which such design is used, hath thereon the word "registered," with the date of registration.

IV. And be it enacted, that unless a design applied to any article of manufacture be registered either as aforesaid or according to the provisions of the said first-mentioned Act, and also after the copyright of such design shall have expired, it shall be unlawful to put on any such article the word "registered," or to advertise the same for sale as a registered article; and if any person shall so unlawfully publish, sell, or expose or advertise for sale any such article of manufacture, he shall forfeit for every such offence a sum not exceeding five pounds nor less than one pound, which may be recovered by any person proceeding for the same by any of the remedies hereby given for the recovery of penalties for pirating any such design. *Penalty for wrongfully using marks denoting a registered design.*

V. And be it enacted, that all such articles of manufacture as are commonly known by the name of floor-cloths or oil-cloths shall henceforth be considered as included in class six in the said first-mentioned Act in that behalf mentioned, and be registered accordingly. *Floor or oil-cloths included in class six.*

VI. And be it enacted, that all and every the clauses and provisions contained in the said first-mentioned Act, so far as they are not repugnant to the provisions contained in this Act, relating respectively to the explanation of the term proprietor, to the transfer of designs, to the piracy of designs, to the mode of recovering penalties, to actions for damages, to cancelling and amending registrations, to the limitation of actions, to the awarding of costs, to the certificate of registration, to the fixing and application of fees of registration, and to the penalty for extortion, shall be applied and extended to this present Act as fully and effectually, and to all intents and purposes, as if the said several clauses and provisoes had been particularly repeated and re-enacted in the body of this Act. *Certain provisions of 5 & 6 Vict. c. 100, to apply to this Act.*

VII. And be it enacted, that so much of the said first-mentioned Act as relates to the appointment of a registrar of designs for ornamenting articles of manufacture, and other officers, as well as to the fixing of the salaries for the payment of the same, shall be and the same is hereby repealed; and for the purpose of carrying into effect the provisions as well of this Act as of the said first-mentioned Act, the Lords of the Committee of the Privy Council for the consideration of all matters of trade and plantations may appoint a person to be registrar of designs for articles of manufacture, and, if the Lords of the said Committee see fit, an assistant registrar and other necessary officers and servants; and such registrar, assistant registrar, officers, and servants shall hold their offices during the pleasure of the Lords of the said Committee; and such registrar shall have a seal of office; *Appointment of registrar, &c.*

and the Commissioners of Her Majesty's Treasury may from time to time fix the salary or other remuneration of such registrar, assistant registrar, and other officers and servants and all the provisions contained in the said first-mentioned Act, and not hereby repealed, relating to the registrar, deputy registrar, clerks, and other officers and servants thereby appointed and therein named, shall be construed and held to apply respectively to the registrar, assistant registrar, and other officers and servants to be appointed under this Act.

Registrar's duties.

VIII. And be it enacted, that the said registrar shall not register any design for the shape or configuration of any article of manufacture as aforesaid, unless he be furnished with two exactly similar drawings or prints of such design, with such description in writing as may be necessary to render the same intelligible according to the judgment of the said registrar, together with the title of the said design and the name of every person who shall claim to be proprietor, or of the style or title of the firm under which such proprietor may be trading, with his place of abode, or place of carrying on

Drawings.

business, or other place of address; and every such drawing or print, together with the title and description of such design, and the name and address of the proprietor aforesaid, shall be on one sheet of paper or parchment, and on the same side thereof; and the size of the said sheet shall not exceed twenty-four inches by fifteen inches; and there shall be left on one of the said sheets a blank space on the same side on which are the said drawings, title, description, name, and address, of the size of six inches by four inches, for the certificate herein mentioned; and the said drawings or prints shall be made on a proper geometric scale; and the said description shall set forth such parts or part of the said design (if any) as shall not be new or original; and the said registrar shall register all such drawings or prints from time to time as they are received by him for that purpose; and on every such drawing or print he shall affix a number corresponding to the order of succession in the register, and he shall retain one drawing or print which he shall file at his office, and the other he shall return to the person by whom the same has been forwarded to him; and in order to give a ready access to the designs so registered, he shall keep a proper index of the titles thereof.

Discretionary power as to registry vested in the registrar.

IX. And be it enacted, that if any design be brought to the said registrar to be registered under the said first-mentioned Act, and it shall appear to him that the same ought to be registered under this present Act, it shall be lawful for the said registrar to refuse to register such design otherwise than under the present Act and in the manner hereby provided; and if it shall appear to the said registrar that the design brought to be registered under the said first-mentioned Act or this Act is not intended to be applied to any article of manufacture, but only to some label, wrapper, or other covering in which such article might be exposed for sale, or that such design is contrary to public morality or order, it shall be lawful for the said registrar in his discretion wholly to refuse to register such design: Provided always, that the Lords *Proviso.* of the said Committee of Privy Council may, on representation made to them by the proprietor of any design so wholly refused to be registered as aforesaid, if they shall see fit, direct the said registrar to register such design, whereupon and in such case the said registrar shall be and is hereby required to register the same accordingly.

X. And be it enacted, That every person shall be at liberty to *Inspection of* inspect the index of the titles of the designs, not being ornamental *index of titles* designs registered under this Act, and to take copies from the *of designs, &c.* same, paying only such fees as shall be appointed by virtue of this Act in that behalf; and every person shall be at liberty to inspect any such design, and to take copies thereof, paying such fee as aforesaid; but no design whereof the copyright shall not have expired shall be open to inspection except in the presence of such registrar, or in the presence of some person holding an appointment under this Act, and not so as to take a copy of such design, not without paying such fee as aforesaid.

XI. And, for the interpretation of this Act, be it enacted, That *Interpretation* the following terms and expressions, so far as they are not *of Act.* repugnant to the context of this Act, shall be construed as follows: (that is to say,) the expression "Commissioners of the Treasury" shall mean the Lord High Treasurer for the time being, or the Commissioners of Her Majesty's Treasury of the United Kingdom of Great Britain and Ireland for the time being, or any three or more of them; and the singular number shall include the plural as well as the singular number; and the masculine gender shall include the feminine gender as well as the masculine gender.

XII. And be it enacted, That this Act may be amended *Alteration of* or repealed by any Act to be passed in the present session of *Act.* Parliament.

---

6 & 7 VICT. c. 68.

An Act for regulating Theatres.

[22nd August, 1843.]

WHEREAS it is expedient that the laws now in force for regulating theatres and theatrical performances be repealed and other provisions be enacted in their stead: Be it enacted by the Queen's

most excellent Majesty, by and with the advice and consent of the
Lords spiritual and temporal, and Commons, in this same parliament

Repeal of
3 Jac. 1, c. 21. assembled, and by the authority of the same, That an Act passed
in the third year of the reign of King James the First, intituled
Part of
10 G. 2, c. 19. an Act to restrain the abuses of players; and so much of an
Act passed in the tenth year of the reign of King George the
Second for the more effectual preventing the unlawful playing of interludes within the precincts of the two universities
in that part of Great Britain called England, and the places
adjacent, as is now in force; and another Act passed in the tenth
10 G. 2, c. 28. year of the reign of King George the Second, intituled an Act to
explain and amend so much of an Act made in the twelfth
year of the reign of Queen Anne, intituled "An Act for reducing
the Laws relating to Rogues, Vagabonds, Sturdy Beggars, and
Vagrants into one Act of Parliament, and for the more effectual
Punishment of such Rogues, Vagabonds, Sturdy Beggars, and
Vagrants, and sending them whither they ought to be sent," as relates
to common players or interludes; and another Act passed in the
twenty-eighth year of the reign of King George the Third, intituled
28 G. 3, c. 30. An Act to enable Justices of the Peace to license theatrical representations occasionally, under the restrictions therein contained, shall
Proviso as to
licences now in
force. be repealed: Provided always, that any licence now in force
granted by the Lord Chamberlain, or granted by any justices
of the peace under the provisions of the last-recited Act, shall
continue in force for the times for which the same were severally
granted, or until revoked by the authority by which they were
severally granted.

All theatres
for the per-
formance of
plays must be
licensed. II. And be it enacted, That, except as aforesaid, it shall not be
lawful for any person to have or keep any house or other place of
public resort in Great Britain, for the public performance of stage
plays, without authority by virtue of letters patent from Her
Majesty, her heirs and successors, or predecessors, or without
licence from the Lord Chamberlain of Her Majesty's household
for the time being, or from the justices of the peace as herein-after
provided; and every person who shall offend against this enactment
shall be liable to forfeit such sum as shall be awarded by the court
in which or the justices by whom he shall be convicted, not
exceeding twenty pounds for every day on which such house or
place shall have been so kept open by him for the purpose aforesaid, without legal authority.

What licences
shall be
granted by the
Lord Cham-
berlain. III. And be it enacted, That the authority of the Lord Chamberlain for granting licences shall extend to all theatres (not being
patent theatres) within the parliamentary boundaries of the cities
of London and Westminster, and of the boroughs of Finsbury and
Marylebone, the Tower Hamlets, Lambeth, and Southwark, and

also within those places where Her Majesty, her heirs and successors, shall, in their royal persons, occasionally reside : Provided always, that, except within the cities and boroughs aforesaid, and the boroughs of New Windsor in the county of Berks, and Brightelmstone in the county of Sussex, licences for theatres may be granted by the justices as herein-after provided, in those places in which Her Majesty, her heirs and successors, shall occasionally reside ; but such licences shall not be in force during the residence there of Her Majesty, her heirs and successors ; and during such residence it shall not be lawful to open such theatres as last aforesaid (not being patent theatres) without the licence of the Lord Chamberlain.

IV. And be it enacted, That for every such licence granted by the Lord Chamberlain, a fee, not exceeding ten shillings for each calendar month during which the theatre is licensed to be kept open, according to such scale of fees as shall be fixed by the Lord Chamberlain, shall be paid to the Lord Chamberlain. *Fee for Lord Chamberlain's licence.*

V. And be it enacted, That the justices of the peace within every county, riding, division, liberty, cinque port, city, and borough in Great Britain beyond the limits of the authority of the Lord Chamberlain, in which application shall have been made to them for any such licence as is herein-after mentioned, shall, within twenty-one days next after such application shall have been made to them in writing signed by the party making the same, and countersigned by at least two justices acting in and for the division within which the property proposed to be licensed shall be situate, and delivered to the clerk to the said justices, hold a special session in the division, district, or place for which they usually act, for granting licences to houses for the performance of stage plays, of the holding of which session seven days notice shall be given by their clerk to each of the justices acting within such division, district, or place ; and every such licence shall be given under the hands and seals of four or more of the justices assembled at such special session, and shall be signed and sealed in open court, and afterwards shall be publicly read by the clerk, with the names of the justices subscribing the same. *Licences may be granted by justices.*

VI. And be it enacted, That for every such licence granted by the justices a fee, not exceeding five shillings for each calendar month during which the theatre is licensed to be kept open, according to such scale of fees as shall be fixed by the justices, shall be paid to the clerk of the said justices. *Fee for justices' licence.*

VII. And be it enacted, That no such licence for a theatre shall be granted by the Lord Chamberlain or justices to any person except the actual and responsible manager for the time being of the theatre in respect of which the licence shall be granted : and *To whom licences shall be granted.*

the name and place of abode of such manager shall be printed on every play bill announcing any representation at such theatre : and such manager shall become bound himself in such penal sum as the Lord Chamberlain or justices shall require, being in no case more than five hundred pounds, and two sufficient sureties, to be approved by the said Lord Chamberlain or justices, each in such penal sum as the Lord Chamberlain or justices shall require, being in no case more than one hundred pounds, for the due observance of the rules which shall be in force at any time during the currency of the licence for the regulation of such theatre, and for securing payment of the penalties which such manager may be adjudged to pay for breach of the said rules, or any of the provisions of this Act.

Rules for the theatres under the control of the Lord Chamberlain.

VIII. And be it enacted, That in case it shall appear to the Lord Chamberlain that any riot or misbehaviour has taken place in any theatre licensed by him, or in any patent theatre, it shall be lawful for him to suspend such licence or to order such patent theatre to be closed for such time as to him shall seem fit; and it shall also be lawful for the Lord Chamberlain to order that any patent theatre or any theatre licensed by him shall be closed on such public occasions as to the Lord Chamberlain shall seem fit ; and while any such licence shall be suspended, or any such order shall be in force, the theatre to which the same applies shall not be entitled to the privilege of any letters patent or licence, but shall be deemed an unlicensed house.

Rules for enforcing order in the theatres licensed by the justices.

IX. And be it enacted, That the said justices of the peace at a special licensing session, or at some adjournment thereof, shall make suitable rules for ensuring order and decency at the several theatres licensed by them within their jurisdiction, and for regulating the times during which they shall severally be allowed to be open, and from time to time, at another special session, of which notice shall be given as aforesaid, may rescind or alter such rules : and it shall be lawful for any one of Her Majesty's principal secretaries of state to rescind or alter any such rules, and also to make such other rules for the like purpose, as to him shall seem fit; and a copy of all rules which shall be in force for the time being shall be annexed to every such licence; and in case any riot or breach of the said rules in any such theatre shall be proved on oath before any two justices usually acting in the jurisdiction where such theatre is situated, it shall be lawful for them to order that the same be closed for such time as to the said justices shall seem fit; and while such order shall be in force the theatre so ordered to be closed shall be deemed an unlicensed house.

Proviso for the universities of Oxford and Cambridge.

X. Provided always, and be it enacted, That no such licence shall be in force within the precincts of either of the Universities of Oxford or Cambridge, or within fourteen miles of the city of

Oxford or town of Cambridge, without the consent of the Chancellor or Vice-Chancellor of each of the said Universities respectively; and that the rules for the management of any theatre which shall be licensed with such consent within the limits aforesaid shall be subject to the approval of the said Chancellor or Vice-Chancellor respectively; and in case of the breach of any of the said rules, or of any condition on which the consent of the Chancellor or Vice-Chancellor to grant any such licence shall have been given it shall be lawful for such Chancellor or Vice-Chancellor respectively to annul the licence, and thereupon such licence shall become void.

XI. And be it enacted, That every person who for hire shall act or present, or cause, permit, or suffer to be acted or presented, any part in any stage play, in any place not being a patent theatre or duly licensed as a theatre, shall forfeit such sum as shall be awarded by the Court in which or the justices by whom he shall be convicted, not exceeding ten pounds for every day on which he shall so offend. *Penalty on persons performing in unlicensed places.*

XII. And be it enacted, That one copy of every new stage play and of every new act, scene, or other part added to any old. stage play, and of every new prologue or epilogue, and of every new part added to an old prologue or epilogue intended to be produced and acted for hire at any theatre in Great Britain, shall be sent to the Lord Chamberlain of Her Majesty's household for the time being, seven days at least before the first acting or presenting thereof, with an account of the theatre where and the time when the same is intended to be first acted or presented, signed by the master or manager, or one of the master or managers, of such theatre; and during the said seven days no person shall for hire act or present the same, or cause the same to be acted or presented; and in case the Lord Chamberlain, either before or after the expiration of the said period of seven days, shall disallow any play, or any act, scene, or part thereof, or any prologue or epilogue, or any part thereof, it shall not be lawful for any person to act or present , the same, or cause the same to be acted or presented, contrary to such disallowance. *No new plays or additions to old ones to be acted until submitted to the Lord Chamberlain.*

XIII. And be it enacted, That it shall be lawful for the Lord Chamberlain to charge such fees for the examination of the plays, prologues, and epilogues, or parts thereof, which shall be sent to him for examination, as to him from time to time shall seem fit, according to a scale which shall be fixed by him, such fee not being in any case morè than two guineas, and such fees shall be paid at the time when such plays, prologues, and epilogues, or parts thereof, shall be sent to the Lord Chamberlain; and the said period of seven days shall not begin to run in any case until the said fee *Fees to be paid for examination of plays, &c.*

shall have been paid to the Lord Chamberlain, or to some officer deputed by him to receive the same.

The Lord Chamberlain may forbid any play. XIV. And be it enacted, That it shall be lawful for the Lord Chamberlain for the time being, whenever he shall be of opinion that it is fitting for the preservation of good manners, decorum, or of the public peace so to do, to forbid the acting or presenting any stage play, or any act, scene, or part thereof, or any prologue or epilogue, or any part thereof, anywhere in Great Britain, or in such theatres as he shall specify, and either absolutely or for such time as he shall think fit.

Penalty for acting plays before they are allowed or after they have been disallowed. XV. And be it enacted, That every person who for hire shall act or present, or cause to be acted or presented, any new stage play, or any act, scene, or part thereof, or any new prologue or epilogue, or any part thereof, until the same shall have been allowed by the Lord Chamberlain, or which shall have been disallowed by him, and also every person who for hire shall act or present, or cause to be acted or presented any stage play, or any act, scene, or part thereof, or any prologue or epilogue, or any part thereof, contrary to such prohibition as aforesaid, shall for every such offence forfeit such sum as shall be awarded by the Court in which or the justices by whom he shall be convicted, not exceeding the sum of fifty pounds; and every licence (in case there be any such) by or under which the theatre was opened, in which such offence shall have been committed, shall become absolutely void.

What shall be evidence of acting for hire. XVI. And be it enacted, That in every case in which any money or other reward shall be taken or charged, directly or indirectly, or in which the purchase of any article is made a condition for the admission of any person into any theatre to see any stage play, and also in every case in which any stage play shall be acted or presented in any house, room, or place in which distilled or fermented exciseable liquor shall be sold, every actor therein shall be deemed to be acting for hire.

Proof of licence in certain cases to lie on the party accused. XVII. And be it enacted, That in any proceedings to be instituted against any person for having or keeping an unlicensed theatre, or for acting for hire in an unlicensed theatre, if it shall be proved that such theatre is used for the public performance of stage plays, the burden of proof that such theatre is duly licensed or authorized shall lie on the party accused, and until the contrary shall be proved such theatre shall be taken to be unlicensed.

Proceedings begun before the passing of this Act may be discontinued. XVIII. And be it enacted, That after the passing of this Act it shall be lawful for any person against whom any action or information shall have been commenced, for the recovery of any forfeiture or pecuniary penalty incurred under the said Act of the tenth year of the reign of King George the Second, to apply to the court in which such action or information shall have been commenced, if such court shall be sitting, or if such court shall not be sitting to any judge of either of the superior courts at Westminster, for an order that such action or information shall be discontinued, upon payment of the costs thereof incurred in the time of such application being made, such costs to be taxed according to the practice of such court; and every such court or judge (as the case may be), upon such application, and proof that sufficient notice has been given to the plaintiff or informer, or to his attorney, of the application, shall make such order as aforesaid; and upon the making such order, and payment or tender of such costs as aforesaid, such action or information shall be forthwith discontinued.

XIX. And be it enacted, That all the pecuniary penalties imposed Penalties how by this Act for offences committed in England may be recovered in to be recoverable. any of her Majesty's courts of record at Westminster, and for offences committed in Scotland by action or summary complaint before the Court of Session or justiciary there, or for offences committed in any part of Great Britain in a summary way before two justices of the peace for any county, riding, division, liberty, city, or borough where any such offence shall be committed, by the oath or oaths of one or more credible witness or witnesses, or by the confession of the offender, and in default of payment of such penalty together with the costs, the same may be levied by distress and sale of the offender's goods and chattels, rendering the overplus to such offender, if any there be above the penalty, costs, and charge of distress; and for want of sufficient distress the offender may be imprisoned in the common gaol or house of correction of any such county, riding, division, liberty, city, or borough for any time not exceeding six calendar months.

XX. And be it enacted, That it shall be lawful for any person Appeal. who shall think himself aggrieved by any order of such justices of the peace to appeal therefrom to the next general or quarter session of the peace to be holden for the said county, riding, division, liberty, city, or borough, whose order therein shall be final.

XXI. And be it enacted, That the said penalties for any offence Appropriation against this Act shall be paid and applied in the first instance of penalties. toward defraying the expenses incurred by the prosecutor, and the residue thereof (if any) shall be paid to the use of Her Majesty, her heirs and successors.

XXII. Provided always, and be it enacted, That no person shall Limitation of be liable to be prosecuted for any offence against this Act unless actions. such prosecution shall be commenced within six calendar months after the offence committed.

Interpretation of Act.

XXIII. And be it enacted, That in this Act the word "stage-play" shall be taken to include every tragedy, comedy, farce, opera, burletta, interlude, melodrama, pantomime, or other entertainment of the stage, or any part thereof: provided always, that nothing herein contained shall be construed to apply to any theatrical representation in any booth or show which by the justices of the peace, or other persons having authority in that behalf, shall be allowed in any lawful fair, feast, or customary meeting of the like kind.

Limits of the Act.

XXIV. And be it enacted, That this Act shall extend only to *Great Britain.*

Act may be amended this session.

XXV. And be it enacted, that this Act may be amended or repealed by any Act to be passed in this Session of Parliament.

---

7 & 8 Vict. c. 12.

An Act to amend the Law relating to International Copyright.

[10th May, 1844.]

1 & 2 Vict. c. 59.

Whereas by an Act passed in the session of Parliament held in the first and second years of the reign of Her present Majesty, intituled "An Act for securing to Authors in certain Cases the Benefit of international Copyright" (and which Act is hereinafter, for the sake of perspicuity, designated as "The International Copyright Act"), Her Majesty was empowered by Order in Council to direct that the authors of books which should after a future time, to be specified in such Order in Council, be published in any foreign country, to be specified in such Order in Council, and their executors, administrators, and assigns, should have the sole liberty of printing and reprinting such books within the British dominions for such term as Her Majesty should by such Order in Council direct, not exceeding the term which authors, being British subjects, were then (that is to say, at the time of passing the said Act), entitled to in respect of books first published in the United Kingdom: and the said Act contains divers enactments securing to authors and their representatives the copyright in the books to which any such Order in Council should extend: And whereas an Act was passed in the session of Parliament held in the fifth and sixth years of the reign

5 & 6 Vict. c. 45.

of her present Majesty, intituled "An Act to amend the Law of Copyright" (and which Act is hereinafter, for the sake of perspicuity, designated as "The Copyright Amendment Act") repealing various Acts therein mentioned relating to the copyright of printed books, and extending, defining, and securing to authors and their repre-

sentatives the copyright of books: And whereas an Act was passed
in the session of Parliament held in the third and fourth years of
the reign of His late Majesty King William the Fourth, intituled:
" An Act to amend the Laws relating to dramatic literary Pro- 3 & 4 W. 4,
perty " (and which Act is hereinafter, for the sake of perspicuity, c. 15.
designated as " The dramatic literary Property Act "), whereby
the sole liberty of representing or causing to be represented any
dramatic piece in any place of dramatic entertainment in any
part of the British dominions, which should be composed and
not printed or published by the author thereof or his assignee,
was secured to such author or his assignee; and by the said Act
it was enacted that the author of any such production which
should thereafter be printed and published, or his assignee, should
have the like sole liberty of representation until the end of twenty-
eight years from the first publication thereof: And whereas by the
said " Copyright Amendment Act" the provisions of the said
" Dramatic literary Property Act" and of the said " Copyright
Amendment Act" were ma e applicable to musical compositions;
and it was thereby also enacted, that the sole liberty of representing
or performing, or causing or permitting to be represented or
performed, in any part of the British dominions, any dramatic piece
or musical composition, should endure and be the property of the
author thereof and his assigns for the term in the said " Copyright
Amendment Act" provided for the duration of the copyright in
books, and that the provisions therein enacted in respect of the
property of such copyright should apply to the liberty of representing or performing any dramatic piece or musical composition:
And whereas under or by virtue of the four several Acts next
hereinafter mentioned, (that is to say,) an Act passed in the eighth
year of the reign of His late Majesty King George the Second,
intituled " An Act for the Encouragement of the Arts of designing, 8 G. 2, c. 13.
engraving, and etching historical and other Prints by vesting the
Properties thereof in the Inventors or Engravers during the Time
therein mentioned;" an Act passed in the seventh year of His late
Majesty King George the Third, intituled " An Act to amend and 7 G. 3, c. 38.
render more effectual an Act made in the Eighth Year of the Reign
of King George the Second, for Encouragement of the Arts of
designing, engraving, and etching historical and other Prints; and
for vesting in and securing to Jane Hogarth, Widow, the Property
in certain Prints ;" an Act passed in the seventeenth year of the reign
of His late Majesty King George the Third, intituled " An Act for 17 G. 3. c. 57.
more effectually securing the Property of Prints to Inventors and
Engravers, by enabling them to sue for and recover Penalties in
certain Cases ;" and an Act passed in the session of Parliament held
in the sixth and seventh years of the reign of His late Majesty

King William the Fourth, intituled "An Act to extend the Protection of Copyright in Prints and Engravings to Ireland;" (and which
said four several Acts are hereinafter, for the sake of perspicuity,
designated as "The Engraving Copyright Acts;") every person
who invents or designs, engraves, etches, or works in mezzotinto
or chiaro-oscuro, or from his own work, design, or invention causes
or procures to be designed, engraved, etched, or worked in mezzotinto or chiaro-oscuro any historical print or prints, or any print or
prints of any portrait, conversation, landscape, or architecture,
map, chart, or plan, or any other print or prints whatsoever, and
every person who engraves, etches, or works in mezzotinto or chiaro-
oscuro, or causes to be engraved, etched, or worked, any print taken
from any picture, drawing, model, or sculpture, either ancient or
modern, notwithstanding such print shall not have been graven or
drawn from the original design of such graver, etcher, or draftsman,
is entitled to the copyright of such print for the term of twenty-
eight years from the first publishing thereof; and by the said several
Engraving Copyright Acts it is provided that the name of the proprietor shall be truly engraved on each plate, and printed on every
such print, and remedies are provided for the infringement of such
copyright: And whereas under and by virtue of an Act passed in
the thirty-eighth year of the reign of His late Majesty King George
the Third, intituled "An Act for encouraging the Art of making,
new Models and Casts of Busts and other Things therein mentioned;" and of an Act passed in the fifty-fourth year of the reign
of His late Majesty King George the Third, intituled "An Act to
amend and render more effectual an Act of His present Majesty, for
encouraging the Art of making new Models and Casts of Busts and
other Things therein mentioned, and for giving further Encouragement to such Arts," (and which said Acts are, for the sake of
perspicuity, hereinafter designated as "The Sculpture Copyright
Acts,") every person who makes or causes to be made any new and
original sculpture, or model or copy or cast of the human figure,
any bust or part of the human figure clothed in drapery or otherwise,
any animal or part of any animal combined with the human figure
or otherwise, any subject, being matter of invention in sculpture,
any alto or basso-relievo, representing any of the matters aforesaid
or any cast from nature of the human figure or part thereof, or of
any animal or part thereof, or of any such subject representing any
of the matters aforesaid, whether separate or combined, is entitled
to the copyright in such new and original sculpture, model, copy,
and cast, for fourteen years from first putting forth and publishing
the same, and for an additional period of fourteen years in case the
original maker is living at the end of the first period; and by the
said Acts it is provided that the name of the proprietor, with the

6 & 7 W. 4,
c. 59.

38 G. 3, c. 71.

54 G. 3, c. 56.

date of the publication thereof, is to be put on all such sculptures, models, copies, and casts, and remedies are provided for the infringement of such copyright : And whereas the powers vested in Her Majesty by the said "International Copyright Act" are insufficient to enable Her Majesty to confer upon authors of books first published in foreign countries copyright of the like duration, and with the like remedies for the infringement thereof, which are conferred and provided by the said "Copyright Amendment Act" with respect to authors of books first published in the British dominions ; and the said "International Copyright Act" does not empower Her Majesty to confer any exclusive right of representing or performing dramatic pieces or musical compositions first published in foreign countries upon the authors thereof, nor to extend the privilege of copyright to prints and sculpture first published abroad ; and it is expedient to invest increased powers in Her Majesty in this respect, and for that purpose to repeal the said "International Copyright Act," and to give such other powers to Her Majesty, and to make such further provisions, as are hereinafter contained : Be it therefore enacted by the Queen's most excellent Majesty, by and with the advice and consent of the Lords spiritual and temporal, and Commons, in this present Parliament assembled, and by the authority of the same, That the said recited Act herein designated as the "International Copyright Act" shall be and the same is hereby repealed. *Repeal of International Copyright Act.*

II. And be it enacted, That it shall be lawful for Her Majesty, by any Order of Her Majesty in Council, to direct that, as respects all or any particular class or classes of the following works, (namely,) books, prints, articles of sculpture, and other works of art, to be defined in such order, which shall after a future time, to be specified in such order, be first published in any foreign country to be named in such order, the authors, inventors, designers, engravers, and makers thereof respectively, their respective executors, administrators, and assigns, shall have the privilege of copyright therein during such period or respective periods as shall be defined in such order, not exceeding however, as to any of the above-mentioned works, the term of copyright which authors, inventors, designers, engravers, and makers of the like works respectively first published in the United Kingdom may be then entitled to under the hereinbefore recited Acts respectively, or under any Acts which may hereafter be passed in that behalf. *Her Majesty, by Order in Council, may direct that authors, &c., of works first published in foreign countries shall have copyright therein within Her Majesty's dominions.*

III. And be it enacted, That in case any such order shall apply to books, all and singular the enactments of the said "Copyright Amendment Act," and of any other Act for the time being in force with relation to the copyright in books first published in this country, shall, from and after the time so to be specified in that *If the order applies to books, the copyright law as to books first published in*

this country
shall apply to
the books to
which the
order relates,
with certain
exceptions.
behalf in such order, and subject to such limitation as to the duration of the copyright as shall be therein contained, apply to and be in force in respect of the books to which such order shall extend, and which shall have been registered as hereinafter is provided, in such and the same manner as if such books were first published in the United Kingdom, save and except such of the said enactments, or such parts thereof, as shall be excepted in such order, and save and except such of the said enactments as relate to the delivery of copies of books at the British Museum, and to or for the use of the other libraries mentioned in the said "Copyright Amendment Act."

If the order
applies to
prints, sculp-
tures, &c., the
copyright law
as to prints or
sculptures first
published in
this country
shall apply to
the prints,
sculptures, &c.,
to which such
order relates.
IV. And be it enacted, That in case any such order shall apply to prints, articles of sculpture, or to any such other works of art as aforesaid, all and singular the enactments of the said "Engraving Copyright Acts," and the said "Sculpture Copyright Acts," or of any other Act for the time being in force with relation to the copyright in prints or articles of sculpture first published in this country, and of any Act for the time being in force with relation to the copyright in any similar works of art first published in this country, shall, from and after the time so to be specified in that behalf in such order, and subject to such limitation as to the duration of the copyright as shall be therein contained respectively, apply to and be in force in respect of the prints, articles of sculpture, and other works of art to which such order shall extend, and which shall have been registered as hereinafter is provided, in such and the same manner as if such articles and other works of art were first published in the United Kingdom, save and except such of the said enactments or such parts thereof as shall be excepted in such order.

Her Majesty
may, by Order
in Council,
direct that
authors and
composers of
dramatic pieces
and musical
compositions
first publicly
represented
and performed
in foreign
countries shall
have similar
rights in the
British
dominions.
V. And be it enacted, That it shall be lawful for Her Majesty, by any Order of Her Majesty in Council, to direct that the authors of dramatic pieces and musical compositions which shall after a future time, to be specified in such order, be first publicly represented or performed in any foreign country to be named in such order, shall have the sole liberty of representing or performing in any part of the British dominions such dramatic pieces or musical compositions during such period as shall be defined in such order, not exceeding the period during which authors of dramatic pieces and musical compositions first publicly represented or performed in the United Kingdom may for the time be entitled by law to the sole liberty of representing and performing the same; and from and after the time so specified in any such last-mentioned order the enactments of the said "Dramatic literary Property Act," and of the said "Copyright Amendment Act," and of any other Act for the time being in force with relation to the liberty of publicly

representing and performing dramatic pieces or musical compositions, shall, subject to such limitation as to the duration of the right conferred by any such order as shall be therein contained, apply to and be in force in respect of the dramatic pieces and musical compositions to which such order shall extend, and which shall have been registered as hereinafter is provided, in such and the same manner as if such dramatic pieces and musical compositions had been first publicly represented and performed in the British dominions, save and except such of the said enactments or such parts thereof as shall be excepted in such order.

VI. Provided always, and be it enacted, That no author of any book, dramatic piece or musical composition, or his executors, administrators, or assigns, and no inventor, designer, or engraver of any print, or maker of any article of sculpture, or other work of art, his executors, administrators, or assigns, shall be entitled to the benefit of this Act, or of any Order in Council to be issued in pursuance thereof, unless, within a time or times to be in that behalf prescribed in each such Order in Council, such book, dramatic piece, musical composition, print, article of sculpture, or other work of art, shall have been so registered, and such copy thereof shall have been so delivered as hereinafter is mentioned; (that is to say,) as regards such book, and also such dramatic piece or musical composition, (in the event of the same having been printed,) the title to the copy thereof, the name and place of abode of the author or composer thereof, the name and place of abode of the proprietor of the copyright thereof, the time and place of the first publication, representation, or performance thereof, as the case may be, in the foreign country named in the Order in Council under which the benefits of this Act shall be claimed, shall be entered in the register book of the Company of Stationers in London, and one printed copy of the whole of such book, and of such dramatic piece or musical composition, in the event of the same having been printed, and of every volume thereof, upon the best paper upon which the largest number or impression of the book, dramatic piece, or musical composition shall have been printed for sale, together with all maps and prints relating thereto, shall be delivered to the officer of the Company of Stationers at the hall of the said company; and as regards dramatic pieces and musical compositions in manuscript, the title to the same, the name and place of abode of the author or composer thereof, the name and place of abode of the proprietor of the right of representing or performing the same, and the time and place of the first representation or performance thereof in the country named in the Order in Council under which the benefit of the Act shall be claimed, shall be entered in the said register book of the said Company of

Particulars to be observed as to registry and to delivery of copies.

2 X

Stationers in London; and as regards prints, the title thereof, the
name and place of abode of the inventor, designer, or engraver
thereof, the name of the proprietor of the copyright therein, and the
time and place of the first publication thereof in the foreign country
named in the Order in Council under which the benefits of the Act
shall be claimed, shall be entered in the said register book of the
said Company of Stationers in London, and a copy of such print,
upon the best paper upon which the largest number of impressions
of the print shall have been printed for sale, shall be delivered to
the officer of the Company of Stationers at the hall of the said
company; and as regards any such article of sculpture or any such
other work of art as aforesaid, a descriptive title thereof, the name
and place of abode of the maker thereof, the name of the proprietor
of the copyright therein, and the time and place of its first publication in the foreign country named in the Order in Council under
which the benefit of this Act shall be claimed, shall be entered in
the said register book of the said Company of Stationers in London;
and the officer of the said Company of Stationers receiving such
copies so to be delivered as aforesaid shall give a receipt in writing
for the same, and such delivery shall to all intents and purposes be
a sufficient delivery under the provisions of this Act.

In case of
books pub-
lished anony-
mously, the
name of the
publisher to
be sufficient.

VII. Provided always, and be it enacted, That if a book be
published anonymously, it shall be sufficient to insert in the
entry thereof in such register book the name and place of abode
of the first publisher thereof, instead of the name and place of
abode of the author thereof, together with a declaration that such
entry is made either on behalf of the author or on behalf of such
first publisher, as the case may require.

The provisions
of the Copy-
right Amend-
ment Act as
regards entries
in the register
book of the
Company of
Stationers, &c.,
to apply to
entries under
this Act.

VIII. And be it enacted, That the several enactments in the
said "Copyright Amendment Act" contained with relation to
keeping the said register book, and the inspection thereof, the
searches therein, and the delivery of certified and stamped copies
thereof, the reception of such copies in evidence, the making of
false entries in the said book, and the production in evidence
of papers falsely purporting to be copies of entries in the said
book, the applications to the courts and judges by persons
aggrieved by entries in the said book, and the expunging and
varying such entries, shall apply to the books, dramatic pieces,
and musical compositions, prints, articles of sculpture, and other
works of art, to which any Order in Council issued in pursuance
of this Act shall extend, and to the entries and assignments of
copyright and proprietorship therein, in such and the same
manner as if such enactments were here expressly enacted in
relation thereto, save and except that the forms of entry prescribed by the said "Copyright Amendment Act" may be varied

to meet the circumstance of the case, and that the sum to be demanded by the officer of the said Company of Stationers for making any entry required by this Act shall be one shilling only.

IX. And be it enacted, That every entry made in pursuance of this Act of a first publication shall be *prima facie* proof of a rightful first publication; but if there be a wrongful first publication, and any party have availed himself thereof to obtain an entry of a spurious work, no order for expunging or varying such entry shall be made unless it be proved to the satisfaction of the court or of the judge taking cognizance of the application for expunging or varying such entry, first, with respect to a wrongful publication in a country to which the author or first publisher does not belong, and in regard to which there does not subsist with this country any treaty of international copyright, that the party making the application was the author or first publisher, as the case requires; second, with respect to a wrongful first publication either in the country where a rightful first publication has taken place, or in regard to which there subsists with this country a treaty of international copyright, that a court of competent jurisdiction in any such country where such wrongful first publication has taken place has given judgment in favour of the right of the party claiming to be the author or first publisher.

As to expunging or varying entry grounded in wrongful first publication.

X. And be it enacted, That all copies of books wherein there shall be any subsisting copyright under or by virtue of this Act, or of any Order in Council made in pursuance thereof, printed or reprinted in any foreign country except that in which such books were first published, shall be and the same are hereby absolutely prohibited to be imported into any part of the British dominions, except by or with the consent of the registered proprietor of the copyright thereof, or his agent authorized in writing, and if imported contrary to this prohibition the same and the importers thereof shall be subject to the enactments in force relating to goods prohibited to be imported by any Act relating to the customs; and as respects any such copies so prohibited to be imported, and also as respects any copies unlawfully printed in any place whatsoever of any books wherein there shall be any such subsisting copyright as aforesaid, any person who shall in any part of the British dominions import such prohibited or unlawfully printed copies, or who, knowing such copies to be so unlawfully imported or unlawfully printed, shall sell, publish, or expose to sale or hire, or shall cause to be sold, published, or exposed to sale or hire, or have in his possession for sale or hire, any such copies so unlawfully imported or

Copies of books wherein copyright is subsisting under this Act printed in foreign countries other than those wherein the book was first published prohibited to be imported.

2 X 2

unlawfully printed, such offender shall be liable to a special action on the case at the suit of the proprietor of such copyright, to be brought and prosecuted in the same courts and in the same manner, and with the like restrictions upon the proceedings of the defendant, as are respectively prescribed in the said "Copyright Amendment Act" with relation to actions thereby authorized to be brought by proprietors of copyright against persons importing or selling books unlawfully printed in the British dominions.

Officer of Stationers' Company to deposit books, &c., in the British Museum.

XI. And be it enacted, That the said officer of the said Company of Stationers shall receive at the hall of the said company every book, volume, or print so to be delivered as aforesaid, and within one calendar month after receiving such book, volume, or print, shall deposit the same in the library of the British Museum.

Second or subsequent editions.

XII. Provided always, and be it enacted, That it shall not be requisite to deliver to the said officer of the said Stationers' Company any printed copy of the second or of any subsequent edition of any book or books so delivered as aforesaid, unless the same shall contain additions or alterations.

Orders in Council may specify different periods for different foreign countries and for different classes of works.

XIII. And be it enacted, That the respective terms to be specified by such Orders in Council respectively for the continuance of the privilege to be granted in respect of works to be first published in foreign countries may be different for works first published in different foreign countries and for different classes of such works; and that the times to be prescribed for the entries to be made in the register book of the Stationers' Company, and for the deliveries of the books and other articles to the said officer of the Stationers' Company, as hereinbefore is mentioned, may be different for different foreign countries and for different classes of books or other articles.

No Order in Council to have any effect unless it states that reciprocal protection is secured.

XIV. Provided always, and be it enacted, That no such order in Council shall have any effect unless it shall be therein stated, as the ground for issuing the same, that due protection has been secured by the foreign power so named in such Order in Council for the benefit of parties interested in works first published in the dominions of Her Majesty similar to those comprised in such order.

Orders in Council to be published in Gazette, and to have same effect as this Act.

XV. And be it enacted, That every Order in Council to be made under the authority of this Act shall as soon as may be after the making thereof by Her Majesty in Council be published in the *London Gazette*, and from the time of such publication shall have the same effect as if every part thereof were included in this Act.

Orders in Council to be laid before Parliament.

XVI. And be it enacted, That a copy of every Order of Her Majesty in Council made under this Act shall be laid before both Houses of Parliament within six weeks after issuing the same, if

Parliament be then sitting, and if not, then within six weeks after the commencement of the then next session of Parliament.

XVII. And be it enacted, That it shall be lawful for Her Majesty by an Order in Council from time to time to revoke or alter any Order in Council previously made under the authority of this Act, but nevertheless without prejudice to any rights acquired previously to such revocation or alteration. Orders in Council may be revoked.

XVIII. Provided always, and be it enacted, That nothing in this Act contained shall be construed to prevent the printing, publication, or sale of any translation of any book the author whereof and his assigns may be entitled to the benefit of this Act (*a*). Translations.

XIX. And be it enacted, That neither the author of any book, nor the author or composer of any dramatic piece or musical composition, nor the inventor, designer, or engraver of any print, nor the maker of any article of sculpture, or of such other work of art as aforesaid, which shall after the passing of this Act be first published out of Her Majesty's dominions, shall have any copyright therein respectively, or any exclusive right to the public representation or performance thereof, otherwise than such (if any) as he may become entitled to under this Act. Authors of works first published in foreign countries not entitled to copyright except under this Act.

XX. And be it enacted, That in the construction of this Act the word "book" shall be construed to include "volume," "pamphlet," "sheet of letter-press," "sheet of music," "map," "chart," or "plan"; and the expression "articles of sculpture" shall mean all such sculptures, models, copies, and casts as are described in the said Sculpture Copyright Acts, and in respect of which the privileges of copyright are thereby conferred; and the words "printing" and "re-printing" shall include engraving and any other method of multiplying copies; and the expression "Her Majesty" shall include the heirs and successors of Her Majesty; and the expressions "Order of Her Majesty in Council," "Order in Council," and "Order," shall respectively mean Order of Her Majesty acting by and with the advice of Her Majesty's most honourable Privy Council; and the expression "officer of the Company of Stationers" shall mean the officer appointed by the said Company of Stationers for the purposes of the said Copyright Amendment Act; and in describing any persons or things any word importing the plural number shall mean also one person or thing, and any word importing the singular number shall include several persons or things, and any word importing the masculine shall include also the feminine gender; unless in any of such cases there shall be something in the subject or context repugnant to such construction. Interpretation clause.

(*a*) This section is repealed so far as it is inconsistent with the provisions contained in 15 & 16 Vict. c. 12.

Act may be repealed this session.

XXI. And be it enacted, That this Act may be amended or repealed by any Act to be passed in this present session of Parliament.

---

7 & 8 VICT. c. 73 (1844).

An Act to reduce, under certain Circumstances, the Duties payable upon Books and Engravings.

Repealed by 9 & 10 Vict. c. 58, s. 1.'

---

8 & 9 VICT. c. 93 (1845).

An Act to regulate the Trade of British Possessions abroad.

Repealed by 16 & 17 Vict. c. 100, s. 358.

---

9 & 10 VICT. c. 58 (1846).

An Act to amend an Act of the seventh and eighth Years of Her present Majesty for reducing, under certain Circumstances, the Duties payable upon Books and Engravings.

Repealed by 24 & 25 Vict. c. 101.

---

10 & 11 VICT. c. 95.

An Act to amend the Law relating to the Protection in the Colonies of Works entitled to Copyright in the United Kingdom.

[22nd July, 1847.]

5 & 6 Vict. c. 45.

WHEREAS by an Act passed in the session of Parliament holden in the fifth and sixth years of Her present Majesty, intituled "An Act to amend the Law of Copyright," it is amongst other things enacted, that it shall not be lawful for any person not being the proprietor of the copyright, or some person authorized by him, to import into any part of the United Kingdom, or into any other part of the British dominions, for sale or hire, any printed book first composed or written or printed or published in any part of the United Kingdom wherein there shall be copyright, and reprinted in any country or place whatsoever out of the British dominions: And whereas by an Act passed in the session of Parliament holden in the eighth and ninth years of the reign of

Her present Majesty, intituled "An Act to regulate the trade of 8 & 9 Vict. the British possessions abroad," books wherein the copyright is c. 93. subsisting, first composed or written or printed in the United Kingdom, and printed or reprinted in any other country, are absolutely prohibited to be imported into the British possessions abroad: And whereas by the said last-recited Act it is enacted, that all laws, bye-laws, usages, or customs in practice, or endeavoured or pretended to be in force or practice in any of the British possessions in America, which are in anywise repugnant to the said Act or to any Act of Parliament made or to be made in the United Kingdom, so far as such Act shall relate to and mention the said possessions, are and shall be null and void to all intents and purposes whatsoever: Now be it enacted, by the Queen's most excellent Majesty, by and with the advice and consent of the Lords spiritual and temporal, and Commons, in this present Parliament assembled, and by the authority of the same, that in Her Majesty case the legislature or proper legislative authorities in any British may suspend possession shall be disposed to make due provision for securing or the prohibition protecting the rights of British authors in such possession, and tion against shall pass an Act or make an ordinance for that purpose, and shall the admission transmit the same in the proper manner, to the Secretary of State, books into the in order that it may be submitted to Her Majesty, and in case Her colonies in Majesty shall be of opinion that such Act or ordinance is sufficient certain cases. for the purpose of securing to British authors reasonable protection within such possession, it shall be lawful for Her Majesty, if she think fit so to do, to express Her royal approval of such Act or ordinance, and thereupon to issue an Order in Council declaring that so long as the provisions of such Act or ordinance continue in force within such colony the prohibitions contained in the aforesaid Acts, and hereinbefore recited, and any prohibitions contained in the said Acts or in any other Acts against the importing, selling, letting out to hire, exposing for sale or hire, or possessing foreign reprints of books first composed, written, printed, or published in the United Kingdom, and entitled to copyright therein, shall be suspended so far as regards such colony; and thereupon such Act or ordinance shall come into operation, except so far as may be otherwise provided therein, or as may be otherwise directed by such Order in Council, anything in the said last-recited Act or in any other Act to the contrary notwithstanding.

II. And be it enacted, That every such Order in Council shall, Orders in Council to be published within one week after the issuing thereof, be published in the lished in *London Gazette*, and that a copy thereof, and of every such colonial *Gazette*. Act or ordinance so approved as aforesaid by Her Majesty, shall be Orders in Council and the laid before both Houses of Parliament within six weeks after the Colonial Acts issuing of such order, if Parliament be then sitting, or if Parliament or ordinances

to be laid
before Parlia-
ment.
be not then sitting, then within six weeks after the opening of the
next session of Parliament.

Act may be
amended, &c.
III. And be it enacted, This Act may be amended or repealed by
any Act to be passed in the present session of Parliament.

---

13 & 14 VICT. c. 104.

*An Act to extend and amend the Acts relating to the Copyright of
Designs.*

[14th August, 1850.]

WHEREAS it is expedient to extend and amend the Acts relating
to the copyright of designs : Be it therefore enacted by the Queen's
most excellent Majesty, by and with the advice and consent of the
Lords spiritual and temporal, and Commons, in this present Parliament assembled, and by the authority of the same :

Certain designs
may be regis-
tered pro-
visionally for
one year.
I. That the registrar of designs, upon application by or on behalf
of the proprietor of any design, not previously published within the
United Kingdom of Great Britain and Ireland or elsewhere, and
which may be registered under the Designs Act, 1842, or under the
Designs Act, 1843, for the provisional registration of such design
under this Act, and upon being furnished with such copy, drawing,
print, or description in writing or in print as in the judgment of
the said registrar shall be sufficient to identify the particular
design in respect of which such registration is desired and the name
of the person claiming to be proprietor, together with his place of
abode or business, or other place of address, or the style or title of
the firm under which he may be trading, shall register such design
in such manner and form as shall from time to time be prescribed
or approved by the Board of Trade ; and any design so registered
shall be deemed "provisionally registered," and the registration
thereof shall continue in force for the term of one year from the
time of the same being registered as aforesaid ; and the said registrar shall certify, under his hand and seal of office, in such form as
the said board shall direct or approve, that the design has been
provisionally registered, the date of such registration, and the name
of the registered proprietor, together with his place of abode or
business, or other place of address.

Benefits con-
ferred by pro-
visional regis-
tration.
II. That the proprietor of any design which shall have been provisionally registered shall, during the continuance of such registration, have the sole right and property in such design; and the
penalties and provisions of the said Designs Act, 1842, for preventing the piracy of designs, shall extend to the acts, matters, and
things next hereinafter enumerated, as fully as if those penalties

and provisions had been re-enacted in this Act, and expressly extended to such acts, matters, and things respectively; that is to say,

1. To the application of any provisionally registered design, or any fraudulent imitation thereof, to any articles of manufacture or to any substance:

2. To the publication, sale, or exposure for sale of any article of manufacture or any substance to which any provisionally registered design shall have been applied.

III. That during the continuance of such provisional regis- *The exhibition* tration neither such registration nor the exhibition or exposure of *of provisionally* any design provisionally registered, or of any article to which any *registered de-* such design may have been or be intended to be applied, in any *signs in certain* place, whether public or private, in which articles are not sold or *defeat copy-* exposed or exhibited for sale, and to which the public are not *right, &c.* admitted gratuitously, or in any place which shall have been previously certified by the Board of Trade to be a place of public exhibition within the meaning of this Act, nor the publication of any account or description of any provisionally registered design exhibited or exposed or intended to be exhibited or exposed in any such place of exhibition or exposure in any catalogue, paper, newspaper, periodical, or otherwise, shall prevent the proprietor thereof from registering any such design under the said Designs Acts at any time during the continuance of the provisional regis- tration, in the same manner and as fully and effectually as if no such registration, exhibition, exposure, or publication had been made; provided that every article to which any such design shall be applied, and which shall be exhibited or exposed by or with the licence or consent of the proprietor of such design, shall have thereon or attached thereto the words " provisionally registered," with the date of registration.

IV. That if during the continuance of such provisional regis- *Sale of articles* tration the proprietor of any design provisionally registered shall *to which pro-* sell, expose, or offer for sale any article, substance, or thing to *visionally re-* which any such design has been applied, such provisional regis- *signs, &c., have* tration shall be deemed to have been null and void immediately *been applied to* before any such sale, offer, or exposure shall have been first made; *right, but* but nothing herein contained shall be construed to hinder or *design itself* prevent such proprietor from selling or transferring the right and *may be sold.* property in any such design.

V. That the Board of Trade may by order in writing with *Extension of* respect to any particular class of designs, or any particular design, *period of pro-* extend the period for which any design may be provisionally *visional re-* registered under this Act, for such term not exceeding the additional *Board of Trade.*

term of six months as to the said board may seem fit; and whenever any such order shall be made, the same shall be registered in
the office for the registration of designs, and during the extended
term the protection and benefits conferred by this Act in case of
provisional registration shall continue as fully as if the original
term of one year had not expired.

Registration of
sculpture,
models, &c.

VI. That the registrar of designs, upon application by or on
behalf of the proprietor of any sculpture, model, copy, or cast
within the protection of the Sculpture Copyright Acts, and upon
being furnished with such copy, drawing, print, or description, in
writing or in print, as in the judgment of the said registrar shall
be sufficient to identify the particular sculpture, model, copy, or
cast in respect of which registration is desired, and the name of the
person claiming to be proprietor, together with his place of abode
or business or other place of address, or the name, style, or title of
the firm under which he may be trading, shall register such
sculpture, model, copy, or cast in such manner and form as shall
from time to time be prescribed or approved by the Board of Trade
for the whole or any part of the term during which copyright in
such sculpture, model, copy, or cast may or shall exist under the
Sculpture Copyright Acts; and whenever any such registration
shall be made, the said registrar shall certify under his hand and
seal of office, in such form as the said board shall direct or approve,
the fact of such registration, and the date of the same, and the
name of the registered proprietor, or the style or title of the firm
under which such proprietor may be trading, together with his
place of abode or business or other place of address.

Benefits con-
ferred by re-
gistration of
sculpture, &c.

VII. That if any person shall, during the continuance of the
copyright in any sculpture, model, copy, or cast which shall have
been so registered as aforesaid, make, import, or cause to be made,
imported, exposed for sale, or otherwise disposed of, any pirated
copy or pirated cast of any such sculpture, model, copy, or cast, in
such manner and under such circumstances as would entitle the
proprietor to a special action on the case under the Sculpture
Copyright Acts, the person so offending shall forfeit for every such
offence a sum not less than five pounds and not exceeding thirty
pounds to the proprietor of the sculpture, model, copy, or cast
whereof the copyright shall have been infringed; and for the
recovery of any such penalty the proprietor of the sculpture, model,
copy, or cast which shall have been so pirated shall have and be
entitled to the same remedies as are provided for the recovery of
penalties incurred under the Designs Act, 1842: Provided always,
that the proprietor of any sculpture, model, copy, or cast which
shall be registered under this Act, shall not be entitled to the benefit
of this Act, unless every copy or cast of such sculpture, model, copy,

or cast which shall be published by him after such registration shall be marked with the word "registered," and with the date of registration.

VIII. That designs for the ornamenting of ivory, bone, papier maché, and other solid substances not already comprised in the classes numbered 1, 2, and 3 in the Designs Act, 1842, shall be deemed and taken to be comprised within the class numbered 4 in that Act, and such designs shall be so registered accordingly.

Designs for ornamenting ivory, &c., may be registered under Designs Act, 1842, for three years.

IX. That the Board of Trade may from time to time order that the copyright of any class of designs or any particular design registered or which may be registered under the Designs Act, 1842, may be extended for such term, not exceeding the additional term of three years, as the said board may think fit, and the said board shall have power to revoke or alter any such order as may from time to time appear necessary; and whenever any order shall be made by the said board under this provision, the same shall be registered in the office for the registration of designs; and during the extended term the protection and benefits conferred by the said Designs Acts shall continue as fully as if the original term had not expired.

Board of Trade may extend copyright in ornamental designs.

X. That the Board of Trade may from time to time make, alter, and revoke rules and regulations with respect to the mode of registration, and the documents and other matters and particulars to be furnished by persons affecting registration and provisional registration under the said Acts and this Act: Provided always, that all such rules and regulations shall be published in the *London Gazette*, and shall forthwith upon the issuing thereof be laid before Parliament, if Parliament be sitting, and if Parliament be not sitting, then within fourteen days after the commencement of the then next session; and such rules and regulations, or any of them, shall be published or notified by the registrar of designs, in such other manner as the Board of Trade shall think fit to direct.

Regulations for the registration of designs may be made by Board of Trade.

XI. That if in any case in which the registration of a design is required to be made under either of the said Designs Acts it shall appear to the registrar that copies, drawings or prints as required by those Acts cannot be furnished, or that it is unreasonable or unnecessary to require the same, the said registrar may dispense with such copies, drawings, or prints, and may allow in lieu thereof such specification or description in writing or in print as may be sufficient to identify and render intelligible the design in respect of which registration is desired; and whenever registration shall be so made in the absence of such copies, drawings, or prints, the registration shall be as valid and effectual to all intents and purposes as if such copies, drawings, or prints had been furnished.

Registrar of designs may dispense with drawings, &c., in certain cases.

XII. That in order to prevent the frequent and unnecessary

Public books

and documents in the Designs Office not to be removed withoutjudge's order.

removal of the public books and documents in the office for the registration of designs, no book or document in the said office shall be removed for the purpose of being produced in any court or before any justice of the peace, without a special order of a judge of the Court of Chancery, or of one of Her Majesty's Superior Courts of Law, first had and obtained by the party who shall desire the production of the same.

Judges may order copies of documents to be furnished to be given in evidence.

XIII. That if application shall be made to a judge of any of Her Majesty's Courts of Law at Westminster by any person desiring to obtain a copy of any registration, entry, drawing, print, or document, of which such person is not entitled as of right to have a copy, for the purpose of being used in evidence in any cause, or otherwise howsoever, and if such judge shall be satisfied that such copy is *bonâ fide* intended for such purpose as aforesaid, such judge shall order the registrar of designs to deliver such copy to the party applying, and the registrar of designs shall, upon payment for the same of such fee or fees as may be fixed according to the provisions of the said Designs Act in this behalf, deliver such copy accordingly.

Copies of documents delivered by the registrar to be sealed, and to be evidence.

XIV. That every copy of any registration, entry, drawing, print, or document delivered by the registrar of designs to any person requiring the same shall be signed by the said registrar, and sealed with his seal of office; and every document sealed with the said seal purporting to be a copy of any registration, entry, drawing print, or document shall be deemed to be a true copy of such registration, entry, drawing, print, or document, and shall, without further proof, be received in evidence before all courts in like manner and to the same extent and effect as the original book, registration, entry, drawing, print, or document would or might be received if tendered in evidence, as well for the purpose of proving the contents, purport, and effect of such book, registration, entry, drawing, print, or document, as also proving the same to be a book, registration, entry, drawing, print, or document of or belonging to the said office, and in the custody of the registrar of designs.

Certain provisions of Designs Act, 1842 and 1843, extended to this Act.

XV. That the several provisions contained in the said Designs Acts (so far as they are not repugnant to the provisions of this Act) relating to the transfer of designs, to cancelling and amending registration, to the refusal of registration in certain cases, to the mode of recovering penalties, to the awarding and recovery of costs, to actions for damages, to the limitation of actions, to the certificate of registration, to penalties for wrongfully using marks, to the fixing and application of fees for registration, and to the penalty for extortion, shall apply to the registration, provisional registration, and transfer of designs, sculptures, models, copies, and casts, and to the designs, sculptures, models, copies, and casts entitled to protection under this Act, and to matters under this Act, as fully and effectually as if those provisions had been re-enacted in this Act with respect to designs, sculptures, models, copies, and casts registered and provisionally registered under this Act; and the forms contained in the Designs Act, 1842, may for the purposes of this Act be varied so as to meet the circumstances of the case.

XVI. That in the interpretation of this Act the following terms Interpretation and expressions shall have the meanings hereinafter assigned to of terms. them, unless such meanings shall be repugnant to or inconsistent with the context or subject matter : that is to say,

> The expression " Designs Act, 1842," shall mean an Act passed in the sixth year of the reign of Her present Majesty intituled " An Act to consolidate and amend the Laws relating to the Copyright of Designs for ornamenting Articles of Manufacture : "
>
> The expression " Designs Act, 1843," shall mean an Act passed in the seventh year of Her present Majesty, intituled " An Act to amend the Laws relating to the Copyright of Designs : "
>
> The expression " Sculpture Copyright Acts " shall mean two Acts passed respectively in the thirty-eighth and fifty-fourth years of the reign of King George the Third, and intituled respectively " An Act for encouraging the Art of making new Models and Casts of Busts and other things herein mentioned," and " An Act to amend and render more effectual an Act for encouraging the Art of making new Models and Casts of Busts and other Things therein mentioned : "
>
> The expression " the Board of Trade " shall mean the Lords of the Committee of Privy Council for the consideration of all matters of trade and plantations :
>
> The expression " Registrar of Designs " shall mean the registrar or assistant registrar of designs for articles of manufacture :
>
> The expression " Proprietor " shall be construed according to the interpretation of that word in the said Designs Act, 1842 :
>
> And words in the singular number shall include the plural, and words applicable to males shall include females.

. XVII. That in citing this Act in other Acts of Parliament, and in Short title. any instrument, document, or proceeding, it shall be sufficient to use the words and figures following, that is to say, " The Designs Act, 1850."

14 Vict. c. 8 (1851).

*An Act to extend the Provisions of the " Designs Act, 1850," and
to give Protection from Piracy to Persons exhibiting new Invention in the Exhibition of the Works of Industry of all Nations
in One thousand eight hundred and fifty-one.*

Spent.

---

15 & 16 Vict. c. 12.

*An Act to enable Her Majesty to carry into effect a Convention
with France on the Subject of Copyright ; to extend and explain
the International Copyright Acts ; and to explain the Acts relating
to Copyright in Engravings.*

[28th May, 1852.]

7 & 8 Vict.
c. 12.

WHEREAS an Act was passed in the seventh year of the reign of
Her present Majesty, intituled " An Act to amend the Law relating
to International Copyright," hereinafter called " The International
Copyright Act : " And whereas a convention has lately been concluded between Her Majesty and the French republic, for extending
in each country the enjoyment of copyright in works of literature
and the fine arts first published in the other, and for certain
reductions of duties now levied on books, prints, and musical works
published in France : And whereas certain of the stipulations on
the part of Her Majesty contained in the said treaty require the
authority of Parliament : And whereas it is expedient that such
authority should be given, and that Her Majesty should be enabled
to make similar stipulations in any treaty on the subject of copyright
which may hereafter be concluded with any foreign power : Be it
enacted by the Queen's most excellent Majesty, by and with the
advice and consent of the Lords spiritual and temporal, and Commons, in this present Parliament assembled, and by the authority of
the same, as follows :

Translations.

I. The eighteenth section of the said Act of the seventh year of
Her present Majesty, chapter twelve, shall be repealed, so far as
the same is inconsistent with the provisions hereinafter contained.

Partial repeal
of 7 & 8 Vict.
c. 12, § 18.

II. Her Majesty may, by Order in Council, direct that the authors
of books which are, after a future time, to be specified in such
order, published in any foreign country, to be named in such order,
their executors, administrators, and assigns, shall, subject to the
provisions hereinafter contained or referred to, be empowered to
prevent the publication in the British dominions of any translations

Her Majesty
may by Order
in Council
direct that the
authors of
books pub-
lished in

of such books not authorized by them, for such time as may be specified in such order, not extending beyond the expiration of five years from the time at which the authorized translations of such books hereinafter mentioned are respectively first published, and in the case of books published in parts, not extending as to each part beyond the expiration of five years from the time at which the authorized translation of such part is first published. *foreign countries may for a limited time prevent unauthorized translations.*

III. Subject to any provisions or qualifications contained in such order, and to the provisions herein contained or referred to, the laws and enactments for the time being in force for the purpose of preventing the infringement of copyright in books published in the British dominions shall be applied for the purpose of preventing the publication of translations of the books to which such order extends which are not sanctioned by the authors of such books, except only such parts of the said enactment as relate to the delivery of copies of books for the use of the British Museum, and for the use of the other libraries therein referred to. *Thereupon the law of copyright shall extend to prevent such translations.*

IV. Her Majesty may, by Order in Council, direct that authors of dramatic pieces which are, after a future time, to be specified in such order, first publicly represented in any foreign country, to be named in such order, their executors, administrators, and assigns, shall, subject to the provisions hereinafter mentioned or referred to, be empowered to prevent the representation in the British dominions of any translation of such dramatic pieces not authorized by them for such time as may be specified in such order, not extending beyond the expiration of five years from the time at which the authorized translations of such dramatic pieces hereinafter mentioned are first published or first publicly represented. *Her Majesty may by Order in Council direct that the authors of dramatic works represented in foreign countries may for a limited time prevent unauthorized translations.*

V. Subject to any provisions or qualifications contained in such last-mentioned order, and to the provisions hereinafter contained or referred to, the laws and enactments for the time being in force for ensuring to the author of any dramatic piece first publicly represented in the British dominions the sole liberty of representing the same shall be applied for the purpose of preventing the representation of any translations of the dramatic pieces to which such last-mentioned order extends, which are not sanctioned by the authors thereof. *Thereupon the law for protecting the representation of such pieces shall extend to prevent unauthorized translations.*

VI. Nothing herein contained shall be so construed as to prevent fair imitations or adaptations to the English stage of any dramatic piece or musical composition published in any foreign country (a). *Adaptations, &c., of dramatic pieces to the English stage not prevented.*

VII. Notwithstanding anything in the said International Copyright Act or in this Act contained, any article of political discussion which has been published in any newspaper or periodical in a foreign country may, if the source from which the same is taken be *All articles in newspapers, &c., relating to politics may be*

(a) See 38 Vict. c. 12, *post*, p. 706.

republished or acknowledged, be republished or translated in any newspaper or
translated; and periodical in this country; and any article relating to any other
also all similar subject which has been so published as aforesaid may, if the source
articles on any
subject, unless from which the same is taken be acknowledged, be republished or
the author has translated in like manner, unless the author has signified his
notified his in-
tention to re- intention of preserving the copyright therein, and the right of
serve the right. translating the same in some conspicuous part of the newspaper
or periodical in which the same was first published, in which case
the same shall, without the formalities required by the next following
section, receive the same protection as is by virtue of the International Copyright Act or this Act extended to books.

No author to   VIII. No author, or his executors, administrators, or assigns,
be entitled to
benefit of this shall be entitled to the benefit of this Act, or of any Order in
Act without   Council issued in pursuance thereof, in respect of the translation
complying   of any book or dramatic piece, if the following requisitions are not
with the requi-
sitions herein complied with: (that is to say,)
specified.

> 1. The original work from which the translation is to be made
>   must be registered and a copy thereof deposited in the
>   United Kingdom in the manner required for original works
>   by the said International Copyright Act, within three
>   calendar months of its first publication in the foreign
>   country.
> 2. The author must notify on the title-page of the original work,
>   or if it is published in parts, on the title-page of the first
>   part, or if there is no title-page, on some conspicuous part
>   of the work, that it is his intention to reserve the right of
>   translating it:
> 3. The translation sanctioned by the author, or a part thereof,
>   must be published, either in the country mentioned in the
>   Order in Council by virtue of which it is to be protected
>   or in the British dominions, not later than one year after
>   the registration and deposit in the United Kingdom of the
>   original work, and the whole of such translation must be
>   published within three years of such registration and
>   deposit:
> 4. Such translation must be registered and a copy thereof
>   deposited in the United Kingdom within a time to be
>   mentioned in that behalf in the order by which it is pro-
>   tected, and in the manner provided by the said International
>   Copyright Act for the registration and deposit of original
>   works:
> 5. In the case of books published in parts, each part of the
>   original work must be registered and deposited in this country
>   in the manner required by the said International Copy-

right within three months after the first publication thereof in the foreign country :

6. In the case of dramatic pieces the translation sanctioned by the author must be published within three calendar months of the registration of the original work :

7. The above requisitions shall apply to articles originally published in newspapers or periodicals if the same be afterwards published in a separate form, but shall not apply to such articles as originally published.

IX. All copies of any works of literature or art wherein there is any subsisting copyright by virtue of the International Copyright Act and this Act, or of any Order in Council made in pursuance of such Acts or either of them, and which are printed, reprinted, or made in any foreign country except that in which such work shall be first published, and all unauthorized translations of any book or dramatic piece the publication or public representation in the British dominions of translations whereof not authorized as in this Act mentioned shall for the time being be prevented under any Order in Council made in pursuance of this Act, are hereby absolutely prohibited to be imported into any part of the British dominions, except by or with the consent of the registered proprietor of the copyright of such work or of such book or piece, or his agent authorized in writing; and the provisions of the Act of the sixth year of Her Majesty " to amend the Law of Copyright," for the forfeiture, seizure, and destruction of any printed book first published in the United Kingdom wherein there shall be copyright, and reprinted in any country out of the British dominions and imported into any part of the British dominions by any person not being the proprietor of the copyright, or a person authorized by such proprietor, shall extend and be applicable to all copies of any works of literature and art, and to all translations the importation whereof into any part of the British dominions is prohibited under this Act. *Pirated copies prohibited to be imported except with consent of proprietor.*

Provisions of 5 & 6 Vict. c. 45, as to forfeiture, &c., of pirated works, &c., to extend to works prohibited to be imported under this Act.

X. The provisions hereinbefore contained shall be incorporated with the International Copyright Act, and shall be read and construed therewith as one Act. *Foregoing provisions and 7 & 8 Vict. c. 12, to be read as one Act.*

XI. And whereas Her Majesty has already, by Order in Council under the said International Copyright Act, given effect to certain stipulations contained in the said convention with the French Republic; and it is expedient that the remainder of the stipulations on the part of Her Majesty in the said convention contained should take effect from the passing of this Act without any further Order in Council : During the continuance of the said convention, and so long as the Order in Council already made under the said Inter- *French translations to be protected as hereinbefore mentioned, without further Order in Council.*

national Copyright Act remains in force, the provisions hereinbefore contained shall apply to the said convention, and to translations of books and dramatic pieces which are, after the passing of this Act, published or represented in France, in the same manner as if Her Majesty had issued Her Order in Council in pursuance of this Act for giving effect to such convention, and had therein directed that such translations should be protected as hereinbefore mentioned for a period of five years from the date of the first publication or public representation thereof respectively, and as if a period of three months from the publication of such translation were the time mentioned in such Order as the time within which the same must be registered and a copy thereof deposited in the United Kingdom.

Reduction of Duties.

Recital of 9 & 10 Vict. c. 58.

XII. And whereas an Act was passed in the tenth year of Her present Majesty, intituled " An Act to amend an Act of the seventh and eighth Years of Her present Majesty, for reducing under certain Circumstances, the Duties payable upon Books and Engravings :" And whereas by the said convention with the French Republic it was stipulated that the duties on books, prints, and drawings published in the territories of the French Republic should be reduced to the amount specified in the schedule to the said Act of the tenth year of Her present Majesty, chapter fifty-eight : And whereas Her Majesty has, in pursuance of the said convention, and in exercise of the powers given by the said Act, by Order in Council declared that such duties shall be reduced accordingly : And whereas by the said convention it was further stipulated that the said rates of duty should not be raised during the continuance of the said conven-tion ; and that if during the continuance of the said convention any reduction of those rates should be made in favour of books, prints, or drawings published in any other country, such reduction shall be at the same time extended to similar articles published in France : And whereas doubts are entertained whether such last-mentioned stipulations can be carried into effect without the authority of Parliament : Be it enacted, That the said rates of duty so reduced as aforesaid shall not be raised during the continuance of the said convention ; and that if during the continuance of the said convention any further reduction of such rates is made in favour of books, prints, or drawings published in any other foreign country, Her Majesty may, by Order in Council, declare that such reduction shall be extended to similar articles published in France ; such order to be made and published in the same manner and to be subject to the same provisions as orders made in pursuance of the said Act of the tenth year of Her present Majesty, chapter fifty-eight.

Rates of duty not to be raised during contin-uance of treaty, and if further reduction is made for other countries it may be ex-tended to France.

XIII. And whereas doubts have arisen as to the construction of the schedule of the Act of the tenth year of Her present Majesty, chapter fifty-eight :

For removal of doubts as to

It is hereby declared, That for the purposes of the said Act every work published in the country of export, of which part has been originally produced in the United Kingdom, shall be deemed to be and be subject to the duty payable on " Works originally produced in the United Kingdom, and published in the country of export," although it contains also original matter not produced in the United Kingdom, unless it shall be proved to the satisfaction of the Commissioners of Her Majesty's Customs by the importer, consignee or other person entering the same that such original matter is at least equal to the part of the work produced in the United Kingdom, in which case the work shall be subject only to the duty on " Works not originally produced in the United Kingdom." *construction of schedule to 9 & 10 Vict. c. 58.*

XIV. And whereas by the four several Acts of Parliament following ; (that is to say,) an Act of the eighth year of the reign of King George the Second, chapter thirteen ; an Act of the seventh year of the reign of King George the Third, chapter thirty-eight : an Act of the seventeenth year of the reign of King George the Third, chapter fifty-seven : and an Act of the seventh year of King William the Fourth, chapter fifty-nine, provision is made for securing to every person who invents, or designs, engraves, etches, or works in mezzotinto or chiaro-oscuro, or from his own work, design, or invention, causes or procures to be designed, engraved, etched, or worked in mezzotinto or chiaro-oscuro, any historical print or prints, or any print or prints of any portrait, conversation, landscape, or architecture, map, chart, or plan, or any other print or prints whatsoever, and to every person who engraves, etches, or works in mezzotinto or chiaro-oscuro, or causes to be engraved, etched, or worked any print taken from any picture, drawing, model, or sculpture, notwithstanding such print has not been graven or drawn from his own original design, certain copyrights therein defined : And whereas doubts are entertained whether the provisions of the said Acts extend to lithographs and certain other impressions, and it is expedient to remove such doubts : *Lithographs, &c.* *Recital of 8 G. 2, c. 13. 7 G. 3, c. 38. 17 G 3, c. 57. 6 & 7 W. 4, c. 59.*

It is hereby declared, That the provisions of the said Acts are intended to include prints taken by lithography, or any other mechanical process by which prints or impressions of drawings or designs are capable of being multiplied indefinitely, and the said Acts shall be construed accordingly. *For removal of doubts as to the provisions of the said Acts including lithographs, prints, &c.*

---

16 & 17 VICT. c. 107 (1853).

An Act to amend and consolidate the Laws relating to the Customs of the United Kingdom and of the Isle of Man, and certain Laws relating to the Trade and Navigation and the British Possessions.

Sects. 44, 46, and 160, repealed 39 & 40 Vict. c. 36.

18 & 19 VICT. o. 96 (1855).

An Act to consolidate certain Acts, and otherwise amend the Laws
of the Customs, and an Act to regulate the Office of the Receipt
of Her Majesty's Exchequer at Westminster.

Sec. 39 and 40 repealed 39 & 40 Vict. c. 36.

---

21 & 22 VICT. c. 70.

An Act to amend the Act of the fifth and sixth Years of Her
present Majesty, to consolidate and amend the Laws relating
to the Copyright of Designs for ornamenting Articles of Manu-
facture.

[2nd August, 1858.]

5 & 6 Vict. c. 100.

WHEREAS by an Act passed in the fifth and sixth years of the reign of Her present Majesty, intituled " An Act to consolidate and amend the Laws relating to the Copyright of Designs for ornamenting Articles of Manufacture," hereinafter called " The Copyright of Designs Act, 1842," there was granted to the proprietor of any new and original design in respect of the application of any such design to ornamenting any article of manufacture contained in the tenth class therein mentioned, with the exceptions therein mentioned, the sole right to apply the same to any articles of manufacture, or any such substances as therein mentioned, for the term of nine calendar months, to be computed from the time of such design being registered according to the said Act : And whereas it is expedient that the term of copyright, in respect of the application of designs to the ornamenting of articles of manufacture comprised in the said tenth class, should be extended, and that some of the provisions of the said Act should be altered, and that further provision should be made for the prevention of piracy, and for the protection of copyright in designs under the Acts in the schedule hereto annexed, and hereinafter called " The Copyright of Designs Acts :" Be it therefore enacted by the Queen's most excellent Majesty, by and with the advice and consent of the Lords Spiritual and Temporal, and Commons, in this present Parliament assembled, and by the authority of the same as follows : that is to say,

Short title.

I. In citing this Act for any purpose whatsoever it shall be sufficient to use the expression " The Copyright of Designs Act, 1858."

Copyright of Designs Acts and this Act to be as one.

II. The said Copyright of Designs Acts and this Act shall be construed together as one Act.

III. In respect of the application of any new and original design for ornamenting any article of manufacture contained in the tenth class mentioned in "The Copyright of Designs Acts, 1842," the term of copyright shall be three years, to be computed from the time of such design being registered, in pursuance of the provisions of "The Copyright of Designs Acts," and of this Act: Provided nevertheless, that the term of such copyright shall expire on the thirty-first of December, in the second year after the year in which such design was registered, whatever may be the day of such registration. *Extension of term of copyright as to the tenth class mentioned in 5 & 6 Vict. c. 100.*

IV. Nothing in the fourth section of "The Copyright of Designs Act, 1842," shall extend or be construed to extend to deprive the proprietor of any new and original design applied to ornamenting any article of manufacture contained in the said tenth class of the benefits of "The Copyright of Designs Acts" or of this Act: Provided there shall have been printed on such articles at each end of the original piece thereof the name and address of such proprietor, and the word "Registered," together with the years for which such design was registered. *Copyright not to be prejudiced if articles marked.*

V. And be it declared, That the registration of any pattern or portion of an article of manufacture to which a design is applied, instead or in lieu of a copy, drawing, print, specification, or description in writing, shall be as valid and effectual to all intents and purposes as if such copy, drawing, print, specification, or description in writing had been furnished to the registrar under "The Copyright of Designs Acts." *Pattern may be registered.]*

VI. The proprietor of such extended copyright shall, on application by or on behalf of any person producing or ‚vending any article of manufacture so marked, give the number and the date of the registration of any article of manufacture so marked; and any proprietor so applied to who shall not give the number and date of such registration shall be subject to a penalty of ten pounds, to be recovered by the applicant, with full cost of suit, in any court of competent jurisdiction. *Proprietor to give the number and date of registration.*

VII. Any person who shall wilfully apply any mark of registration to any article of manufacture in respect whereof the application of the design thereto shall not have been registered, or after the term of copyright shall have expired, or who shall, during the term of copyright, without the authority of the proprietor of any registered design, wilfully apply the mark printed on the piece of any article of manufacture, or who shall knowingly sell or issue any article of manufacture to which such mark has been wilfully and without due authority applied, shall be subject to a penalty of ten pounds, to be recovered by the proprietor of such design, with full costs of suit, in any court of competent jurisdiction. *Penalty on issuing articles not so marked.*

Proceedings for prevention of piracy may be instituted in the County Courts.

VIII. Notwithstanding anything in "The Copyright of Designs Acts," it shall be lawful for the proprietor of copyright in any design under the "Copyright of Designs Acts" or this Act, to institute proceedings in the county court of the district within which the piracy is alleged to have been committed, for the recovery of damages which he may have sustained by reason of such piracy: Provided always, that in any such proceedings the plaintiff shall deliver with his plaint a statement of particulars as to the date and title or other description of the registration whereof the copyright is alleged to be pirated, and as to the alleged piracy; and the defendant, if he intends at the trial to rely as a defence on any objection to such copyright, or to the title of the proprietor therein, shall give notice in the manner provided in the seventy-sixth section of the Act of the ninth and tenth Victoria, chapter ninety-five, of his intention to rely on such special defence, and shall state in such notice the date of publication and other particulars of any designs whereof prior publication is alleged, or of any objection to such copyright, or to the title of the proprietor to such copyright; and it shall be lawful for the judge of the county court, at the instance of the defendant or plaintiff respectively, to require any statement or notice so delivered by the plaintiff or of the defendant respectively to be amended in such a manner as the said judge may think fit.

The proceedings of County Courts Acts applicable to proceedings for designs.

IX. The provisions of an Act of the ninth and tenth Victoria, chapter ninety-five, and of the twelfth and thirteenth Victoria, chapter one hundred, as to proceedings in any plaint, and as to appeal, and as to writs of prohibition, shall, so far as they are not inconsistent with or repugnant to the provisions of this Act, be applicable to any proceedings for piracy of copyright of designs under the said Copyright of Designs Acts or this Act.

SCHEDULE REFERRED TO IN THE FOREGOING ACT.

5 & 6 Vict. c. 100. [10 Aug. 1842.]	An Act to consolidate and amend the Laws relating to the Copyright of Designs for ornamenting Articles of Manufacture.
6 & 7 Vict. c. 65. [22 Aug. 1843.]	An Act to amend the Laws relating to the Copyright of Designs.
13 & 14 Vict. c. 104. [14 Aug. 1850.]	An Act to extend and amend the Acts relating to the Copyright of Designs.
14 Vict. c. 8. [11 April, 1851.]	An Act to extend the Provisions of the Designs Act, 1850, and to give Protection from Piracy to Persons exhibiting new Inventions in the Exhibition of the Works of Industry of all Nations in One thousand eight hundred and fifty-one.

24 & 25 VICT. C. 73.

An Act to amend the Law relating to the Copyright of Designs.

[6th August, 1861.]

WHEREAS by an Act passed in the session holden in the fifth and sixth years of the reign of Her present Majesty, chapter one hundred, intituled "An Act to consolidate and amend the Laws relating to the Copyright of Designs for ornamenting Articles of Manufacture," it was enacted, that the proprietor of every such design as therein mentioned, not previously published either within the United Kingdom of Great Britain and Ireland or elsewhere, should have the sole right to apply the same to any articles of manufacture, or to any such substances as therein mentioned, provided the same were done within the United Kingdom of Great Britain and Ireland, for the respective terms therein mentioned, and should have such copyright in such designs as therein provided : And whereas divers Acts have since been passed extending or amending the said recited Acts : And whereas it is expedient that the provisions of the said recited Act, and of all Acts extending or amending the same should apply to designs, and to the application of such designs, within the meaning of the said Acts, whether such application be effected within the United Kingdom or elsewhere : Be it enacted by the Queen's most excellent Majesty, by and with the advice and consent of the Lords Spiritual and Temporal, and Commons, in this present Parliament assembled, and by the authority of the same, as follows :

5 & 6 Vict. c. 100.

1. That the said recited Act, and all Acts extending or amending the same, shall be construed as if the words "provided the same be done within the United Kingdom of Great Britain and Ireland" had not been contained in the said recited Act ; and the said recited Act, and all Acts extending or amending the same, shall apply to every such design as therein referred to, whether the application thereof be done within the United Kingdom or elsewhere and whether the inventor or proprietor of such design be or be not a subject of Her Majesty.

5 & 6 Vict. c. 100, and other Acts relating to copyright of designs extended.

2. That the said several Acts shall not be construed to apply to the subjects of Her Majesty only.

Application of Acts.

---

25 & 26 VICT. C. 68.

An Act for amending the Law relating to Copyright in Works of the Fine Arts, and for repressing the Commission of Fraud in the Production and Sale of such Works.

[29th July, 1862.]

WHEREAS by law, as now established, the authors of paintings, drawings, and photographs have no copyright in such their works,

and it is expedient that the law should in that respect be amended :
Be it therefore enacted by the Queen's most excellent Majesty, by
and with the advice and consent of the Lords Spiritual and Temporal, and Commons, in this present Parliament assembled, and by
the authority of the same, as follows :

Copyright in works here-after made or sold to vest in the author for his life and for seven years after his death. I. The author, being a British subject or resident within the
dominions of the Crown, of every original painting, drawing, and
photograph which shall be or shall have been made either in the
British dominions or elsewhere, and which shall not have been sold
or disposed of before the commencement of this Act, and his assigns
shall have the sole and exclusive right of copying, engraving,
reproducing, and multiplying such painting or drawing, and the
design thereof, or such photograph, and the negative thereof, by any
means and of any size, for the term of the natural life of such author
and seven years after his death ; provided that when any painting
or drawing, or the negative of any photograph, shall for the first
time after the passing of this Act be sold or disposed of, or shall be
made or executed for or on behalf of any other person for a good or a
valuable consideration, the person so selling or disposing of or making
or executing the same shall not retain the copyright thereof,
unless it be expressly reserved to him by agreement in writing
signed, at or before the time of such sale or disposition, by the
vendee or assignee of such painting or drawing, or of such negative
of a photograph, or by the person for or on whose behalf the same
shall be so made or executed, but the copyright shall belong to the
vendee or assignee of such painting or drawing, or of such negative
of a photograph, or to the person for or on whose behalf the same
shall have been made or executed ; nor shall the vendee or assignee
thereof be entitled to any such copyright, unless, at or before the
time of such sale or disposition, an agreement in writing, signed by
the person so selling or disposing of the same, or by his agent duly
authorized, shall have been made to that effect.

Copyright not to prevent the representation of the same subjects in other works. II. Nothing herein contained shall prejudice the right of any
person to copy or use any work in which there shall be no copyright
or to represent any scene or object, notwithstanding that there
may be copyright in some representation of such scene or object.

Assignments, licences, &c., to be in writing. III. All copyright under this Act shall be deemed personal or
moveable estate, and shall be assignable at law, and every assign-
ment thereof, and every licence to use or copy by any means or
process the design or work which shall be the subject of such copyright, shall be made by some note or memorandum in writing, to
be signed by the proprietor of the copyright, or by his agent
appointed for that purpose in writing.

Register of proprietors of IV. There shall be kept at the hall of the Stationers' Company,
by the officer appointed by the said company for the purposes of

the Act passed in the sixth year of Her present Majesty, intituled copyright in paintings, drawings, and photographs to be kept at Stationers' Hall as in 5 & 6 Vict. c. 45. "An Act to amend the Law of Copyright," a book or books intituled "The Register of Proprietors of Copyright in Paintings, Drawings, and Photographs," wherein shall be entered a memorandum of every copyright to which any person shall be entitled under this Act, and also of every subsequent assignment of any such copyright; and such memorandum shall contain a statement of the date of such agreement or assignment, and of the names of the parties thereto, and of the name and place of abode of the person in whom such copyright shall be vested by virtue thereof, and of the name and place of abode of the author of the work in which there shall be such copyright, together with a short description of the nature and subject of such work, and in addition thereto, if the person registering shall so desire, a sketch, outline, or photograph of the said work; and no proprietor of any such copyright shall be entitled to the benefit of this Act until such registration, and no action shall be sustainable nor any penalty be recoverable in respect of anything done before registration.

V. The several enactments in the said Act of the sixth year of Certain enactments of 5 & 6 Vict. c. 45, to apply to the books to be kept under this Act. Her present Majesty contained, with relation to keeping the register book thereby required, and the inspection thereof, the searches therein, and the delivery of certified and stamped copies thereof, the reception of such copies in evidence, the making of false entries in the said book, and the production in evidence of papers falsely purporting to be copies of entries in the said book, the application to the courts and judges by persons aggrieved by entries in the said book, and the expunging and varying such entries, shall apply to the book or books to be kept by virtue of this Act, and to the entries and assignments of copyright and proprietorship therein under this Act, in such and the same manner as if such enactments were here expressly enacted in relation thereto, save and except that the forms of entry prescribed by the said Act of the sixth year of Her present Majesty may be varied to meet the circumstances of the case, and that the sum to be demanded by the officer of the said Company of Stationers for making any entry required by this Act shall be one shilling only.

VI. If the author of any painting, drawing, or photograph in Penalties on infringement of copyright. which there shall be subsisting copyright, after having sold or disposed of such copyright, or if any other person, not being the proprietor for the time being of copyright in any painting, drawing, or photograph, shall, without the consent of such proprietor, repeat, copy, colourably imitate, or otherwise multiply for sale, hire, exhibition, or distribution, or cause or procure to be repeated, copied, colourably imitated, or otherwise multiplied for sale, hire, exhibition, or distribution, any such work or the design thereof, or knowing that any such repetition, copy, or other imitation has been unlawfully made shall import into any part of the United Kingdom, or sell, publish, let to hire, exhibit, or distribute, or offer for sale, hire, exhibition, or distribution, or cause or procure to be imported, sold, published, let to hire, distributed, or offered for sale, hire, exhibition or distribution, any repetition, copy, or imitation of the said work, or of the design thereof, made without such consent as aforesaid, such person for every such offence shall forfeit to the proprietor of the copyright for the time being a sum not exceeding ten pounds; and all such repetitions, copies, and imitations made without such consent as aforesaid, and all negatives of photographs made for the purpose of obtaining such copies, shall be forfeited to the proprietor of the copyright.

Penalties on fraudulent productions and sales.

VII. No person shall do or cause to be done any or either of the following acts: that is to say,

First, no person shall fraudulently sign or otherwise affix, or fraudulently cause to be signed or otherwise affixed, to or upon any painting, drawing, or photograph, or the negative thereof, any name, initials, or monogram:

Secondly, no person shall fraudulently sell, publish, exhibit, or dispose of, or offer for sale, exhibition or distribution, any painting, drawing, or photograph, or negative of a photograph, having thereon the name, initials, or monogram of a person who did not execute or make such work:

Thirdly, no person shall fraudulently utter, dispose of, or put off, or cause to be uttered or disposed of, any copy or colourable imitation of any painting, drawing, or photograph, or negative of a photograph, whether there shall be subsisting copyright therein or not, as having been made or executed by the author or maker of the original work from which such copy or imitation shall have been taken:

Fourthly, where the author or maker of any painting, drawing, or photograph, or negative of a photograph, made either before or after the passing of this Act, shall have sold or otherwise parted with the possession of such work, if any alteration shall afterwards be made therein by any other person, by addition or otherwise, no person shall be at liberty, during the life of the author or maker of such work, without his consent, to make or knowingly to sell or publish or offer for sale, such work or any copies of such work so altered, as aforesaid, or of any part thereof, as or for the unaltered work of such author or maker:

Penalties

Every offender under this section shall, upon conviction, forfeit to the person aggrieved a sum not exceeding ten pounds, or not exceeding double the full price, if any, at which all such copies, engravings, imitations, or altered works shall have been sold or offered for sale; and all such copies, engravings, imitations, or altered works shall be forfeited to the person, or the assigns or legal representatives of the person, whose name, initials, or monogram shall be so fraudulently signed or affixed thereto, or to whom such spurious or altered work shall be so fraudulently or falsely ascribed as aforesaid : Provided always, that the penalties imposed by this section shall not be incurred unless the person whose name, initials, or monogram shall be so fraudulently signed or affixed, or to whom such spurious or altered work shall be so fraudulently or falsely ascribed as aforesaid, shall have been living at or within twenty years next before the time when the offence may have been committed.

VIII. All pecuniary penalties which shall be incurred, and all such unlawful copies, imitations, and all other effects and things as shall have been forfeited by offenders, pursuant to this Act, and pursuant to any Act for the protection of copyright engravings, may be recovered by the person hereinbefore and in any such Act as aforesaid empowered to recover the same respectively, and hereinafter called the complainant or the complainer, as follows : Recovery of pecuniary penalties:

In England and Ireland, either by action against the party offending, or by summary proceeding before any two justices having jurisdiction where the party offending resides: In England and Ireland;

In Scotland, by action before the Court of Session in ordinary form, or by summary action before the sheriff of the county where the offence may be committed or the offender resides, who, upon proof of the offence or offences, either by confession of the party offending, or by the oath or affirmation of one or more credible witnesses, shall convict the offender, and find him liable to the penalty or penalties aforesaid, as also in expenses; and it shall be lawful for the sheriff, in pronouncing such judgment for the penalty or penalties and costs, to insert in such judgment a warrant, in the event of such penalty or penalties and costs not being paid, to levy and recover the amount of the same by poinding: Provided always, that it shall be lawful to the sheriff, in the event of his dismissing the action and assoilzieing the defender, to find the complainer liable in expenses, and any judgment so to be pronounced by the sheriff in such summary application shall be final and conclusive, and not subject to review by avocation, suspension, reduction, or otherwise. In Scotland.

IX. In any action in any of Her Majesty's superior Courts of Record at Westminster and in Dublin for the infringement of any Superior Courts of Record in which any action is pending may make an order for an injunction, inspection, or account.

such copyright as aforesaid, it shall be lawful for the court in which such action is pending, if the court be then sitting, or if the court be not sitting then for a judge of such court, on the application of the plaintiff or defendant respectively, to make such order for an injunction, inspection, or account, and to give such direction respecting such action, injunction, inspection, and account and the proceedings therein respectively, as to such court or judge may seem fit.

Importation of pirated works prohibited.

X. All repetitions, copies, or imitations of paintings, drawings, or photographs, wherein or in the design whereof there shall be subsisting copyright under this Act, and all repetitions, copies, and imitations of the design of any such painting or drawing, or of the negative of any such photograph, which, contrary to the provisions of this Act, shall have been made in any foreign state, or in any part of the British dominions, are hereby absolutely prohibited to be imported into any part of the United Kingdom, except by or with the consent of the proprietor of the copyright thereof, or his agent

Application in such cases of Customs Acts.

authorized in writing; and if the proprietor of any such copyright, or his agent, shall declare that any goods imported are repetitions, copies, or imitations of any such painting, drawing, or photograph, or of the negative of any such photograph, and so prohibited as aforesaid, then such goods may be detained by the officers of Her Majesty's Customs.

Saving of right to bring action for damages.

XI. If the author of any painting, drawing, or photograph, in which there shall be subsisting copyright, after having sold or otherwise disposed of such copyright, or if any other person, not being the proprietor for the time being of such copyright, shall, without the consent of such proprietor, repeat, copy, colourably imitate, or otherwise multiply, or cause or procure to be repeated, copied, colourably imitated, or otherwise multiplied, for sale, hire, exhibition, or distribution, any such work or the design thereof, or the negative of any such photograph, or shall import or cause to be imported into any part of the United Kingdom, or sell, publish, let to hire, exhibit, or distribute, or offer for sale, hire, exhibition, or distribution, or cause or procure to be sold, published, let to hire, exhibited, or distributed, or offered for sale, hire, exhibition, or distribution, any repetition, copy, or imitation of such work, or the design thereof, or the negative of any such photograph, made without such consent as aforesaid, then every such proprietor, in addition to the remedies hereby given for the recovery of any such penalties, and forfeiture of any such things as aforesaid, may recover damages by and in a special action on the case, to be brought against the person so offending, and may in such action recover and enforce the delivery to him of all unlawful repetitions, copies, and imitations, and negatives of photographs, or may recover damages for the retention or conversion thereof: Provided that nothing herein contained, nor any proceeding, conviction, or judgment, for any act hereby forbidden, shall affect any remedy which any person aggrieved by such act may be entitled to either at law or in Equity.

XII. This Act shall be considered as including the provisions of the Act passed in the session of Parliament held in the seventh and eighth years of Her present Majesty, intituled " An Act to amend the Law relating to International Copyright," in the same manner as if such provisions were part of this Act. *Provisions of 7 & 8 Vict. c. 12, to be considered as included in this Act.*

---

32 & 33 VICT. C. 24.

An Act to repeal certain Enactments relating to Newspapers, Pamphlets, and other Publications, and to Printers, Typefounders, and Reading Rooms.

[12th July, 1869.]

BE it enacted by the Queen's most excellent Majesty, by and with the advice and consent of the Lords Spiritual and Temporal, and Commons, in this present Parliament assembled, and by the authority of the same, as follows:

1. The Acts and parts of Acts described in the first schedule to this Act are hereby repealed, but the provisions of the said Acts which are set out in the second schedule to this Act shall continue in force in the same manner as if they were enacted in the body of this Act : and this Act shall not affect the validity or invalidity of anything already done or suffered, or any right or title already acquired or accrued, or any remedy or proceeding in respect thereof, and all such remedies and proceedings may be had and continued in the same manner as if this Act had not passed. *Acts and parts of Acts in first schedule repealed, except as in second schedule.*

2. This Act may be cited as " The Newspapers, Printers, and Reading Rooms Repeal Act, 1869." *Short title.*

[FIRST SCHEDULE

FIRST SCHEDULE.

DATE OF ACT.	TITLE OF ACT, AND PART REPEALED.	
36 Geo. 3, c. 8.	An Act for the more effectually preventing seditious meetings and assemblies.	
39 Geo. 3, c. 79, in part.	An Act for the more effectual suppression of societies established for seditious and treasonable purposes, and for better preventing treasonable and seditious practices – –	In part, namely,—sections fifteen to thirty-three, both inclusive, and so much of sections thirty-four to thirty-nine as relates to the above-mentioned sections.
51 Geo. 3, c. 65.	An Act to explain and amend an Act passed in the thirty-ninth year of His Majesty's reign, intituled "An Act for the more effectual suppression of societies established for seditious and treasonable purposes, and for better preventing treasonable and seditious practices," so far as respects certain penalties on printers and publishers.	
55 Geo. 3, c. 101, in part.	An Act to regulate the collection of stamp duties and matters in respect of which licences may be granted by the Commissioner of Stamps in Ireland –	In part, namely,—section thirteen.
60 Geo. 3 & 1 Geo. 4, c. 9.	An Act to subject certain publications to the duties of stamps upon newspapers, and to make other regulations for restraining the abuses arising from the publication of blasphemous and seditious libels.	
11 Geo. 4 & 1 Will. 4, c. 73.	An Act to repeal so much of an Act of the sixtieth year of His late Majesty King George the Third, for the more effectual prevention and punishment of blasphemous and seditious libels, as relates to the sentence of banishment for the second offence, and to provide some further remedy against the abuse of publishing libels.	
6 & 7 Will. 4, c. 76, in part.	An Act to reduce the duties on newspapers and to amend the laws relating to the duties on newspapers and advertisements –	In part, namely,— Except sections one to four (both inclusive), sections thirty-four and thirty-five, and the schedule.
2 & 3 Vict. c. 12.	An Act to amend an Act of the thirty-ninth year of King George the Third, for the more effectual suppression of societies established for seditious and treasonable purposes, and for preventing treasonable and seditious practices, and to put an end to certain proceedings now pending under the said Act.	

DATE OF ACT.	TITLE OF ACT, AND PART REPEALED.	
5 & 6 Vict. c. 82, in part.	An Act to assimilate the stamp duties in Great Britain and Ireland, and to make regulations for collecting and managing the same until the tenth day of October, One thousand eight hundred and forty-five —	In part, namely,— The following words in section twenty : " and also licence to any person to keep any printing presses and types for printing in Ireland."
9 & 10 Vict. c. 33, in part.	An Act to amend the laws relating to corresponding societies and the licensing of lecture rooms —	In part, namely,— So far as it relates to any proceedings under the enactments repealed by this schedule.
16 & 17 Vict. c. 59, in part.	An Act to repeal certain stamp duties and to grant others in lieu thereof, to amend the laws relating to stamp duties, and to make perpetual certain stamp duties in Ireland. —	In part, namely,— So much of section twenty as makes perpetual the provisions of 5 & 6 Vict. c. 82, repealed by this Act.

SECOND SCHEDULE.

The enactments in this Schedule, with the exception of sect. 19 of 6 & 7 Will. 4, c. 76, do not apply to Ireland.

39 Geo. 3, c. 79.   Section 28.

Nothing in this Act contained shall extend or be construed to extend to any papers printed by the authority and for the use of either House of Parliament.

Not to extend to papers printed by authority of Parliament.

Section 29.

Every person who shall print any paper for hire, reward, gain, or profit, shall carefully preserve and keep one copy (at least) of every paper so printed by him or her, on which he or she shall write, or cause to be written or printed, in fair and legible characters, the name and place of abode of the person or persons by whom he or she shall be employed to print the same ; and every person printing any paper for hire, reward, gain, or profit who shall omit or neglect to write, or cause to be written or printed as aforesaid, the name and place of his or her employer on one of such printed papers, or to keep or preserve the same for the space of six calendar months next after the printing thereof, or to produce and shew the same to any justice of the peace who within the said space of six calendar months shall require to see the same, shall for every such omission, neglect, or refusal forfeit and lose the sum of twenty pounds.

Printers to keep a copy of every paper they print, and write thereon the name and abode of their employer. Penalty of 20l. for neglect or refusing to produce the copy within six months.

SECOND SCHEDULE—*continued.*

Section 31.

Not to extend to impressions of engravings or the printing names and addresses.

Nothing herein contained shall extend to the impression of any en-graving, or to the printing by letter-press of the name, or the name and address, or business or profession, of any person, and the articles in which he deals, or to any papers for the sale of estates or goods by auction or otherwise.

Section 34.

Prosecutions to be commenced within three months after penalty is incurred.

No person shall be prosecuted or sued for any penalty imposed by this Act, unless such prosecution shall be commenced, or such action shall be brought, within three calendar months next after such penalty shall have been incurred.

Part of Section 35.

Recovery of penalties.

And any pecuniary penalty imposed by this Act, and not exceeding the sum of twenty pounds, shall and may be recovered before any justice or justices of the peace for the county, stewartry, riding, division, city, town, or place. in which the same shall be incurred, or the person having in-curred the same shall happen to be, in a summary way.

Section 36.

Application of penalties.

All pecuniary penalties hereinbefore imposed by this Act shall, when recovered in a summary way before any justice, be applied and disposed of in manner hereinafter mentioned ; that is to say, one moiety thereof to the informer before any justice, and the other moiety thereof to His Majesty, his heirs and successors.

51 Geo. 3, c. 65.   Section 3.

Name and residence of printers not required to be put to bank notes, bills,&c., or to any paper printed by authority of any public board or public office.

Nothing in the said Act of the thirty-ninth year of King George the Third, chapter seventy-nine, or in this Act contained, shall extend or be construed to extend to require the name and residence of the printer to be printed upon any bank note, or bank post bill of the Governor and Company of the Bank of England, upon any bill of exchange, or promis-sory note, or upon any bond or other security for payment of money, or upon any bill of lading, policy of insurance, letter of attorney, deed, or agreement, or upon any transfer or assignment of any public stocks, funds, or other securities, or upon any transfer or assignment of the stocks of any public corporation or company authorized or sanctioned by Act of Parliament, or upon any dividend warrant of or for any such public or other stocks, funds, or securities, or upon any receipt for money or goods, or upon any proceeding in any court of law or equity, or in any inferior court, warrant, order, or other papers printed by the authority of any public board or public officer in the execution of the duties of their respec-tive offices, notwithstanding the whole or any part of the said several securities, instruments, proceedings, matters, and things aforesaid shall have been or shall be printed.

SECOND SCHEDULE—*continued*.

6 & 7 Will. 4, c. 76. Section 19.

If any person shall file any bill in any court for the discovery of the **Discovery of** name of any person concerned as printer, publisher, or proprietor of any **proprietors,** newspaper, or of any matters relative to the printing or publishing ˙of any **printers, or** newspaper, in order the more effectually to bring or carry on any suit or **publishers of** action for damages alleged to have been sustained by reason of any slan- **newspapers** derous or libellous matter contained in any such newspaper respecting **may be en-** such person, it shall not be lawful for the defendant to plead or demur to **forced by bill,** such bill, but such defendant shall be compellable to make the discovery **&c.** required: Provided always, that such discovery shall not be made use of as evidence or otherwise in any proceeding against the defendant, save only in that proceeding for which the discovery is made.

2 & 3 Vict. c. 12, Section 2.

Every person who shall print any paper or book whatsoever which shall **Penalty upon** be meant to be published or dispersed, and who shall not print upon the **printers for not** front of every such paper, if the same shall be printed on one side only, or **printing their** upon the first or last leaf of every paper or book which shall consist of **name and resi-** more than one leaf, in legible characters, his or her name and usual place **dence on every** of abode or business, and every person who shall publish or disperse, or **and on persons** assist in publishing or dispersing, any printed paper or book on which the **publishing the** name and place of abode of the person printing the same shall not be **same.** printed as aforesaid, shall for every copy of such paper so printed by him or her forfeit a sum not more than five pounds: Provided always, that nothing herein contained shall be construed to impose any penalty upon any person for printing any paper excepted out of the operation of the said Act of the thirty-ninth year of King George the Third chapter seventy-nine, either in the said Act or by any Act made for the amendment thereof.

Section 3.

In the case of books or papers printed at the University Press of Oxford **As to books or** or the Pitt Press of Cambridge, the printer, instead of printing his name **papers printed** thereon, shall print the following words: "Printed at the University **at the Univer-** Press, Oxford," or "The Pitt Press. Cambridge," as the case may be. **sity presses.**

Section 4.

Provided always, that it shall not be lawful for any person or persons **No actions for** whatsoever to commence, prosecute, enter, or file, or cause or procure to be **penalties to be** commenced, prosecuted, entered, or filed, any action, bill, plaint, or infor- **commenced** mation in any of Her Majesty's courts, or before any justice or justices of **except in the** the peace, against any person or persons for the recovery of any fine, **name of the** penalty, or forfeiture made or incurred or which may hereafter be incurred **Attorney or** under the provisions of this Act, unless the same be commenced, prosecuted, **Solicitor** entered, or filed in the name of Her Majesty's Attorney-General of **General in** Solicitor-General in that part of Great Britain called England, or Her **England or the** Majesty's Advocate for Scotland (as the case may be respectively); and if **Queen's Ad-** any action, bill, plaint, or information shall be commenced, prosecuted, or **vocate in Scotland.**

2 z

SECOND SCHEDULE—*continued.*

filed in the name or names of any other person or persons than is or are in that behalf before mentioned, the same and every proceeding thereupon had are hereby declared and the same shall be null and void to all intents and purposes.

9 & 10 Vict. c. 33. Section 1.

Proceedings shall not be commenced unless in the name of the law officers of the Crown.

It shall not be lawful for any person or persons to commence, prosecute, enter, or file, or cause or procure to be commenced, prosecuted, entered, or filed, any action, bill, plaint, or information in any of Her Majesty's courts or before any justice or justices of the peace, against any person or persons for the recovery of any fine which may hereafter be incurred under the provisions of the Act of the thirty-ninth year of King George the Third, chapter seventy-nine, set out in this Act, unless the same be commenced, prosecuted, entered, or filed in the name of Her Majesty's Attorney-General or Solicitor-General in England or Her Majesty's Advocate in Scotland; and every action, bill, plaint, or information which shall be commenced, prosecuted, entered, or filed in the name or names of any other person or persons than is in that behalf before mentioned, and every proceeding thereupon had, shall be null and void to all intents and purposes.

---

38 Vict. c. 12.

An Act to amend the Law relating to International Copyright.
[13th May, 1875].

WHEREAS by an Act passed in the fifteenth year of the reign of Her present Majesty, chapter 12, intituled " An Act to enable Her Majesty to carry into effect a convention with France on the subject of Copyright; to extend and explain the International Copyright Acts; and to explain the Acts relating to copyright in engravings," it is enacted that " Her Majesty may, by Order in Council, direct that authors of dramatic pieces which are, after a future time to be specified in such order, first publicly represented in any foreign country, to be named in such order, their executors, administrators, and assigns, shall, subject to the provisions therein-after mentioned or referred to, be empowered to prevent the represen-tation in the British Dominions of any translation of such dramatic pieces not authorized by them for such time as may be specified in such order, not extending beyond the expiration of five years from the time at which the authorized translations of such dramatic pieces are first published and publicly represented:" And whereas by the same Act it is further enacted, " that, subject to any provisions or qualifications contained in such order, and to the provisions in the said Acts contained or referred to, the law and enactments for the time being in force for ensuring to the author of any dramatic

piece, first publicly represented in the British Dominions the sole
liberty of representing the same shall be applied for the purposes
of preventing the representation of any translations of the
dramatic pieces to which such order extends, which are not
sanctioned by the authors thereof :" And whereas by the sixth
section of the said Act it is provided that " nothing in the said act
contained shall be so construed as to prevent fair imitations or
adaptation to the English stage of any dramatic piece or musical
composition published in any foreign country :"

And whereas it is expedient to alter or amend the last mentioned
provisions under certain circumstances :

Be it therefore enacted by the Queen's most excellent Majesty,
by and with the advice and consent of the Lords spiritual and
temporal, and Commons, in this present Parliament assembled,
and by the authority of the same, as follows : viz.,

1. In any case in which, by virtue of the enactments hereinbefore *Section 6 of*
recited, any Order in Council has been or may hereafter be made *recited Act not*
for the purpose of extending protection to the translations of *to apply to*
dramatic pieces first publicly represented in any foreign country, it *pieces in cer-*
shall be lawful for Her Majesty by Order in Council to direct that the *tain cases.*
sixth section of the said Act shall not apply to the dramatic pieces
to which protection is so extended ; and thereupon the said recited
Act shall take effect with respect to such dramatic pieces, and to
the translations thereof as if the said sixth section of the said Acts
were hereby repealed.

---

38 & 39 VICT. c. 53.

*An Act to give effect to an Act of the Parliament of the Dominion
of Canada respecting Copyright.*   [*2nd August*, 1875.]

WHEREAS by an Order of Her Majesty in Council, dated the 7th
day of July 1868, it was ordered that all prohibitions contained in
Acts in the Imperial Parliament against the importing into the
Province of Canada, or against the selling, letting out to hire,
exposing for sale or hire, or possessing therein foreign reprints
of books first composed, written, printed, or published in the
United Kingdom, and entitled to copyright therein, should be
suspended so far as regarded Canada :

And whereas the Senate and House of Commons of Canada did,
in the second session of the third Parliament of the Dominion of
Canada, held in the thirty-eighth year of Her Majesty's reign, pass
a Bill intituled " An Act respecting Copyrights," which Bill has
been reserved by the Governor-General for the signification of Her
Majesty's pleasure thereon :

And whereas by the said reserved Bill provision is made, subject to such conditions as in the said Bill are mentioned, for securing in Canada the rights of authors in respect of matters of copyright, and for prohibiting the importation into Canada of any work for which copyright under the said reserved Bill has been secured; and whereas doubts have arisen whether the said reserved Bill may not be repugnant to the said Order in Council, and it is expedient to remove such doubts and to confirm the said Bill:

Be it enacted by the Queen's most excellent Majesty, by and with the advice and consent of the Lords spiritual and temporal, and Commons, in this present Parliament assembled, and by the authority of the same, as follows:

Short title of Act.

1. This Act may be cited for all purposes as The Canada Copyright Act, 1875.

Definition of terms.

2. In the construction of this Act the words " book " and " copyright," shall have respectively the same meaning as in the Act of the fifth and sixth years of Her Majesty's reign, chapter forty-five, intituled " An Act to amend the Law of Copyright."

Her Majesty may assent to the Bill in schedule.

3. It shall be lawful for Her Majesty in Council to assent to the said reserved Bill as contained in the schedule to this Act annexed, and if Her Majesty shall be pleased to signify Her assent thereto, the said Bill shall come into operation at such time and in such manner as Her Majesty may by Order in Council direct; anything in the Act of the twenty-eighth and twenty-ninth years of the reign of Her Majesty, chapter ninety-three, or in any other Act to the contrary notwithstanding.

Colonial reprints not to be imported into United Kingdom.

4. Where any book in which, at the time when the said reserved Bill comes into operation, there is copyright in the United Kingdom, or any book in which thereafter there shall be such copyright, becomes entitled to copyright in Canada in pursuance of the provisions of the said reserved Bill, it shall be unlawful for any person not being the owner, in the United Kingdom, of the copyright in such book, or some person authorised by him, to import into the United Kingdom any copies of such book reprinted or republished in Canada; and for the purposes of such importation the seventeenth section of the said Act of the fifth and sixth years of the reign of Her Majesty, chapter forty-five, shall apply to all such books in the same manner as if they had been reprinted out of the British Dominions.

Order in Council of 7th July, 1868, to continue in force subject to this Act.

5. The said Order in Council, dated the seventh day of July one thousand eight hundred and sixty-eight, shall continue in force so far as relates to books which are not entitled to copyright for the time being, in pursuance of the said reserved Bill.

SCHEDULE.

[38 & 39 VICT. c. 53].'

An Act respecting Copyrights.

Her Majesty, by and with the advice and consent of the Senate and House of Commons of Canada, enacts as follows :—

1. The Minister of Agriculture shall cause to be kept in his office books to be called the " Registers of Copyrights," in which proprietors of literary, scientific, and artistic works or compositions may have the same registered in accordance with the provisions of this Act.

2. The Minister of Agriculture may, from time to time, subject to the approval of the Governor in Council, make such rules and regulations and prescribe such forms as may appear to him necessary and expedient for the purposes of this Act : such regulations and forms, being circulated in print for the use of the public, shall be deemed to be correct for the purposes of this Act, and all documents executed and accepted by the said Minister of Agriculture shall be held valid so far as relates to all official proceedings under this Act.

3. If any person prints or publishes, or causes to be printed or published, any manuscript whatever, the said manuscript having not yet been printed in Canada or elsewhere, without the consent of the author or legal proprietor first obtained, such person shall be liable to the author or proprietor for all damages occasioned by such publication, to be recovered in any court of competent jurisdiction.

4. Any person domiciled in Canada, or in any part of the British Possessions, or being a citizen of any country having an international copyright treaty with the United Kingdom, who is the author of any book, map, chart, or musical composition, or of any original painting, drawing, statue, sculpture, or photograph, or who invents, designs, etches, engraves, or causes to be engraved, etched, or made from his own design, any print or engraving, and the legal representatives of such person, shall have the sole right and liberty of printing, reprinting, publishing, reproducing, and vending such literary, scientific, or artistic works or compositions, in whole or in part, and of allowing translations to be printed or reprinted and sold, of such literary works from one language into other languages, for the term of twenty-eight years from the time of recording the copyright thereof in a manner herein-after directed:

(2.) The condition for obtaining such copyright shall be that the said literary, scientific, or artistic works be printed and published, or reprinted or republished in Canada, or in the case of works of art that it be produced or reproduced in Canada, whether they be so published or produced for the first time or contemporaneously with or subsequently to publication or production elsewhere: provided that in no case the exclusive privilege in Canada shall continue to exist after it has expired anywhere else.

(3.) No immoral, or licentious, or irreligious, or treasonable, or seditious literary, scientific, or artistic work shall be the legitimate subject of such registration or copyright.

5. If at the expiration of the aforesaid term of twenty-eight years, such author, or any of the authors when the work has been originally composed

and made by more than one person, be still living, or being dead has left a widow or a child or children living, the same exclusive right shall be continued to such author, or, if dead, then to such widow and child or children (as the case may be) for the further term of fourteen years; but in such case within one year after the expiration of the first term the title of the work secured shall be a second time recorded, and all other regulations herein required to be observed in regard to original copyrights shall be complied with in respect to such renewed copyright.

6. In all cases of renewal of copyright under this Act the author or proprietor shall, within two months from the date of such renewal cause a copy of the record thereof to be published once in the "Canada Gazette."

7. No person shall be entitled to the benefit of this Act unless he has deposited in the office of the Minister of Agriculture two copies of such book, map, chart, musical composition, photograph, print, cut, or engraving, and in case of paintings, drawings, statuary, and sculpture, unless he has furnished a written description of such works of art, and the Minister of Agriculture shall cause the copyright of the same to be recorded forthwith in a book to be kept for that purpose, in the manner adopted by the Minister of Agriculture, or prescribed by the rules and forms which may be made from time to time as hereinbefore provided.

8. The Minister of Agriculture shall cause one of the two copies of such book, map, chart, musical composition, photograph, print, cut, or engraving aforesaid, to be deposited in the Library of the Parliament of Canada.

9. No person shall be entitled to the benefit of this Act unless he gives information of the copyright being secured, by causing to be inserted in the several copies of every edition published during the term secured, on the title page, or the page immediately following, if it be a book, or if a map, chart, musical composition, print, cut, engraving, or photograph, by causing to be impressed on the face thereof, or if a volume of maps, charts, music, engravings, or photographs, upon the title page or frontispiece thereof, the following words, that is to say: "Entered according to Act of Parliament of Canada, in the year   , by A.B., in the office of the Minister of Agriculture." But as regards paintings drawings, statuary, and sculptures, the signature of the artist shall be deemed a sufficient notice of such proprietorship.

10. Pending the publication or republication in Canada of a literary, scientific, or artistic work, the author, or his legal representatives or assigns, may obtain an interim copyright by depositing in the office of the Minister of Agricuture a copy of the title, or a designation of such work intended for publication or republication in Canada, the said title or designation to be registered in an interim copyright register in the said office, to secure to the author aforesaid, or his legal representatives or assigns, the exclusive rights recognised by this Act, previous to publication or republication in Canada: the said interim registration, however, not to endure for more than one month from the date of the original publication elsewhere, within which period the work shall be printed or reprinted and published in Canada.

(2.) In all cases of interim registration under this Act, the author or proprietor shall cause notice of such registration to be inserted once in the "Canada Gazette."

(3.) A literary work intended to be published in pamphlet or book form,

but which is first published in separate articles in a newspaper
or periodical, may be the subject of registration within the
meaning of this Act while it is so preliminarily published, provided that the title of the manuscript and a short analysis of the
work are deposited in the office of the Minister of Agriculture,
and that every separate article so published is preceded by the
words "Registered in accordance with the Copyright Act of
1875;" but the work when published in book or pamphlet form
shall be subject, besides, to the other requirements of this Act.

(4.) The importation of newspapers and magazines published in foreign
countries, and containing, together with foreign original matter,
portions of British copyright works republished with the consent
of the author or his assigns or under the law of the country where
such copyright exists, shall not be prohibited.

11. If any other person after the interim registration of the title of any
book according to this Act within the term herein limited, or after the
copyright is secured, and for the term or terms of its duration, prints, publishes, or reprints, or republishes, or imports, or causes to be so printed,
published, or imported, any copy or any translation of such book without
the consent of the person legally entitled to the copyright thereof first had
and obtained by assignment, or knowing the same to be so printed or imported publishes, sells, or exposes for sale, or causes to be published, sold,
or exposed for sale, any copy of such book without such consent, such
offender shall forfeit every copy of such book to the person then legally
entitled to the copyright thereof; and shall forfeit and pay for every such
copy which may be found in his possession, either printed or printing,
published, imported, or exposed for sale, contrary to the intent of this Act,
such sum not being less than ten cents nor more than one dollar as the
court shall determine: of which penalty one moiety shall be to the use of
Her Majesty, and the other to the legal owner of such copyright, and
such penalty may be recovered in any court of competent jurisdiction.

12. If any person after the recording of any painting, drawing, statue,
or other work of art within the term or terms limited by this Act, reproduces in any manner, or causes to be reproduced, made, or sold, in whole
or in part, copies of the said works of art without the consent of the proprietor or proprietors, such offender or offenders shall forfeit the plate or
plates on which such reproduction has been made, and also every sheet
thereof so copied, printed, or photographed, to the proprietor or proprietors
of the copyright thereof, and shall further forfeit for every sheet of the
same reproduction so published or exposed for sale, contrary to the true
intent and meaning of this Act, such sum, not being less than ten cents nor
more than one dollar, as the court shall determine; and one moiety of such
forfeiture shall go to the proprietor or proprietors, and the other moiety to
the use of Her Majesty, and such forfeiture may be recovered in any court
of competent jurisdiction.

13. If any person, after the recording of any print, cut, or engraving,
map, chart, musical composition, or photograph, according to the provisions
of this Act, within the term or terms limited by this Act, engraves, etches,
or works, sells or copies, or causes to be engraved, etched, or copied, made
or sold, either in the whole or by varying, adding to, or diminishing the
main design with intent to evade the law, or prints, or reprints, or imports

for sale, or causes to be so printed or imported for sale, any such map, chart, musical composition, print, cut, or engraving, or any part thereof, without the consent of the proprietor or proprietors of the copyright thereof first obtained as aforesaid, or knowing the same to be so printed or imported without such consent, publishes, sells, or exposes for sale, or in any manner disposes of any such map, chart, musical composition, engraving, cut, photograph, or print without such consent as aforesaid, such offender or offenders shall forfeit the plate or plates on which such map, chart, musical composition, engraving, cut, photograph, or print has been copied, and also every sheet thereof so copied or printed as aforesaid, to the proprietor or proprietors of the copyright thereof, and shall further forfeit for every sheet of such map, musical composition, print, cut, or engraving which may be found in his or their possession, printed or published or exposed for sale contrary to the true intent and meaning of this Act, such sum not being less than ten cents nor more than one dollar as the court shall determine; and one moiety of such forfeiture shall go to the proprietor or proprietors, and the other moiety to the use of Her Majesty, and such forfeiture may be recovered in any court of competent jurisdiction.

14. Nothing herein contained shall prejudice the right of any person to represent any scene or object, notwithstanding that there may be copyright in some other representation of such scene or object.

15. Works of which the copyright has been granted and is subsisting in the United Kingdom, and copyright of which is not secured or subsisting in Canada under any Canadian or Provincial Act, shall, upon being printed and publis ed or reprinted and republished in Canada, be entitled to copyright under this Act; but nothing in this Act shall be held to prohibit the importation from the United Kingdom of copies of such works legally printed there.

(2.) In the case of the reprinting of any such copyright work subsequent to its publication in the United Kingdom, any person who may have previous to the date of entry of such work upon the registers of copyright imported any foreign reprints, shall have the privilege of disposing of such reprints by sale or otherwise; the burden of proof, however, in such a case will lie with such person to establish the extent and regularity of the transaction.

16. Whenever the author of a literary, scientific, or artistic work or composition which may be the subject of copyright has executed the same for another person or has sold the same to another person for due consideration, such author shall not be entitled to obtain or to retain the proprietorship of such copyright, which is by the said transaction virtually transferred to the purchaser who may avail himself of such privilege, unless a reserve of the said privilege is specially made by the author or artist in a deed duly executed.

17. If any person, not having legally acquired the copyright of a literary, scientific, or artistic work, inserts in any copy thereof printed, produced, reproduced, or imported, or impresses on any such copy that the same hath been entered according to this Act, or words purporting to assert the existence of a Canadian copyright in relation thereto, every person so offending shall incur a penalty not exceeding three hundred dollars (one moiety whereof shall be paid to the person who sues for the same, and the other moiety to the use of Her Majesty), to be recovered in any court of competent jurisdiction.

(2.) If any person causes any work 'to be inserted in the Register of Interim Copyright and fails to print and publish or reprint and republish the same within the time prescribed, he shall incur a penalty not exceeding one hundred dollars (one moiety whereof shall be paid to the person who sueth for the same, and the other moiety to the use of Her Majesty), to be recovered in any court of competent jurisdiction.

18. The right of an author of a literary, scientific, or artistic work to obtain a copyright, and the copyright when obtained, shall be assignable in law, either as to the whole interest or any part thereof, by an instrument in writing made in duplicate, and to be recorded in the office of the Minister of Agriculture, on production of both duplicates and payment of the fee herein-after provided. One of the duplicates shall be retained in the office of the Minister of Agriculture, and the other returned, with the certificate of registration, to the party depositing it.

19. In case of any person making application to register as his own the copyright of a literary, scientific, or artistic work already registered in another person's name, or in case of simultaneous conflicting applications, or of an application made by any person other than the person entered as proprietor of a registered copyright, to cancel the said copyright, the party so applying shall be notified that the question is to be settled before a court of competent jurisdiction, and no further proceedings shall be had concerning the subject before a judgment is produced, maintaining, cancelling, or otherwise settling the matter; and this registration, or cancellation, or adjustment of the said right shall then be made by the Minister of Agriculture in accordance with such decision.

20. Clerical errors happening in the framing or copying of any instrument drawn in the office of the Minister of Agriculture shall not be construed as invalidating the same, but when discovered they may be corrected under the authority of the Minister of Agriculture.

21. All copies or extracts certified from the officer of the Minister of Agriculture shall be received in evidence without further proof, and without production of the originals.

22. Should a work copyrighted in Canada become out of print, a complaint may be lodged by any person with the Minister of Agriculture who, on the fact being ascertained to his satisfaction, shall notify the copyright owner of the complaint and of the fact; and if, within a reasonable time, no remedy is applied by such owner, the Minister of Agriculture may grant a license to any person to publish a new edition or to import the work, specifying the number of copies, and the royalty to be paid on each to the copyright owner.

23. The application for the registration of an interim copyright, of a temporary copyright, and of a copyright may be made in the name of the author or of his legal representative by any person purporting to be the agent of the said author, and any fraudulent assumption of such authority shall be a misdemeanor, and shall be punished by fine and imprisonment accordingly; and any damage caused by a fraudulent or an erroneous assumption of such authority shall be recoverable before any court of competent jurisdiction.

24. If any person shall wilfully make or cause to be made any false entry in the registry books of the Minister of Agriculture, or shall wilfully

produce or cause to be tendered in evidence any paper falsely purporting to be a copy of an entry in the said books, he shall be guilty of a misdemeanor, and shall be punished accordingly.

25. If a book be published anonymously it shall be sufficient to enter it in the [name of the first publisher thereof, either on behalf of the unnamed author or on behalf of such first publisher, as the case may be.

26. It shall not be requisite to deliver any printed copy of the second or of any subsequent edition of any book or books unless the same shall contain very important alterations or additions.

27. No act or prosecution for the recovery of any penalty under this Act shall be commenced more than two years after the cause of action arose.

The following fees shall be payable to the Minister of Agriculture before an application for any of the purposes herein-after mentioned shall be entertained ; that is to say,

	Dol.	c.
On registering a copyright	1	00
On registering an interim copyright .	0	50
On registering a temporary copyright . .	0	50
On recording an assignment	1	00
On certified copy of registration . .	0	50
On registering any decision of a court of justice, for every folio	0	50

On office copies of documents not above mentioned, the following charges shall be made :

	Dol.	c.
For every single or first folio certified copy .	0	50
For every subsequent one hundred words (fractions from and under fifty being not counted, and over fifty being counted for one hundred).	0	25

(2.) The said fees shall be in full of all services performed under this Act by the Minister of Agriculture, or by any person employed by him in pursuance of this Act.

(3.) All fees received under this Act shall be paid over to the Receiver General and form part of the Consolidated Revenue Fund of Canada. No fees shall be made the subject of exemption in favour of any person, and no fee exacted by this Act, once paid, shall be returned to the person who paid it.

28. "The Copyright Act of 1868," being the Act thirty-first Victoria, chapter fifty-four, and all other Acts or parts of Acts inconsistent with the provisions of this Act, are hereby repealed, subject to the provisions of the next following section.

29. All copyrights heretofore acquired under the Acts or parts of Acts repealed shall, in respect of the unexpired terms thereof, continue unimpaired, and shall have the same force and effect as regards the province or provinces to which they now extend, and shall be assignable and renewable, and all penalties and forfeitures incurred and to be incurred under the same may be sued for and enforced, and all prosecutions commenced before the passing of this Act for any such penalties or

forfeitures already incurred may be continued and completed as if such Acts were not repealed.

30. In citing this Act it shall be sufficient to call it "The Copyright Act of 1875."

---

38 & 39 VICT. c. 93.

An Act to Amend the Copyright of Designs Act. [13th August, 1875.]

BE it enacted by the Queen's most excellent Majesty, by and with the advice and consent of the Lords spiritual and temporal, and Commons, in this present Parliament assembled, and by the authority of the same, as follows:

1. This Act shall come into operation on the first day of January one thousand eight hundred and seventy-six, which day is in this Act referred to as the commencement of this Act. Commencement of Act.

2. On and after the commencement of this Act all powers, duties, and authorities vested in, imposed on, or to be exercised by the Board of Trade under the Acts mentioned in the Schedule to this Act shall be transferred to, vested in, and imposed on the Commissioners of Patents for Inventions, and the said Acts shall be construed as if the said Commissioners of Patents were throughout substituted for the Board of Trade or the Lords of the Committee of the Privy Council for the consideration of all matters of trade and plantations. Transfer to commissioners of patents of powers and duties of Board of Trade under Copyright of Designs Acts.

3. The said Commissioners of Patents may from time to time make, and when made, revoke and alter, general rules for regulating registration under the Acts mentioned in the Schedule hereto, and this Act, and on and after the commencement of this Act any discretion or power vested in the registrar under the said Acts shall be subject to the control of the Commissioners of Patents and shall be exercised by him in such manner and with such limitations and restrictions (if any) as may be prescribed by the said general rules, and any provisions contained in the said Act as to the copies, drawings, prints, descriptions, information, matters, and particulars to be furnished to the registrar, and generally as to any Act or thing to be done by the registrar, may be modified by such general rules in such manner as the Commissioners of Patents may think Expedient. Power for commissioners to make general rules.

General rules made in pursuance of this section shall be laid before parliament within one month after they are made if Parliament be then sitting, or if not, within one month after the commencement of the then next session; and if either House of Parliament resolve within one month after such rules have been laid before such House that any of such rules ought not to continue in force, any rule in respect of which such resolution has been passed shall, after the date of such resolution, cease to be of any force, without prejudice nevertheless to the making of any other rule in its place, or to anything done in pursuance of any such rules before the date of such resolution.

Transfer of duties of registrar to officers of Commissioners of Patents.

The office of registrar under the Acts mentioned in the Schedule to this Act shall cease to exist as a separate paid office, and the Commissioners may from time to time make arrangements as to the mode in which and the person or persons by whom the duties of registrar and other duties under the said Acts are to be performed and may from time to time delegate to any such person or persons all or any of the duties of the registrar, and any person or persons to whom such duties may be delegated shall, in so far as delegation extends, be deemed to be the registrar within the meaning of the said Acts.

Any arrangement or delegation of duties to the clerk or other officer of the Commissioners of Patents made by the Board of Trade shall be as valid as it would have been if this Act had been passed at the date of such arrangement or delegation and the same had been made by the Commissioners of Patents.

Short title of Acts.

5. Each of the Acts mentioned in the Schedule to this Act may be cited as the Copyright of Designs Act of the year in which it was passed, and the said Acts may, together with this Act, be cited as the Copyright of Designs Act 1842 to 1875, and this Act may be cited as the Copyright of Designs Act, 1875.

SESSION AND CHAPTER.	TITLE.
5 & 6 Vict. c. 100.	An Act to consolidate and amend the Laws relating to the Copyright of Designs for ornamenting Articles of Manufacture.
6 & 7 Vict. c. 65.	An Act to amend the Laws relating to the Copyright of Designs.
13 & 14 Vict. c. 104.	An Act to extend and amend the Acts relating to the Copyright of Designs.
21 & 22 Vict. c. 70.	An Act to amend the Act of the 5th and 6th year of Her present Majesty to consolidate and amend the Law relating to the Copyright of Designs for ornamenting Articles of Manufacture.
24 & 25 Vict. c. 73.	An Act to amend the Law relating to the Copyright of Designs.

39 & 40 VICT. c. 36.

[24th July 1876.]

" The Customs Consolidation Act, 1876."

42. The goods enumerated and described in the following table of prohibitions and restrictions incurred are hereby prohibited to be imported or brought into the United Kingdom, save as thereby excepted, and if any goods so enumerated and described shall be imported or brought into the United Kingdom contrary to the prohibitions or restrictions contained therein, such goods shall be forfeited, and may be destroyed or otherwise disposed of as the Commissioners of Customs may direct.

A Table of Prohibitions and Restrictions inwards.
Goods prohibited to be imported.

Books wherein the copyright shall be first subsisting, first composed, or written or printed, in the United Kingdom, and printed or reprinted in any other country, as to which the proprietor of such copyright or his agent shall have given to the Commissioners of Customs a notice in writing, duly declared, that such copyright subsists, such notice also stating when such copyright will expire.

The Commissioners of Customs shall cause to be made, and to be publicly exposed at the Custom Houses in the several ports in the United Kingdom, lists of all books wherein the copyright shall be subsisting, and as to which the proprietor of such copyright, or his agent, shall have given notice in writing to the said commissioners that such copyright exists, stating in such notice when such copyright expires, accompanied by a declaration made and subscribed before a collector of customs or a justice of the peace, that the contents of such notice are true.

45. If any person shall have cause to complain of the insertion of any book in such lists, it shall be lawful for any judge at chambers, on the application of the person so complaining, to issue a summons, calling upon the person upon whose notice such book shall have been so inserted to appear before any such judge at a time to be appointed in such summons, to show cause why such book shall not be expunged from such lists, and any such judge shall at the time so appointed proceed to hear and determine upon the matter of such summons, and make his order thereon in writing; and upon service of such order, or a certified copy thereof, upon the Commissioners of Customs or their secretary for the time being, the said commissioners shall expunge such book from the list, or

retain the same therein, according to the tenor of such order; and in case such books shall be expunged from such lists, the importation thereof shall not be deemed to be prohibited. If at the time appointed in any such summons the person so summoned shall not appear before such judge, then upon proof by affidavit that such summons, or a true copy thereof, has been personally served upon the person so summoned, or sent to him by post to or left at his last known place of abode or business, any such judge may proceed ex parte to hear and determine the matter; but if either party be dissatisfied with such order, he may apply to a superior court to review such decision and to make such further order thereon as the court may see fit: Provided always, that nothing herein contained shall affect any proceeding at law or in equity which any party aggrieved by reason of the insertion of any book pursuant to any such notice, or the removal of any book from such list pursuant to any such order, or by reason of any false declaration under this Act, might or would otherwise have against any party giving such notice or obtaining such order, or making such false declaration.

As to the Channel Islands and other Possessions.

Foreign re-
prints of books
under copy-
right pro-
hibited.
152. Any books wherein the copyright shall be subsisting, first composed or written or printed in the United Kingdom, and printed or reprinted in any other country, shall be and are hereby absolutely prohibited to be imported into the British Possessions abroad: provided always, that no such books shall be prohibited to be imported as aforesaid, unless the proprietor of such copyright, or his agent, shall have given notice in writing to the Commissioners of Customs that such copyright subsists, and in such notice shall have stated when the copyright will expire; and the said commissioners shall cause to be made and transmitted to the several ports in the British Possessions abroad, from time to time to be publicly exposed there, lists of books respecting which such notice shall have been duly given, and all books imported contrary thereto shall be forfeited; but nothing herein contained shall be taken to prevent Her Majesty from exercising the powers vested in her by 10 & 11 Vict. c. 95, intituled " An Act to amend the Law relating to the protection in the Colonies of works entitled to copyright in the United Kingdom," to suspend in certain cases such prohibition.

APPENDIX (B).

———◦◦◦———

Revised Statute of the United States being the Act of July 8th, 1870, as contained in the Revised Statutes, Second Edition, 1878.

Copyrights to be under charge of Librarian of Congress.

4948. All records and other things relating to copyrights and required by law to be preserved, shall be under the control of the Librarian of Congress, and kept and preserved in the Library of Congress ; and the Librarian of Congress shall have the immediate care and supervision thereof, and, under the supervision of the joint committee of Congress on the Library, shall perform all acts and duties required by law touching copyrights.

Seal of Office.

4949. The seal provided for the office of the Librarian of Congress shall be the seal thereof, and by it all records and papers issued from the office and to be used in evidence shall be authenticated.

Bond of Librarian.

4950. The Librarian of Congress shall give a bond, with sureties to the Treasurer of the United States, in the sum of five thousand dollars, with the condition that he will render to the proper officers of the Treasury a true account of all moneys received by virtue of his office.

Annual Report.

4951. The Librarian of Congress shall make an annual report to Congress of the number and description of copyright publications for which entries have been made during the year.

What Publications may be entered for Copyright.

4952. Any citizen of the United States or resident therein, who shall be the author, inventor, designer, or proprietor of any book, map, chart, dramatic or musical composition, engraving, cut, print,

or photograph or negative thereof, or of a painting, drawing,
chromo, statue, statuary, and of models or designs intended to be
perfected as works of the fine arts, and the executors, administrators,
or assigns of any such person shall, upon complying with the provisions of this chapter have the sole liberty of printing, reprinting,
publishing, completing, copying, executing, finishing, and vending
the same; and, in the case of a dramatic composition, of publicly
performing or representing it, or causing it to be performed or represented by others. And authors may reserve the right to
dramatise or to translate their own works.

Terms of Copyright.

4953. Copyrights shall be granted for the term of twenty-eight
years from the time of recording the title thereof, in the manner
hereinafter directed.

Continuance of Term.

4954. The author, inventor, or designer, if he be still living and
a citizen of the United States or resident therein, or his widow or
children, if he be dead, shall have the same exclusive right continued for the further term of fourteen years, upon recording the
title of the work or description of the article so secured a second
time, and complying with all other regulations in regard to original
copyrights, within six months before the expiration of the first
term. And such person shall, within two months from the date of
said renewal, cause a copy of the record thereof to be published in
one or more newspapers, printed in the United States, for the space
of four weeks.

Assignment of Copyrights and recording.

4955. Copyrights shall be assignable in law, by any instrument
of writing, and such assignment shall be recorded in the office of
the Librarian of Congress within sixty days after its execution; in
default of which it shall be void as against any subsequent purchaser or mortgagee for a valuable consideration, without notice.

Deposit of Title and published Copies.

4956. No person shall be entitled to a copyright unless he shall,
before publication, deliver at the office of the Librarian of Congress
or deposit in the mail addressed to the Librarian of Congress, at
Washington, district of Columbia, a printed copy of the title of the
book or other article, or a description of the painting, drawing,
chromo, statue, statuary, or a model or design for a work of the
fine arts for which he desires a copyright, nor unless he shall also,

within ten days from the publication thereof, deliver at the office of the Librarian of Congress or deposit in the mail addressed to the Librarian of Congress, at Washington, District of Columbia, two copies of such copyright, book or other article, or in case of a painting, drawing, statue, statuary, model, or design for a work of the fine arts, a photograph of the same.

Book of Entry and attested Copy.

4957. The Librarian of Congress shall record the name of such copyright book or other article, forthwith, in a book to be kept for that purpose, in the words following: "Library of Congress, to wit: Be it remembered that on the   day of   , A. B., of   , hath deposited in this office the title of a book (map, chart, or otherwise, as the case may be, or description of the article), the title or description of which is in the following words, to wit (here insert the title or description); the right whereof he claims as author, (originator, or proprietor as the case may be), in conformity with the laws of the United States respecting copyrights. C. D., Librarian of the Congress." And he shall give a copy of the title or description, under the seal of the Librarian of Congress, to the proprietor whenever he shall require it.

Fees.

4958. The Librarian of Congress shall receive, from the persons to whom the services designated are rendered, the following fees:—

First. For recording the title or description of any copyright book or other article, fifty cents.

Second. For every copy under seal of such record actually given to the person claiming the copyright, or his assigns, fifty cents.

Third. For recording any instrument of writing for the assignment of a copyright, fifteen cents for every one hundred words.

Fourth. For every copy of an assignment, ten cents for every one hundred words.

All fees so received shall be paid into the Treasury of the United States.

Copies of Copyright Works to be furnished to Librarian of Congress.

4959. The proprietor of every copyright book or other article shall deliver at the office of the Librarian of Congress, or deposit in the mail addressed to the Librarian of Congress at Washington, District of Columbia, within ten days after its publication, two complete printed copies thereof, of the best edition issued or description or photograph of such article as hereinbefore required,

3 A

and a copy of every subsequent edition wherein any substantial changes shall be made.

Penalty for omission.

4960. For every failure on the part of the proprietor of any copyright to deliver or deposit in the mail either of the published copies or description or photograph, required by sections four thousand nine hundred and fifty-six, and four thousand nine hundred and fifty-nine, the proprietor of the copyright shall be liable to a penalty of twenty-five dollars, to be recovered by the Librarian of Congress, in the name of the United States, in an action in the nature of an action of debt, in any district court of the United States within the jurisdiction of which the delinquent may reside or be found.

Postmaster to give Receipts.

4961. The postmaster to whom such copyright book, title, or other article is delivered, shall, if requested, give a receipt therefor; and when so delivered he shall mail it to its destination.

Publication of Notice of Entry for Copyright prescribed.

4962. No person shall maintain an action for the infringement of his copyright unless he shall give notice thereof by inserting in the several copies of every edition published, on the title-page or the page immediately following, if it be a book; or if a map, chart, musical composition, print, cut, engraving, photograph, painting, drawing, chromo, statue, statuary, or model or design intended to be perfected and completed as a work of the fine arts, by inscribing upon some portion of the face or front thereof, or on the face of the substance on which the same shall be mounted the following words: "Entered according to the Act of Congress in the year   , by A. B., in the office of the Librarian of Congress at Washington."

Penalty for false Publication of Notice of Entry.

4963. Every person who shall insert or impress such notice, or words of the same purport, in or upon any book, map, chart, musical composition, print, cut, engraving, or photograph, or other article, for which he has not obtained a copyright, shall be liable to a penalty of one hundred dollars, recoverable one half for the person who shall sue for such penalty, and one half to the use of the United States.

Damages for violation of Copyright of Books.

4964. Every person who after the recording of the title of any book as provided by this chapter shall, within the term limited, and without the consent of the proprietor of the copyright first obtained in writing, signed in presence of two or more witnesses, print, publish, or import, or knowing the same to be so printed, published, or imported, shall sell or expose to sale any copy of such book, shall forfeit every copy thereof to such proprietor, and shall also forfeit and pay such damages as may be recovered in a civil action by such proprietor in any court of competent jurisdiction.

For violating Copyright of Maps, Charts, Prints, &c.

4965. If any person, after the recording of the title of any map, chart, musical composition, print, cut, engraving, or photograph, or chromo, or of the description of any painting, drawing, statue, statuary, or model or design intended to be perfected and executed as a work of the fine arts, as provided by this chapter, shall, within the term limited and withou tthe consent of the proprietor of the copyright first obtained in writing, signed in presence of two or more witnesses, engrave, etch, work, copy, print, publish, or import, either in whole or in part, or by varying the main design with intent to evade the law, or, knowing the same to be so printed published, or imported, shall sell or expose to sale any copy of such map or other article as aforesaid, he shall forfeit to the proprietor all the plates on which the same shall be copied, and every sheet thereof, either copied, or printed, and shall further forfeit one dollar for every sheet of the same found in his possession, either printing, printed, copied, published, imported, or exposed for sale; and in case of a painting, statue or statuary, he shall forfeit ten dollars for every copy of the same in his possession, or by him sold or exposed for sale; one half thereof to the proprietor and the other half to the use of the United States.

For violating Copyright of Dramatic Compositions.

4966. Any person publicly performing or representing any dramatic composition for which a copyright has been obtained without the consent of the proprietor thereof, or his heirs or assigns, shall be liable for damages therefor, such damages in all cases to be assessed at such sum, not less than one hundred dollars for the first, and fifty dollars for every subsequent performance, as to the court shall appear to be just.

Damages for printing or publishing any Manuscript without consent of Author, &c.

4967. Every person who shall print or publish any manuscript whatever, without the consent of the author or proprietor first

obtained, if such author or proprietor is a citizen of the United
States, or resident therein, shall be liable to the author or proprietor
for all damages occasioned by such injury.

Limitation of Action in Copyright Cases.

4968. No action shall be maintained in any case of forfeiture or
penalty under the copyright laws, unless the same is commenced
within two years after the cause of action has arisen.

Defences to Action in Copyright Cases.

4969. In all actions arising under the laws respecting copyrights,
the defendant may plead the general issue, and give the special
matter in evidence.

Injunctions in Copyright Cases.

4970. The circuit courts, and district courts having the jurisdiction of circuit courts, shall have power, upon bill in equity, filed by
any party aggrieved, to grant injunctions to prevent the violation
of any right secured by the laws respecting copyrights, according
to the course and principles of courts of equity, on such terms as
the court may deem reasonable.

Aliens and Non-Residents not Privileged.

4971. Nothing in this chapter shall be construed to prohibit
the printing, publishing, importation, or sale of any book, map,
chart, dramatic or musical composition, print, cut, engraving, or
photograph, written, composed, or made by any person not a citizen
of the United States nor resident therein.

ACT OF JUNE 18, 1874.

(18 U.S. St. at L. 78.)

*An Act to amend the Law relating to Patents, Trade-marks and
Copyrights.*

Be it enacted by the Senate and House of Representatives of
the United States of America in Congress assembled, That no person
shall maintain an action for the infringement of his copyright
unless he shall give notice thereof by inserting in the several copies
of every edition published, on the title-page or the page immediately
following, if, it be a book; or if a map, chart, musical composition,
print, cut, engraving, photograph, painting, drawing, chromo, statue,
statuary or model, or design intended to be perfected and completed
as a work of the fine arts, by inscribing upon some visible portion

thereof or of the substance on which the same shall be mounted, the following words, viz.: "Entered according to Act of Congress, in the year   , by A. B., in the office of the Librarian of Congress, at Washington;" or at his option the word "Copyright," together with the year the copyright was entered, and the name of the party by whom it was taken out; thus: "Copyright 18   , by A. B."

Fees for recording and certifying Assignments of Copyright.

2. That for recording and certifying any instrument of writing for the assignment of a copyright, the Librarian of Congress shall receive from the persons to whom the service is rendered, one dollar; and for every copy of an assignment, one dollar; said fee to cover, in either case, a certificate of the record under seal of the Librarian of Congress; and all fees so received shall be paid into the Treasury of the United States.

Restrictions on application of Words "Engraving,' " Cut," and "Print."

3. That in the construction of this Act, the words "engraving," "cut," and "print," shall be applied only to pictorial illustrations or works connected with the fine arts, and no prints or labels designed to be used for any other articles of manufacture shall be entered under the copyright law, but may be registered in the Patent Office. And the Commissioner of Patents is hereby charged with the supervision and control of the entry or registry of such prints or labels in conformity with the regulations provided by law as to copyright of prints, except that there shall be paid for recording the title of any print or label not a trade-mark, six dollars, which shall cover the expense of furnishing a copy of the record under the seal of the Commissioner of Patents, to the party entering the same.

Repeal of inconsistent Laws.

4. That all laws and parts of laws inconsistent with the for ‐ going provisions be and the same are hereby repealed.

5. That this Act shall take effect on and after the first day of August, eighteen hundred and seventy-four.

Approved, June 18, 1874.

OFFICIAL REGULATIONS.

DIRECTIONS for securing COPYRIGHTS under the REVISED ACT of CONGRESS which took effect 1st August, 1874.

Printed Title for Entry before Publication.

1. A printed copy of the title of the book, map, chart, dramatic or musical composition, engraving, cut, print, photograph, or a description of the painting, drawing, chromo, statue, statuary, or model or design for a work of the fine arts, for which copyright is desired, must be sent by mail or otherwise, prepaid, addressed—

LIBRARIAN OF CONGRESS,
Washington, D. C.

This must be done before publication of the book or other article.

Copyright Fees.

2. A fee of 50 cents, for recording the title of each book or other article, must be enclosed with the title as above, and 50 cents in addition (or one dollar in all) for each certificate of copyright under seal of the Librarian of Congress, which will be transmitted by return mail.

What is required to perfect Copyright.—Penalty.

3. Within ten days after publication of each book or other article, two complete copies of the best edition issued must be sent, to perfect the copyright, with the address—

LIBRARIAN OF CONGRESS,
Washington, D. C.

It is optional with those sending books and other articles to perfect copyright to send them by mail or express, but in either case the charges are to be prepaid by the senders. Without the deposit of copies above required the copyright is void, and a penalty of 25 dollars is incurred. No copy is required to be deposited elsewhere.

Notice of Copyright to be given by Imprint.

4. No copyright is valid unless notice is given by inserting in every copy published, on the title page or the page following, if it be a book; or if a map, chart, musical composition, print, cut, engraving, photograph, painting, drawing, chromo, statue, statuary, or model or design intended to be perfected as a work of the fine arts, by inscribing upon some portion thereof, or on the substance on which the same is mounted, the following words, viz.: "*Entered according to Act of Congress, in the year   , by   , in the office of the Librarian of Congress at Washington;*" or, at the option of the person entering the copyright, the words "*Copyright, 18 , by   .*"

The law imposes a penalty of 100 dollars upon any person who has not obtained copyright who shall insert the notice "*Entered according to Act of Congress,*" or "*Copyright,*" &c., or words of the same import, in or upon any book or other article.

Translations, &c.

5. Any author may reserve the right to translate or to dramatise his own work. In this case notice should be given by printing the words " *Right of translation reserved*," or " *All rights reserved*," below the notice of copyright entry, and notifying the Librarian of Congress of such reservation, to be entered upon the record.

Duration of Copyright.—Renewals.

6. Each copyright secures the exclusive right of publishing the book or article copyrighted for the term of 28 years. At the end of that time the author or designer, or his widow or children, may secure a renewal for the further term of 14 years, making 42 years in all. Applications for renewal must be accompanied by explicit statement of ownership in the case of the author, or of relationship in the case of his heirs, and must state definitely the date and place of entry of the original copyright.

Time of Publication.

7. The time within which any work copyrighted may be issued from the press is not limited by any law or regulation, but depends upon the discretion of the proprietor. A copyright may be secured for a projected work as well as for a completed one.

Assignments.

8. Any copyright is assignable in law by any instrument of writing, but such assignment must be recorded in the office of the Librarian of Congress within 60 days from its date. The fee for this record and certificate is one dollar, and for a certified copy of any record of assignment, one dollar.

Copies, or Duplicate Certificates.

9. A copy of the record (or duplicate certificate) of any copyright entry will be furnished under seal, at the rate of 50 cents each.

Serials or separate Publications to be copyrighted separately.

10. In the case of books published in more than one volume, or of periodicals published in numbers, or of engravings, photographs, or other articles published with variations, a copyright is to be taken out for each volume or part of a book, or number of a periodical, or variety, as to size, title, or inscription, of any other article.

Copyrights for Works of Art.

11. To secure a copyright for a painting, statue, or model or design intended to be perfected as a work of the fine arts, so as to prevent infringement by copying, engraving, or vending such design, a definite description must accompany the application for copyright, and a photograph of the same, at least of " cabinet size," must be mailed to the Librarian of Congress within 10 days from the completion of the work.

No Labels copyright.

12. Copyrights cannot be granted upon trade-marks, or labels intended to be used with any article of manufacture. If protection for such prints or labels is desired, application must be made to the Patent Office, where they are registered at a fee of six dollars for labels, and 25 for trade-marks.

Full Name of Proprietor required.

13. Every applicant for a copyright must state distinctly the name and residence of the claimant, and whether the right is claimed as author, designer, or proprietor. No affidavit or formal application is required.

Office of the Librarian of Congress,
        Washington, 1874.

APPENDIX (C).

*Her Majesty's Orders in Council consequent upon the Arrange-
ment and Settlement of an International Copyright Treaty with
Prussia. (Similar orders were issued on the adjustment of the
convention with Brunswick, 24th April, 1847, with Hanover,
30th October, 1847, with the Thuringian Union, 10th August,
1847, &c.)*

At the Court at Osborne House, Isle of Wight, the 27th day of
August, 1846.

Present—

THE QUEEN'S MOST EXCELLENT MAJESTY IN COUNCIL.

WHEREAS a treaty has been concluded between Her Majesty and
His Majesty the King of Prussia, whereby due protection has been
secured within the Prussian dominions for the authors of books,
dramatic works, or musical compositions, and the inventors,
designers, or engravers of prints, and articles of sculpture, and the
authors, inventors, designers, or engravers of any other works
whatsoever of literature and the fine arts, in which the laws of
Great Britain and of Prussia do now, or may hereafter, give their
respective subjects the privileges of copyright, and for the lawful
representatives or assigns of such authors, inventors, designers, or
engravers, with regard to any such works first published within the
dominions of Her Majesty.

Now, therefore, Her Majesty, by and with the advice and consent
of Her Privy Council, and by virtue of the authority committed to
her by an Act passed in the session of Parliament holden in the
seventh and eighth years of ·her reign, intituled "An Act to
amend the Law relating to International Copyright," doth order,
and it is hereby ordered, that, from and after the first day of
September, one thousand eight hundred and forty-six, the authors,
inventors, designers, engravers, and makers of any of the following
works (that is to say), books, prints, articles of sculpture, dramatic

works, musical compositions, and any other works of literature and the fine arts, in which the laws of Great Britain give to British subjects the privilege of copyright, and the executors, administrators, and assigns of such authors, inventors, designers, engravers, and makers respectively, shall, as respects works first published within the dominions of Prussia, after the said first day of September one thousand eight hundred and forty-six, have the privilege of copyright therein for a period equal to the term of copyright which authors, inventors, designers, engravers, and makers of the like works respectively, first published in the United Kingdom, are by law entitled to; provided such books, dramatic pieces, musical compositions, prints, articles of sculpture, or other works of art, have been registered, and copies thereof have been delivered, according to the requirements of the said recited Act, within twelve months after the first publication thereof in any part of the Prussian dominions. And it is hereby further ordered, that the authors of dramatic pieces and musical compositions, which shall, after the said first day of September, one thousand eight hundred and forty-six, be first publicly represented or performed within the dominions of Prussia shall have the sole liberty of representing or performing in any part of the British dominions such dramatic pieces or musical compositions, during a period equal to the period during which authors of dramatic pieces and musical compositions first publicly represented or performed in the United Kingdom are entitled by law to the sole liberty of representing or performing the same; provided such dramatic pieces, or musical compositions, have been registered, and copies thereof have been delivered according to the requirements of the said recited Act, within twelve calendar months after the time of their being first represented or performed in any part of the Prussian dominions.

And the Right Honourable the Lords Commissioners of Her Majesty's Treasury are to give the necessary orders herein accordingly.

(Signed)

C. C. GREVILLE.

————

At the Court at Osborne House, Isle of Wight, the 27th day of August, 1846.

Present—

THE QUEEN'S MOST EXCELLENT MAJESTY IN COUNCIL.

WHEREAS by an Act passed in the present session of Parliament, intituled "An Act to amend an Act of the seventh and eighth years of Her present Majesty, for reducing, under certain circumstances, the duties payable upon Books and Engravings," it is enacted, that whenever Her Majesty has, by virtue of any authority vested in her for that purpose, declared that the authors, inventors, designers, engravers, or makers of any books, prints, or other works of art first published in any foreign country or countries, shall have the privilege of copyright therein, it shall be lawful for Her Majesty, if she thinks fit, from time to time, by any Order in Council, to declare that from and after a day to be named in such Order, in lieu of the customs, from time to time payable, on the importation into the United Kingdom of books, prints, and drawings, there shall be payable only such duties of customs as are mentioned in the said Act.

And whereas Her Majesty hath this day, by virtue of the authority vested in her for that purpose, declared that the authors, inventors, designers, engravers, and makers of books, prints, and certain other works of art, first published within the dominions of Prussia, shall have the privilege of copyright therein.

Now, therefore, Her Majesty, by and with the advice and consent of her Privy Council, and in virtue of the authority committed to her by the said recited Act, doth order, and it is hereby ordered, that, from and after the first day of September, one thousand eight hundred and forty-six, in lieu of the duties now payable upon books, prints, and drawings, published at any place within the dominion of Prussia, there shall be payable only the duties of customs following (that is to say):

On books originally produced in the United Kingdom, and republished at any place within the dominions of Prussia, a duty of two pounds ten shillings per hundred-weight. On prints or drawings, plain or coloured, published at any place within the dominions of Prussia:

	s.	d.
Single, each	0	0½
Bound or sewn, the dozen . .	0	1½

And the Right Honourable the Lords Commissioners of Her Majesty's Treasury are to give the necessary orders herein accordingly.

(Signed)

C. C. GREVILLE.

APPENDIX (D).

—◆◆—

DIRECTIONS ISSUED BY THE BOARD OF TRADE FOR REGISTRATION OF
DESIGNS.

ORNAMENTAL DESIGNS.

Directions for Registering and Searching.

PERSONS proposing to register a design for ornamenting an article of
manufacture, must bring or send to the Designs Office :

1. Two EXACTLY SIMILAR *copies, drawings* (or *tracings*), NOT IN PENCIL,
   photographs, or *prints* thereof, with the proper fees.
2. THE NAME AND ADDRESS of the proprietor or proprietors, or the
   title of the firm under which he or they may be trading, together
   with their place of abode, or place of carrying on business,
   distinctly written or printed.
3. THE NUMBER of the class in respect of which such registration is
   intended to be made, except it be for sculpture.

The aforesaid *copies* may consist of portions of the manufactured articles
(*except carpets, oil-cloths, and woollen shawls*), when such can conveniently be done (as in the case of *paper-hangings, calico, prints, &c.*),
which, as well as the *drawings* or *tracings* (which must be fixed), or
prints of the design, to be furnished when the article is of such a nature
as not to admit of being pasted in a book, *must,* whether coloured or not,
be facsimiles of each other.

Should paper-hangings or furnitures exceed 42 inches in length by 23
inches in breadth, drawings will be required, but they must not exceed
these dimensions.

Applications for registering may be made in the following form :—

Application to register.
(Blank Forms may be obtained at the Office.)

C.D. Works,   188 .

You are hereby requested to register, provisionally (*a*) the accompanying
ornamental designs (*in Class* 1, [2, 3, 4, &c.,]) (*or for sculpture* (*b*))

(*a*) If not provisionally, strike out the word " provisionally."
(*b*) Here insert " for sculpture," if for sculpture, or the class or classes.

in the name of ((*a*) *A. B. of*   , *of*   ,) *or* (*A. B. of*   ,
and C. D. of   , *&c., trading under the style or firm of B. D. & Co.,
of   , of   , of*   ), who claim to be the proprietors
thereof, and to return the same (*if sent by post*), directed to   (*if
brought by hand*), to the bearer of the official acknowledgment for the
same.

 To the Registrar of Designs,   (Signed) B. D. & Co.,
   Designs Office, London.   by J. F.

 The person bringing a design must take an acknowledgment for it,
which will be delivered to him on payment of the proper fees. This
acknowledgment must be produced on application for the certified copy,
which will be returned in exchange for the same.

 A design may be registered in respect of one or more of the above
classes according as it is intended to be employed in one or more species
of manufacture, but a separate fee must be paid, and two exactly similar
copies supplied, on account of each separate class, and all such registrations must be made at the same time.

 After the design has been registered, one of the two copies, drawings
(or tracings), or prints will be filed at the office, and the other returned to
the proprietor, with a certificate annexed, on which will appear the *mark
to be placed* on each article of manufacture to which the design shall have
been applied.

 If the design is for an article registered under Class 10, no mark is
required, but there must be printed on such article, at each end of the
original piece thereof, the name and address of the proprietor, and the
word "registered," together with the years for which the design is
registered.

 If the design is for sculpture, no mark is required to be placed thereon
after registration, but merely the word "registered" and the date of
registration.

 If the design is for provisional registration, no mark is required to be
placed thereon after registration, but merely the words "provisionally
registered" and the date of registration.

 Any person who shall put the registration mark on any design not
registered, or after the copyright thereof has expired, *is liable to forfeit for
every such offence* £5.

Transfers.

 In case of the transfer of a design, registered, whether provisionally or
completely, the certified copy thereof must be transmitted to the registrar,
together with the fee and forms of application (which may be procured
at the office), properly filled up and signed. The transfer will then be
registered and the certified copy returned.

Extension of Copyright.

 The copyright may be extended in certain cases in provisional registration, for a term not exceeding the additional term of six months, and in

---

 (*a*) Insert here the name and address of the proprietor, in the form in which it is to be
entered on the certificate.

complete registration for a term not exceeding the additional term of three years, as the Board of Trade may think fit.

In case of extension, the certified copy, together with the proper fee, should be delivered at the Designs Office for registration, *prior to the expiration of the existing copyright.*

Searches.

All designs of which the copyright has expired may be inspected at the Designs Office, on the payment of the proper fee; but *no design, the copyright of which is existing,* is in general open to inspection. Any person however, may, by application at the office, and on production of the registration mark, except in Class X., of any particular design, be furnished with a certificate of search, stating whether the copyright be in existence, and in respect to what particular article of manufacture it exists: also, the term of such copyright and the date of registration, and the name and address of the registered proprietor thereof.

Any party may also, on the production of a piece of the manufactured article with the pattern thereon, together with the registration mark, be informed whether such pattern, supposed to be registered, is really so or not.

As this mark is not applied to a provisionally registered design, *or to articles registered under Class X.,* certificates of search for such designs will be given on production of the design, or a copy or drawing thereof with the number and date of registration.

Persons bringing designs to be registered, on delivering them, must compare such designs together, count them, and see that the name and address and number of class is correctly written, and examine their certificates previous to leaving the office, to see that the name, &c., is correctly entered, as no error can afterwards be rectified.

An acknowledgment of its receipt will be delivered, on payment of the fees, to the person bringing a design, and *no certified copy of a design,* will be returned, except to the bearer of this acknowledgment, which must be produced on application at the office for the certified copy, and given in exchange for the same.

All communications for the registration of designs may be made either through the General Post Office, directed to "The Registrar of Designs, Designs Office, London, S.W.," or by any other mode of conveyance; and provided the carriage be paid, and the proper fees, or a Post Office Order for the amount, payable at the Post Office, Charing Cross, to J. H. Bowen, Esq., be inclosed, the designs will be duly registered, and the certified copies returned to the proprietors free of expense.

Postage-stamps, orders upon bankers or other persons, country and Scotch bank-notes, and light gold, cannot be received in payment of fees.

The Designs Office, No. 1, Whitehall, S.W., is open every day, between the hours of 10 in the morning and 4 in the afternoon, during which time inquiries and searches may be made. Designs and transfers are registered from 11 until 3.

Directions for registering designs for articles of utility may be procured at the office.

By Order of the Registrar.

ORNAMENTAL DESIGNS.

1. Registration of Ornamental Designs under these Acts may be either Complete or Provisional.

Conditions of Complete Registration.

2. Under the Designs Act, 1842, 5 & 6 Vict. c. 100, and the amending Acts, the author or proprietor of "any new and original design, whether such design be applicable to the ornamenting of any article of manufacture. or of any substance, artificial or natural, or partly artificial and partly natural, and that whether such design be so applicable for the pattern, or for the shape or configuration, or for the ornament thereof, or for any two or more of such purposes," may obtain a copyright or property in such design for various terms, according to the class to which the article of manufacture or substance belongs.

3. The design *should not have been published, either within the United Kingdom of Great Britain and Ireland, or elsewhere,* previous to its registration.

4. Articles of manufacture and substances to which designs may be applied are divided into 13 classes given in the following table. Opposite to each class are placed the respective terms for which copyright in each class may be obtained, and the registration fees payable on each design:—

CLASS.	ARTICLE.				COPYRIGHT.	Registration Fees.	
						£	s.
1.	Articles composed wholly or chiefly of metal				5 years	1	0
2.	Do.	do.	do.	wood	3 ,,	1	0
3.	Do.	do.	do.	glass	3 ,,	1	0
4.	Do. do. do. earthenware, bone, ivory, papier-mâché or other solid substances not comprised in Classes 1, 2, and 3				3 ,,	1	0
5.	Paper hangings				3 ,,	0	10
6.	Carpets, floor-cloths, or oil-cloths				3 ,,	1	0
7.	Shawls (patterns printed, &c., &c.)				9 months	0	1
	Do.	do.	extended term of 9	,,		0	6
	Do.	do.	for the whole term of 18	,,		0	7
8.	Shawls (not comprised in Class 7)				3 years	1	0
9.	Yarn, thread, or warp (printed, &c., &c.)				9 months	0	1
(a) 10.	Woven fabrics (patterns printed, &c., &c.), except those included in Class 11				3 years	0	1
11.	Woven fabrics, technically called furnitures (patterns printed, &c., &c.), the repeat of the pattern exceeding 12 inches by 8 inches				3 ,,	0	5
12.	Woven fabrics (not comprised in any preceding class)				12 months	0	5
	Do.	do.	extended term of	1 year		0	8
	Do.	do.	extended term of	2 years		0	16
	Do.	do.	whole term of	3 ,,		1	0
13.	Lace and any other articles not comprised in any preceding class				12 months	0	5

(a) See proviso 21 & 22 Vict. c. 70, s. 3.

Transfers, &c.

Transfer (see paragraph 24) . . . . ⎫
Certifying former registration (to proprietor of design) ⎬ Same as
Cancellation or substitution (according to decree or ⎭ Registration Fee.
    order in Chancery) . . . .

5. A design may be registered in respect of one or more of the above classes, according as it is intended to be employed in one or more species of manufacture, but a separate fee must be paid, and two exactly similar copies supplied, on account of each separate class, and all such registrations must be made at the same time.

6. Persons proposing to register a design must bring or send to the Designs Office—

(1.) Two exactly similar copies, drawings, tracings (not in pencil), photographs, or prints of the design, with the prescribed fees.

(2.) The name and address of the proprietor or proprietors, or the title of the firm under which he or they may be trading, together with his or their place of abode or place of carrying on business, distinctly written or printed.

(3.) The number of the class in respect of which registration is intended to be effected.

The two facsimile copies of the design to be furnished may consist of portions of the manufactured articles, when such can conveniently be sent, as in the case of paper hangings, calico prints, &c. Portions of carpets, however, will not be received. When drawings or tracings are furnished they must be "fixed." In the case of designs applied to articles which from their nature are incapable of being pasted into books, photographs or prints of such designs may be furnished.

7. Should paper hangings or furnitures exceed 42 inches in length, by 23 inches in breadth, drawings will be required, which must not exceed those dimensions.

8. Applications to register may be made in the following form (blank Forms may be obtained at the Office):—

Application to Register.

Form.   188 .

You are hereby requested to register the accompanying Design in Class , in the name of ((*a*) *A. B. of*   , *of*   ) or (*A. B. of*   , *and* *C. D. of*   , &c., *trading under the style or firm of B. D. and Co., of* *of*   , *of*   ,) who claim to be the proprietors thereof, and to return the same (*if sent by post*), directed to   , (*if brought by hand*) to the bearer of the official acknowledgment for the same.

                           (Signed)   B. D. & Co.,

To the Registrar of Designs,   by J. F.
    Designs Office, London.

9. The person bringing a design must take an acknowledgment for it, which will be delivered to him on payment of the prescribed fees. This acknowledgment must be produced on application for the certified copy, which will be returned in exchange for the same.

    (*a*) Insert here legibly the name & address of the proprietor, in the form in which it is to be entered on the certificate.

10. After complete registration, every article of manufacture published by the proprietor thereof, to which such design shall have been applied, must have thereon or attached thereto a particular mark, which will be exhibited on the certificate of registration.

11. If the design is for an article registered under Class 10, there must be printed on such article, at each end of the original piece thereof, the name and address of the proprietor, and the word " Registered," together with, the years for which the design is registered.

12. Any person who shall put the registration mark on any design not registered, or after the copyright thereof has expired, is liable to forfeit for every such offence 5*l.* See " Designs Act, 1842," section 11, also the " Merchandise Marks Act, 1862," section 7.

13. Persons bringing designs to be registered must, on delivering them, compare such designs together, count them and see that the name and address and number of class are correctly given, and examine their certificates previous to leaving the office, to see that the name and other particulars are correctly entered.

14. The above conditions being observed, the right of the proprietor is protected from piracy by a penalty of from 5*l.* to 30*l.* for each offence, each illegal publication or sale of a design constituting a separate offence. This penalty may be recovered by the aggrieved party either by action in the superior or county courts, or by a summary proceeding before two magistrates. See Designs Act, 1842, section 8.

15. If a design be executed by the author on behalf of another person, for a valuable consideration, the latter is entitled to be registered as the proprietor thereof; and every person purchasing either the exclusive or partial right to use the design is in the same way equally entitled to be registered; and for the purpose of facilitating the transfer thereof a short form (copies of which may be procured at the Designs Office) is given in the Act.

Provisional Registration.

16. The author or proprietor of any original design for ornamenting any article of manufacture or substance may obtain, under the Designs Act, 1850, 13 & 14 Vict. c. 104, a Provisional Registration, giving a copyright of one year. During such term the proprietor of the design may sell the right to apply the same to an article of manufacture, but must not, under the penalty of nullifying the copyright, sell any article with the design applied thereto until after complete registration, which must be effected prior to the expiration of the provisional registration. No mark is placed upon a design provisionally registered, but merely the words " Provisionally Registered " and the date of registration.

17. *The following Fees are payable for Provisional Registration.*

Registration irrespective of classes, one year 1*s.* each Design.

Transfer (see paragraph 24)	5*s.*	„
Certifying former registration (to proprietor of Design) - - -	1*s.*	
Cancellation or substitution (according to Decree, or Order in Chancery)	5*s.*	„

18. Applications should be made in the same manner as for complete registration, but omitting the reference to classes, and substituting the word " Provisionally " in its place (see paragraph 8).

3 B

19. If the proprietor of any design so provisionally registered wishes to obtain complete registration for such design, he must, prior to the expiration of provisional registration, comply with the conditions for complete registration already set out in paragraphs 1–13.

Sculpture.

20. The proprietor of any sculpture, model, copy, or cast within the protection of the Sculpture Copyright Acts may obtain registration, under the Designs Act of 1850, for the term, or unexpired part of the term, during which copyright in such sculptures, models, copies, or casts may or shall exist under the Sculpture Copyright Acts.

21. No *mark* is required to be placed on sculpture, &c., after registration, but merely the word " Registered " and the date of registration. The Act 54 Geo. III. c. 56, is still in force, and requires the name of the proprietor and date of publication to be placed upon the design.

22. The *following Fees are payable in regard to Designs for Sculpture:*

	£	s.
Each design -	5	0
Transfer (see paragraph 24) -	- 1	0
Certifying former registration (to proprietor of design)	1	0
Cancellation or substitution (according to Decree or Order in Chancery) -	- 1	0

23. Applications should be made in the same manner as for complete registration of ornamental designs, but omitting the reference to classes, and substituting the words " for Sculpture " in its place (see paragraph 8).

Transfers of Designs.

24. In the case of the transfer of a design (whether registered provisionally or completely. or for sculpture), the certified copy thereof must be transmitted to the Registrar, together with the fee and forms of application (which may be procured at the office), properly filled up and signed. The transfer will then be registered and the certified copy returned.

Searches.

25. All designs of which the copyright has *expired* may be inspected at the Designs Office, on the payment of the prescribed fee. Any person may, by application at the office, and on production of the registration mark of any design (except in Class X.), be furnished with a certificate of search, stating in respect to what particular article of manufacture the copyright exists, the term of such copyright, the date of registration, and the name and address of the registered proprietor thereof.

26. Any person may also, on the production of a piece of the manufactured article, with the pattern thereon, together with the registration mark, be informed whether such pattern, supposed to be registered, is really so registered or not.

27. As the Registration mark is not applied to a provisionally registered design, or to articles registered under Class X., certificates of search for such designs will be given on production of the design, or a copy or drawing thereof, with the number and date of registration.

28. *Inspections, &c., of Provisional and Complete Registrations and Sculpture.*

	s.
Search -	2
Inspection of all the designs of which the copyright has expired, each quarter or part of quarter of an hour, each class - - -	1
Taking copies of expired designs, each hour or part of an hour, each copy -	1
Taking copies of unexpired designs (according to Judge's order), for each hour or part of an hour, each copy - -	2

29. All communications for the registration of designs may be made either through the General Post Office, directed to "The Registrar of Designs, Designs Office, London, W.C.," or by any other mode of conveyance ; and provided the carriage be paid, and the proper fees, or a Post Office Order for the amount, payable at the Post Office, Chancery Lane, W.C., to H. Reader Lack, Esq., be enclosed, the designs will be duly registered, and the certified copies returned to the proprietors free of expense.

30. *Postage stamps, orders upon bankers or other persons, country and Scotch bank notes, and light gold, cannot be received in payment of fees.*

31. The Designs Office, No. 25, Southampton Buildings, Chancery Lane, W.C., is open every day between the hours of 10 in the morning and 4 in the afternoon, during which time inquiries and searches may be made. Designs and transfers are registered from 11 until 3.

32. Directions for registering designs for articles of utility may be procured at the Office.

By order,

1st May, 1879.　　　　　　　　H. READER LACK,
　　　　　　　　　　　　　　　　Registrar.

USEFUL DESIGNS.

COPYRIGHT OF DESIGNS FOR ARTICLES OF UTILITY.

1. Under the Designs Act, 1843, 6 & 7 Vict. c. 65, the author or proprietor of any new or original design for the shape or configuration either of the whole or of any part of any article of manufacture, such shape or configuration having reference to some purpose of utility, may by registration obtain a copyright for such design, whether the article of manufacture be made in metal or any other substance.

2. Such registration may be either provisional or complete.

3. To obtain this protection it is necessary—

(a.) That the design should not have been published, either within the United Kingdom of Great Britain and Ireland or elsewhere, previous to its registration.

(b.) That after registration, or provisional registration, every article of manufacture made according to such design, or to which such design is applied, should have upon it the word "Registered," or the words "Provisionally Registered," with the date of registration.

3 B 2

4. By Provisional Registration (13 & 14 Vict. c. 104), a copyright is obtained for one year.

5. During such term the proprietor of the design may sell the right to apply the same to an article of manufacture, but must not, under the penalty of nullifying the copyright, sell any article with the design applied thereto until after complete registration.

6. Complete registration under the Designs Act, 1843, 6 & 7 Vict. c. 65, gives a copyright of three years.

7. Provisional registration is not such a publication of a design as will prevent its being further protected by complete registration, 13 & 14 Vict. c. 104. s. 3 ; and in order to obtain such further registration of a design already provisionally registered, application should be made *during the continuance of the provisional registration.*

8. In case of piracy of a design so registered, the same remedies are given, and the same penalties imposed (from 5*l*. to 30*l*. for each offence), as in the case of ornamental designs registered under the Designs Act, 1842 (5 & 6 Vict. c. 100), and all the provisions contained in the latter Act relating to the transfer of ornamental designs, in case of purchase or devolution of a copyright, are made applicable to those useful designs registered under the Designs Acts, 1843 and 1850.

9. In addition to this, a penalty of not more than 5*l*. nor less than 1*l*. is imposed upon all persons marking, selling, or advertising for sale any article as "Registered," unless the design for such article has been registered under one of the above mentioned Acts.

DIRECTIONS FOR REGISTERING.

10. Persons proposing to register a design for purposes of utility, must bring or send to the Designs Office two exactly similar drawings, photographs, or prints thereof, not in pencil, made on a proper geometric scale, marked with letters, figures, or colours, to be referred to as hereinafter mentioned, together with the following particulars, in the order set out in the annexed form :—

(*a.*) The title of the design.

(*b.*) The name and address of the proprietor or proprietors, or the title of the firm under which he or they may be trading, together with their place of abode or place of carrying on business, distinctly written or printed.

(*e.*) A statement in the following form, viz. : " The purpose of utility to which the shape or configuration of (the new parts of) this design has reference is," &c., &c.

(*d.*) A description to render the representation of the design intelligible, distinguishing its several parts by reference to letters, figures, or colours.

NOTE.—No description of the parts of the drawings which are old will be admitted, except such as may be absolutely necessary to render the purpose of utility of the shape of the new parts intelligible.

(*e.*) A short and distinct statement as regards the shape or configuration thereof, which must be in the following form, viz. :—(if the whole design is new state)—" The whole of this design is new in so far as regards the shape or configuration thereof." (If there are any old parts, state)—" Protection is sought for the shape or configuration of the parts marked (A., B., C., &c.) or coloured (blue, green, &c.), which are new and original; the remainder is old."

NOTE.—The above particulars must be given in the aforesaid order under their several heads, and in distinct and separate paragraphs, which must be strictly confined to what is here required to be contained in each.

Specimen Form, 24 inches by 15 inches.

(Title of the design.)

....

(Name of the proprietor.)

....

(Address of the proprietor.)

....

(The drawing to be inserted here.)

(Statement of utility.)

The purpose of utility to which the shape or configuration of (the new parts of) this design has reference is ....

(Description.)

(If the whole design is new, state—)

The whole of this design is new in so far as regards the shape or configuration thereof.

(If there are any old parts, state—)

Protection is sought for the shape or configuration of the parts marked A., B., C., &c., or coloured (blue, green, &c.), which are new and original. The remainder is old.

6 in.   6 in.

4 in.   4 in.

24 inches.

15 inches.

11. Each drawing or print, together with the whole of the above particulars, must be drawn, written, or printed on one side of a sheet of paper or parchment, not exceeding in size 24 inches by 15 inches ; and on one of the said sheets, on the same side on which are the said drawings and particulars, there must be left two blank spaces, each of the size of 6 inches by 4 inches, for the certificates of registration.

Notice.

12. Parties are strongly recommended to read the Designs Acts, 1843 and 1850, 6 & 7 Vict. c. 65, and 13 & 14 Vict. c. 104, before determining to register their designs, in order that they may be satisfied as to the nature, extent, and comprehensiveness of the protection afforded ; and further, that their designs come within the meaning and scope of the Acts, of which facts the registration will not constitute any guarantee.

13. As these Acts give protection only to the shape or configuration of articles of utility (and not to any mechanical action, principle, contrivance, application, or adaptation, or to the material of which the article may be composed), no design will be registered, the description of, or statement respecting which, shall contain any wording suggestive of the registration being for any such mechanical action, principle, contrivance, application or adaptation, or for the material of which the article may be composed.

14. With this exception, and those mentioned in the Designs Act, 1843, s. 9, all designs, the drawings and descriptions of which are properly prepared and made out, will, on payment of the proper fee, be registered without reference to the nature or extent of the copyright sought to be thereby acquired, as proprietors of designs must use their own discretion in judging whether or not the design proposed for registration be for the shape or configuration of an article of utility coming within the meaning and scope of the Acts above mentioned.

15. After the design has been registered, one of the drawings will be filed at the Office, and the other returned to the proprietor, duly stamped and certified.

16. An acknowledgment of its receipt will be delivered, on payment of the fees, to the person bringing a design, and no certified copy of a design will be returned except to the bearer of this acknowledgment which must be produced on application at the office for the certified copy, and given in exchange for the same.

17. Persons bringing designs to be registered should, on delivering their designs and on examining their certificates previous to leaving the office, see that the titles, names, &c., are correct.

Transfers.

18. In case of the transfer of a completely registered design, a copy thereof (or the certified copy, provided there is space sufficient thereon for the certificate) made on one sheet of paper, with a blank space left for the certificate, must be transmitted to the registrar, together with the forms of application (which may be procured at the office), properly filled up and signed ; the transfer will then be registered, and the certified copy returned.

19. For the transfer of a design provisionally registered a new copy will not be required, but the certified copy must be transmitted to the Registrar with the above-mentioned forms.

Searches.

20. An index of the titles and names of the proprietors of all the registered designs for articles of utility is kept at the Designs Office, and may be inspected by any person, and extracts made from it.

21. Designs, the copyright of which is expired, may be inspected and copied at the office.

22. Designs, the copyright of which is unexpired, may also be inspected but not copied, except according to a Judge's order.

---

23. TABLES OF FEES.

Provisional Registration (Optional).

	Fee. s.
Registering design	10
Certifying former registration (to proprietor of design) . .	5
Registering and certifying transfer	10
Cancellation or substitution (*according to Decree or Order in Chancery*)	5

Complete Registration.

	Stamp. £	Fee. £	Total. £
Registering design	5	5	10
Certifying former Registration (*to proprietor of designs*)	5	1	6
Registering and certifying transfer. . . .	5	1	6
Cancellation or substitution (*according to Decree or Order in Chancery*)	0	1	1

Inspections, &c., of Provisional and Complete Registrations.

			Fee. s.
Inspecting register, index of titles and names, for each quarter or part of quarter of an hour.			1
Inspecting designs, unexpired copyright, each design . . . c.py.	ditto	ditto ditto	2
Inspecting designs, expired copyright, each volume	ditto	ditto ditto	1
Inspecting the register of Inventions, under the " Protection of Inventions Act, 1851.".	ditto	ditto ditto	1
Taking copies of designs, unexpired copyright (*according to Judge's order*), for each hour or part of an hour, each copy			2
Taking copies of designs, expired copyright, each copy	ditto	ditto ditto	1

24. All communications for the registration of designs, either for ornamental or useful purposes, may be made either through the General Post Office, directed to "The Registrar of Designs, Designs Office, London, W.C.," or by any other mode of conveyance ; and provided the carriage be paid, and the proper fees, or a Post Office Order for the amount, payable at the Post Office, Chancery Lane, W.C., to H. Reader Lack, Esq., be enclosed, the designs will be duly registered, and the certified copies returned to the proprietor free of expense.

25. *Postage stamps, orders upon bankers or other persons, Scotch and country bank notes, and light gold, cannot be received in payment of fees.*

26. The Designs Office, No. 25, Southampton Buildings, Chancery Lane, W.C., is open every day, between the hours of 10 in the morning and 4 in the afternoon, during which time inquiries and searches may be made. Designs and transfers are registered from 11 until 3.

27. Directions for registering ornamental designs may also be procured at the office.

1st. May, 1879.　　　　　　　　By order,

　　　　　　　　　　　　　　　H. READER LACK,
　　　　　　　　　　　　　　　　　Registrar.

APPENDIX (E).

FORMS USED AT STATIONERS' HALL.

A.

(FORM OF REQUIRING ENTRY OF PROPRIETORSHIP.)

Fee 5s.

To the Registering Officer appointed by the Stationers' Company,

I, of , do hereby certify, That I am the proprietor of the copyright of a book, intitled ; and I hereby require you to make entry in the Register Book of the Stationers' Company of my proprietorship of such copyright, according to the particulars under-written.

(*Every particular given must be clearly written.*)

Title of Book.	Name of Publisher, and Place of Publication.	Name and Place of Abode of the Proprietor of the Copyright.	Date of First Publication.

Dated this day of , 188 .

Witness (Signed)

N.B.—Office Hours from Ten to Four.

B.

(FORM OF CONCURRENCE OF THE PARTY ASSIGNING IN ANY BOOK PREVIOUSLY REGISTERED.)

Fee 5s.

To the Registering Officer appointed by the Stationers' Company.

I, of , being the assigner of the copyright of the

book hereunder described, do hereby require you to make entry of the assignment of the copyright therein.

Title of Book.	Assigner of the Copyright.	Assignee of Copyright. (a)
₊ The date of the previous registration or assignment must be given here		(a) Qy. abode. See Sec. 13.

[Form for *all* assignment of books (including music, dramatic compositions) under English Act, and for assignment of every description of copyright under International Acts.]

Dated this   day of   , 188 .

(Signed)

N.B.—Office Hours from Ten to Four.

C.

(FORM OF REQUIRING ENTRY OF PROPRIETORSHIP OF DRAMATIC PIECE OR MUSICAL COMPOSITION.)

Fee 5*s*.

To the Registering Officer appointed by the Stationers' Company.

I,   of   , do hereby certify, That I am the proprietor of the *Liberty of Representation or Performance of a Dramatic Piece or Musical Composition*, intituled   ; and I hereby require you to make entry in the Register Book of the |Stationers' Company of my proprietorship of such *Liberty of Representation or Performance*, according to the particulars underwritten.

(*Every particular given must be clearly written.*)

Title of Dramatic Piece or Musical Composition.	Name and Place of Abode of the Author or Composer.	Name and Place of Abode of the Proprietor of the Liberty of Representation or Performance.	Time and Place of First Representation or Performance.

Dated this   day of   , 188 .

Witness   (Signed)

N.B.—Office Hours from Ten to Four.

D.

(FORM OF CONCURRENCE OF THE PARTY ASSIGNING ANY PIECE OR
COMPOSITION PREVIOUSLY REGISTERED.)

Fee 5s.

To the Registering Officer appointed by the Stationers' Company.

I,   of   , being the assigner of the *Liberty of Representation
or Performance of a Dramatic Piece or Musical Composition* hereunder
described, do hereby require you to make entry of the assignment of such
Liberty of Representation or Performance.

Title of Dramatic Piece or Musical Composition.	Assigner of the Liberty of Representation or Performance.	Assignee of the Liberty of Representation or Performance.
*** The date of the previous registration or assignment must be given here.		

Parties must attend in Person or by Agent. Dated this   day of   188 .
No correspondence entered into.   Witness   (Signed)

N.B.—*Office Hours from Ten to Four.*

E.

(MEMORANDUM FOR REGISTRATION UNDER COPYRIGHT (WORKS OF
ART) ACT.)

Fee 1s.

To the Registering Officer appointed by the Stationers' Company.

I,   of   , do hereby certify, That I am entitled to the copyright in the undermentioned work; and I hereby require a Memorandum
of such copyright [*or,* the assignment of such copyright] to be entered in
the Register of Proprietors of Copyright in Paintings, Drawings, and
Photographs, kept at Stationers' Hall, according to the particulars under-
written.

(*Every particular given must be clearly written.*)

Description of Work.	Date of Agreement or Assignment.	Names of Parties to Agreement.	Name and Place of abode of Proprietor of Copyright	Name and Place of Abode of Author of Work.

Dated this   day of   , 188 .

(Signed)

N.B.—*Office Hours from Ten to Four.*

F.

(LA FORME POUR REQUÉRIR L'ENREGISTREMENT DE PROPRIÉTÉ À
STATIONERS' HALL, LONDON.)

A Monsieur le Registraire, nommé par la Corporation des Libraires.

Moi,   de   je certifie par ceci, que je suis le Propriétaire du
Droit d'Auteur d'un Livre, intitulé   et je vous requiers par ceci d'inscrire,
sur le Livre d'Enregistrement de la Corporation des Libraires, ma Propriété
de tel Droit d'Auteur, selon les détails ci-dessous écrits.

Le Titre du Livre.	Le Nom et la Demeure d'Auteur ou du Compositeur.	Le Nom et la Demeure du Propriétaire du Droit d'Auteur.	L'Epoque et le Lieu de la première Publication.

Daté ce   jour de   188 .
Témoin,   (Signé)

N.B.—Il faut que tous les détails soient écrits très clairement.

Original entry.
Form under International Copyright Act.

This Form is at present used for every work, whether book, print, piece
of sculpture; whether French, German, &c, &c.

APPENDIX (F).

———◆———

No. 1.—Agreement for Sale of Copyright in a Work.

MEMORANDUM OF AGREEMENT made the   day of   188 . Between A. B., of   , of the one part, and C. D., and E. F. (hereinafter called D. & F.), publishers, of the other part.

1. The said A. B. agrees to write and edit a work to be entitled   , to prepare the same for the press, together with a full and comprehensive Index and Table of Cases and Contents to the same, by the   day of   , to correct the proof-sheets, and to sell and assign all his copyright and interest in the said work to the said D. & F., their executors, administrators, and assigns, for the sum of money hereinafter mentioned.

2. The said D. & F., for themselves, their executors, administrators, and assigns, agree to print and publish and bear all the charges of printing and publishing the said work, and to pay to the said A. B., for his copyright and interest in the said work the sum of   pounds, on the day of publication of the said work,

3. The said A. B. to have   copies of the said work free of charge. In witness whereof the said parties have hereunto set their hands the day and year first above written.

———

No. 2.—Half-profit Agreement between Author and Publisher.

MEMORANDUM OF AGREEMENT made the   day of   188 . Between A. B., of   , of the one part, and C. D., of   , publisher, of the other part.

1. It is agreed that the said C. D. shall, at his own expense and risk, print and publish, a work entitled   , and, after deducting from the produce of the sale thereof the charges for printing, paper, advertisements, embellishments (if any), and other incidental expenses, including the allowance of   per cent. on the gross amount of the sale for commission and risk of bad debts, the profits remaining of every edition that shall be printed of the work shall be divided into two equal parts, one moiety to be paid to the said A. B., and the other moiety to be retained by the said C.D.

2. The books sold shall be accounted for at the trade sale price, reckoning 25 copies as 24, unless it be thought advisable to dispose of any copies, or of the remainder, at a lower price, which shall be left to the judgment and discretion of the said C. D.

3. It is understood between the aforesaid parties, that ⁣ copies of the said book are to be presented to the said A. B. free of charge. (a)　*In witness, &c.*

(a) See a similar agreement: *Reade* v. *Bentley* (3 K. & J. 271).

No. 3.—*Another Form of Agreement.*

MEMORANDUM OF AGREEMENT made the　　day of　　188 . Between A. B., of　　　, the author of　　　, of the one part, and C. D. & E. F. (hereinafter called D. & F.) publishers, of the other part.

1. The said A. B. shall fully prepare the whole of the said book for the press, on or before the　　day of　, and shall correct the proof-sheets, and superintend the printing thereof.

2. The said D. & F. shall direct the mode of printing the said book, and shall bear and pay all the charges thereof, and of publishing the same (except as hereinafter mentioned), and shall take all the risk of the publication on themselves.

3. The said E. & F. shall, out of the produce of the sale of the said book, in the first instance, be refunded all the cost and expenses which they shall have incurred respecting the said book, after which the profits shall be equally divided between the said A. B. and D. & F.

4. The accounts shall be made up at the end of every year, and the profits, if any, be then divided.

5. The said D. & F. shall account for all the copies which they shall sell of the said book at the wholesale bookseller's price, deducting therefrom a commission of　, they taking the risk of the credit which they shall give on the same.

6. The alterations and corrections in the proof-sheets, and revises, which shall exceed the charge of　　per sheet, shall be borne and paid by the said A. B., and shall be deducted out of his share of the profits.

7. In case all the copies of the said book shall have been sold off, and a second or any subsequent edition of the said book be required by the public, the said A. B. shall make all necessary alterations and additions thereto, and the said D. & F. shall print and publish the said second and every subsequent edition of the said book on the above conditions.

8. In case all the copies of any edition of the said work shall not be sold off within　　years after the time of publication, the said D. & F. shall be at full liberty to dispose of the remaining copies, so unsold, either by public auction or private contract, or in such manner as they may deem most advisable, so that the account may be finally settled and closed. (a)　*In witness, &c.*

(a) See *Stevens* v. *Benning* (6 D. M. & G. 223).

No. 4.— Licence to print one Edition of a Work.

MEMORANDUM OF AGREEMENT made the   day of   188 . Between A. B., of   , of the one part, and C. D , of   , of the other part.

1. Whereas the said A. B. has in preparation a work to be called   . Now THIS AGREEMENT WITNESSETH: that the said A. B. for the consideration hereinafter expressed, doth hereby authorize the said C. D. to print, publish, and sell an edition of   copies of the said work, the said A. B. hereby reserving to himself the general copyright in the said work. And the said A. B., in consideration of the payments hereinafter agreed to be made by the said C. D., doth hereby agree with the said C. D. that he will furnish to the printer, to be employed by him, a fair copy of the said work, and will superintend the printing, and correct the proofs thereof in the usual manner, and that he will register his title under the "Literary Copyright Act, 1842," and will not authorize any person to print, publish, or sell, and will not himself print, publish, or sell, any other copies until the whole of the said   copies have been disposed of by the said C. D., provided the said   copies are sold within   years from the date hereof. *And* the said C. D., in consideration of the aforesaid authority and agreement, doth hereby agree with the said A. B. that he will pay him, the said A. B. the sum of   for each and every copy of the said   copies, payable half-yearly, as fast as the said copies shall be sold, or otherwise disposed of, he rendering to the said A. B. an account of sales of the said work, at the expiration of every six months from the day of the first publication, until the whole shall be sold, and that he will also give to the said A. B.   copies of the said work, bound, and free of charge, as soon as conveniently may be done, after the manuscript copy has been furnished by the said A. B. *And* the said C. D., in consideration also of the aforesaid authority and agreement, doth further agree with the said A. B. that he will not print, publish, or sell, any more than the said   copies, until authorized by the said A. B., or his legal representatives, it being clearly understood that the licence herein contained extends only to one edition of the number above specified. *In witness, &c.*

No. 5.— Limited Assignment by an Author of a new Edition of his Work.

A. B., of   , having prepared a new edition of   , and C. D., of   , being desirous of purchasing the same, it is agreed that   copies of the work shall be printed in type and page corresponding with   , at the sole cost of the said C. D., and the said C. D. shall pay to the said A. B. for the said   edition, the sum of   . The work to be divided into   volumes, and to be sold to the public for   in boards ; but should the said work exceed   sheets, or   pages, a proportionate increase is to be made in the charge to the public, and a proportionate addition made to the consideration to be paid by C. D. to A. B.   copies in boards to be delivered to the said A. B. free from all charge or expense. (*a*)

(*a*) See *Sweet* v. *Cater* (11 Sim. 572).

No. 6.—Agreement to enlarge a second Edition of a Book, and correct Proof of same.

THIS AGREEMENT, made the day of 188 . Between A. B., of , of the one part, and C. D., of , of the other part.

Witnesseth, that the said A. B., in consideration of the sum of , agrees to examine, correct, and enlarge the work known as , to furnish additional manuscript matter for the second edition of the work, and to enlarge the index, and make it full and complete. IT IS AGREED that the new edition of the work shall be of the same sized page as the present work, and contain an equal amount of matter on each page, and that the additional matter furnished shall enlarge the work not less than pages, and shall be furnished to the said C. D. at not less than pages per day, commencing on the instant. *And* the said A. B. is to examine and to correct the proof-sheets so soon as they shall be furnished, and to complete the index within a reasonable time after the whole signatures of the text shall be ready for him for that purpose. *And* the said C. D. on his part agrees to print the said work as the matter shall be supplied, to provide the said A. B. with a copy of the work, by signatures, as each signature shall be worked off, for the purpose of arranging the index; to furnish the said A. B. bound copies of the work, as soon as they can be conveniently furnished, and to pay the said A. B. the sum of on the day the last proof-sheet is corrected for the press. *In witness, &c.*

No. 7.—Agreement between an Author and Publisher for the sale of a Work where a Sum is paid for the Copyright; with variation where the Profits are divided. (a)

THIS AGREEMENT made the day of 188 . Between A. B., [*author*] of , of the one part, and C. D., [*publisher*] of , of the other part.

Whereas the said A. B. has written and composed a certain work entitled , and the same is now ready for the press, and the said C. D. has contracted for the purchase of the copyright of the said work at or for the price or sum of £ , to be paid in the manner hereinafter mentioned. NOW THESE PRESENTS WITNESS that the said A. B. agrees to sell, and the said C. D. agrees to purchase *all that* the said work and premises and the copyright thereof. AND IT IS HEREBY AGREED that the said work shall consist of sheets [*size*]. *And* that the said A. B. shall correct the said sheets of the said work through the press, and compose a good and sufficient index thereto, and in every respect prepare the same for publication, and complete the same within calendar months from the date hereof. *And* shall and will, within days after the publication thereof, or at any time or times thereafter, if so required by the said C. D. assign and

(a) Where the profits are to be divided between the author and publishers, leave out the portions of the precedent within brackets and add: " And it is hereby agreed that after paying and defraying all such expenses as aforesaid, the net proceeds and profits as well of the [first as of every other succeeding edition shall be equally divided between the said A. B. and C. D."

make over the said work and all his right, title and interest in the copy-right thereof unto the said C. D., his executors, administrators, or assigns in such manner and form as may be by him or them reasonably required. [*And* that the said C. D. shall pay the said sum of £   in the manner hereinafter mentioned (that is to say) the sum of £   on the day of the publication of the said work, and the sum of £   (the residue thereof) within three months after the publication thereof]. *And* shall and will cause the said work to be printed on good paper and pay and defray all the costs, expenses of printing and advertising the said work, and all other expenses attending its publication. *And* shall and will allow   copies of the said work to the said A. B. *And* shall and will exert himself to the utmost in procuring, and advancing the sale of the said work. [AND IT IS HEREBY AGREED that in case a second, third, or any other succeeding edition of the said work shall at any time be called for, the said A. B. agrees to make all necessary additions, alterations, and corrections to such edition and to make the same as complete as possible. *And* shall from time to time within   days after the publication thereof, or at any time or times thereafter, if so required by the said C. D. assign and make over the said second, third, or other succeeding edition of the said work, and all his right title and interest in the copyright thereof unto the said C. D., his executors, administrators, or assigns in such manner and as may be by him or them reasonably required. *And* the said C. D., shall pay the sum of £   to the said A. B. on the day of the publication of such second, third, and every subsequent edition, and shall and will pay and sustain all the costs and charges of such second, third, and every subsequent edition in the same manner as is hereinbefore agreed upon respecting the first edition. AND IT IS HEREBY AGREED that in case the said A. B. should refuse to edit such second, third, or subsequent edition or neglect so to edit the same after six months' notice to him for that purpose given by the said C. D. it shall be lawful for the said C. D. to engage with any other person or persons to edit the same]. *In witness, &c.* .

No. 8.—Agreement between an Author and Publisher for the sale of a Work by Commission.

THIS AGREEMENT made the   day of   188 . Between A. B. [*author*] of   , of the one part, and C. D. [*publisher*] of   , of the other part.

Whereas the said A. B. is the author and proprietor of a certain work entitled   ; *and Whereas* there is now a demand for a new edition of such work being the   edition. NOW THESE PRESENTS WITNESS that the said A. B. doth hereby agree with the said C. D. that he the said C. D. shall be the sole publisher of the said edition of the said work at a commission of   pounds per cent. *And* that he the said A. B. will within   days next hereafter deliver to such printer as the said C. D. shall name a portion of the copy of the said work and continue to supply him with copy thereof until the whole is completed ; *And* that the said C. D. shall indemnify the said A. B. from all losses to be incurred as well in the printing and publishing of the said work as after its publication or by reason of the said work not selling. AND IT IS HEREBY AGREED that it

3 C

shall be lawful for the said C. D. out of the profits and proceeds of the
said work in the first place to deduct and repay himself the expenses of
the paper, printing, advertisements, warehouse-room, insurance money, and
commission after the rate aforesaid. *And* that he the said C. D. will
render a full and faithful account to the said A. B. on the   day of
          and on the   day of   in every year of the sale and proceeds
of the said edition. *In witness, &c.*

---

*No. 9.—Agreement for the editing of a Work between the Publisher and
Editor, with variations where for translating a Work.* (a)

THIS AGREEMENT made the   day of   188 , Between A. B.,
of [*publisher*] &c., of the one part, and C. D. [*editor*] of &c., of
the other part.

Whereas the said A. B. some time since published a certain
work written and composed by C. D., and entitled   . *And whereas*
there is a demand for a new edition of the said work. And *whereas*
the said A. B. has agreed with the said C. D. to edit and make ready
for publication as hereinafter is mentioned, a new edition (being the
,) of the said work [to be contained in   volumes] for the sum of
pounds. NOW THEREFORE THESE PRESENTS WITNESS that the said C. D.,
in consideration of the sum of £   , to be paid to him by the said A. B. in
manner hereinafter mentioned, agrees with the said A. B. that he will
edit and prepare for publication the   edition of the said work. *And*
will also examine and correct the proof sheets of the said work in its
progress through the press. *And* that he will complete and render fit for
publication the [first volume of the] said work by the   day of
next [the second volume by the   day of   &c. (*according to the
number of volumes*.)] *And* further that the said C. D. will render the said
          edition of the said work as complete as possible, and will make all
necessary and proper additions, and corrections, and add such observations
and information to the said work as shall occur to him, and exert himself
to the utmost to render the said work valuable and popular. *And* the
said A. B. agrees to pay unto the said C. D. for editing the said
volumes the said sum of £   in the proportions and at the times hereinafter mentioned (that is to say) the sum of £   being one   part
thereof on the first of the said volumes being ready for publication, and
the like sum of £   on each of them the said second and third of the
said three volumes (*or according to the number of volumes*) being ready for
publication. *In witness, &c.*

(a) Where the agreement is for translating a work, leave out the recitals of the precedent
above and insert: "Whereas a certain work has lately been published in Germany in
the German language entitled   . And *whereas* the said A. B. is desirous that a
translation of the said work should be made and perfected by the said C. D. NOW THESE
PRESENTS WITNESS that in consideration of the payment of the sum hereinafter mentioned to
him the said C. D., he the said C. D. agrees that he will well and faithfully translate the
said work into English, and will complete the same on or before the   day of   ," &c.

No. 10.—Agreement between a Publisher and Engraver for the engraving of a Painting.

THIS AGREEMENT made the   day of   188 . Between A. B. [*publisher*] of &c., of the one part, and C. D. [*engraver*] of &c., of the other part.

Whereas the said A. B. is desirous of publishing a line [*or* mezzotinto] engraving of a certain painting called   , and painted by Mr.   . Now THEREFORE THESE PRESENTS WITNESS that in consideration of the sum of £ to be paid in the manner hereinafter mentioned, he the said C. D. agrees that he will at his own cost and charges engrave and execute a perfect and correct line [*or* mezzotinto] engraving on copper [*or* steel] plate of the said painting called . *And* the said engraving shall be   inches long and   inches broad, and that the copper [*or* steel] on which the same shall be engraved shall be   inches long, and   inches broad. *And* that the said C. D. will complete the same on or before the   day of   . *And* shall at his own expense take off and print   complete impressions from the said plate, on good and proper paper and deliver them to the said A. B. *And* the said A. B. agrees to pay the said sum of £   in manner hereinafter mentioned (that is to say) the sum of £   on the   day of   , and the sum of £   (the residue thereof) on the   day of   , if the said work shall be completed at such last mentioned time. *And* it is hereby agreed that the said C. D. shall be allowed to retain   complete impressions of the said engraving for the use of himself and friends, but it shall not be lawful for the said C. D. to sell or dispose of the same. *In witness, &c.*

No. 11.—Agreement between an Artist and a Purchaser respecting a Painting, and the Copyright therein, under the 25 & 26 Vict. c. 68. The purchase money being payable by Instalments.

ARTICLES OF AGREEMENT made the   day of   188 . Between A. B. [*artist*] of &c., of the one part, and C. D. [*purchaser*] of &c., of the other part.

Whereas the said A. B. is the artist of and is now engaged in finishing an original drawing or painting called or intended to be called or known as   . AND WHEREAS the said C. D. hath contracted and agreed with the said A. B. for the absolute purchase of the said drawing or painting, and the copyright thereof, or the sole and exclusive right of copying, engraving, reproducing and multiplying such drawing or painting and the design thereof by any means and of any size whatsoever at the price or sum of £   to be paid by the several instalments and in manner hereinafter appearing. Now THESE PRESENTS WITNESS, and it is hereby agreed and declared by and between the parties hereto as follows:—

1. The said A. B. shall forthwith proceed to complete and finish the said drawing or painting called or intended to be called or known as   to the satisfaction in all respects of the said C. D. and deliver the same to him, his executors, administrators, or assigns, or his or their order, completely finished and perfected on or before the   day of   next.

2. The copyright in the said drawing or painting and the sole and exclusive

3 C 2

right of copying, engraving, reproducing and multiplying such drawing, or painting, and the design thereof by any means, and of any size whatsoever, shall upon the execution of these presents become and be vested in the said C. D., his executors, administrators, and assigns, and should the said C.D., his executors, administrators, or assigns at any time hereafter during the existence of the said copyright require a more formal assignment, the said A. B. shall duly assign unto the said C. D. his executors, administrators, and assigns the said copyright, and do or cause to be done all such acts and assurances as may be by him or them deemed necessary or advisable for vesting the said copyright in the said C. D., his executors, administrators and assigns.

3. The said C. D. shall and will on the execution hereof pay or cause to be paid unto the said A. B. the sum of £   , part of the said purchase money, or sum of £   , and shall and will pay or cause to be paid unto the said A. B. his executors, administrators, or assigns the sum of £ by equal payments or instalments of £   to be paid by equal yearly payments on the   day of   in each year until the whole of the said purchase moneys shall be satisfied, and this without any deduction or abatement on any account whatsoever, the first of such annual instalments to be made on the   day of   . *And* shall and will also pay or cause to be paid unto the said A. B., his executors, administrators, or assigns, interest on the said sum of £   or the balance of the said purchase money for the time being remaining unpaid at the rate of £   per centum per annum to be computed from the   day of   next.

4. Any formal assignment which may be required by the said C. D. under the provisions hereinbefore contained shall contain covenants on the part of the said A. B., his heir, executors, and administrators, that he the said A. B. hath good right to assign and assure the said copyright and premises unto the said C. D., his executors, administrators, and assigns free from any charge or incumbrance whatsoever, that the same shall and may during the term specified in the first section of the 25 & 26 Vict. c. 68, be exercised and enjoyed accordingly by the said C .D., his executors, administrators, and assigns without any lawful interruption or disturbance, and also a covenant for further assurance in the ordinary and usual form.

5. *The ordinary arbitration clause. In witness, &c.*

No. 12.—*Agreement to write an Opera.*

MEMORANDUM OF AN AGREEMENT made the   day of   · Between A. B., of the one part, and C. D., of the other part.

Mr. C. D. engages to write a full opera for musical performance at one of the large theatres, on the following terms :—

1. That the copyright of the said opera shall remain the property of the said C. D. except as hereinafter mentioned.

2. That the price for the performance of the said opera to be charged by C. D. to managers of country theatres (that is, of all theatres in the United Kingdom, except those in, or within five miles of, London) shall not exceed the sum of twenty shillings nightly. (*a*)

(*a*) The object of this stipulation being that the amount of the charge should not prevent the performance of the opera.

3. That the sum to be paid the said C. D. by the said A. B. for writing the said opera shall be   pounds, lawful money of Great Britain, to be paid in the following manner, viz.,   pounds on the signature of the present agreement, a second sum of   pounds within a month of this date,   pounds on the delivery of the complete manuscript óf the said opera, and the remaining sum of   pounds on the day following the first night of the performance of the said opera.

4. That the said A. B. shall have all the profits and benefits arising from the right of representation of the said opera in London, or within five miles thereof, and shall be at liberty to make arrangements with any manager for its performance within the aforesaid distance from London.

5. That the said A. B. shall have the entire and exclusive right of publishing, with the music, all the poetry or words of the vocal portions of the said opera, for the sole benefit of the said A. B., but not the right of publishing such poetry or words independently of the music.

And the said A. B. doth hereby agree for the purchase of the said opera, at the price and under the regulations aforesaid, the said C. D. also agreeing to deliver the complete manuscript of the said opera within six months of the present date, under the penalty of one hundred pounds.

Provided always, that the said C. D. is not prevented completing the manuscript by the necessity of alterations or additions suggested by the composer of the music of the said opera, which alterations or additions the said C. D., however, engages to make (to any reasonable extent) previous to the first performance of the said opera.

(Signed)   A. B.

Witness   .

APPENDIX (G).

FORMS WHICH MAY BE USED UNDER THE 25 & 26 VICT. c. 68.

*No. 1.—Form for entire reservation of Copyright by the Author where his Work
has been Commissioned.*

MEMORANDUM OF AGREEMENT made the   day of   188 .
Between A. B., of   , of the one part, and C. D., of ' , of the
other part.

Whereas the said A. B. has at the request of the said C. D. made for
him at the price of £   a drawing [*or painting or photograph*] being
[*shortly describe the subject*]. NOW THIS AGREEMENT WITNESSETH that at
or before the time of the sale or disposition of such drawing [*or painting
or photograph,*] it was agreed between the said parties hereto that all
the copyright in such work (including the making repetitions thereof)
should be the property of the said A. B., and that he should be entitled to
sell or otherwise dispose of all sketches and studies made, designed, or
executed in connection with the said work. *In witness, &c.*

---

*No. 2.—Form for entire reservation of Copyright by Author, where he first
sells his non-commissioned Work.*

MEMORANDUM OF AGREEMENT made the   day of   188 .
Between A. B., of   , of the one part, and C. D., of   , of the
other part.

Whereas the said C. D. hath agreed to purchase from the said A. B. at
the price of £   a drawing [*or painting or photograph*] being [*shortly
describe the subject*].   NOW THIS AGREEMENT WITNESSETH that at or before
the time of the sale of such drawing [*or painting or photograph*] it
was agreed between the said parties hereto that all the copyright in such
work (including the making of repetitions thereof), should be the property
of the said A. B., and that he should be entitled to sell or otherwise dispose
of all sketches and studies made, designed, or executed in connection with
the said work. *In witness, &c.*

No. 3.—Form for partial reservation of Copyright by the Author where his Work has been Commissioned.

MEMORANDUM OF AGREEMENT made the   day of   188 .
Between A. B., of   , of the one part, and C. D., of   , of the other part.

Whereas the said A. B. has at the request of the said C. D. made for him at the price of £ a painting [*or drawing or photograph*] being [*shortly describe the subject*]. NOW THIS AGREEMENT WITNESSETH that at or before the time of the sale of the said painting [*or drawing or photograph*] it was agreed between the said parties hereto that all copyright thereof for the purpose of making all engravings and photographs therefrom should be the property of the said A. B. And that the said A. B. should be entitled to sell or otherwise dispose of all sketches and studies made, designed, or executed in connection with the said work. *In witness, &c.*

No. 4.—Form for Partial Reservation of Copyright by the Author where he first sells his non-commissioned Work.

MEMORANDUM OF AGREEMENT made the   day of   188 .
Between A. B., of   , of the one part, and C. D., of   , of the other part.

Whereas the said C. D. has agreed to purchase from the said A. B. at the price of £ a painting [*or drawing or photograph*] being [*shortly describe the subject*]. NOW THIS AGREEMENT WITNESSETH that at or before the time of the sale of the said painting [*or drawing or photograph*] it was agreed between the said parties hereto that all copyright thereof for the purpose of making all engravings or photographs therefrom should be the property of the said A. B., and that the said A. B. should be entitled to sell or otherwise dispose of all sketches and studies made, designed, or executed in connection with the said work. *In witness, &c.*

No 5.—Licence by Proprietor of Copyright.

I, A. B., of   , being the proprietor of the copyright in a painting [*or drawing or photograph*] in consideration of the sum of £ paid to me by C. D. of   , do hereby grant to the said C. D. the sole and exclusive liberty and licence to copy, use, and apply the design of such work for all purposes of engraving and photographing the same. [*Any additional terms may be here mentioned.*]

A. B.

To Mr. C. D.

APPENDIX (H).

┝──◦◦──┥

FORMS OF INJUNCTIONS.

LITERARY COPYRIGHT.

No. 1.—*Restraining publication of Poems.*

That the defendant, &c., be restrained from printing, reprinting, publishing, or exposing to sale any copy or edition of a certain book or poem, entitled 'Paradise Lost,' composed by John Milton, or of the life of the said John Milton, or of the notes of various authors upon the said poem, compiled by Dr. Thomas Newton, until the hearing of this cause; and it is further ordered that the plaintiffs do speed their cause.—Eldon, L.C., in *Tonson* v. *Walker*, 3 Swan. 681.

No. 2.—*Topographical Dictionary.*

Let the defendant, his agents, servants, and workmen be restrained from further printing, publishing, selling, or otherwise disposing of any copy or copies of a book called 'A New and Comprehensive Gazetteer' containing any articles or article, passages or passage, copied, taken, or colourably altered from a book called 'The Topographical Dictionary of England,' published by the plaintiffs.—*Lewis* v. *Fullarton*, 2 Beav. 6, 14.

No. 3.—*Order restraining publication of Books, awarding Damages, and directing an Account.*

That the defendants be restrained from printing, publishing, and selling any copies or copy of a third or any subsequent edition of the plaintiff's book called 'The Practice of Photography.' It was ordered that the defendants deliver to the plaintiff all copies of the third edition of the plaintiff's book in the pleadings mentioned, the defendants offering to pay 25*l.* to the plaintiff in full of all claims for profit upon the sale of the said edition. If the plaintiff accept such offer, it was ordered that the defendants pay the same accordingly; but if the plaintiff does not accept such offer, then it was ordered that the usual accounts be taken of the gains and profits received by the defendants from the third edition of the plaintiff's book.—Wood, V.C., in *Delfe* v. *Delamotte*, 3 K. & J., 581.

No. 4.—*Use of Name—Injury to Employer's Property.*

That the defendant be restrained from publishing, issuing, or circulating any such advertisements, circulars, or letters as aforesaid, containing any statement or representation that the defendant is interested or concerned in any annual, book, or publication, other than 'Beeton's Christmas Annual' so published from year to year by the plaintiffs, or that the defendant's connection with the plaintiff's firm is terminated, or that the use of the defendant's name by the plaintiffs for the purposes of their said 'Beeton's Christmas Annual' is improper or unauthorized.—Malins, V.C., in *Ward* v. *Beeton*, L. R. 19 Eq. 211.

No. 5.—Publication of a Magazine as a continuation of Plaintiff's Magazine.

That the defendants &c., be restrained from publishing or exposing to sale any copy or copies of the defendant's said work, and from printing, publishing, or exposing to sale any other work or publication as or being a continuation of the plaintiff's work, or of the defendant's work which had been so published as such continuation as aforesaid, and from printing all or any part or parts of the plaintiff's said work; and that the injunction shall be continued as to any letters, &c., admitted by the answer to have been received from correspondents by the defendant, while publishing for the plaintiff.—Lord Eldon, C., in *Hogg* v. *Kirby*, 8 Ves. 215.

No. 6.—Publication of Magazine in Breach of Contract.

That the defendant, his servants, agents, and workmen be restrained from carrying on, or conducting the 'Temple Bar Magazine,' in the plaintiff's bill mentioned, but the order to be without prejudice to the publication of the said magazine until the hearing of the cause, so as that the name of the defendant Bentley do not appear on the title page or any other part of the said publication or in any advertisements of the said publication, and this order to be without prejudice to the right (if any) of the plaintiff to damages or profits in respect to any publication of the said work.—Wood, V.C., in *Ainsworth* v. *Bentley*, 14 W. R. 632.

No. 7.—Name and Title-page of Song.

That the defendants, &c., be restrained from printing, publishing, selling, exposing for sale, or otherwise disposing of the said song 'Minnie Dale,' or any copy or copies thereof, or any other publication containing a colourable imitation of the name, title, or title page of the plaintiff's said song.— Wood, V.C., in *Chappell* v. *Sheard*, 2 K. & J. 122.

TITLES.

No. 8.—Name of Newspaper.

That the defendants, their servants, workmen, and agents be restrained from printing, publishing or continuing to print or publish any newspaper or other periodical paper with or under the name or style of the Penny 'Bell's Life and Sporting News;' or with or under any name or style of which the name, style, or words of 'Bell's Life' shall form a part, or in any way occur; and from using the said name, style, or title of 'Bell's Life' by way of name, style, or title to any newspaper or periodical without the licence or consent of the plaintiff.—Stuart, V.C., in *Clement* v. *Maddick*, 1 Giff. 101.

No. 9.—Name of Newspaper—Soliciting Customers.

That the defendant, &c., be restrained from printing, or publishing, or exposing for sale, or procuring to be printed or sold, the newspaper publication called the 'True Britannia,' or any other newspaper or publication by way of a continuation or imitation of 'The Britannia,' and from soliciting custom in the name of the plaintiff's trade and business for 'The Britannia' newspaper, and from pledging the plaintiff's credit, and from excluding the plaintiff from the accounts and particulars of the plaintiff's trade and business, and from concealing from the plaintiff the names of the subscribers to, and advertisers in, the plaintiff's newspaper 'The Britannia,' or any of them, or the amounts of their respective debts, or any particulars relating thereto.—Stuart, V.C., in *Prowett* v. *Mortimer*, 2 Jur. (N.S.) 414.

No. 10.—Name of Newspaper.—Injury to Periodical.

That the defendant, &c., be restrained from printing, publishing, or selling any newspaper or other periodical under the name of 'The Daily London Journal,' or under any other name or style of which the words 'London Journal' shall form part, and from doing or committing any act or default that may tend to lessen or diminish the sale or circulation of the plaintiff's periodical called, 'The London Journal.'—Wood, V.C., in *Ingram* v. *Stiff*, 5 Jur. (N.S.) 947.

DRAMATIC AND MUSICAL COPYRIGHT.

No. 11.—As to an Operatic Magazine.

Let an injunction be awarded against the defendant to restrain him, his servants, agents, and workmen until, &c., from selling or otherwise disposing of the portion of No. 111 in the 'Pianista and Italian Opera Promenade Concert Magazine of Pianoforte and Vocal Music,' containing three pianoforte solos from Mendelssohn's original composition of music to Shakespeare's 'Midsummer Night's Dream,' called respectively the 'Scherzo,' the 'Notturno,' and the 'Wedding March,' and also from reprinting or multiplying any further copies of the said No. 111 of the 'Pianista' which shall contain the said pieces, or any of them, and also from printing, publishing, or selling any portion of the said work or composition of music to Shakespeare's 'Midsummer Night's Dream,' composed and arranged by Felix Mendelssohn-Bartholdy, except the overture thereof.—*Buxton* v. *James*, 5 De G. & Sm. 80.

ENGRAVINGS AND ETCHINGS.

No. 12.—Collection of Etchings.

That the defendant, W. S., his servants, agents, and workmen, be restrained from exhibiting the gallery or collection of etchings in the bill mentioned, or any of such etchings, and from making or permitting to be made any engravings or copies of the same or any of them; and from publishing the same or any of them, or parting with or disposing of the same or any of them ; and from selling or in any manner publishing, and from printing the descriptive catalogue in the plaintiff's bill mentioned.—Knight Bruce, V.C., in *Prince Albert* v. *Strange*, 2 De G. & Sm. 656.

No. 13.—*Etchings improperly obtained and published ; Catalogues improperly published—Decree—Delivery up.*

By the decree it was declared that the plaintiff was entitled to have delivered to him the impressions (by the answer of defendant Judge admitted to be in his possession) of such of the several etchings in the pleadings mentioned, as in the catalogue, and in the pleadings were stated to have been etched by the plaintiff; that is to say [they were described by reference to the numbers in the catalogue]; and it was ordered that Judge should, within four days after the service of the decree, deliver up the impressions above specified on oath, and leave them with the Clerk of Records and Writs, at the Record Office. And it was ordered that the defendant Strange should, within four days after service of the decree, deliver to the Clerk of Records and Writs, at the said office, the twenty-three copies of the catalogue, being the same as were mentioned in the decree in the other suit of even date. And the decree contained similar directions as to six copies of the catalogue admitted by Judge to be in his possession, and the Clerk of Records and Writs was ordered to destroy these copies of the catalogue, giving notice to the solicitors of the several parties of the time and place at which he intended to do so. And it was ordered that the defendants, their servants, &c., should be restrained from making, or permitting to be made, any engraving or copy of such etchings, or any of them; and from publishing the same ; and from parting with, or disposing of them, or any of them, except in obedience to the decree : and from selling or in any manner publishing the catologue or any work being or purporting to be a catalogue of the etchings made by the plaintiff. Provision made for costs. Liberty to apply reserved.—Knight Bruce, V.C., in *Prince Albert* v. *Strange*, 2 De G. & Sm. 717.

No. 14.—*Illustrated Book.*

That the defendants, their agents, and servants be restrained from printing or publishing or selling or exposing for sale or hire, or otherwise disposing of, or causing, procuring, or permitting to be printed, published, sold, exposed for sale or hire, or otherwise disposed of, any further or other copies or copy of a book called ' The Comical History and Tragical End of Reynard the Fox,' or any other book, work, publication, or thing, containing any passage, article, print, wood-cut, engraving, illustration, matter, or thing taken or copied, or colourably altered from any passage, article, print, wood-cut, engraving, matter, or thing contained in a book of the plaintiff's, entitled ' The Comical Creatures from Wurtemberg, including the story of Reynard the Fox, with twenty illustrations drawn from the stuffed animals contributed by Hermann Ploucquet, of Stuttgart, to the Great Exhibition,' wherein copyright subsisted or belonged to the plaintiff.—Parker, V.C., in *Bogue* v. *Houlston*, 16 Jur. 372.

DESIGNS.

No. 15.—As to Catalogue of Designs.

Let a perpetual injunction be awarded to restrain the defendant, his servants, agents, and printers, from publishing, printing, selling, delivering, or otherwise disposing of the sheet of monumental designs in the bill mentioned, or any other sheet in the compilation of which the plaintiff's book of monumental designs has been used, and from copying or pirating any part of the said book.—*Grace* v. *Newman*, L. R. 19 Eq. 623.

No. 16.—As to Woven Fabrics, and delivery up of Articles.

That the injunctions awarded on the   day of   , against the defendants, restraining them, and each of them, their workmen, servants, and agents, from selling or disposing of any of the articles of manufacture to which the plaintiff's design, in the plaintiff's bill mentioned, or a fraudulent imitation thereof, had been applied, as in the said bill mentioned, and from applying the plaintiff's said design or any fraudulent imitation thereof, to any woven fabrics or articles of manufacture, be continued until over the   day of   , and that the defendants should forthwith deliver up to the plaintiffs, for the purpose of being destroyed, the drawing or drawings, point paper, and the several cards used in applying the design in the plaintiff's bill mentioned; and also the articles manufactured by the defendants to which the said plaintiff's design had been applied, the same to be verified by affidavit, and that such costs, when taxed, be paid by the defendants: and on payment thereof, that all further proceedings in this suit should be stayed, unless the defendants committed any breach of the injunction already awarded; and any of the parties were to be at liberty to apply to the Court, as there should be occasion.—Knight Bruce, V.C., in *MacRae* v. *Holdsworth*, 2 De G. & Sm. 499.

Places where various Forms of other Injunctions may be found.

17. Injunctions staying publishing of newspaper 'The Real John Bull.' —*Edmonds* v. *Benbow*, cited Seton on Decrees.

18. Injunctions as to partial infringement.—*Bainbridge* v. *Briggs*, cited Seton.

19. Injunctions as to Selections from Poems, 'Book of the Poets.' —*Campbell* v. *Scott*, 11 Sim. 31 ; Pemberton's Judgments, 287.

20. Injunction as to Handbook.—*Colburn* v. *Simms*, 2 Hare, 543 ; Pemberton's Judgments, 289.

21. Injunctions as to Directories.—*Kelly* v. *Morris*, Wood, V.C., L. R. Eq. 697 ; Pemberton's Judgments, 286.

22. Injunctions as to portions of work. 'The Guardian Angel.' —*Low* v. *Ward*, L. R. 6 Eq. 415 ; Pemberton's Judgments, 287.

23. Injunctions against piracy of book, and order as to damages, "The Pedigree of the English People.'—*Pike* v. *Nicholas*, L. R. 5 Ch. 251; Pemberton's Judgments, 288.

24. Injunction as to Directory—not to extend to advertisements, 'The Merchants' and Manufacturers' Pocket Directory of London, 1868.' 'The Business Directory of London.'—*Morris* v. *Ashbee*, L. R. 7 Eq. 34; Pemberton's Judgments, 286.

25. Injunctions against printing a dramatised novel. 'Lady Audley's Secret,' 'Aurora Floyd.'—*Tinsley* v. *Lacy*, 32 L.J. (Ch.) 535; Pemberton's Judgments, 292.

26. Injunction against piracy of maps, and inquiry as to damages, 'Bird's-eye View or Plan of Paris and its Fortifications.'—*Stannard* v. *Harrison.* Bacon, V.C. Pemberton's Judgments, 288.

27. Injunction under Designs Act as to Mantilla Shawls.—*Norton* v. *Nicholas*, 4 K. & J. 475; Pemberton's Judgments, 297.

28. Judgments making injunction perpetual as to Copyright.—*Macklin* v. *Richardson*, Ambl. 694; Seton 944.

APPENDIX (I).

JAMES, L.J. :—

The question before us resolves itself into this—whether this pattern for working in Berlin wool is a piratical copy of the print of which the defendants are the proprietors. It appears to me that the Vice-Chancellor fell into (if I may venture so to call it) the error of supposing that the case was within the Act, 8 Geo. 2. c. 13, which gave a protection, not to a mere engraver, but to a man of genius who by his industry, pains, and expense, invented a design, "or engraved, etched, or worked, or from his own work and invention caused to be designed and engraved, etched, or worked," and so on, "any historical print."

Those words were intended to give protection for the genius exhibited in the invention of the design, and the protection was commensurate with the invention and design. That Act was afterwards extended to embrace the case of persons engraving from something which was not the design of the engraver. Now it appears to me that the protection given by the subsequent Acts to the mere engraver was intended to be, and was commensurate with that which the engraver did, that the engraver did not acquire against anybody in the world any right to that which was the work of the original painter, did not acquire any right to the design, did not acquire any right to the grouping or composition, because that was not his work but the work of the original painter. What, as it seems to me, the Act gave him and intended to give him, was protection for that which was his own meritorious work. The art of the engraver is often of the very highest character, as in the print before me. It is difficult to conceive any skill or art much higher than that which has by a wonderful combination of lines and touches reproduced the very texture and softness of the hair, the very texture and softness of the dress, and the expression of love and admiration in the eyes of the lady looking up at her lover. That art or skill was the thing which, as I believe, was intended to be protected by the Acts of Parliament, and what we have to consider is, whether the wool pattern before us (the maker of which must have been aided in the production of it by having before him the defendants' print, or some kind of copy of it, because the wool pattern follows the print in some particulars in which the print differs from the picture) is a copy of the engraver's work? It appears to me that without going into any etymological definition of the word " copy," and using the word in the ordinary sense of mankind as applied to the subject-matter, the question is, Is this a copy, is it a piracy, is it a piratical imitation of the engraving—of that which was the engraver's meritorious work in the print? I am of opinion, as a matter of fact, that the wool pattern is not a copy, is not a piratical imitation, with colourable variations of the defendants' engraving. The alleged copy is not a thing intended as a print in the ordinary sense of the word. It was intended to be printed, and was printed, as a pattern for Berlin wool, not put forward in any way fraudulently or as a sham, but really in truth intended solely for that purpose. Now, I am of opinion that, whatever may be the similarities between the one and the other, the attempt not to reproduce the print, but to produce something which has some distant resemblance to the print, not by anything in the nature of the engraver's work, but by what I may call a mosaic of coloured parallelograms, is not in any sense of the word a piratical imitation of the print. Nobody would ever take it to be the print, nobody would ever buy it instead of the print, nobody would ever suppose that it was, to use the language of the first Act, a base copy of the print. It is a work of a different class, intended for a different purpose, and, in my opinion, no more calculated to injure the print *quâ* print, or the reputation of the engraver, or the commercial value of the engraving in the hands of the proprietor, than if the same group were reproduced from the same engraving by waxwork at Madame Tussaud's, or in a plaster of Paris cast, or in a painting on porcelain. I cannot conceive that such a reproduction of the subject in tapestry, or Berlin wool, or upon china, or in earthenware, is within the meaning of the Act of Parliament. Whether dealing with it as a matter of law, or dealing with it, as we must do, as a matter of fact, I am satisfied that the appellants' pattern is not a copy or piracy of any part of that which constituted the real merit and labour of the engraver of the defendants' print.

BAGGALLAY, L.J.:—

I also am of opinion that the Berlin wool pattern is not a copy of the defendants' print within the meaning of the statutes. Reliance has been placed upon the very general words of the 17 Geo. 3, c. 57, which refer to engraving, etching, or working, or causing or procuring to be engraved, etched or worked in mezzo-tinto, or chiaroscuro, or otherwise or in any other manner copying in the whole or in part any print. Now, it is perfectly clear that those words must receive some limitation, for they cannot have been intended to apply to a lady copying a print or a part of a print upon a china plate, or to a person who for his own amusement makes an etching, drawing, or water-colour sketch from an engraving. If, then, we are to limit the meaning of the word " copy," how are we to judge of the extent to which it is to be limited? I think we can only do that by having regard to the preambles to the several statutes. We find an important preamble in the first Act, and then in the second and third of the Acts it is stated that the former Act has not been sufficient for effectuating the desired purpose. Now I think that in *Gambart* v. *Ball* (a) the object of the Acts was well pointed out as being of twofold character, first, the protection of the reputation of the engraver; and, secondly, his protection against any invasion of his commercial property in the print. It seems to me idle to suggest that in this case the reputation of the engraver from whose hands this beautiful engraving proceeded will suffer from the publication of a print intended for the purpose of ladies or others working in Berlin wool from it, and as regards his commercial property it appears to me almost as absurd to imagine that the commercial position of the owner of the print could suffer by the sale or the publication of this article.

I do not mean to say that a representation of this print in chromo-lithography, executed with that high skill and art with which works in chromo-lithography are now executed, could not be treated as a copy of the print prohibited by the statute. I do not say that it would be so, but I consider it a fairly arguable question. Here, however, though we have, no doubt, a young man and a young woman standing up in the centre of the picture in the same attitudes as in the print, in other respects the two designs have hardly anything in common. Again, this pattern cannot be called a work of art. The wool-work eventually to be made might probably be a work of art, but as for this pattern you might almost as well call a representation of the king and queen on a ginger-bread stall at a fair a work of art.

I am of opinion, therefore, that this pattern cannot be looked upon as a copy of the engraving within the intent and meaning of the Acts.

BRAMWELL, L.J. :—

I am of the same opinion and should add nothing were it not that I do not like differing from the learned Judge in the Court

(a) 14 C. B. (N.S.) 306.

below without showing that I have done my best to form an opinion upon the matter.

I should have thought it tolerably plain, as has been said by the Lord Justice James, that the object of these statutes was to protect the engraver, and that what the Legislature contemplated was that his work as an engraver should not be pirated, that there should not be another plate made—another engraving, the engraver of which availed himself of what had been done by his predecessor. That this is the true construction of the Act of Parliament, is, I think, shewn by the expressions that are used, for instance, that the pirated plate is to be destroyed; and I am very much inclined to think that the omission of the words "or otherwise copy" from the 7 Geo. 3, c. 38, was the result of an opinion on the part of its framer that that was the meaning of the first Act; and though the words "or otherwise copy" occur in the first Act and in the third, I think the intention was only to prohibit a piratical reproduction of the original engraving. I do not at all mean to say that the words "or otherwise copy" are to have no meaning; I think they were put in with a view to the possibility that, by some means other than engraving, a copy might be made, the maker of which would be taking the benefit of the engraver's work, and produce a sort of equivalent or substitute for the engraving of what I may call an engraving character. I think that a strong argument in support of this view is furnished by the following considerations. It has been held that these statutes were partly for the protection of the fame of the artist. Now, how can his fame be injured, except by the circulation of something which might be taken to be his work? Is it conceivable that anybody could confound this pattern with an artistic engraving, and say, "Oh! that must be the engraver's production!" To my mind, that consideration furnishes a strong argument that what the Legislature had in view was a new engraving, or something which could be taken as an engraving or an equivalent to it.

Now, what are the facts of this particular case? There is a picture of which the defendants are not the owners. It is conceded that anybody might have gone to that picture and made a fresh engraving of it upon a fresh plate unless there had been some bargain which precluded his having a right to do so. It is conceded à *multo fortiori* that the persons who prepared this pattern might have gone to the picture and taken from it the materials for producing that pattern. A further fact that I may mention is this: I have very little doubt, and I should find it as a fact if necessary, that this pattern was either mediately or immediately got from the engraving, since it follows the engraving in particulars in which the engraving differs from the original picture.

3 D

But if the pattern might with these trifling variations have been taken from the original picture without infringing the engraving, how can it be possible to say that because the man who prepared it instead of going to the picture thought it more convenient to take this engraving, or possibly a smaller one, or possibly the etching (for any one of them would have served his purpose, because all he wanted was the outline), the case is brought within the Act? I do not say that if this were an ordinary engraving with no picture, a lithograph taken from it would not be a copy. I think that a photograph taken from it would be a copy. I do not say that if this were an original engraving with no picture and a copy were made of it and afterwards coloured, there might not be some ground for saying that there was a piracy of the art and skill of the engraver. I should have very great misgiving about it, because I doubt whether the statutes were not intended to protect the artist's skill as an engraver only and not as a draftsman. I give no opinion on the point, and I only mention it for the purpose of shewing that this particular case is not that which I have supposed, but is a case in which the man might have done everything that he has done by going to the picture instead of using the more convenient, more accessible, and more manageable thing, the engraving. I cannot but think, therefore, with great submission to the learned Judge in the Court below, that this is not a copy within the statutes of Mr. Barlow's most beautiful engraving.

APPENDIX (K).

INTERNATIONAL CONVENTIONS.

CONVENTION BETWEEN HER MAJESTY AND THE KING OF PRUSSIA FOR THE ESTABLISHMENT OF INTERNATIONAL COPYRIGHT. *Signed at Berlin, May* 13, 1846.

Art. I. The authors of books, dramatic works, or musical compositions, and the inventors, designers, or engravers of prints, and articles of sculpture; and the authors, inventors, designers, or engravers of any other works whatsoever of literature and the fine arts, in which the laws of Great Britain and of Prussia do now or may hereafter give their respective subjects the privilege of Copyright, shall, with regard to any such works or articles first published in either of the two States, enjoy in the other the same privilege of Copyright as would by law be enjoyed by the author, inventor, designer, or engraver of a similar work, if first published in such other State; together with the same legal remedies and protection against piracy and unauthorised republication.

The lawful representatives or assigns of authors, inventors, designers, or engravers, shall, in all these respects, be treated on the same footing as the authors, inventors, designers, or engravers themselves.

Art. II. No person shall, in either country, be entitled to the protection stipulated by the preceding Article, unless the work in respect of which Copyright is claimed shall have been registered by the original producer, or by his lawful representatives or assigns, in the manner following :—

First. If the work be one that has first appeared in the dominions of His Majesty the King of Prussia, it must have been registered in the register-book of the Company of Stationers in London.

Secondly. If the work be one that has first appeared in the dominions of Her Britannic Majesty, it must have been registered in the catalogue to be kept for that purpose at the office of His Prussian Majesty's Minister for Ecclesiastical, Educational, and Medical Affairs.

3 D 2

Nor shall any person be entitled to such protection as aforesaid, unless the laws and regulations of the respective States in regard to the work in respect of which it may be claimed shall have been duly complied with; nor, in cases where there are several copies of the work, unless one copy of the best edition, or in the best state, shall have been delivered gratuitously at the place appointed by law for that purpose in the respective countries.

A certified copy of the entry in the said register-book of the Company of Stationers in London shall be valid in the British dominions, as proof of the exclusive right of republication, until a better right shall have been established by any other party before a court of justice:—and the certificate given under the laws of Prussia, of the registration of any work in that country, shall be valid for the same purpose in the Prussian dominions.

Art. III. The authors of dramatic and musical works which shall have been first publicly represented or performed in either of the two countries, as well as the lawful representatives or assigns of such authors, shall likewise be protected in regard to the public representation or performance of their works in the other country, to the full extent in which native subjects would be protected in respect of dramatic and musical works first represented or performed in such country; provided they shall previously have duly registered their copyright in the offices mentioned in the preceding Article, in conformity with the laws of the respective States.

Art. IV. In lieu of the rates of duty which may at any time, during the continuance of this convention, be payable upon the importation into the United Kingdom of foreign books, prints, and drawings, there shall be charged upon the importation of books, prints, or drawings, published within the dominions of Prussia, and legally importable into the United Kingdom, only the rates of duty specified in the table hereto annexed; that is to say—

		£	s.	d.
Duties on books, viz.—				
Works originally produced in the United Kingdom and republished in Prussia . . . . . the cwt.		2	10	0
Works not originally produced in the United Kingdom . . . . the cwt.		0	15	0
Prints or drawings:—				
—— plain or coloured, single . . . . . each		0	0	0½
—— bound or sewed . . . . . . the dozen		0	0	1½

It is understood that all works, of which any part was originally produced in the United Kingdom, will be considered as " works originally produced in the United Kingdom, and republished in Prussia," and will be subject to the duty of fifty shillings per cwt., although the same may contain also original matter produced elsewhere; unless such original matter shall be at least equal in bulk to the part of the work originally produced in the United Kingdom, in which case the work will be subject only to the duty of fifteen shillings per cwt.

Art. V. It is agreed that stamps shall be provided according to a pattern to be made known to the Custom-house officers of the United Kingdom, and that the municipal or other authorities of the several towns in Prussia shall affix such stamps to all books intended for exportation to the United Kingdom. And no books shall, for the purposes of this convention, so far as the same relates to the rates of duty at which such books are to be entered, be deemed to have been published in Prussia, except such as appear by their title-page to have been published at some town or place within the dominions of Prussia, and which have been duly stamped by the proper municipal or other authority of any such town or place.

Art. VI. Nothing in this convention shall be construed to affect the right of either of the two high contracting parties to prohibit the importation into its own dominions, of such books as, by its internal law, or under its treaties with other States, are declared to be piracies, or infringements of Copyright.

Art. VII. In case either of the two high contracting parties shall conclude a treaty of International Copyright with any third power, a stipulation similar to that contained in the preceding Article shall be inserted in such treaty.

Art. VIII. Those German States which, together with Prussia, compose the Customs and Commercial Union, or which may hereafter join the said Union, shall have the right of acceding to the present convention; and books, prints, and drawings, published in any State so becoming a party to this convention, and exported from any other State also being a party to the same, shall be considered, for the purposes of this convention, to have been exported from the country of their publication.

Art. IX. The present convention shall come into operation on the 1st of September, 1846. It shall remain in force for five years from that date, and further, until the expiration of a year's notice, which may be given by either party, at any time after the 1st of September, 1851.

Art. X. The present convention shall be ratified, and the ratifications shall be exchanged at Berlin, at the expiration of two months, or sooner if possible.

Protocol signed by the two Plenipotentiaries on the conclusion of the preceding Convention.

The undersigned plenipotentiaries of Her Majesty the Queen of Great Britain and Ireland, and of His Majesty the King of Prussia, met together this day in order to sign the treaty drawn up on the basis of the negotiations which have taken place for the reciprocal protection of the right of authors against piracy and unauthorized reproduction.

The two original copies of the treaty having been examined and found to correspond in form and contents with the concerted stipulations, the plenipotentiaries proceeded to sign the same, under the following conditions; such conditions, though not appearing of a nature to be admitted into the text of the treaty, nevertheless to be considered, on the ratification of the treaty, as thereby agreed to and ratified:—

1. With respect to Article II.:—Both Governments engage that the fees which may at any time be levied for the registering of a single work in the register-book of the Company of Stationers in London, or in the catalogue of the office of His Prussian Majesty's Minister for Ecclesiastical, Educational, and Medical Affairs, shall not exceed the sum of one shilling sterling, or of ten silver groschen, as has been already declared on the part of Great Britain in a letter from the Board of Trade of the 2nd April, 1844, letter E.

2. With reference to the same Article:—The delivery of a copy gratuitously shall take place in Great Britain at the Stationers' Company in London, and in Prussia at the office of the Minister of Ecclesiastical, Educational, and Medical Affairs in Berlin.

3. With reference to Article IV.:—Both Governments agree, that the duty on musical works imported from Prussia into Great Britain shall not be greater than the duty on books imported from Prussia into Great Britain.

4. With reference to Article V.:—It is understood that the stamping agreed to in this Article will be confined to books and musical works (according to the interpretation of the word "books" given in Article II. of the Act of Parliament 5 & 6 Vict. c. 45, of 1st of July, 1842); whereas all other objects mentioned in Article I. of the convention this day signed, will not require to be stamped in order to enable them to be imported into Great Britain at the rate of duty fixed for these objects by Article IV. of the present treaty.

ACCESSION OF THE KING OF SAXONY TO THE CONVENTION CON-
CLUDED MAY 13, 1846, BETWEEN GREAT BRITAIN AND
PRUSSIA, FOR THE ESTABLISHMENT OF INTERNATIONAL COPY-
RIGHT. *Signed at Berlin, August 24, 1846.*

Her Majesty the Queen of the United Kingdom of Great Rritain
and Ireland, and His Majesty the King of Prussia, having concluded at Berlin, on the 13th of May, 1846, a convention for the
reciprocal protection of Copyright against piracy; and it having
been stipulated in Article VIII. of that convention, that those
German States which, together with Prussia, compose the German
Union of Customs, or which may hereafter join that Union, should
have the right of acceding to the said convention; their Britannic
and Prussian Majesties have addressed to His Majesty the King of
Saxony the invitation to accede thereto;

And His Majesty the King of Saxony being desirous of availing
himself of the opportunity thus afforded to him of acceding to the
said convention;

The plenipotentiary of His Majesty the King of Saxony in consequence declares, in virtue of his full powers, that His said Majesty
accedes both to the convention of the 13th May, 1846, containing
ten Articles, and ·of which a printed copy is annexed to the present
Act, and to the special provisions contained in ss. 1–4 of the
separate protocol signed on the same day, of which a copy is also
hereunto annexed; promising that the stipulations of the said
convention, which shall come into operation in the Kingdom of
Saxony, from and after the 1st of September, 1846, as well as those
of the separate protocol, shall be carried into execution by His
Majesty the King of Saxony in all points, so far as they may be
applicable to the relations which subsist between the Saxon Government and the British Government and its subjects; subject, however, to the express reservation, that Article II. of the convention
shall be modified, with regard to Saxony, in the following manner,
that is to say:

No person in either of the two countries, either in the United
Kingdom of Great Britain and Ireland, or in the Kingdom of
Saxony, shall be entitled to the protection stipulated by Article I. of
the convention, unless the work to be protected against piracy
shall have been registered by the author or his agents in the following manner :—

1. If the work has first appeared in the dominions of His Majesty
the King of Saxony, it must have been registered in the register-
book of the Company of Stationers in London.

2. If the work ·has first appeared in the dominions of Her

Britannic Majesty, it must have been registered in the register-book kept by the Royal Direction of the Circle (*die Bücherrolle*) at Leipzig.

Nor shall any person be entitled to the protection aforesaid, unless the laws and regulations of the respective States shall have been duly observed in regard to the work to be protected; nor, in cases where there are several copies of the work, unless one copy of the best edition, or in the best state, shall have been delivered gratuitously to the authorities appointed for that purpose by the laws of the respective countries.

A certified copy of the registration in the aforesaid register-book of the Company of Stationers in London, shall be valid in the British dominions, as proof of the exclusive right of publication, until a better right shall be established by any other party before a court of justice; and the certificate given under the laws of Saxony, of the registration of any work in the aforesaid register-book at Leipzig, shall be equally valid in the dominions of His Saxon Majesty.

The plenipotentiaries of Her Majesty the Queen of the United Kingdom of Great Britain and Ireland and of His Majesty the King of Prussia, in virtue of their full powers, accept the accession of His Majesty the King of Saxony; promising that the stipulations of the convention of the 13th of May, 1846, as well as the special provisions which are contained in the protocol of the same date, and those which form the reservation above mentioned, shall be carried into execution by their respective sovereigns in all points, with regard to the Saxon Government and its subjects in the same manner as between the British and Prussian Governments and their subjects.

Accession of the States forming the Thuringian Union, to the Convention concluded May 13, 1846, between Great Britain and Prussia, for the establishment of International Copyright. *Signed at Berlin, July* 1, 1847.

Her Majesty the Queen of the United Kingdom of Great Britain and Ireland, and His Majesty the King of Prussia, having concluded at Berlin, on the 13th of May, 1846, a convention for the reciprocal protection of Copyright against piracy; and having stipulated in Article VIII. of that convention, that those German States which, together with Prussia, compose the German Union of Customs, or which may hereafter join that Union, should have the right of acceding to the said convention; their Britannic and Prussian Majesties have addressed to the States forming the Thuringian Union, that is to say, His Royal Highness the Grand Duke of Saxe-Weimar-Eisenach, their Royal Highnesses (*Hoheiten*) the Dukes of Saxe-Altenburg, Saxe-Coburg-Gotha, and Saxe-Meiningen, and their Serene Highnesses the Princes of Schwarzburg-Rudolstadt and Schwarzburg-Sondershausen, Reuss-Greitz, Reuss-Lobenstein-Eberdorf, and Reuss-Schleitz, the invitation to accede thereto ;

And the said States being desirous of availing themselves of the opportunity thus afforded to them of acceding to the said convention;

The plenipotentiary of His Royal Highness the Grand Duke of Saxe-Weimar-Eisenach, as well as the plenipotentiary of their Royal Highnesses the Dukes of Saxe-Altenburg, Saxe-Coburg-Gotha, and Saxe-Meiningen, and of their Serene Highnesses the Princes of Schwarzburg-Rudolstadt and Schwarzburg-Sondershausen, Reuss-Greitz, Reuss-Lobenstein-Ebersdorf, and Reuss-Schleitz, in consequence declare, in virtue of their full powers, that their said Royal and Serene Highnesses accede both to the convention of the 13th May, 1846, containing ten Articles, and of which a printed copy is annexed to the present Act, and to the special provisions contained in ss. 1-4 of the separate protocol signed on the same day, of which a copy is also hereunto annexed ; promising that the stipulations of the said convention, which shall come into operation in the States of the Thuringian Union from and after the 15th of July, 1847, as well as those of the separate protocol, shall be carried into execution by their said Royal and Serene Highnesses in all points, so far as they may be applicable to the relations which subsist between the States of the Thuringian Union and the British Government and its subjects; and declaring that English works registered, in virtue of Article II. of the convention, in the register-book kept at Berlin, shall be entitled also to protection against piracy in the said States.

The plenipotentiaries of Her Majesty the Queen of the United Kingdom of Great Britain and Ireland, and of His Majesty the King of Prussia, in virtue of their full powers, accept the accession of their said Royal and Serene Highnesses; promising that the stipulations of the convention of the 13th of May, 1846, as well as the special provisions which are contained in the protocol of the same date, shall be carried into execution by their respective sovereigns in all points, with regard to the States of the Thuringian Union and their subjects, in the same manner as between the British and Prussian Governments and their subjects.

Note addressed by the British Plenipotentiary to the Prussian Plenipotentiary on the signature of the preceding Act of Accession.

The Act of Accession of the States forming the Thuringian Union of German Customs, to the convention concluded on the 13th of May, 1846, between Great Britain and Prussia, for the reciprocal protection of Copyright, having been this day signed by the respective plenipotentiaries, the undersigned, Envoy Extraordinary and Minister Plenipotentiary of Her Britannic Majesty, in accepting the proposition, according to which it will for the present be sufficient for the purpose of securing protection to an English work within the States of the said Union, that it should have been registered in the register-book kept at Berlin, gives at the same time, in the name of his Government, the formal assurance, that if hereafter, more than one other place, besides Berlin and Leipzig, should be selected by the members of the Zollverein who may accede to the convention of the 13th of May, 1846, for the registration of English books to be protected against piracy, the town of Weimar shall likewise be made a place of registration.

In making the present declaration, the undersigned avails himself, &c.

Berlin, July 1, 1847.

(Signed) WESTMORLAND.

His Excellency the Baron de Canitz,
&c. &c.

Convention between Her Majesty and the King of Hanover, for the establishment of International Copyright. *Signed at London, August* 4, 1847.

Art. I. The authors of books, dramatic works, or musical compositions, and the inventors, designers, or engravers of prints and articles of sculpture; and the authors, inventors, designers, or engravers of any other works whatsoever of literature and the fine arts, in which the laws of Great Britain and of Hanover do now or may hereafter give their respective subjects the privilege of copyright, shall, with regard to any such works or articles first published in either of the two States, enjoy in the other the same privilege of copyright as would by law be enjoyed by the author, inventor, designer, or engraver of a similar work, if first published in such other State, together with the same legal remedies and protection against piracy and unauthorized republication.

The lawful representatives or assigns of authors, inventors, designers, or engravers, shall, in all these respects, be treated on the same footing as the authors, inventors, designers, or engravers themselves.

Art. II. No person shall in either country be entitled to the protection stipulated by the preceding Article, unless the work in respect of which copyright is claimed shall have been registered by the original producer, or by his lawful representatives or assigns, in the manner following :—

First. If the work be one that has first appeared in the dominions of His Majesty the King of Hanover, it must have been registered in the register-book of the Company of Stationers in London.

Secondly. If the work be one that has first appeared in the dominions of Her Britannic Majesty, it must have been registered in the Catalogue to be kept for that purpose at the office of His Hanoverian Majesty's Minister of the Interior.

Nor shall any person be entitled to such protection as aforesaid unless the laws and regulations of the respective States in regard to the work in respect of which it may be claimed, shall have been duly complied with, nor unless one copy of the work, or, in cases where there are several copies of the work, unless one copy of the best edition, or in the best state, shall have been delivered gratuitously at the place appointed by law for that purpose in the respective countries.

A certified copy of the entry in the said register-book of the Company of Stationers in London shall be valid in the British dominions, as proof of the exclusive right of republication, until a better right shall have been established by any other party before a court of justice; and the certificate given under the laws of Hanover of the registration of any work in that country shall be valid for the same purpose in the Hanoverian dominions.

Art. III. The authors of dramatic and musical works which shall have been first publicly represented or performed in either of the two countries, as well as the lawful representatives or assigns of such authors, shall likewise be protected in regard to the public representation or performance of their works in the other country, to the full extent in which native subjects would be protected in respect of dramatic and musical works first represented or performed in such country; provided they shall previously have duly registered their copyright in the offices mentioned in the preceding Article, in conformity with the laws of the respective States.

Art. IV. In lieu of the rates of duty which may at any time, during the continuance of this convention, be payable upon the importation into the United Kingdom of foreign books, musical works, prints, and drawings, there shall be charged upon the importation of books, musical works, prints, or drawings, published within the dominions of Hanover, and legally importable into the United Kingdom, only the rates of duty specified in the table hereto annexed, that is to say—

Duties on books and musical works, viz. :—	£	s.	d.
Works originally produced in the United Kingdom and republished in Hanover . . . . the cwt.	2	10	0
Works not originally produced in the United Kingdom . . . . the cwt.	0	15	0
Prints or drawings, plain or coloured . single, each	0	0	0½
——— bound or sewed . . . . . . the dozen	0	0	1½

It is understood, that all works of which any part was originally produced in the United Kingdom, will be considered as " works originally produced in the United Kingdom, and republished in Hanover," and will be subject to the duty of fifty shillings per cwt., although the same may contain also original matter produced elsewhere, unless such original matter shall be at least equal in bulk to the part of the work originally produced in the United Kingdom, in which case, the work will be subject only to the duty of fifteen shillings per cwt.

Art. V. It is agreed that stamps shall be provided according to a pattern to be made known to the Custom-house officers of the United Kingdom, and that the municipal or other authorities of the several towns in Hanover shall affix such stamps to all books intended for exportation to the United Kingdom. And no books shall, for the purposes of this convention, so far as the same relates to the rates of duty at which such books are to be entered, be deemed to have been published in Hanover, except such as appear by their title-page to have been published at some town or place within the dominions of Hanover, and which have been duly stamped by the proper municipal or other authority.

It is understood that the stamping agreed to in this Article will be confined to books and musical works (according to the interpretation of the word " books," given in section 2 of the Act of Parliament 5 & 6 Victoria, cap. 45, of July 1, 1842), whereas all other objects mentioned in Article IV. will not require to be stamped in order to enable them to be imported into Great Britain, at the rate of duty fixed for those objects by the said Article.

Art. VI. Nothing in this convention shall be construed to affect the right of either of the two high contracting parties to prohibit the importation into its own dominions of such books as, by its internal law, or under its treaties with other States, are declared to be piracies or infringements of copyright.

Art. VII. In case either of the two high contracting parties shall conclude a treaty of International Copyright with any third power, a stipulation similar to that contained in the preceding Article shall be inserted in such treaty.

Art. VIII. Any German State which may choose to accede to the present convention, shall be admitted to it. Books, musical works, prints, and drawings, published in any State so becoming a party to this convention, and exported from any other State, also being a party to the same, shall be considered, for the purposes of the convention, to have been exported from the country of their publication.

Art. IX. The present convention shall come into operation one calendar month after the exchange of the ratifications. It shall remain in force until the 1st of September, 1851 ; and further, until the expiration of a year's notice, which may be given by either party, at any time after the 1st of September, 1851.

Art. X. The present convention shall be ratified, and the ratifications shall be exchanged at Hanover, at the expiration of two months, or sooner if possible.

Protocol signed by the Plenipotentiaries on the conclusion of the preceding Convention.

The undersigned plenipotentiaries of Her Majesty the Queen of the United Kingdom of Great Britain and Ireland, and of His Majesty the King of Hanover, met together this day in order to sign the treaty drawn up on the basis of the negotiations which have taken place for the reciprocal protection of the rights of authors against piracy and unauthorized republication.

The two original copies of the treaty having been examined and found to correspond in form and contents with the concerted stipulations, the plenipotentiaries proceeded to sign the same, under the following conditions : such conditions, though not appearing of a nature to be admitted into the text of the treaty, nevertheless to be considered, on the ratification of the treaty, as thereby agreed to and ratified :—

1. It is understood that no clause of the present convention shall affect or alter the exclusive rights and privileges subsisting at this time in the Kingdom of Hanover, for the publication of calendars and almanacks, psalm-books, catechisms, &c.

2. With respect to Article II :—Both Governments engage that the fees which may at any time be levied for the registering of a single work in the register-book of the Company of Stationers in London, or in the Catalogue of the office of His Hanoverian Majesty's Minister of the Interior, shall not exceed the sum of one shilling sterling, or of eight gutegroschen.

3. With reference to the same Article :—The delivery of one copy gratuitously shall take place in Great Britain at the Hall of the Stationers' Company in London, and in Hanover at the office of the Minister of Ecclesiastical and Educational Affairs. The value of any copy besides, demanded on behalf of any library in either country, shall be paid to the publisher.

PALMERSTON.

London, August 4, 1847.   H. LABOUCHERE.

A. KIELMANSEGGE.

ACCESSION OF THE GRAND DUKE OF OLDENBURG TO THE CONVENTION CONCLUDED AUGUST 4, 1847, BETWEEN GREAT BRITAIN AND HANOVER, FOR THE ESTABLISHMENT OF INTERNATIONAL COPYRIGHT. *Signed at Hanover, December 28, 1847.*

Her Majesty the Queen of the United Kingdom of Great Britain and Ireland, and His Majesty the King of Hanover, having concluded at London, on the 4th of August, 1847, a convention for the reciprocal protection of Copyright against piracy; and it having been stipulated in Article VIII. of that convention, that any German State which may choose to accede to the said convention should be admitted to it; Their Britannic and Hanoverian Majesties have addressed to His Royal Highness the Grand Duke of Oldenburg the invitation to accede thereto;

And His Royal Highness the Grand Duke of Oldenburg, being desirous to avail himself of the opportunity thus afforded to him of acceding to the said convention;

The plenipotentiary of His Royal Highness the Grand Duke of Oldenburg in consequence declares, in virtue of his full powers, that His Royal Highness accedes both to the convention of the 4th of August, 1847, containing ten Articles, and of which a printed copy is annexed to the present Act, and to the special provisions contained in the separate protocol signed on the same day, of which a copy is also hereunto annexed; promising that the stipulations of the said convention, which shall come into operation in the Grand Duchy of Oldenburg from and;after the day of the signature of the present Act, as well as those of the separate protocol, shall be carried into execution by His Royal Highness the Grand Duke of Oldenburg, in all points, so far as they may be applicable to the relations which subsist between the Government of Oldenburg and the British Government and its subjects; subject, however, to the express reservation,—

1. That Article II. of the convention shall be modified, with

regard to the Grand Duchy of Oldenburg, in the following manner ; that is to say,—

No person in either of the two countries, either in the United Kingdom of Great Britain and Ireland, or in the Grand Duchy of Oldenburg, shall be entitled to the protection stipulated by Article I. of the convention, unless the work to be protected against piracy shall have been registered by the author or his agents, in the following manner :—

If the work has first appeared in the dominions of His Royal Highness the Grand Duke of Oldenburg, it must have been registered in the register-book of the Company of Stationers in London.

If the work has first appeared in the dominions of Her Britannic Majesty, it must have been registered in the register-book kept by the Grand-Ducal Department of State and Cabinet at Oldenburg.

Nor shall any person be entitled to the protection aforesaid, unless the laws and regulations of the respective States shall have been duly observed in regard to the work to be protected ; nor, in cases where there are several copies of the work, unless one copy of the best edition, or in the best state, shall have been delivered gratuitously to the authorities appointed for that purpose by the laws of the respective countries.

A certified copy of the registration in the aforesaid register-book of the Company of Stationers in London, shall be valid in the British dominions, as proof of the exclusive right of publication, until a better right shall be established by any other party before a court of justice ; and the certificate given under the laws of Oldenburg, of the registration of any work in the aforesaid register-book at Oldenburg, shall be equally valid in the dominions of His Royal Highness the Grand Duke of Oldenburg.

2. That the stipulations of s. 1 of the separate protocol shall not apply to the Grand Duchy of Oldenburg.

3. And that the stipulations of the present Act shall extend to the principalities of Lubeck and Birkenfeld, as forming part of the Grand Duchy of Oldenburg.

The plenipotentiaries of Her Majesty the Queen of the United Kingdom of Great Britain and Ireland, and of His Majesty the King of Hanover, in virtue of their full powers, accept the accession of His Royal Highness the Grand Duke of Oldenburg ; promising that the stipulations of the convention of the 4th of August, 1847, as well as the special provisions which are contained in the protocol of the same date, and those which form the reservation above mentioned, shall be carried into execution by their respective Sovereigns in all points, with regard to the Government of Oldenburg and its subjects, in the same manner as between the British and Hanoverian Governments and their subjects.

CONVENTION BETWEEN HER MAJESTY AND THE FRENCH RE-
PUBLIC, FOR THE ESTABLISHMENT OF INTERNATIONAL COPYRIGHT.
Signed at Paris, November 3, 1851.

Art. I. From and after the date on which, according to the provisions of Article XIV., the present convention shall come into
operation, the authors of works of literature or of art, to whom the
laws of either of the two countries do now or may hereafter give
the right of property, or copyright, shall be entitled to exercise that
right in the territories of the other of such countries for the same
term, and to the same extent, as the authors of works of the same
nature, if published in such other country, would therein be entitled to exercise such right; so that the republication or piracy in
either country, of any work of literature or of art, published in the
other, shall be dealt with in the same manner as a republication or
piracy of a work of the same nature first published in such other
country; and so that such authors in the one country shall have
the same remedies before the courts of justice in the other country,
and shall enjoy in that other country the same protection against
piracy and unauthorized republication, as the law now does or
may hereafter grant to authors in that country.

The terms "works of literature or of art," employed at the beginning of this Article, shall be understood to comprise publications
of books, of dramatic works, of musical compositions, of drawing,
of painting, of sculpture, of engraving, of lithography, and of any
other works whatsoever of literature and of the fine arts.

The lawful representatives or assigns of authors, translators,
composers, painters, sculptors, or engravers, shall in all respects
enjoy the same rights which by the present convention are granted
to the authors, translators, composers, painters, sculptors, or engravers themselves.

Art. II. The protection granted to original works is extended to
translations; it being, however, clearly understood, that the intention of the present Article is simply to protect a translator in
respect of his own translation, and that it is not intended to confer
upon the first translator of any work the exclusive right of translating that work, except in the case and to the extent provided for
in the following Article.

Art. III. The author of any work published in either of the two
countries, who may choose to reserve the right of translating it,

shall, until the expiration of five years from the date of the first publication of the translation thereof authorized by him, be, in the following cases, entitled to protection from the publication in the other country of any translation of such work not so authorized by him :

§ 1. If the original work shall have been registered and deposited in the one country within three months after its first publication in the other.

§ 2. If the author has notified on the title-page of his work his intention to reserve the right of translating it.

§ 3. Provided always, that at least a part of the authorized translation shall have appeared within a year after the registration and deposit of the original, and that the whole shall have been published within three years after the date of such deposit.

§ 4. And provided that the publication of the translation shall take place within one of the two countries, and that it shall be registered and deposited according to the provisions of Article VIII.

With regard to works which are published in parts, it will be sufficient if the declaration of the author that he reserves the right of translation, shall appear in the first part. But with reference to the period of five years limited by this Article for the exercise of the exclusive right of translation, each part shall be treated as a separate work, and each part shall be registered and deposited in the one country within three months after its first publication in the other.

Art. IV. The stipulations of the preceding Articles shall also be applicable to the representation of dramatic works, and to the performance of musical compositions, in so far as the laws of each of the two countries are or shall be applicable in this respect to dramatic and musical works first publicly represented or performed therein.

In order, however, to entitle the author to legal protection in regard to the translation of a dramatic work, such translation must appear within three months after the registration and deposit of the original.

It is understood that the protection stipulated by the present Article is not intended to prohibit fair imitations, or adaptations of dramatic works to the stage in England and France respectively, but is only meant to prevent piratical translations.

The question whether a work is an imitation or a piracy, shall in all cases be decided by the courts of justice of the respective countries, according to the laws in force in each.

Art. V. Notwithstanding the stipulations of Articles I. and II. of the present convention, articles extracted from newspapers or periodicals published in either of the two countries, may be re-

3 E

published or translated in the newspapers or periodicals of the other country, provided the source from whence such articles are taken be acknowledged.

Nevertheless, this permission shall not be construed to authorize the republication in one of the two countries, of articles from newspapers or periodicals published in the other country, the authors of which shall have notified in a conspicuous manner in the journal or periodical in which such articles have appeared, that they forbid the republication thereof.

Art. VI. The importation into and the sale in either of the two countries of piratical copies of works which are protected from piracy under Articles I., II., III., and V. of the present convention, are prohibited, whether such piratical copies originate in the country where the work was published, or in any other country.

Art. VII. In the event of an infraction of the provisions of the foregoing Articles, the pirated works or articles shall be seized and destroyed; and the persons who may have committed such infraction shall be liable in each country to the penalties and actions which are or may be prescribed by the laws of that country for such offences, committed in respect of a work or production of home origin.

Art. VIII. Neither authors, nor translators, nor their lawful representatives or assigns, shall be entitled in either country to the protection stipulated by the preceding Articles, nor shall copyright be claimable in either country, unless the work shall have been registered in the manner following, that is to say:—

1. If the work be one that has first appeared in France, it must be registered at the Hall of the Company of Stationers in London.

2. If the work be one that has first appeared in the dominions of Her Britannic Majesty, it must be registered at the *Bureau de la Librairie* of the Ministry of the Interior at Paris.

No person shall be entitled to such protection as aforesaid, unless he shall have duly complied with the laws and regulations of the respective countries in regard to the work in respect of which such protection may be claimed. With regard to books, maps, prints, or musical publications, no person shall be entitled to such protection, unless he shall have delivered gratuitously, at one or other of the places mentioned above, as the case may be, one copy of the best edition, or in the best state, in order to its being deposited at the place appointed for that purpose in each of the two countries; that is to say, in Great Britain, at the British Museum at London; and in France, at the National Library at Paris.

In every case, the formality of deposit and registration must be fulfilled within three months after the first publication of the work in the other country. With regard to works published in parts, the period of three months shall not begin to run until the date of the publication of the last part, unless the author shall have notified his intention to reserve the right of translating it, as provided in Article III.; in which case each part shall be treated as a separate work.

A certified copy of the entry in the register-book of the Company of Stationers in London shall confer, within the British dominions, the exclusive right of republication, until a better right shall have been established by any other party before a court of justice.

The certificate given under the laws of France, proving the registration of any work in that country, shall be valid for the same purpose throughout the territories of the French Republic.

A certificate or certified copy of the registration of any work so registered in either country, shall, if required, be delivered at the time of registration; and such certificate shall state the exact date at which the registration was made.

The charge for the registration of a single work, under the stipulations of this Article, shall not exceed one shilling in England, nor one franc and twenty-five centimes in France; and the further charge for a certificate of such registration shall not exceed the sum of five shillings in England, nor six francs and twenty-five centimes in France.

The provisions of this Article shall not extend to articles which may appear in newspapers or periodicals; which shall be protected from republication or translation simply by a notice from the author, as prescribed by Article V. But if any article or work which has originally appeared in a newspaper or periodical, shall afterwards be published in a separate form, it shall then become subject to the stipulations of the present Article.

Art. IX. With regard to any article other than books, prints, maps, and musical publications, in respect to which protection may be claimable under Article I. of the present convention, it is agreed, that any other mode of registration than that prescribed in the preceding Article, which is or may be applicable by law in one of the two countries to any work or article first published in such country, for the purpose of affording protection to copyright in such work or article, shall be extended on equal terms to any similar work or article first published in the other country.

Art. X. During the continuance of this convention, the duties now payable upon the lawful importation into the United Kingdom of Great Britain and Ireland of books, prints, drawings, or musical works, published throughout the territories of the French Republic, shall be reduced to and fixed at the rates hereinafter specified; that is to say—

3 E 2

1. Duties on books and musical works, viz.—

	£	s.	d.
(a) Works originally produced in the United Kingdom, and republished in France the cwt.	2	10	0
(b) Works not originally produced in the United Kingdom . . . . the cwt.	0	15	0

2. Prints or drawings :—

	£	s.	d.
(a) Coloured or plain, single . . . each	0	0	0½
(b) Bound or sewed . . . the dozen	0	0	1½

It is agreed that the rates of duty above specified shall not be raised during the continuance of the present convention: and that if hereafter, during the continuance of this convention, any reduction of those rates should be made in favour of books, prints, drawings, or musical works published in any other country, such reduction shall be at the same time extended to similar articles published in France.

It is moreover understood that all works published in France, of which any part may have been originally produced in the United Kingdom, shall be considered as " works originally produced in the United Kingdom, and republished in France," and as such shall be subject to the duty of fifty shillings per cwt., although the same may contain also original matter not produced in the United Kingdom; unless such original matter shall be at least equal in bulk to the part of the work originally produced in the United Kingdom, in which case the work shall be subject only to the duty of fifteen shillings per cwt.

Art. XI. In order to facilitate the execution of the present convention, the two high contracting parties engage to communicate to each other the laws and regulations which may hereafter be establishsd in their respective territories, with respect to copyright in works or productions protected by the stipulations of the present convention.

Art. XII. The stipulations of the present convention shall in no way affect the right which each of the two high contracting parties expressly reserves to itself, of controlling or of prohibiting, by measures of legislation or of internal police, the sale, circulation, representation, or exhibition of any work or production, in regard to which either country may deem it expedient to exercise that right.

Art. XIII. Nothing in this convention shall be construed to affect the right of either of the two high contracting parties to prohibit the importation into its own dominions, of such books as, by its internal law, or under engagements with other States, are or may be declared to be piracies, or infringements of copyright.

Art. XIV. Her Britannic Majesty engages to recommend to Parliament to pass an Act to enable her to carry into execution such of the arrangements contained in the present convention as require the sanction of an Act of the Legislature. When such an Act shall have been passed, the convention shall come into operation from and after a day to be then fixed upon by the two high contracting parties. Due notice shall be given beforehand in each country, by the Government of that country, of the day which may be so fixed upon; and the stipulations of the convention shall apply only to works or articles published after that day.

The convention shall continue in force for ten years from the day on which it may come into operation : and if neither party shall, twelve months before the expiration of the said period of ten years, give notice of its intention to terminate its operation, the convention shall continue in force for a year longer, and so on from year to year, until the expiration of a year's notice from either party for its termination.

The high contracting parties, however, reserve to themselves the power of making by common consent, in this convention, any modifications which may not be inconsistent with its spirit and principles, and which experience of its working may shew to be desirable.

Art. XV. The present convention shall be ratified, and the ratifications shall be exchanged at Paris as soon as may be within three months from the date of signature.

Procès-Verbal of the exchange of Ratifications.

The undersigned having met together in order, on the part of Her Majesty the Queen of the United Kingdom of Great Britain and Ireland, and of the President of the French Republic, to proceed to the exchange of the respective ratifications of the convention between Great Britain and France, signed at Paris on the 3rd of November last, for the mutual protection, in the two countries, of copyright in works of literature and of art; the respective instruments of ratification were produced, and after having been carefully compared and found to be exactly conformable to each other, were exchanged in the usual form.

1. Notwithstanding, however, that by the terms of Article XIV., it is stipulated that none of the arrangements of the convention shall come into operation until after the time when such of those arrangements as require to be confirmed in Great Britain by an Act of the Legislature, shall have been so sanctioned; it was mutually agreed, that such of those arrangements as do not require that sanction, and as the present state of the law enables the British

Crown to carry at once into execution, shall on either side receive their full and entire effect as soon as possible.

2. It was also agreed, that the stipulations contained in Article V., which forbid the republication in either of the two countries, of articles from newspapers or periodicals published in the other, the authors of which shall have notified in the newspaper or periodical in which such articles have appeared, that they forbid the republication thereof,—shall not be applicable to articles of political discussion.

The preceding interpretations and explanations shall have the same force and validity as if they had been inserted in the convention itself.

In witness whereof the undersigned have signed the present *procès-verbal*, in duplicate, at Paris, the eighth day of January, in the year of our Lord one thousand eight hundred and fifty-two.

(L.S.)　NORMANBY.

(L.S.)　TURGOT.

ACCESSION OF THE DUKES OF ANHALT TO THE CONVENTION CONCLUDED MAY 13, 1846, BETWEEN GREAT BRITAIN AND PRUSSIA, FOR THE ESTABLISHMENT OF INTERNATIONAL COPYRIGHT. *Signed at Berlin, February 8, 1853.*

Her Majesty the Queen of the United Kingdom of Great Britain and Ireland, and His Majesty the King of Prussia, having concluded at Berlin, on the 13th of May, 1846, a convention for the reciprocal protection of Copyright against piracy, and it having been stipulated in Article VIII. of that convention that those German States which, together with Prussia, compose the German Union of Customs, or which may hereafter join that Union, should have the right of acceding to the said convention, their Britannic and Prussian Majesties have addressed to their Serene Highnesses the Dukes of Anhalt-Dessau and Anhalt-Bernbourg the invitation to accede thereto;

And their Serene Highnesses being desirous of availing themselves of the opportunity thus afforded to them of acceding to the said convention;

The plenipotentiary of their Serene Highnesses the Dukes of Anhalt-Dessau and Anhalt-Bernbourg in consequence declares, in virtue of his full powers, that their said Serene Highnesses accede both to the convention of the 13th May, 1846, containing ten Articles, and of which a printed copy is annexed to the present Act, and to the special provisions contained in ss. 1-4 of the separate protocol signed on the same day, of which a copy is also hereunto annexed, promising that the stipulations of the said convention, which shall come into operation in the Duchies of Anhalt from and after the 1st of April, 1853, as well as those of the separate protocol, shall be carried into execution by their Serene Highnesses the Dukes of Anhalt-Dessau and Anhalt-Bernbourg, in all points, so far as they may be applicable to the relations which subsist between the Governments of the two Duchies and the British Government and its subjects, and declaring that English works registered, in virtue of Article II. of the convention, in the register kept at Berlin, shall be entitled also to protection against piracy in the Duchies of Anhalt.

The plenipotentiaries of Her Majesty the Queen of the United Kingdom of Great Britain and Ireland, and of His Majesty the King of Prussia, in virtue of their full powers, accept the accession of their Serene Highnesses the Dukes of Anhalt-Dessau and Anhalt-Bernbourg; promising that the stipulations of the convention of the 13th of May, 1846, as well as the special provisions which are contained in the protocol of the same date, shall be carried into execution by their respective Sovereigns on all points, with regard to the Governments of the Duchies of Anhalt and of their subjects, in the same manner as between the British and Prussian Governments and their subjects.

CONVENTION BETWEEN HER MAJESTY AND THE FREE HANSEATIC CITY OF HAMBURG, FOR THE ESTABLISHMENT OF INTERNATIONAL COPYRIGHT. *Signed at Hamburg, August 16, 1853.*

Art. I. The authors of works of literature or of art, to whom the laws of either of the two States do now or may hereafter give the right of property or copyright, shall be entitled to exercise that right in the territories of the other of such States for the same term, and to the same extent, as the authors of works of the same nature, if published in such other State, would therein be entitled to exercise such right; so that the republication or piracy in either State of any work of literature or of art published in the other shall be dealt with in the same manner as the republication or piracy of a work of the same nature first published in such other State, and so that such authors in the one State shall have the same remedies before the courts of justice in the other State, and shall enjoy in that other State the same protection against piracy and unauthorized republication as the law now does or may hereafter grant to authors in that State.

The terms "works of literature or of art" employed at the beginning of this Article shall be understood to comprise publications of books, of dramatic works, of musical compositions, of drawing, of painting, of sculpture, of engraving, of lithography, and of any other works whatsoever of literature and of the fine arts.

The lawful representatives or assigns of authors, translators, composers, painters, sculptors, or engravers shall, in all respects, enjoy the same rights which by the present convention are granted to the authors, translators, composers, painters, sculptors, or engravers themselves.

Art. II. The protection granted to original works is extended to translations, it being however clearly understood that the intention of the present Article is simply to protect a translator in respect of his own translation, and that it is not intended to confer upon the first translator of any work the exclusive right of translating that work, except in the case and to the extent provided for in the following Article.

Art. III. The author of any work published in either of the two States, who may choose to reserve the right of translating it, shall, until the expiration of five years from the date of the first publication of the translation thereof authorized by him, be, in the following cases, entitled to protection from the publication in the other State of any translation of such work not so authorized by him.

§ 1. If the original work shall have been registered and deposited in the one State within three months after its first publication in the other.

§ 2. If the author has notified on the title-page of his work his intention to reserve the right of translating it.

§ 3. Provided always that at least a part of the authorized translation shall have appeared within a year after the registration and deposit of the original, and that the whole shall have been published within three years after the date of such deposit.

§ 4. And provided that the publication of the translation shall take place within one of the two States, and that it shall be registered and deposited according to the provisions of Article VII.

With regard to works which are published in parts, it will be sufficient if the declaration of the author that he reserves the right of translation, shall appear in the first part. But with reference to the period of five years limited by this Article for the exercise of the exclusive right of translation, each part shall be treated as a separate work, and each part shall be registered and deposited in the one State within three months after its first publication in the other.

Art. IV. The stipulations of the preceding Article shall also be applicable to the representation of dramatic works, and to the performance of musical compositions, in so far as the laws of each of the two States are or shall be applicable in this respect to dramatic and musical works first publicly represented or performed therein.

In order, however, to entitle the author to legal protection in regard to the translation of a dramatic work, such translation must appear within three months after the registration and deposit of the original.

It is understood that the protection stipulated by the present Article is not intended to prohibit fair imitations or adaptations of dramatic works to the stage of England and Hamburgh respectively, but is only meant to prevent piratical translations.

The question whether a work is an imitation or a piracy shall in all cases be decided by the courts of justice of the respective States, according to the laws in force in each.

Art. V. The importation into, and the sale in either of the two States of piratical copies of works, which are protected from piracy under Articles I., II., and III. of the present convention, are prohibited, whether such piratical copies originate in the country where the work was published or in any other country.

Art. VI. In the event of an infraction of the provisions of the foregoing Articles, the pirated works or articles shall be seized and destroyed; and the persons who may have committed such infraction shall be liable in each State to the penalties and actions which are or may be prescribed by the laws of that State for such offences, committed in respect of a work or production of home origin.

Art. VII. Neither authors, nor translators, nor their lawful representatives or assigns, shall be entitled in either State to the protection stipulated by the preceding Articles, nor shall copyright be claimable in either State unless the work shall have been registered in the manner following, that is to say :—

1. If the work be one that has first appeared in Hamburgh, it must be registered at the Hall of the Company of Stationers in London ;

2. If the work be one that has first appeared in the dominions of Her Britannic Majesty, it must be registered in the Catalogue kept for that purpose at the Office of the Public Library at Hamburgh.

No person shall be entitled to such protection as aforesaid, unless he shall have duly complied with the laws and regulations of the respective States in regard to the work in respect of which such protection may be claimed. With regard to books, maps, and prints, and also with regard to dramatic works and musical compositions, unless such dramatic works and musical compositions shall be in manuscript only, no person shall be entitled to such protection, unless he shall have delivered gratuitously, at one or other of the places mentioned above, as the case may be, one copy of the best edition, or in the best state, in order to its being deposited at the place appointed for that purpose in each of the two States, that is to say, in Great Britain at the British Museum at London; and in Hamburgh at the Public Library of that city.

In every case the formality of deposit and registration must be fulfilled within three months after the first publication of the work in the other State. With regard to works published in parts, the period of three months shall not begin to run until the date of the publication of the last part, unless the author shall have notified his intention to reserve the right of translating it, as provided in Article III., in which case each part shall be treated as a separate work.

A certified copy of the entry in the register-book of the Company of Stationers in London shall confer, within the British dominions, the exclusive right of republication, until a better right shall have been established by any other party before a court of justice.

The certificate given under the laws of Hamburgh, proving the registration of any work in that State, shall be valid for the same purpose throughout the territory of Hamburgh.

A certificate or certified copy of the registration of any work so registered in either State, shall, if required, be delivered at the time of registration, and such certificate shall state the exact date at which the registration was made.

The charge for the registration of a single work, under the stipulations of this Article, shall not exceed one shilling in England, nor twelve shillings currency in Hamburgh; and the further charge for a certificate of such registration shall not exceed the sum of five shillings in England, nor four marks currency in Hamburgh.

Art. VIII. With regard to any article other than books, prints, maps, and musical publications, in respect to which protection may be claimable under Article I. of the present convention, it is agreed that any other mode of registration than that prescribed in the preceding Article, which is or may be applicable by law in one of the two States to any work or article first published in such State, for the purpose of affording protection to copyright in such work or article, shall be extended on equal terms to any similar work or article first published in the other State.

Art. IX. During the continuance of this convention, the duties now payable upon the lawful importation into the United Kingdom of Great Britain and Ireland of books, prints, drawings, or musical works, published throughout the Republic of Hamburgh, shall be reduced to and fixed at the rates hereinafter specified, that is to say :

1. Duties on books and musical works, viz. :

		£	s.	d.
(a.) Works originally produced in the United Kingdom, and republished in Hamburgh	the cwt.	2	10	0
(b.) Works not originally produced in the United Kingdom.	the cwt.	0	15	0

2. Prints or drawings :

		£	s.	d.
(a.) Coloured or plain, single	each	0	0	0½
(b.) Bound or sewed	the dozen	0	0	1½

It is agreed that the rates of duty above specified shall not be raised during the continuance of the present convention, and that if hereafter, during the continuance of this convention, any reduction of those rates should be made in favour of books, prints, drawings, or musical works published in any other country, such reduction shall be at the same time extended to similar articles published in Hamburgh.

It is moreover understood that all works published in Hamburgh, of which any part may have been originally produced in the United Kingdom, shall be considered as works originally produced in the United Kingdom and republished in Hamburgh, and as such shall be subject to the duty of fifty shillings per cwt., although the same may contain also original matter not produced in the United Kingdom, unless such original matter shall be at least equal in bulk to the part of the work originally produced in the United Kingdom, in which case the work shall be subject only to the duty of fifteen shillings per cwt.

It is further agreed that during the continuance of this convention, the rate of duties now payable on the importation into the territories of Hamburgh of books, prints, drawings, and musical works published throughout the dominions of Her Britannic Majesty, shall not be raised, and shall not exceed the rates of duty which are or may be levied on the importation into the United Kingdom of similar works published in the territory of Hamburgh.

Art. X. It is agreed that all books, prints, and drawings, published within the dominions of any other State that has concluded or concludes, or has acceded or accedes to, a Copyright Convention with Great Britain, and which may be legally imported into the United Kingdom, shall, if exported from Hamburgh, be considered, for the purposes of this convention, to have been exported from the country of their publication.

Art. XI. It is further agreed, that stamps shall be provided at Hamburgh according to a pattern to be made known to the Custom-house officers of the United Kingdom, and that such stamps shall be affixed to all books intended for exportation to the United Kingdom, unless they be already provided with the stamps of the States mentioned in the foregoing Article X.

Art. XII. In order to facilitate the execution of the present convention, the two high contracting parties engage to communicate to each other the laws and regulations which may hereafter be established in their respective territories, with respect to copyright in works or productions protected by the stipulations of the present convention.

Art. XIII. The stipulations of the present convention shall in no way affect the right which each of the two high contracting parties expressly reserves to itself, of controlling or of prohibiting, by measures of legislation or of internal police, the sale, circulation, representation, or exhibition of any work or production, in regard to which either State may deem it expedient to exercise that right.

Art. XIV. Nothing in this convention shall be construed to affect the right of either of the two high contracting parties to prohibit the importation into its own dominions of such books as, by its internal law, or under engagements with other States, are or may be declared to be piracies or infringements of copyright.

Art. XV. The present convention shall come into operation as soon as possible after the exchange of the ratifications. Due notice shall be given beforehand in each State, by the Government of that State, of the day which may be fixed upon for its coming into operation, and the stipulations of the convention shall apply only to works or articles published after that day.

The convention shall continue in force for ten years from the day on which it may come into operation; and if neither party shall, twelve months before the expiration of the said period of ten years, give notice of its intention to terminate its operation, the convention shall continue in force for a year longer, and so on from year to year, until the expiration of a year's notice from either party for its termination.

The high contracting parties, however, reserve to themselves the power of making, by common consent in this convention, any modifications which may not be inconsistent with its spirit and principles, and which experience of its working may show to be desirable.

Art. XVI. The present convention shall be ratified, and the ratifications shall be exchanged at Hamburgh as soon as may be within three months from the date of the signature.

CONVENTION BETWEEN HER MAJESTY AND THE KING OF THE
BELGIANS, FOR THE ESTABLISHMENT OF INTERNATIONAL
COPYRIGHT. *Signed at London, August* 12, 1854.

Art. I. From and after the date on which, according to the
provisions of Article XV., the present convention shall come into
operation, the authors of works of literature or of art, to whom the
laws of either of the two countries do now or may hereafter give
the right of property or copyright, shall be entitled to exercise that
right in the territories of the other of such countries for the same
term, and to the same extent, as the authors of works of the same
nature, if published in such other country, would therein be
entitled to exercise such right; so that the republication or piracy
in either country, of any work of literature or of art, published in
the other, shall be dealt with in the same manner as the republication or piracy of a work of the same nature first published in
such other country ; and so that such authors in the one country
shall have the same remedies before the courts of justice in the
other country, and shall enjoy in that other country the same
protection against piracy and unauthorized republication, as the
law now does or may hereafter grant to authors in that country.

The terms "works of literature or of art," employed at the
beginning of this Article, shall be understood to comprise publications of books, of dramatic works, of musical compositions, of
drawing, of painting, of sculpture, of engraving, of lithography, and
of any other works whatsoever of literature and of the fine arts.

The lawful representatives or assigns of authors, translators,
composers, painters, sculptors, or engravers, shall, in all respects,
enjoy the same rights which by the present convention are granted
to the authors, translators, composers, painters, sculptors, or
engravers themselves.

Art. II. The protection granted to original works is extended to
translations; it being, however, clearly understood that the intention of the present Article is simply to protect a translator in
respect of his own translation, and that it is not intended to confer
upon the first translator of any work the exclusive right of translating that work, except in the case and to the extent provided for
in the following Article.

Art. III. The author of any work published in either of the two
countries, who may choose to reserve the right of translating it,
shall, until the expiration of five years from the date of the first
publication of the translation thereof authorized by him, be, in the
following cases, entitled to protection from the publication in the

other country of any translation of such work not so authorized by him;

§ 1. If the original work shall have been registered and deposited in the one country within three months after its first publication in the other.

§ 2. If the author has notified on the title-page of his work his intention to reserve the right of translating it.

§ 3. Provided always, that at least a part of the authorized translation shall have appeared within a year after the registration and deposit of the original, and that the whole shall have been published within three years after the date of such deposit.

§ 4. And provided that the publication of the translation shall take place within one of the two countries, and that it shall be registered and deposited according to the provisions of Article VIII.

With regard to works which are published in parts, it will be sufficient if the declaration of the author that he reserves the right of translation, shall appear in the first part. But with reference to the period of five years limited by this Article for the exercise of the exclusive right of translation, each part shall be treated as a separate work, and each part shall be registered and deposited in the one country within three months after its first publication in the other.

Art. IV. The stipulations of the preceding Articles shall also be applicable to the representation of dramatic works, and to the performance of musical compositions, in so far as the laws of each of the two countries are or shall be applicable in this respect to dramatic and musical works first publicly represented or performed therein.

In order, however, to entitle the author to legal protection in regard to the translation of a dramatic work, such translation must appear within three months after the registration and deposit of the original.

It is understood that the protection stipulated by the present Article is not intended to prohibit fair imitations, or adaptations of dramatic works to the stage in England and Belgium respectively, but is only meant to prevent piratical translations.

The question whether a work is an imitation or a piracy, shall in all cases be decided by the courts of justice of the respective countries, according to the laws in force in each.

Art. V. Notwithstanding the stipulations of Articles I. and II. of the present convention, articles extracted from newspapers or periodicals published in either of the two countries, may be republished or translated in the newspapers or periodicals of the other country, provided the source from whence such articles are taken be acknowledged.

Nevertheless, such permission shall not be construed to authorize the republication in one of the two countries, of articles from newspapers or periodicals published in the other country, the authors of which shall have notified in a conspicuous manner in the journal or periodical in which such articles have appeared, that they forbid the republication thereof.

This last stipulation shall not, however, apply to articles of political discussion.

Art. VI. The introduction, circulation, sale, and exhibition, in either of the two countries, of unauthorized republications of works or articles defined in the preceding Articles I., II., III., IV., are prohibited, whether such unauthorized republications originate in either of the two countries, or whether they originate in any foreign country.

Art. VII. In the event of an infraction of the provisions of the foregoing Articles, the pirated works or articles shall be seized and destroyed ; and the persons who may have committed such infraction shall be liable in each country to the penalties and actions which are or may be prescribed by the laws of that country for such offences, committed in respect of a work or production of home origin.

Art. VIII. Neither authors nor translators, nor their lawful representatives or assigns, shall be entitled in either country to the protection stipulated by the preceding Articles, nor shall copyright be claimable in either country, unless the work shall have been registered in the manner following, that is to say :

1. If the work be one that has first appeared in Belgium, it must be registered at the Hall of the Company of Stationers in London.

2. If the work be one that has first appeared in the dominions of Her Britannic Majesty, it must be registered at the office of the Minister of the Interior at Brussels.

No person shall be entitled to such protection as aforesaid, unless he shall have duly complied with the laws and regulations of the respective countries in regard to the work in respect of which such protection may be claimed. With regard to books, maps, and prints, and also with regard to dramatic works and musical publications, unless such dramatic works and musical publications shall be in manuscript only, no person shall be entitled to such protection, unless he shall have delivered gratuitously, at one or other of the places mentioned above, as the case may be, one copy of the best edition, or in the best state, in order to its being deposited at the place appointed for that purpose in each of the two countries : that is to say, in Great Britain, at the British Museum at London ; and in Belgium, at the Royal Library at Brussels.

In every case the formality of deposit and registration must be fulfilled within three months after the first publication of the work in the other country. With regard to works published in parts, each part shall be treated as a separate work.

A certified copy of the entry in the register-book of the Company of Stationers in London shall confer, within the British dominions, the exclusive right of republication, until a better right shall have been established by any other party before a court of justice.

The certificate given under the laws of Belgium, proving the registration of any work in that country, shall be valid for the same purpose throughout the territories of the kingdom of Belgium.

A certificate or certified copy of the registration of any work so registered in either country shall, if required, be delivered at the time of registration ; and such certificate shall state the exact date at which the registration was made.

The charge for the registration of a single work, under the stipulations of this Article, shall not exceed one shilling in England, nor one franc and twenty-five centimes in Belgium ; and the further charge for a certificate of such registration shall not exceed the sum of five shillings in England, nor six francs and twenty-five centimes in Belgium.

The provisions of this Article shall not extend to articles which may appear in newspapers or periodicals ; which shall be protected from republication or translation simply by a notice from the author, as prescribed by Article V. But if any article or work which has originally appeared in a newspaper or periodical, shall afterwards be published in a separate form, it shall then become subject to the stipulations of the present Article.

Art. IX. With regard to any work of literature or of art other than books, prints, maps, and musical publications, in respect to which protection may be claimable under Article I. of the present convention, it is agreed, that any other mode of registration than that prescribed in the preceding Article, which is or may be applicable by law in one of the two countries to any work or article first published in such country, for the purpose of affording protection to copyright in such work or article, shall be extended on equal terms to any similar work or article, first published in the other country.

Art. X. During the continuance of this convention, the duties now payable upon the lawful importation into the United Kingdom of Great Britain and Ireland of books, prints, drawings, or musical works, published throughout the territories of the Kingdom of Belgium, shall be reduced to and fixed at the rates hereinafter specified ; that is to say :

                                              £ s. d.
1. On books and musical works . . the cwt. 0 15 0
2. On prints or drawings, coloured or plain,
   the lb. 0 0 1½

It is agreed that the rates of duty above specified shall not be
raised during the continuance of the present convention ; and that
if hereafter, during the continuance of this convention, any reduction of those rates should be made in favour of books, prints,
drawings, or musical works published in any other country, such
reduction shall be at the same time extended to similar articles
published in Belgium.

During the continuance of the present convention, the duties
now payable on the lawful importation into Belgium, of books,
musical works, prints, and maps or charts published throughout
the United Kingdom of Great Britain and Ireland, shall be reduced
to and fixed at the uniform rate of ten francs the hundred kilo-
grammes.

Art. XI. It is agreed that no books shall, for the purposes of this
convention, so far as relates to the rate of duty at which such books
are to be entered, be deemed to have been published in Belgium,
except such as appear by their title-page to have been published at
some town or place within the dominions of Belgium.

Art. XII. In order to facilitate the execution of the present convention, the two high contracting parties engage to communicate
to each other the laws and regulations which may hereafter be
established in their respective territories, with respect to copyright
in works or productions protected by the stipulations of the present
convention.

Art. XIII. The stipulations of the present convention shall in no
way affect the right which each of the two high contracting parties
expressly reserves to itself, of controlling and of prohibiting, by
measures of legislation or of internal police, the sale, circulation,
representation, or exhibition of any work or production, in regard
to which either country may deem it expedient to exercise that right.

Art. XIV. Nothing in this convention shall be construed to affect
the right of either of the two high contracting parties to prohibit
the importation into its own dominions, of such books as, by its
internal law, or under engagements with other States, are or may
be declared to be piracies, or infringements of copyright.

Art. XV. The present convention shall come into operation as
soon as possible after the exchange of the ratifications. Due notice
shall be given beforehand in each country, by the Government of
that country, of the day which may be fixed upon for that purpose,
and the stipulations of the convention shall be applicable only to

                                                      3 F

works and articles published, and to dramatic works or musical compositions represented or executed for the first time in either of the two countries, after the convention shall have come into operation.

The convention shall continue in force for ten years from the day on which it may come into operation; and if neither contracting party shall, twelve months before the expiration of the said period of ten years, give notice of its intention to terminate its operation, the convention shall continue in force for a year longer, and so on from year to year, until the expiration of a year's notice from either contracting party for its termination.

The high contracting parties, however, reserve to themselves the power of making by common consent, in this convention, any modifications which may not be inconsistent with its spirit and principles, and which experience of its working may show to be desirable.

Art. XVI. The present convention shall be ratified, and the ratifications shall be exchanged at London as soon as may be within six months from the date of signature.

CONVENTION BETWEEN HER MAJESTY AND THE KING OF PRUSSIA, ADDITIONAL TO THE CONVENTION CONCLUDED AT BERLIN, MAY 13, 1846, FOR THE ESTABLISHMENT OF INTERNATIONAL COPYRIGHT. *Signed at London, June 14, 1855.*

Art. I. It is agreed that all books, prints, and drawings published within the dominions of any other State that has concluded or may conclude, or which has acceded or may accede to, a Copyright Convention with Great Britain, shall, if exported from Prussia, Saxony, Saxe-Weimar, Saxe-Meiningen, Saxe-Altenburg, Saxe-Coburg-Gotha-Brunswick, Anhalt-Dessau-Cöthen, Anhalt-Bernburg, Schwarzburg-Rudolstadt, Schwarzburg-Sondershausen, or Reuss, be considered, for the purposes of this convention, to have been exported from the country of their publication.

Art. II. The protection granted by the convention which was concluded between the high contracting parties on the 13th of May, 1846, to original works, is extended to translations; it being, however, clearly understood that the intention of the present Article is simply to protect a translator in respect of his own translation, and that it is not intended to confer upon the first translator of any work the exclusive right of translating that work, except in the case and to the extent provided for in the following Article.

Art. III. The author of any work published in either of the two countries, who may choose to reserve the right of translating it, shall, until the expiration of five years from the date of the first publication of the translation thereof authorized by him, be, in the following cases, entitled to protection from the publication in the other country of any translations of such work not so authorized by him :

§ 1. If the original work shall have been registered and deposited in the one country within three months after its first publication in the other ;

§ 2. If the author has notified on the title-page of his work his intention to reserve the right of translating it;

§ 3. Provided always, that at least a part of the authorized translation shall have appeared within a year after the registration and deposit of the original, and that the whole shall have been published within three years after the date of such deposit;

§ 4. And provided that the publication of the translation shall take place within one of the two countries, and that it shall be registered and deposited in conformity with the stipulations of Article II. of the convention of the 13th of May, 1846.

With regard to works which are published in parts, it will be sufficient if the declaration of the author that he reserves the right of translation shall appear in the first part. But with reference to the period of five years, limited by this Article for the exercise of the exclusive right of translation, each part shall be treated as a separate work, and each part shall be registered and deposited in the one country within three months after its first publication in the other.

Art. IV. The stipulations of the preceding Articles shall also be applicable to the representation of dramatic works, and to the performance of musical compositions, in so far as the laws of each of the two countries are or shall be applicable in this respect to dramatic and musical works first publicly represented or performed therein.

In order, however, to entitle the author to legal protection in regard to the translation of a dramatic work, such translation must appear within three months after the registration and deposit of the original.

It is understood that the protection stipulated by the present Article is not intended to prohibit fair imitations, or adaptations of dramatic works to the stage in England and Prussia respectively, but is only meant to prevent piratical translations.

The question whether a work is an imitation or a piracy, shall in all cases be decided by the courts of justice of the respective countries, according to the laws in force in each.

3 F 2

Art. V. Notwithstanding the stipulations of Article I. of the convention of the 13th of May, 1846, and of Article II. of the present additional convention, articles extracted from newspapers or periodicals published in either of the two countries, may be republished or translated in the newspapers or periodicals of the other country, provided the source from whence such articles are taken be acknowledged.

Nevertheless, this permission shall not be construed to authorize the republication or translation in one of the two countries, of articles from newspapers or periodicals published in the other country, the authors of which shall have notified in a conspicuous manner in the journal or periodical in which such articles have appeared, that they forbid the republication thereof.

This last stipulation shall not, however, apply to articles of political discussion.

Art. VI. The present additional convention shall come into operation as soon as possible after the exchange of the ratifications thereof. Due notice shall be given beforehand in each country by the Government of that country; of the day which may be fixed upon for its so coming into operation, and its stipulations shall apply only to works published after that day.

Art. VII. The present additional convention shall have the same duration as the convention of the 13th May, 1846. It shall be ratified, and the ratifications shall be exchanged at London as soon as may be within two months from the date of signature.

CONVENTION BETWEEN HER MAJESTY AND THE QUEEN OF SPAIN, FOR THE ESTABLISHMENT OF INTERNATIONAL COPYRIGHT. *Signed at Madrid, July 7, 1857.*

Art. I. From and after the date on which, according to the provisions of Article XIII., the present convention shall come into operation, the authors of works of literature or of art, to whom the laws of either of the two countries do now or may hereafter give the right of property, or copyright, shall be entitled to exercise that right in the territories of the other of such countries for the same term, and to the same extent, as the authors of works of the same nature, if published in such other country, would therein be entitled to exercise such right; so that the republication or piracy, in either country, of any work of literature or of art published in the other shall be dealt with in the same manner as the republication or piracy of a work of the same nature first published in such other country; and so that such authors in the one country shall have the same remedies before the courts of justice in the other country, and shall enjoy in that other country the same protection against piracy and unauthorized republication, as the law now does or may hereafter grant to authors in that country.

The terms "works of literature or of art," employed at the beginning of this Article, shall be understood to comprise publications of books, of dramatic works, of musical compositions, of drawing, of painting, of sculpture, of engraving, of lithography, and of any other works whatsoever of literature and of the fine arts.

The lawful representatives or assigns of authors, translators, composers, painters, sculptors, or engravers, shall, in all respects, enjoy the same right which by the present convention are granted to the authors, translators, composers, painters, sculptors, or engravers themselves.

Art. II. The protection granted to original works is extended to translations, it being, however, clearly understood that the intention of the present Article is simply to protect a translator in respect of his own translation, and that it is not intended to confer upon the first translator of any work the exclusive right of translating that work, except in the case and to the extent provided for in the following Article.

Art. III. The author of any work published in either of the two countries, who may choose to reserve the right of translating it, shall, until the expiration of five years from the date of the first publication of the translation thereof authorized by him, be, in the following cases, entitled to protection from the publication in the other country of any translation of such work not so authorized by him :—

§ 1. If the original work shall have been registered and deposited in the one country within three months after its first publication in the other;

§ 2. If the author has notified on the title-page of his work his intention to reserve the right of translating it;

§ 3. Provided always, that at least a part of the authorized translation shall have appeared within a year after the registration and deposit of the original, and that the whole shall have been published within three years after the date of such deposit;

§ 4. And provided that the publication of the translation shall take place within one of the two countries, and that it shall be registered and deposited according to the provisions of Article VIII.

With regard to works which are published in parts, it will be sufficient if the declaration of the author that he reserves the right . of translation shall appear in the first part. But with reference to the period of five years limited by this Article for the exercise of the exclusive right of translation, each part shall be treated as a separate work, and each part shall be registered and deposited in the one country within three months after its first publication in the other.

Art. IV. The stipulations of the preceding Articles shall also be applicable to the representation of dramatic works, and to the performance of musical compositions, in so far as the laws of each of the two countries are or shall be applicable in this respect to dramatic and musical works first publicly represented or performed therein.

In order, however, to entitle the author to legal protection in regard to the translation of a dramatic work, such translation must appear within three months after the registration and deposit of the original.

It is understood that the protection stipulated by the present Article is not intended to prohibit fair imitations or adaptations of dramatic works to the stage in England and Spain respectively, but is only meant to prevent piratical translations.

The question whether a work is an imitation or a piracy shall in all cases be decided by the courts of justice of the respective countries, according to the laws in force in each.

Art. V. Notwithstanding the stipulations of Articles I. and II. of the present convention, articles extracted from newspapers or periodicals published in either of the two countries may be republished or translated in the newspapers or periodicals of the other country, provided the source from whence such articles are taken be acknowledged.

Nevertheless, this permission shall not be construed to authorize the republication in one of the two countries of articles other than those of political discussion, from newspapers or periodicals published in the other country, the authors of which shall have notified in a conspicuous manner in the journal or periodical in which such articles have appeared, that they forbid the republication thereof.

Art. VI. The importation into and the sale in either of the two countries of piratical copies of works which are protected from piracy under Articles I., II., III., and V. of the present convention are prohibited, whether such piratical copies originate in the country where the work was published or in any other country.

Art. VII. In the event of an infraction of the provisions of the foregoing articles, the pirated works or articles shall be seized and destroyed; and the persons who may have committed such infraction shall be liable in each country to the penalties and actions which are or may be prescribed by the laws of that country for such offences, committed in respect of a work or production of home origin.

Art. VIII. Neither authors, nor translators, nor their lawful representatives or assigns, shall be entitled in either country to the protection stipulated by the preceding Articles, nor shall copyright be claimable in either country, unless the work shall have been registered in the manner following, that is to say :—

1. If the work be one that has first appeared in Spain it must be registered at the Hall of the Company of Stationers in London ;

2. If the work be one that has first appeared in the dominions of Her Britannic Majesty, it must be registered at the Ministry of Public Works (*Ministerio de Fomento*) at Madrid.

No person shall be entitled to such protection as aforesaid unless he shall have duly complied with the laws and regulations of the respective countries in regard to the work in respect of which such protection may be claimed. With regard to books, maps, and prints, and also with regard to dramatic works and musical compositions (unless such dramatic works and musical compositions shall be in manuscript only), no person shall be entitled to such protection unless he shall have delivered gratuitously, at one or other of the places mentioned above, as the case may be, one copy of the best edition, or in the best state, in order to its being deposited at the place appointed for that purpose in each of the two countries: that is to say, in Great Britain, at the British Museum at London; and in Spain, at the National Library at Madrid.

In every case the formality of deposit and registration must be fulfilled within three months after the first publication of the work in the other country. With regard to works published in parts, each part shall be treated as a separate work.

A certified copy of the entry in the register-book of the Company of Stationers in London shall confer, within the British dominions, the exclusive right of republication until a better right shall have been established by any other party before a court of justice.

The certificate given under the laws of Spain, proving the registration of any work in that country, shall be valid for the same purpose throughout the territories of Her Catholic Majesty.

A certificate or certified copy of the registration of any work so registered in either country shall, if required, be delivered at the time of registration, and such certificate shall state the exact date at which the registration was made.

The charge for the registration of a single work, under the stipulations of this Article, shall not exceed one shilling in England, nor five rials vellon in Spain; and the further charge for a certificate of such registration shall not exceed the sum of five shillings in England, nor twenty-five rials vellon in Spain.

The provisions of this Article shall not extend to articles which may appear in newspapers or periodicals, which shall be protected from republication or translation simply by a notice from the author, as prescribed by Article V. But if any article or work which has originally appeared in a newspaper or periodical shall afterwards be published in a separate form, it shall then become subject to the stipulations of the present Article.

Art. IX. With regard to any article other than books, prints, maps, and musical publications, in respect to which protection may be claimable under Article I. of the present convention, it is agreed that any other mode of registration than that prescribed in the preceding Article, which is or may be applicable by law in one of the two countries to any work or article first published in such country, for the purpose of affording protection to copyright in such work or article, shall be extended on equal terms to any similar work or article first published in the other country.

Art. X. In order to facilitate the execution of the present convention, the two high contracting parties engage to communicate to each other the laws and regulations which may hereafter be established in their respective territories, with respect to copyright in works or productions protected by the stipulations of the present convention.

Art. XI. The stipulations of the present convention shall in no way affect the right which each of the two high contracting parties expressly reserves to itself, of controlling or of prohibiting, by measures of legislation or of internal police, the sale, circulation, representation or exhibition of any work or production in regard to which either country may deem it expedient to exercise that right.

Art. XII. Nothing in this convention shall be construed to affect the right of either of the two high contracting parties to prohibit the importation into its own dominions of such books as, by its internal law, or under engagements with other States, are or may be declared to be piracies, or infringements of copyright.

Art. XIII. The present convention shall come into operation as soon as possible after the exchange of the ratifications. Due notice shall be given beforehand in each country, by the Government of that country, of the day which may be fixed upon for its coming into operation; and the stipulations of the convention shall apply only to works or articles published after that day.

The convention shall continue in force for six years from the day on which it may come into operation; and if neither party shall, twelve months before the expiration of the said period of six years, give notice of its intention to terminate its operation, the convention shall continue in force for a year longer, and so on from year to year, until the expiration of a year's notice from either party for its termination (a).

The high contracting parties, however, reserve to themselves the power of making by common consent, in this convention, any modifications which may not be inconsistent with its spirit and principles, and which experience of its working may show to be desirable.

Art. XIV. The present convention shall be ratified, and the ratifications shall be exchanged at Madrid as soon as may be within three months from the date of signature.

Declaration.

The undersigned plenipotentiaries of Her Majesty the Queen of the United Kingdom of Great Britain and Ireland, and of Her Majesty the Queen of Spain, authorized for this purpose by their respective Sovereigns, declare, for the purpose of facilitating the customs service in the execution of a part of the convention for the protection of literary property which they have this day signed, that, in order to make the origin of works published in either of the two countries evident, there shall appear in their title-page the city or place of their publication.

(L.S.)   HOWDEN.

(L.S.)   EL. MARGS. DE PIAL.

CONVENTION BETWEEN HER MAJESTY AND THE KING OF SARDINIA, FOR THE ESTABLISHMENT OF INTERNATIONAL COPYRIGHT. *Signed at Turin, November* 30, 1860.

Art. I. From and after the date on which, according to the provisions of Article XIV., the present convention shall come into operation, the authors of works of literature or of art, to whom the laws of either of the two countries do now or may hereafter give the right of property, or copyright, shall be entitled to exercise that right in the territories of the other of such countries for the same term, and to the same extent, as the authors of works of the same nature, if published in such other country, would therein be entitled to exercise such right; so that the republication or piracy, in either country, of any work of literature or of art published in the other, shall be dealt with in the same manner as the republication or piracy of a work of the same nature first published in such other country; and so that authors in the one country shall have the same remedies before the courts of justice in the other country,

(a) This treaty expired on the 17th March, 1880, and a new treaty has been entered into, but is not yet printed.

and shall enjoy in that other country the same protection against piracy and unauthorized republication, as the law now does or may hereafter grant to authors in that country.

The terms " works of literature or of art," employed at the beginning of this Article, shall be understood to comprise publications of books, of dramatic works, of musical compositions, of drawing, of painting, of sculpture, of engraving, of lithography, and of any other works whatsoever of literature and of the fine arts.

The lawful representatives or assigns of authors, translators, composers, painters, sculptors, or engravers, shall, in all respects, enjoy the same rights which by the present convention are granted to the authors, translators, composers, painters, sculptors, or engravers themselves.

Art. II. The protection granted to original works is extended to translations; it being, however, clearly understood that the intention of the present Article is simply to protect a translator in respect of his own translation, and that it is not intended to confer upon the first translator of any work the exclusive right of translating that work, except in the case and to the extent provided for in the following Article.

Art. III. The author of any work published in either of the two countries, who may choose to reserve the right of translating it, shall, until the expiration of five years from the date of the first publication of the translation thereof authorized by him, be, in the following cases, entitled to protection from the publication in the other country of any translation of such work not so authorized by him :—

1. If the original work shall have been registered and deposited in the one country within three months after its first publication in the other;

2. If the author has notified on the title-page of his work his intention to reserve the right of translating it;

3. Provided always, that at least a part of the authorized translation shall have appeared within a year after the registration and deposit of the original, and that the whole shall have been published within three years after the date of such deposit;

4. And provided that the publication of the translation shall take place within one of the two countries, and that it shall be registered and deposited according to the provisions of Article VIII.

With regard to works published in parts, it will be sufficient if the declaration of the author that he reserves the right of translation shall appear in the first part. But with reference to the period of five years limited by this Article for the exercise of the exclusive right of translation, each part shall be treated as a separate work, and each part shall be registered and deposited in the one country within three months after its first publication in the other.

Art. IV. The stipulations of the preceding Articles shall also be applicable to the representation of dramatic works, and to the performance of musical compositions, in as far as the laws of each of the two countries are or shall be applicable in this respect to dramatic and musical works first publicly represented or performed therein.

In order, however, to entitle the author to legal protection in regard to the translation of a dramatic work, such translation must appear within three months after the registration and deposit of the original.

It is understood that the protection stipulated by the present Article is not intended to prohibit fair imitations or adaptations of dramatic works to the stage of the respective countries, but is only meant to prevent piratical translations.

The question whether a work is an imitation or a piracy shall in all cases be decided by the courts of justice of the respective countries, according to the laws in force in each.

Art. V. Notwithstanding the stipulations of Articles I. and II. of the present convention, articles extracted from newspapers or periodicals published in either of the two countries may be republished or translated in the newspapers or periodicals of the other country, provided the source from whence such articles are taken be acknowledged.

Nevertheless, this permission shall not be construed to authorize the republication in one of the two countries of articles other than those of political discussion, from newspapers or periodicals published in the other country, the authors of which shall have notified in a conspicuous manner in the journal or periodical in which such articles have appeared that they forbid the republication thereof.

Art. VI. The importation into and the sale in either of the two countries of piratical copies of works which are protected from piracy under Articles I., II., III., and V. of the present convention are prohibited, whether such piratical copies originate in the country where the work was published or in any other country.

Art. VII. In the event of an infraction of the provisions of the foregoing Articles, the pirated works or articles shall be seized and destroyed; and the persons who may have committed such infraction shall be liable in each country to the penalties and actions which are or may be prescribed by the laws of that country for such offences, committed in respect of a work or production of home origin.

Art. VIII. Neither authors, nor translators, nor their lawful representatives or assigns, shall be entitled in either country to the protection stipulated by the preceding Articles, nor shall copyright be claimable in either country, unless the work shall have been registered in the manner following, that is to say:—

1. If the work be one that has first appeared in the dominions of His Sardinian Majesty, it must be registered at the Hall of the Company of Stationers in London (*Stationers' Hall*);

2. If the work be one that has first appeared in the dominions of Her Britannic Majesty, it must be registered at the Ministry of the Interior (*Ministero dell' Interno*) at Turin.

No person shall be entitled to such protection as aforesaid, unless he shall have duly complied with the laws and regulations of the respective countries in regard to the work in respect of which such protection may be claimed. With regard to books, maps, and prints, and also with regard to dramatic works and musical compositions (unless such dramatic works and musical compositions shall be in manuscript only), no person shall be entitled to such protection unless he shall have delivered gratuitously, at one or other of the places mentioned above, as the case may be, one copy of the best edition, or in the best state, in order to its being deposited at the place appointed for that purpose in each of the two countries: that is to say, in the dominions of Her Britannic Majesty, at the British Museum in London; and in the dominions of His Sardinian Majesty, at the Ministry of the Interior (*Ministero dell' Interno*) at Turin.

In every case, the formality of deposit and registration must be fulfilled within three months after the first publication of the work in the other country. With regard to works published in parts, each part shall be treated as a separate work.

A certified copy of the entry in the register book of the Company of Stationers in London shall confer, within the British dominions, the exclusive right of republication, until a better right shall have been established by any other party before a court of justice.

The certificate given under the laws of the States of His Sardinian Majesty, proving the registration of any work in that country, shall be valid for the same purpose throughout the above-mentioned States.

A certificate or certified copy of the registration of any work so registered in either country shall, if required, be delivered at the time of registration; and such certificate shall state the exact date at which the registration was made.

The charge for the registration of a single work, under the stipulations of this Article, shall not exceed one shilling in England, nor one franc twenty-five centimes in the States of His Sardinian

Majesty; and the further charge for a certificate of such registration shall not exceed the sum of five shillings in England, nor six francs and twenty-five centimes in the States of His Sardinian Majesty.

The provisions of this Article shall not extend to articles which may appear in newspapers or periodicals; which shall be protected from republication or translation simply by a notice from the author, as prescribed by Article V. But if any article or work which has originally appeared in a newspaper or periodical shall afterwards be published in a separate form, it shall then become subject to the stipulations of the present Article.

Art. IX. With regard to any article other than books, prints, maps, and musical publications, in respect to which protection may be claimable under Article I. of the present convention, it is agreed, that any other mode of registration than that prescribed in the preceding Article, which is or may be applicable by law in one of the two countries to any work or article first published in such country, for the purpose of affording protection to copyright in such work or article, shall be extended on equal terms to any similar work or article first published in the other country.

Art. X. It is agreed that if by any convention for the protection of copyright in works of literature or of art, greater favours than those stipulated by the present convention should be accorded by either of the high contracting parties to a third power, the same advantages shall be extended to the other party on the same conditions.

Art. XI. In order to facilitate the execution of the present convention, the two high contracting parties engage to communicate to each other the laws and regulations which may hereafter be established in their respective territories, with respect to copyright in works or productions protected by the stipulations of the present convention.

Art. XII. The stipulations of the present convention shall in no way affect the right which each of the two high contracting parties expressly reserves to itself, of controlling or prohibiting, by measures of legislation or of internal police, the sale, circulation, representation, or exhibition of any work or production in regard to which either country may deem it expedient to exercise that right.

Art. XIII. Nothing in this convention shall be construed to affect the right of either of the two high contracting parties to prohibit the importation into its own dominions of such books as, by its internal law, or under engagements with other States, are or may be declared piracies, or infringements of copyright.

Art. XIV. The present convention shall come into operation as soon as possible after the exchange of the ratifications. Due notice shall be given beforehand in each country, by the Government of

that country, of the day which may be fixed upon for its coming
into operation : and the stipulations of the convention shall apply
only to works or articles published after that day.

The convention shall continue in force for six years from the
day on which it may come into operation ; and if neither party
shall, twelve months before the expiration of the said period of six
years, give notice of its intention to terminate its operation, the
convention shall continue in force for a year longer, and so on from
year to year, until the expiration of a year's notice from either party
for its termination.

The high contracting parties, however, reserve to themselves
the power of making by common consent, in this convention, any
modifications which may not be inconsistent with its spirit and
principles, and which experience of its working may show to be
desirable.

Art. XV. The present convention shall be ratified, and the
ratifications shall be exchanged at Turin, as soon as may be within
three months from the date of signature.

INDEX.

Abridgment—*continued.*
    extent to which held good in America, 205
    suggestions of Copyright Commissioners as to, 62, note (*a*)

'Abridgment of Cases in Equity,' 207

Abroad,
    publication, prevents copyright in this country, 112, 113, 323, 324, 331,
        472, 505
        except under International treaties, 331
        simultaneous, and in this country, 113, 117, note (*e*), 125, note (*a*)
    work composed, by Englishmen, protected if first published here, 115
    residence, by Englishmen at time of publication does not affect copyright,
        114
    whether foreigner resident, can obtain copyright here, 116, 117, 118, 125,
        note (*a*), 170.
    assignment by foreigner, to an Englishman, 168
    articles sold, without registration mark, 429.

Abstract,
    an, no piracy, 59, note (*b*)
    of title, copyright in, 46, note (*b*)

Account,
    incident to remedy in equity, 268
    need not be specifically prayed, 270
    right to, dependent on right to injunction, 269, 270
    usually waived, 268, 271
    has reference to past as well as future transactions, 270
    plaintiff entitled to profits from sales on commission of piratical copies,
        270
    defendant ordered to pay net profits in equity, 261, 270
    when ordered to be kept by defendant, 254
    between authors and publishers, 612

Acquiescence,
    not presumed where there is no knowledge, 134
    in infringement fatal to subsequent action, 134
    plaintiff may forfeit rights by delay or laches, 248, 249
          ”   ”   five months' delay, 249
          ”   ”   tendency of modern decisions, 250
        right not prejudiced by custom, 82, 83, 194, 196, 248
        not responsible for delay when ignorant of piracy, 134
    delay may be explained, 249
    injunction not granted generally where there has been, 252, 266
    no proof of assignment, 266

Action : *see also* Damages (Action for)
    for importing pirated copies, 217–221, 638
    for recovery of penalties, 223, 224, 641
        ”   of copies pirated 225, 640
        ”   of value of copies sold, 225
        ”   of damages for performing play, 230, 627
    for infringing airs in an opera, 230
    for false representation as to the registry of a design, 427, note (*a*)
    for damages under Designs Act, 441

ARTICLES : *see also* ENCYCLOPEDIAS ; NEWSPAPERS; PERIODICAL PUBLICATIONS.
    copyright in, for reviews, &c., 75, 76, 593, 638
        newspapers, 470, 638
    for newspapers may be withdrawn, 51
        but need not be preserved by editors, 52
    of political discussion may be translated from foreign newspapers, 480,
        687
    exhibited at exhibitions, 451
    registration of design by sample of, 417, 418
    provisionally registered: *see* PROVISIONAL REGISTRATION.

ARTISTS'
    sketches and studies, 407, 408
    replicas of, 408

ARTS: *See* DESIGNS; DRAWINGS; ENGRAVINGS; FINE ARTS; PAINTINGS;
    PHOTOGRAPHS ; SCULPTURE.

ASSIGNEES
    of copyright, 115, 157, 158, 159
    of manuscript, 8, note (*a*)
    of foreign authors, 117, note (*e*), 118
    of works first published abroad not protected, 116
    of author before publication, right to publish, 11, 117, and note (*e*)
    who are, 158
    difference between licensees and, 161, note (*b*), 171
    rights of, under a commission in bankruptcy, 157, 158
    registration by, 140
    title should be stated in bill for injunction, 235
    what passes to, by assignment under 22nd section of 5 & 6 Vict. c. 45 ..
        317, 318
    claim by, what must be shewn, 265
    instance where, by parol obtained injunction, 265, note (*a*)
    may claim penalties under 3 Will. 4, c. 15, though assignment not by
        deed, 316
    may maintain action for piracy of engravings, 375
    may sue for penalties under 25 & 26 Vict. c. 68, before assignment has
        been registered, 395
        though previous assignments have not been registered, 395

ASSIGNMENT OF COPYRIGHT,
    Literary Copyright,
        will not be presumed, 159
        may be limited to licence for particular purpose, 392
        agreement for division of profits not an, 595, 596
        not effected by mortgage of share in newspaper, 466
        under the statute of Anne, 161
        by a foreigner, 117, note (*e*), 118, 168
        does not prevent assignor selling stock on hand, 170, 606, 608
        by entry on register under 5 & 6 Vict. c. 45 ..136, 164, 636
        stamp, 136, 164
        by delivery of manuscript, 158
        as to whether need be in writing, 159, 160, 165
        instance where person claiming under parol, obtained an injunction,
        265, note (*a*)
        licence to publish is not an, 171
        difference between, and licence, 161 note (

3 H

IMPORTATION—*continued.*
    penalties, forfeitures and damages for, in case of engravings and prints, 616, 699
    of paintings, drawings, and photographs protected by 25 & 26 Vict. c. 68 ., 406, 700
    prohibited by International Copyright Act, 492, 675, 689
    from colonies, 679, 708, 718
    first Act making unlawful, 615

IMPORTER
    cannot plead want of knowledge of piracy, 225

IMPROVEMENTS : *see* ADDITIONS.

INCIDENTS : *see* SCENES.

INDECENT PUBLICATIONS : *see* IMMORAL WORKS.

INDIA,
    copyright in, 506
       ,,   term of, 506
       ,,   ,,   in book published after author's death, 506
       ,,   registration of, 506
               ,,   fees payable on, 506
       ,,   ,,   certificated copies of, 506

INDICES OF TITLE
    copyright in, 46, note (*b*)

INFRINGEMENT OF COPYRIGHT,
    In Books.
        considerations for judging of an, 172, 175
           ,,   the *animus furandi* not to be relied on, 173 and note (*b*)
        plagiarism not necessarily an, 173, 197, 201
        the latter work to be an, need not serve as a substitute for the former, 174
        modes adopted for, 186
        by reproducing the whole *verbatim*, 186
           ,,   verbatim a part, 186
        by piratical criticism, 191, 192
        by imitation of wrapper, 72
        by quotation, 188
        by reviewing, 194, 196
        by reproduction in an abridged form, 201
        by copying general arrangement, 215
        by way of digest, 208
        by translation, 211, 214
        by abridgment, 56, 60
        by gratuitous distribution of copies, 216, 217
        by importation, 217, 221
           ,,   offence committed though no copy sold, 218
        in directories, 15, 177
        in dictionaries, 181
        in reports, 194
        in titles : *see* TITLES.
        quantity but slight criterion, 61, 187
        substantial identity test of, 200
        ignorance no excuse for, 67, 82, 83, 194, 196, 248, 253, 305

JAPAN,
　　copyright in, 567
　　　　„　　duration of, 567
　　　　„　　translations in, 567

JEFFERYS v. BOOSEY, celebrated case of, 31, 118, 122, 166, 167

JOINT AUTHORSHIP, WHAT IS, 130, 131, 133, note (a), 321
　　　　　　　　　what is not, in a musical arrangement, 129, 321
　　adventure, what is a, 599
　　　　　　　not assignable, 601
　　　　　　　terminable by notice, 602, 603
　　owners may contract between themselves as to printing and publishing
　　　599, note (a)

'JOHN BULL' (The), 73

JOHNSON'S (DR.) 'RASSELAS' abridged, 60, 203
　　opinion as to imitations, 196, 197, 201

JUDICATURE ACTS, effect of, 222, 257

JUDICIAL COMMITTEE OF PRIVY COUNCIL,
　　may license republication of books, 109, 633

JUDICIAL DECISIONS : see JUDGMENTS.

JUDGMENTS,
　　right of using, in text-books, 63
　　belong to the government, 126
　　making injunction perpetual as to copyright, 765
　　of the Lords Justices in late case of Dicks v. Brooks, 766

'JUDY,' 72, 247

JURISDICTION : see REMEDIES FOR INFRINGEMENT OF COPYRIGHT.

'JURIST' (The), 77, 463

JUSTICE,
　　sales of original compositions founded on natural, 2
　　no copyright in works parodying, 92

'JUSTICE OF THE PEACE,' (Burn's), 584

'KATHLEEN MAVOUREEN,' 232, note (a)

'KING'S WAGER,' (The), 131, 321

KING'S INN AT DUBLIN,
　　delivery of copies of books to, 153

KNOWLEDGE OF PIRACY,
　　ignorance no defence for piracy generally, 67, 305, 367
　　printer or importer of books without, liable under 5 & 6 Vict. c. 45..218,
　　　225
　　must be shewn in seller, 225
　　seller of engravings and prints not liable to penalties and forfeitures under
　　　8 Geo. 2, c. 13, when ignorant of piracy, 367, 368, 614　　　·
　　but is liable to damages under 17 Geo. 3, c. 57..367, 368, 622

MAPS—*continued*.
    degree of originality necessary in, 42, 65, note (*a*), 183, 184
    copyright in, 41, 110
    published separately, protected under Engraving Acts, and also Literary
        Copyright Act, 360
        with letter-press protected by the Act of 1842 , 360
    registration of, 147–151, 360
    protected as engravings, 360

MARGINAL NOTES: *see* SIDE NOTES.

' MARINO FALIERO,' BYRON'S, 33

MARK OF REGISTRATION, 414, 427, 647
    no, required in sculpture, 427
    wrongfully using, 427, 652
    on articles provisionally registered, 427
    articles sold abroad, 429

MARTIN'S PICTURE, ' BELSHAZZAR'S FEAST,' 374

MATERIALS, COMMON,
    no copyright in, 42, 214, 215 : *see also* COMPILATIONS.

MATHEMATICAL TABLES,
    copyright in, 43

MAURITIUS,
    adopts the provisions of the 10 & 11 Vict. c. 95 .. 499

MAXIMS,
    copyright in collections of, 43

MEANING : *see* CONSTRUCTION ; DEFINITIONS.

' MELBOURNE ARGUS,' 101

MELVILLE'S (LORD) TRIAL, 284

' MEMOIR OF HARRIETTE WILSON,' 93

' MEMOIRS OF THE LIFE OF MRS. BELLAMY,' 204

MENDELSSOHN'S MUSIC TO SHAKESPEARE'S ' MIDSUMMER NIGHT'S DREAM,' 762

' MERCHANTS' AND MANUFACTURERS' POCKET DIRECTORY OF LONDON,' 764 :
    see Morris v. *Ashbee*.

MERIT : *see* VALUE.

METAL,
    copyright in designs as applied to, 412, 646, 735

MEXICO,
    copyright in, 567
        perpetual, 567
    registration of protected works in, 567
    right of representation in, 567
    artistic copyright in, 567

PAPIER MÂCHE, '
  copyright in designs applied to, 412, 683, 735

' PARADISE LOST,' 28, 243, 760

PARAGUAY,
  no copyright law in, 568

PARIS,
  purchase by, of Agave, 2

PARLIAMENT,
  ordinance of the Long, 21
  Acts of : *see* STATUTES.
  petition to, to protect copyright, 25

' PARLOUR LIBRARY,' (The), 78

PAROL assignment not sufficient to pass copyright, 165, 318

PART,
  there may be copyright in, of work, 126
  infringement of copyright by copying, 242, 243
  injunction as to, 242, 243
  of compilation, not new, not protected, 42
  a title taken, 73
  of work published in this country protected, 124

PARTIAL
  assignment of copyright, 166, 167, 168
  infringement of copyright, 242, 243
    as to registration of, 168

PARTICULARS OF OBJECTIONS, 227, and note (*b*)

PARTNERSHIP,
  not constituted between authors and publishers by agreement to divide
    profits, 601, 602

PASSAGES may be selected from reports, 63

PATENT,
  no copyright in specifications of, 96

PATENTS, COMMISSIONERS OF, 413, 715
  empowered to extend time for protection of designs, 413
  orders made by, to be registered, 413, 715
  registrar and officers to be appointed by, 416, 425
  to exercise power of Board of Trade, 715
  transfer of duties of registrar to officers of, 716

PATTERN,
  persons have to register, under Designs Act, 417
    when advisable so to register, 417
      when not so, 418
  when registration by, what protected, 418, 425

PATTERN FOR BERLIN WOOLWORK,
  design for a, not a piracy of an engraving, 372, 373, 766

PROPERTY—*continued.*
in a stream of water, 6
in private and commercial letters, 43
in the paper on which letters written, 43
in lectures, 17
in the Bible, 274, 276
production the principle of one source of, 3
value of, in musical composition, 17, 293, note (*a*)
considered as the right to profits of work, 84
    „   „   publish or withhold, 85
no, in works of libellous, immoral, or obscene nature, 84

PROPRIETARY RIGHTS
ideas not the subject of, 5

PROPRIETORS : *see also* AUTHORS ; PUBLISHERS.
of copyright, who, 158
copyright of articles in, of periodicals, 593, 639
of periodicals, right to publish articles, 51, 52, 75, 78
how can, of periodicals interfere with editor, 594
name and abode of, to appear in register, 82, 639
may sue for recovery of copies pirated, 225, 640
    otherwise at Common Law, 225
    value of pirated copies sold, 225
    in Equity entitled to nett profits only, 261
of designs, may have pirated copies delivered up, 226 '
meaning of word, 648

PROTECTION
obtained by the Universities, 35, 618
    „   registration of sample : *see* DESIGNS ; REGISTRATION.

PROTECTOR-LABEL
not a proper subject of registration, 439

PROVERBS,
copyright in collections of, 43

PROVISIONAL REGISTRATION, 427, 450, 680, 737 : *see also* SCULPTURE.
on what terms may be obtained, 737
no mark necessary, 427, 737
what necessary to furnish registrar, 448, note (*a*)
same protection afforded a, as to designs completely registered, 450
of articles exhibited, 450, 451, 681
fees on, 451, 737
transfer of designs provisionally registered, 738
    fees on, 737
cancellation of, 737
provisions as to searches, 738
    „   inspection of register, 739
    fees on, 739

PRUSSIA,
international convention with England, 505, 729, 730 ; Appendix (K.)

PUBLIC
offices, letters addressed to, 53
documents, copyright in, 126
    „   publication of, may be prevented by Government, 53, 54
libraries : *see* BRITISH MUSEUM ; UNIVERSITIES.

REMEDIES FOR INFRINGEMENT OF COPYRIGHT—*continued.*
  At Law—continued.
    Engravings, Prints, and Lithographs—continued.
      summary proceedings for recovery of penalties, 377, 699
           in England, 377, 699
           in Ireland, 377, 699
           in Scotland, 377, 699
      order for inspection and injunction or account, 378, 700
      evidence on behalf of plaintiff, 378
      not necessary to produce plate, 378
    Sculptures and Busts,
      action for damages given by 54 Geo. 3, c. 56 .. 385, 625
      penalty imposed on offender, 385, 625
      remedy provided by the 13 & 14 Vict. c. 104 .. 385, 682
    Paintings, Drawings, and Photographs,
      action only maintainable as to offence after registration, 395, 695
      assignee may sue though prior assignments not registered, 395
      who is an aggrieved person, 396
      expunging entry in registry, 397
      penalties on infringement, 397, 699
      penalties cumulative, 400
      forfeiture of copies, 401, 700
         suggestions of Copyright Commissioners as to this, 401, 402
      Penalties imposed for :—
        fraudulently signing painting, drawing, or photograph, 402, 698
        „   selling, publishing, or exhibiting same, 403, 698
        „   selling any copy or colourable imitation, 403, 698
        knowingly selling work having altered it without author's consent, 403, 698
        to whom penalty is payable, 404
        penalties imposed as a punishment for a criminal offence, 404
        „   cannot be escaped by a composition deed, 404, 405, 406
        importing piratical copies, 406, 700
    Designs,
      manufacturer bound to inquire where design registered, 436
      notice as provided by 7th section of 5 & 6 Vict. c. 100 .. 436, 437, 649
      what necessary to prove, 437
      ignorance of registration no excuse, 438
      action for damages under sect. 9 of 5 & 6 Vict. c. 100 .. 441, 652
      forfeiture under the 8th s. of 5 & 6 Vict. c. 100 .. 442, 649
         in England, 442, 650
         in Scotland, 443, 651
         in Ireland, 443, 652
      limitation of actions, 444, 653
      justices may order payment of costs in cases of summary proceedings, 444, 653
      same remedies for infringement of useful as ornamental designs, 444, 659
      proceedings may be taken in the county court, 444, 694
      considerations affecting choice of remedy, 445
      no provision for delivery up of pirated articles, 445
        „   but order made on one occasion, 445
      proceedings may be taken in Chancery Division of High Court of Justice in all cases, 446

Representation—*continued.*
    right of, does not pass by assignment of copyright with registration, 316, 640
    express assignment of, need not be registered, 317, 318
    effect of assignment of right of, in London, 350
    penalties for assignment violated only in those taking part in, 305
    suggestion of the Copyright Commissioners as to the right of, 325

Reprinting,
    invasion of copyright by, the whole, 186
        ,,   ,,   a part, 186 *et seq.*
    in colonies : *see* Foreign Reprints Act.
        provision in Canadian Act as to, 708
        Customs Consolidated Act, 1876 .. 718

Republication of Books, by order of Privy Council, 109, 633

Requisites for securing Copyright : *see* Registration.

Resemblance between Works,
    not amounting to piracy, 196, 197
    amounting to substantial identity test of piracy, 200
    in general appearance, 246, 247
    see Originality; Similarity.

Reservation,
    of copyright in paintings, 390, 747, 755
        ,,   in one country on sale in respect of another, 116
    of separate publication of articles written for periodicals, 76
    form for entire, of copyright under the 25 & 26 Vict. c. 68 .. 758
        partial, of copyright, under the 25 & 26 Vict. c. 68 .. 759

Residence,
    proprietor's place of, must be entered in registry book, 136
    abroad, by Englishmen, does not affect copyright, 114, 115, 139
    necessary in British dominions for alien to obtain copyright here, 116, 117
        note (*a*), and 122
    meaning of, in United States, 569
    as to the, of an assignee, 139

Restraints of Press removed, 21

Restrictions,
    on importation of pirated copies, 217, 218, 219, 220, 679, 700
    contained in Customs Consolidated Act, 1876 .. 219, 220, 717

Result in Compilation must be original, 42, 174, 178, 181, 198, 215

Reviews : *see* Periodical Publications.
    copyright in articles written for, 75, *etc.*, 638, 639
    when, are invasions of copyright, 188, 140, 191
    registration of title of, 81, 144, 639
    extracting whole stories for, 194, 196

Revised Edition : *see* Editions.

Reward due to an Author, 36, 576, 577.

Right : *see also* Property.
    of action : *see* Actions.

SALES—*continued.*
    forms of, under Literary Copyright Act, 749, 750, 752
        „   „   the 25 & 26 Vict. c. 68..755, 758, 759
    restraining sales: *see* INJUNCTIONS.

SAMPLE,
    permissible to register by, 417
    when advisable to register by, 417
    when not advisable to register by, 418
    what protected when registration by, 418–425

SARDINIA,
    convention between, and Austria, 506
        „   „   this country, 506, Appendix (K.)

SAXONY,
    joins the international convention, 506, Appendix (K.)

SCANDALOUS WORK,
    no copyright in, 92

SCENES,
    piracy by taking of certain, of play, 313, 314, 315, 327–330

SCENIC ENTERTAINMENT,
    included in definition of dramatic piece, 5 & 6 Vict. c. 45..632

SCHOOL BOOKS,
    cópyright in, 46, note (*b*), 65, 179, 180

SCIENCE (GUIDE TO): *see* BREWER (DR.)

SCORE,
    copyright in a pianoforte, 342
    distinction between pianoforte, and original, 343, 344

SCORING TABLET,
    copyright in, 100, 139

SCOTLAND,
    early decisions as to author's common law rights in, 30, note (*a*)
    principles upon which Court of Session in, have acted in issuing injunc-
        tions, 49, 240
    remedy in, under the Copyright (Works of Art) Act, 377, 699
        „   under Designs Act, 443, 651

SCOTT (SIR WALTER),
    works infringed, 103, 104, 215, 216

SCRIPTURES : *see also* BIBLE.
    work denying truth of, not protected, 88

SCULPTURE AND BUSTS
    construction of Aets relating to, 381
    copyright in, 379
        extent of, 381, 624
        term of, 382, 624, 625
        term of, suggestion of Copyright Commissioners as to, 383, note (*b*)
            when date from, 382

918   INDEX.

WORKS OF LITERATURE AND ART REFERRED TO—*continued.*
    Musical and Dramatic Works—continued.
        Other Music,
            'What an Afternoon !' 232, note (*b*)
            Bellini's 'Sonnambula,' 166
            'The Burlesque Valse,' 293, note (*a*)
            'The Cornflower Valse' 293, note (*a*)
            'Fra Diavolo,' 142, 241
            Auber's 'Lestocq,' 209
            Offenbach's 'Vert-vert,' 476
            'Popular Favourites for the Pianoforte,' 293, note (*a*)
            'Prince Imperial Galop,' 293, note (*a*)
            'The Serious Family Polka,' 75
            'The Sweetly Pretty Valse,' 293, note (*a*)
    Works of Art,
            'Belshazzar's Feast,' 374
            'Death of Chatterton,' 34
            Landseer's 'Eve of the Battle of Edgehill,' 403, 404
            Frith's 'Railway Station,' 405
            Eddis's 'Going to Work,' 392
            'Holiday Time,' 392, 393
            Rosa Bonheur's 'Horse Fair,' 371
            Millais' 'Huguenot,' 372, 373
            Hunt's 'Light of the World,' 371, Appendix (I.)
            'Ordered on Foreign Service,' 394
            'My First Sermon,' 394
            'My Second Sermon,' 394
            Thompson's 'Roll-Call' 397
            'The Young Cricketer,' 395, note (*c*)

WOVEN FABRICS,
    copyright in designs as applied to, 412, 646, 693, 735

WRAPPERS,
    may be rejected by registrar under Designs Acts, 449
    imitation of, 72

'WREATH' (The), 216

WRITING : *see also* LETTERS ; MANUSCRIPT.
    as to whether assignment of copyright must be in, 159, 161, 165, 318
    contracts between authors and publishers should be in, 578

YARN,
    copyright in designs as applied to, 412, 646, 735

YATES,
    arguments against literary property, 6, 7

'YOUNG CRICKETER' (The), 395, note (*c*)

LONDON : PRINTED BY WILLIAM CLOWES AND SONS, LIMITED, STAMFORD STREET
AND CHARING CROSS.